CHANGZHOU STATISTICAL YEARBOOK

常州统计年鉴 2013

（总第23期 No.23）

常州市统计局
国家统计局常州调查队 编

Compiled by Changzhou Municipal Statistics Bureau and
Changzhou Investigation Team of the national Bureau of Statistics

中国统计出版社
China Statistics Press

地区生产总值

Gross Domestic Product

单位：亿元(100 million yuan)

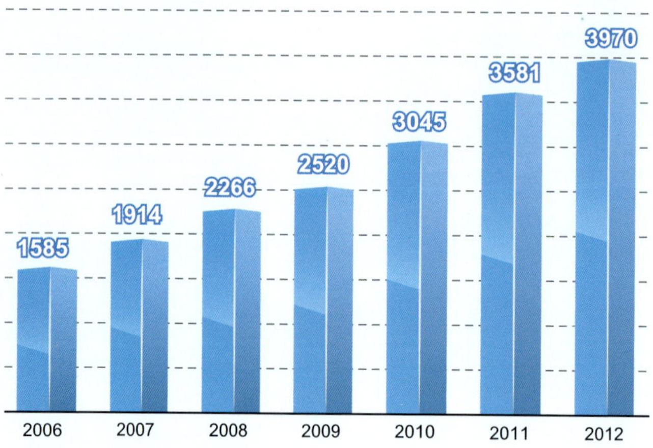

国民经济三次产业结构

Proportions in Gross Domestic Product

单位：%

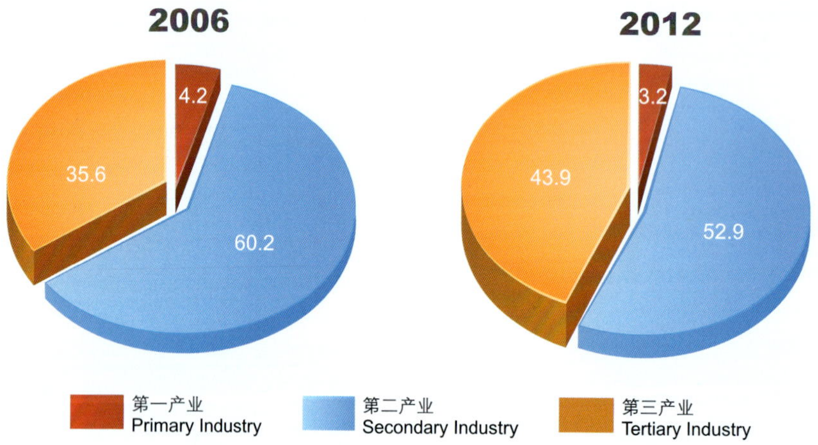

人均地区生产总值

Per Capita of Gross Domestic Product

单位：元(yuan)

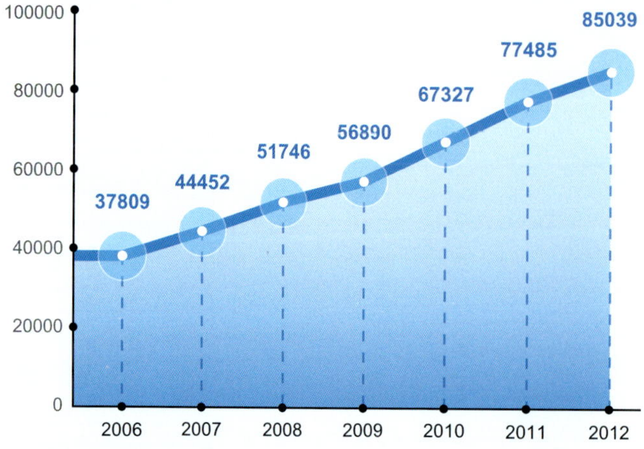

全社会固定资产投资完成额

Total Completed Investment in Fixed Assets

单位：亿元(100 million yuan)

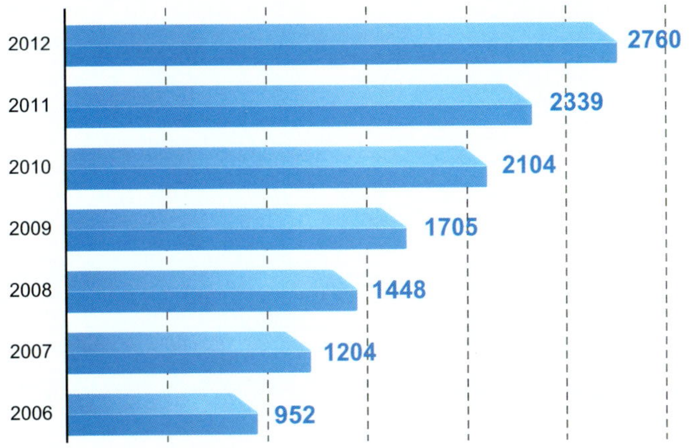

全社会固定资产投资构成

Total Investment in Fixed Assets

单位：%

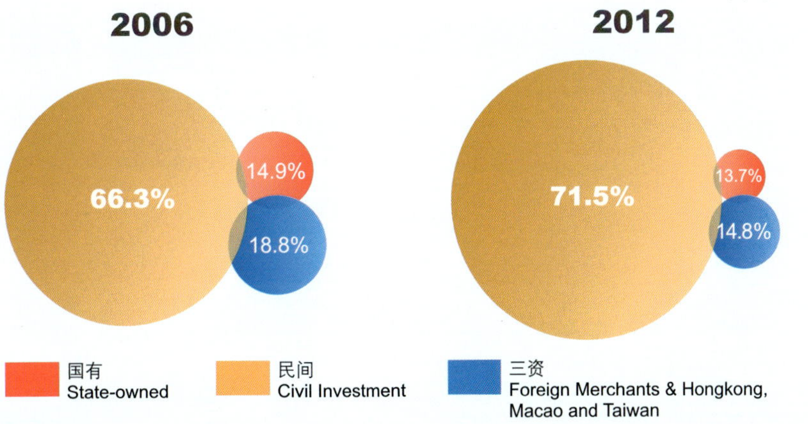

社会消费品零售总额

Total Retail Sales of Consumer Goods

单位：亿元(100 million yuan)

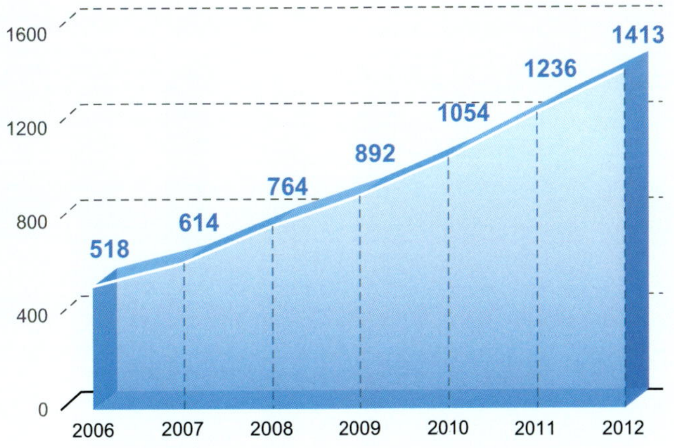

农林牧渔业总产值(现价)

Gross Output Value of Farming, Forestry,Animal Husbandry and Fishery (Current)

单位：亿元(100 million yuan)

农村三次产业从业人员比重

Proportion of Employment in Tertiary Industry in Rural Area

单位：%

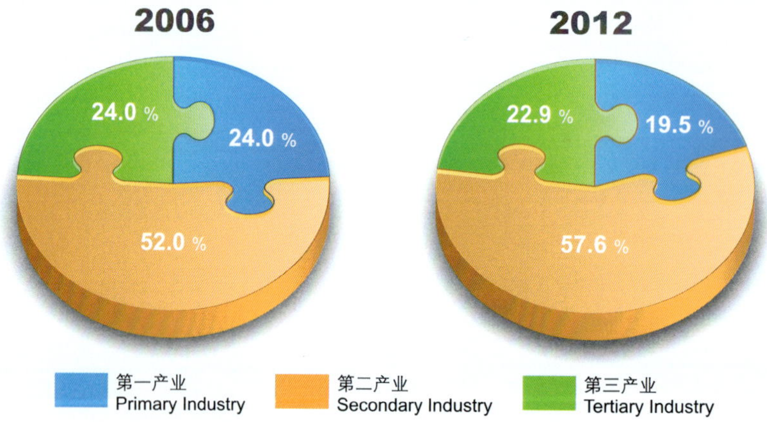

水稻单产

Per Hectare of Paddy Rice

单位：公斤/公顷(kg/hectare)

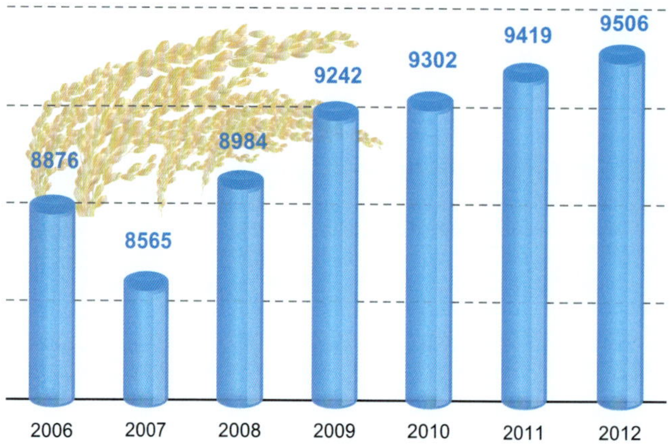

工业生产发展指数（以2000年为100）

Indices of Gross Industrial Output

(Calculated by Comparable Price:2000=100)

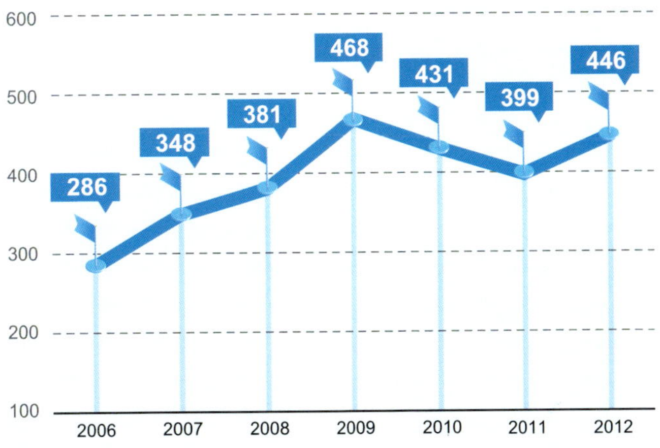

规模以上工业实现利润

Profit of Industries above Dseignated Size

单位：亿元(100 million yuan)

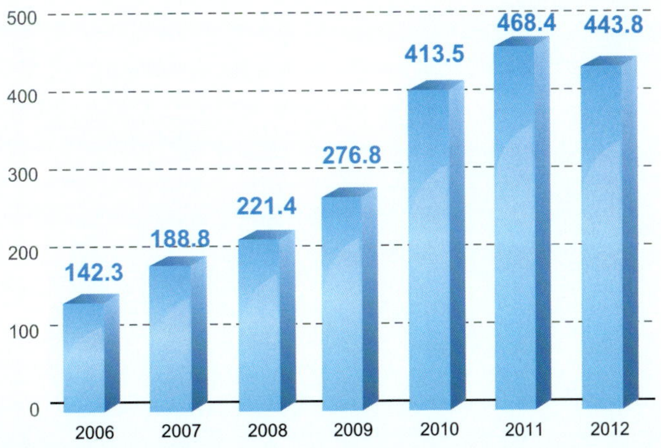

工业主要行业构成

Main Industry Structure

单位：%

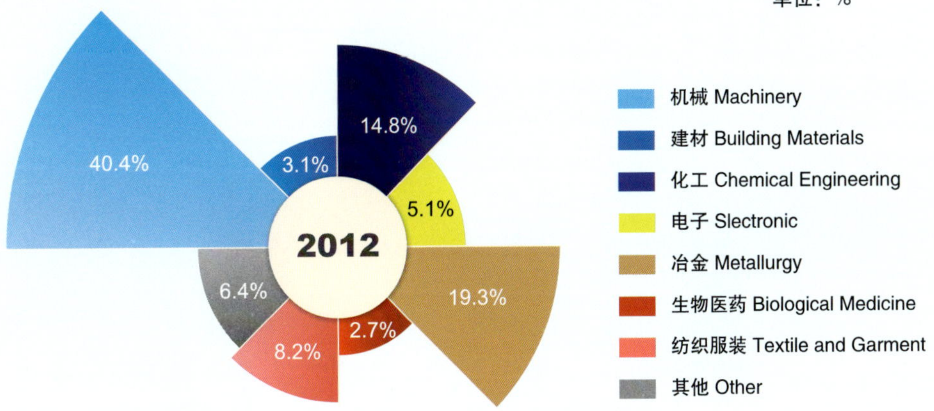

私营企业注册资本

Registered Capital of Private Enterprises

单位：亿元(100 million yuan)

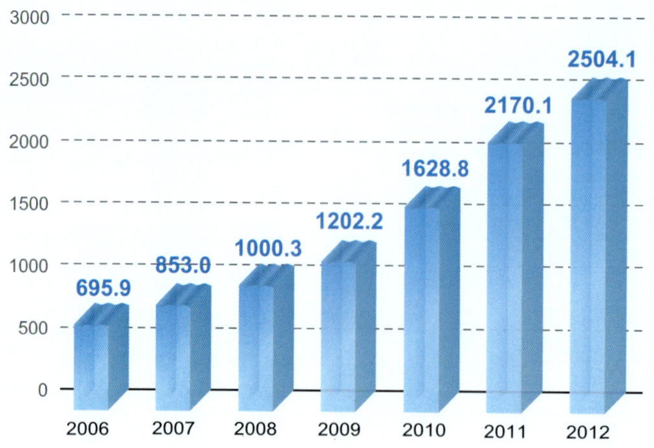

个私企业从业人数

Number of Employees in Individual and Private Enterprises at Year-end

单位：万人(10000 persons)

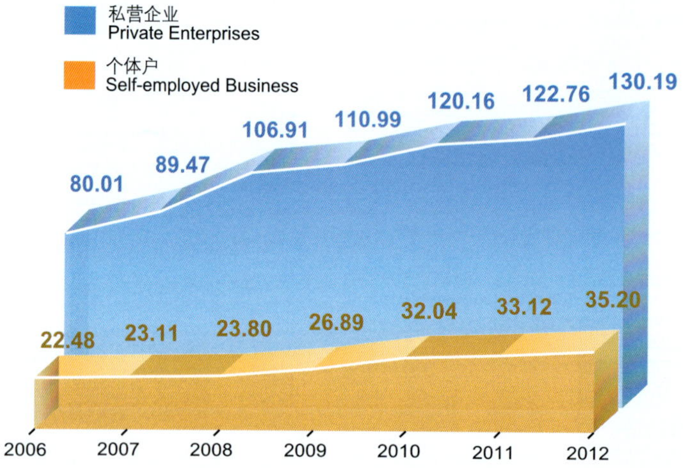

个私企业户数

Number of Individual and Private Economy at Year-end

单位：户(unit)

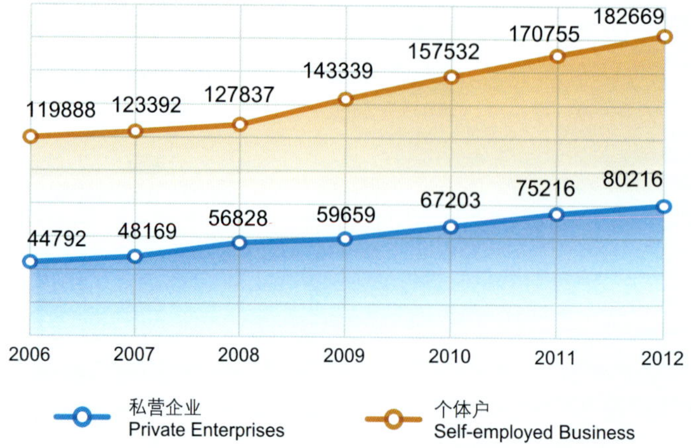

进出口总额
Total Imports and Exports

单位：亿美元(USD 100 million)

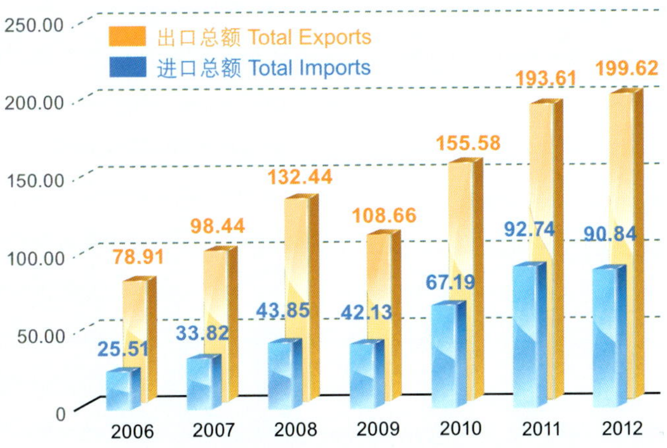

实际利用外资金额
Total Amount of Foreign Investment Actually Utilized

单位：亿美元(USD 100 million)

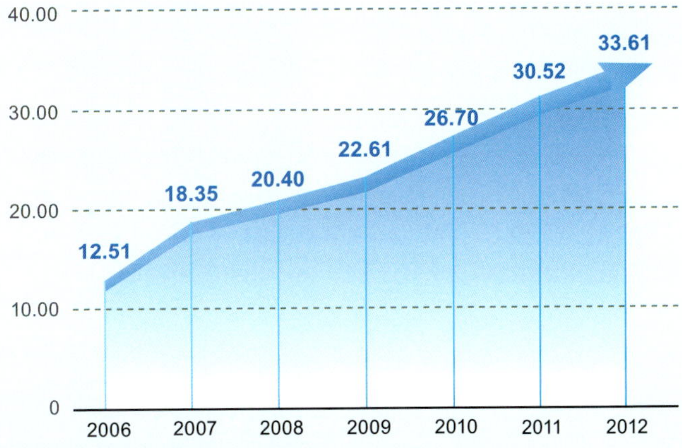

规模以上三资企业工业总产值
Total Output Value of Foreign-funded Industrial Enterprises Above Designated Size

单位：亿元(100 million yuan)

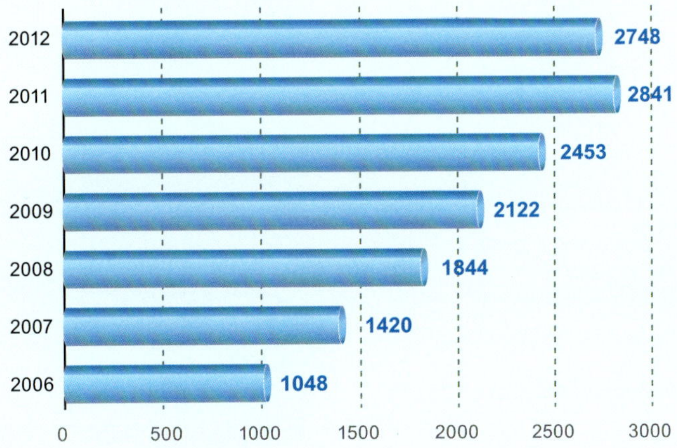

财政总收入和支出

Total Financial Revenue & Finacial Expenditure

单位：亿元（100 million yuan）

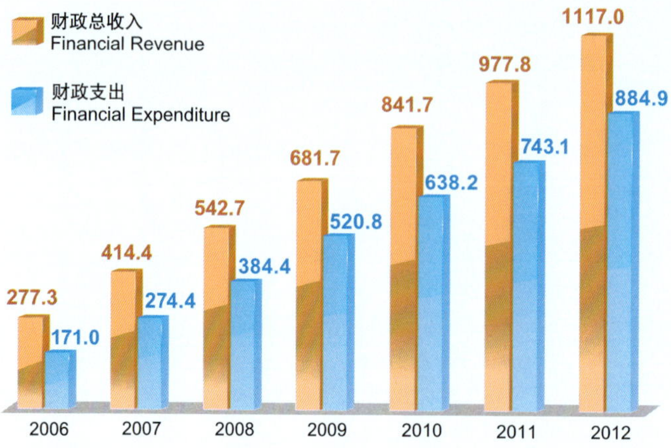

财政收入占GDP比重

Proportion of Revenue in GDP

单位：%

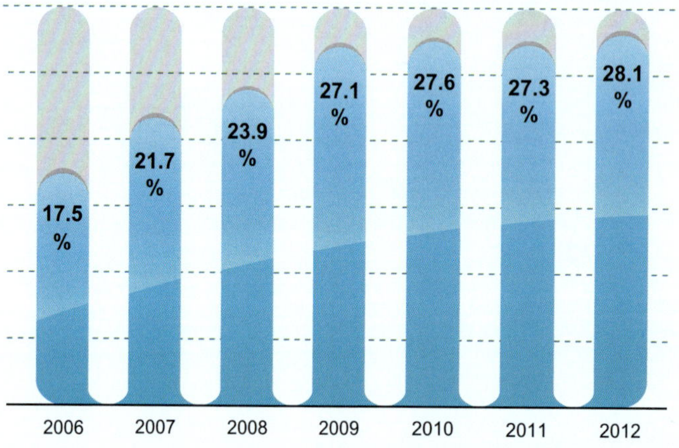

金融机构存贷款余额

Deposit and Loan Balance of National Banking Institutions

单位：亿元（100 million yuan）

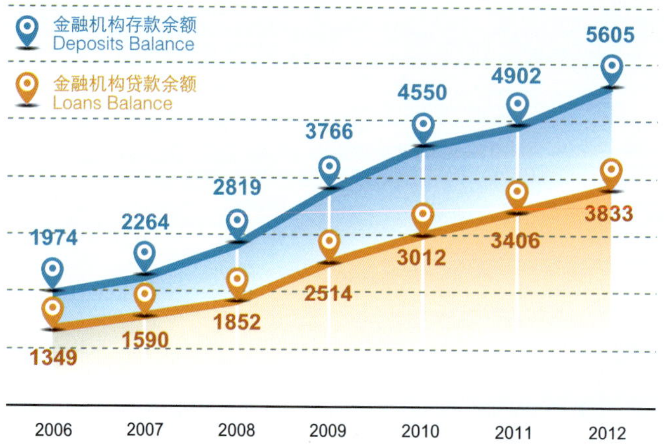

市区居民人均可支配收入、农民人均纯收入
Per Capita Disposable Income and Net Income of Rural Residents

单位：元（yuan）

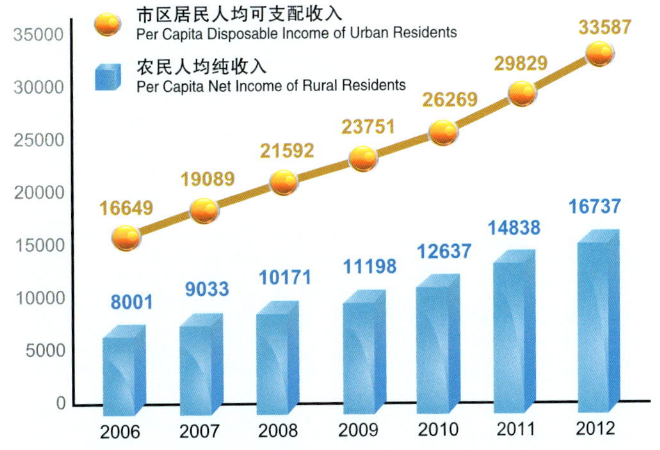

城镇、农村居民恩格尔系数
Engel Coefficient of Urban and Rual Residents

单位：%

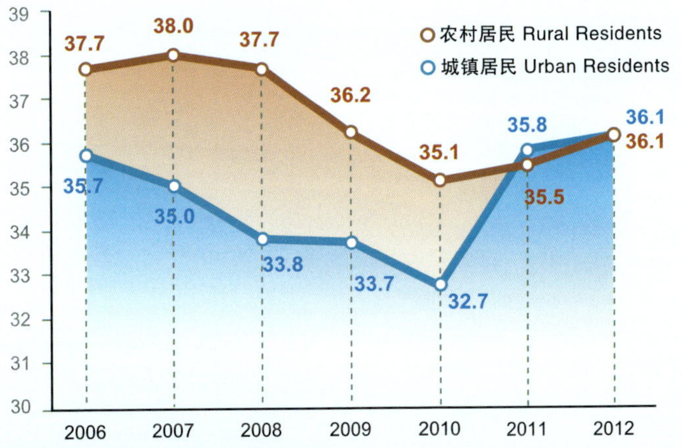

城乡居民人均储蓄存款余额
Per Capita Deposits of Urban and Rural Residents

单位：元(yuan)

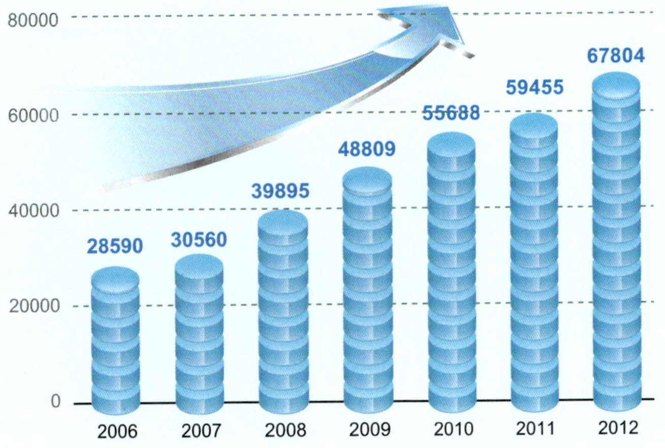

普通高等院校在校学生数
Students Enrollmed of Institutions of Higher Education

单位：人（person）

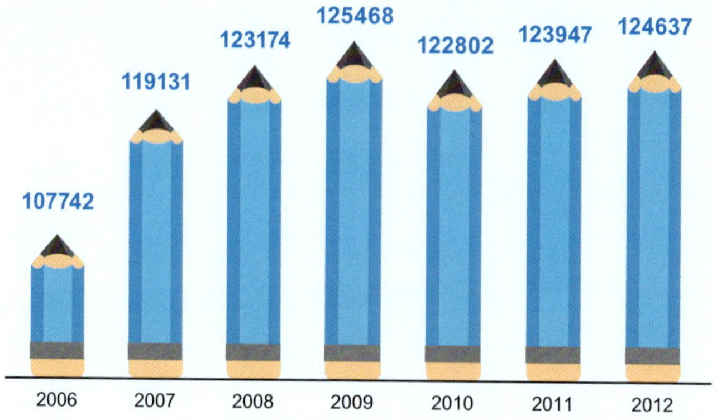

专利申请量、专利授权量
Number of Patent Authorizaions Examined and Granted

单位：项（unit）

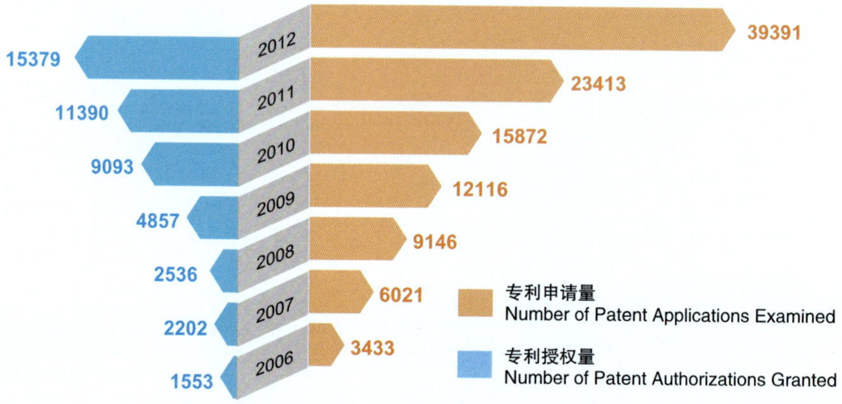

全社会卫生机构床位数
Beds of Health Care Institutions

单位：张（bed）

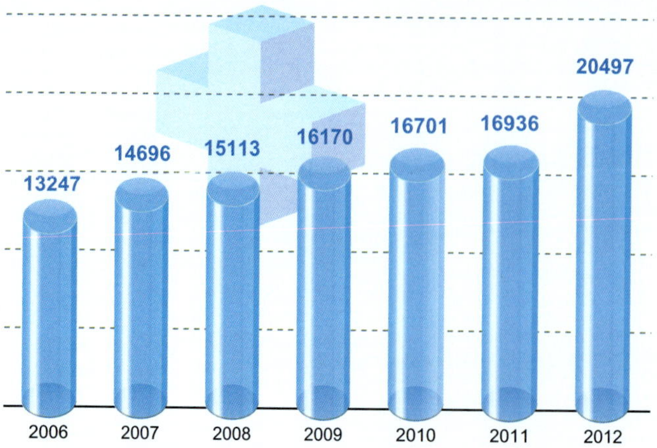

人均拥有道路面积
Per Capita Area of Roads

单位：平方米（sq.m）

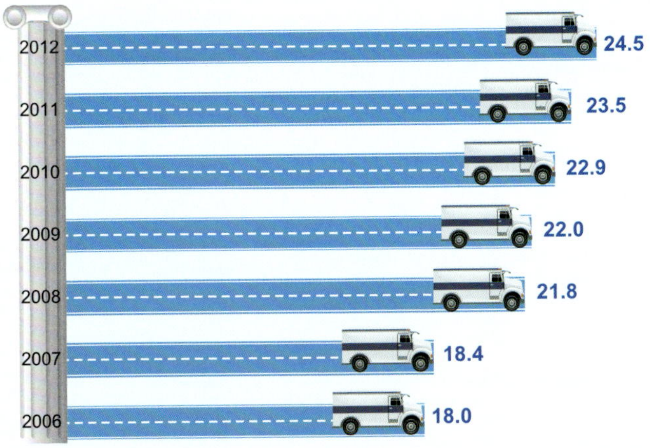

人均公园绿地面积
Per Capita Green Area of Parks

单位：平方米（sq.m）

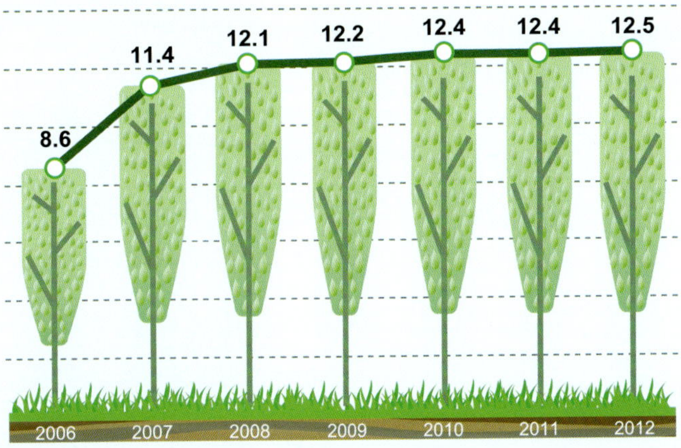

建成区面积
Area of Constructed Regions

单位：平方公里（sq.km）

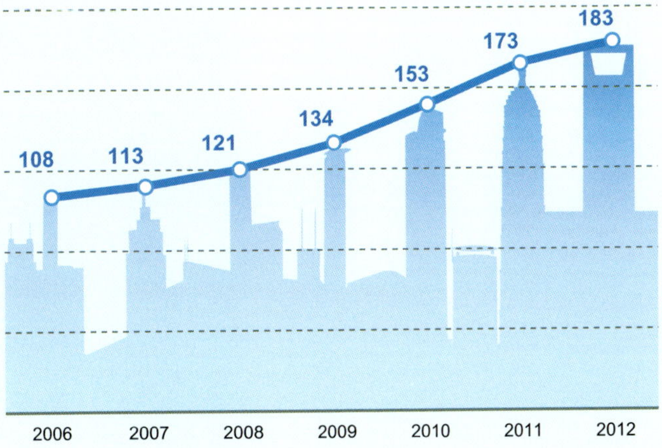

常州统计年鉴

2013 STATISTICAL YEARBOOK

编 者 说 明

一、《常州统计年鉴—2013》是一本信息高度密集的资料和工具书。它以翔实的统计数据反映了2012年常州经济、科技、社会各方面的发展变革情况，以及历史年份和改革开放以来大量的统计数据。

二、全书内容分为22部分，即：1. 概述；2. 排名榜；3. 行政区划、自然概况；4. 综合；5. 人口；6. 从业人员、工资总额；7. 物价指数；8. 人民生活；9. 固定资产投资；10. 农业；11. 工业；12. 建筑业；13. 交通运输、邮电通信；14. 贸易、住宿餐饮业；15. 个体、私营经济；16. 对外经济、旅游；17. 能源消费；18. 财政、金融、保险；19. 城市建设、环境保护；20. 科技、教育、文化；21. 卫生、体育；22. 民政、司法、其他。书末附有主要统计指标解释等附录资料。

三、本书中所使用的度量衡单位采用国际统一标准计量单位，价值量指标凡未表明何种价格的，均为以现行价格计算。

四、本书中的简称和符号使用说明：年主营业务收入2000万元以上的法人工业企业，简称“规模以上”工业企业；“…”表示数据不足本表最小单位数；“空格”表示数据不详或无该项数据；“#”表示其中数。

《常州统计年鉴》公开出版以来，受到社会各界关心和支持，并提出了许多宝贵意见，对此，我们深表谢意。热忱欢迎读者继续对年鉴的不足之处批评指正，帮助我们进一步提高编辑水平。

Preface

I. Changzhou Statistical Yearbook-2013 is a reference book, which reflects the economic, scientific and technological, social development in Changzhou city in 2012 by means of full and accurate statistical data. It also provides abundant statistical data about past years and the years since reform and opening-up.

II. This book contains the following twenty-three parts: 1.General Description; 2.List of Top Strengths; 3. Division of Administration Areas and Natural Resources; 4.General Survey; 5.Population; 6.Employment and Total Wages; 7.Price Indices; 8.People' s Livelihood; 9.Investment in Fixed Assets; 10.Agriculture; 11.Industry; 12.Construction; 13.Transportation, Post and Telecommunications; 14.Trade, Accommodation and Catering Trade; 15.Individual and Private Economy; 16.Foreign Economy and Tourism; 17.Energy Consumption; 18. Public Finance, Banking and Insurance; 19.Urban Construction and Environmental Protection; 20.Science Technology, Education and Culture; 21.Health and Sports; 22.Givil Administration Judicature and Others. In addition, Explanatory Notes on Main Statistical Indicators are provided at the end of each part.

III. The units of measurement used in this book are internationally standard measurement units. Those undefined price indices should be calculated in accordance with current prices.

IV. Abbreviations and Notations used in this book:

Corporate industrial enterprises with main business income of 20 million yuan and above are referred to the statistical coverage of industrial enterprises "above designated size" for short. "…" indicates that the figure is not big enough to be measured with the smallest unit in the table, "(blank)" indicates that the data are not available, "#" indicates the items of the total.

Here we' d like to express our sincere thanks to the readers who have offered us so many invaluable suggestions on content selection and compilation of the yearbook. Our thanks also go to those friends in all circles of society who have shown their support and care to the publication of the yearbook. We welcome any suggestions and comments from readers so as to help us to further improve our work of compilation.

目 录

CONTENTS

第一篇 概 述

CHAPTER 1 GENERAL DESCRIPTION

第二篇 排名榜

CHAPTER 2 LIST OF TOP STRENGTHS

第三篇 行政区划 自然概况

CHAPTER 3 ADMINISTRATIVE DIVISION AND NATURAL RESOURCES

第四篇 综 合

CHAPTER 4 GENERAL SURVEY

第五篇 人 口

CHAPTER 5 POPULATION

第六篇 从业人员 工资总额

CHAPTER 6 EMPLOYMENT AND TOTAL WAGES

第七篇 物价指数

CHAPTER 7 PRICE INDEX

第八篇 人民生活

CHAPTER 8 PEOPLE'S LIVELIHOOD

第九篇 固定资产投资

CHAPTER 9 INVESTMENT IN FIXED ASSETS

第十篇　农　业

CHAPTER 10 AGRICULTURE

第十一篇 工 业

CHAPTER 11 INDUSTRY

第十二篇 建筑业

CHAPTER 12 CONSTRUCTION

第十三篇 交通运输 邮电通信

CHAPTER 13 TRANSPORTATION, POST AND TELECOMMUNICATIONS

第十四篇 贸易 住宿餐饮业

CHAPTER 14 TRADE, ACCOMMODATION AND CATERING TRADE

第十五篇 个体 私营经济

CHAPTER 15 INDIVIDUAL AND PRIVATE ECONOMY

第十六篇 对外经济 旅游

CHAPTER 16 FOREIGN ECONOMY AND TOUEISM

第十七篇 能源消费

CHAPTER 17 CONSUMPTION OF ENERGY

第十八篇 财政 金融 保险

CHAPTER 18 PUBLIC FINANCE, BANKING AND INSURANCE

第十九篇 城市建设 环境保护
CHAPTER 19 URBAN CONSTRUCTION AND ENVIRONMENTAL PROTECTION

第二十篇 科技 教育 文化
CHAPTER 20 SCIENCE, TECHNOLOGY, EDUCATION AND CULTURE

第二十一篇 卫生 体育

CHAPTER 21 HEALTH AND SPORTS

第二十二篇 民政 司法 其他

CHAPTER 22 CIVIL ADMINISTRATION, JUDICATURE AND OTHERS

附 录

APPENDIX

1

CHAPTER 1

概 述

GENERAL DESCRIPTION

常州市
2012年国民经济和社会发展统计公报

2012年，面对严峻复杂的国际经济形势和国内经济下行压力，全市上下认真贯彻中央和省的决策部署，大力实施“创新驱动加速年”活动，深入推进“八项工程”建设，统筹做好稳增长、调结构、抓创新、惠民生、促和谐等各项工作，经济社会发展保持稳中有进的态势，在基本现代化建设新征程上迈出了新的步伐。

一、经济运行

【综　合】产业结构继续优化。全年实现地区生产总值（GDP）3969.9亿元，按可比价计算增长11.5%，其中第一产业完成增加值126.4亿元，增长4.7%；第二产业完成增加值2100.8亿元，增长11.7%；第三产业完成增加值1742.7亿元，增长11.6%。全市一、二、三次产业比重由上年的3.1：54.5：42.4调整为3.2：52.9：43.9，服务业增加值在全市经济总量中所占比重较上年提高1.5个百分点。全市按常住人口计算的人均生产总值达85039元，按平均汇率折算达13472美元。

财政收入增势平稳。全年实现公共财政预算收入379.0亿元，比上年增长8.0%，其中增值税25%及营改增增值税、营业税、个人所得税分别入库51.6亿元、83.8亿元和19.9亿元，分别增长6.2%、13.1%和3.8%，企业所得税40.7亿元，下降7.7%。财政支出继续向民生领域倾斜，全年公共财政预算支出391.2亿元，比上年增长8.1%，其中教育支出66.1亿元，社会保障和就业支出41.7亿元，农林水事务支出28.6亿元，医疗卫生支出22.8亿元，分别比上年增长20.4%、14.6%、11.5%和15.7%。

【农业与农村经济】农业生产保持稳定。全市实现农林牧渔业总产值219.6亿元，比上年增长12.8%。全市粮食播种面积155.65千公顷，比上年下降2.4%。粮食总产量114.8万吨，比上年下降0.4%。粮食单产达到491.7公斤，比上年增加10.6公斤，水稻单产633.7公斤，比上年增加5.8公斤，蝉联全省“十连冠”。全市蔬菜播种面积41.13万亩、产量89.26万吨，分别比上年增长1.0%、8.6%；出栏生猪88.58万头，家禽4941万羽。花木产业提升工程成效显著，全市新增设施花木3.5万亩，总面积达36.4万亩，总产值达27亿元，分别比上年增长10.6%、22.0%，实现花木基地面积、花木产能、经济总量的“三提升”。

农业现代化建设稳步推进。全市高标准农田比重达58.7%，高效设施农（渔）业面积占比达20.5%，农业综合机械化水平达83.0%，全市优质农产品基地占耕地面积的比重达90.0%，农业信息化覆盖率达98.5%，持证农业劳动力占比达29.6%，工商登记农户入社率94.7%，农业适度规模经营比重73.2%。农业系统全年实施市级以上农业科技项目43项，引进、示范、推广农业新品种56个、新技术72项。全市新增1家国家级生猪核心育种场、2家省级青虾良种繁育场。优质高产多抗粳稻新品种——武运粳23号的育成与推广获市科技进步一等奖，农业科技进步贡献率超过64.5%。

农业生态显著改善。绿化造林6.7万亩，新创省级村庄绿化示范村、标准化绿化示范村85个，林木覆盖率达24.0%。天目湖通过国家湿地公园建设试点批准。开展“江之情、湖之恋、河之爱”系列放鱼活动，投放鱼苗2550万尾，水域生态持续改善。农业面源污染治理取得积极成果，全市农业废弃物综合利用率达95.5%。创成3个江苏省最具魅力休闲乡村，全市农游景点接待游客突破700万人次，实现旅游收入12.5亿元。

【工　业】工业生产稳中有进。全年完成规模以上工业产值9031.3亿元，同比增长12.1%，其中轻工业1730.6亿元，增长12.8%；重工业7300.7亿元，增长12.0%。规模以上工业中，民营企业完成产值5932.0亿元，增长17.4%，其中私营企业5354.9亿元，增长17.4%；外商及港澳台商投资企业完成产值2809.6亿元，增长3.6%。重点行业平稳运行，机械、冶金、化工、纺织服装、电子行业全年完成产值3424.8亿元、2142.1亿元、1239.2亿元、787.1亿元和388.7亿元，同比分别增长9.7%、9.3%、28.7%、12.4%和18.1%。全年完成高新技术产业产值3555.2亿元，占规模以上工业总产值的比重达到39.4%，比上年提高2.1个百分点。企业经济效益低位开局、逐步向好，规模以上工业企业全年完成主营业务收入8980.3亿元，同比增长11.9%，实现利税、利润703.4亿元、428.2亿元，同比增长4.0%、0.8%。规模以上工业经济效益综合指数为

250.4%，成本费用利润率为5.0%，产品销售率为97.9%。

重点企业支撑良好。2012年，全市产值超亿元企业1292家，超10亿元企业达124家，分别比上年增加55家和7家，超100亿元企业8家，其中，华润包装材料有限公司和常州市盛洲铜业有限公司产值首次超100亿元。全市产值排位前50强企业共完成产值3456亿元，同比增长16.8%，增速高于全市平均水平4.5个百分点，对全市工业经济发展支撑作用良好。

【建筑业】建筑行业稳步发展。全年实现建筑业增加值200.2亿元，比上年增长10.1%；建筑企业全年完成施工产值1071.7亿元，比上年增长19.1%；施工面积8765.1万平方米，增长14.5%；竣工面积3067.9万平方米，增长8.3%。建筑业按施工产值计算的全员劳动生产率达26.3万元/人，比上年提高5.6%。

【国内贸易】消费品市场运行平稳。全年实现社会消费品零售总额1413.3亿元，比上年增长14.3%，扣除价格因素，实际增长12.4%。其中批发零售业实现零售额1293.2亿元，增长14.1%；住宿餐饮业实现零售额120.2亿元，增长17.5%。城乡市场呈现同步发展态势，城镇地区实现零售额1319.4亿元，增长14.3%；乡村地区实现零售额94.0亿元，增长15.2%。限额以上批发零售企业建筑及装潢材料类、体育娱乐用品类、家俱类、金银珠宝类和汽车类商品零售额增长较快，零售额分别比上年增长27.1%、21.3%、24.0%、20.2%和19.0%。

商品市场繁荣兴旺。全市亿元以上商品交易市场59家，商品成交额1890.88亿元，比上年增长16.5%。全市有7家市场年成交额突破百亿元，分别是江苏凌家塘市场、江苏长江塑料化工交易市场、江苏湖塘纺织城、常州市武进汽车城投资发展有限公司、常州市武进夏溪花木市场发展有限公司、常州钢材现货交易市场、常州淮都金属城有限公司，成交额分别达到234.07亿元、214.65亿元、204.21亿元、118.13亿元、115.61亿元、110.54亿元和110亿元。

【交通运输和邮电通讯】交通运能稳步提升。全年完成公路客运量16542万人，比上年增长12.3%，公路旅客周转量102.6亿人公里。全年完成货运量17794万吨，增长15.2%，其中公路货运量16075万吨，水路货运量1719万吨；货物周转量133.5亿吨公里，其中公路货物周转量104.7亿吨公里，水路货物周转量28.7亿吨公里。铁路客运量（含常州、戚墅堰、常州北站）1099.7万人，其中常州北站客运量119.1万人。常州机场全年旅客吞吐量突破100万人次，达到107.8万人次，比上年增长15.5%，跻身全国中等机场行列；货物吞吐量1.1万吨，增长32.2%；起降航班22367架次，其中运输起降11384架次。全年港口货物吞吐量8998.0万吨，其中常州长江港货物吞吐量2666.0万吨。年末全市机动车拥有量达95.5万辆，比上年末增长8.3%；民用汽车拥有量72.7万辆，比上年末增长29.8%，其中私人汽车54.0万辆，增长24.3%。

通信行业平稳发展。全年邮政业务总收入6.7亿元，比上年增长14.1%；发送函件1.1亿件，特快专递506.2万件，分别增长14.0%、23.8%。全年通信业务收入59.2亿元，比上年增长9.9%。年末本地网电话用户161.6万户，移动电话用户519.4万户，其中3G用户达到87.9万户；互联网用户数达127.9万户，比年初增长22.2%，其中宽带网用户117.4万户，增长25.9%。

【金融保险业】金融服务能力提升。年末全市金融机构人民币存款余额5604.9亿元，比年初增加702.9亿元，增长14.3%；贷款余额3832.8亿元，比年初增加426.5亿元，增长12.5%。各项贷款余额中，短期贷款2095.4亿元，比年初增长13.9%，其中个人贷款及透支211.7亿元，增长26.1%，单位经营贷款1669.9亿元，增长13.3%；中长期贷款1618.7亿元，比年初增长9.2%，其中个人贷款641.5亿元，增长11.4%，单位经营贷款138.6亿元，增长43.5%。全市新增股份制商业银行分支机构2家、科技支行4家，成立村镇银行1家。

保险业务平稳增长。截止年末，全市共有保险公司61家，比上年增加4家，其中寿险公司35家，产险公司26家。全年实现保费总收入109.4亿元，比上年增长16.9%，其中寿险75.6亿元，增长18.3%，财产险33.8亿元，增长13.7%；全年保险赔款支出21.2亿元，比上年增长27.7%，其中寿险2.2亿元，比上年增长8.7%，财产险19.0亿元，比上年增长30.4%；寿险其它各类给付支出8.8亿元，比上年增长1.9%。

证券交易持续低迷。全市24个证券营业部全年证券交易总额3493.8亿元，比上年下降27.8%，其中债券成交额102.9亿元，比上年增加96.1亿元，股票、基金分别成交3338.2亿元、52.7亿元，分别下降30.2%和0.5%。截至年底，全市资金账户62.6万户，增长17.0%，持有A股股票市值301.8亿元，增长3.0%。

企业上市稳步推进。年内新增2家上市企业，其中裕兴股份登陆深圳创业板，募集资金8.4亿元；新城发展在香港联交所主板上市，募集资金16.5亿元。截至年底，全市企业上市股票34只，共筹集资金276.7亿元，比上年增长9.9%。

【旅游业】旅游产业快速发展。全年实现旅游总收入520.34

亿元，旅游接待总人数4003.84万人，分别比上年增长22.2%、17.7%。全市接待国内游客3958.27万人次，国内旅游收入490.37亿元，分别比上年增长17.8%和23.1%；接待入境游客45.57万人次，旅游外汇收入4.74亿美元，分别比上年增长10.3%和12.6%。中华恐龙园魔幻雨林4D过山车、春秋淹城旅游区百灵水世界、环球动漫嬉戏谷中华龙塔、南山竹海二期历史文化区，天宁宝塔因缘果报殿等一批旅游新项目提档升级，为全市旅游发展注入新的动力。截至年底，全市共有国家5A级旅游区1家，国家4A级旅游区12家；全国工农业旅游示范点17家，江苏省四星级乡村旅游点15家，江苏省工业旅游点3家，江苏省自驾游基地6家。旅行社发展到120家，其中2家旅行社进入全省旅行社20强，1家旅行社进入全国旅行社100强；星级酒店发展到65家，其中五星级酒店6家，四星级酒店26家。

【固定资产投资】固定资产投资稳定增长。全年完成全社会固定资产投资2760.1亿元，比上年增长18.0%。第一产业完成投资5.8亿元，比上年下降42.1%，第二、三次产业分别完成投资1534.0亿元和1220.4亿元，分别增长18.4%和18.1%。工业投资保持稳定增长，全年完成投资1526.0亿元，增长18.0%，对全社会投资增长的贡献率达55.2%，高于上年0.6个百分点。工业投资中，设备购置投资845.7亿元，增长18.2%。

房地产开发投资有所放缓。列统房地产开发企业全年完成投资597.0亿元，比上年增长5.5%，其中住宅完成投资416.1亿元，增长3.3%，占房地产开发投资的比重达到69.7%；商业营业用房完成投资89.4亿元，增长8.3%；办公楼投资21.8亿元，下降23.0%。全年商品房屋施工面积4314.4万平方米，增长9.9%，其中本年新开工面积1100.2万平方米，下降24.2%。

二、改革开放

【民营经济】民营经济稳步发展。民营经济全年完成增加值2663.5亿元，按可比价计算增长11.6%，在全市经济总量中所占比重由上年的66.8%提高到67.1%；上缴税收385.18亿元，比上年增长6.2%，在全市税收总收入中所占比重为62.4%。截至年底，全市共有个体工商户18.3万户，从业人员35.2万人，注册资金86.0亿元，其中年内新增个体工商户3.5万户，注册资金25.2亿元。全市私营企业累计达到8万户，雇工人数114.2万人，注册资金2504.1亿元，其中年内新增私营企业9778户，注册资金224.6亿元。

【开放型经济】对外贸易克难求进。全年实现进出口贸易总额290.5亿美元，比上年增长1.4%，其中出口199.6亿美元，增长3.1%；进口90.7亿美元，下降2.2%。全年机电产品出口105.5亿美元，增长2.1%；高新技术产品出口39.7亿美元，下降3.2%，其中光伏产品出口比上年减少14.8亿美元。新兴国家和地区出口比重有所上升，全市对东盟、拉美、俄罗斯、非洲等新兴市场出口分别增长19.5%、17.3%、12.1%和7.1%。

外资引进质量提高。全年注册外资实际到帐33.6亿美元，比上年增长10.1%；新增工商登记注册外资54.2亿美元，比上年增长0.2%。外资大项目有所增加，全年新增工商登记注册外资超3000万美元项目44个（其中制造业项目28个），比上年度增加1个，其中超亿美元项目4个，比上年度增加2个。全市新增世界500强企业投资项目6个，其中德国蒂森克虏伯、瑞士ABB首次在我市投资。博世力士乐、普利司通自行车等6家世界500强企业年内实现增资。投资性公司和功能性机构建设有所突破，香港瑞声集团在我市投资设立的瑞声（中国）投资有限公司注册资本达1亿美元，成为继光宝科技之后落户我市的第二家投资性公司。

对外合作不断深化。全年新签外经合同额6.0亿美元，比上年增长3.2%；完成外经营业额5.4亿美元，比上年增长9.1%。截至年底，全市拥有服务外包企业405家，从业人员近3万人，全年完成服务外包合同额3.4亿美元，比上年增长24.1%，执行额2.9亿美元，增长16.1%；完成服务外包离岸合同额2.6亿美元，增长15.9%，离岸执行额2.2亿美元，增长10.7%。

【开发区建设】开发区经济平稳运行。全市开发区当年完成全社会固定资产投资1573.9亿元，其中工业投入954.5亿元，基础设施建设投入196.2亿元；完成公共财政预算收入234.4亿元，工业产品销售收入7869.2亿元。开发区利用外资主阵地作用进一步显现，全市开发区当年完成工商登记协议注册外资45.1亿美元，实际到账外资28.0亿美元，新增工商登记注册外资3000万美元以上外资项目41个，占全市的93.2%，其中制造业项目27个，占全市的96.4%。

【外事】外事活动日益活跃。全年接待外宾138批、945人次，其中副部长以上团组7批、79人次；接待来常考察访问的外国驻华使、领馆官员37批、278人次，接待来访外国记者19批、78人次。年内与比利时罗莫尔市正式缔结了友好城市关系，至年底，已有16个外国城市与我市结为友好城市，友好城市年内来访团组36批、289人次，组织24个团组、160人次出访友好城市。在

“2012全国百城论坛”和“2012中国国际友好城市大会”上，我市分别荣获“友城战略发展奖”和“国际友好交流与合作奖”。

三、社会事业

【科技事业】创新能力持续加强。全年政府科技经费投入19.33亿元，比上年增长39.4%。新认定国家高新技术企业208家，累计达797家；争取省级以上科技项目451项，获得经费支持4.9亿元；成功举办“5.18”展洽会，组织产学研重大活动13次，新增产学研合作项目316项。全年完成专利申请39391件，同比增长68.4%，其中发明专利10123件；专利授权15379件，其中发明专利授权1188件，万人发明专利拥有量由上年的4.77件增加到7.59件。常州高新区、武进高新区成为首批省级科技金融合作创新示范区，武进高新区升格为国家级高新区。

创新体系不断完善。着力加快创新载体建设，“一核八园”入库企业932家，全年营业总收入突破1000亿元，增长44.8%。科教城研发机构总数达101家，高科技创业企业达635家，各类研发人才超过1.5万人。全年新增“两站三中心”150家，累计775家。企业创新力度加大，全市有620家大中型工业企业建有研发机构，覆盖率超过90%。孵化器、加速器建设加快，常州生物医药孵化器全面启用，常州创意产业基地获得全省唯一、全国地级市唯一首批国家文化和科技融合示范基地授牌。全市市级以上孵化器、加速器累计达64家，其中国家级孵化器10家，省级孵化器22家，省级加速器2家。产学研用结合更显特色，成功举办“5.18”展洽会，签约34个重大项目，其中16个重大产业化项目的技术合同总金额达2.39亿元。

创新人才加快集聚。截至年底，共有396个领军人才签约我市创新创业。全市累计引进领军人才1200名，其中国家“千人计划”108名，省“双创”145名，形成了“搭建平台，引进人才，孵化企业，培育产业”的良好创新创业氛围。成立常州市高新技术企业协会，加强企业家之间的互动与交流。设立专项培训科技企业家，共组织2批115名高企负责人参加市科技型企业家培训班。

【教育事业】教育事业扎实推进。年末全市共有各类学校617所，在校学生73.59万人，教职工5.26万人，其中专任教师4.13万人。学前教育加快发展，全市新建扩建幼儿园32所，公办幼儿园比例提高，占比达75%以上，市级以上优质园占比率、就读率分别达80%、90%以上。各辖市、区全面建立学前教育生均公用经费财政拨款制度。义务教育更加均衡，热点普通高中统招名额分配到各初中的比例达70%，全市公办学校吸纳流动就业人员随迁子女比例达88.91%，义务教育阶段省优质学校占比达84.2%、就读率达86.7%。实施高中质量提升工程，启动创新人才培养实验项目及课程基地建设，遴选、确定4所学校6个项目为市级普通高中创新人才培养项目，高考本二上线率56.34%（含体育、艺术）（其中市区63.11%），较上年提高近6个百分点。推进省职业教育创新发展实验区建设，殷村职教园开工建设，参加省技能大赛获一等奖54个（31个为项目一等奖第一名），国家中等职业教育改革发展示范学校增至5所，省级品牌、特色专业增至20个，职业学校单招高考和本专科录取率全省十三连冠。加强终身教育服务，有国家级社区教育示范区、实验区各1个，国家级社区教育示范乡镇（街道）增至7个，省级社区培训学院和社区教育实验区实现全覆盖，省级社区教育中心增至22个，省级社区教育示范乡镇（街道）增至8个，命名10个市民终身学习服务基地，市级标准化成人教育中心校增至24所，市级标准化村民（居民）学校增至103所。推进教育信息化，确定市“e学习”项目学校40所，13所学校成为省“e学习”试点校。切实加大帮困助学力度，落实政府政策资助2.23亿元，接受社会捐赠735万元。推进教育国际化，天合国际学校顺利招生，确定首批常州市国际理解教育试点学校25所。

【文化事业】精品创作卓有成效。原创舞剧《格桑花•茉莉花》荣获剧目金奖，并包揽7个单项奖。电影《秋之白华》、儿童剧《留守小孩》和广播剧《君子史良》荣获全国“五个一工程”奖；市滑稽剧团创排的《飞扬少年》成功入选第九届全国儿童剧展演；市锡剧院大型原创交响锡剧《天涯歌女》获省“五个一”工程奖；市曲艺团首部常州方言长篇评话《常州白泰官》获得中国曲艺最高奖“牡丹奖”文学奖。

文化服务扎实推进。常州市图书馆建成全省首家电视图书馆，覆盖终端用户突破100万户。各类免费开放公益文化单位全年举办各类文化艺术展览超过500场。全年送戏300场，送电影超过1万场，城市“15分钟公共文化圈”、农村“十里文化圈”更加完善。“智慧社区”第一批建设任务基本完成，惠及市民10万户。广播电视和新闻出版稳步推进，全市共有1080家印刷企业、894家书报刊发行企业、351家音像制品经营单位，印刷行业年产值超过70亿元，实现电影票房近两亿元。作品版权登记增长30%以上，总计超过700件。全市广播、电视节目综合覆盖率均为100%，全市数字电视用户达到109.0万户，比上年增长2.1%，《常州日报》、《常州晚报》年发行量分别达3083.2万份和3516.3万份。

文物保护成效明显。在武进太湖湾成功发掘钱一本墓，象墩遗址发掘和环太湖艺术城地块考古勘探顺利推进。截至年底，全市拥有不可移动文物1677处，其中全国重点文物保护单位5处，省级文物保护单位50处，市、县级文物保护单位235处。省级历史文化街区3处，历史建筑48处。“国家历史文化名城申报”工作全力推进。

【卫生事业】卫生服务水平不断提升。年末全市共有各级各类医疗卫生机构1128个，拥有总床位20497张，卫生技术人员2.53万人，其中执业（助理）医师10094人、注册护士10192人，全市每千常住人口拥有卫生技术人员5.39人、总床位4.37张。新农合保障水平得到提升，参合率100%，人均筹资标准达360元，比2011年提高55元。县乡两级政策范围内住院补偿比达76.13%，住院实际补偿比达51.98%。全面推进门诊总额预付制改革，3个地区推进住院费用混合支付方式改革。公共卫生服务逐步均等，按人均45元补助标准落实专项经费，10类41项基本公共卫生服务和7大类重大公共卫生服务项目全面开展。基层卫生服务不断强化，新创省示范乡镇卫生院6家、国家和省示范社区卫生服务中心各1家。基础建设顺利推进，一院综合病房大楼封顶，二院（阳湖院区）投入使用，四院（新北院区）投入试运行，儿童医院病房楼交付使用，七院门急诊病房综合楼完成外装。

【体育事业】体育事业继续发展。年内全市承办国际级比赛7项、国家级比赛14项、省级比赛19项。常州籍运动员全年在重大比赛中获得40项冠军，其中世界冠军2项，亚洲冠军3项，全国冠军35项。全民健身扎实推进，全市新增社区健身活动场所83个，比上年增加20个，城市社区“十分钟体育健身圈”建设初见成效，连续16年获得全国全民健身活动优秀组织奖。全年发行体育彩票13.2亿元，比上年增长22.1%。

四、人口、民生与社会保障

【人口与就业】人口规模基本稳定。截至年末，全市户籍人口达364.8万人，比上年末增长0.5%。户籍人口中，男性181.6万人，增长0.4%，男女性别比为99.1：100；60岁以上人口达77.2万人，占总人口的比重达21.2%。年末全市暂住人口155.0万人，比上年末增长16.5%。全市计划生育率达98.9%，节育率达86.7%，独生子女率为77.4%；全市人口出生率9.4‰，人口死亡率7.9‰，人口自然增长率为1.5‰。

就业创业扎实推进。全年新增就业10.5万人，援助困难群体实现再就业10532人，及时援助城乡零就业家庭，常州籍高校毕业生充分就业和特困家庭毕业生100%就业。扶持创业6875人，带动就业41250人。年末城镇登记失业率为2.37%。成功创建8个省级充分就业示范社区，入选“全国创业先进城市”。2012年新安置就业残疾人1271人。

【人民生活】居民收入稳步增长。全年城镇居民人均可支配收入33587元，比上年增长12.6%，扣除价格因素实际增长9.9%；人均消费性支出20519元，比上年增长8.6%，其中人均食品消费7406元，增长9.6%，居民恩格尔系数为36.1%，比上年上升0.3个百分点。农民人均纯收入16737元，比上年增长12.8%；人均生活消费支出12027元，增长7.3%，居民恩格尔系数36.1%，比上年上升0.6个百分点。截至年末，全市居民储蓄存款余额2473.3亿元，比年初增加315.9亿元，增长14.6%。

住房保障工作积极推进。2012年全市新开工各类保障房25103套（户），其中公共租赁住房（含廉租房）13414套，经济适用住房869套，限价商品房3566套，城市棚户区危旧房改造安置住房7254套。竣工各类保障性住房7371套（户），其中公共租赁住房（含廉租房）3575套，经济适用住房859套，限价商品房1515套，城市棚户区危旧房改造安置住房1422套。年内新增廉租住房租金补贴家庭642户。全市共安排1775户廉租住房和公共租赁住房实物配租家庭，其中廉租住房实物配租家庭375户，公共租赁住房保障家庭1400户。

【市场物价】物价水平温和上涨。全年居民消费价格指数（CPI）102.5。八大类商品和服务价格“六涨二跌”，其中食品类上涨4.9%、烟酒类上涨3.3%、衣着类上涨1.6%、家庭设备用品及维修服务类上涨7.2%、娱乐教育文化用品及服务类上涨1.0%；居住类上涨2.5%，医疗保健和个人用品类价格下降0.4%，交通和通信类价格下降0.6%。

【社会保障】社会保障不断完善。全市企业养老、医疗、失业、工伤、生育五大保险分别扩面净增6.32万人、7.99万人、6.18万人、11.04万人、6.56万人。截至年末，共有121.13万人参加企业养老保险，比上年末增长6.5%；95.98万人参加失业保险，增长7.9%；162.87万人参加城镇职工基本医疗保险，增长7.3%。五大保险基金总收入153.33亿元，比上年增长29.3%；支出114.94亿元，增长22.8%。市区企业离退休人员月人均养老金水平提高至

1849元，城乡居民社会养老保险基础养老金提高到110元/月。职工医保、城镇居民医保政策范围内住院医疗费用报销比例分别在89.3%和70.5%。

【社会福利与救济】社会救助不断完善。年末全市拥有各类养老机构178个，比上年增加86个。养老床位数达24678张，收养人数达17442人。全市28628户、52526人纳入低保范围，其中城镇低保对象10035户、18287人，农村低保对象18593户，34239人，累计发放保障金1.4亿元。全市共有28786人得到医疗救助，比上年增加13204人；救助金额达2300万元。全年发行福利彩票10.6亿元，增长14.3%。法律援助工作不断完善，全年共受理各类法律援助案件3633件，比上年增长27.5%，接受各类法律咨询2.5万人次，比上年增长27%。

慈善救助深入展开。全市各级慈善会共发放各类救助金1.16亿元，8万人次困难群众从中受益。其中，市慈善总会（含4分会）全年发放各类慈善救助金4439.25万元，救助困难群众3.33万余人次，全年助老、助孤、助学、助困、助残、助医活动分别发放救助金77.2万元、79.48万元、196.54万元、326.96万元、74.95万元、933.86万元。市慈善总会“大病关爱——常州慈善救助”项目获得全国民政系统为民服务优秀服务品牌。

五、城乡建设

【基础设施建设】基础设施建设不断推进。全年完成交通建设投资74.3亿元，年内新增高速公路里程20.2公里，改扩建国省公路41公里，新改建农村公路210公里、桥梁111座；完成各类水利建设土方1497.1万立方米，恢复治理水土流失面积25平方公里；完成农村水利建设投资4.3亿元。泰州大桥南接线工程建成通车，常溧高速公路启动建设，“三纵三横”路网建设进度加快，大明路、劳动东路东段等已完成通车，龙城大道隧道、玉龙路等建设工程加快实施。江边污水厂三期扩建、魏村自来水厂装机备用工程完工投运。花博会主场馆及配套设施建设、现代传媒中心建设、青果巷改造工程等重大公共基础设施建设项目顺利推进。城市轨道交通建设规划获国家批准。新城建设加快实施，凤凰新城、钟楼新城等城市新片区建设全面推进，东大门建设工程顺利推进。

【公用事业】公交线网不断完善。截至年底，市区公交线路197条，公交营运车辆2590辆。市区新增、更新公交车辆200辆，新增、优化线路47条，全年公交客运量41190万人次，市区公交日均客流量达到120万人次，城市公交分担率达到26.4%。金坛、武进19个镇的镇村公交顺利开通，“镇村公交”线路累计达到213条，实现镇村公交全覆盖。

公共服务能力提升。全年全社会用电量351.5亿千瓦时，比上年增长6.0%，其中城乡居民生活用电32.2亿千瓦时，增长14.8%。城区供水总量2.74亿立方米，其中居民生活用水1.17亿立方米，供水普及率100%。年末城区天然气用户达50.24万户，比上年末增长1.1%，城市燃气普及率达99.7%。城区生活污水日处理能力63.5万吨，生活污水处理率达95.5%。年底城区路灯总数17.3万盏，比上年末增长5.9%。全年生活垃圾清运量91.4万吨，生活垃圾无害化处理率达100%。

六、环境保护与资源节约

【环境保护与治理】生态文明扎实推进。全面启动国家生态文明示范市建设，河道水环境整治和水源地建设保护工作得到加强，三条入太湖河道和主要湖泊水质进一步好转，完成41条黑臭河道整治，全年市区空气质量优良天数达337天。着力推进城乡生态协调发展，年内8个镇通过国家级生态镇核查验收，新建省级生态街道2个，省级生态村23个。

【城市绿化】绿化水平不断提升。年末建成区绿地面积达7072公顷，其中公园绿地面积1759公顷，分别比上年末增长6.4%和3.3%；城区人均公园绿地达到12.5平方米；建成区绿化覆盖率达42.21%，比上年提高0.04个百分点，建成区绿地率38.59%，比上年提高0.19个百分点。荷园廉政文化主题公园建设工程年内完工，武进中国花博会主展区常州园建设工程进场施工，丁塘河湿地公园、凤凰公园、新区新龙国家森林公园建设顺利推进。实施花都花城建设工程，年内完成机场路、中吴大道景观提升和月季种植工程。积极推进农村村庄环境整治工程，村庄绿化覆盖率达到30%以上。

注：公报中各项统计数据除注明按可比价格计算外，均按现行价格计算。

STATISTICAL COMMUNIQUE OF CHANGZHOU ON THE 2012 NATIONAL ECONOMIC AND SOCIAL DEVELOPMENT

In 2012, faced with severe and complicated international economic situation and the downward pressure on the domestic economy, Changzhou conscientiously implemented the decisions and arrangements of the Central Government and Jiangsu Province, vigorously carried out the program called The Year of Innovation-Driven Acceleration, further promoted the construction of the Eight Projects, and well organized the tasks of maintaining steady growth, adjusting economic structure, focusing on innovation, benefiting people's livelihood, promoting social harmony, etc. With stable and advancing economic and social development, Changzhou has taken a new step in the course towards the goal of basic modernization.

I. Economic Development

Economic Aggregate

Industrial structure kept improving. The gross domestic product (GDP) of Changzhou reached 396.99 billion yuan, increased by 11.5% over 2012 calculated on comparable prices. The value added of primary industry, secondary industry and tertiary industry made 12.64 billion yuan, 210.08 billion and 174.27 billion respectively, up 4.7%, 11.7% and 11.6% respectively over the previous year. The ratio of the outputs of the three sectors was adjusted to 3.2 : 52.9 : 43.9 from 3.1 : 54.5 : 42.4 of last year, and the proportion of the value added of the tertiary industry to the city's total economic output increased 1.5 percentage points over the previous year. The per capita GDP based on resident population reached 85,039 yuan, approximately 13,472 US dollars based on the average exchange rate.

Financial income increased stably. The revenue of local general budget in year 2012 achieved 37.90 billion yuan, increased by 8% over 2012, of which the value-added tax accounted for 25%. The replacement of business tax with value-added tax, business tax, and individual income tax made respectively 5.16 billion yuan, 8.38 billion yuan and 1.99 billion yuan, up 6.2%, 13.1% and 3.8% respectively; while the corporate income tax was 4.07 billion yuan, down 7.7%. The investment of people's livelihood kept increasing. All the year through, the fiscal expenditure of general budget hit 39.12 billion yuan, up 8.1%, of which 6.61 billion yuan was spent on education, 4.17 billion yuan was paid for social security and other programs in fields of employment, 2.86 billion yuan was expended on agriculture, forestry and water affairs, and 2.28 billion yuan was used in health and medical services, increased by 20.4%, 14.6%, 11.5%, and 15.7% respectively.

Agriculture and Rural Economy

Agricultural production remained stable. The total output value of agriculture, forestry, animal husbandry and fishery achieved 21.96 billion yuan, up 12.8% over 2012. The total sown areas of the whole city reached 155.65 thousand hectares, down 2.4% over the previous year. Grain yield made 491.7 kilograms per mu, an increase of 10.6 kilograms. Rice output hit 633.7 kilograms per mu, increased by 5.8 kilograms over the previous year, ranking the first in Jiangsu province for 10 straight years. The city's vegetable sown area reached 411,300 mu, with an output of 892,600 tons, up 1.0% and 8.6% respectively. The production of live pigs and poultry made respectively 885,800 and 4,941,000. The flower and plant industry achieved significant results in upgrading. With the newly added 35,000 mu of protected trees and flowers, the total planting area reached 364,000 mu and the total output value made 2.7 billion yuan, increased by 10.6% and 22.0% respectively, realizing 'triple-upgrading' of planting area, capacity and economic output.

The construction of agricultural modernization advanced smoothly. The proportion of high-standard farmland reached 58.7%; areas of high-efficiency protected agriculture (fishery)accounted for 20.5%; comprehensive agricultural mechanization level achieved 83.0%; high-quality agricultural products bases accounted for 90.0% of arable land; coverage of agricultural information realized 98.5%; agricultural workers holding certificates accounted for 29.6%;94.7% of the farmers joining cooperatives had registered at industrial and commercial authority; and the moderate scale management of agriculture accounted for 73.2%. In 2012, the agricultural sector implemented 43 agricultural technology projects at or above municipal level, and introduced, demonstrated and promoted 56 new agricultural varieties and 72 new agricultural technologies. One national key pig breeding farm and two provincial freshwater shrimp breeding farms were newly constructed. A new variety of high-yielding and multi-resistant japonica hybrid rice---Wuyun Japonica Hybrid Rice No. 23 was successfully bred and widely promoted, winning the Municipal Science & Technology Progress Award. Agricultural science and technology contribution rate reached more than 64.5%.

Agricultural ecology achieved significant improvement. Changzhou completed afforestation of 6.7 mu, newly built 85 provincial model green villages and standardized model green villages, and achieved forest coverage rate of 24.0%. Tianmu Lake tourist resort was approved as a pilot construction site of National Wetland Park. The serial fish release activities called A Love for River released 25.5 million fish fries. Water ecosystems were continuously improved. Agricultural nonpoint source (NPS)pollution control achieved positive results, and the city's agricultural waste comprehensive utilization rate reached 95.5%. Three villages were titled as the Most Attractive Leisure Villages in Jiangsu Province, while the city's agricultural tour attractions received more than 7 million tourists, making 1.25 billion yuan in tourism income.

Industry

Industrial production was stable and progressing. The above-scale industrial output value achieved 903.13 billion yuan all the year around, an increase of 12.1% over the previous year, of which the light industry contributed 173.06 billion yuan, up 12.8%; and the heavy industry produced 730.07 billion yuan, up 12.0%. Among the above-scale industries, non-government companies achieved the output value of 593.20 billion yuan, increased by 17.4%, of which private enterprises made 535.49 billion yuan, up 17.4%; while the foreign invested and Hong Kong-, Macao- or Taiwan- funded industrial enterprises achieved the output value of 280.96 billion yuan, an increase of 3.6%. Key industries maintained stable operation. Machinery, metallurgy, chemicals, textiles and garments, and electronics industries respectively achieved annual output value of 342.48 billion yuan, 214.21 billion yuan, 123.92 billion yuan, 78.71 billion yuan and 38.87 billion yuan, increased by 9.7%, 9.3%, 28.7%, 12.4% and 18.1% respectively. In 2012, the high-tech industry output value reached 355.52 billion yuan, accounting for 39.4% of the above-scale industrial output value, an increase of 2.1 percentage points over the previous year. The economic efficiency of enterprises started low and grew gradually. The industrial enterprises above designated size accomplished the main business income of 898.03 billion yuan, a year-on-year growth of 11.9%, and achieved pre-tax profits of 70.34 billion yuan and the profits of 42.82 billion yuan, up 4.0% and 0.8% respectively. The overall efficiency index for above-scale industry was 250.4%, with the cost margin of 5.0% and the sales ratio of 97.9%.

Key enterprises provided good support. In 2012, 1,292 companies each achieved output value of over 100 million yuan and 124 enterprises each made output value of above one billion yuan, the number of which increased by 55 and seven respectively compared with 2012. Eight companies each reached 10 billion yuan in output value, among which China Resources Packaging Materials Co., Ltd. and Changzhou Shengzhou Copper Limited achieved output value of over 10 billion yuan for the first time. The city's top 50 companies in output value made total output value of 345.6 billion yuan, a year-on-year increase of 16.8%, and the growth rate was 4.5 percentage points higher than the city’s average, playing a good supporting role in the city's industrial and economic development.

Architecture Industry

Architecture industry was in a stage of steady development. The value added of architecture industry reached 20.02 billion yuan, up 10.1%; the construction output of architecture companies achieved 107.17 billion yuan, up 19.1%; the construction area reached 87.651 million square meters, increased by 14.5%; the completed construction area reached 30.679 million square meters, an increase of 8.3%. All-personnel labor productivity hit 263,000 yuan / person calculated on its output value, up 5.6% over the previous year.

Domestic Trade

The consumer goods market ran stably. The total of social retail goods reached 141.33 billion yuan, increased by 14.3% (actual increase of 12.4% deducting price factors)over the previous year, of which wholesale and retail industry contributed 129.32 billion yuan, up 14.1%; the sales of the catering industry made 12.02 billion yuan, up 17.5%. The urban and rural markets developed simultaneously, of which the retail sales of consumer goods in urban area achieved 131.94 billion yuan, up 14.3%, while that in the rural area reached 9.40 billion yuan, up 15.2%. The retail sales of wholesale and retail enterprises above designated size in construction and decoration materials, sports and recreation articles, furniture, gold and silver jewelry and automobiles have witnessed a rapid increase, which were up by 27.1%, 21.3%, 24.0%, 20.2% and 19.0% respectively.

The commodity market was prosperous. There were 59 products trading markets of which sales achieved over 100 million yuan. The volume of business reached 189.088 billion yuan, up 16.5% over last year. Seven markets each achieved 10 billion yuan in turnover, namely Jiangsu Lingjiatang Market (23.407 billion yuan), Jiangsu Yangtze River Plastic and Chemistry Trade Market (21.465 billion yuan), Jiangsu Hutang Textile City (20.421 billion yuan), Changzhou Wujin Automobile Town Investment and Development Co. Ltd. (11.813 billion yuan), Changzhou Wujin Xiaxi Flowers & Trees Market Development Co. Ltd. (11.561 billion yuan), Changzhou Steel Spot Market (11.054 billion yuan), and Changzhou Huaidu Metal Town Co. Ltd.(11 billion yuan).

Transportation and Postal & Telecommunications

The traffic capacity was in a stage of steady growth. The highway passenger volume hit 165.42 million, up 12.3%, and the highway passenger circulation volume reached 10.26 billion persons / km. The total volume of cargo transportation amounted to 177.94 million tons, up 15.2%, of which highway cargo transportation volume achieved 160.75 million tons and waterway cargo transportation volume reached 17.19 million. The cargo circulation volume reached 13.35 billion tons / km, of which highway cargo circulation volume hit 10.47 billion tons / km and waterway cargo circulation volume achieved 2.87 billion tons / km. The railway passenger volume (including Changzhou, Qishuyan, and Changzhou North Stations)hit 10.997 million, of which the passenger volume in Changzhou North Station amounted to 1.191 million. The passenger throughput in Changzhou Airport surpassed one million, which is 1.078 million, up 15.5%, becoming one of the national medium airports. The cargo throughput achieved 11,000, up 32.3%. Flights taking off and landing reached 22,367 sorties, of which 11,384 sorties are for transportation. The volume of freight handled at ports achieved 89.98 million tons, of which Yangtze River Changzhou Port made 26.66 million tons. By the end of 2012, the amount of vehicles reached 955,000 sets, up 8.3%; while the amount of private vehicles reached 727,000 sets, a rise of 29.8%, including 540,000 sets of private cars, up 24.3%.

Telecommunication services made a steady development. The income of post business reached 670 million yuan all the year around, up 14.1% over the previous year. The amounts of letter and express mail services were 110 million pieces and 5.062 million pieces respectively, a rise of 14.0% and 23.8% respectively. The income of communication business reached 5.92 billion yuan, up 9.9% over the previous year. By the end of this year, the number of local telephone subscribers was 1.616 million, and the number of mobile phone subscribers was 5.194 million, including 879,000 3G phone subscribers. The number of Internet subscribers reached 1.279 million, an increase of 22.2% over the beginning of this year, of which the number of broadband network subscribers was 1.174 million, up 25.9%.

Finance and Insurance

The financial-service capability has been upgrading. By the end of this year, the balance of deposits among financial institutions reached 560.49 billion yuan, 70.29 billion yuan more and 14.3% higher than that at the beginning of 2012; while the balance of loans achieved 383.28 billion yuan, increasing 42.65 billion yuan and up 12.5% over the beginning of this year. In various kinds of balance of loans, short-term loans reached 209.54 billion yuan, 13.9% higher than that at the beginning of this year, of which personal loans and overdrafts contributed 21.17 billion yuan, up 26.1%; business operating loans made RMB 166.99 billion yuan, up 13.3%; medium and long-term loans achieved 161.87 billion yuan, increased by 9.2% comparing with that at the beginning of this year, of which personal loans contributed 5 billion yuan, up 11.4% and business operating loans were 13.86 billion yuan, up 43.5%. Two branches of joint-stock commercial banks and four branches of science and technology banks were newly established. One rural bank was founded.

Insurance business increased steadily. By the end of 2012, Changzhou had a total of 61 insurance institutions, an increase of four institutions over last year, among which there were 35 life insurance institutions and the rest were property insurance institutions. The gross income of insurance amounted to 10.94 billion yuan, an increase of 16.9%, including 7.56 billion yuan of life insurance and 3.38 billion yuan of property insurance, increased by 18.3% and 13.7% respectively. The expenditure of insurance indemnity reached 2.12 billion yuan, increased by 27.7%, of which 220 million yuan was spent on life insurance, a rise of 8.7%, and 1.9 billion yuan was spent on property insurance, an increase of 30.4%. 880 million yuan was spent on other insurance indemnity, increased by 1.9%.

The securities and exchange continued to slump. The turnover of various securities in 24 security-exchange offices reached 349.38 billion yuan, decreased by 27.8%, of which the turnover of bond exchange contributed 10.29 billion yuan, an increase of 9.61 billion yuan; the turnover of stock exchange and fund exchange made 333.82 billion yuan and 5.27 billion yuan respectively, dropped by 30.2% and 0.5% respectively. By the end of this year, the number of cash accounts was 626,000, up 17.0%, including A-share stock market value of 30.18 billion yuan, increased by 3.0%.

Listed companies were steadily promoted. Two more listed companies were added, of which the Yuxing shares got listed on Shenzhen GEM, raising funds of 840 million yuan; Metro Development listed on the Hong Kong Main Board of the Stock Exchange, raising funds of 1.65 billion yuan. By the end of this year, 34 enterprises in Changzhou got listed on the stock market, raising a total of 27.67 billion yuan, up 9.9% over the previous year.

Tourism

Tourism industry developed in a fast pace. The total tourism income of the city achieved 52.034 billion yuan and the total number of visitors hit 40.0384 million all the year around, up 22.2% and 17.7% respectively over the previous year. The city received 39.5827 million person-times of domestic tourists, contributing 49.037 billion yuan, up 17.8% and 23.1% respectively; and received 455,700 person-times of overseas tourists, producing foreign exchange earnings from tourism of 474 million US dollars, up 10.3% and 12.6% respectively. A group of programs such as 4D Roller Coaster in the Magical Rainforest of China Dinosaur Park, the Amusement Park of Yancheng Remains of Spring & Autumn Period, the Chinese Dragon Tower of Global Animation Joyland, the historical and cultural area of Nanshan Bamboo Forest Phrase II, the Tianning Pagoda Karma Palace, and so on have been advanced and improved, injecting new vitality into the tourism industry of the city. By the end of this year, Changzhou had one National

AAAAA Tourist Attraction, 12 National AAAA Scenic Spots, 17 National Demonstration Scenic Spots of Industry and Agriculture, 15 Jiangsu Provincial AAAA Rural Scenic Spots, three Provincial Industrial Scenic Spots and six Jiangsu Provincial Bases for Self-driving Tour. There are 120 travel agencies, two of which were ranked among the Top 20 Travel Agencies of Outstanding Contribution in Jiangsu Province; one of which were ranked among the Top 100 Travel Agencies for Outstanding Contribution in China; and 65 hotels with stars, including six five-star hotels and 26 four-star hotels.

Investment in Fixed Assets

The investment in Fixed Assets had stable growth. The amount of overall social investment in fixed assets hit 276.01 billion yuan, up 18.0% over the previous year. The investment in the primary industry reached 580 million yuan, decreased by 42.1%; the investment in secondary and tertiary industries made 153.4 billion yuan and 122.04 billion yuan respectively, up 18.4% and 18.1% respectively. The industrial investment structure was optimized, making 152.6 billion yuan, up 18.0%, contributing 55.2% to the social investment growth, 0.6 percentage points higher than that of last year. In the industrial investment, the investment in equipments and tools and instruments made 84.57 billion yuan, an increase of 18.2%.

The development of investment in real estate slowed down. Real estate companies completed investment of 59.70 billion yuan all the year around, up 5.5% over the previous year, among which the residential investment contributed 41.61 billion yuan, up 3.3% and took up 69.7% of the real estate investment; the investment of commercial business contributed 8.94 billion yuan, a rise of 8.3%. The investment of office buildings was 2.18 billion yuan, a fall of 23.0%. The area of commercial residential building under construction reached 43.144 million square meters, an increase of 9.9%, of which the newly commenced construction took an area of 11.002 million square meters, decreased by 24.2%.

II.Reform and Opening-up

Private Economy

Private economy maintained steady development. The total added value of private economy in the city achieved 266.35 billion yuan, 11.6% higher than that of the previous year calculated on comparable prices, the proportion of that to the city's total economic output increased from 66.8% to 67.1%; while the tax revenue of private economy reached 38.518 billion yuan, up 6.2%, and its proportion to the city's total tax revenue increased to 62.4%. By the end of 2012, the individually-owned businesses in Changzhou reached 183,000, with 352,000 employees, and the total registered capital of individually-owned businesses reached 8.6 billion yuan, including newly added 35,000 individually-owned businesses and 2.52 billion yuan registered capital. The number of newly added private enterprises reached 9,778, amounting to 80,000 with 1.142 million people employed in private enterprises, whose total amount of registered capital made 250.41 billion yuan, newly increased with 22.46 billion yuan.

Open Economy

Foreign trade obtained progress while overcoming difficulties. During the whole year, the total volume of imports and exports reached USD 29.03 billion, up 1.4%. The total export volume achieved USD 19.96 billion, up 3.1%; while the total import volume made USD 9.07 billion, decreased by 2.2%. The annual export of electromechanical products reached USD 10.55 billion, up 2.1%; the annual export of hi-tech products achieved USD 3.97 billion, dropped by 3.2%, including a decrease of USD 1.48 billion in photovoltaic products compared with the previous year. The ratio of the export to new developing countries and regions made increase. The growth rate of export to Eastern Europe, Latin America, Russia and Africa markets reached 19.5%, 17.3%, 12.1% and 7.1% respectively.

The quality of introduced Foreign Investment was improved. In the year of 2012, the paid-in registered foreign capital was USD 3.36 billion, an increase of 10.1% over the previous year; the industrial and commercial registered foreign capital newly increased USD 5.42 billion, up 0.2%. The number of foreign-invested projects relatively increased. The city added 44 projects each with industrial and commercial registered foreign capital above USD 30 million (containing 28 manufacturing projects), one more than that of previous year. Among these projects, four of them each made foreign capital above USD 100 million, the number of which was two more than that of the previous year. Six Fortune 500 Companies newly invested in Changzhou, among which, ThyssenKrupp AG and ABB invested in our city for the first time. Another six Fortune 500 Companies, including Bosch Rexroth and Bridgestone Cycle, added investment by the end of the year. The structure of investment companies and functional organizations made some progress. Changzhou AAC Acoustic Technologies Holdings INC, invested by AAC Technologies Holdings INC in Hong Kong, with USD 100 million registered capital, became the second investment company settled down in Changzhou, following the Lite-On Technology.

Foreign cooperation was further deepened. All the year around, the amount of newly contracted foreign investment was USD 600 million, an increase of 3.2% over the previous year; and the foreign trade turnover made USD 540 million, increased by 5.5%. By the end of 2012, there were 405 service outsourcing enterprises and nearly 30,000 employees. The service outsourcing contract value achieved USD 340 million with executed value of USD 290 million, up 24.1% and 16.1% respectively. The offshore service outsourcing contract value reached USD 260 million with offshore executed value of USD 220 million, up 15.9% and 10.7% respectively.

Construction of Development Zones

Economy of development zones moved forward smoothly. In 2012, the total fixed assets investment in development zones reached 157.39 billion yuan, among which the investment in industry reached 95.45 billion yuan and the investment in infrastructure construction achieved 19.62 billion yuan; the public finance budget revenue reached 23.44 billion yuan and industrial products sales revenue made 786.92 billion yuan. Foreign capital made a significant effect as playing a major role in development zones. The agreed industrial and commercial registered foreign investment of development zones reached USD 4.51 billion, while the paid-in foreign investment achieved USD 2.8 billion. Besides, 41 new projects each made industrial and commercial registered capital of more than USD 30 million, accounting for 93.2% of the city's total amount, among which there were 27 manufacturing projects, accounting for 96.4%.

Foreign Affairs

Foreign affairs became increasingly active. In 2012, the city received 138 foreign delegations with total 945 visitors, including seven delegations with total 79 members at vice-minister level and above; 37 investigation missions with total 278 officials from foreign embassies and consulates; and 19 journalist delegations with total 78 members. Changzhou had established sister-city relationship with 16 foreign cities, including a new sister city, Lommel of Belgium. By the end of the year, the city had received 36 delegations with total 289 visitors from sister cities and sent 24 delegations with total 160 members to visit them. Changzhou was honored the Award for 'International Sister City Strategic Development' at the 2012 China Cities Forum and the Award for 'International Friendly Communication and Cooperation' at the 2012 China International Friendship Cities Conference.

III. Social Undertaking

Science and Technology

Technological innovation was continuously strengthened. In 2012, the government invested 1.933 billion yuan in science and technology research, increased by 39.4%. The city had recognized 797 hi-tech enterprises, including 208 newly added ones; and had obtained 451 science and technology projects above provincial level, receiving funding of 490 million yuan; and successfully held the Changzhou Exhibition for Advanced Manufacturing Technology Achievements, organized 13 significant production-teaching-research activities and added 316 production-teaching-research cooperation programs. During the whole year, the number of patent applications achieved 39,391, increased by 68.4% over 2012, among which 10,123 were patent of invention applications; and the number of patent authorizations made 15,379, among which 1,188 were patent of invention authorizations. Besides, the amount of ownership of invention patent per 10,000 people grew from 4.77 to 7.59. Changzhou National Development Zone and Wujin Hi-tech Development Zone were classified among the first batch of Jiangsu Provincial Demonstration Zones for Science-technology-finance Cooperation Innovation, and Wujin Hi-tech Development Zone was promoted as one of the National Development Zones.

Innovation system was constantly optimized. Changzhou worked hard to accelerate the construction of innovative foundations. The program called 'One Scientific Center & Eight Industrial Parks' had attracted 932 industries to settle in, and the total sales volume broke 100 billion yuan, up 44.8%. The number of R&D agencies in Changzhou Science and Education Town amounted to 101. And the number of hi-tech industries reached 635, which employed more than 15,000 various kinds of R&D personnel. In 2012, the city newly built 150 projects referred as 'Two Stations and Three Centers', and the total number reached 775. The city strengthened the innovation in industries. There were 620 large-and-medium-sized industrial enterprises with R&D agencies, occupying 90% of the total. The construction of incubators and accelerators was speeded up, among which Changzhou Biopharmaceutical Business Incubator was widely applied and Changzhou Creative Industries Park was entitled as the only prefecture-level city and the only Jiangsu city among the first batch of National Demonstration Bases for Culture-technology Integration. Besides, the city had newly added 10 state incubators, 33 provincial incubators and two provincial accelerators, amounting to 64 incubators and accelerators above municipal level in total. The characteristic of the cooperation of enterprises, universities and research institutes was highlighted. In 2012, the city successfully hosted Changzhou Exhibition for Advanced Manufacturing Technology Achievements and signed contracts of 34 key projects, of which the technology contracts of 16 key industrial projects amounted to 239 million yuan.

The gathering of creative talents was speeded up. By the end of the year, there were 396 leading talents signing to start their businesses in Changzhou. The city had introduced 1,200 leading talents, including 108 selected from the National One Thousand Talents Introduction Plan and 145 from the Jiangsu Provincial Innovation and Entrepreneurship Talents, fostering a good atmosphere for innovation and entrepreneurship through the concept of 'Providing a platform, introducing talents, incubating enterprises and cultivating industries'. The city established Changzhou Hi-tech Enterprises Association to strengthen the interaction and exchange between entrepreneurs. Besides, Changzhou set up special projects to produce technological entrepreneurs, and organized two groups of leading officials of hi-tech enterprises with total 115 members to participate in training courses for technological entrepreneurs.

Education

Educational undertakings were steadily advanced. By the end of the year, Changzhou had a total of 617 various kinds of full-time schools, 735,900 full-time students, and 52,600 faculty members, among which 41,300 were full-time teachers. The development of preschool education was quickened. There were 32 kindergartens newly constructed or renovated, and the proportion of public kindergartens had increased, accounting for 75%, the proportion and enrollment rate of municipal quality kindergartens reached over 80% and 90% respectively. All county-level cities and districts under the administration of Changzhou had established the Allocation System of Public Funds per Student for Preschool Education and Tuition. Compulsory education was further balanced. 70% admission quota of hot high schools was allocated to all junior high schools, and 88.91% children of migrant employees were enrolled into public schools. The number of proportion and enrollment rate of quality schools at the preschool education stage reached 84.2% and 86.7% respectively. The city implemented the project of Improving High School Quality and initiated the Pilot Project and Curriculum Base for Creative Talents Training. Four schools and six projects passed the examination and were selected as Municipal Projects for Training High School Creative Talents. The admission rate of second-tier undergraduate college entrance examination (including sport and art)reached 56.34% (63.11% in urban city), an increase of 6% over previous year. The construction of Provincial Innovation & Development Experimental Zone for Vocational Education was further improved, and the construction of Yincun Vocational Education Park was launched. In 2012, the students participated in provincial skills competitions won 54 first prizes (including 31 champions of first prizes for projects). The city totally owned five National Secondary Vocational Education Reform & Development Demonstration Schools and 20 Provincial Renowned Special Major Programs. The acceptance rate of higher vocational education entrance examination and undergraduate or associate college admission ranked the first place for 13 consecutive years. The programs for lifelong learning was further enhanced. By the end of 2012, Changzhou had one National Community Education Demonstration Area, one National Community Education Experimental Site and seven National Demonstration Towns (Sub-districts)of Community Education, and achieved full coverage of Provincial Community Training Schools and Education Experimental Sites. The city owned 22 Provincial Community Education Centers and eight Provincial Demonstration Towns (Sub-districts)of Community Education, and established 10 Lifelong Learning Service Bases for the public. The city had 24 municipal-level standardized Adult Education Centers and 103 municipal-level standardized Villagers' (Residents')Schools. The informationization of education was advanced. 40 schools were recognized as Municipal E-learning Project Schools and 13 schools were selected as Provincial E-learning Experimental Spots. Changzhou also strengthened the assistance for students in straitened situation. A total of 223 million yuan allocated from government and 7.35 million yuan funded through social donation were used to help these students. The internationalization of education made new progress. Changzhou Trina International School succeeded in its first-year enrollment, and 25 schools were recognized as the first batch of Changzhou Pilot International Schools for Understanding of Education.

Culture

The creation of excellent works achieved marked results. The original dancing drama Kelsang Flowers & Jasmine Flowers claimed the gold award of drama and other seven individual awards. The film The Seal of Love, the children's drama Left-behind Children and the broadcasting drama Shi Liang won the national prize of the Five-one Project; and Youthful Teenagers, created by Changzhou Farce Troupe, was successfully selected into the 9th National Children's Drama Performance; and the original symphony Xi Ju (opera)The Wandering Songstress, created by Changzhou Xi Ju Theater, won the provincial prize of the Five-one Project; the first Changzhou dialect long story Changzhou Bai Tai Guan, created by Changzhou Folk Art Group, won the Literature Award of the Peony Award, which is the highest fork art award in China.

Cultural service was effectively promoted. Changzhou Library was established as the first TV Library in Jiangsu Province, covering over 1 million end-users. In 2012, various kinds of open-free and non-profit cultural units held over 500 various cultural and art exhibitions. Last year, 300 showing-times dramas and more than 10,000 showing-times movies were open for free. The programs of One Public Cultural Sphere per 15-minute Walk in urban areas and One Cultural Sphere Every Five Kilometers in rural areas were further optimized. The first-phase construction of Smart Community was basically finished, benefiting 100,000 households. Broadcasting, television, and press and publishing maintained steady development. The city owned 1,080 printing enterprises, 894 publishing enterprises and 351 audio-video products operating entities. The annual value of printing enterprises was over 7 billion yuan and the box-office performance obtained nearly 200 million yuan. Besides, the registration of works' copyright increased by 30%, amounting to more than 700 pieces. The comprehensive coverage rate of radio and TV programs reached 100%. And the number of digital TV subscribers reached 1.09 million, up 2.1% over the previous year. During 2012, Changzhou Daily and Changzhou Evening published 30.832 million and 35.163 million copies respectively.

The protection of cultural relics made remarkable achievements. The tomb of Qian Yiben was successfully discovered at Wujin Taihu Lake Bay. The exploration of Xiangdun Ruins and the archaeological survey and exploration in the Taihu Lake Art Town was successfully advanced. By the end of the year, the city had owned 1,677 immovable cultural heritages, including five National

Cultural Relic Protection Units, 50 Provincial Cultural Relic Protection Units and 235 Municipal and Prefectural Cultural Relic Protection Units. Besides, there were three Provincial Historical and Cultural Blocks and 48 Historical Architectures in Changzhou. Tasks concerning the Declaration of National Historical and Cultural City were in full progress.

Health Care

The level of health service was constantly improved. By the end of the year, the city had owned 1,128 medical and health institutions of various kinds, with a total of 20,497 hospital beds and 25,300 health technical personnel including 10,094 medical practitioners (or mediatinus)and 10,192 registered nurses. For per 1,000 permanent residents, there were 5.39 health technical personnel and 4.37 hospital beds. The security of new-type rural cooperative medical care system was improved, with 100% coverage rate and capital funding of 360 yuan per person, a rise of 55 yuan over 2011. The hospitalization subsidy rate on the range of county and township policy was 76.13%, and the actual hospitalization subsidy rate was 51.98%. The Total Outpatient Prospective Payment Reform was fully implemented. Three regions implemented the Hospitalization Costs Mixed Payment Reform. Public health services were gradually equitable. The standardized subsidy of 45 yuan per person was used in special funds, and 10 categories with 41 sections of basic public health services and seven categories of major public health services were fully progressed. The basic health services was constantly strengthened with six newly recognized provincial example township hospitals and one national and provincial demonstration community health services centers. Besides, the infrastructure was successfully implemented, among which, the floors of comprehensive building of Changzhou No.1 People's Hospital was filled, Changzhou No.2 People's Hospital (Yanghu Branch)was applied into practice, Changzhou No.4 Hospital (Xinbei Branch)started trial operation, the ward building of Children's Hospital of Changzhou was placed in operation, and the exterior construction of the outpatient and emergency comprehensive ward building of Changzhou No.7 Hospital was finished.

Sports

Sports undertaking was continuously developed. In 2012, Changzhou held seven world-class sporting events, as well as 14 national tournaments and 19 provincial competitions. Through the year, Changzhou athletes won 40 champions in major competitions, including two world champions, three Asian champions and 35 national champions. The nationwide fitness campaign was effectively promoted. The city newly built 83 community fitness centers, 20 more than that of previous year. The program of One Sports and Fitness Site within 10-minute Walk in urban communities had achieved progress, which was rewarded the Outstanding Organization Award of National Nationwide Fitness Activities for 16 consecutive years. The sales volume of sports lottery in the whole year reached 1.32 billion yuan, a year-on-year increase of 22.1% .

IV. Population, Livelihood and Social Security

Population & Employment

The population size remained stable. By the end of the year, the registered household population of Changzhou totaled 3.648 million, 0.5% higher than the same period of last year. In the whole registered household population, the male population reached 1.816 million, up 0.4%; while the ratio of male to female was 99.1:100; the population aged above 60 reached 772,000, occupying 21.2% of total. The population of temporary residents reached 1.55 million, up 16.5% over the previous year. The planned birth rate was 98.9%, while the controlled birth rate and one-child per family rate reached 86.7% and 77.4% respectively. In 2012, the newly-born population rate was 9.4%, while the death population rate was 7.9%. The natural population growth rate was 1.5%.

The process of employment and entrepreneurship was effectively advanced. 105,000 workers were employed and 10,532 workers who used to have difficulties in getting jobs were assisted to be reemployed. Zero-employment families were given a priority. Changzhou higher educated graduates were fully employed and the graduates from most needy families were 100% employed. 6,875 people who started their own businesses received government support, which in turn created 41,250 jobs. By the end of the year, the unemployment rate registered in urban areas was within 2.37%. The city successfully established eight Provincial Demonstration Communities of Full Employment. As a result, Changzhou won the title of National Advanced City for Entrepreneurship. 1,271 disable people were resettled to be employed in 2012.

People's Lives

The residents' income and expenditure maintained steady growth. Urban residents' annual per capita disposable income reached 33,587 yuan, increased by 12.6% year-on-year, a 9.9% growth in real terms after deducting the price factor; while the per capita expenditure on consumption amounted to 20,519 yuan, a rise of 9.6%, including 7,406 yuan consumption of food, up 9.6%. The urban residents' Engel coefficient (the proportion of food expenditure in consumer expenditure)reached 36.1%, 0.3% higher than that of previous year. The per capita net income of rural residents made 16,737 yuan, an increase of 12.8%. The per capita living expenditure achieved 12,027 yuan, grew by 7.3%. The rural residents' Engel coefficient reached 36.1%, 0.6% higher than that of previous year. By the end of the year, the balance of savings of deposits of residents surged to 247.33 billion yuan, an increase of 31.59 billion yuan over that of the beginning of the year, up 14.6%.

Housing security was actively boosted. In 2012, there were 25,103 security houses newly came into establishment in the whole city, including 13,414 public rental houses (which contained low-rent houses), 869 economically affordable houses, and 3,566 low-cost commercial residential buildings, as well as 7,254 resettlement houses which were reconstructed based on the dilapidated buildings in shanty areas. Construction of 7,371 security houses were completed, including 3,575 public rental houses (which contained low-rent houses), 859 economically affordable houses and 1,515 low-cost commercial residential buildings, as well as 1,422 resettlement houses which were renovated based on the dilapidated building in shanty areas. An addition of 642 families received subsidies for low-rent housing. 1,175 low-rent houses and public rental houses were allocated by the government to 375 low-rent housing families and 1,400 public rental housing families.

Market Prices

The price level increased mildly. The CPI (Consumer Price Index)of the whole year was 102.5. Among the prices of eight major categories of commodities and services, 'Six of them rose while two of them fell'. The food prices increased by 4.9%; the prices of tobacco and wine grew by 3.3%; the prices of clothing went up 1.6%; the prices of household appliances and maintenance rose by 7.2%; entertainment, education, cultural products and services prices climbed by 1.0%; housing prices increased by 2.5%; the prices of medical care and personal items decreased by 0.4%; and the prices of transportation and telecommunications dropped by 0.6%.

Social Security

Social security was continuously optimized. In 2012, the coverages of five major types of insurance, i.e. pension, medical, unemployment, occupational injury and maternity insurances, increased by 63,200, 79,900, 61,800, 110,400 and 65,600 people respectively. By the end of the year, 1,211,300 people joined the pension insurance, up 6.5% over the same period of last year; 959,800 people joined the unemployment insurance, 7.9% higher than previous year; 1,628,700 people joined the medical insurance for workers in urban and township areas, 7.3% higher than last year. The total income of the funds of five major types of insurance achieved 15,333 billion yuan, 29.3% higher than last year, while the expenses made 11.494 billion yuan, 22.8% higher than previous year. The average monthly pension of urban enterprise employees increased to 1,849 yuan. The basic monthly pension of social endowment insurance of urban and rural residents increased to 110 yuan/per month. The proportions of medi-care insured employees and urban residents applying for reimbursement of hospitalization within the prescribed limit reached 89.3% and 70.5% respectively.

Social Welfare and Relief

Social aid was constantly promoted. By the end of 2012, the number of various nursing homes reached 178, an increase of 86 over last year. The total number of beds in nursing homes reached 24,678, taking care of 17,442 eld. 28,628 households and 52,526 residents were included in the subsistence allowance system, among which there were 10,035 households and 18,287 residents in urban areas and 18,593 households and 34,239 residents in rural areas. 140 million yuan of subsistence allowance was issued. In 2012, 28,786 person-times received medical aid, 13,204 more than last year, and the amount of aid funding reached 23 million yuan. Welfare lottery tickets worth 1.06 billion yuan were released throughout the year, up 14.3% over the previous year. Legal aid work was continuously optimized. 3,633 various legal-aid cases were accepted, an increase of 27.5% over last year, while a variety of legal consulting services was provided to 25,000 person-times, a rise of 27% over last year.

Charitable Aid was further implemented. During the whole year, all levels of charity foundations allocated a total of 116 million yuan of aid funds and supported 80,000 person-times of people in straitened situation, among which, Changzhou Charity Federation (including four branches)distributed total funding of 44.3925 million yuan and benefited more than 33,300 person-times of people in straitened situation. Last year, the activities for aiding people who need help respectively funded 772,000 yuan for old people, 794,800 yuan for orphans, 1,965,400 yuan for students, 3,269,600 yuan for poor people, 749,500 yuan for disabled people and 9,338,600 yuan for people in medical treatment. The Caring for People with Severe Diseases---- Changzhou Charitable Aid program raised by Changzhou Charity Federation was entitled the Award of Service Excellence of National Civil Affairs System.

V. Urban and Rural Construction

Infrastructure Construction

Infrastructure construction was steadily advancing. The investment in transportation construction achieved 7.43 billion yuan. Newly built highway within this year reached 20.2 km; renovation and expansion of national and provincial highways were 41 km; newly remodeled rural roads were 210 km and the number of newly built bridges were 111; water conservancy construction earthworks were 14.971 million cubic meters; 25 square kilometers water and soil erosion area were restored; and the investment in water conservancy construction in rural areas was 430 million yuan. The south terminal program of Taizhou Bridge was finished and opened to traffic. The Changzhou-Liyang highway was under construction. The construction of 'three vertical and three horizontal' road network was accelerated. Daming Road and the eastern section of East Laodong Road were completed. The construction of Longcheng Avenue tunnel and Yulong Road was speeded up. The expansion of the Riverside Sewage Treatment Plant Phase Ⅲ and the spare installed project of Weicun Water Plant were finished. Major public under-built infrastructures such as the construction of main venues of Flower Expo and its supporting facilities, the construction of Modern Media Center, and the renovation of Qingguo Lane were actively promoted. The urban rail transit construction plan was approved by the State. The implementation of Metro construction was speeded up: the construction of new sections, such as Phoenix Metro and Zhonglou Metro, was promoted comprehensively, and the construction of the East Gate Project was in smooth progress.

Public Utility

The public transportation network was constantly improved. At the end of year, there were 197 urban bus lines with 2,590 buses. The city added or updated 200 buses and increased or optimized 47 bus lines. The total transport capacity made 411.90 million passengers, with daily transport capacity of 1.2 million passengers. The rate of public transportation reached 26.4%. The public transportation in 19 towns and villages of Jintan and Wujin has been successfully launched. Bus lines for towns and villages achieved a total of 213, realizing the full coverage in towns and villages.

The public services system kept improving. The total consumption of electricity in Changzhou reached 35.15 billion kwh the whole year, up 6%, among which the household electricity consumption of urban and rural residents amounted to 3.22 billion kwh, increased by 14.8%. The total urban water supply amount reached 274 million cubic meters, including domestic water use of 117 million cubic meters, with the coverage rate of running water reaching 100%. By the end of this year, 502,400 families became users of natural gas, up 1.1% over the end of last year. The rate of liquefied gas supply of the whole city reached 99.7%. The daily treatment capacity of domestic sewage achieved 635,000 tons, and sewage water treatment rate in the urban area made 95.5%. By the end of the year, the number of street lamps was 173,000, increased by 5.9% compared with the end of last year. The annual clearance volume of household garbage was 914,000 tons and the non-hazardous treatment ratio of household garbage reached 100%.

VI.Environmental Protection and Resource Conservation

Environmental Protection and Treatment

The ecological civilization made solid progress. The construction of National Ecological Civilization Model City was comprehensively launched. The water environment treatment in river course and the protection of water source construction has been enhanced. The quality of the three water channels flowing into Taihu Lake, as well as the other lakes was further improved. The renovations for 41 black and odorous water channels in suburban area were finished. There were 337 days with air quality above the good level this year. Focus has been put on to promote the coordinated ecological development in urban and rural areas, 8 National Ecological Towns create the smooth passage of national acceptance within this year, and newly built 2 provincial Eco-Streets and 23 provincial Eco-Villages .

Urban Greening

The green level was continually improved. By the end of 2012, the green areas of built-up regions covered 7,072 hectares, including park green lands of 1,759 hectares, up 6.4% and 3.3% respectively; and the per capita park green area in urban Changzhou achieved 12.5 square meters. The rate of greenery coverage of built up area was 42.21%, an increase of 0.04 percentage points over last year; meanwhile, the rate of green land coverage of built up area was 38.59%, up 0.19 percentage points over the previous years. The construction of the Theme Garden of Culture Against Corruption at Lotus Park was finished within the year. Changzhou Venue in the main exhibition area of the China Flower Expo (Wujin)started construction. The construction of Dingtang River Wetland Park, Phoenix Park and Xinlong National Forest Park in Xinbei District progressed smoothly. To implement the project of building the "Flower City", the landscape upgrading and rose planting of Airport Road and Zhongwu Avenue was completed. The environmental restoration project in rural area was finished, where the green coverage rate reached more than 30% .

Note:The statistical data in the communiqué are calculated on current price except those calculated on comparable price as specially defined.

2

CHAPTER 2

排 名 榜

LIST OF TOP STRENGTHS

常州统计年鉴

2-1 工业企业主营业务收入前 100 名单位（2012 年）
TOP 100 INDUSTRIAL ENTERPRISES BY MAIN BUSINESS INCOME（2012）

序号 No.	企业名称 Name of Enterprises	序号 No.	企业名称 Name of Enterprises
1	中天钢铁集团有限公司	26	国茂减速机集团有限公司
2	江苏申特钢铁有限公司	27	百兴集团有限公司
3	亚邦投资控股集团有限公司	28	常州东昊化工有限公司
4	江苏新时代控股集团有限公司	29	常柴股份有限公司
5	常州金源铜业有限公司	30	江苏蓝色星球环保科技股份有限公司
6	常州东方特钢有限公司	31	常州东风农机集团有限公司
7	常州市盛洲铜业有限公司	32	国电常州发电有限公司
8	江苏上上电缆集团有限公司	33	常州龙源港机重工集团有限公司
9	华润包装材料有限公司	34	现代（江苏）工程机械有限公司
10	江苏国强镀锌实业有限公司	35	常州市英中电气有限公司
11	常州亚邦化学有限公司	36	常州华利达服装集团有限公司
12	常州天合光能有限公司	37	江苏常宝钢管股份有限公司
13	江苏江南实业集团有限公司	38	江苏诚达石化工业有限公司
14	常州新日化学有限公司	39	常州海杰冶金机械制造有限公司
15	新誉集团有限公司	40	江苏华电戚墅堰发电有限公司
16	新华昌集团有限公司	41	常州岩松金属制品有限公司
17	瑞声声学科技（常州）有限公司	42	天合光能（常州）科技有限公司
18	江苏华鹏变压器有限公司	43	江苏常发农业装备股份有限公司
19	南车戚墅堰机车有限公司	44	常州神力电机股份有限公司
20	常州安凯特电缆有限公司	45	常州市亚达铜业有限公司
21	光宝科技（常州）有限公司	46	小松（常州）工程机械有限公司
22	江苏今创投资经营有限公司	47	江苏常隆化工有限公司
23	江苏鸿开有色金属有限公司	48	常州老三集团有限公司
24	江苏新科数字技术股份有限公司	49	常州格力博工具有限公司
25	江苏旷达汽车织物集团股份有限公司	50	江苏正昌集团有限公司

2-1 续表 continued

序号 No.	企业名称 Name of Enterprises	序号 No.	企业名称 Name of Enterprises
51	常州常松金属复合材料有限公司	76	卡尔迈耶（中国）有限公司
52	江苏金昇实业股份有限公司	77	梅特勒-托利多（常州）测量技术有限公司
53	东华纺织集团有限公司	78	常州市名杰建材设备制造有限公司
54	莱尼电气线缆（常州）有限公司	79	江苏武进不锈钢管厂集团有限公司
55	常州亿晶光电科技有限公司	80	金坛正信光伏电子有限公司
56	江苏金峰水泥集团有限公司	81	常州明谛树脂有限公司
57	江苏中东化肥股份有限公司	82	常州世鑫化工有限公司
58	中电装备东芝（常州）变压器有限公司	83	常州宝菱重工机械有限公司
59	溧阳市宏峰水泥有限公司	84	常州赛迪电气制造有限公司
60	常州西电变压器有限责任公司	85	常州东奥服装有限公司
61	江苏顺风光电科技有限公司	86	常林股份有限公司
62	常州亿禾铝业有限公司	87	今创集团股份有限公司
63	溧阳市新金峰水泥有限公司	88	盘固水泥集团有限公司
64	常州市正和电磁线有限公司	89	江苏常发制冷股份有限公司
65	南车戚墅堰机车车辆工艺研究所有限公司	90	江苏沙钢集团鑫瑞特钢有限公司
66	溧阳市万兴特种建材有限公司	91	常州龙宇颜料化学有限公司
67	江苏正信新能源科技集团有限公司	92	常州星宇车灯股份有限公司
68	中盐常州化工股份有限公司	93	常州昌瑞汽车部品制造有限公司
69	江苏安格特科技发展有限公司	94	常州市牛塘化工厂有限公司
70	常州兆阳光能科技有限公司	95	江苏华威世纪电子集团有限公司
71	森萨塔科技（常州）有限公司	96	江苏安格特新材料科技有限公司
72	常州常发动力机械有限公司	97	溧阳市宏瑞精密铸造有限公司
73	江苏新鸿联集团有限公司	98	常州豪爵铃木摩托车有限公司
74	江苏金牛线缆集团有限公司	99	中韩科技有限公司
75	常州协鑫光伏科技有限公司	100	常州华日升反光材料有限公司

2-2 工业企业实现利税前 100 名单位（2012 年）
TOP 100 INDUSTRIAL ENTERPRISES BY PROFITS AND TAXES（2012）

序号 No.	企业名称 Name of Enterprises	序号 No.	企业名称 Name of Enterprises
1	江苏申特钢铁有限公司	26	江苏金峰水泥集团有限公司
2	新誉集团有限公司	27	今创集团股份有限公司
3	常州市盛洲铜业有限公司	28	溧阳市新金峰水泥有限公司
4	瑞声声学科技（常州）有限公司	29	黑牡丹集团股份有限公司
5	江苏新时代控股集团有限公司	30	江苏恒立高压油缸股份有限公司
6	亚邦投资控股集团有限公司	31	华润包装材料有限公司
7	中天钢铁集团有限公司	32	常州市英中电气有限公司
8	江苏国强镀锌实业有限公司	33	常州四药制药有限公司
9	常州东方特钢有限公司	34	百兴集团有限公司
10	江苏华电戚墅堰发电有限公司	35	常州海杰冶金机械制造有限公司
11	江苏江南实业集团有限公司	36	现代（江苏）工程机械有限公司
12	江苏华鹏变压器有限公司	37	江苏武进不锈钢管厂集团有限公司
13	江苏蓝色星球环保科技股份有限公司	38	创生医疗器械（中国）有限公司
14	新华昌集团有限公司	39	常州港华燃气有限公司
15	国电常州发电有限公司	40	江苏正信新能源科技集团有限公司
16	常州龙源港机重工集团有限公司	41	常州神力电机股份有限公司
17	常州安凯特电缆有限公司	42	安费诺（常州）连接系统有限公司
18	常州亿禾铝业有限公司	43	常州星宇车灯股份有限公司
19	溧阳市宏峰水泥有限公司	44	盘固水泥集团有限公司
20	卡尔迈耶（中国）有限公司	45	常州金源铜业有限公司
21	江苏今创投资经营有限公司	46	溧阳市万兴特种建材有限公司
22	国茂减速机集团有限公司	47	梅特勒-托利多（常州）测量技术有限公司
23	江苏上上电缆集团有限公司	48	常州华利达服装集团有限公司
24	江苏旷达汽车织物集团股份有限公司	49	常州制药厂有限公司
25	江苏常发农业装备股份有限公司	50	常州科研试制中心有限公司

2-2 续表 continued

序号 No.	企业名称 Name of Enterprises	序号 No.	企业名称 Name of Enterprises
51	溧阳罗地亚稀土新材料有限公司	76	中盐金坛盐化有限责任公司
52	安费诺（常州）高端连接器有限公司	77	森萨塔科技（常州）有限公司
53	安费诺—泰姆斯（常州）通讯设备有限公司	78	常州市亚达铜业有限公司
54	金坛市飞达柴油机配件厂	79	江苏金昇实业股份有限公司
55	江苏斯达工业科技有限公司	80	常州常宝精特钢管有限公司
56	常州千红生化制药股份有限公司	81	常州市康辉医疗器械有限公司
57	常州市荣立机械有限公司	82	金坛市科宇合金铸钢有限公司
58	常州首创服饰有限公司	83	普利司通（常州）汽车配件有限公司
59	常州市名杰建材设备制造有限公司	84	常州盘石水泥有限公司
60	常州市武进凤市电子集团有限公司	85	常州市联中混凝土有限公司
61	常州亚邦化学有限公司	86	南车戚墅堰机车车辆工艺研究所有限公司
62	金坛市海林稀土有限公司	87	常州市同和纺织机械制造有限公司
63	江苏兴荣美乐铜业有限公司	88	江苏常隆化工有限公司
64	江苏安格特科技发展有限公司	89	溧阳市三维铸造有限公司
65	常州博瑞电力自动化设备有限公司	90	常州旷达织物整理有限公司
66	江苏中东化肥股份有限公司	91	江苏春江农化有限公司
67	常州市正和电磁线有限公司	92	南车戚墅堰机车有限公司
68	常州润源电力建设有限公司	93	金坛市金冠化工有限公司
69	常州常发动力机械有限公司	94	江苏裕兴薄膜科技股份有限公司
70	常州赛迪电气制造有限公司	95	常州乐士雷利电机有限公司
71	溧阳市宏瑞精密铸造有限公司	96	江苏领航材料科技有限公司
72	江苏溧阳南方水泥有限公司	97	空气化工产品（常州）有限公司
73	中电装备东芝（常州）变压器有限公司	98	常州侨裕旅游用品有限公司
74	江苏常宝钢管股份有限公司	99	常州市华菱涂料有限公司
75	江苏正昌集团有限公司	100	江苏智思机械集团有限公司

2-3 工业企业实现利润前 100 名单位（2012 年）
TOP 100 INDUSTRIAL ENTERPRISES BY PROFITS（2012）

序号 No.	企业名称 Name of Enterprises	序号 No.	企业名称 Name of Enterprises
1	新誉集团有限公司	26	江苏今创投资经营有限公司
2	江苏新时代控股集团有限公司	27	今创集团股份有限公司
3	江苏申特钢铁有限公司	28	常州港华燃气有限公司
4	常州市盛洲铜业有限公司	29	江苏金峰水泥集团有限公司
5	江苏国强镀锌实业有限公司	30	溧阳市新金峰水泥有限公司
6	瑞声声学科技（常州）有限公司	31	新华昌集团有限公司
7	常州安凯特电缆有限公司	32	创生医疗器械（中国）有限公司
8	常州龙源港机重工集团有限公司	33	盘固水泥集团有限公司
9	江苏华电戚墅堰发电有限公司	34	江苏武进不锈钢管厂集团有限公司
10	常州亿禾铝业有限公司	35	常州华利达服装集团有限公司
11	江苏华鹏变压器有限公司	36	常州星宇车灯股份有限公司
12	江苏蓝色星球环保科技股份有限公司	37	安费诺（常州）高端连接器有限公司
13	国电常州发电有限公司	38	江苏正信新能源科技集团有限公司
14	卡尔迈耶（中国）有限公司	39	梅特勒–托利多（常州）测量技术有限公司
15	常州东方特钢有限公司	40	常州神力电机股份有限公司
16	中天钢铁集团有限公司	41	华润包装材料有限公司
17	国茂减速机集团有限公司	42	常州海杰冶金机械制造有限公司
18	黑牡丹集团股份有限公司	43	常州市英中电气有限公司
19	亚邦投资控股集团有限公司	44	常州千红生化制药股份有限公司
20	江苏常发农业装备股份有限公司	45	常州市荣立机械有限公司
21	江苏恒立高压油缸股份有限公司	46	常州制药厂有限公司
22	溧阳市宏峰水泥有限公司	47	安费诺–泰姆斯（常州）通讯设备有限公司
23	江苏上上电缆集团有限公司	48	常州亚邦化学有限公司
24	江苏江南实业集团有限公司	49	金坛市飞达柴油机配件厂
25	江苏旷达汽车织物集团股份有限公司	50	常州科研试制中心有限公司

2-3 续表 continued

序号 No.	企业名称 Name of Enterprises	序号 No.	企业名称 Name of Enterprises
51	安费诺（常州）连接系统有限公司	76	常州金源铜业有限公司
52	江苏常宝钢管股份有限公司	77	光宝科技（常州）有限公司
53	常州市亚达铜业有限公司	78	常州东风农机集团有限公司
54	常州市武进凤市电子集团有限公司	79	常州市名杰建材设备制造有限公司
55	江苏斯达工业科技有限公司	80	金坛市望胜合金铸钢有限公司
56	金坛市科宇合金铸钢有限公司	81	江苏春江农化有限公司
57	百兴集团有限公司	82	常州市新东方电缆有限公司
58	常州四药制药有限公司	83	普利司通（常州）汽车配件有限公司
59	常州首创服饰有限公司	84	常州市联中混凝土有限公司
60	常州博瑞电力自动化设备有限公司	85	金坛市成龙橡塑制品有限公司
61	溧阳罗地亚稀土新材料有限公司	86	常州赛迪电气制造有限公司
62	江苏溧阳南方水泥有限公司	87	江苏正昌集团有限公司
63	常州润源电力建设有限公司	88	常州乐士雷利电机有限公司
64	江苏安格特科技发展有限公司	89	常州旷达织物整理有限公司
65	江苏裕兴薄膜科技股份有限公司	90	空气化工产品（常州）有限公司
66	常州市同和纺织机械制造有限公司	91	溧阳市三维铸造有限公司
67	溧阳市万兴特种建材有限公司	92	常州市正和电磁线有限公司
68	江苏常隆化工有限公司	93	金坛市金冠化工有限公司
69	常州市康辉医疗器械有限公司	94	东华纺织集团有限公司
70	常州常发动力机械有限公司	95	常州侨裕旅游用品有限公司
71	柳工常州挖掘机有限公司	96	江苏领航材料科技有限公司
72	森萨塔科技（常州）有限公司	97	梅特勒-托利多（常州）精密仪器有限公司
73	江苏省激素研究所股份有限公司	98	常州亚细制衣有限公司
74	常州常宝精特钢管有限公司	99	布勒（常州）机械有限公司
75	金坛市海林稀土有限公司	100	江苏长海复合材料股份有限公司

2-4 批发贸易业企业商品销售总额前 10 名单位（2012 年）
TOP TEN WHOLESALE TRADE ENTERPRISES BY COMMODITIES SALES VOLUME（2012）

序号 No.	单位名称 Name of Units	序号 No.	单位名称 Name of Units
1	江苏省烟草公司常州市公司	6	江苏沙兴钢材销售有限公司
2	常州市化工轻工材料总公司	7	常州市联众商贸有限公司
3	常州市大江铜业有限公司	8	江苏和瑞升金属资源有限公司
4	常州大华进出口（集团）有限公司	9	常州圣玛隆国际贸易有限公司
5	常州天悦薄板有限公司	10	江苏中铜铜业有限公司

2-5 批发贸易业企业利税总额前 10 名单位（2012 年）
TOP TEN WHOLESALE TRADE ENTERPRISES BY PROFITS AND TAXES（2012）

序号 No.	单位名称 Name of Units	序号 No.	单位名称 Name of Units
1	江苏省烟草公司常州市公司	6	常州国电常发能源有限公司
2	常州万恒国际贸易有限公司	7	江苏和瑞升金属资源有限公司
3	梅特勒–托利多（常州）称重系统设备有限公司	8	常州老三集团进出口有限公司
4	常州正华物资回收有限公司	9	常州苏南物资再生利用有限公司
5	常州天悦薄板有限公司	10	江苏绿能再生资源有限公司

2-6 零售贸易业企业商品销售总额前 10 名单位（2012 年）
TOP TEN RETAIL TRADE ENTERPRISES BY COMMODITIES SALES VOLUME（2012）

序号 No.	单位名称 Name of Unitss	序号 No.	单位名称 Name of Units
1	江苏明都汽车集团有限公司	6	常州宝尊汽车销售服务有限公司
2	常州药业股份有限公司	7	常州市凯歌汽车销售有限公司
3	江苏万帮明都汽车有限公司	8	常州金店有限公司
4	国药控股常州有限公司	9	常州市五星电器有限公司
5	常州百货大楼股份有限公司	10	常州苏宁电器有限公司

2-7　零售贸易业企业利税总额前 10 名单位（2012 年）
TOP TEN RETAIL TRADE ENTERPRISES BY PROFITS AND TAXES（2012）

序号 No.	单位名称 Name of Units	序号 No.	单位名称 Name of Units
1	常州百货大楼股份有限公司	6	常州泰富百货集团有限责任公司
2	常州新世纪商城有限公司	7	常州外汽星豪汽车销售服务有限公司
3	常州药业股份有限公司	8	常州市五星电器有限公司
4	常州金店有限公司	9	金坛大统华购物中心有限公司
5	溧阳八佰伴商贸中心有限公司	10	江苏明都汽车集团有限公司

2-8　批发零售贸易业企业利润总额前 10 名单位（2012 年）
TOP TEN WHOLESALE AND RETAIL TRADE ENTERPRISES BY PROFITS （2012）

序号 No.	单位名称 Name of Units	序号 No.	单位名称 Name of Units
1	江苏省烟草公司常州市公司	6	常州药业股份有限公司
2	常州百货大楼股份有限公司	7	常州新世纪商城有限公司
3	常州天悦薄板有限公司	8	常州国电常发能源有限公司
4	梅特勒–托利多（常州）称重系统设备有限公司	9	常州正华物资回收有限公司
5	江苏和瑞升金属资源有限公司	10	常州外汽星豪汽车销售服务有限公司

2-9　餐饮业企业营业收入前 10 名单位（2012 年）
TOP TEN CATERING TRADE ENTERPRISES BY BUSINESS INCOME（2012）

序号 No.	单位名称 Name of Unitss	序号 No.	单位名称 Name of Units
1	大娘水饺餐饮集团股份有限公司	6	常州锦湖酒店管理有限公司
2	常州丽华快餐集团有限公司	7	溧阳泰丰餐饮有限公司
3	常州福记餐饮投资管理有限公司	8	常州富都青枫苑宾馆有限公司
4	常州市福记逸高酒店有限公司	9	常州奥体明都国际饭店有限公司
5	常州听松楼花园酒店有限公司	10	常州市长兴楼饭店有限公司

2-10 餐饮业企业利税总额前 10 名单位（2012 年）
TOP TEN CATERING TRADE ENTERPRISES BY PROFITS AND TAXES（2012）

序号 No.	单位名称 Name of Units	序号 No.	单位名称 Name of Units
1	大娘水饺餐饮集团股份有限公司	6	常州奥体明都国际饭店有限公司
2	常州丽华快餐集团有限公司	7	常州锦湖酒店管理有限公司
3	溧阳泰丰餐饮有限公司	8	常州听松楼花园酒店有限公司
4	常州福记餐饮投资管理有限公司	9	常州国安大酒店有限公司
5	常州市福记逸高酒店有限公司	10	常州湟里金鼎国际大酒店有限公司

2-11 住宿业企业营业收入前 10 名单位（2012 年）
TOP TEN HOTELS BY BUSINESS INCOME（2012）

序号 No.	单位名称 Name of Units	序号 No.	单位名称 Name of Units
1	常州富都大酒店有限公司	6	常州阳光国际大酒店有限公司
2	常州涵田度假村酒店管理有限公司	7	常州富都花园酒店有限公司
3	江苏天目湖宾馆有限公司	8	常州锦江国际大酒店有限公司
4	溧阳宾馆有限公司	9	常州大酒店有限公司
5	常州波尔曼旅游投资发展有限公司	10	常州万豪花都国际大酒店有限公司

2-12 住宿业企业利税总额前 10 名单位（2012 年）
TOP TEN HOTELS BY PROFITS AND TAXES（2012）

序号 No.	单位名称 Name of Unitss	序号 No.	单位名称 Name of Units
1	江苏天目湖宾馆有限公司	6	常州市明都大饭店管理有限公司
2	常州富都大酒店有限公司	7	金坛市九九宾馆有限公司
3	常州涵田度假村酒店管理有限公司	8	常州市和平假日大饭店有限公司
4	溧阳宾馆有限公司	9	溧阳市扬子国际大酒店有限公司
5	常州万豪花都国际大酒店有限公司	10	溧阳市公路运输有限公司皇廷国际大酒店

2-13　住宿餐饮企业利润总额前 10 名单位（2012 年）
TOP TEN ACCOMMODATION AND CATERING TRADE ENTERPRISES BY PROFITS（2012）

序号 No.	单位名称 Name of Units	序号 No.	单位名称 Name of Units
1	大娘水饺餐饮集团股份有限公司	6	常州国安大酒店有限公司
2	江苏天目湖宾馆有限公司	7	常州丽华快餐集团有限公司
3	溧阳泰丰餐饮有限公司	8	溧阳宾馆有限公司
4	常州富都大酒店有限公司	9	常州福记餐饮投资管理有限公司
5	常州涵田度假村酒店管理有限公司	10	常州奥体明都国际饭店有限公司

2-14　成交额超亿元市场前 10 名单位（2012 年）
TOP TEN MARKETS BY TANSACTION VOLUME ABOVE RMB100 MILLION （2012）

序号 No.	单位名称 Name of Units	序号 No.	单位名称 Name of Units
1	江苏凌家塘市场发展有限公司	6	常州钢材现货交易市场有限公司
2	江苏长江塑料化工交易市场有限公司	7	常州淮都金属城有限公司
3	江苏湖塘纺织城投资发展有限公司	8	江苏苏浙皖边界市场发展有限公司
4	常州市武进汽车城投资发展有限公司	9	常州龙成钢材城有限公司
5	常州市武进夏溪花木市场发展有限公司	10	江苏亚邦物流市场

2-15　出口额前 10 名单位（2012 年）
TOP TEN ENTERPRISES BY EXPORT VALUE（2012）

序号 No.	单位名称 Name of Unitss	序号 No.	单位名称 Name of Units
1	常州天合光能有限公司	6	常州亿晶光电科技有限公司
2	常州迈捷克物流有限公司	7	常州华利达服装集团有限公司
3	常州赣运捷物流有限公司	8	天合光能（常州）科技有限公司
4	华润包装材料有限公司	9	常州对外贸易有限公司
5	常州大华进出口（集团）有限公司	10	常州机械设备进出口有限公司

2-16 驰名商标和著名商标一览
RENOWNED AND DISTINGUISHED BRANDS

企业名称 Name of Enterprises	商标名称 Brand Name	主要产品 Mostly Product	颁布时间 Time of Release	所在地区 Region
驰名商标 Renowned Brand				
常柴股份有限公司	CHANGCHAI及图; 常柴CC及图	柴油机	1995年	钟楼区
常州东风农机集团有限公司	东风及图；DF及图	拖拉机	1999年	钟楼区
新科电子集团有限公司	新科Shinco	影碟机	1999年	武进区
江苏正昌集团有限公司	正　昌	饲料机械	2000年	溧阳市
常州常发动力机械有限公司	常　发	柴油机	2002年	武进区
黑牡丹（集团）股份有限公司	黑牡丹HEIMUDAN及图	牛仔布、色织布	2005年	天宁区
江苏华鹏变压器有限公司	华鹏HUA PENG	变压器	2005年	溧阳市
江苏庄臣同大有限公司	全无敌	杀虫剂、蚊香	2006年	新北区
江苏上上电缆集团有限公司	上上及图	电线、电缆	2006年	溧阳市
江苏新鸿联集团有限公司	红联及图	灯　具	2006年	武进区
亚邦投资控股集团有限公司	亚邦及图	染料、涂料	2007年	武进区
江苏兰陵化工集团有限公司	兰陵及图	防腐涂料、防火涂料	2008年	武进区
顶呱呱彩棉服饰有限公司	顶呱呱	内衣等	2008年	武进区
江苏天容集团股份有限公司	溧化LIHUA及图	农　药	2008年	溧阳市
亚邦投资控股集团有限公司	光辉GUANGHUI及图	油漆、耐酸漆	2009年	武进区
江苏庄臣同大有限公司	爱家及图	空气清新剂、杀害虫剂等	2009年	新北区
常州市武进五洋纺织机械有限公司	五洋WYFJ及图	针织机械、编织机	2010年	武进区
江苏迪邦三星轴承有限公司	三鑫SANXIN及图	圆柱滚子轴承、四列圆锥滚子轴承	2010年	武进区
江苏旷达汽车织物集团股份有限公司	旷　达	装饰布	2010年	武进区
江海环保股份有限公司	江海及图	水质稳定剂	2010年	武进区
国茂减速机集团有限公司	国茂GUOMAO及图	减速机	2010年	武进区
江苏洛基木业有限公司	洛基LODGI及图	地板、铺地木材、非金属地板等	2010年	武进区
江苏开利地毯股份有限公司	天目湖及图	地　毯	2010年	溧阳市
江苏天容集团股份有限公司	天容及图	杀害虫剂、除草剂、消灭有害植物剂	2010年	溧阳市
常州光洋轴承股份有限公司	NRB	轴承（机器零件）、传动轴承	2011年	新北区
常州银河电器有限公司	BILIN	晶体管（电子）、半导体器件、晶片（锗片）	2011年	新北区
常州市常欣电子衡器有限公司	常欣CHANGXIN及图	超载限制器	2011年	新北区
灵通投资集团有限公司	LING TONG及图	金属陈列架	2011年	武进区
常州迪邦纺织有限公司	迪邦DiBang	纱、线、棉线和棉纱	2011年	武进区
江苏太阳宝新能源有限公司	太阳宝	太阳能热水器	2011年	武进区

2-16 续表 1 continued 1

企业名称 Name of Enterprises	商标名称 Brand Name	主要产品 Mostly Product	颁布时间 Time of Release	所在地区 Region
江苏亚示照明集团有限公司	YASHIPS	灯、照明器	2011年	武进区
江苏裕成电子有限公司	裕成YUCHENG及图	自行车发动机	2011年	武进区
常州玉宇电光器件有限公司	玉 宇	灯泡、电灯	2011年	武进区
常州市武进五洋纺织机械有限公司	柳绿LLPJ及图	纺织织物、布、编织织物	2011年	武进区
今创集团股份有限公司	KTK及图	车辆行李架、车辆座位、车辆内装饰品	2011年	武进区
新城控股集团有限公司	新城及图	建筑、砖石建筑、商业摊位及商店的建筑	2011年	武进区
江苏省激素研究所股份有限公司	金珠及图	农 药	2012年	金坛市
冶建新材料股份有限公司	天虎及图	涂 料	2012年	溧阳市
江苏瑞阳化工股份有限公司	瑞阳RUI YANG及图	季戊四醇、盐类	2012年	溧阳市
常州市国宇环保科技有限公司	玉宇及图	硝酸银、催化剂	2012年	武进区
江苏晨光涂料有限公司	晨光CHENGUANG及图	氯磺化聚乙烯工业涂料	2012年	武进区
常州华通焊业股份有限公司	華通HUATONG及图	金属焊丝	2012年	武进区
常州市润源经编机械有限公司	润源及图	纺织工业用机器	2012年	武进区
常州市钱璟康复器材有限公司	钱璟及图	按摩器械等	2012年	武进区
江苏众恒染整有限公司	众恒ZHONGHENG及图	针织牛仔布	2012年	武进区
江苏天香集团有限公司	香雪及图	味 精	2012年	武进区
江苏金鼎电动工具集团有限公司	金鼎及图	电动手工具等	2012年	武进区
江苏长海复合材料股份有限公司	常海CHANGHAI及图	热敷胶粘纤维布等	2012年	武进区
江苏南洋木业有限公司	第1330307号图形	成品木材等	2012年	武进区
亚邦化工集团有限公司	金囤及图	农 药	2012年	武进区
常州远东连杆集团有限公司	滆湖GH及图	连杆总成	2012年	武进区
江苏华光粉末有限公司	剑亮及图	粉末涂料	2012年	武进区
常州方圆制药有限公司	创成及图	化学药物制剂	2012年	新北区
江苏华冠电器集团有限公司	华程HUACHENG HC	配电柜等	2012年	新北区
常州市康辉医疗器械有限公司	康辉及图	外科器械	2012年	新北区
江苏久信医用净化工程有限公司	久信JIU XIN及图	空气净化等	2012年	新北区
常州市瑞悦车业有限公司	富满及图	车辆内装饰品等	2012年	新北区
常州星宇车灯股份有限公司	星宇及图	照明防护装置等	2012年	新北区
江苏三恒科技集团有限公司	三 恒	报警器等	2012年	新北区
江苏华达化工集团有限公司	常恒CHANGHENG及图	胶粘剂等	2012年	新北区
常州市常蒸蒸发器有限公司	常蒸及图	蒸发器	2012年	新北区

2-16 续表 2 continued 2

企业名称 Name of Enterprises	商标名称 Brand Name	主要产品 Mostly Product	颁布时间 Time of Release	所在地区 Region
吟飞科技（江苏）有限公司	吟飞Ringway	乐 器	2012年	新北区
大娘水饺餐饮集团股份有限公司	吴大娘WU DA NIANG 及图	餐厅等	2012年	天宁区
常州亚玛顿股份有限公司	亞瑪頓	光学玻璃等	2012年	天宁区
常州东风农机集团有限公司	DFAM及图	拖拉机等	2012年	钟楼区
常州祥兴电机有限公司	第965963号图形	马达及其部件	2012年	戚墅堰区
著名商标 Distinguished Brand				
南京化工学院常州市武进水质稳定剂厂	颂歌及图形	水质稳定剂	2010	武进区
常州市国宇环保科技有限公司	玉宇及图形	硝酸银、催化剂、工业用纤维素醚等	2010	武进区
江苏猴王涂料有限公司	猴王牌及图形	涂 料	2010	武进区
金隆化工集团有限公司	华隆及图形	染 料	2010	武进区
江苏玉兰木业有限公司	图 形	金属地板、建筑用金属框架	2010	武进区
江苏双菱链传动有限公司	双菱及图形	滚子链条	2010	武进区
常州市武进五菱柴油机有限公司	五菱牌及图形	柴油机	2010	武进区
常州钢筘有限公司	蓝箭及图形	梳理机用齿条、钢筘	2010	武进区
常州远东连杆集团有限公司	滆湖及图形	泵油扳手总成、连杆总成	2010	武进区
江苏常嘉电器有限公司	吉诺尔及图形	洗衣机	2010	武进区
常州市永安电机有限公司	图 形	电 机	2010	武进区
江苏省范群干燥设备厂	范群及图形	食品加工机（电动）、制药加工工业用机器、化学工业用电力机械等	2010	武进区
常州常发农业装备有限公司	常发及图形	泵（机器）、液压泵、发电机（组）等	2010	武进区
江苏智思机械集团有限公司	ZS及图形	工业用卷烟机、烟草加工机	2010	武进区
常州东吴链传动制造有限公司	東傳及图形	非陆地车辆传动链、机器传动装置、机器转动装置等	2010	武进区
常州欧凯电器有限公司	OUCK	马达和引擎起动器、发电机、冰箱电机等	2010	武进区
常州联发机械有限公司	常联发及图形	柴油机、农业机械、汽油机等	2010	武进区
常州市润源经编机械有限公司	润源及图形	纺织机、编织机、缝编机等	2010	武进区
江苏金牛线缆集团有限公司	金牛及图形	电缆、电线、绝缘铜线等	2010	武进区
创生医疗器械（江苏）有限公司	创生及图形	骨科手术器械	2010	武进区
江苏康进医疗器材有限公司	康进及图形	医用导管、医用注射器、医疗器械和仪器等	2010	武进区
常州西武暖通设备有限公司	真乐及图形	散热器、空气调节设备	2010	武进区
常州市凯凯照明电器有限公司	图 形	照明灯（照明灯笼）、照明防护装置、弧光灯等	2010	武进区
普罗斯电器（江苏）有限公司	Plusrite	灯、照明防护装置、照明器械及装置等	2010	武进区
常州常发农业装备有限公司	常发及图形	拖车（车辆）、拖拉机、陆地车辆动力装置	2010	武进区

2-16 续表 3　continued 3

企业名称 Name of Enterprises	商标名称 Brand Name	主要产品 Mostly Product	颁布时间 Time of Release	所在地区 Region
今创集团有限公司	KTK	车辆卧铺、车辆行李架、车辆内装饰品等	2010	武进区
常州华日升反光材料有限公司	通明及图形	反光膜	2010	武进区
江苏润德医用材料有限公司	润德及图形	密封橡皮圈、橡皮塞子、垫片（密封垫）等	2010	武进区
常州市欧太装饰材料有限公司	欧运及图形	非金属地板、非金属建筑材料、非金属门等	2010	武进区
江苏尼高科技有限公司	尼高科技及图形	建筑灰浆、非金属建筑材料、涂面材料等	2010	武进区
常州市佳安装饰材料有限公司	好佳好HAOJIAHAO	地板、贴面板、半成品木材等	2010	武进区
常州迪邦纺织有限公司	迪邦DiBang	纱、线、棉线和绵纱等	2010	武进区
常州市武进五洋纺织机械有限公司	柳绿及图形	纺织织物、布、编织织物等	2010	武进区
江苏长海复合材料股份有限公司	常海及图形	热敷胶粘纤维布、纺织用玻璃纤维织物等	2010	武进区
江苏天香集团有限公司	香雪及图形	酱油、味精	2010	武进区
常州市立华畜禽有限公司	雪山及图形	活动物、活家禽、种家禽等	2010	武进区
常州市翟家果品专业合作社	常溪及图形	鲜水果、鲜葡萄、杏仁（水果）等	2010	武进区
常州市武进夏溪花木市场发展有限公司	夏溪花木市场及图形	树木评估、组织商业或广告交易会、推销等	2010	武进区
新城控股集团有限公司	新城及图形	建筑、砖石建筑、商业摊位及商店的建筑等	2010	武进区
常州华钛化学股份有限公司	图　形	工业用化学品、紫外线吸收剂、光引发剂	2010	金坛市
江苏省激素研究所股份有限公司	金珠及图形	农　药	2010	金坛市
金坛柴油机有限公司	天鹅及图形	柴油机、发电机组	2010	金坛市
金坛市旺达喷灌机有限公司	大网及图形	排水机、农业用排灌机、泵等	2010	金坛市
常州而今太阳能设备制造有限公司	而今ERJIN	太阳能收集器、太阳能热水器、淋浴器	2010	金坛市
江苏省金坛密封件厂	JMP及图形	橡皮圈、密封用橡皮圈、橡皮减震器等	2010	金坛市
盘固水泥集团有限公司	盘固及图形	水　泥	2010	金坛市
金坛市博天鞋业有限公司	博天BOTIAN	鞋	2010	金坛市
江苏茅山青锋茶叶有限公司	金鹿及图形	茶　叶	2010	金坛市
金坛市方麓茶场有限公司	百园春及图形	茶　叶	2010	金坛市
江苏鑫品茶业有限公司	鑫品及图形	茶、茶叶代用品	2010	金坛市
金坛市御庭春茶业有限公司	天壶及图形	茶、茶叶代用品	2010	金坛市
江苏瑞阳化工股份有限公司	瑞阳及图形	季戊四醇、甲酸等	2010	溧阳市
江苏江南农化有限公司	巨能及图形	农药、杀虫剂、灭杂草剂等	2010	溧阳市
江苏竹箦阀业有限公司	竹机ZJ	闸　阀	2010	溧阳市
江苏省社渚轴承有限公司	球星牌及图形	轴　承	2010	溧阳市
溧阳市重型机械厂有限公司	麦重及图形	破碎机、喂料机等	2010	溧阳市

2-16 续表 4 continued 4

企业名称 Name of Enterprises	商标名称 Brand Name	主要产品 Mostly Product	颁布时间 Time of Release	所在地区 Region
江苏保龙机电制造有限公司	保龙及图形	刨削机、刨花机、风力机和其配件等	2010	溧阳市
江苏省溧阳市汽车座椅调角器总厂	力乐及图形	汽车配件（汽车座椅调角器）	2010	溧阳市
江苏金峰水泥集团有限公司	金峰牌JINFENGPAI	水 泥	2010	溧阳市
江苏天目湖宾馆有限公司	天目湖及图形	鱼制食品等	2010	溧阳市
江苏省前峰茶厂	前峰及图形	茶 叶	2010	溧阳市
溧阳市天目湖玉莲珍稀茶果场	玉莲及图形	茶、茶叶代用品	2010	溧阳市
重庆啤酒集团常州天目湖啤酒有限公司	天目湖及图形	啤酒、汽水	2010	溧阳市
江苏华能建设工程集团有限公司	苏华及图形	锅炉清垢与修理、供暖设备的安装和修理等	2010	溧阳市
常州亚玛顿光伏玻璃有限公司	亚玛顿	光学玻璃、太阳能电池、表面覆有带电导体的玻璃等	2010	天宁区
常州新华陵汽车电器有限公司	超灵及图形	汽车配件	2010	天宁区
江苏恒利集团有限公司	恒利及图形	棉布、色织布、牛仔布等	2010	天宁区
常州丽华快餐集团有限公司	丽华快餐	餐厅、快餐馆、流动饮食供应等	2010	天宁区
常州红梅乳业有限公司	红梅及图形	牛奶、牛奶饮料（以牛奶为主的）及制品等	2010	钟楼区
常州千红生化制药股份有限公司	怡 开	人用药、原料药、生化药品等	2010	新北区
常州市常欣电子衡器有限公司	常欣及图形	超载限制器	2010	新北区
常州银河电器有限公司	BILIN	晶体管（电子）、半导体器件、晶片等	2010	新北区
江苏三恒科技集团有限公司	三 恒	报警器、监视器（计算机硬件）等	2010	新北区
常州市康辉医疗器械有限公司	康辉及图形	外科器械、止血缝合器械	2010	新北区
常州市常蒸蒸发器有限公司	常蒸及图形	蒸发器	2010	新北区
常州亨达车业部件有限公司	一帆顺YIFANSHUN	汽车照明设备、车灯、车辆反光镜等	2010	新北区
江苏贝德莱特太阳能科技有限公司	BadeLite	太阳能热水器、太阳能集热器、空气调节设备等	2010	新北区
常州市曙光车业有限公司	知音及图形	车辆油箱盖（气）、车内装饰品、车辆信号灯等	2010	新北区
江苏华生塑业有限公司	华生及图形	塑料管、管子接头、非金属软管	2010	新北区
常州丰盛光电科技股份有限公司	Julite	半加工塑料物质、有机玻璃、塑料板等	2010	新北区
常州市宏发纵横新材料科技有限公司	PGTEX	纺织织物、航空气球用不透气织物等	2010	新北区
常州市祥兴电机有限公司	图 形	马达及其部件	2010	戚墅堰区
常州市同和纺织机械制造有限公司	TONGHE	纺织工业用机器、纺织机、精纺机等	2010	戚墅堰区
江苏凯隆电器有限公司	KRAO及图形	断路器、高低压开关板、工业操作遥控电器设备等	2010	戚墅堰区
常州亚联灯具有限公司	FANOYA	路灯、探照灯、安全灯等	2010	戚墅堰区
常州制药厂有限公司	常药及图形	西药、原料药	2010	市 属
常州金源铜业有限公司	金线及图形	金属杆、金属板条	2010	市 属

2-16 续表 5　continued 5

企业名称 Name of Enterprises	商标名称 Brand Name	主要产品 Mostly Product	颁布时间 Time of Release	所在地区 Region
常林股份有限公司	常林及图形	装载机	2010	市　属
常林股份有限公司	CHANGLIN	装载机；压路机；平地机等	2010	市　属
常州能源设备总厂有限公司	CEEF及图形	载热体加热炉	2010	市　属
月星集团有限公司	图　形	家具、非纺织品壁饰（家具），陈列架等	2010	市　属
常州月兔调味食品有限公司	月兔牌及图形	味　精	2010	市　属
常州神龙饲料有限公司	水神及图形	饲料（包括非医用饲料添加剂及催化剂）	2010	市　属
江苏常宝钢管股份有限公司	环球及图形	钢管、钢带、钢坯	2011	常州市
常州东风农机集团有限公司	常拖及图形	内燃机（不包括汽车、拖拉机、谷物联合收割机等）	2011	常州市
常州天马集团有限公司	天马及图形	纺织用玻纤织物、纺织品用玻纤织物	2011	常州市
常州耀春格瑞纺织品有限公司	春格儿及图形	床罩、被子、床单等	2011	常州市
常州市丽岛金属材料制造有限公司	丽岛LIDAO	建筑用金属包层、金属地板、金属建筑材料等	2011	钟楼区
江苏洛克电气有限公司	洛克及图形	电　机	2011	钟楼区
江苏中江焊丝有限公司	鲀鱼及图形	金属焊丝；金焊锡；锡焊锡等	2011	新北区
常州市第八纺织机械有限公司	华发及图形	纺织机械及零件、针织机械及零件	2011	新北区
常州市西夏墅工具研究所有限公司	合力HL	刀具（机器零件）、切削工具（包括机械刀片）	2011	新北区
常州宝隆冶金设备制造有限公司	常　冶	输送机、包装机、轧钢机滚筒等	2011	新北区
常州市南港港口机械有限公司	NGPMC及图形	起重机、装卸设备	2011	新北区
常州天山重工机械有限公司	TS·HI及图形	机器传动装置、非陆地车辆变速箱、齿轮传动装置等	2011	新北区
常州太平洋电力设备（集团）有限公司	常太及图形	配电箱（电）、配电盘、配电控制台（电）等	2011	新北区
常州太平电器有限公司	太平通信TAIPING	光通信设备、分线盒（电）、电源材料等	2011	新北区
常州市永光车业有限公司	永兆YONGZHAO及图形	汽车灯、车辆灯	2011	新北区
常州星宇车灯股份有限公司	星宇及图形	荧光灯、照明防护装置等	2011	新北区
常州市瑞悦车业有限公司	富满及图形	车门、车辆轮辐、后视镜等	2011	新北区
吟飞科技（江苏）有限公司	吟飞及图形	手风琴、钢琴、乐器等	2011	新北区
常州市墅乐厨具有限公司	墅乐及图形	家用压面机	2011	新北区
常州中华恐龙园有限公司	恐龙及图形	帘子布、无纺布、纺织品壁挂等	2011	新北区
常州市牛塘化工厂有限公司	牛塘及图形	氰尿酸聚丁脂、癸二酸二酰肼等	2011	武进区
江苏江海化工集团有限公司	江海及图形	水质稳定剂	2011	武进区
常州市源恩合成材料有限公司	源恩及图形	工业用粘合剂、鞋粘合剂、皮革粘合剂等	2011	武进区
常州市方鑫化工物资有限公司	方鑫FANGXIN及图形	未加工环氧树脂、合成树脂、人造树脂等	2011	武进区
常州市南方卫生器材厂有限公司	妙手及图形	外科敷料，医用橡皮膏，医用胶布等	2011	武进区

2-16 续表 6 continued 6

企业名称 Name of Enterprises	商标名称 Brand Name	主要产品 Mostly Product	颁布时间 Time of Release	所在地区 Region
江苏聚荣制药集团有限公司	聚荣及图形	人用药	2011	武进区
常州市运河焊材有限公司	大运河及图形	焊 丝	2011	武进区
江苏武进液压启闭机有限公司	五叶 WY 及图形	液压启闭机	2011	武进区
常州市武起汽车电机有限公司	常乐及图形	起动机电机	2011	武进区
江苏恒力电机集团股份有限公司	WUDIAN 及图形	直流起动机、发电机、发动机等	2011	武进区
常州市华立液压润滑设备有限公司	华润 HUARUN 及图形	液压润滑设备、液压元件、油箱等	2011	武进区
江苏金鼎电动工具集团有限公司	金鼎及图形	机械操纵手持工具、电动手工操作钻孔器等	2011	武进区
常州市永明机械制造有限公司	常明 CHANGMING 及图形	纺织工业用机器、压平机、马达和引擎起动器等	2011	武进区
江苏洛凯机电制造集团有限公司	洛凯及图形	非陆地车辆传动马达、定子、引擎用风扇等	2011	武进区
江苏武东机械有限公司	武东及图形	机器、马达和引擎调速器、联轴器等	2011	武进区
常州市传动输送机械有限公司	霸宇及图形	传动装置（机器）、机器、马达和引擎调速器等	2011	武进区
江苏容天乐机械股份有限公司	WJT	自动加油轴承、滚珠轴承、机器轴承托架等	2011	武进区
江苏昌盛电缆集团有限公司	昌盛 CHANGSHENG 及图形	防火线缆、电线、电缆	2011	武进区
江苏华鑫合金有限公司	热工及图形	热电耦丝、补偿导线	2011	武进区
江苏宏事达电气制造有限公司	宏事达	电子计算机及外部设备、计时装置等	2011	武进区
江苏南方通信科技有限公司	精科及图形	电缆、电线、电源材料等	2011	武进区
江苏英特曼电器有限公司	Etman 及图形	插头、插座、电开关、电器接插件等	2011	武进区
常州市钱璟康复器材有限公司	钱璟及图形	按摩器械、振动按摩器、医用体育活动器械等	2011	武进区
常州市云涛洁具有限公司	云涛及图形	玛瑙浴缸、脸盆、澡盆等	2011	武进区
新科电子集团有限公司	Shinco	空调、电热水器、冷藏箱（集装箱）等	2011	武进区
江苏常嘉电器有限公司	首都 CAPITAL	照明灯、卫生器械及设备、水净化装置等	2011	武进区
江苏环球龙圣环境科技发展有限公司	宇球及图形	水冷却装置、冷却设备和装置	2011	武进区
江苏亚示照明集团有限公司	YASHIPS	灯、照明器、灯泡等	2011	武进区
江苏海鸥冷却塔股份有限公司	图 形	水冷却装置、冷却设备和装置	2011	武进区
江苏友奥电器有限公司	YOAU	制冰机和设备；空气调节设备；干燥设备等	2011	武进区
常州玉宇电光器件有限公司	Yuyu	照明器、灯泡、灯等	2011	武进区
江苏裕成电子有限公司	裕成 YUCHENG 及图形	陆地车辆传送马达、联动机件、动力装置等	2011	武进区
江苏逸盛投资集团有限公司	逸盛 CES	车辆轮胎、汽车轮胎、飞机轮胎等	2011	武进区
常州市宇锋车辆厂	宇锋及图形	机动自行车、电动车辆、小型机动车等	2011	武进区
常州市铭锦弹簧有限公司	铭锦及图形	车辆减震器、减震弹簧、机动车减震器等	2011	武进区
常州精科实业有限公司	CONTIN	钟表及其零部件、计时器（时钟）等	2011	武进区

2-16 续表 7 continued 7

企业名称 Name of Enterprises	商标名称 Brand Name	主要产品 Mostly Product	颁布时间 Time of Release	所在地区 Region
江苏恒耐炉料集团有限公司	恒耐及图形	耐火材料	2011	武进区
常州市洁丽木业有限公司	洁丽及图形	地板、护墙板、已加工木材等	2011	武进区
江苏博大木业有限公司	博瑞得及图形	地板、胶合板、耐火材料等	2011	武进区
江苏贝尔装饰材料有限公司	贝尔BeiEr	木材、铺地木材、制家用器具用木材等	2011	武进区
江苏玉兰木业有限公司	帕伦克及图形	地板、拼花地板条、贴面板等	2011	武进区
江苏中鑫德赛木业有限公司	荣登及图形	木地板；铺地木材；地板等	2011	武进区
江苏欧龙地板有限公司	伊恩YIEN	半成品木材、地板、耐火材料等	2011	武进区
常州市锦纶厂有限公司	威美WEIMEI及图形	丙纶丝、锦纶丝	2011	武进区
常州市棱光化工材料有限公司	棱光及图形	铝鞋眼	2011	武进区
江苏吉祥贺盛食品有限公司	贺盛及图形	味精、调味品等	2011	武进区
常州四药制药有限公司	奥 克	西 药	2011	天宁区
常州航月纺织机件有限公司	航月及图形	纺织机、纺纱车、纺织工业用机器等	2011	天宁区
常州亚泰纺织染整有限公司	SYT及图形	织物、布、棉织品等	2011	天宁区
大娘水饺餐饮集团股份有限公司	WUDANIANG及图形	馅饼、饺子、八宝饭等	2011	天宁区
常州市宏达机床数控设备有限公司	宏瑞达	机械台架、切削工具（包括机械刀片）、刀座	2011	戚墅堰区
常州市新东方电缆有限公司	神鸡及图形	电线、电缆	2011	戚墅堰区
常州普灵仕制衣有限公司	蓝豹及图形	服装、女衣裤、内衣等	2011	戚墅堰区
江苏竹溪活性炭有限公司	竹溪及图形	活性炭	2011	溧阳市
江苏天容集团股份有限公司	瑞禾及图形	杀害虫剂、除草剂、除莠剂等	2011	溧阳市
江苏溧阳南方水泥有限公司	苏特SUTE	水 泥	2011	溧阳市
溧阳市天目湖玉枝特种茶果园艺场	玉枝及图形	茶、茶叶代用品	2011	溧阳市
江苏天目湖生态农业有限公司	富子fz	茶	2011	溧阳市
江苏天目湖集团公司	天目湖及图形	观光旅游；安排游览；旅行预订等	2011	溧阳市
江苏金源锻造股份有限公司	金石Jinshi	研磨加工；金属锻造；金属冶炼等	2011	溧阳市
中盐金坛盐化有限责任公司	金赛盐业及图形	岩盐、原盐、工业用盐	2011	金坛市
江苏丰登农药有限公司	丰登及图形	农 药	2011	金坛市
常州金土木工程仪器有限公司	金土木	信号遥控电子启动设备、声波定位仪器、观测仪器等	2011	金坛市
江苏华兴电子有限公司	FY及图形	磁铁、扼流圈（阻抗）、半导体器件等	2011	金坛市
常州亿晶光电科技有限公司	EGNG及图形	单晶硅、多晶硅、碳电极等	2011	金坛市
常州市龙泉太阳能设备厂	龍全及图形	太阳能热水器、浴用加热器、太阳能集热器等	2011	金坛市
金坛市明日春花盆有限公司	树春及图形	花和植物用盆（花展用）、花盆、非纸制花盆套	2011	金坛市

2-16 续表 8 continued 8

企业名称 Name of Enterprises	商标名称 Brand Name	主要产品 Mostly Product	颁布时间 Time of Release	所在地区 Region
江苏鸿瑞昌泰纺织有限公司	HRCT及图形	织物、纺织织物、毛织品等	2011	金坛市
常州金松时装有限公司	G&P	服装、女紧身衣裤、连裤内衣等	2011	金坛市
江苏波仕曼制衣有限公司	波仕曼及图形	服装、袜、游泳衣等	2011	金坛市
溧阳市幽香苏茶有限公司	幽香苏及图形	茶，茶叶代用品	2011	金坛市
金坛丰登酒业有限公司	丰登及图形	酒	2011	金坛市
江苏力合粘合剂有限公司	力合及图形	粘合剂	2012	金坛市
溧阳市利达有机硅科技有限公司	科达及图	工业用粘合剂和胶	2012	溧阳市
常州嘉仁禾化学有限公司	嘉仁禾CARINVER及图	盐类（化学制剂）、硬脂酸盐类等	2012	溧阳市
常茂生物化学工程股份有限公司	图　形	酸、酒石酸等	2012	新北区
常州武帆合金有限公司	武　帆	铝锰铁复合脱氧剂	2012	武进区
江苏中东化肥股份有限公司	中东ZHONGDONG及图	农业肥料、农业用肥、混合肥料等	2012	武进区
江苏安格特新材料科技有限公司	安格特AGT	未加工塑料、聚丙烯、聚氯乙烯树脂等	2012	武进区
江苏卓云豆宝食品有限公司	康力KANGLI及图	防水浆消泡剂、葡萄糖酸盐、葡萄糖酸内酯等	2012	新北区
冶建新材料股份有限公司	天虎及图	涂　料	2012	溧阳市
江苏晨光涂料有限公司	晨光CHENGUANG	油漆、底漆、刷墙用白浆（白垩灰浆）等	2012	武进区
常州市长润石油有限公司	江	各种机油、工业脂、高温脂	2012	武进区
江苏省健尔康医用敷料有限公司	JIANERKANG及图形	卫生绷带、外科用纱布等	2012	金坛市
常州佳尔科药业集团有限公司	佳尔科JIAERKE及图	人用药、医用激素等	2012	武进区
常州方圆制药有限公司	创成及图	医药制剂、化学药物制剂	2012	新北区
常州华联保健敷料有限公司	华联及图	医用敷料、医用胶布、止血栓等	2012	武进区
江苏常隆化工有限公司	天　宁	农　药	2012	新北区
江苏国强镀锌实业有限公司	图　形	建筑用金属柱、金属护栏等	2012	溧阳市
常州华通焊业股份有限公司	華通HUATONG及图	金属焊丝、金属焊条等	2012	武进区
中天钢铁集团有限公司	ZENITH及图	未加工或半加工普通金属、铸钢等	2012	武进区
江苏圣乐机械有限公司	圣盛SHENGSHENG及图	金属铸模、铁路金属材料等	2012	武进区
常州腾龙汽车零部件股份有限公司	CZTL及图形	压缩空气管用金属配件、金属管等	2012	武进区
常州常松金属复合材料有限公司	常松及图	金属片和金属板、钢板等	2012	钟楼区
溧阳市四方不锈钢制品有限公司	利洋四方LYSF	金属管道弯头、金属管道接头、金属阀门等	2012	溧阳市
江苏丰顺新材料科技有限公司	FENGSHUN及图	金属建筑材料、建筑用金属板、铝塑板（以铝为主）等	2012	武进区
常州永盛包装有限公司	永盛及图	包装机械、胶带分配机	2012	戚墅堰区
常州市科沛达超声工程设备有限公司	科沛达KePeida	电焊机、清洗设备等	2012	戚墅堰区

2-16 续表 9　continued 9

企业名称 Name of Enterprises	商标名称 Brand Name	主要产品 Mostly Product	颁布时间 Time of Release	所在地区 Region
常州弹簧厂有限公司	四环牌及图	弹　簧	2012	天宁区
常州市骠马涂装系统工程有限公司	骠马涂装	涂漆机、油漆喷枪 等	2012	天宁区
常州市腾田液压机械有限公司	腾田TENT及图形	液压机、活塞（机器或发动机部件）等	2012	武进区
江苏先锋干燥工程有限公司	先锋XIANFENG及图	化学工业用电动机械、制药加工工业用机器等	2012	武进区
常州市武进广宇花辊机械有限公司	广宇及图	轧花机、织机（机器）等	2012	武进区
常州市长力冲压机床有限公司	万	内燃机配件、机器飞轮等	2012	新北区
常州东风轴承有限公司	DFB	传动轴轴承、滚珠轴承（滚柱）等	2012	新北区
江苏峨嵋动力机械有限公司	金田JINTIAN及图	柴油机、汽油机、发动机喷油嘴等	2012	金坛市
江苏金动动力机械有限公司	金动JINDONG及图	柴油机、汽油机	2012	金坛市
常州凯达轧辊集团有限公司	凯　达	铸铁轧辊	2012	武进区
常州市武进协昌机械有限公司	协昌xiechang及图	橡胶塑料工业设备	2012	武进区
常州一步干燥设备有限公司	一步YIBU及图	食品工业用机械及部件、制药工业用机械及部件、林产化学设备等	2012	武进区
常州机械设备进出口有限公司	亚美柯AMEC及图	柴油机、汽油机、发电机等	2012	钟楼区
常州瑞华电力电子器件有限公司	申社及图形	半导体器件、控制板（电）等	2012	金坛市
江苏苏宏医疗器械有限公司	苏　宏	秤、衡器	2012	武进区
常州速骏电子有限公司	QUICK	电焊设备、电测量仪器等	2012	武进区
常州海弘电子有限公司	长江及图	线路板	2012	新北区
江苏德春电力科技有限公司	成玥 CHENGYUE	电开关、接线盒（电）等	2012	新北区
江苏华冠电器集团有限公司	华程HUACHENG及图	配电柜（电）、配电控制台（电）等	2012	新北区
江苏山湖电缆有限公司	山湖牌及图	电缆、电线、接线盒	2012	溧阳市
常州特种变压器有限公司	稳福WENFU及图	变压器（电）、配电箱（电）	2012	天宁区
江苏上能变压器有限公司	上能Sunel	变压器、高压防爆配电设备、电器联接器等	2012	天宁区
常州市薛巷电讯元件有限公司	桑乐SANGLE及图	电线、电器接插件、电连接器等	2012	武进区
江苏日盈电器有限公司	图　形	电器接插件、电线、电线连接物等	2012	武进区
常州联力自动化科技有限公司	联力LIANLI及图	用于计算器操作仪器的机械装置、工业操作遥控电力装置、工业操作遥控电器设备	2012	新北区
中韩科技有限公司	中　韩	冰柜；冰箱；饮水机等	2012	武进区
特瑞斯能源装备有限公司	TRUBILITY	煤气管道用调节和安全附件、煤气设备用的调节和安全附件等	2012	新北区
江苏三信环保设备有限公司	SANXIN及图	加热装置、锅炉（非机器部件）、熔炉进料装置等	2012	新北区
常州晶雪冷冻设备有限公司	晶　雪	冷藏室、空气调节器	2012	武进区
常州九鼎车业有限公司	JUDNG	车辆灯、汽车照明设备等	2012	新北区
江苏恒鑫富奥汽车零部件有限公司	恒鑫HENGXIN及图	汽车零部件（不包括轮胎）、摩托车零部件（不包括轮胎）	2012	武进区

2-16 续表 10 continued 10

企业名称 Name of Enterprises	商标名称 Brand Name	主要产品 Mostly Product	颁布时间 Time of Release	所在地区 Region
常州昊邦汽车零部件有限公司	HAOB	车辆座位、车辆减震器等	2012	钟楼区
江苏凯灵汽车电器有限公司	凯　灵	汽车综合开关、汽车地板	2012	金坛市
江苏常武起动电机有限公司	常威changwei及图	汽车发动机、汽车起动机	2012	武进区
江苏龙城精锻有限公司	图　形	陆地车辆传动齿轮、陆地车辆传动马达、陆地车辆传动轴等	2012	武进区
常州市飞拓模塑有限公司	飞拓FEITUO及图	后视镜、车辆内装饰、车辆保险杆等	2012	新北区
常州市盛扬电动自行车有限公司	盛扬SHENGYANG及图	电动车辆、机动自行车、三轮运货车等	2012	新北区
常州金店有限公司	皆是缘JIESHIYUAN	玉雕首饰、黄金首饰、铂金首饰等	2012	钟楼区
常州吉春包装有限公司	吉春jichun	纸板盒或纸盒、纸板或纸制瓶封套等	2012	武进区
常州市河马塑胶有限公司	河马HEMA及图	塑料管、管子接头、非金属软管	2012	武进区
常州市瑞腾塑胶有限公司	特丽隆TELILONG	防水卷材、建筑用塑料板等	2012	溧阳市
江苏双奇地板有限公司	双　奇	木地板、非金属地板等	2012	武进区
江苏凯莱木业有限公司	凯莱KAILAI	地板、非金属建筑材料等	2012	武进区
江苏红日防静电地板有限公司	红日及图	地板、建筑用木材、铺地木材	2012	武进区
常州市赛力木业有限公司	圣力及图	地板、镶花地板等	2012	武进区
江苏科利达装饰材料有限公司	科利达KLD	木材、地板、非金属建筑材料等	2012	武进区
常州新鸿联家具有限公司	鸿联及图	家具、金属家具、办公用家具等	2012	武进区
常州工业技术玻璃有限公司	长江CHANGJIANG及图	车窗玻璃、钢化玻璃	2012	新北区
常州宝丽丝纤维有限公司	博　洋	纱、丝纱等	2012	溧阳市
江苏阳湖纺织集团股份有限公司	阳湖及图	棉纱和棉线等	2012	武进区
常州旭荣针织印染有限公司	NEW WIDE及图	布、织物等	2012	天宁区
江苏飞洋鱼制衣有限公司	飞洋鱼	针织衣服、衬衫、套服等	2012	金坛市
常州环球地毯制造有限公司	环球HUANQIU及图	地　毯	2012	钟楼区
常州恐龙园文化创意有限公司	恐龙宝贝	游戏机、玩具、扑克牌等	2012	新北区
金坛市江南制粉有限公司	沁雪及图形	谷类制品、米、生糯粉等	2012	金坛市
金坛市江南春米业有限公司	蘇及图形	米、面粉、谷类制品等	2012	金坛市
江苏金唐农业科技有限公司	绿坛及图	鲜水果、新鲜蔬菜等	2012	金坛市
常州保纳商业广场经营管理有限公司	保　纳	推销（替他人）、商业管理咨询等	2012	新北区
常嘉建设集团有限公司	图　形	建筑、商业摊位及商店的建筑等	2012	天宁区
江苏久信医用净化工程有限公司	久信 JIUXIN及图形	空气净化、水净化等	2012	新北区
常州马複兴餐饮管理有限公司	马複兴	备办宴席、饭店、快餐馆等	2012	钟楼区

2-17　名牌产品一览
GENERAL VIEW OF FAMOUS BRAND PRODUCTS

企业名称 Name of Enterprises	产品名称 Product Name	颁布时间 Time of Release
中国名牌产品　China Top Brand Products		
江苏上上电缆集团	上上牌交联聚乙烯电力电缆	2004年
黑牡丹（集团）股份有限公司	黑牡丹牌牛仔布	2005年
常州月夜灯芯绒有限公司	月夜牌灯芯绒	2005年
常柴股份有限公司	常柴牌单缸柴油机	2005年
江苏常发集团常州常发动力机械有限公司	常发牌单缸柴油机	2005年
江苏华鹏变压器有限公司	华鹏牌干式电力变压器	2005年
江苏华鹏变压器有限公司	华鹏牌110KV及以下油浸式电力变压器	2005年
常州华电变压器集团公司常州变压器厂	常州牌110KV及以下油浸式电力变压器	2005年
常州天马集团有限公司	天马牌无碱玻璃纤维短切原丝毡	2005年
江苏多棱数控机床股份有限公司	SDL牌重型数控镗铣床	2006年
常州东风农机集团有限公司	东风牌手扶拖拉机	2006年
江苏常发集团常州常发动力机械有限公司	常发牌手扶拖拉机	2006年
新科电子集团有限公司	新科、Shinco牌激光视盘机	2006年
江苏康泰氟化工有限公司	蓝色星球牌HFC-134A制冷剂	2006年
江苏常隆化工有限公司	天宁牌吡虫啉杀虫剂	2006年
江苏同大股份有限公司	全无敌牌气雾杀虫剂	2006年
月星集团有限公司	月星牌实木家具	2006年
江苏鸿联集团有限公司	红联牌室内灯具	2006年
常州天马集团有限公司	天马牌玻璃纤维土工格栅	2006年
江苏金鼎电动工具集团有限公司	金鼎牌电动工具	2007年
常州市永明机械制造有限公司	常明牌PP编织物机	2007年
常州市武进不锈钢管厂有限公司	阳湖牌锅炉用不锈钢无缝钢管	2007年
江苏常隆化工有限公司	天宁牌乙草胺	2007年
常林股份有限公司	常林牌装载机	2007年
新科电子集团有限公司	新科、Shinco牌家用分体空调	2007年

2-17 续表 1 continued 1

企业名称 Name of Enterprises	产品名称 Product Name	颁布时间 Time of Release
江苏名牌产品 Jiangsu Famous Brand Products		
江苏裕成电子有限公司	（YC字样图案）牌微型动圈式受话器/扬声器	2010年
常州星海电子有限公司	灵杰牌硅半导体二极管	2010年
常州天合光能有限公司	天合光能牌太阳能电池组件	2010年
常州成业服饰有限公司	CY牌短裤	2010年
江苏波仕曼制衣有限公司	波仕曼牌羽绒服装	2010年
顶呱呱彩棉服饰有限公司	顶瓜瓜牌天然彩棉内衣	2010年
江苏旷达汽车织物集团股份有限公司	旷达牌汽车内饰面料	2010年
江苏中东集团有限公司	中东牌复混肥料	2010年
常州亚邦化学有限公司	亚邦牌顺丁烯二酸酐	2010年
江苏省激素研究所股份有限公司	金珠牌除草剂、杀虫剂、植物生长调节剂	2010年
江苏丰登农药有限公司	丰登牌三唑类杀菌剂	2010年
江苏瑞邦农药厂有限公司	瑞邦牌75%苯磺隆水分散粒剂	2010年
常州市国宇环保科技有限公司	玉宇牌硝酸银	2010年
江苏天容集团股份有限公司	溧化牌苄嘧磺隆除草剂；天容牌杀虫双（单）、杀螟丹、精噁唑禾草灵	2010年
江苏恒立高压油缸有限公司	恒立牌液压油缸	2010年
金坛市农用水泵厂	国农牌自吸泵	2010年
常州市永安电机有限公司	M牌房间空调器用电动机	2010年
常州市武起汽车电机有限公司	常乐牌汽车用起动机	2010年
常州市武进五洋纺织机械有限公司	五洋牌GE-288A型中绒双针床经编机	2010年
江苏金鼎电动工具集团有限公司	金鼎牌电动工具	2010年
江苏鑫和泰机械集团有限公司	常动牌单缸柴油机铸铁机体	2010年
常柴股份有限公司	常柴牌柴油机	2010年
常州常发动力机械有限公司	常发牌柴油机、常发系列旋耕机	2010年
常州亚美柯机械设备有限公司	亚美柯牌柴油机	2010年
江苏保龙机电制造有限公司	保龙牌木材加工机械	2010年
常州联发凯迪机械有限公司	联发凯迪牌轮式拖拉机	2010年
常州太平洋电力设备（集团）有限公司	常太牌常太牌高低压开关柜	2010年
江苏安靠超高压电缆附件有限公司	安靠牌高压及超高压交联聚乙稀绝缘电力电缆附件系列产品	2010年

2-17 续表 2　continued 2

企业名称 Name of Enterprises	产品名称 Product Name	颁布时间 Time of Release
常州市拓源电气制造有限公司	常州拓源（图形）牌低压成套开关设备和控制设备	2010年
国茂减速机集团有限公司	国茂牌减速机	2010年
常州市永明机械制造有限公司	常明牌PP编织物机	2010年
常州市润源经编机械有限公司	润源牌经编机	2010年
江苏南方轴承股份有限公司	南方牌滚针轴承	2010年
盘固水泥集团有限公司	盘固牌通用硅酸盐水泥	2010年
江苏扬子水泥有限公司	长荡湖牌PO42.5水泥	2010年
江苏长海复合材料股份有限公司	常海牌薄型玻璃纤维短切毡	2010年
常州而今太阳能设备制造有限公司	而今牌家用太阳热水系统	2010年
江苏太阳宝新能源有限公司	太阳宝牌太阳能热水器	2010年
溧阳军荣旅游用品有限公司	JUNRONG牌旅行箱包	2010年
江苏力强化工有限公司	力洋牌酚醛模塑料	2010年
江苏凯灵汽车电器有限公司	凯灵牌汽车组合开关	2010年
江苏洛基木业有限公司	洛基牌浸渍纸层压木质地板	2010年
常州市佳安装饰材料有限公司	好佳好牌浸渍纸层压木质地板	2010年
常州市赛力木业有限公司	圣力牌浸渍纸层压木质地板	2010年
江苏科利达装饰材料有限公司	科利达牌浸渍纸层压木质地板	2010年
常州市赛欧地板有限公司	大欧牌浸渍纸层压木质地板	2010年
常州市森尼装饰材料有限公司	森尼牌浸渍纸层压木质地板	2010年
常州市欧太装饰材料有限公司	欧运牌浸渍纸层压木质地板	2010年
江苏太平洋印刷有限公司	小白豚牌相册	2010年
常州速派奇车业有限公司	速派奇牌电动自行车	2010年
江苏武进不锈钢管厂集团有限公司	阳湖牌锅炉用不锈钢无缝钢管	2010年
常州灵通展览用品有限公司	灵通LINGTONG牌展览展示器材	2010年
江苏国强镀锌实业有限公司	国强牌镀锌焊接钢管、高速公路波形梁护栏	2010年
常州制药厂有限公司	常药牌卡托普利系列、盐酸多西环素、复方利血平片	2010年
常州四药制药有限公司	奥克牌奥美拉唑系列、兰苏牌盐酸氨溴索系列、缬克牌缬沙坦胶囊	2010年
江苏康友医用器械有限公司	康友牌一次性使用无菌注射器	2010年
江苏康进医疗器材有限公司	康进牌一次性使用无菌注射器、输液器（带针）	2010年

2-17 续表 3 continued 3

企业名称 Name of Enterprises	产品名称 Product Name	颁布时间 Time of Release
常州医疗器材总厂有限公司	乐伦牌一次性使用无菌注射器输液器	2010年
常州千红生化制药股份有限公司	常生千红牌肝素系列产品及其制剂、怡开牌胰激肽原酶及其制剂系列产品	2010年
江苏省前峰茶厂	前峰牌绿茶	2010年
金坛市方麓茶场有限公司	百园春牌金坛雀舌茶	2010年
江苏德盛食品有限公司	德盛牌米果	2010年
江苏常州城北国家粮食储备库	诚百牌大米	2010年
江苏南顺食品有限公司	满天星牌小麦粉、挂面	2010年
金坛市江南制粉有限公司	沁雪牌水磨糯米粉	2010年
常州长江水产有限公司冷冻加工厂	江南牌太湖冻银鱼	2010年
金坛市绿野农业服务中心	碧润牌无节水芹	2010年
江苏吉祥贺盛食品有限公司	贺盛牌鸡精调味料	2010年
常州市康乐农牧有限公司	中东牌商品猪	2010年
江苏正平技术服务事务所有限公司	江苏服务业名牌	2010年
常州市维益专利事务所	江苏服务业名牌	2010年
常州大华进出口（集团）有限公司	江苏服务业名牌	2010年
常州中华恐龙园有限公司	江苏服务业名牌	2010年
江苏南方通信科技有限公司	精科牌铜芯聚烯烃绝缘铝塑综合护套市内通信电缆	2011年
常州金松时装有限公司	G&P牌衬衫	2011年
江苏华达化工集团有限公司	常恒牌1-萘胺、1-萘酚系列产品	2011年
冶建新材料股份有限公司	天虎牌TH-2型硅酸锌车间底漆	2011年
常州华日升反光材料有限公司	通明牌反光膜	2011年
常州市源恩合成材料有限公司	源恩牌聚氨酯胶粘剂	2011年
江苏华盛天龙光电设备股份有限公司	华盛天龙牌DRF系列直拉式单晶炉	2011年
金坛天鹅喷灌机械有限公司	天鹅牌轻小型喷灌机	2011年
常州联凯动力机械有限公司	常联发牌单缸柴油机	2011年
金坛柴油机有限公司	天鹅牌单缸柴油机	2011年
江苏海鸥冷却塔股份有限公司	海鸥牌冷却塔	2011年
金坛市旺达喷灌机有限公司	大网牌轻小型喷灌机	2011年
常州市第八纺织机械有限公司	华发牌整经机	2011年

2-17 续表 4　continued 4

企业名称 Name of Enterprises	产品名称 Product Name	颁布时间 Time of Release
江苏峨嵋动力机械有限公司	金田牌单缸柴油机	2011年
江苏天元工程机械有限公司	teeyer牌蒸压加气混凝土切割机	2011年
常州常瑞天力动力机械有限公司	常瑞牌单缸燃气机	2011年
江苏省社渚轴承有限公司	球星牌圆锥滚子轴承	2011年
江苏华阳电器有限公司	华阳huayang牌BYJ系列减速永磁步进电动机	2011年
常州亚玛顿股份有限公司	亞瑪頓牌太阳能电池用光伏镀膜玻璃	2011年
江苏丰顺新材料科技有限公司	丰顺牌建筑幕墙用铝塑复合板	2011年
江苏红日防静电地板有限公司	红日牌防静电活动地板	2011年
江苏欧龙地板有限公司	欧塞牌浸渍纸层压木质地板	2011年
江苏中鑫德赛木业有限公司	荣登牌浸渍纸层压木质地板	2011年
江苏亿家美木业有限公司	申嘉牌浸渍纸层压木质地板	2011年
常州市零点木业有限公司	零点牌浸渍纸层压木质地板	2011年
常州市东家装饰材料有限公司	东家牌浸渍纸层压木质地板	2011年
百兴集团有限公司	百兴牌聚氯乙烯硬片、膜	2011年
江苏南洋木业有限公司	南洋牌实木地板	2011年
江苏友奥电器有限公司	友奥牌移动式空调器	2011年
江苏德莱仕电器有限公司	中韩牌冷藏冷冻箱	2011年
常州市常蒸蒸发器有限公司	常蒸牌蒸发器、冷凝器（高效节能换热器）	2011年
常州华通焊丝有限公司	华通牌碳钢焊丝	2011年
江苏吉景金属科技有限公司	吉景牌连续热镀锌钢带	2011年
江苏康华医疗器材有限公司	常宝牌一次性使用无菌注射器、输液器	2011年
江苏润德医用材料有限公司	润德（+图形）牌注射液用卤化丁基橡胶塞	2011年
金坛市江南春米业有限公司	蘇牌大米	2011年
金坛市碧润水芹专业合作社	碧润牌无节水芹	2011年
常州市常洛果品专业合作社	苏常鲜牌绿色食品（葡萄）	2011年
金坛市后渎特种水产养殖场有限公司	苏标牌长荡湖中华绒螯蟹	2011年
江苏新城房产股份有限公司	江苏服务业名牌	2011年
常州市春秋乐园旅游发展有限公司	江苏服务业名牌	2011年
江苏凌家塘市场发展有限公司	江苏服务业名牌	2011年

2-17 续表 5 continued 5

企业名称 Name of Enterprises	产品名称 Product Name	颁布时间 Time of Release
常州华威电子有限公司	CHANG牌铝电解电容器	2012年
黑牡丹（集团）股份有限公司	黑牡丹牌色织牛仔布	2012年
溧阳新元窗帘制品有限公司	新元牌窗帘	2012年
江苏开利地毯股份有限公司	天目湖牌地毯	2012年
江苏鸿瑞昌泰纺织有限公司	HRCT（图形）牌毛毯	2012年
江苏常隆化工有限公司	天宁牌农药	2012年
江苏亚邦染料股份有限公司	亚邦牌分散染料	2012年
江苏春江农化有限公司	江润禾牌高效氯氟氰菊酯	2012年
江苏兰陵化工集团有限公司	兰陵牌涂料	2012年
常州光辉化工有限公司	光辉牌油漆涂料	2012年
中盐金坛盐化有限责任公司	金赛盐业牌盐	2012年
常州市宏发纵横新材料科技股份有限公司	PGTEX牌连续树脂基预浸料用多轴向经编增强复合材料	2012年
南京化工学院常州市武进水质稳定剂厂	颂歌牌水处理剂	2012年
江苏竹溪活性炭有限公司	竹溪牌活性炭	2012年
华润包装材料有限公司	华蕾牌聚对苯二甲酸二甲酯	2012年
江苏瑞阳化工股份有限公司	瑞阳牌工业用季戊四醇	2012年
江苏蓝色星球环保科技股份有限公司	蓝色星球牌工业用1,1,1,2-四氟乙烷（HFC-134a）	2012年
常州天马集团有限公司（原建材二五三厂）	天马牌不饱和聚酯树脂、玻璃纤维制品	2012年
江苏晨光涂料有限公司	晨光牌内外墙涂料	2012年
常州华钛化学股份有限公司	RUNTECURE牌光引发剂	2012年
江苏竹箦阀业有限公司	ZJ牌阀门	2012年
常州市华立液压润滑设备有限公司	华润牌稀油润滑装置	2012年
江苏上上电缆集团有限公司	上上牌电线电缆	2012年
江苏金牛线缆集团有限公司	金牛牌电线电缆	2012年
梅特勒–托利多（常州）测量技术有限公司	METTLERTOLEDO牌电子衡器	2012年
江苏金动动力机械有限公司	金动牌柴油机	2012年
金坛鑫田柴油机有限公司	鑫田牌单缸柴油机	2012年
常州市骠马涂装系统工程有限公司	骠马涂装牌乘用车清洁涂装自动化生产线	2012年
江苏常发制冷股份有限公司	常发牌冰箱、空调用蒸发器、冷凝器	2012年

2-17 续表 6　continued 6

企业名称 Name of Enterprises	产品名称 Product Name	颁布时间 Time of Release
常州宝菱重工机械有限公司	BLHI牌冷（连）轧机组、连铸机	2012年
溧阳市重型机械厂有限公司	麦重牌破碎机	2012年
常州市铭锦弹簧有限公司	锦弹、铭锦牌冷卷圆柱螺旋弹簧	2012年
常州东风农机集团有限公司	东风牌拖拉机	2012年
江苏常发农业装备股份有限公司	常发、CF字母图形牌轮式拖拉机	2012年
江苏裕成电子有限公司	裕成牌电动自行车用轮毂电机	2012年
江苏龙城精锻有限公司	（图形）汽车发电机转子用精锻爪极	2012年
常州市墅乐厨具有限公司	墅乐牌家用制面机	2012年
江苏正昌集团有限公司	正昌牌成套工程、饲料压制机、粉碎机	2012年
布勒（常州）机械有限公司	布勒牌饲料机械	2012年
江苏华鹏变压器有限公司	华鹏牌电力变压器	2012年
江苏上齿集团有限公司	上溧牌汽车及工程车螺旋锥齿轮	2012年
江苏华冠电器集团有限公司	华程牌高低压开关设备	2012年
江苏新洛凯机电有限公司	洛凯牌智能电网断路器操作机构	2012年
常州光洋轴承股份有限公司	NRB牌滚动轴承	2012年
常州市南港港口机械有限公司	NGPMC（图形）牌港口装卸设备	2012年
常州联力自动化科技有限公司	联力牌矿用隔爆兼本质安全型真空组合开关	2012年
江苏金峰水泥集团有限公司	金峰牌通用硅酸盐水泥	2012年
常州市龙泉太阳能设备厂	龙全牌太阳能热水器	2012年
常州市洁丽木业有限公司	洁丽牌实木地板	2012年
江苏博大木业有限公司	博瑞得牌热固性树脂浸渍纸高压装饰层积板	2012年
江苏贝尔装饰材料有限公司	BBL牌浸渍纸层压木质地板	2012年
江苏玉兰木业有限公司	东方玉兰牌（图形）浸渍纸层压木质地板	2012年
江苏凯莱木业有限公司	凯莱牌浸渍纸层压木质地板	2012年
江苏双奇地板有限公司	双奇牌浸渍纸层压木质地板	2012年
江苏好佳好木业有限公司	斯比诺牌浸渍纸层压木质地板	2012年
金坛市鑫隆防水塑胶制品有限公司	隆坛牌高分子防水材料	2012年
江西洪都航空工业集团常州洪都电动车有限公司	洪都牌电动自行车	2012年

2-17 续表 7 continued 7

企业名称 Name of Enterprises	产品名称 Product Name	颁布时间 Time of Release
常州星宇车灯股份有限公司	星宇牌汽车车灯	2012年
江苏亚示照明灯具有限公司	YASHIPS牌室外灯具	2012年
常州市云涛洁具有限公司	云涛牌玻璃纤维增强塑料浴缸	2012年
常州晶雪冷冻设备有限公司	晶雪牌组合冷库用隔热夹芯板	2012年
中天钢铁集团有限公司	ZENITH牌热轧带肋钢筋、热轧光圆钢筋	2012年
江苏常宝钢管股份有限公司	环球牌石油油套管、高压锅炉管等无缝钢管	2012年
常州方圆制药有限公司	创成牌硫酸依替米星	2012年
常州千红生化制药股份有限公司	怡开、常生千红牌胰激肽原酶、肝素钠	2012年
常州市南方卫生器材厂有限公司	妙手牌一次性伤口敷料	2012年
江苏省健尔康医用敷料有限公司	JIANERKANG牌脱脂纱布	2012年
常州环球地毯制造有限公司	环球牌阿克明斯特地毯	2012年
金坛市金土地有机稻米专业合作社	黄金村牌有机软米	2012年
江苏立华牧业有限公司	雪山牌雪山鸡	2012年
常州阳湖新月茶业有限公司	阳湖新月牌绿茶	2012年
江苏茅山青锋茶叶有限公司	金鹿牌茅山青锋	2012年
江苏鑫品茶业有限公司	鑫品牌金坛雀舌茶	2012年
金坛市茅麓茶厂	巨鹿牌绿茶	2012年
常州市盛丰园果品专业合作社	景丰牌葡萄	2012年
常州神龙饲料有限公司	水神牌水产饲料	2012年
重庆啤酒集团常州天目湖啤酒有限公司	天目湖牌天目湖啤酒	2012年
金坛丰登酒业有限公司	丰登牌黄酒（封缸酒）	2012年
江苏艺林园花木有限公司	厚余牌樟树苗木	2012年
常州市建筑科学研究院股份有限公司	江苏服务业名牌	2012年
常州三晶世界科技产业发展有限公司	江苏服务业名牌	2012年
大娘水饺餐饮集团股份有限公司	江苏服务业名牌	2012年
常州丽华快餐集团有限公司	江苏服务业名牌	2012年
常州国旅旅行社有限公司	江苏服务业名牌	2012年
常州港华燃气有限公司	江苏服务业名牌	2012年

2-17 续表 8　continued 8

企业名称 Name of Enterprises	产品名称 Product Name	颁布时间 Time of Release
常州名牌产品　Changzhou Famous Brand Products		
江苏德盛食品有限公司	米果、豆果	2012年
溧阳市太云白茶生态庄园	绿　茶	2012年
溧阳市桂林茶场	绿　茶	2012年
溧阳市天目湖环湖茶场	环湖翠柏茶	2012年
溧阳天目湖亳上瓜果专业合作社	草　莓	2012年
江苏天目湖生态农业有限公司	葡　萄	2012年
溧阳市天目湖燕山种鸡场	鸡　蛋	2012年
溧阳市天目湖茶场	绿　茶	2012年
溧阳市天目湖满山跑绿壳蛋鸡散养场	绿壳鸡蛋	2012年
常州天目湖生物科技有限公司	风　鹅	2012年
溧阳市竹箦北山茶场	绿　茶	2012年
溧阳市天目湖小胖子腌制食品厂	咸　鹅	2012年
溧阳市松溪生态农业有限公司	鸡　蛋	2012年
江苏常州城北国家粮食储备库	大　米	2012年
常州市高露达饮用水有限公司	瓶（桶）装天然矿泉水、天然泉水、矿物质水、纯净水	2012年
常州市鑫灿食品有限公司	糕　点	2012年
常州月兔调味食品有限公司	味精、鸡精、汤料	2012年
常州正大面粉有限公司	小麦粉（通用）	2012年
常州市康惠保健品有限公司	肉松、鸡爪	2012年
江苏艺林园花木有限公司	樟树苗木	2012年
常州市盛丰园果品专业合作社	无公害鲜食葡萄	2012年
坛市鑫园粉茶有限公司	超微绿茶粉	2012年
江苏三德利牧业发展有限公司	商品活鸡	2012年
江苏八达畜禽有限公司	家　禽	2012年
金坛市金土地有机稻米专业合作社	有机软米、彩色稻米	2012年
常州市西湖山庄水产科技有限公司	淡水龙虾	2012年
常州金英王生态农业有限公司	瓜果蔬菜	2012年
常州市科丰葡萄专业合作社	鲜食葡萄	2012年
江苏名仁生态农产品销售有限公司	农产品	2012年

2-17 续表 9 continued 9

企业名称 Name of Enterprises	产品名称 Product Name	颁布时间 Time of Release
常州红谷粮食贸易有限公司	常金大米	2012年
常州金海棠茶果专业合作社	茶 叶	2012年
常州红梅乳业有限公司	鲜牛奶	2012年
常州五星禾绿蔬菜食品有限公司	豆芽菜	2012年
常州市阳光营养食品有限公司	阳光月饼	2012年
常州五星禽蛋有限公司	鸡 蛋	2012年
常州新区怡泰食品有限公司	固体饮料	2012年
溧阳市天目湖羽韵茶场	白 茶（绿茶）	2012年
溧阳市金山茶业有限公司	绿 茶	2012年
溧阳市欣龙生态农业发展有限公司	白 茶	2012年
溧阳市天目湖新峰茶场	绿 茶	2012年
溧阳华晶电子材料有限公司	双向拉伸聚酰亚胺膜	2012年
江苏保龙机电制造有限公司	木材加工机械	2012年
江苏力强化工有限公司	酚醛模塑料	2012年
江苏金峰水泥集团有限公司	通用硅酸盐水泥	2012年
江苏国强镀锌实业有限公司	波型梁护栏	2012年
常州宝丽丝纤维有限公司	纱 线	2012年
江苏华冠电器集团有限公司	高低压开关设备	2012年
常州星宇车灯股份有限公司	汽车车灯	2012年
江苏常胜电器有限公司	热保护器	2012年
吟飞科技（江苏）有限公司	电子乐器	2012年
常州千红生化制药股份有限公司	胰激肽原酶、肝素钠及其制剂	2012年
江苏凯特汽车部件有限公司	汽车铝合金车轮	2012年
常州市正阳焊接材料有限公司	气体保护焊丝	2012年
常州市五一灯具有限公司	前组合灯	2012年
常州市永光车业有限公司	摩托车灯具	2012年
常州市莱赛激光工程有限公司	激光扫平仪、激光标线仪	2012年
江苏华达化工集团有限公司	1-萘胺、1-萘酚系列产品	2012年
常州华碧宝特种新材料有限公司	玻璃纤维壁布	2012年
常州工业技术玻璃有限公司	汽车用安全玻璃	2012年

2-17 续表 10　continued 10

企业名称 Name of Enterprises	产品名称 Product Name	颁布时间 Time of Release
常州太平洋电力设备（集团）有限公司	高低压开关柜	2012年
常州能源设备总厂有限公司	有机热载体炉	2012年
常州亚邦化学有限公司	顺酐、富马酸	2012年
常茂生物化学工程股份有限公司	酒石酸	2012年
常州制药厂有限公司	卡托普利系列产品	2012年
常州制药厂有限公司	沙利度胺片	2012年
常州制药厂有限公司	复方硫酸双肼屈嗪片	2012年
常州天马集团有限公司	不饱和聚酯树脂、玻璃纤维制品	2012年
常州科研试制中心有限公司	无极绳连续牵引车	2012年
常州环球地毯制造有限公司	阿克敏斯特机织地毯	2012年
常州市武进中天机房设备有限公司	抗静电活动地板	2012年
江苏德哲木业有限公司	浸渍纸层压木质地板	2012年
常州市威德达耐火板有限公司	热固性树脂浸渍纸高压装饰层积板	2012年
常州双鑫木业有限公司	浸渍纸层压木质地板	2012年
常州市洛景木业有限公司	浸渍纸层压木质地板	2012年
常州市琪豪纺织有限公司	针织面料	2012年
江苏欧龙地板有限公司	浸渍纸层压木质地板	2012年
江苏双奇地板有限公司	浸渍纸层压木质地板	2012年
常州远东连杆集团有限公司	内燃机连杆	2012年
常州普江不锈钢管有限公司	不锈钢无缝钢管	2012年
江苏智思机械集团有限公司	烟草加工机械	2012年
江苏金球链传动有限公司	链　条	2012年
常州玉宇电光器件有限公司	数字电影机用氙灯	2012年
常州市铭锦弹簧有限公司	冷卷螺旋弹簧、拉伸簧、扭簧、卡簧、弹簧补偿器	2012年
常州金海防静电地板有限公司	防静电PVC地板	2012年
常州市武进恒通金属钢丝有限公司	铝包钢、铜包钢、钢丝系列、铝包钢丝护栏网	2012年
江苏双菱链传动有限公司	板式链	2012年
常州市富利华车业有限公司	自行车	2012年
金坛博源电力设备有限公司	低压成套开关设备	2012年
江苏金洋造船有限公司	内河钢质船舶	2012年

2-17 续表 11 continued 11

企业名称 Name of Enterprises	产品名称 Product Name	颁布时间 Time of Release
常州博瑞油泵油嘴有限公司	喷油嘴偶件	2012年
江苏亚邦强生药业有限公司	头孢类口服固体制剂	2012年
江苏力合粘合剂有限公司	粘合剂	2012年
金坛市微特电机有限公司	永磁直流电动机	2012年
常州日晟服装有限公司	衬　衫	2012年
中韩科技有限公司	冰　箱	2012年
常州市新盛电器有限公司	PLC光功率分配器	2012年
常州杨氏电机有限公司	直流电动机	2012年
常州市国宇环保科技有限公司	白　银	2012年
常州凯达重工科技有限公司	铸钢轧辊、铸铁轧辊	2012年
常州常矿起重机械有限公司	起重机	2012年
常州市福兴电器有限公司	节能灯、卤素灯、LED灯、JDD、玻罩等	2012年
江苏胜大石油设备制造股份有限公司	油套管	2012年
江苏安普特防爆科技有限公司	阻隔防爆橇装式加油装置	2012年
江苏圣贤锻造有限责任公司	锻件产品	2012年
常州市科协减速机制造有限公司	摆线针轮减速机	2012年
常州市传动输送机械有限公司	电筒滚筒	2012年
江苏丰顺包装容器有限公司	铁　桶	2012年
常州市武进第一水利机械有限公司	启闭机、水工金属结构、起重机	2012年
常州神龙管业有限公司	不锈钢焊管、钛焊管、钛合金焊管	2012年
江苏新洛凯机电有限公司	智能电网断路器操作机构	2012年
常州市永新华立纺织复合材料有限公司	土工格栅系列	2012年
常州市旺月新材料技术有限公司	酚醛泡沫建筑保温板	2012年
常州市双进电子有限公司	印制线路板	2012年
常州市华岳电子有限公司	无极荧光灯	2012年
江苏恒茂机械制造有限公司	甲醛成套设备	2012年
常州市新亚不锈钢管有限公司	不锈钢无缝钢管	2012年
常州阿斯顿木业有限公司	浸渍纸层压木质地板	2012年
常州市双马医疗器材有限公司	一次性使用输液器 带针	2012年
常州市泛亚微透科技有限公司	微电声元件防尘网胶圈阻尼薄膜	2012年

2-17 续表 12　continued 12

企业名称 Name of Enterprises	产品名称 Product Name	颁布时间 Time of Release
常州倍安特动力机械有限公司	风冷柴油机	2012年
江苏卡特新能源有限公司	环氧脂肪酸甲酯	2012年
常州电站辅机总厂有限公司	阀门电动装置	2012年
常州中进医疗器材有限公司	康复轮椅	2012年
常州市新星原制冷设备有限公司	组合冷库用隔热夹芯板	2012年
江苏聚荣制药集团有限公司	安神补脑液	2012年
常州华迪特种变压器有限公司	干式变频调速用变压器（H级移相整流变压器）	2012年
江苏朗生生命科技有限公司	透析器	2012年
江苏丽岛新材料股份有限公司	彩色涂层铝材	2012年
常州钟恒新材料有限公司	双向拉伸聚酯薄膜	2012年
常州第二电子仪器有限公司	激光测距仪	2012年
常州常松金属复合材料有限公司	镀锌板、彩涂板、镀铝锌板	2012年
常州达立电池有限公司	电　池	2012年
江苏阳湖电缆有限公司	电线电缆	2012年
常州市明景电子有限公司	室外智能高速球型摄像机、红外一体化智能高速云台摄像机等	2012年
常州爱斯特空调设备有限公司	屋顶式空调	2012年
常州市中航复合材料有限公司	铝蜂窝板、石材蜂窝板、蜂窝制品	2012年
常州市嘉鹏塑料制品有限公司	聚乙烯薄膜	2012年
常州市骠马涂装系统工程有限公司	乘用车清洁涂装自动化生产线	2012年
常州市科信燃气设备有限公司	城镇燃气调压箱	2012年
常州新华陵汽车电器有限公司	汽车电器、组合开关	2012年
常州好特曼时装有限公司	西装、西裤	2012年
常州霸狮腾特种纺织品有限公司	遮阳布	2012年
江苏上能新特变压器有限公司	10KV系列干式变压器	2012年
常州纺兴精密机械有限公司	喷丝板	2012年
常州市恒丰铜材有限公司	镀银丝及绞线	2012年
常州联力自动化科技有限公司	矿用隔爆兼本质安全型真空组合开关	2012年
常州市宏光机械有限公司	钣金件	2012年
江苏宏微科技有限公司	IGBT模块	2012年
常州常捷科技有限公司	金属化薄膜电容器	2012年

2-17 续表 13 continued 13

企业名称 Name of Enterprises	产品名称 Product Name	颁布时间 Time of Release
常州市第一橡塑设备有限公司	平板硫化机	2012年
常州东风轴承有限公司	轴 承	2012年
常州华生制药有限公司	奥氮平片	2012年
常州君合科技有限公司	太阳能硅片清洗剂	2012年
常州有则科技有限公司	太阳能级硅片	2012年
常州市云豪车辆部件有限公司	汽车内外饰塑料装饰件	2012年
常州声泰龙电子音响有限公司	扬仕苹果时尚音响	2012年
常州银河世纪微电子有限公司	硅塑封微型贴片半导体分立器件	2012年
江苏久信医用净化工程有限公司	洁净数字化手术室系统	2012年
常州汉森机械有限公司	拖拉机前置装载机	2012年
常州市申宏电力设备有限公司	高低压配电柜、预装式箱式变电站	2012年
常州市西夏墅工具研究所有限公司	可转位面铣刀	2012年
江苏浩峰汽车附件有限公司	汽车空调电机PWM控制模块	2012年
常州市海力工具有限公司	整体硬质合金直柄立铣刀	2012年
常州新区金康精工机械有限公司	双头自动绑线机	2012年
常州普莱克红梅色母料有限公司	塑料色母料系列产品	2012年
江苏叶迪车灯有限公司	系列车灯	2012年
常州常荣电器有限公司	压缩机内置式过载保护器	2012年
特瑞斯信力（常州）燃气设备有限公司	燃气调压箱	2012年
常茂生物化学工程股份有限公司	阿斯巴甜	2012年
江苏维尔利环保科技股份有限公司	膜生化反应器加纳滤组合系统装备	2012年
常州市宝菱重工机械有限公司	冶金刀片、连铸设备、轧制设备和制管工具	2012年
江苏威司顿印刷科技有限公司	预涂感光版	2012年
常州博尼特种钢管有限公司	不锈钢无缝钢管	2012年
溧阳市濑江防火门有限公司	防火门	2012年
布勒（常州）机械有限公司	饲料机械	2012年
溧阳市天目助剂有限公司	工业甲醛溶液	2012年
溧阳中南化工有限公司	井冈·苯醚甲（12%可湿性粉剂）	2012年
江苏省奥谷生物科技有限公司	高转化率糖化酶	2012年

2-17 续表 14　continued 14

企业名称 Name of Enterprises	产品名称 Product Name	颁布时间 Time of Release
溧阳市东晨服饰制伞有限公司	雨　具	2012年
江苏海水冷却塔有限公司	方形横流式冷却塔	2012年
溧阳市金昆锻压有限公司	锻件产品	2012年
溧阳康达威实业有限公司	密封胶	2012年
江苏国强镀锌实业有限公司	低压流体输送管道用螺旋缝埋弧焊钢管	2012年
常州亚泰焊割科技有限公司	数控切割机	2012年
溧阳市虹翔机械制造有限公司	铸件产品	2012年
凡登（常州）新型金属材料技术有限公司	切割钢线	2012年
江苏蓝色星球环保科技股份有限公司	HFC-134a制冷剂	2012年
金坛市金旺包装科技有限公司	全自动水平式袋装机	2012年
江苏晨洋电缆有限公司	电线电缆	2012年
金坛市鸿图橡塑制品有限公司	O型圈橡胶密封圈	2012年
常州市立华生物肥料有限公司	有机肥料	2012年
常州市利来密封件有限公司	旋转轴唇形密封圈	2012年
金坛市新华门窗装璜有限公司	建筑外窗	2012年
江苏柚山建材有限公司	42.5通用硅酸盐水泥	2012年
金坛市利益建材有限公司	实木复合门	2012年
常州翔宇资源再生科技有限公司	电子废弃物的处理和再生利用	2012年
常州金店有限公司	黄铂金、珠宝首饰销售服务	2012年
常州渔蒙家餐饮管理有限公司	餐饮服务	2012年
常州饭店有限公司	餐饮服务	2012年
江苏网泰信息有限公司	药店GSP认证进销存综合信息管理系统软件服务	2012年
常州西普信息科技有限公司	西普物流软件服务	2012年
常州买东西网络科技有限公司	电子商务服务	2012年
江苏世轩科技股份有限公司	世轩电子病历系统软件服务	2012年
常州大江网络工程有限公司	大江治安管理系统软件服务	2012年
溧阳市天目湖南山竹海旅游有限公司	景区游览服务	2012年
溧阳市天目湖南山竹海温泉度假有限公司	温泉服务	2012年
常州市建筑科学研究院股份有限公司	建设工程质量检测服务	2012年

3

CHAPTER 3

行政区划　自然概况

ADMINISTRATIVE DIVISION AND NATURAL RESOURCES

3 行政区划　自然概况
ADMINISTRATIVE DIVISION AND NATURAL RESOURCES

行政区划　自然概况

行政区划

常州市下辖溧阳、金坛两市及武进、新北、天宁、钟楼、戚墅堰五区。溧阳、金坛二市下辖17辖个镇、67个居民委员会（社区居委会）和332个村民委员会；武进、新北、天宁、钟楼、戚墅堰区下辖 21个街道办事处、 20个镇，287个居民委员会（社区居委会）和445个村民委员会。

位　置

常州地处江苏省南部，沪宁线中段，属长江三角洲沿海经济开放区。位于北纬31° 09'至32° 04'，东经119° 08'至120° 12'之间，北倚长江天堑，南与安徽省交界，东濒太湖与无锡市相连，西与南京、镇江两市接壤。

常州水陆空交通便利。沪宁铁路、沪宁与宁杭高速公路、312国道、京杭大运河穿境而过。全市水网纵横交织，连江通海。长江常州港为一类口岸，常州民航站已开通至北京、广州、大连、厦门、深圳、海口、西安等国内近20个大中城市的航线。

地　势

常州地貌类型属高沙平原，山丘平圩兼有。南为天目山余脉，西为茅山山脉，北为宁镇山脉尾部，中部和东部为宽广的平原、圩区。境内地势西南略高，东北略低，高低相差1.5～2米左右。

面　积

常州市总面积4372平方公里，市区面积为1862平方公里。

河　流

常州境内河道纵横交织，湖塘星罗棋布。著名的有泊洮湖（长荡湖）、滆湖、太湖三大天然湖泊，并有沙河（天目湖）、大溪两大人工水库，贯通全境的京杭大运河更是支流密布，脉脉相连，形成江河相通，三湖相连的水系网络。

Administrative Division and Natural Resources

Administrative Division

Changzhou has jurisdiction over two county-level cities and five districts. There are 17 towns, 67 neighborhood committees (community committees), and 332 villagers' committees under the jurisdiction of Jintan city and Liyang city; and Wujin district, Xinbei district, Tianning district, Zhonglou district, Qishuyan district totally administer 21 subdistrict offices, 20 towns, 287 neighborhood committees (community committees) and 445 villagers' committees.

Location

Changzhou, located in the southeast of Jiangsu province and the central section of Shanghai-Nanjing railway, belongs to the coastal economic open zone. Between north latitude 31° 09' to 32° 04' and east longitude 119° 08' to 120° 12', bordering the great Yangtze River in the north, Anhui province in the south and facing Taihu Lake and Wuxi city in the east and neighboring Nanjing city, Zhenjiang city in the west.

Changzhou is easily accessed by water, land and air since it is traversed by railways and expressways, including Shanghai-Nanjing Railway, Shanghai-Nanjing expressway, Nanjing-Hangzhou Expressway, Yangtze Riverside Expressway, Wuxi-Yixing Expressway, Yangzhou-Liyang Expressway, National Highway 312 and Beijing-Hangzhou Grand Canal; Besides, it owns the crisscross network of waters, connecting Yangtze River and leading to the sea. Changzhou Port of the Yangtze River is listed as the state category-1 port; and Changzhou civil airport has scheduled flights to nearly 20 large and medium size domestic cities, such as Beijing, Guangzhou, Dalian, Xiamen, Shenzhen, Haikou and Xi'an, etc.

Topography

The relief type of Changzhou is combined with plain and hills and polders. It has Tianmu Mountain ranges in the south, Maoshan Mountain ranges in the west, Tailing edge of Ningzhen Mountain in the north, vast plain and polder in the central section and east. The terrain is relatively higher in southwest and relatively lower in the northeast with a difference of 1.5 ~ 2 meters.

Area

The total area of Changzhou is 4372sq.km, The urban area covers1862sq.km.

Rivers

The rivers cross the city in a crisscross pattern, and lakes spread all over the city like the stars in the sky and scattered like the pieces on a chessboard.There are three famous natural lakes, such as Taohu Lake (Changdang Lake), Gehu Lake, Taihu Lake and two artificial reservoirs, namely, Shahe (Tianmu), Daxi reservoirs. The Beijing-Hangzhou Grand Canal goes through the city properly with many branches interlinked with rivers, which forms the water system network of canal, rivers interlinked and three lakes connected.

3-1 行政区划和土地面积（2012 年底）
ADMINISTRATIVE DIVISION AND LAND AREA（END OF 2012）

单位：个（unit）

地 区	Region	镇 Town	村民委员会 Villagers Committee	街 道 Subdistrict	居民委员会（社区居委会） Neighborhood Committee（Community Committee）	土地面积（平方公里） Area of Land（sq.km）
全 市	**Whole Municipality**	**37**	**777**	**21**	**354**	**4372.15**
市 区	**Urban Area**	**20**	**445**	**21**	**287**	**1861.96**
武进区	Wujin District	14	246	2	121	1245.84
新北区	Xinbei District	6	115	3	45	452.60
天宁区	Tianning District		34	6	63	65.03
钟楼区	Zhonglou District		41	7	51	66.81
戚墅堰区	Qishuyan District		9	3	7	31.68
县级市	**Cities at Country Level**	**17**	**332**		**67**	**2510.20**
溧阳市	Liyang City	10	175		51	1534.52
金坛市	Jintan City	7	157		16	975.68

3-2 行政区划（1983-2012 年）
ADMINISTRATIVE DIVISION（1983-2012）

单位：个（unit）

年 份 Year	街道办事处 Urban Subdistrict Office	居民委员会（社区居委会） Neighborhhood Committee（Community Committee）	镇人民政府 Town Governments	乡人民政府 Township Governments	村民委员会 Villagers Committee
1983	18	236	7	136	1868
1984	18	265	7	136	1886
1985	19	288	16	125	1914
1986	18	303	16	125	1922
1987	18	329	22	119	1918
1988	19	336	35	106	1922
1989	18	339	39	102	1969
1990	18	363	39	102	1920
1991	18	375	48	93	1919
1992	18	388	49	88	1913
1993	20	414	65	72	1913
1994	19	429	71	66	1915
1995	18	450	74	63	1908
1996	18	460	81	56	1907
1997	19	471	81	56	1903
1998	19	482	81	55	1902
1999	20	505	70	9	1900
2000	23	344	70	9	1888
2001	25	336	70	9	1104
2002	22	339	70	9	1103
2003	27	273	65		1085
2004	27	273	65		1092
2005	24	293	64		1092
2006	16	289	64		1092
2007	20	291	37		1078
2008	20	304	37		1073
2009	21	292	37		940
2010	21	323	37		807
2011	21	359	37		782
2012	21	354	37		777

3-3 分地区镇、街道数及名称（2012年底）
NUMBER AND NAME OF SUBDISTRICT AND TOWN BY REGION（END OF 2012）

单位：个（unit）

指标	Item	镇、街道数 Number of Subdistricts and Towns	镇、街道名称 Names of Subdistricts and Towns
总 计	**Total**	**58**	
街 道	**Subdistrict**	**21**	
按地区分	By Region		
武进区	Wujin District	2	南夏墅、西湖
新北区	Xinbei District	3	河海、三井、龙虎塘
天宁区	Tianning District	6	天宁、兰陵、茶山、雕庄、红梅、青龙
钟楼区	Zhonglou District	7	南大街、荷花池、新闸、五星、永红、北港、西林
戚墅堰区	Qishuyan District	3	戚墅堰、丁堰、潞城
镇	**Town**	**37**	
按地区分	By Region		
市 区	Urban Area	20	
武进区	WujinDistrict	14	湖塘、前黄、洛阳、遥观、横林、横山桥、郑陆、牛塘、奔牛、嘉泽、湟里、雪堰、邹区、礼嘉
新北区	Xinbei District	6	春江、新桥、孟河、西夏墅、薛家、罗溪
溧阳市	Liyang City	10	溧城、社渚 、南渡、上兴、别桥、上黄、竹箦、戴埠、埭头、天目湖
金坛市	Jintan City	7	金城、薛埠、尧塘、直溪、儒林、朱林、指前

4

CHAPTER 4

综 合

GENERAL SURVEY

4 综 合
GENERAL SURVEY

从统计数字看 2012 年的常州
CHANGZHOU IN STATISTICS OF 2012

一、常州的人口
POPULATION OF CHANGZHOU

年末常住人口	Permanent Population at Year-end	468.68 万人	(10000 persons)
#城镇人口	Urban Population	310.31 万人	(10000 persons)
人口密度	Density of population	1072 人/平方公里	(person/sq.km)

二、常州在全省的地位
POSITION OF CHANGZHOU IN JIANGSU PROVINCE

地区生产总值	Gross Domestic Product	居全省第 6 位	No. 6in Jiangsu
人均地区生产总值	Per Capita GDP	居全省第 4 位	No.4in Jiangsu
公共财政预算收入	Public Finance Budget Revenue	居全省第 5 位	No.5 in Jiangsu
进出口总额（海关数）	Total Imports and Exports	居全省第 4 位	No.4 in Jiangsu
#出 口	Exports	居全省第 4 位	No.4 in Jiangsu
城镇居民人均可支配收入	Per Capita Disposable Income of Urban and Town Residents	居全省第 4 位	No.4 in Jiangsu
农民人均纯收入	Average Net Income Per Farmer	居全省第 3 位	No.3 in Jiangsu

三、常州市区的市政建设和公用事业
URBAN CONSTRUCTION AND PUBLIC UTILITIES OF CHANGZHOU

年末建成区面积	Total Area of the Constructed Regions at Year-end	183.24 平方公里	(sq.km)
年末城市道路长度	Length of Roads at Year-end	1891.59 公里	(km)
年末城市道路面积	Area of Roads at Year-end	3451 万平方米	(10000 sq.m)
年末城市桥梁数	Number of Bridges in Urban Area at Year-end	1029 座	(unit)
公共汽车客运总数	Total Volume of Passengers Traffic by Public Buses	41190 万人次	(10000 person-times)
年末供水综合生产能力	Production Capacity of Water Supply at Year-end	197.5 万吨/日	(10000 tons/day)
居民家庭用水	Family Water Consumption	8729.06 万立方米	(10000 m^3)
年末家庭燃气用户数	Number of Consumer of Gas and LPG at Year-end	49.85 万户	(10000 household)
燃气普及率	Percentage of Population with Access to Gas and LGP	99.7%	
年末城市园林绿地面积	Total Area of Parks,Gardens and Green Area in City at Year-end	7914 公顷	(hectare)
建城区绿化覆盖率	Coverage Rate of Green Area in the Constructed Area	42.2%	

四、常州的经济

ECONOMIC OF CHANGZHOU

	2012年实绩 Achievements in 2012	人均水平 Per Capita	日均水平 Per Dialy
地区生产总值 Gross Domestic Produc	3969.87亿元 （100 million yuan）	85039元 （yuan）	108466万元 （10000 yuan）
#第三产业 Tertiary Industry	1742.74亿元 （100 million yuan）	37331元 （yuan）	47616万元 （10000 yuan）
农林牧渔业总产值 Total Output Value of Farming,forestry,Animal Husbandry and Fishing	219.85亿元 （100 million yuan）	6035元 （yuan）	5999万元 （10000 yuan）
#农　业 Agriculture	120.82亿元 （100 million yuan）	3321元 （yuan）	3301万元 （10000 yuan）
规模以上工业总产值 Gross Output Value of Industrial Enterprises above Designated Size	8970.30亿元 （100 million yuan）	246559元 （yuan）	24509万元 （10000 yuan）
社会消费品零售总额 Total Retail Sales of Consumer Goods	1413.33亿元 （100 million yuan）	38847元 （yuan）	38616万元 （10000 yuan）
进出口总额 Total Imports and Exports	290.46亿美元 （USD 100 million）	7979美元 （USD）	7936万美元 （USD 10000）
#出　口 Exports	199.62亿美元 （USD 100 million）	5486美元 （USD）	5454万美元 （USD 10000）
实际到帐注册外资 Foreign Capital Actually Utilized	33.61亿美元 （USD 100 million）	924美元 （USD）	918万美元 （USD 10000）
全社会固定资产投资额 Total Investment in Fixed Assets	2760.14亿元 （100 million yuan）	75866元 （yuan）	75414万元 （10000 yuan）
房地产开发企业竣工住宅建筑面积 Completed Housing Area by Real Estate Development Enterrpises	642.50万平方米 （10000 sq.m）	1.77平方米 （sq.m）	17555平方米 （sq.m）
财政总收入 Financial Revenue	1117.03亿元 （100 million yuan）	30703元 （yuan）	30520万元 （10000 yuan）
#公共财政预算收入 Public Finance Budget Revenue	378.99亿元 （100 million yuan）	10417元 （yuan）	10355万元 （10000 yuan）
邮电业务收入 Revenue from Post & Telecommunication Services	65.93亿元 （100 million yuan）	1812元 （yuan）	1806万元 （10000 yuan）
全社会用电量 Total Electricity Consumed	351.51亿千瓦时 （100 million kw.h）	9662千瓦时 （kw.h）	9604万千瓦时 （10000 kw.h）

注：人均地区生产总值、人均第三产业增加值按常住人口计算。
Note: Per capita of gross regional product and per capita value added of tertiary industry are calculated as per permanent population.

4-1 历年地区生产总值
GROSS DOMESTIC PRODUCT OVER THE YEARS

单位：万元（10000 yuan）

年 份 Year	地区生产总值 Gross Domestic Product	其中 of which				
		第一产业 Primary Industry	第二产业 Secondary Industry	其中 of which		第三产业 Tertiary Industry
				工业 Industry	建筑业 Construction	
1949	24979	17434	3193	3129	64	4352
1950	28470	18951	4463	4339	124	5056
1951	31080	19497	5310	5114	196	6273
1952	34493	21086	6620	5980	640	6787
1953	38228	21944	8331	7865	466	7953
1954	37536	20704	8482	7978	504	8350
1955	37985	21262	7539	6959	580	9184
1956	42016	21606	9713	8849	864	10697
1957	41120	20269	11410	10565	845	9441
1958	50377	20110	19284	17632	1652	10983
1959	53880	16766	24578	22848	1730	12536
1960	62495	18720	27681	26005	1676	16094
1961	45580	16215	16742	16001	741	12623
1962	46409	19128	15090	14311	779	12191
1963	49362	22345	15418	14513	905	11599
1964	53181	24631	17678	16711	967	10872
1965	62909	29268	21549	20524	1025	12092
1966	68993	31178	25295	24176	1119	12520
1967	63602	30983	20405	19306	1099	12214
1968	62681	27946	22896	21798	1098	11839
1969	71965	29154	29640	28420	1220	13171
1970	81090	27892	39166	37189	1977	14032
1971	96559	33300	48162	45761	2401	15097
1972	108835	33843	56735	53487	3248	18257
1973	122521	35367	67591	63108	4483	19563
1974	125285	35160	70303	66170	4133	19822
1975	131084	30945	78314	74137	4177	21825
1976	144282	35323	86637	81957	4680	22322
1977	154405	30472	99584	94311	5273	24349
1978	175707	38525	112468	105407	7061	24714
1979	201753	49760	122481	112412	10069	29512
1980	227642	48897	142729	133235	9494	36016

4-1 续表 continued

单位：万元（10000 yuan）

年 份 Year	地区生产总值 Gross Domestic Product	其中 of which 第一产业 Primary Industry	第二产业 Secondary Industry	其中 of which 工业 Industry	建筑业 Construction	第三产业 Tertiary Industry
1981	247378	51946	158129	147001	11128	37303
1982	260487	62795	160469	147281	13188	37223
1983	298476	70682	180162	166110	14052	47632
1984	387700	97530	218908	203098	15810	71262
1985	495896	105195	304811	280504	24307	85890
1986	547374	117724	328039	297125	30914	101611
1987	664549	125279	412259	376766	35493	127011
1988	821138	153477	505986	461754	44232	161675
1989	872397	165070	521667	483264	38403	185660
1990	948687	176805	579610	540600	39010	192272
1991	1021751	160573	656120	610693	45427	205058
1992	1443961	190338	929968	859302	70666	323655
1993	2238962	250531	1481661	1366806	114855	506770
1994	3149332	338176	2009160	1861541	147619	801996
1995	3697000	398160	2206420	2028562	177858	1092420
1996	4311541	455496	2465057	2236314	228743	1390988
1997	4701069	443684	2658167	2400789	257378	1599218
1998	5045974	444352	2810279	2526923	283356	1791343
1999	5387217	440113	2995019	2689386	305633	1952085
2000	6006573	451378	3366847	3019891	346956	2188348
2001	6729008	471137	3807601	3416841	390760	2450270
2002	7606035	488378	4315041	3877933	437108	2802616
2003	9014200	471800	5202500	4689100	513400	3339900
2004	11021900	541900	6618600	5929600	689000	3861400
2005	13081800	596200	7990500	7199500	791000	4495100
2006	15851100	660700	9544500	8750400	794100	5645900
2007	19135000	743200	11351300	10476100	875200	7040500
2008	22663200	845000	13170500	12094000	1076500	8647700
2009	25199300	917500	14297300	13016300	1281000	9984500
2010	30448900	997800	16836800	15308600	1528200	12614300
2011	35809900	1117800	19508400	17689100	1819300	15183700
2012	39698700	1263700	21007600	19005500	2002100	17427400

注：2000-2003年数据根据第一次经济普查结果进行了调整，2005-2007年数据根据第二次经济普查结果进行了调整。

Note: The data collected during 2000-2003 were adjusted according to the record of the first Economic Census; and the data collected during 2005-2007 were adjusted according to the record of the second Economic Census.

4-2 地区生产总值指数（1978-2012 年，上年 =100）
GROSS DOMESTIC PRODUCT INDEX NUMBER（1978-2012， PRECEDING YEAR=100）

按可比价格计算 Calculated by comparable price

年份 Year	地区生产总值 Gross Domestic Product	其中 of which 第一产业 Primary Industry	第二产业 Secondary Industry	其中 of which 工业 Industry	第三产业 Tertiary Industry	人均地区生产总值 Per Capita Gross Domestic Product
1978	100.0	100.0	100.0	100.0	100.0	100.0
1979	108.6	104.4	108.0	106.2	117.9	107.8
1980	112.2	97.4	116.4	118.1	115.2	111.3
1981	108.5	103.2	111.3	110.9	102.2	107.6
1982	104.1	113.5	102.9	101.8	98.9	103.1
1983	114.8	108.4	113.9	114.4	127.8	113.8
1984	126.6	131.0	120.7	121.4	146.0	125.7
1985	122.8	97.9	133.7	132.4	110.1	122.2
1986	105.9	103.2	105.4	103.8	110.5	105.2
1987	116.3	96.0	121.1	122.1	114.3	115.1
1988	110.6	99.7	113.9	113.6	104.1	109.3
1989	94.7	102.9	92.8	94.0	98.3	93.5
1990	107.9	98.8	110.8	111.6	101.3	106.5
1991	107.3	88.8	114.6	114.9	102.2	106.4
1992	134.8	107.9	136.5	136.4	150.6	134.0
1993	133.9	110.1	137.8	139.5	135.6	133.4
1994	116.6	114.2	112.3	112.7	130.2	116.1
1995	113.6	109.6	113.1	113.1	116.5	112.8
1996	110.8	105.6	109.6	108.8	116.0	109.8
1997	109.1	101.3	108.5	108.3	113.1	108.2
1998	110.8	100.0	111.3	111.4	112.8	110.3
1999	110.2	104.6	110.6	110.7	110.6	110.1
2000	111.0	104.3	111.3	111.3	112.1	110.9
2001	112.0	105.7	112.9	113.1	112.0	111.7
2002	112.4	105.2	113.4	113.5	112.3	112.1
2003	114.5	102.4	116.5	117.3	113.3	113.7
2004	115.5	102.7	117.6	118.1	114.1	114.6
2005	115.1	105.0	116.3	116.5	114.8	113.6
2006	115.2	105.0	115.8	117.6	115.5	112.0
2007	115.6	103.5	116.2	117.3	116.0	112.6
2008	112.4	103.8	112.1	112.6	113.7	110.4
2009	111.7	104.7	110.8	110.4	114.1	110.5
2010	113.1	104.3	113.2	113.3	113.6	110.7
2011	112.2	103.9	112.2	112.6	112.8	109.8
2012	111.5	104.7	111.7	111.7	111.6	110.4

4-3 地区生产总值指数（1978-2012 年，1978=100）
GROSS DOMESTIC PRODUCT INDEX NUMBER（1978-2012，1978=100）

按可比价格计算 Calculated by comparable price

年份 Year	地区生产总值 Gross Domestic Product	其中 of which 第一产业 Primary Industry	第二产业 Secondary Industry	其中 of which 工业 Industry	第三产业 Tertiary Industry	人均地区生产总值 Per Capita Gross Domestic Product
1978	100.0	100.0	100.0	100.0	100.0	100.0
1979	108.6	104.4	108.0	106.2	117.9	107.8
1980	121.8	101.7	125.7	125.4	135.8	120.0
1981	132.1	105.0	139.9	139.1	138.8	129.1
1982	137.5	119.2	144.0	141.6	137.3	133.1
1983	157.8	129.2	164.0	162.0	175.5	151.5
1984	199.7	169.2	197.9	196.7	256.2	190.4
1985	245.2	165.6	264.6	260.4	282.1	232.7
1986	259.7	170.9	278.9	270.3	311.7	244.8
1987	302.0	164.1	337.8	330.0	356.2	281.7
1988	334.0	163.6	384.7	374.9	370.9	307.9
1989	316.3	168.3	357.0	352.4	364.5	287.9
1990	341.3	166.3	395.6	393.3	369.3	306.6
1991	366.2	147.7	453.4	451.9	377.4	326.2
1992	493.7	159.4	618.8	616.4	568.4	437.2
1993	661.0	175.5	852.8	859.9	770.8	583.2
1994	770.7	200.4	957.6	969.1	1003.5	677.1
1995	875.6	219.6	1083.1	1096.0	1169.1	763.7
1996	970.1	231.9	1187.1	1192.5	1356.2	838.6
1997	1058.4	234.9	1288.0	1291.5	1533.9	907.4
1998	1172.7	234.9	1433.5	1438.7	1730.2	1000.8
1999	1292.3	245.7	1585.5	1592.6	1913.6	1101.9
2000	1434.5	256.3	1764.7	1772.6	2145.1	1222.0
2001	1606.6	270.9	1992.3	2004.8	2402.5	1365.0
2002	1805.8	285.0	2259.3	2275.4	2698.0	1530.2
2003	2067.6	291.8	2632.1	2669.0	3056.8	1739.8
2004	2388.1	299.7	3095.3	3152.1	3487.8	1993.8
2005	2748.7	314.7	3599.8	3672.2	4000.5	2265.0
2006	3166.5	330.4	4168.6	4267.1	4620.6	2536.8
2007	3660.5	342.0	4843.9	5005.3	5359.8	2856.4
2008	4114.4	356.4	5430.0	5636.0	6094.2	3153.5
2009	4595.8	373.1	6016.4	6227.8	6953.3	3484.6
2010	5197.8	389.1	6810.6	7056.1	7898.9	3857.5
2011	5832.0	404.3	7641.5	7945.2	8910.0	4235.5
2012	6502.7	423.3	8535.5	8874.8	9943.6	4676.0

4-4 历年地区生产总值构成
PROPORTIONS IN GROSS DOMESTIC PRODUCT OVER THE YEARS

单位：%

年 份 Year	地区生产总值 Gross Domestic Product	其 中 of which				
		第一产业 Primary Industry	第二产业 Secondary Industry	其 中 of which		第三产业 Tertiary Industry
				工 业 Industry	建筑业 Construction	
1949	100	69.8	12.8	12.5	0.3	17.4
1950	100	66.6	15.7	15.2	0.4	17.8
1951	100	62.7	17.1	16.5	0.6	20.2
1952	100	61.1	19.2	17.3	1.9	19.7
1953	100	57.4	21.8	20.6	1.2	20.8
1954	100	55.2	22.6	21.3	1.3	22.2
1955	100	56.0	19.8	18.3	1.5	24.2
1956	100	51.4	23.1	21.1	2.1	25.5
1957	100	49.3	27.7	25.7	2.1	23.0
1958	100	39.9	38.3	35.0	3.3	21.8
1959	100	31.1	45.6	42.4	3.2	23.3
1960	100	30.0	44.3	41.6	2.7	25.8
1961	100	35.6	36.7	35.1	1.6	27.7
1962	100	41.2	32.5	30.8	1.7	26.3
1963	100	45.3	31.2	29.4	1.8	23.5
1964	100	46.3	33.2	31.4	1.8	20.4
1965	100	46.5	34.3	32.6	1.6	19.2
1966	100	45.2	36.7	35.0	1.6	18.1
1967	100	48.7	32.1	30.4	1.7	19.2
1968	100	44.6	36.5	34.8	1.8	18.9
1969	100	40.5	41.2	39.5	1.7	18.3
1970	100	34.4	48.3	45.9	2.4	17.3
1971	100	34.5	49.9	47.4	2.5	15.6
1972	100	31.1	52.1	49.1	3.0	16.8
1973	100	28.9	55.2	51.5	3.7	16.0
1974	100	28.1	56.1	52.8	3.3	15.8
1975	100	23.6	59.7	56.6	3.2	16.6
1976	100	24.5	60.0	56.8	3.2	15.5
1977	100	19.7	64.5	61.1	3.4	15.8
1978	100	21.9	64.0	60.0	4.0	14.1
1979	100	24.7	60.7	55.7	5.0	14.6
1980	100	21.5	62.7	58.5	4.2	15.8

4-4 续表 continued

单位：%

年 份 Year	地区生产总值 Gross Domestic Product	其中 of which 第一产业 Primary Industry	第二产业 Secondary Industry	其中 of which 工 业 Industry	建筑业 Construction	第三产业 Tertiary Industry
1981	100	21.0	63.9	59.4	4.5	15.1
1982	100	24.1	61.6	56.5	5.1	14.3
1983	100	23.7	60.4	55.7	4.7	16.0
1984	100	25.2	56.5	52.4	4.1	18.4
1985	100	21.2	61.5	56.6	4.9	17.3
1986	100	21.5	59.9	54.3	5.6	18.6
1987	100	18.9	62.0	56.7	5.3	19.1
1988	100	18.7	61.6	56.2	5.4	19.7
1989	100	18.9	59.8	55.4	4.4	21.3
1990	100	18.6	61.1	57.0	4.1	20.3
1991	100	15.7	64.2	59.8	4.4	20.1
1992	100	13.2	64.4	59.5	4.9	22.4
1993	100	11.2	66.2	61.0	5.1	22.6
1994	100	10.7	63.8	59.1	4.7	25.5
1995	100	10.8	59.7	54.9	4.8	29.5
1996	100	10.6	57.2	51.9	5.3	32.3
1997	100	9.4	56.5	51.1	5.5	34.0
1998	100	8.8	55.7	50.1	5.6	35.5
1999	100	8.2	55.6	49.9	5.7	36.2
2000	100	7.5	56.1	50.3	5.8	36.4
2001	100	7.0	56.6	50.8	5.8	36.4
2002	100	6.4	56.8	51.0	5.8	36.8
2003	100	5.2	57.7	52.0	5.7	37.1
2004	100	4.7	58.8	53.1	5.7	36.5
2005	100	4.6	61.0	55.0	6.0	34.4
2006	100	4.2	60.2	55.2	5.0	35.6
2007	100	3.9	59.3	54.7	4.6	36.8
2008	100	3.7	58.1	53.4	4.7	38.2
2009	100	3.6	56.8	51.7	5.1	39.6
2010	100	3.3	55.3	50.3	5.0	41.4
2011	100	3.1	54.5	49.4	5.1	42.4
2012	100	3.2	52.9	47.9	5.0	43.9

注：2000-2003年数据根据第一次经济普查结果进行了调整，2005-2007年数据根据第二次经济普查结果进行了调整。
Note: The data collected during 2000-2003 were adjusted according to the record of the first Economic Census; and the data collected during 2005-2007 were adjusted according to the record of the second Economic Census.

4-5 历年分地区人均生产总值
PER CAPITA OF GROSS DOMESTIC PRODUCT BY REGION OVER THE YEARS

单位：元（yuan）

年 份 Year	全 市 Whole Municipality	市 区 Urban Area	溧阳市 Liyang City	金坛市 Jintan City	年 份 Year	全 市 Whole Municipality	市 区 Urban Area	溧阳市 Liyang City	金坛市 Jintan City
1949	144	183	73	83	1981	832	1088	432	482
1950	163	208	89	84	1982	867	1120	454	545
1951	174	223	98	88	1983	985	1276	518	599
1952	190	238	117	105	1984	1272	1615	748	781
1953	206	262	114	116	1985	1620	2101	901	905
1954	198	252	112	110	1986	1775	2271	1007	1071
1955	196	249	115	109	1987	2134	2722	1231	1273
1956	213	279	118	98	1988	2606	3225	1597	1778
1957	205	264	119	106	1989	2732	3404	1618	1859
1958	243	321	135	103	1990	2935	3709	1662	1917
1959	253	342	128	87	1991	3136	4000	1740	1959
1960	291	400	123	96	1992	4404	5568	2499	2853
1961	211	289	80	92	1993	6806	8569	4075	4208
1962	212	285	90	106	1994	9532	11714	6121	6313
1963	219	283	120	116	1995	11117	13870	7912	7612
1964	229	290	126	147	1996	12847	15369	9294	9486
1965	264	343	139	151	1997	13892	16204	8174	8420
1966	283	373	140	155	1998	14842	16962	8869	9472
1967	256	323	143	173	1999	15834	18323	9431	10399
1968	247	327	124	138	2000	17635	20744	10344	11648
1969	279	375	133	147	2001	19704	23370	11563	13392
1970	308	429	126	147	2002	22215	26744	13005	15662
1971	358	485	198	153	2003	26149	31920	15415	18648
1972	397	529	245	165	2004	31665	38601	18968	22594
1973	441	583	264	205	2005	32116	34874	24456	27986
1974	445	604	239	188	2006	37809	40574	29658	33008
1975	462	645	221	166	2007	44452	46994	36039	38771
1976	504	696	261	181	2008	51746	53788	43186	43486
1977	535	739	273	189	2009	56890	60756	48488	47863
1978	605	810	309	305	2010	67327	71812	56784	56127
1979	689	914	334	395	2011	77485	81897	66934	65946
1980	771	1000	405	470	2012	85039	90107	73768	67129

注：1.2005年起人均地区生产总值按常住人口计算。
2.2000-2003年数据根据第一次经济普查结果进行了调整，2005-2007年数据根据第二次经济普查结果进行了调整。

Note: 1.Per capita regional GDP is calculated as per permanent population since 2005.
2.The data collected during 2000-2003 were adjusted according to the record of the first Economic Census; and the data collected during2005-2007 were adjusted according to the record of the second Economic Census.

4-6 分地区生产总值（2012年）
GROSS DOMESTIC PRODUCT BY REGION（2012）

单位：亿元（100 million yuan）

指标	Item	全市 Whole Municipality	其中 of which 市区 Urban Area	溧阳市 Liyang City	金坛市 Jintan City
地区生产总值	**Gross Domestic Product**	**3969.87**	**3021.64**	**559.20**	**373.81**
第一产业	Primary Industry	126.37	59.70	39.02	27.64
第二产业	Secondary Industry	2100.76	1633.15	306.58	197.81
工　业	Industry	1900.55	1517.22	278.79	169.68
建筑业	Construction	200.21	115.93	27.79	28.13
第三产业	Tertiary Industry	1742.74	1328.79	213.60	148.36
交通运输业和仓储业	Transport and Storage	164.17	116.41	42.07	26.82
信息传输、计算机服务和软件业	Information Transmission, Computer Servcie and Software Industries	52.15	36.67	3.94	4.84
批发和零售业	Retail and Wholesale Industries	441.89	367.87	49.06	24.02
住宿和餐饮业	Hoteling and Cateries	111.97	89.40	12.13	6.00
金融业	Financial	227.46	178.58	27.12	12.54
银行及其他金融活动	Banking and Other Financing Activities	218.78	171.25	26.74	11.16
保险业	Insurance	8.68	7.33	0.38	1.38
房地产业	Real Estate	215.58	163.19	25.12	10.49
房地产开发经营业	Real Estate Development Industry	121.98	111.10	13.98	3.08
物业管理、中介服务业和其他房地产	Property Management, Agency Service Industry and Other Real Estate	17.36	15.00	1.13	1.94
居民自有住房服务业	Resident Private House Service Industry	76.24	37.09	10.01	5.47
租赁和商务服务业	Leasehold and Business in Services	185.06	140.89	10.76	10.75
科学研究、技术服务和地质勘查业	Scientific Research, Technology Service and Geological Prospecting	22.76	19.92	1.21	2.70
水利、环境和公共设施管理业	Water Conservancy, Environment and Public Facility Management	36.15	18.92	2.22	17.93
居民服务和其他服务业	Community Service and Other Service	51.58	27.42	3.99	3.04
教　育	Education	79.28	61.10	10.45	9.14
卫生、社会保障和社会福利业	Health, Social Security and Welfare	38.21	29.73	3.67	4.70
文化、体育和娱乐业	Culture, Sports and Entertainment	29.01	19.33	5.05	4.47
公共管理和社会组织	Public Administration and Social Organizations	87.47	59.36	16.81	10.92

4-7 主要年份社会经济主要指标 MAJOR SOCIAL AND ECONOMIC INDICATORS IN MAIN YEARS

指　标	Item	1990	1995	2000	2005	2010	2012
人口与就业	**Population and Employment**						
人　口	**Population**						
年末总人口（万人）	Year-end Population （10000 persons）	324.85	333.65	341.48	351.63	360.80	364.77
#非农业人口	Non-agricultural Population	81.40	120.48	147.81	160.56	161.68	196.94
就　业	**Employment**						
从业人员（万人）	Employment（10000 persons）	186.06	188.78	179.36	222.31	272.00	280.99
在岗职工人（万人）	Number of Fully Employed Staff and Workers（10000 persons）	56.17	54.42	40.39	35.11	36.70	46.80
宏观经济	**Macroeconomy**						
国民经济核算	**National Accounting**						
地区生产总值（亿元）	Gross Domestic Products （100 million yuan）	94.87	369.70	600.66	1308.18	3044.89	3969.87
第一产业	Primary Industry	17.68	39.82	45.14	59.62	99.78	126.37
第二产业	Secondary Industry	57.96	220.64	336.68	799.05	1683.68	2100.76
#工　业	Industy	54.06	202.86	301.99	719.95	1530.86	1900.55
第三产业	Tertiary Industry	19.23	109.24	218.83	449.51	1261.43	1742.74
固定资产投资	**Investment in Fixed Assets**						
全社会固定资产投资完成额（亿元）	Total Investment in Fixed Assets（100 million yuan）	22.71	115.06	163.43	769.80	2103.55	2760.14
#房地产开发	Real Estate Investment	0.95	18.47	29.98	114.27	446.96	597.01
财　政	**Government Finance**						
财政总收入（亿元）	Financial Revenue （100 million yuan）	13.10	28.50	60.23	220.45	841.67	1117.03
#公共财政预算收入	Public Finance Budget Revenue			32.25	94.99	286.18	378.99
公共财政预算支出	Public Finance Budget Expenditure			31.83	97.85	281.44	391.22
#用于教育	Education Expenditure			6.12	13.47	40.61	66.11
吸收外资	**Forign Capital Inducement**						
新签外资项目数（个）	The number of new foreign investment projects signed （unit）	40	292	167	509	327	298
协议（合同）外资金额（亿美元）	Amount of Foreign Capital in the Newly Signed Agreements（USD 100 million）	0.18	8.87	10.03	28.51	47.42	47.49
实际到帐注册外资（亿美元）	Foreign Capital Actually Utilized（USD 100 million）	0.07	3.29	7.00	7.31	26.70	33.61

4-7　续表 1　continued 1

指　标	Item	1990	1995	2000	2005	2010	2012
产　业	**Industries**						
农　业	**Agriculture**						
耕地面积（千公顷）	Cultivated Areas（1000 hectares）	204.54	200.88	204.25	176.32	150.39	149.71
从业人员（万人）	Employment（10000 persons）	135.80	136.31	128.67	126.86	133.95	129.93
农林牧渔业总产值（亿元）	Gross Output Value of Agriculture（100 million yuan）	29.06	74.74	85.88	104.10	174.09	219.58
主要农副产品产量	Output of Major Farm and Sideline Products						
粮　食（万吨）	Grain（10000 tons）	164.50	159.57	136.22	98.06	115.16	114.80
油　料（吨）	Oil-Bearing Crop（ton）	63899	72786	91629	85960	40035	37684
水产品（吨）	Aquatic Products（ton）	53149	90571	111188	130198	147938	181240
蚕　茧（吨）	Silkworm Cocoons（ton）	8726	10055	4815	2843	671	469
水　果（吨）	Fruits（ton）	9670	22716	29639	67275	99565	117431
茶　叶（吨）	Tea（ton）	3730	2550	2680	2762	3464	3502
工　业	**Industry**						
规模以上工业企业主要经济指标	**Major Economy Indictors of Industrial Enterprises above Designated Size**						
工业总产值（亿元）	Gross Output Value of Industry（100 million yuan）	196.20	579.62	874.63	2504.19	7396.09	8970.30
固定资产原价（亿元）	Original Value of Fixed Assets（100 million yuan）	80.42	252.19	395.90	796.70	2219.00	3353.34
主营业务收入（亿元）	Main Business Income（100 million yuan）	160.85	542.82	836.10	2459.56	7274.88	9097.95
实现利税（亿元）	Total Pre-tax Profits（100 million yuan）	13.21	34.65	59.64	161.84	620.18	730.30
建筑业	**Construction**						
建筑业总产值（亿元）	Gross Output Value of Construction（100 million yuan）	8.64	30.93	123.18	283.48	735.61	1050.20
房屋竣工建筑面积（万平方米）	Floor Space of Buildings Completed（10000 sq.m）	193.97	194.70	630.28	1588.83	2659.14	3067.89
交通运输、邮电通信	**Transportation,Post and Telecommunications**						
货物运输量（万吨）	Freight Traffic（10000 tons）	4375	5804	4696	6032	13109	17154
旅客发送量（万人次）	Number of Passenger Despatched（10000 person-times）	5048	7270	10196	15235	29361	17257
邮电业务收入（亿元）	Total Busines Volume of Post and Telecommunications（100 million yuan）	0.65	5.46	16.84	34.36	55.69	65.93
年末固定电话用户（万户）	Number of Fixed Telephone Subscribers at Year-end（10000 Subscribers）	15.57	19.79	75.88	202.08	159.58	161.61

4-7 续表 2 continued 2

指 标	Item	1990	1995	2000	2005	2010	2012
年末移动电话用户（万户）	Number of Mobile Telephone Subscribers at Year-end （10000 Subscribers）		1.80	56.68	207.46	501.39	519.35
电话交换机容量（万门）	Capacity of Telephone Exchanges （10000 line）	5.16	29.79	118.30	160.33	284.41	365.80
国内商业	**Domestic Trade**						
社会消费品零售总额（亿元）	Total Retail Sales of Consumer Goods （100 million yuan）	38.19	131.78	202.31	444.94	1054.39	1413.33
对外经济贸易	**Foreign Trade**						
进出口总额（亿美元）	Total Exports and Imports （USD 100 million）	0.62	9.93	28.22	83.34	222.78	290.46
进 口	Imports	0.12	2.24	9.62	22.09	67.19	90.84
出 口	Exports	0.50	7.69	18.60	61.24	155.58	199.62
国际旅游	**International Tourism**						
来常旅游人数（万人次）	Number of Tourists from Abroad （10000 person-times）	0.70	1.95	3.31	18.20	35.91	45.57
旅游外汇收入（亿美元）	Foreign Exchange Earnings from Tourism （USD 100 million）		0.10	0.24	1.44	3.47	4.74
金融保险	**Banking & Insurance**						
金融机构存款余额（亿元）	Deposit Balance of Financial Institutions （100 million yuan）	59.37	257.61	629.36	1649.61	4550.47	5604.90
金融机构贷款余额（亿元）	Loans Balance of Financial Institutions （100 million. yuan）	74.24	211.88	389.26	1113.25	3011.67	3832.80
保险费收入（亿元）	Income From Insurances （100 million yuan）	1.00	4.44	12.10	37.88	86.53	109.44
保险赔（结）款支出（亿元）	Expenditure for Insurance Claims （100 million yuan）	0.25	1.28	3.59	10.42	18.76	29.93
教育、科技	**Education,Science and Technology**						
教 育	**Education**						
专任教师数（万人）	Full-time Teachers （10000 persons）	2.52	2.74	2.82	3.16	3.46	3.48
#普通高等学校	Institutions of Higher Education	0.07	0.10	0.12	0.45	0.54	0.52
普通中学	Regular Secondary Schools	0.91	0.96	1.04	1.29	1.39	1.39
小 学	Primary Schools	1.31	1.36	1.30	1.14	1.19	1.23
在校学生数（万人）	Students Enrollment （10000 persons）	46.10	50.19	57.10	64.88	60.39	59.69
#普通高等学校	Institutions of Higher Education	0.51	1.16	2.00	9.54	12.28	12.46
普通中学	Regular Secondary Schools	14.90	15.86	18.23	22.07	18.84	16.91
小 学	Primary Schools	27.70	27.16	30.01	24.46	22.15	23.43

4-7 续表 3 continued 3

指　标	Item	1990	1995	2000	2005	2010	2012
科　技	**Science and Technology**						
专利申请量（项）	Number of Patent Applications Examined（unit）		547	837	2696	15872	39391
专利授权量（项）	Number of Patent Authorizations Granted（unit）		255	731	1240	9093	15379
家庭、生活、环境	**Family, Livelihood and Environment**						
家　庭	**Family**						
家庭总户数（万户）	Total Number of Household（10000 households）	106.91	114.00	117.89	121.97	127.11	128.75
平均每户家庭人口（人）	Average Number of Household Size（person）	3.04	2.93	2.90	2.88	2.84	2.83
婚　姻	**Marriages and Divorces**						
准予登记结婚（对）	Marriage Leagally Registered（couple）	24093	31889	23916	26536	33182	37719
准予登记离婚数（对）	Divorce Leagally Registered（couple）	604	1399	2203	5001	7795	8678
住　宅	**Housing**						
农村居民人均住房面积（平方米）	Per Capita Living Space Of Rural Residents（sq.m）	31.66	35.90	49.27	56.20	58.40	60.31
生　活	**People's Livelihood**						
农村居民人均纯收入（元）	Per Capita Net Income Of Rural Residents（yuan）	1401	3397	4430	7002	12637	16737
农村居民人均生活消费支出（元）	Per Capita Living Expenditure of Rural Residents（yuan）	1231	2952	3243	5712	9924	12027
城乡居民储蓄存款余额（亿元）	Balance of Saving Deposits in Urban and Rural Residents（100 million yuan）	34.29	128.65	355.57	865.39	2009.24	2473.27
工　资	**Wages**						
在岗职工工资总额（亿元）	Total Wages of Fully Employde Staff and Workers（100 million yuan）	12.90	38.68	48.97	78.57	161.50	259.01
卫　生	**Health Care**						
医　院（包括卫生院，个）	Hospitals（include Township Hospitals,unit）	163	161	117	113	91	109
医　生（人）	Doctors（person）	6144	7073	7779	8356	9962	10943
医院床位数（包括卫生院，张）	Number of Hospital Beds（include Township Hospitals,unit）	9495	10339	10730	11734	15263	19140
火灾、交通事故	**Fire Loss and Road Accidents**						
火灾发生数（起）	Number of Fire Disasters（time）	262	229	1371	2209	340	394
火灾损失额（万元）	Fire Loss（10000 yuan）	140	430	507	460	637	286
道路交通事故发生数（起）	Number of Road Accidents（time）	1163	1425	3405	2993	1409	1293
道路交通事故损失额（万元）	Loss of Road Accidents（10000 yuan）	144	765	1301	770	247	304

4-8 主要年份市区社会经济主要指标
MAJOR SOCIAL AND ECONOMIC INDICATORS OF URBAN DISTRICTS IN MAIN YEARS

指标	Item	1990	1995	2000	2005	2010	2012
人口与就业	Population and Employment						
人口	Population						
年末总人口（万人）	Year-end Population（10000 persons）	195.24	202.20	208.18	220.76	227.75	230.47
#非农业人口	Non-agricultural Population	64.74	84.50	104.39	110.38	121.96	135.52
就业	Employment						
从业人员（万人）	Employment（10000 persons）	117.84	118.01	111.55	148.55	186.92	193.86
在岗职工人数（万人）	Number of Fully Employed Staff and Workers（10000 persons）	45.19	42.44	29.90	25.36	26.22	34.68
宏观经济	Macroeconomy						
国民经济核算	National Accounting						
地区生产总值（亿元）	Gross Domestic Products （100 million yuan）	72.06	279.19	430.89	981.45	2316.26	3021.64
第一产业	Primary Industry	9.07	20.95	22.75	27.03	47.64	59.70
第二产业	Secondary Industry	48.54	179.22	256.10	620.51	1316.20	1633.15
#工业	Industy	45.91	170.20	239.46	571.46	1229.12	1517.22
第三产业	Tertiary Industry	14.44	79.02	152.04	333.91	952.42	1328.79
固定资产投资	Investment in Fixed Assets						
全社会固定资产投资完成额（亿元）	Total Investment in Fixed Assets（100 million yuan）	17.09	85.23	126.90	609.75	1649.98	2166.09
#房地产开发	Real Estate Investment	0.78	14.62	25.46	97.76	401.22	531.74
财政	Government Finance						
财政总收入（亿元）	Financial Revenue （100 million yuan）	11.66	23.99	50.77	182.12	710.11	930.51
#公共财政预算收入	Public Finance Budget Revenue			27.60	79.14	239.15	315.38
公共财政预算支出	Public Finance Budget Expenditure			25.41	79.80	225.81	313.66
#用于教育	Education Expenditure			4.05	9.55	28.40	48.22
价格	Price						
居民消费价格指数（上年=100）	Consumer Price Index（preceding year=100）	104.2	114.9	99.5	102.8	103.4	102.5
商品零售价格指数（上年=100）	Retail Price Index（preceding year=100）	103.4	112.8	98.0	101.3	102.7	101.7
吸收外资	Forign Capital Inducement						
新签外资项目数（个）	The number of new foreign Investment projects Signed （unit）	39	243	132	355	208	218
协议（合同）外资金额（亿美元）	Amount of Foreign Capital in the Newly Signed Agreements（USD 100 million）	0.15	7.05	4.78	20.33	31.61	33.41

注：本表资料1990、1995、2000年数据除城市建设外均按新行政区划作了调整，2005年起均为新行政区划数据。
Note: The data of 1990, 1995 and 2000 in this table had been adjusted according to the new administrative division, except those of urban construction. The data are all under new administrative division since 2005.

4-8 续表 1 continued 1

指　标	Item	1990	1995	2000	2005	2010	2012
产　业	**Industries**						
农　业	**Agriculture**						
耕地面积（千公顷）	Cultivated Areas（1000 hectares）	97.01	94.80	88.75	64.27	59.25	58.37
从业人员（万人）	Employment（10000 persons）	76.65	75.96	71.22	75.19	81.99	77.61
农林牧渔业总产值（亿元）	Gross Output Value of Agriculture（100 million yuan）	15.48	39.34	43.81	47.90	78.39	97.99
主要农副产品产量	Output of Major Farm and Sideline Products						
粮　食（万吨）	Grain（10000 tons）	89.07	81.30	66.11	39.28	34.22	32.02
油　料（吨）	Oil-Bearing Crop（ton）	11710	12068	17412	8489	3922	3228
水产品（吨）	Aquatic Products（ton）	16049	45321	35588	57173	52783	69184
水　果（吨）	Fruits（ton）	6038	18527	21811	49747	56204	75751
工　业	**Industry**						
规模以上工业企业主要经济指标	Major Economy Indictors of Industrial Enterprises above Designated Size						
工业总产值（亿元）	Gross Output Value of Industry（100 million yuan）	163.78	474.76	730.74	2032.39	5873.16	7043.25
固定资产原价（亿元）	Original Value of Fixed Assets（100 million yuan）	69.40	215.79	339.76	660.42	1859.81	2790.69
主营业务收入（亿元）	Main Business Income（100 million yuan）	136.76	446.40	704.23	2016.20	5789.68	7156.86
实现利税（亿元）	Total Pre-tax Profits（100 million yuan）	11.67	28.13	50.94	119.96	442.32	562.24
建筑业	**Construction**						
建筑业总产值（亿元）	Gross Output Value of Construction（100 million yuan）			46.65	154.51	375.25	438.82
房屋竣工建筑面积（万平方米）	Floor Space of Buildings Completed（10000 sq.m）		80.50	320.17	830.89	1191.62	1264.54
交通运输、邮电通信	**Transportation,Post and Telecommunications**						
货物运输量（万吨）	Freight Traffic（10000 tons）	2349	4483	3100	3857	8933	11707
旅客发送量（万人次）	Number of Passenger Despatche（10000 person-times）	2849	4383	6924	10308	20625	12396
邮电业务收入（亿元）	Total Busines Volume of Post and Tele-communications（100 million yuan）	0.55	4.42	14.11	27.74	44.48	52.24
年末固定电话用户（万户）	Number of Fixed Telephone Subscribers at Year-end（10000 Subscribers）	2.46	11.68	53.43	145.97	112.63	118.05
年末移动电话用户（万户）	Number of Mobile Telephone Subscribers at Year-end（10000 Subscribers）		1.35	46.96	162.58	383.62	395.03
电话交换机容量（万门）	Capacity of Telephone Exchanges（10000 line）	4.23	21.53	82.45	114.35	202.74	284.30
国内商业	**Domestic Trade**						
社会消费品零售总额（亿元）	Total Retail Sales of Consumer Goods（100 million yuan）	26.21	84.99	133.88	329.21	790.65	1058.35

4-8 续表 2 continued 2

指 标	Item	1990	1995	2000	2005	2010	2012
对外经济贸易	**Foreign Trade**						
进出口总额（亿美元）	Total Exports and Imports（USD 100 million）	0.61	9.43	25.15	76.03	199.49	263.13
进 口	Imports	0.11	2.22	8.81	21.11	63.43	85.71
出 口	Exports	0.50	7.21	16.34	54.92	136.06	177.41
国际旅游	**International Tourism**						
来常旅游人数（万人次）	Number of Tourists from Abroad（10000 person-times）	0.65	1.90	3.11	17.28	34.25	43.54
旅游外汇收入（亿美元）	Foreign Exchange Earnings from Tourism（USD 100 million）		0.09	0.23	1.38	3.31	4.53
金融保险	**Banking & Insurance**						
金融机构存款余额（亿元）	Deposit Balance of Financial Institutions（100 million yuan）	46.24	205.93	511.00	1375.25	3800.47	4558.74
金融机构贷款余额（亿元）	Loans Balance of Financial Institutions（100 million yuan）	58.52	170.12	324.19	966.84	2518.92	3109.26
保险费收入（亿元）	Income From Insurances（100 million yuan）	0.84	4.38	10.27	30.54	73.12	92.13
保险赔（结）款支出（亿元）	Expenditure for Insurance Claims（100 million yuan）	0.19	1.16	3.04	8.97	15.39	24.91
教育、科技	**Education,Science and Technology**						
教 育	**Education**						
专任教师数（万人）	Full-time Teachers（10000 persons）	1.59	1.76	1.82	2.15	2.42	2.47
#普通高等学校	Institutions of Higher Education	0.07	0.10	0.12	0.45	0.54	0.52
普通中学	Regular Secondary Schools	0.56	0.60	0.64	0.79	0.86	0.88
小 学	Primary Schools	0.75	0.78	0.75	0.71	0.76	0.81
在校学生数（万人）	Students Enrollment（10000 persons）	28.82	15.94	37.33	46.45	46.28	46.73
#普通高等学校	Institutions of Higher Education	0.51	1.16	2.00	9.54	12.22	12.39
普通中学	Regular Secondary Schools	9.17	9.84	11.11	13.52	12.37	11.55
小 学	Primary Schools	16.46	15.95	17.69	15.95	15.89	17.21
科 技	**Science and Technology**						
专利申请量（项）	Number of Patent Applications Examined（unit）				1976	12278	31742
专利授权量（项）	Number of Patent Authorizations Granted（unit）				1021	7559	11737
家庭、生活、环境	**Family, Livelihood and Environment**						
家 庭	**Family**						
家庭总户数（万户）	Total Number of Household（10000 households）	63.65	67.67	70.77	74.36	79.54	81.31
平均每户家庭人口（人）	Average Number of Household Size（person）	3.07	2.98	2.94	2.97	2.86	2.83

4-8 续表 3 continued 3

指　标	Item	1990	1995	2000	2005	2010	2012
婚　姻	**Marriages and Divorces**						
准予登记结婚（对）	Marriage Leagally Registered（couple）	11058	19048	14848	17002	19730	23094
准予登记离婚数（对）	Divorce Leagally Registered（couple）	496	1165	1280	3494	5084	5464
住　宅	**Housing**						
城市居民人均使用面积（平方米）	Per Capita Usable Floor Space of Urban Residents（sq.m）	13.22	15.04	15.19	21.04	24.91	26.50
生　活	**People's Livelihood**						
市区居民人均可支配收入（元）	Per Capita Disposable Income Of Urban Residents（yuan）	1769	5632	8540	14589	26269	33587
市区居民人均生活消费支出（元）	Per Capita Living Expenditure of Urban Residents（yuan）	1498	4426	6759	10718	17124	20519
城乡居民储蓄存款余额（亿元）	Balance of Saving Deposits in Urban and Rural Residents（100 million yuan）	25.45	96.92	268.11	671.82	1567.26	1911.14
工　资	**Wages**						
在岗职工工资总额（亿元）	Total Wages of Fully Employed Staff and Workers（100 million yuan）	10.82	31.91	38.59	60.26	124.85	203.32
卫　生	**Health Care**						
医　院（包括卫生院，个）	Hospitals（include Township Hospitals,unit）	90	91	64	61	47	61
医　生（人）	Doctors（person）	4636	5146	5616	4751	5771	8050
医院床位数（包括卫生院，张）	Number of Hospital Beds（include Township Hospitals,unit）	6506	7236	7774	8467	11151	14286
城市建设	**Urban construction**						
自来水供水量（万吨）	Annual Consumption of Tap Water（100 million tons）	25994	11257	16631	32384	21981	21801
城市排水管道长度（公里）	Length of Sewer Piplelines of Urban Districts（km）	231	698	929	2918	3627	4214
用电量（亿千瓦时）	Electric Power Consumption（100 milliom kwh）	14.72	22.44	32.74	143.21	215.17	254.14
城市煤气供应量（万立方米）	Goal Gas Supply of Urban Districts（10000 m^3）	1601	1783	4256	8030	48099	55209
年末出租车运营数（辆）	Number of Operating Taxi at Year-end（coach）	137	592	1443	1842	2542	2542
年末运营公交车辆数（辆）	Number of Public Transit Vehicles at Year-end（coach）	232	307	1572	2105	2518	2590
铺装道路长度（公里）	Length of Paved Roads（km）	336	483	697	3584	1753	1892
公园绿地面积（公顷）	Green Space of Park（hectare）	121	283	458	1568	1632	1759
火灾、交通事故	**Fire Loss and Road Accidents**						
火灾发生数（起）	Number of Fire Disasters（time）	162	139	1119	1605	244	303
火灾损失额（万元）	Fire Loss（10000 yuan）	93	317	370	383	475	237
道路交通事故发生数（起）	Number of Road Accidents（time）	702	925	2339	2074	1016	862
道路交通事故损失额（万元）	Loss of Road Accidents（10000 yuan）	92	557	868	506	155	140

4-9 主要年份社会经济主要指标增长速度
GROWTH RATE OF MAJOR SOCIAL AND ECONOMIC INDICATORS IN MAIN YEARS

单位：%

指　标	Item	2012年比下列各年增长 Growth Rates of 2012 over Following Years				
		1978	1990	2000	2010	2011
人口与就业	**Population and Employment**					
年末总人口	Total Population at year-end	25.4	12.3	6.8	1.1	0.5
从业人员	Number of Employed Persons	88.0	51.0	56.7	3.3	1.2
宏观经济	**Macroeconomy**					
地区生产总值	Gross Domestic Product	64.0倍	18.1倍	3.5倍	25.1	11.5
第一产业	Primary Industry	3.2倍	1.5倍	65.2	8.8	4.7
第二产业	Secondary Industry	84.4倍	20.6倍	3.8倍	25.3	11.7
#工　业	Industry	87.7倍	21.6倍	4.0倍	25.8	11.7
第三产业	Tertiary Industry	98.4倍	25.9倍	3.6倍	25.9	11.6
全社会固定资产投资完成额	Total Investment in Fixed Assets	3117.1倍	120.5倍	15.9倍	31.2	18.0
财政总收入	Total Financial Revenue	178.9倍	84.3倍	17.5倍	32.7	14.2
#公共财政预算收入	Public Finance Budget Revenue			10.8倍	32.4	8.0
公共财政预算支出	Public Finance Budget Expenditure			11.3倍	39.0	8.1
新签外资项目数	The number of new foreign investment projects Signed		6.5倍	78.4	-8.9	-3.2
协议（合同）外资金额	Amount of Foreign Capital in the Newly Signed Agreements		270.2倍	3.7倍	0.2	2.5
实际到帐注册外资	Foreign Capital Actually Utilized		503.6倍	3.8倍	25.9	10.1
产　业	**Industries**					
农林牧渔业总产值	Gross Output Value of Agriculture	30.5倍	6.6倍	1.6倍	26.1	12.8
建筑业总产值	Gross Output Value of Construction		120.6倍	7.5倍	42.8	18.8
货物运输量	Freight Traffic		2.9倍	2.7倍	30.9	9.7
邮电业务收入	Total Busines Volume of Post and Telecommunications		100.4倍	2.9倍	18.4	10.0
社会消费品零售总额	Total Retail Sales of Consumer Goods	292.0倍	36.0倍	6.0倍	34.0	14.3
进出口总额	Total Exports and Imports		470.8倍	9.3倍	30.3	1.4

注：地区生产总值按可比价计算。
Note:GDP can be calculated by comparable price.

4-9 续表 continued　　　　单位：%

指　标	Item	2012年比下列各年增长 Growth Rates of 2012 over Following Years				
		1978	1990	2000	2010	2011
进　口	Imports		767.5倍	8.4倍	35.0	-2.2
出　口	Exports		400.4倍	9.7倍	28.3	3.1
来常旅游人数	Number of Tourists from Abroad		64.1倍	12.8倍	26.9	10.3
旅游外汇收入	Foreign Exchange Earnings from Tourism			18.8倍	36.6	12.6
金融机构存款余额	Deposit Balance of Financial Institutions		93.4倍	7.9倍	23.2	14.3
#储蓄存款	Savings Deposits	3434.1倍	71.1倍	6.0倍	23.1	14.6
金融机构贷款余额	Loans Balance of Financial Institutions		50.6倍	8.8倍	27.3	12.5
保费收入	Income From Insurances		108.4倍	8.0倍	26.4	10.2
保险赔（结）款支出	Expenditure for Insurance Claims		83.7倍	4.9倍	59.5	18.9
教育、科技	**Education,Science and Technology**					
在校学生数	Students Enrollment	-0.3	29.5	4.5	-1.2	-0.6
#普通高等学校	Institutions of Higher Education	286.2倍	23.5倍	5.2倍	1.5	0.6
普通中学	Regular Secondary Schools	-21.5	13.4	-7.3	-10.3	-4.8
小　学	Primary Schools	-38.2	-15.4	-21.9	5.8	2.3
专利申请量	Number of Patent Applications Examined			46.1倍	148.2	68.2
专利授权量	Number of Patent Authorizations Granted			20.0倍	69.1	35.0
家庭、生活、环境	**Family,Livelihood and Environment**					
市区居民人均可支配收入	Per Capita Net Income of Urban Residents		18.0倍	2.9倍	27.9	12.6
市区居民人均生活消费支出	Per Capita Living Expenditure of Urban Residents		12.7倍	203.6	19.8	8.6
医　生	Doctors	2.6倍	78.1	40.7	9.8	5.5
医院、卫生院床位数	Number of Hospital Beds	1.7倍	95.4	78.4	25.4	22.8
自来水供水量	Annual Volume of Tap Water Supply	5.9	-16.1	32.2	-0.01	0.6
城市排水管道长度	Length of Sewer Piplelines of Urban Districts	29.1倍	17.2倍	3.5倍	16.2	10.7
用电量	Electric Power Consumption		11.0倍	3.7倍	20.7	6.0
城市煤气供应量	Goal Gas Supply of Urban Districts		33.5倍	12.0倍	14.8	5.5

4-10 主要时期社会经济主要指标平均增长率
AVERAGE GROWTH RATE OF MAJOR SOCIAL AND ECONOMIC INDICATORS OF MAIN PERIOD

单位：%

指 标	Item	"九五"时期 "Ninth Five-Year Plan" Period	"十五"时期 "Tenth Five-Year Plan" Period	"十一五"时期 ""Eleventh Five-Year Plan" Period	1979～2012
年末总人口	Year-end Population	0.5	0.6	0.5	0.7
从业人员	Number of Employed Persons	-1.0	3.3	4.1	1.9
地区生产总值	Gross Domestic Product	10.4	13.9	13.6	13.1
第一产业	Primary Industry	3.1	4.2	4.3	4.3
第二产业	Secondary Industry	10.3	15.3	13.6	14.0
第三产业	Tertiary Industry	12.9	13.3	14.6	14.5
全社会固定资产投资完成额	Financial in Fixed Assets	7.3	36.3	22.3	26.7
财政总收入	Total Government Revenue	16.1	29.6	30.7	16.5
地方财政支出	Local Expenditure	19.5	34.0	35.4	22.4
新签外资项目数	The number of new foreign investment projects Signed	-10.6	25.0	-8.5	
协议（合同）外资金额	Amount of Foreign Capital in the Newly Signed Agreements	-13.0	36.9	10.7	
实际到帐注册外资	Foreign Capital Actually Utilized	16.4	5.5	29.6	
农林牧渔业总产值	Total Output value of Farming,Forestry,Animal Husbandry and Fishing	2.8	3.9	10.8	10.7
规模以上工业总产值	Total Output Value of Industry above Designated Size	8.6	23.4	24.2	
货物运输量	Freight Traffic	-4.1	5.1	16.8	
旅客发送量	Number of Passenger Despatched	7.0	8.4	13.9	
邮电业务收入	Total Busines Volume of Post and Telecommunications	25.3	15.3	10.1	
社会消费品零售总额	Total Retail Sales of Consumer Goods	9.0	17.0	18.8	18.2
进出口总额	Total Exports and Imports	23.2	24.2	21.7	
进 口	Imports	33.8	18.1	24.9	
出 口	Exports	19.3	26.9	20.5	
市区居民人均可支配收入	Per Capita Dispoable Income of Urban Household	8.7	11.3	12.5	
市区居民人均消费性支出	Per Capita Living Expenditures of Urban Household	8.8	9.7	9.8	
农村居民人均纯收入	Per Capita Net Income of Rural Residents	5.5	9.6	12.5	
农村居民人均生活消费支出	Per Capita Living Expenditure of Rural Residents	1.9	12.0	11.7	
在岗职工年平均工资	Average Annual Wage of Fully Employed Staff and Workers	10.2	14.8	14.0	14.7
平均每人储蓄存款余额	Per Capita Balance of Savings Deposits	22.0	18.8	17.7	26.2
医 生	Doctors	1.9	1.4	3.6	3.9
在校学生数	Students Enrollment	2.6	2.6	-1.4	0.0
#高等学校	Institutions of Higher Education	11.4	36.7	5.2	18.1

4-11　主要年份社会经济发展结构指标
STRUCTURAL INDICATORS ON ECONOMIC AND SOCIAL DEVELOPMENT IN MAIN YEARS

单位：%

指　标	Item	1990	1995	2000	2005	2010	2012
人　口	**Population**						
农业非农业结构	Agricultural and Non-agricultural Structure	100.0	100.0	100.0	100.0	100.0	100.0
农　业	Agriculture	74.9	63.9	56.7	54.3	50.4	54.0
非农业	Non-agricultural	25.1	36.1	43.3	45.7	49.6	46.0
性别结构	Sexual Structure	100.0	100.0	100.0	100.0	100.0	100.0
男	Male	51.5	51.4	50.8	50.5	50.0	49.8
女	Female	48.5	48.6	49.2	49.5	50.0	50.2
就　业	**Employment**						
从业人员产业结构	Industrial Structure	100.0	100.0	100.0	100.0	100.0	100.0
第一产业	Primary Industry	35.9	29.4	28.9	13.5	8.7	7.7
第二产业	Secondary Industry	45.6	47.3	43.6	53.4	55.5	55.4
第三产业	Tertiary Industry	18.5	23.3	27.5	33.1	35.7	36.9
国民经济核算	**National Accounting**						
地区生产总值产业结构	Industrial Structure	100.0	100.0	100.0	100.0	100.0	100.0
第一产业	Primary Industry	18.6	10.8	7.5	4.3	3.3	3.2
第二产业	Secondary Industry	61.1	59.7	56.1	61.1	55.3	52.9
第三产业	Tertiary Industry	20.3	29.5	36.4	34.6	41.4	43.9
固定资产投资	**Investment in Fixed Assets**						
全社会固定资产投资结构	Investment Structure of Fixed Assets	100.0	100.0	100.0	100.0	100.0	100.0
#工业投资	Industrial investment	70.4	47.7	36.3	59.7	56.1	55.3
第三产业投资	Investment in Tertiary Industry	27.4	50.5	59.9	39.5	43.2	44.2
#房地产开发	Real Estate Development	4.1	16.1	18.3	14.8	21.2	21.6
财　政	**Government Finance**						
公共财政预算收入结构	Public Finance Budget Expenditure			100.0	100.0	100.0	100.0
#税收收入	Income from Taxes			92.1	84.1	83.1	80.2
吸收外资	**Utilization of Foreign Capital**						
实际吸收外资结构	Structure of Foreign Capital Actually Utilized		100.0	100.0	100.0	100.0	100.0
#合资企业	Joint-ventures		86.4	51.5	22.1	24.5	16.7
合作企业	Cooperative Enterprises		4.2	9.1	4.0	0.1	0.6
独资企业	Foreign Funded Enterprises		9.4	39.4	73.9	75.4	82.2
农　业	**Agriculture**						
农林牧渔业总产值结构	Structure of Gross Agricultural Output Value	100.0	100.0	100.0	100.0	100.0	100.0
农　业	Planting	61.9	59.7	59.8	48.2	54.6	55.0
林　业	Forestry	0.6	0.7	1.0	1.2	0.7	0.7
牧　业	Animal Husbandry	28.5	23.4	15.1	18.0	15.7	15.6

4-11 续表 1 continued 1 单位：%

指 标	Item	1990	1995	2000	2005	2010	2012
渔 业	Fishery	8.9	16.1	24.1	27.9	24.4	23.9
农林牧渔服务业	Service Industry for Planting, Forestry, Animal Husbandry and Fishery				4.7	4.6	4.8
工 业	**Industry**						
工业总产值结构	Structure of Gross Industrial Output Value	100.0	100.0	100.0	100.0	100.0	100.0
轻工业	Light Industry	49.5	40.0	41.4	34.9	21.6	21.9
重工业	Heavy Industry	50.5	60.0	58.6	65.1	78.4	78.1
建筑业	**Construction**						
建筑业企业总产值结构	Structure of Total Output Value of Construction Enterprises		100.0	100.0	100.0	100.0	100.0
#房屋土木工程建筑业	Building and Civil Engineering Construction		78.6	75.1	79.7	79.2	79.9
建筑安装业	Installation		11.7	13.8	11.2	12.4	11.8
建筑装饰业	Decoration		9.6	11.1	5.2	6.5	7.2
运输业	**Transportation**						
货运量结构	Structure of Freight Traffic	100.0	100.0	100.0	100.0	100.0	100.0
铁 路	Railways	2.9	3.2	4.7	4.9	1.7	1.1
公 路	Highways	67.3	61.2	71.0	82.1	88.5	89.4
水 运	Waterway	29.9	35.6	24.2	13.0	9.8	9.4
民用航空	Civil Aviation	…	…	…	…	…	…
国内商业	**Domestic Trade**						
社会消费品零售总额结构	Total Retail Sale of Consumer Goods		100.0	100.0	100.0	100.0	100.0
市的零售额	Retail Prices of Urban Districts		62.2	67.6	89.7	93.3	93.4
县以下零售额	Retail Prices of County Level and Below		37.8	32.4	10.3	6.7	6.6
对外经济贸易	**Foreign Trade**						
进出口结构	Structure of Imports and Exports	100.0	100.0	100.0	100.0	100.0	100.0
出 口	Exports	80.8	77.5	65.9	73.5	69.8	68.7
进 口	Imports	19.2	22.5	34.1	26.5	30.2	31.1
国际旅游	**International Tourism**						
来常旅游人数结构	Structure of Foreign Tourists	100.0	100.0	100.0	100.0	100.00	100.00
外国人	Foreigners	47.1	61.9	66.8	73.4	86.7	87.5
港澳台同胞	Compartiots from Hongkong, Macao,Taiwan	52.9	38.1	33.2	26.6	13.3	12.5
金 融	**Banking**						
金融机构存款结构	Structure of Savings Deposits in Banking Institutions	100.0	100.0	100.0	100.0	100.00	100.00
储蓄存款	Savings Deposits	57.8	49.9	56.5	52.5	44.2	44.1
金融机构贷款结构	Structure Loans in Banking Institutions		100.0	100.0	100.0	100.0	100.0
#短期贷款	Short-term Loans		74.3	82.0	63.7	50.5	54.7
中长期贷款	Medium-term and Long-term Loans		11.8	8.5	26.0	46.7	42.2

4-11 续表2 continued 2

单位：%

指标	Item	1990	1995	2000	2005	2010	2012
教 育	**Education**						
在校学生结构	Structure of Student Enrollment	100.0	100.0	100.0	100.0	100.0	100.0
#大学生	College and University Students	1.1	2.3	3.5	14.7	20.3	20.9
中学生	Secondary School Students	38.8	43.6	43.9	47.6	43.0	39.7
小学生	Primary School Students	60.1	54.1	52.6	37.7	36.7	39.3
专任教师结构	Full-time Teachers by Type	100.0	100.0	100.0	100.0	100.0	100.0
#高等教育	Higher Education	2.8	3.5	4.4	14.3	15.6	15.1
普通中学	Regular Secondary Schools	35.9	35.2	36.7	40.8	40.2	49.5
小 学	Primary Schools	51.9	49.6	46.0	36.2	34.4	35.2
生 活	**Livelihood**						
市区居民消费结构	Consumption Structure of Urban Residents	100.0	100.0	100.0	100.0	100.0	100.0
食品类	Food	61.6	54.9	40.1	35.9	32.7	36.1
衣着类	Clothing	11.1	10.4	7.9	9.7	9.5	9.7
家庭设备、用品及服务	Household Appliances	5.0	5.7	10.5	6.5	6.6	6.7
医疗保健	Health Care	1.5	1.4	6.1	7.6	6.5	7.1
交通和通信	Transportation and Communication	3.0	4.7	5.9	12.2	17.1	15.9
娱乐、教育、文化服务	Recreational,Educational and Cultural Services	6.7	9.7	12.2	13.8	15.0	15.1
居 住	Housing	7.5	8.6	11.0	9.9	8.2	6.4
杂项商品和服务	Miscellaneous Commodities and Services	3.6	4.6	6.3	4.3	4.3	3.0
农村居民消费结构	Consumption Structure of Rural Residents		100.0	100.0	100.0	100.0	100.0
食品类	Food		49.9	43.1	39.8	35.1	36.1
衣着类	Clothing		7.1	5.5	6.5	7.7	7.4
居 住	Housing		15.8	17.8	14.0	11.5	11.6
家庭设备、用品及服务	Household Appliances		8.5	5.1	6.1	5.6	7.0
医疗保健	Health Care		2.0	5.5	6.6	7.4	7.6
交通和通信	Transportation and Communication		1.8	8.1	11.6	13.9	12.7
文教娱乐用品及服务	Recreational,Educational and Cultural Services		12.4	11.8	13.1	16.2	15.3
其他商品和服务	Other Commodities and Services		2.5	3.1	2.4	2.6	2.3
卫 生	**Public Health**						
卫生机构数结构	Number of Health Institutions	100.0	100.0	100.0	100.0	100.0	100.0
#医院（包括卫生院）	Hospitals（include Township Hospitals）	18.3	18.8	15.0	8.9	8.4	9.7
门诊部、所	Clinics	77.1	76.0	79.2	36.9	30.6	32.7
卫生技术人员结构	Structure of Medical Technical Personnel	100.0	100.0	100.0	100.0	100.0	100.0
#医 生	Doctors	47.5	47.3	46.5	46.8	45.4	43.3
护师、护士	Nurses	26.5	28.0	29.7	32.8	35.5	40.3
卫生技术人员结构	Structure of Medical Technical Personnel	100.0	100.0	100.0	100.0	100.0	100.0
#医 生	Doctors	47.5	47.3	46.5	46.8	45.4	43.3
护师、护士	Nurses	26.5	28.0	29.7	32.8	35.5	40.3

4-12 主要年份社会经济发展相对指标
RELATIVE INDICATORS ON ECONOMIC AND SOCIAL DEVELOPMENT IN MAIN YEARS

指 标	Item	1990	1995	2000	2005	2010	2012
人 口	**Population**						
出生率（‰）	Birth Rate（‰）	15.1	11.7	12.6	8.3	7.8	9.4
死亡率（‰）	Death Rate（‰）	6.4	6.4	6.8	6.2	8.5	7.9
自然增长率（‰）	Natural Growth Rate（‰）	8.7	5.3	5.8	2.1	-0.7	1.6
国民经济核算	**National Accounting**						
经济增长贡献率（%）	Growth Rate of Economy（%）						
第一产业	Primary Industry	15.4	11.0	1.8	2.6	1.5	3.8
第二产业	Secondary Industry	76.0	36.0	60.0	66.6	48.4	38.6
#工 业	Industy	75.2	30.5	53.4	61.6	43.7	33.9
第三产业	Tertiary Industry	8.7	53.0	38.2	30.8	50.1	57.7
人均地区生产总值（元）	Per Capita Gross Domestic Product（yuan）	2935	11117	17635	32116	67327	85039
固定资产投资	**Investment in Fixed Assets**						
全社会固定资产投资占地区生产总值比例（%）	Proportion of Total Investment in Fixed Assets to GDP（%）	23.9	31.1	27.2	58.8	69.1	69.5
财 政	**Government Finance**						
全市财政收入占地区生产总值比例（%）	Proportion of Government Revenue to GDP（%）	13.8	7.7	10.0	16.9	27.6	28.1
公共财政预算收入占地区生产总值比例（%）	Proportion of to Public Finance Budget Revenue to GDP（%）			5.4	7.3	9.4	9.5
吸收外资	**Utilization of Foreign Capital**						
实际利用外资额占签订利用外资比例（%）	Proportion of Foreign Capital Actually Utilized（%）	38.0	37.0	69.8	25.6	56.3	70.8
农 业	**Agriculture**						
平均每个农村人口占有耕地（平方米）	Cultivated Land per Rural Population（sq.m）	844	840	862	749	633	648
每公顷耕地农业机械总动力（千瓦）	Total Power of Agricultural Machinery per Hectare of Cultivated Land（kw）	5.72	6.83	8.21	9.19	9.99	10.59
农民人均农产品产量（公斤）	Output of Farm Products per Agricultural Laborer（kg）						

4-12　续表 1　continued 1

指　标	Item	1990	1995	2000	2005	2010	2012
粮　食	Grain	506.40	478.25	398.90	278.88	319.17	314.71
油　料	Oil-bearing Crops	19.67	21.82	26.83	24.45	11.10	10.33
茶　叶	Tea	1.15	0.76	0.79	0.79	0.96	0.96
水　果	Fruits	2.98	6.81	8.68	19.13	27.60	32.19
猪　肉	Pork	21.55	26.97	18.83	18.46	16.57	18.24
水产品	Aquatic Products	16.36	27.15	32.51	37.03	41.00	49.67
每公顷播种面积农产品产量（公斤）	Output of Farm Crops per Hectare of Sown Area（kg）						
粮　食	Grain	5720	6666	6982	6772	7131	7375
棉　花	Cotton	552	577	967	764	843	865
油　料	Oil-bearing Crops	1594	1644	1850	1952	2030	2187
工　业	**Industry**						
资产负债率（%）	Asstes-Liability Ratio（%）		64.82	61.70	65.61	59.89	61.01
成本费用利润率（%）	Ratio of Pre-tax Profits to Gross Output Value （%）		2.23	3.13	4.06	6.13	5.15
工业产品销售率（%）	Ratio of Industrial Products Sales（%）		96.13	97.12	97.77	98.45	98.99
全员劳动生产率（元/人）	Overall Labor Productivity（yuan/person）		23586	44066	98345	182977	240278
建筑业	**Construction**						
全员劳动生产率（元/人,按施工产值计算）	Overall Labor Productivity（yuan/person, In Terms of Construction Output Value）	11326	39838	77513	163100	220627	257574
交通、通信业	**Transportation and Telecommunication Services**						
每万人拥有公共车辆（标台）	Number of Public Transit Vehicles Owned per 10000 Persons（set）	4.30	4.80	15.60	9.02	13.10	14.60
住宅电话普及率（部/百人）	Access to Home Telephone（set/100 persons）		11.88	18.81	32.30	26.00	23.51
移动电话普及率（部/百人）	Access to Mobile Telephone（set/100 persons）		0.54	16.64	45.50	138.97	138.58
国内商业	**Domestic Trade**						
人均消费品零售额（元）	Per Capita Consumption Retail Sale（yuan）	1182	3963	5940	12702	29264	38847

4-12 续表 2 continued 2

指 标	Item	1990	1995	2000	2005	2010	2012
对外经济贸易	**Foreign Trade and Economic Cooperation**						
进出口总额占地区生产总值比例（%）	Ratio of Total Imports and Exports and Gross Domestic Product（%）	3.10	22.43	38.89	52.18	49.53	46.16
出口总额占地区生产总值比例（%）	Ratio of Total Exports and Gross Domestic Product（%）	2.51	17.38	25.64	38.35	34.59	31.74
教 育	**Education**						
学龄儿童入学率（%）	Rate of School-age Children Enrollment（%）	100.00	99.65	100.00	100.00	100.00	100.00
中学毕业生升学率（%）	Rate of Secondary School Graduates Entering Higher Level Schools（%）	49.02	72.53	90.28	96.51	99.90	99.94
平均每个教师负担学生数（人）	Number of Students Burdened Per Teacher（person）	18.28	18.32	20.22	20.51	17.45	17.16
高等学校	Institutions of Higher Education	7.30	12.17	16.23	21.13	22.75	23.74
普通中学	Regular Secondary School	16.46	16.45	17.61	17.12	13.54	12.12
小 学	Primary School	21.17	19.97	23.08	21.37	18.62	19.12
婚 姻	**Marriage**						
离婚率（‰）	Divorce Rate（‰）	0.19	0.42	0.65	1.43	2.16	2.39
生 活	**Livelihood**						
城市与农村居民收入比例	Proportion of Income of Urban Residents to Income of Rural Residents	1.26:1	1.66:1	1.93:1	2.08:1	2.08:1	2.01:1
卫 生	**Health Care**						
每万人拥有医院数（包括卫生院，个）	Number of Hospitals Per 10000 Persons（unit）	0.50	0.48	0.34	0.32	0.26	0.30
每万人拥有医生数（人）	Number of Doctors Per 10000 Persons（person）	18.91	21.20	22.78	23.76	27.61	30.00
每万人拥有医院床位数（包括卫生院，张）	Number of Hospital Beds Per 10000 Persons（bed）	29.23	30.99	31.42	33.37	42.30	52.47
城市建设	**Urban Construction**						
人均公园绿地面积（平方米）	Per Capita Green Area of Park（sq.m）	1.83	4.10	5.64	7.10	12.35	12.49
建成区绿化覆盖率（%）	Coverage Rate of Green Areas（%）	15.13	29.80	31.69	38.80	42.15	42.21
人均拥有道路面积（平方米）	Per Capita Area of Road（sq.m）	5.50	6.50	10.68	17.90	22.88	24.50

4-13　常州国民经济主要指标占全省的比重（2012 年）
PERCENTAGE OF CHANGZHOU'S MAJOR NATIONAL ECONOMIC INDICATORS IN THE PROVINCE（2012）

指　标	Item	常州市 Changzhou City	江苏省 Jiangsu Province	常州市占全省的比重（%） Percentage of Changzhou in Jiangsu
土地面积（平方公里）	Area of Land （sq.km）	4372.15	102600	4.3
常住人口（万人）	Permanent Populationn（10000 persons）	468.68	7920.00	5.9
全社会从业人员（万人）	Social Employment（10000 persons）	280.99	4759.53	5.9
地区生产总值（亿元）	Gross Domestic Product（100 million yuan）	3969.87	54058.22	7.3
第一产业	Primary Industry	126.37	3418.34	3.7
第二产业	Secondary Industry	2100.76	27121.92	7.7
第三产业	Tertiary Industry	1742.74	23517.96	7.4
固定资产投资完成额（亿元）	Investment in Fixed Assets（100 million yuan）	2621.56	31707.20	8.3
公共财政预算收入（亿元）	Public Finance Budget Revenue（100 million yuan）	378.99	5860.69	6.5
公共财政预算支出（亿元）	Public Finance Budget Expenditure（100 million yuan）	391.22	7027.67	5.6
城镇居民人均可支配收入（元）	Per Capita Disposable Income of Urban Residents （yuan）	33587	29677	高出全省3910元
农民人均纯收入（元）	Per Capita Net Income of Rural Residents （yuan）	16737	12202	高出全省4535元
城乡居民储蓄存款余额（亿元）	Balance Amount of Saving Deposits of Urban and Rural Residents（100 million yuan）	2473.27	30057.19	8.2
粮食产量（万吨）	Output of Grain （10000 tons）	114.80	3372.50	3.4
油料产量（万吨）	Output of Oil-bearing Crops（10000 tons）	3.77	146.95	2.6
社会消费品零售总额（亿元）	Total Retail Sales of Consumer Goods（100 million yuan）	1413.33	18331.30	7.7
进出口总额（亿美元）	Total Exports & Imports（USD 100 million）	290.46	5480.93	5.3
#出　口	Exports	199.62	3285.38	6.1
实际到帐注册外资（亿美元）	Foreign Capital Actually Utilized（USD 100 million）	33.61	357.60	9.4

4-14 五区社会经济主要指标（2012 年）
MAJOR SOCIAL AND ECONOMIC INDICATORS OF FIVE DISTRICTS（2012）

指 标	Item	武进区 wujin District	新北区 Xinbei District	天宁区 Tianning District	钟楼区 Zhonglou District	戚墅堰区 Qishuyan District
人口与就业	**Population and Employment**					
年末总户数（万户）	Total Number of Households at Year-end （10000 households）	36.33	15.13	13.87	13.12	2.86
年末户籍总人口（万人）	Total Population at Year-end （10000 persons）	102.62	46.94	37.40	35.62	7.89
年末常住人口（万人）	Permanent Population at Year-end（10000 persons）	160.40	61.75	52.33	51.63	10.70
#城镇人口	Non-agricultural Population	89.88	35.40	52.33	51.63	10.70
年末在岗职工人数（万人）	Number of Staff & Workers Employed at Year-end （10000 persons）	11.74	6.79	9.05	5.20	1.91
年末私营企业从业人员（万人）	Employees of Urban Private Enterprises at Year-end （10000 persons）	49.97	21.79	8.53	6.52	2.38
年末个体从业人员（万人）	Urban Self-employed Individuals at Year-end （10000 persons）	11.88	4.99	4.90	3.98	0.71
城镇登记失业人员（人）	Urban Registered Unemployed Persons at Year-end （person）	7627	1486	10443	6059	1699
综合经济	**Aggregative Economy**					
地区生产总值（亿元）	Gross Domestic Product （100 million yuan）	1536.69	700.32	393.20	360.14	90.12
第一产业	Primary Industry	46.07	13.41	0.06	0.13	0.02
第二产业	Secondary Industry	921.89	436.90	125.73	168.10	62.79
#工　业	Industry	875.14	415.13	111.64	151.29	59.46
第三产业	Tertiary Industry	568.73	250.01	267.41	191.91	27.31
地区生产总值指数（上年=100）	Gross Domestic Product Index Number （Preceding Year=100）	112.0	111.9	110.6	110.6	111.3
第一产业	Primary Industry	105.1	104.9	66.7	94.0	104.7
第二产业	Secondary Industry	112.0	111.7	108.4	109.8	111.0
#工　业	Industry	112.0	112.3	107.8	109.5	110.8
第三产业	Tertiary Industry	112.6	112.7	111.8	111.4	112.3
固定资产投资	**Investment in Fixed Assets**					
全社会固定资产投资完成额（亿元）	Total Investment in Fixed Assets（100 million yuan）	844.85	597.52	279.56	269.55	69.71
#工业投资	Industrial investment	514.97	370.14	35.39	53.17	35.04
房地产投资	Investment in Real Estate	134.83	147.94	120.68	105.55	22.75
财　政	**Finance**					
财政总收入（亿元）	Total Financial Revenue （100 million yuan）	338.14	192.33	68.65	54.68	19.97

4-14　续表 1　continued 1

指　标	Item	武进区 wujin District	新北区 Xinbei District	天宁区 Tianning District	钟楼区 Zhonglou District	戚墅堰区 Qishuyan District
#公共财政预算收入	Public Finance Budget Revenue	117.05	82.66	40.07	33.50	9.59
#各项税收	Taxes	95.07	66.26	34.23	27.61	8.20
财政支出（亿元）	Fiscal Expenditure（100 million yuan）	250.06	99.58	19.95	20.78	6.52
#公共财政预算支出	Public Finance Budget Expenditure	111.92	48.34	18.92	18.57	5.79
工　业	**Industry**					
规模以上工业企业主要经济指标	**Main Indicators of Enterprises Above Designated Size**					
企业单位数（个）	Number of Enterprises Above Designated Size（unit）	1731	853	227	244	97
内资企业	Domestic-funded Enterprises	1489	582	156	190	83
港、澳、台商投资企业	Enterprises with Investment from Hongkong,Macao and Taiwan	113	85	34	18	7
外商投资企业	Enterprises with Foreign Investment	129	186	37	36	7
工业总产值（亿元）	Gross Industrial Output Value（100 million yuan）	3559.02	1782.52	704.84	720.03	276.84
内资企业	Domestic-funded Enterprises	2941.01	858.58	354.85	535.25	199.52
港、澳、台商投资企业	Enterprises with Investment from Hongkong,Macao and Taiwan	347.69	277.92	118.29	87.81	28.67
外商投资企业	Enterprises with Foreign Investment	270.32	646.02	231.70	96.97	48.65
#制造业	Manufacturing	3541.13	1748.14	687.00	720.03	245.82
#重工业	Heavy Industry	2600.38	1480.11	336.91	643.98	257.67
总资产（亿元）	Total Assets（100 million yuan）	2717.48	1609.24	439.67	408.30	246.85
固定资产原价（亿元）	Original Value of Fixed Assets（100 million yuan）	704.40	439.93	97.79	115.51	78.29
负债合计（亿元）	Total Liabilities（100 million yuan）	1641.79	949.86	235.62	242.58	133.48
主营业务收入（亿元）	Main Business Income（100 million yuan）	3630.13	1766.22	722.24	747.20	291.06
利税总额（亿元）	Total Pre-tax Profits（100 million yuan）	280.33	122.77	61.47	61.95	35.72
利润总额（亿元）	Total Profits（100 million yuan）	168.14	66.50	41.38	39.27	26.51
贸易、外经	**Trade, Foreign Trade**					
社会消费品零售总额（亿元）	Total Retail Sales of Consumption Goods（100 million yuan）	362.46	184.90	292.18	203.70	15.11
进出口总额（亿美元）	Total Imports & Exports（USD 100 million）	90.01	114.05	28.27	23.44	5.66
#出　口	Exports	55.86	71.43	23.82	20.12	4.58

4-14 续表 2 continued 2

指　标	Item	武进区 wujin District	新北区 Xinbei District	天宁区 Tianning District	钟楼区 Zhonglou District	戚墅堰区 Qishuyan District
新签外资项目数（个）	The number of new foreign investment projects signed（unit）	90	80	10	29	9
协议（合同）外资金额（亿美元）	Amount of Foreign Capital in the Newly Signed Agreements（USD 100 million）	14.10	14.10	4.19	4.37	1.72
实际到帐注册外资（亿美元）	Foreign Capital Actually Utilized（USD 100 million）	9.00	8.46	1.20	2.29	0.64
教育、卫生	**Education and Public Health**					
普通中学学校数（个）	Number of Regular Secondary Schools（unit）	49	17	3	3	3
小学学校数（个）	Number of Primary Schools（unit）	47	22	22	21	4
普通中学在校学生数（人）	Number of Student Enrollment of Regular Secondary Schools（person）	55018	16087	2385	2160	3032
小学在校学生数（人）	Number of Student Enrollment of Primary Schools（person）	84991	29285	26180	26502	5187
普通中学专任教师数（人）	Number of Full-time Teachers of Regular Secondary Schools（person）	4120	1364	214	141	225
小学专任教师数（人）	Number of Full-time Teachers of Primary Schools（person）	3740	1402	1408	1263	294
幼儿园数（个）	Number of Kindergartens（unit）	54	27	24	25	5
入园儿童数（人）	Number of Newly Enrolled in Kindergartens（persons）	33514	16195	10023	12906	2327
卫生机构数（个）	Number of Health Institutions（unit）	340	117	170	86	18
#医院、卫生院	Hospitals	30	13	12	5	1
卫生机构床位数（张）	Number of Beds in Health Institutions（unit）	4935	1155	8371	1051	347
#医院、卫生院	Hospitals	4649	918	7542	865	312
卫生技术人员（人）	Number of Medical Personnel（person）	4487	1031	7953	1072	437
#医　生	Doctors	2460	753	3729	871	237
#执业（助理）医师	Practicing（Assistant）Doctors	1811	433	2681	357	147
人民生活	**People's Livelihood**					
城镇居民人均可支配收入（元）	Per Capita Disposable Income of Urban Residents（yuan）	34971				
农民人均纯收入（元）	Per Capita Net Income of Rural Residents（yuan）	18444	16572			
社会治安	**Security of Society**					
刑事案件立案数（件）	Number of Criminal Cases Registered（case）	1504	506	620	512	81
犯罪人数（人）	Number of Criminals（person）	2280	748	964	740	148
民事案件发案数（人）	Number of Civil Cases Arised（person）	8383	5221	4496	4987	585

5

CHAPTER 5

人　口

POPULATION

常州统计年鉴

5 人　口 POPULATION

2012 年主要统计指标 MAJOR STATISTICAL INDICATORS OF 2012

年底总户数	Total Households	128.75万户	(10000 households)
比上年增长	Over the Previous Year	0.5%	
年底总人口	Total Population	364.77万人	(10000 persons)
比上年增长	Over the Previous Year	0.5%	
年底市区人口	Urban Districts Population	230.47万人	(10000 persons)
比上年增长	Over the Previous Year	0.7%	
年底常住人口	Permanent population	468.68万人	(10000 persons)
比上年增长	Over the Previous Year	0.8%	
年底暂住人口	Temporary Resident Population At Year-end	155.04万人	(10000 persons)
比上年增长	Over the Previous Year	16.5%	
暂住一个月以上人口	Temporary Resident Population Over One Month	139.02万人	(10000 persons)
比上年增长	Over the Previous Year	12.9%	

5-1　历年年末户籍户数、人口数
YEAR-END HOUSEHOLDS AND POPULATION OVER THE YEARS

年　份 Year	总户数（万户） Total Number of Households（10000 households）	总人口（万人） Total Population（10000 persons）	城镇人口（万人） Urban Population（10000 persons）	年平均人口（万人） Average Population Per Year（10000 persons）	平均每户人口（人） Average Person Per Household（person）
1949	40.88	173.89	33.77	173.89	4.25
1950	42.37	176.45	31.86	175.17	4.16
1951	43.52	179.87	30.44	178.16	4.13
1952	44.23	183.34	31.31	181.61	4.15
1953	45.76	187.99	32.46	185.67	4.11
1954	45.86	191.54	34.38	189.77	4.18
1955	46.96	196.35	36.82	193.95	4.18
1956	47.03	198.34	37.45	197.35	4.22
1957	47.94	203.70	38.79	201.02	4.25
1958	48.60	211.66	48.22	207.68	4.36
1959	50.31	214.43	49.18	213.05	4.26
1960	50.87	215.49	50.04	214.96	4.24
1961	52.86	215.57	45.10	215.53	4.08
1962	53.18	222.13	39.49	218.85	4.18
1963	54.67	229.31	39.15	225.72	4.19
1964	55.26	235.39	38.84	232.35	4.26
1965	55.78	240.79	39.48	238.09	4.32
1966	56.20	246.69	40.12	243.74	4.39
1967	57.60	250.36	41.10	248.53	4.35
1968	59.10	256.51	43.01	253.44	4.34
1969	60.47	260.19	36.82	258.35	4.30
1970	61.93	266.82	37.58	263.51	4.31
1971	63.33	272.22	38.61	269.52	4.30
1972	64.16	275.67	39.00	273.95	4.30
1973	65.71	279.95	41.97	277.81	4.26
1974	66.81	282.61	40.86	281.28	4.23
1975	68.01	284.69	40.74	283.65	4.19
1976	69.98	287.32	42.25	286.01	4.11
1977	71.63	289.64	42.75	288.48	4.04
1978	73.23	291.00	45.22	290.32	3.97
1979	74.41	294.42	51.79	292.71	3.96
1980	77.19	295.92	53.48	295.17	3.83

5-1 续表 continued

年 份 Year	总户数 （万户） Total Number of Households (10000 households)	总人口 （万人） Total Population (10000 persons)	城镇人口 （万人） Urban Population (10000 persons)	年平均人口 （万人） Average Population Per Year (10000 persons)	平均每户人口 （人） Average Person Per Household (person)
1981	79.93	298.75	55.17	297.34	3.74
1982	81.59	301.98	57.68	300.37	3.70
1983	83.73	304.26	59.47	303.12	3.63
1984	85.60	305.48	61.46	304.87	3.57
1985	88.21	306.87	64.20	306.18	3.48
1986	91.06	309.74	67.92	308.31	3.40
1987	93.67	313.22	69.21	311.48	3.34
1988	100.32	317.06	75.08	315.14	3.16
1989	104.80	321.65	79.32	319.36	3.07
1990	106.91	324.85	81.40	323.25	3.04
1991	108.61	326.87	82.80	325.86	3.01
1992	110.41	328.57	97.58	327.72	2.98
1993	111.63	329.33	115.11	328.95	2.95
1994	111.84	331.44	116.02	330.39	2.96
1995	114.00	333.65	120.48	332.55	2.93
1996	114.73	337.54	124.71	335.60	2.94
1997	115.69	339.23	128.47	338.39	2.93
1998	116.57	340.75	130.43	339.99	2.92
1999	117.44	339.71	139.43	340.23	2.89
2000	117.89	341.48	147.81	340.60	2.90
2001	118.65	341.52	152.40	341.50	2.88
2002	119.74	343.24	157.82	342.38	2.86
2003	121.04	346.22	201.01	344.73	2.86
2004	121.63	348.96	206.75	347.59	2.87
2005	121.97	351.63	212.56	350.30	2.88
2006	122.32	354.67	223.99	353.15	2.90
2007	122.21	357.38	264.84	356.03	2.92
2008	123.40	358.74	268.66	358.06	2.91
2009	125.47	359.82	272.27	359.28	2.87
2010	127.11	360.80	293.74	360.31	2.84
2011	128.10	362.86	303.16	361.83	2.83
2012	128.75	364.77	310.31	363.82	2.83

注：2003年前城镇人口为非农业人口数据，2006年起城镇人口按常住人口计算。

Note：The data of urban population belong to the data of non-agricultural before the year of 2003，the urban population is calculated as permanent population since 2006.

5-2 历年人口自然变动情况
POPULATION NATURAL CHANGE OVER THE YEARS

年 份 Year	出生人数（人） Birth Population (person)	出生率（‰） Birth Rate (‰)	死亡人数（人） Death Population (person)	死亡率（‰） Death Rate (‰)	自然增长人数（人） Natural Growth Population (person)	自然增长率（‰） Natural Growth Rate (‰)
1949	68233	39.2	28572	16.4	39661	22.8
1950	69811	39.9	28921	16.5	40890	23.3
1951	73147	41.1	28458	16.0	44689	25.1
1952	76275	42.0	28956	15.9	47319	26.1
1953	79065	42.6	28832	15.2	50233	27.1
1954	74832	39.4	23251	12.3	51581	27.2
1955	70118	36.2	21094	10.9	49024	25.3
1956	70379	35.7	23938	12.1	46441	23.5
1957	73364	36.5	19413	9.7	53951	26.8
1958	64609	31.1	18203	8.8	46406	22.3
1959	44026	20.7	26971	12.7	17055	8.0
1960	44985	20.9	32791	15.3	12194	5.7
1961	46124	21.4	26508	12.3	19616	9.1
1962	80239	36.7	20515	9.4	59724	27.3
1963	89412	39.6	18889	8.4	70523	31.2
1964	83705	36.0	18644	8.0	65061	28.0
1965	77946	32.7	18188	7.6	59758	25.1
1966	73364	30.1	16995	7.0	56369	23.1
1967	73418	29.5	16405	6.6	57013	22.9
1968	75064	29.6	15607	6.2	59457	23.5
1969	71259	27.6	14611	5.7	56648	21.9
1970	70116	26.6	16094	6.1	54022	20.5
1971	66295	24.6	16815	6.2	49480	18.4
1972	56287	20.5	16850	6.2	39437	14.4
1973	46210	16.6	17319	6.2	28891	10.4
1974	43963	15.6	17964	6.3	25999	9.2
1975	42669	15.0	17906	6.3	24763	8.7
1976	40004	14.0	17748	6.2	22256	7.8
1977	42121	14.6	18985	6.6	23136	8.0
1978	41310	14.2	18293	6.3	23017	7.9
1979	37548	12.8	18392	6.3	19156	6.5
1980	35260	11.9	19086	6.5	16174	5.5

5-2 续表 continued

年 份 Year	出生人数（人） Birth Population (person)	出生率（‰） Birth Rate (‰)	死亡人数（人） Death Population (person)	死亡率（‰） Death Rate (‰)	自然增长人数(人) Natural Growth Population (person)	自然增长率（‰） Natural Growth Rate (‰)
1981	46288	15.6	18865	6.3	27423	9.2
1982	46030	15.3	18086	6.0	27944	9.3
1983	32485	10.7	19710	6.5	12775	4.2
1984	29331	9.6	19340	6.3	9991	3.3
1985	30971	10.1	19082	6.2	11889	3.9
1986	40329	13.1	19067	6.2	21262	6.9
1987	47636	15.3	19274	6.2	28362	9.1
1988	48901	15.5	20204	6.4	28697	9.1
1989	50730	15.9	19115	6.0	31615	9.9
1990	48772	15.1	20595	6.4	28177	8.7
1991	41384	12.7	20412	6.3	20972	6.4
1992	39676	12.1	20979	6.4	18697	5.7
1993	37130	11.3	20176	6.1	16954	5.2
1994	35638	10.8	20248	6.1	15390	4.7
1995	38830	11.7	21292	6.4	17538	5.3
1996	33464	10.0	22239	6.6	11225	3.3
1997	48469	14.3	20008	5.9	28461	8.4
1998	40230	11.8	22255	6.5	17975	5.3
1999	31975	9.4	20355	6.0	11620	3.4
2000	42845	12.6	22998	6.8	19847	5.8
2001	28713	8.4	18720	5.5	9993	2.9
2002	30949	9.0	19746	5.8	11203	3.2
2003	25490	7.4	19867	5.8	5623	1.6
2004	27992	8.1	24266	7.0	3726	1.1
2005	29049	8.3	21624	6.2	7425	2.1
2006	28166	8.0	21465	6.1	6701	1.9
2007	27236	7.7	23811	6.7	3425	1.0
2008	25273	7.1	24734	6.9	539	0.2
2009	26142	7.3	27577	7.7	-1435	-0.4
2010	27950	7.8	30510	8.5	-2560	-0.7
2011	29007	8.0	22144	6.1	6863	1.9
2012	34352	9.4	28625	7.9	5727	1.6

5-3 分地区户数和人口情况（2012 年底）
NUMBER OF HOUSHOLD AND POPULATION BY REGION（END OF 2012）

地 区 Region		总户数（户）Total Number of Households（household）	户籍人口（人）Household register Population（person）	按性别分 By Sex 男 Male	女 Female	按年龄分 By Age # 18岁以下 Age 18 and Under	# 60岁以上 Age 60 and Over	常住人口（万人）permanent population（10000 persons）	其中 of which # 城镇人口 Urban Population
总 计	**Total**	**1287467**	**3647719**	**1815859**	**1831860**	**478029**	**772148**	**468.68**	**310.31**
市 区	Urban Area	813122	2304677	1140540	1164137	311219	487642	336.81	239.94
武进区	Wujin District	363327	1026151	506640	519511	131684	229801	160.40	89.88
新北区	Xinbei District	151321	469397	232953	236444	69179	85646	61.75	35.40
天宁区	Tianning District	138669	374031	183733	190298	51849	78191	52.33	52.33
钟楼区	Zhonglou District	131226	356179	177150	179029	49222	75043	51.63	51.63
戚墅堰区	Qishuyan District	28579	78919	40064	38855	9285	18961	10.70	10.70
溧阳市	Liyang City	264905	789928	399711	390314	105940	164290	76.03	40.23
金坛市	Jintan City	209440	553114	275762	277352	60870	120216	55.84	30.14

5-4 分地区暂住人口情况（2012 年底）
TEMPORARY RESIDENT POPULATION BY REGION（END OF 2012）

单位：人（person）

指 标 Item		全 市 Whole Municipality	其 中 of which 市 区 Urban Area	溧阳市 Liyang City	金坛市 Jintan City
总 计	**Total**	**1550404**	**1365428**	**63976**	**121000**
按时间分	By Time				
# 一个月以上	Over One Month	1390201	1230602	52413	107186
# 一年以上	Over One Year	229224	184571	6030	38623
按活动类型分	By Active Type				
# 务 工	Engaged into Industry or Project	1116481	1018886	37788	59807
务 农	Engaged into Agriculture	80823	64388	2452	13983
经 商	Business	152534	137617	6826	8091
服 务	Service	96690	85201	3854	7635

5-5 分地区人口自然增长和迁移情况（2012 年）
NATURAL GROWTH AND MIGRATION OF POPULATION BY REGION（2012）

地 区	Region	出生人数（人）Birth Population（person）	出生率（‰）Birth Rate（‰）	死亡人数（人）Death Population（person）	死亡率（‰）Death Rate（‰）
总 计	**Total**	**34352**	**9.4**	**28625**	**7.9**
市 区	Urban Area	20940	9.1	15998	7.0
武进区	Wujin District	8600	8.4	7761	7.6
新北区	Xinbei District	5352	11.5	3198	6.9
天宁区	Tianning District	3069	8.2	2224	6.0
钟楼区	Zhonglou District	3310	9.3	2218	6.3
戚墅堰区	Qishuyan District	609	7.7	597	7.6
溧阳市	Liyang City	7502	9.5	5939	7.5
金坛市	Jintan City	5910	10.7	6688	12.1

5-5 续表 continued

地 区	Region	自然增长人数（人）Natural Growth Population（person）	自然增长率（‰）Natural Growth Rate（‰）	迁入人数（人）Number of the Transferred From Outside（person）	迁出人数（人）Number of the Transferred to Outside（person）
总 计	**Total**	**5727**	**1.6**	**38713**	**24805**
市 区	Urban Area	4942	2.2	29082	19128
武进区	Wujin District	839	0.8	11762	10049
新北区	Xinbei District	2154	4.6	6232	1939
天宁区	Tianning District	845	2.3	4446	2869
钟楼区	Zhonglou District	1092	3.1	5246	3791
戚墅堰区	Qishuyan District	12	0.2	1396	480
溧阳市	Liyang City	1563	2.0	4156	2465
金坛市	Jintan City	-778	-1.4	5475	3212

5-6　预期寿命
LIFE EXPECTANCY

单位：岁（age）

年　代	year	平均预期寿命 Average Life Expectancy	其　中 of which 男 性 Male	女 性 Female
全　市	**Whole Municipality**			
第三次人口普查（1982 年）	The Third Census （1982）	67.8	66.5	73.2
第四次人口普查（1990 年）	The Forth Census （1990）	72.2	70.1	74.3
第五次人口普查（2000 年）	The Fifth Census （2000）	75.5	73.3	77.8
第六次人口普查（2010 年）	The Sixth Census （2010）	77.6	75.8	79.7
市　区	**Urban Area**			
第一次人口普查（1953 年）	The First Census （1953）	63.3	62.9	66.6
第二次人口普查（1964 年）	The Second Census （1964）	57.1	54.3	60.7
第三次人口普查（1982 年）	The Third Census （1982）	71.6	69.1	74.4
第四次人口普查（1990 年）	The Forth Census （1990）	74.7	72.7	76.6
第五次人口普查（2000 年）	The Fifth Census （2000）	77.8	75.8	79.8
第六次人口普查（2010 年）	The Sixth Census （2010）	79.0	77.7	80.5

5-7　分地区计划生育情况（2012 年）
STATISTICS ON BIRTH CONTROL BY REGION（2012）

指　标	Item	全　市 Whole Municipality	其　中 of which 市　区 Urban Area	溧阳市 Liyang City	金坛市 Jintan City
计划生育率（%）	Family Planning Rate （%）	98.7	98.8	98.0	98.1
独生子女率（%）	Only-child Rate （%）	77.4	76.8	75.1	82.8
育龄妇女人数（万人）	Number of Woman of Child-bearing Age （10000 persons）	110.06	73.18	21.52	15.36
#已婚育龄妇女数	Number of Married Woman of Child-bearing Age	82.33	54.47	15.62	12.24
有效领独生子女证人数（万人）	Number of Only-child Certificare Obtained （10000 persons）	28.58	20.24	4.25	4.08
晚婚率（%）	Deferred Marriage Rate （%）	71.4	79.4	55.5	67.0
现家庭只有一个孩子的妇女人数（万人）	Number of Woman Owns One-child in Family （10000 persons）	63.73	41.85	11.74	10.14

6
CHAPTER 6

从业人员　工资总额
EMPLOYMENT AND TOTAL WAGES

6 从业人员 工资总额
EMPLOYMENT AND TOTAL WAGES

2012 年主要统计指标
MAJOR STATISTICAL INDICATORS OF 2012

年底社会从业人员数	Number of Employment	280.99万人	(10000 persons)
比上年增长	Over the Previous Year	1.2%	
城镇非私营单位年底在岗职工人数	Number of Fully Employed Staff and Workers of Urban Non-Private Entities by the End of Year	46.80万人	(10000 persons)
比上年增长	Over the Previous Year	-3.1%	
城镇非私营单位在岗职工平均工资	Average Wage of On-Post Employees of Urban Non-Private Entities	55764元	(yuan)
比上年增长	Over the Previous Year	12.1%	
私营单位从业人员平均工资	Average Wage of Employees of Private Entities	33865元	(yuan)
比上年增长	Over the Previous Year	15.6%	

6-1　历年年末从业人员及构成
NUMBER AND COMPOSITION OF EMPLOYED PERSONS OVER THE YEARS

年份 Year	年末从业人员（万人） Number of Employed persons (10000 persons)	其中 of which 第一产业 Primary Industry	第二产业 Secondary Industry	第三产业 Tertiary Industry	构成（%） Composition (%)	其中 of which 第一产业 Primary Industry	第二产业 Secondary Industry	第三产业 Tertiary Industry
1949	67.24	56.96	4.08	6.20	100	84.7	6.1	9.2
1950	70.06	58.53	5.46	6.07	100	83.5	7.8	8.7
1951	72.82	61.64	5.49	5.69	100	84.6	7.5	7.8
1952	78.04	65.81	6.44	5.79	100	84.3	8.3	7.4
1953	80.06	66.77	7.46	5.83	100	83.4	9.3	7.3
1954	82.70	69.68	7.38	5.64	100	84.3	8.9	6.8
1955	84.64	72.22	6.85	5.57	100	85.3	8.1	6.6
1956	84.81	71.67	7.13	6.01	100	84.5	8.4	7.1
1957	84.80	71.31	7.41	6.07	100	84.1	8.7	7.2
1958	87.44	62.17	18.78	6.49	100	71.1	21.5	7.4
1959	87.82	63.36	17.30	7.16	100	72.1	19.7	8.2
1960	89.23	67.06	14.61	7.61	100	75.2	16.4	8.5
1961	91.28	69.54	13.28	8.47	100	76.2	14.5	9.3
1962	98.92	80.91	8.98	9.03	100	81.8	9.1	9.1
1963	101.81	84.14	8.93	8.74	100	82.6	8.8	8.6
1964	100.72	82.34	10.05	8.33	100	81.8	10.0	8.3
1965	106.33	85.77	11.36	9.21	100	80.7	10.7	8.7
1966	106.80	85.30	12.60	8.90	100	79.9	11.8	8.3
1967	110.36	88.85	12.78	8.73	100	80.5	11.6	7.9
1968	115.08	92.74	13.39	8.95	100	80.6	11.6	7.8
1969	118.59	95.82	14.13	8.64	100	80.8	11.9	7.3
1970	127.24	100.81	16.10	10.33	100	79.2	12.7	8.1
1971	131.32	101.71	18.83	10.78	100	77.5	14.3	8.2
1972	134.45	101.22	21.40	11.83	100	75.3	15.9	8.8
1973	136.12	100.92	22.72	12.48	100	74.1	16.7	9.2
1974	138.01	100.05	24.71	13.25	100	72.5	17.9	9.6
1975	138.69	97.10	27.79	13.80	100	70.0	20.0	10.0
1976	140.81	97.19	30.58	13.04	100	69.0	21.7	9.3
1977	144.43	93.53	36.11	14.79	100	64.8	25.0	10.2
1978	149.35	90.36	40.20	18.79	100	60.5	26.9	12.6
1979	151.59	92.75	43.17	15.67	100	61.2	28.5	10.3
1980	155.45	90.25	49.18	16.02	100	58.1	31.6	10.3

6-1 续表 continued

年份 Year	年末从业人员（万人）Number of Employed persons (10000 persons)	其中 of which 第一产业 Primary Industry	第二产业 Secondary Industry	第三产业 Tertiary Industry	构成（%）Composition (%)	其中 of which 第一产业 Primary Industry	第二产业 Secondary Industry	第三产业 Tertiary Industry
1981	157.23	87.90	51.84	17.49	100	55.9	33.0	11.1
1982	160.65	84.48	55.32	20.85	100	52.6	34.4	13.0
1983	168.92	87.09	59.26	22.57	100	51.6	35.1	13.4
1984	173.73	78.25	67.98	27.50	100	45.0	39.1	15.8
1985	178.64	70.19	77.50	30.96	100	39.3	43.4	17.3
1986	181.69	67.84	80.62	33.23	100	37.3	44.4	18.3
1987	187.00	65.96	84.95	36.09	100	35.3	45.4	19.3
1988	185.59	65.24	86.90	33.44	100	35.2	46.8	18.0
1989	184.55	66.88	84.09	33.58	100	36.2	45.6	18.2
1990	186.06	66.82	84.83	34.42	100	35.9	45.6	18.5
1991	187.39	67.33	84.15	35.90	100	35.9	44.9	19.2
1992	187.00	65.03	84.80	37.17	100	34.7	45.3	19.9
1993	188.65	63.70	86.56	38.39	100	33.8	45.9	20.3
1994	187.19	61.42	85.75	40.02	100	32.8	45.8	21.5
1995	188.78	55.51	89.23	44.04	100	29.4	47.3	23.3
1996	188.75	53.68	88.02	47.05	100	28.4	46.6	24.9
1997	185.23	54.69	84.05	46.49	100	29.5	45.4	25.1
1998	183.96	55.04	80.17	48.75	100	29.9	43.6	26.5
1999	185.60	54.38	79.64	51.57	100	29.3	42.9	27.8
2000	179.36	51.82	78.13	49.41	100	28.9	43.6	27.5
2001	189.11	49.81	85.26	54.04	100	26.3	45.1	28.6
2002	192.14	46.22	88.47	57.45	100	24.1	46.0	29.9
2003	199.74	38.77	98.92	62.05	100	19.4	49.5	31.1
2004	217.42	34.57	114.52	68.32	100	15.9	52.7	31.4
2005	222.31	30.01	118.71	73.58	100	13.5	53.4	33.1
2006	225.81	27.32	123.52	74.97	100	12.1	54.7	33.2
2007	233.18	25.88	129.65	77.65	100	11.1	55.6	33.3
2008	242.71	24.76	136.16	81.79	100	10.2	56.1	33.7
2009	251.56	24.40	140.87	86.29	100	9.7	56.0	34.3
2010	272.00	23.66	151.23	97.10	100	8.7	55.6	35.7
2011	277.72	22.26	153.21	102.25	100	8.0	55.2	36.8
2012	280.99	21.76	155.59	103.66	100	7.7	55.4	36.9

6-2　历年年末市区从业人员及构成
NUMBER AND COMPOSITION OF URBAN EMPLOYED PERSONS OVER THE YEARS

年份 Year	年末从业人员（万人）Number of Employed persons (10000 persons)	其中 of which 第一产业 Primary Industry	第二产业 Secondary Industry	第三产业 Tertiary Industry	构成（%）Composition (%)	其中 of which 第一产业 Primary Industry	第二产业 Secondary Industry	第三产业 Tertiary Industry
1949	43.68	34.17	3.90	5.61	100	78.2	8.9	12.8
1950	45.54	34.97	5.23	5.34	100	76.8	11.5	11.7
1951	47.35	37.35	5.14	4.85	100	78.9	10.9	10.2
1952	51.91	41.19	6.02	4.70	100	79.3	11.6	9.1
1953	53.59	41.93	7.04	4.63	100	78.2	13.1	8.6
1954	53.81	42.60	6.87	4.34	100	79.2	12.8	8.1
1955	54.73	43.91	6.43	4.39	100	80.2	11.7	8.0
1956	53.90	42.58	6.70	4.63	100	79.0	12.4	8.6
1957	52.50	41.04	6.87	4.59	100	78.2	13.1	8.7
1958	53.07	34.97	14.01	4.09	100	65.9	26.4	7.7
1959	55.92	37.84	13.18	4.92	100	67.7	23.6	8.8
1960	56.96	39.81	11.64	5.51	100	69.9	20.4	9.7
1961	57.20	41.78	9.29	6.13	100	73.0	16.2	10.7
1962	62.26	48.25	8.02	5.99	100	77.5	12.9	9.6
1963	63.92	49.93	8.03	5.96	100	78.1	12.6	9.3
1964	60.98	45.89	9.22	5.87	100	75.3	15.1	9.6
1965	65.26	48.38	10.46	6.42	100	74.1	16.0	9.8
1966	65.42	47.52	11.65	6.25	100	72.6	17.8	9.6
1967	67.77	49.87	11.79	6.11	100	73.6	17.4	9.0
1968	71.56	53.15	12.30	6.11	100	74.3	17.2	8.5
1969	73.98	55.02	12.94	6.01	100	74.4	17.5	8.1
1970	81.33	59.44	14.62	7.27	100	73.1	18.0	8.9
1971	83.32	58.76	16.77	7.80	100	70.5	20.1	9.4
1972	84.70	58.52	18.14	8.04	100	69.1	21.4	9.5
1973	85.32	57.38	19.46	8.48	100	67.3	22.8	9.9
1974	86.40	56.37	21.05	8.98	100	65.2	24.4	10.4
1975	86.86	53.75	23.96	9.15	100	61.9	27.6	10.5
1976	88.70	53.48	26.57	8.65	100	60.3	30.0	9.8
1977	90.55	50.47	30.04	10.03	100	55.7	33.2	11.1
1978	94.91	48.72	32.99	13.19	100	51.3	34.8	13.9
1979	96.41	49.59	36.63	10.19	100	51.4	38.0	10.6
1980	98.05	46.67	40.30	11.08	100	47.6	41.1	11.3

6-2 续表 continued

年份 Year	年末从业人员（万人） Number of Employed persons (10000 persons)	其中 of which			构成（%） Composition (%)	其中 of which		
		第一产业 Primary Industry	第二产业 Secondary Industry	第三产业 Tertiary Industry		第一产业 Primary Industry	第二产业 Secondary Industry	第三产业 Tertiary Industry
1981	99.87	45.00	42.99	11.89	100	45.1	43.0	11.9
1982	101.92	43.42	43.84	14.66	100	42.6	43.0	14.4
1983	109.08	45.74	47.34	16.01	100	41.9	43.4	14.7
1984	112.35	40.25	52.73	19.39	100	35.8	46.9	17.3
1985	115.20	34.77	58.77	21.66	100	30.2	51.0	18.8
1986	116.71	33.34	59.93	23.45	100	28.6	51.3	20.1
1987	116.23	32.10	62.60	21.55	100	27.6	53.9	18.5
1988	118.03	31.43	63.55	23.06	100	26.6	53.8	19.5
1989	117.61	32.25	62.14	23.22	100	27.4	52.8	19.7
1990	117.84	31.57	62.92	23.35	100	26.8	53.4	19.8
1991	118.96	31.41	63.04	24.51	100	26.4	53.0	20.6
1992	118.19	30.20	61.99	26.00	100	25.6	52.4	22.0
1993	118.37	29.08	62.96	26.33	100	24.6	53.2	22.2
1994	116.74	27.84	61.58	27.32	100	23.8	52.7	23.4
1995	118.01	23.96	55.52	38.53	100	20.3	47.0	32.6
1996	116.51	23.05	61.52	31.94	100	19.8	52.8	27.4
1997	112.56	23.73	58.27	30.56	100	21.1	51.8	27.1
1998	111.80	24.04	55.21	32.55	100	21.5	49.4	29.1
1999	115.00	24.11	54.88	36.01	100	21.0	47.7	31.3
2000	111.55	22.68	53.67	35.20	100	20.3	48.1	31.6
2001	119.33	20.55	59.71	39.07	100	17.2	50.0	32.7
2002	123.33	19.84	62.59	40.90	100	16.1	50.7	33.2
2003	132.88	18.03	70.91	43.94	100	13.2	53.5	33.1
2004	148.11	16.73	81.80	49.57	100	11.3	55.2	33.5
2005	148.55	14.56	80.81	53.18	100	9.8	54.4	35.8
2006	149.48	12.56	83.26	53.66	100	8.4	55.7	35.9
2007	156.23	11.87	87.96	56.40	100	7.6	56.3	36.1
2008	164.24	11.33	93.45	59.45	100	6.9	56.9	36.2
2009	170.09	11.06	96.10	62.93	100	6.5	56.5	37.0
2010	186.92	10.65	104.68	71.59	100	5.7	56.0	38.3
2011	193.55	9.6	107.97	75.98	100	5.0	55.8	39.3
2012	193.86	9.18	107.45	77.25	100	4.7	55.4	39.8

6-3 主要年份城镇非私营单位在岗职工人数和工资情况
THE NUMBER AND THE WAGES OF FULLY EMPLOYED STAFF AND WORKERS OF URBAN NON-PRIVATE ENTITIES IN MAIN YEARS

年 份 Year	年底在岗职工人数（万人） Number of Fully Employed Staff and Workers by the End of Year (10000 persons)	在岗职工工资总额（万元） Total Wages of Fully Employed Staff and Workers (10000 yuan)	在岗职工年平均工资（元） Average Annual Wage of Fully Employed Staff and Workers (yuan)	年 份 Year	年底在岗职工人数（万人） Number of Fully Employed Staff and Workers by the End of Year (10000 persons)	在岗职工工资总额（万元） Total Wages of Fully Employed Staff and Workers (10000 yuan)	在岗职工年平均工资（元） Average Annual Wage of Fully Employed Staff and Workers (yuan)
1949	3.91	1472	376	1989	55.12	112962	2052
1952	6.44	3077	508	1990	56.17	128994	2333
1957	11.03	4854	573	1991	56.14	144208	2558
1962	16.51	7942	531	1992	56.15	178846	3147
1965	18.51	8266	572	1993	57.53	242714	4216
1970	13.45	9988	499	1994	55.52	325767	5887
1971	24.83	12021	512	1995	54.42	386820	7098
1972	26.03	12895	500	1996	53.70	430388	7984
1973	26.44	13423	507	1997	49.69	456656	8594
1974	27.21	13836	512	1998	46.67	455656	9570
1975	28.35	14341	517	1999	44.75	479067	10514
1976	30.26	14899	508	2000	40.39	489699	11542
1977	31.94	15343	493	2001	37.66	518441	13108
1978	36.63	19255	534	2002	35.90	552293	14907
1979	39.14	22002	580	2003	34.67	607812	17259
1980	40.99	27169	690	2004	34.84	698249	19985
1981	42.61	28835	697	2005	35.11	785656	22990
1982	44.24	32000	737	2006	35.47	928432	26553
1983	46.31	34859	764	2007	35.51	1076918	30413
1984	47.97	45634	973	2008	35.92	1253405	34834
1985	50.27	58411	1196	2009	35.97	1410417	39220
1986	51.89	71936	1417	2010	36.70	1615042	44214
1987	53.80	83035	1588	2011	48.31	2271309	49755
1988	55.44	102877	1902	2012	46.80	2590106	55764

注：根据国家统计局规定，从2011年起，在岗职工人数中包含了劳务派遣人员，在岗职工工资中包括了用人单位使用的劳务派遣人员工资。
Note:According to the provisions of the National Bureau of Statistics, starting from 2011, the number of dispatched workers is included in the number of Fully Employed Staff and Workers; and the wages of dispatched workers are included in the salaries of Fully Employed Staff and Workers.

6-4 分地区城镇非私营单位从业人员（2012 年底）
NUMBER OF EMPLOYED PERSONS OF URBAN NON-PRIVATE ENTITIES BY REGION (END OF 2012)

单位：人（person）

指标	Item	全市 Whole Municipality	其中 of which 市区 Urban Area	溧阳市 Liyang City	金坛市 Jintan City
总计	**Total**	**488632**	**362175**	**65174**	**61283**
#女性	Female	227500	167062	29992	30446
按企业、事业、机关分	**Grouped by Character of the Units**				
企业	Enterprises	355557	266355	43944	45258
事业	Institutions	97893	71398	14477	12018
机关	Government Agencies	35020	24422	6591	4007
按登记注册类型分	**Grouped by Type of Registration**				
内资	Domestic-funded	359132	267220	51908	40004
国有	State-owned	156054	114599	24778	16677
集体	Collective-owned	14171	10510	794	2867
股份合作	Share-holding Cooperative	9574	3666	2439	3469
联营	Joint Ownership	1612	1086	526	
有限责任公司	Limited Liability Corporations	106930	77220	19764	9946
股份有限公司	Share-holding Corporations Ltd.	40657	33712	2043	4902
其他	Others	30134	26427	1564	2143
港澳台商投资	Investment from Hongkong, Macao and Taiwan	70602	58061	4115	8426
外商投资	Foreign Investment	58898	36894	9151	12853
按国民经济行业分	**Grouped by Economic Sector**				
农林牧渔业	Farming,Forestry,Animal Husbandry and Fishery	703	97	439	167
采矿业	Mining	310			310
制造业	Manufacturing	224908	162008	27859	35041
电力、热力、燃气及水的生产和供应业	Production and Supply of Electricity, Heat, Gas and Water Industry"	6732	5206	967	559
建筑业	Construction	35199	26230	5849	3120
批发和零售业	Wholesale and Retail Trade	21225	18016	2241	968
交通运输、仓储和邮政业	Transportation , Storage and Post	19085	15020	2401	1664
住宿和餐饮业	Accommodation and Catering Services	8145	5891	2104	150
信息传输、软件和信息技术服务业	Information Transmission, Software and IT Services Industry	4497	3667	524	306
金融业	Banking	19574	17627	1063	884
房地产业	Real Estate Industry	4585	3588	491	506
租赁和商务服务业	Rent and Business Services	6501	3876	562	2063
科学研究和技术服务	Scientific Researches and Technical Services	6778	6104	307	367
水利、环境和公共设施管理业	Water Conservancy, Environment and Public Facilities Management	9450	5940	1647	1863
居民服务、修理和其他服务业	Residential Services, Repairing and other Services Industry	392	331	36	25
教育	Education	48134	34469	7974	5691
卫生和社会工作	Health and Social Work	28494	21661	3651	3182
文化、体育和娱乐业	Culture, Sports and Entertainment	4443	4126	164	153
公共管理、社会保障和社会组织	Public Administration, Social Security and Social Organizations	39477	28318	6895	4264

注：从业人员中包含了劳务派遣人员。
Note:Dispatched workers are included in Employed Persons.

6-5　分地区城镇非私营单位从业人员工资总额（2012 年）
TOTAL LABOR REWARD OF PERSONS EMPLOYED BY URBAN NON- PRIVATE ENTITIES BY REGION（2012）

单位：万元（10000 yuan）

指标	Item	全市 Whole Municipality	其中 of which 市区 Urban Area	溧阳市 Liyang City	金坛市 Jintan City
总计	**Total**	**2660521**	**2088090**	**307719**	**264712**
按企业、事业、机关分	**Grouped by Character of the Units**				
企业	Enterprises	1686523	1346362	173373	166788
事业	Institutions	691563	537408	84802	69353
机关	Government Agencies	281977	204320	49085	28572
按登记注册类型分	**Grouped by Type of Registration**				
内资	Domestic-funded	2072270	1628248	257907	186115
国有	State-owned	1122060	863065	154295	104699
集体	Collective-owned	72937	58952	3743	10242
股份合作	Share-holding Cooperative	41829	15211	14122	12496
联营	Joint Ownership	5767	4565	1201	
有限责任公司	Limited Liability Corporations	432981	325838	73339	33804
股份有限公司	Share-holding Corporations Ltd.	274101	248587	6598	18916
其他	Others	122595	112029	4608	5958
港澳台商投资	Investment from Hongkong, Macao and Taiwan	297828	252825	14158	30846
外商投资	Foreign Investment	290423	207017	35655	47752
按国民经济行业分	**Grouped by Economic Sector**				
农林牧渔业	Farming,Forestry,Animal Husbandry and Fishery	3199	414	2267	519
采矿业	Mining	1273			1273
制造业	Manufacturing	1001547	765943	106883	128721
电力、热力、燃气及水的生产和供应业	Production and Supply of Electricity, Heat, Gas and Water Industry	59234	46634	8791	3809
建筑业	Construction	98477	72005	18799	7673
批发和零售业	Wholesale and Retail Trade	93472	82044	7145	4284
交通运输、仓储和邮政业	Transportation , Storage and Post	88963	73443	10042	5478
住宿和餐饮业	Accommodation and Catering Services	26722	18870	7482	370
信息传输、软件和信息技术服务业	Information Transmission, Software and IT Services Industry	40265	34316	4447	1502
金融业	Banking	203192	189209	6242	7741
房地产业	Real Estate Industry	22826	17284	2962	2580
租赁和商务服务业	Rent and Business Services	24494	16460	2243	5791
科学研究和技术服务	Scientific Researches and Technical Services	49143	44030	1864	3249
水利、环境和公共设施管理业	Water Conservancy, Environment and Public Facilities Management	35873	23663	7382	4829
居民服务、修理和其他服务业	Residential Services, Repairing and other Services Industry	2298	1979	181	137
教育	Education	361775	275406	49391	36978
卫生和社会工作	Health and Social Work	205365	166535	20192	18638
文化、体育和娱乐业	Culture, Sports and Entertainment	32081	30659	696	726
公共管理、社会保障和社会组织	Public Administration, Social Security and Social Organizations	310323	229197	50711	30416

注：从业人员工资中包含了劳务派遣人员工资。
Note: The wages of dispatched workers are included in the salaries of Employed Persons.

6-6 分地区城镇非私营单位从业人员平均工资（2012 年）
AVERAGE WAGE OF EMPLOYED PERSONS OF URBAN NON- PRIVATE ENTITIES BY REGION（2012）

单位：元（yuan）

指标	Item	全市 Whole Municipality	其中 of which 市区 Urban Area	溧阳市 Liyang City	金坛市 Jintan City
总计	Total	55027	58711	46976	42463
按企业、事业、机关分	Grouped by Character of the Units				
企业	Enterprises	47976	51554	39173	36164
事业	Institutions	71315	76477	58585	56721
机关	Government Agencies	80956	84329	74259	71572
按登记注册类型分	Grouped by Type of Registration				
内资	Domestic-funded	58524	62269	49577	45865
国有	State-owned	72357	76077	62276	62136
集体	Collective-owned	51802	56543	46387	35974
股份合作	Share-holding Cooperative	42849	41278	57948	34330
联营	Joint Ownership	41308	51238	23788	
有限责任公司	Limited Liability Corporations	41853	44306	36850	33773
股份有限公司	Share-holding Corporations Ltd.	67704	74305	32406	37877
其他	Others	41087	43020	29573	26611
港澳台商投资	Investment from Hongkong , Macao and Taiwan	42613	44429	33001	35467
外商投资	Foreign Investment	48796	55559	38781	36555
按国民经济行业分	Grouped by Economic Sector				
农林牧渔业	Farming,Forestry,Animal Husbandry and Fishery	45316	42639	51290	31060
采矿业	Mining	41331			41331
制造业	Manufacturing	44332	47243	38106	36013
电力、热力、燃气及水的生产和供应业	Production and Supply of Electricity, Heat, Gas and Water Industry	85908	87723	86272	68012
建筑业	Construction	32548	34378	31521	22924
批发和零售业	Wholesale and Retail Trade	43490	44803	32243	44389
交通运输、仓储和邮政业	Transportation , Storage and Post	46507	48728	41720	33197
住宿和餐饮业	Accommodation and Catering Services	32454	31513	35663	25014
信息传输、软件和信息技术服务业	Information Transmission, Software and IT Services Industry	90645	94927	84857	49571
金融业	Banking	104641	108014	60602	88875
房地产业	Real Estate Industry	49774	48078	59236	52554
租赁和商务服务业	Rent and Business Services	38634	44105	39909	28305
科学研究和技术服务	Scientific Researches and Technical Services	73468	73164	59369	91000
水利、环境和公共设施管理业	Water Conservancy, Environment and Public Facilities Management	39155	40651	44682	28591
居民服务、修理和其他服务业	Residential Services, Repairing and other Services Industry	58312	59438	50333	54800
教育	Education	74982	80582	62095	60452
卫生和社会工作	Health and Social Work	74091	79644	55214	59150
文化、体育和娱乐业	Culture, Sports and Entertainment	74364	76705	42439	47444
公共管理、社会保障和社会组织	Public Administration, Social Security and Social Organizations	79069	81617	73313	71600

注：从业人员工资中包含了劳务派遣人员工资。
Note: The wages of dispatched workers are included in the salaries of Employed Persons.

6-7 分地区城镇非私营单位在岗职工人数（2012 年底）
NUMBER OF ON-POST STAFF AND WORKERS OF URBAN NON-PRIVATE ENTITIES BY REGION（END OF 2012）

单位：人（person）

指标	Item	全市 Whole Municipality	其中 of which 市区 Urban Area	溧阳市 Liyang City	金坛市 Jintan City
总　计	**Total**	**468040**	**346830**	**63001**	**58209**
按企业、事业、机关分	**Grouped by Character of the Units**				
企　业	Enterprises	341802	254969	43146	43687
事　业	Institutions	91739	67741	13409	10589
机　关	Government Agencies	34337	24120	6284	3933
按登记注册类型分	**Grouped by Type of Registration**				
内　资	Domestic-funded	340430	253485	49878	37067
国　有	State-owned	150361	111236	23221	15904
集　体	Collective-owned	12308	9598	775	1935
股份合作	Share-holding Cooperative	9364	3465	2430	3469
联　营	Joint Ownership	1605	1080	525	
有限责任公司	Limited Liability Corporations	100591	71157	19608	9826
股份有限公司	Share-holding Corporations Ltd.	37440	30858	1783	4799
其　他	Others	28761	26091	1536	1134
港澳台商投资	Investment from Hongkong, Macao and Taiwan	69405	56910	4107	8388
外商投资	Foreign Investment	58205	36435	9016	12754
按国民经济行业分	**Grouped by Economic Sector**				
农林牧渔业	Farming,Forestry,Animal Husbandry and Fishery	681	78	436	167
采矿业	Mining	310			310
制造业	Manufacturing	222724	160205	27777	34742
电力、热力、燃气及水的生产和供应业	Production and Supply of Electricity, Heat, Gas and Water Industry	6693	5186	948	559
建筑业	Construction	30217	22298	5820	2099
批发和零售业	Wholesale and Retail Trade	19709	16842	1934	933
交通运输、仓储和邮政业	Transportation , Storage and Post	18765	14854	2276	1635
住宿和餐饮业	Accommodation and Catering Services	7177	5076	1951	150
信息传输、软件和信息技术服务业	Information Transmission, Software and IT Services Industry	4400	3660	520	220
金融业	Banking	17082	15151	1062	869
房地产业	Real Estate Industry	3962	3042	486	434
租赁和商务服务业	Rent and Business Services	6401	3785	553	2063
科学研究和技术服务	Scientific Researches and Technical Services	6245	5580	301	364
水利、环境和公共设施管理业	Water Conservancy, Environment and Public Facilities Management	7702	5152	1481	1069
居民服务、修理和其他服务业	Residential Services, Repairing and other Services Industry	378	317	36	25
教　育	Education	45749	33228	7339	5182
卫生和社会工作	Health and Social Work	26993	20526	3402	3065
文化、体育和娱乐业	Culture, Sports and Entertainment	4293	4004	154	135
公共管理、社会保障和社会组织	Public Administration, Social Security and Social Organizations	38559	27846	6525	4188

注：城镇非私营单位在岗职工人数中包含了劳务派遣人员。
Note：The number of dispatched workers is included in the number of Fully Employed Staff and Workers of non-private companies in urban areas.

6-8 分地区城镇非私营单位在岗职工工资总额（2012 年）
TOTAL WAGES OF ON-POST STAFF AND WORKERS OF URBAN NON-PRIVATE ENTITIES BY REGION（2012）

单位：万元（10000 yuan）

指 标	Item	全 市 Whole Municipality	其中 of which 市 区 Urban Area	溧阳市 Liyang City	金坛市 Jintan City
总 计	**Total**	**2590106**	**2033237**	**301357**	**255512**
按企业、事业、机关分	**Grouped by Character of the Units**				
企 业	Enterprises	1637375	1303075	171529	162771
事 业	Institutions	672585	526631	81379	64575
机 关	Government Agencies	279688	203532	47991	28166
按登记注册类型分	**Grouped by Type of Registration**				
内 资	Domestic-funded	2017525	1588441	251751	177333
国 有	State-owned	1102699	852818	149423	100458
集 体	Collective-owned	69066	56606	3690	8770
股份合作	Share-holding Cooperative	41072	14514	14062	12496
联 营	Joint Ownership	5751	4551	1200	
有限责任公司	Limited Liability Corporations	420719	314283	72929	33506
股份有限公司	Share-holding Corporations Ltd.	259065	234555	5889	18621
其 他	Others	119154	111115	4557	3482
港澳台商投资	Investment from Hongkong , Macao and Taiwan	294125	249254	14135	30736
外商投资	Foreign Investment	278456	195541	35471	47443
按国民经济行业分	**Grouped by Economic Sector**				
农林牧渔业	Farming,Forestry,Animal Husbandry and Fishery	3113	338	2256	519
采矿业	Mining	1273			1273
制造业	Manufacturing	984002	749514	106632	127856
电力、热力、燃气及水的生产和供应业	Production and Supply of Electricity, Heat, Gas and Water Industry	59019	46466	8744	3809
建筑业	Construction	90380	66577	18648	5155
批发和零售业	Wholesale and Retail Trade	88624	78081	6323	4219
交通运输、仓储和邮政业	Transportation , Storage and Post	88263	73126	9695	5442
住宿和餐饮业	Accommodation and Catering Services	25372	17666	7336	370
信息传输、软件和信息技术服务业	Information Transmission, Software and IT Services Industry	39692	34060	4418	1214
金融业	Banking	190407	176487	6239	7682
房地产业	Real Estate Industry	21553	16195	2940	2418
租赁和商务服务业	Rent and Business Services	24078	16080	2207	5791
科学研究和技术服务	Scientific Researches and Technical Services	47250	42152	1853	3245
水利、环境和公共设施管理业	Water Conservancy, Environment and Public Facilities Management	32701	22013	6936	3751
居民服务、修理和其他服务业	Residential Services, Repairing and other Services Industry	2252	1934	181	137
教 育	Education	353376	271861	47486	34030
卫生和社会工作	Health and Social Work	200060	162754	19382	17924
文化、体育和娱乐业	Culture, Sports and Entertainment	31664	30305	681	679
公共管理、社会保障和社会组织	Public Administration, Social Security and Social Organizations	307026	227628	49399	29999

注：在岗职工工资总额中包含了劳务派遣人员的工资。
Note：The wages of dispatched workers are included in the salaries of Fully Employed Staff and Workers.

6-9　分地区城镇非私营单位在岗职工平均工资（2012 年）
AVERAGE WAGE OF ON-POST STAFF AND WORKERS OF URBAN NON-PRIVATE ENTITIES BY REGION（2012）

单位：元（yuan）

指 标	Item	全 市 Whole Municipality	其中 of which 市 区 Urban Area	溧阳市 Liyang City	金坛市 Jintan City
总 计	**Total**	**55764**	**59441**	**47577**	**43249**
按企业、事业、机关分	**Grouped by Character of the Units**				
企 业	Enterprises	48234	51797	39469	36635
事 业	Institutions	74162	79150	60685	60098
机 关	Government Agencies	81864	84978	76055	72147
按登记注册类型分	**Grouped by Type of Registration**				
内 资	Domestic-funded	59870	63660	50352	47334
国 有	State-owned	73897	77547	64323	62723
集 体	Collective-owned	56482	59422	46831	45820
股份合作	Share-holding Cooperative	42985	41622	57916	34330
联 营	Joint Ownership	41375	51366	23812	
有限责任公司	Limited Liability Corporations	42460	45247	36943	33900
股份有限公司	Share-holding Corporations Ltd.	69714	76911	33138	38104
其 他	Others	42041	43254	29784	31003
港澳台商投资	Investment from Hongkong, Macao and Taiwan	42847	44739	33011	35532
外商投资	Foreign Investment	47314	53097	39147	36593
按国民经济行业分	**Grouped by Economic Sector**				
农林牧渔业	Farming,Forestry,Animal Husbandry and Fishery	45504	43372	51378	31060
采矿业	Mining	41331			41331
制造业	Manufacturing	44014	46792	38136	36091
电力、热力、燃气及水的生产和供应业	Production and Supply of Electricity, Heat, Gas and Water Industry	86084	87738	87439	68012
建筑业	Construction	33200	34886	31479	23274
批发和零售业	Wholesale and Retail Trade	44427	45640	33107	45370
交通运输、仓储和邮政业	Transportation , Storage and Post	46909	49048	42409	33572
住宿和餐饮业	Accommodation and Catering Services	34948	34282	37449	25014
信息传输、软件和信息技术服务业	Information Transmission, Software and IT Services Industry	91225	94375	84960	54694
金融业	Banking	113129	118075	60635	89843
房地产业	Real Estate Industry	54194	52977	59390	56894
租赁和商务服务业	Rent and Business Services	38593	44175	39917	28305
科学研究和技术服务	Scientific Researches and Technical Services	76530	76474	60156	91653
水利、环境和公共设施管理业	Water Conservancy, Environment and Public Facilities Management	44227	43913	46678	41915
居民服务、修理和其他服务业	Residential Services, Repairing and other Services Industry	59255	60611	50333	54800
教 育	Education	77082	82590	64880	60680
卫生和社会工作	Health and Social Work	76584	82482	56838	60126
文化、体育和娱乐业	Culture, Sports and Entertainment	76043	78205	44221	50274
公共管理、社会保障和社会组织	Public Administration, Social Security and Social Organizations	80080	82384	75396	72148

注：在岗职工工资中包含了劳务派遣人员的工资。
Note：The wages of dispatched workers are included in the salaries of Fully Employed Staff and Workers.

6-10 分地区城镇非私营单位从业人员和工资（2012 年）
THE PERSONS EMPLOYED BY AND THE WAGES OFFERED BY URBAN NON-PRIVATE ENTITIES BY REGION（2012）

地 区	Region	年底从业人员人数（人）Number of Persons Employed at Year-end (person)	年底在岗职工人数（人）umber of Fully Employed Staff and Workers by the End of Year (person)	从业人员工资总额（万元）Total Wages of Persons Employed (10000 yuan)
全 市	**Whole Municipality**	**488632**	**468040**	**2660521**
市 区	Urban Area	362175	346830	2088090
武进区	Wujin Distric	121423	117416	621389
新北区	New District	69120	67853	435967
天宁区	Tianning District	95919	90474	612886
钟楼区	Zhonglou District	55350	51999	302872
戚墅堰区	Qishuyan District	20363	19088	114975
溧阳市	Liyang City	65174	63001	307719
金坛市	JintanCity	61283	58209	264712

6-10 续表 1 continued 1

地 区	Region	在岗职工工资总额（万元）Total Wages of Fully Employed Staff and Workers (10000 yuan)	从业人员平均工资（元）Average Wage of Persons Employed (yuan)	在岗职工平均工资（元）Average Wages of Staff and Workers with Post (yuan)
全 市	**Whole Municipality**	**2590106**	**55027**	**55764**
市 区	Urban Area	2033237	58711	59441
武进区	Wujin Distric	611493	53741	53927
新北区	New District	425208	62916	62916
天宁区	Tianning District	592273	63925	65577
钟楼区	Zhonglou District	291711	54888	56579
戚墅堰区	Qishuyan District	112551	57122	58590
溧阳市	Liyang City	301357	46976	47577
金坛市	JintanCity	255512	42463	43249

注：在岗职工人数、从业人员中包含了劳务派遣人员，在岗职工工资中包含了劳务派遣人员的工资。
Note: The number of dispatched workers is included in the number of Fully Employed Staff and Workers and the number of Employed Persons; and the wages of dispatched workers are included in the salaries of Fully Employed Staff and Workers.

6-11　分地区城镇就业和失业变动情况（2012 年）
URBAN EMPLOMENT AND UNEMPLOYMENT CHANGE BY REGION（2012）

单位：人（person）

指　标	Item	全　市 Whole Municipality	其　中 of which 市　区 Urban Area	溧阳市 Liyang City	金坛市 Jintan City
上年末结转失业人数	Number of Unemployed Persons Carried Forward at Previous Year-end	32650	26813	3362	2475
本年新登记失业人数	Number of Newly Registered Unemployed Persons at This Year	82967	73273	3849	5845
#女　性	Female	42971	38512	1656	2803
#由就业转失业人数	Number of Employed Persons Changed to Unemployed	54303	48439	2540	3324
本年失业人员就业数	Number of Employment of Former Unemployed Persons	78734	70279	3729	4726
#女　性	Female	40988	36877	1613	2498
年末实有登记失业人数	Actual Registered Unemployed Persons at Year-end	34013	27314	3482	3217
#女　性	Female	15210	12321	1474	1415
#由就业转失业人数	Long-term Unemployed Persons	8836	4177	2728	1931
登记失业率（%）	Registered Unemployment Rate（%）	2.37	2.43	1.92	2.44

6-12　失业人员安置情况（2007-2012 年）
UNEMPLOYED PERSONS ALLOCATION （2007-2012）

单位：人（person）

指　标	Item	2007	2008	2009	2010	2012
当年登记失业人数	Number of Registered Unem ployed Persons at This Year	56683	48063	67464	87152	82967
当年已安置就业人数	Number of Arranged Empl oyed Persons at This Year	52651	48649	65387	84142	78734
年末实有登记失业人数	Actual Number of Registered Unemployed Persons at Year-end	32777	30811	31454	32650	34013
登记失业率（%）	Registered Unemployment Rate（%）	2.91	2.71	2.60	2.60	2.37

7

CHAPTER 7

物价指数

PRICE INDEX

常州统计年鉴

7 物价指数
PRICE INDEX

2012 年主要统计指标
MAJOR STATISTICAL INDICATORS OF 2012

市区居民消费价格指数（以上年价格为100）	Consumer Price Index of Urban Residents（Preceding Year=100）	102.5
#食　品	Food	104.9
市区商品零售价格指数（以上年价格为100）	Retail Price Index of Urban Commodities（Preceding Year=100）	101.7
#食　品	Food	105.1

7-1　市区居民消费价格指数（1984-2012 年，以上年价格为 100）
CONSUMER PRICE INDEX OF URBAN RESIDENTS（1984-2012, PRECEDING YEAR=100）

年份 Year	居民消费价格指数 Consumer Price Index	其中 食品类 Food	其中 of which 粮食 Grain	肉禽及其制品 Meat and Poultry	水产品 Aquatic Products	菜类 Vegetables	其中 of which 鲜菜 Fresh Vegetables	衣着类 Clothing
1984	102.6	103.9	99.9	105.3	127.9		101.2	99.5
1985	112.9	119.0	100.7	118.1	148.5		160.7	100.1
1986	106.1	108.5	98.4	111.4	102.3		116.9	101.0
1987	116.2	112.9	104.1	115.5	118.1		128.2	108.0
1988	123.3	130.2	102.2	135.3	129.3		153.0	120.3
1989	116.1	112.9	101.2	115.5	119.9		98.3	125.6
1990	104.2	102.3	101.8	101.2	102.7		105.9	110.0
1991	108.4	111.3	155.9	97.9	107.4		139.8	105.6
1992	108.2	109.9	159.2	103.0	112.1		99.7	103.5
1993	121.7	123.0	153.1	112.6	142.0		138.8	111.6
1994	122.4	131.1	159.0	140.9	119.1	134.8	137.2	115.3
1995	114.9	117.9	129.1	122.9	115.6	121.0	122.8	118.0
1996	110.2	108.9	107.4	105.6	105.0	131.7	133.7	114.1
1997	101.9	98.7	83.6	105.3	97.1	94.6	93.1	102.1
1998	101.6	97.8	101.7	90.5	92.6	105.2	105.7	101.5
1999	98.3	94.0	97.7	84.9	90.6	95.3	94.8	97.8
2000	99.5	95.5	80.5	96.1	95.2	110.4	110.9	95.3
2001	100.1	97.4	91.4	97.4	95.3	93.3	92.0	94.4
2002	98.5	97.8	96.1	97.7	93.0	111.1	109.7	99.5
2003	100.7	102.8	102.8	104.6	98.9	110.5	111.4	97.4
2004	104.3	113.2	140.2	122.1	119.2	93.8	93.3	98.5
2005	102.8	104.7	99.7	106.2	101.3	107.7	108.5	97.1
2006	101.8	104.7	103.9	99.2	108.2	108.0	108.9	99.7
2007	103.3	110.4	104.2	125.1	111.8	116.4	117.1	100.4
2008	105.2	112.3	113.9	121.1	112.6	104.7	103.6	102.4
2009	99.5	101.3	106.9	91.0	102.0	115.8	116.9	102.6
2010	103.4	107.4	119.8	101.5	114.3	114.8	115.3	102.4
2011	105.0	111.7	116.0	121.6	113.9	107.6	106.6	101.6
2012	102.5	104.9	105.3	103.0	107.0	105.5	106.2	101.6

of which								
家庭设备及用品类 Household Appliances	医疗保健及个人用品 Health Care and Personal Articles	交通和通讯工具类 Means of Transportation and Commun -ication	娱乐教育文化用品类 Recreational, Educational and Cultural Goods	居住类 Housing	服务项目类 Service	其中 of which 学杂保育费 Tuition and Children Care	修理及其他服务费 Repair and Other Services	医疗保健服务 Medical and Health Care Services
98.6	106.3		99.7		104.3	116.4	106.9	100.0
101.0	102.4		100.5		109.8	127.3	118.1	100.0
102.6	100.8		101.5		106.6	104.4	113.5	102.3
106.9	104.9		103.2		108.5	100.0	115.4	105.4
111.0	117.5		107.7		117.6	100.4	133.7	100.0
114.7	112.2		121.3		115.7	148.3	123.4	100.0
101.3	101.0		97.2		114.1	102.7	109.6	332.4
102.1	101.5		96.1		111.5	100.0	115.4	100.0
103.7	109.6		90.4		121.1	148.0	103.2	100.0
112.2	108.9		102.3		140.3	130.1	148.2	231.5
111.8	103.3	105.7	109.6	113.5	117.6	117.1	120.0	114.4
105.3	103.9	103.8	105.8	111.9	121.6	128.7	123.8	100.0
101.6	108.7	97.2	113.0	126.0	112.3	115.7	100.4	101.4
101.9	102.1	100.1	103.6	109.7	113.2	127.3	100.2	100.1
95.9	98.7	100.5	101.5	117.7	112.8	109.2	108.3	138.7
98.4	102.4	102.7	98.0	106.5	108.5	122.1	100.9	118.9
99.7	101.8	97.6	101.7	103.8	111.7	128.7	100.0	108.8
98.5	101.6	97.6	112.8	99.7	110.5	138.5		116.9
97.5	100.3	98.2	97.5	100.7	99.5	102.3		100.0
93.9	98.2	98.9	99.4	103.7	101.1	103.7		100.0
98.3	93.6	100.2	99.2	103.3	100.8	100.0		100.0
100.2	100.2	99.7	103.6	106.5	104.9	112.5		101.0
101.6	101.1	99.3	96.2	106.3	101.8	99.0		103.4
101.4	100.9	96.8	96.2	104.2	99.4	97.5		100.0
103.8	102.0	99.2	97.9	106.5	102.0	101.1		100.0
101.3	100.4	94.9	98.6	97.9	99.5	100.0		100.3
101.8	101.5	100.1	99.7	104.1	102.2	100.1		102.1
106.3	102.4	100.0	101.5	104.4	103.0	100.7		102.4
107.2	99.6	99.4	101.0	102.5	103.0	102.0		100.0

7-2　市区商品零售价格指数（1984-2012 年，以上年价格为 100）
RETAIL PRICE INDEX OF URBAN COMMODITIES（1984-2012, PRECEDING YEAR=100）

年份 Year	商品零售价格指数 Retail Price Index of commodities	其中 of which 食品类 Food	其中 of which 粮食 Grain	肉禽蛋 Meat,Poultry and Eggs	水产品 Aquatic Products	鲜菜 Fresh Vegetables	饮料烟酒类 Beverages, Tobacco and Liquor	服装鞋帽类 Clothing, Shoes and Hats	纺织品类 Textiles
1984	102.5	103.9	99.9	105.3	127.9	101.2	99.3	99.6	99.2
1985	113.2	119.0	100.7	118.1	148.5	160.7	100.8	100.1	100.0
1986	106.1	108.5	98.4	114.4	102.3	116.9	101.9	100.8	101.3
1987	110.4	112.9	104.1	115.5	118.1	128.2	107.2	109.8	104.2
1988	123.8	130.2	102.2	135.3	129.3	153.0	124.1	120.9	118.9
1989	116.1	112.9	101.2	115.5	119.9	98.3	109.9	124.6	128.4
1990	103.4	102.3	101.8	101.2	102.7	105.9	97.6	109.8	110.5
1991	108.1	111.3	155.9	97.9	107.4	139.8	104.8	106.1	103.4
1992	107.0	109.9	159.2	103.0	112.1	99.7	111.3	104.3	101.3
1993	119.9	123.0	153.1	112.6	142.0	138.8	107.8	114.4	100.8
1994	118.9	134.9	154.7	135.6	121.2	137.6	108.2	118.3	111.6
1995	112.8	123.2	130.1	125.0	115.4	127.6	108.1	119.0	113.4
1996	107.8	109.4	111.8	105.7	105.4	132.2	107.8	117.8	112.4
1997	100.2	97.0	82.3	101.6	97.8	93.5	97.7	102.8	105.8
1998	98.8	98.4	101.6	93.4	93.1	106.3	99.1	102.7	100.7
1999	97.3	93.3	98.0	85.5	91.5	95.3	99.6	98.6	99.6
2000	98.0	94.0	80.6	94.3	95.7	110.4	95.9	97.2	94.1
2001	97.3	98.6	105.5	99.2	94.2	94.7	98.3	90.8	90.3
2002	99.0	99.3	97.2	99.0	94.2	105.6	94.2	100.8	106.0
2003	100.8	103.0	103.3	105.0	98.9	111.4	105.0	98.0	98.3
2004	103.7	114.0	139.2	123.9	119.5	92.8	101.6	97.3	100.0
2005	101.3	104.7	99.8	105.9	101.3	109.1	101.3	96.0	100.8
2006	100.6	104.4	102.9	98.6	108.2	108.9	97.3	97.0	99.9
2007	102.4	110.6	103.3	125.8	111.7	117.1	101.1	100.1	102.2
2008	104.7	112.6	113.9	121.8	111.8	103.6	103.9	102.7	103.7
2009	99.6	101.8	107.1	92.7	101.7	116.9	101.5	103.2	101.9
2010	102.7	107.8	120.0	100.8	114.1	115.3	100.5	102.5	109.5
2011	104.4	111.5	116.0	120.3	114.2	106.6	103.9	103.4	132.1
2012	101.7	105.1	105.3	103.3	107.8	106.2	103.3	105.6	131.5

of which									
中西药品类 Traditional Chinese and Western Medicines	化妆品类 Cosmetics	书报杂志类 Newspapers and Magazines	文化体育用品类 Cultural and Sports Goods	日用品类 Articles for Daily Use	家用电器类 Household Appliances	首饰类 Jewelry	燃料类 Fuels	建筑装璜材料类 Building Decoration Materials	机电产品类 Mechanical and Electrical Products
106.3		100.0	99.5	100.5	98.4		100.0		
102.4		116.3	101.7	103.4	99.2		100.0		
100.8		125.4	106.9	102.1	101.3		100.0		
104.9		100.0	115.9	112.4	100.3		100.0		
117.5		116.2	108.2	115.7	107.7		100.0	127.8	
112.2		198.4	112.6	117.9	118.5		100.0	120.6	
101.0		110.9	109.5	107.4	96.2		161.9	101.7	
101.5		100.3	101.6	102.5	96.5		143.9	100.3	
109.6		108.1	100.7	105.8	91.4		141.8	100.8	
108.9		105.9	105.4	113.4	104.5		201.9	125.8	
103.7	133.0	135.2	107.4	114.0	105.9	114.2	124.5	103.5	
103.3	109.4	126.8	103.9	109.0	100.9	99.6	107.9	100.1	92.6
106.9	102.1	138.1	102.1	106.5	99.6	99.0	111.8	99.1	94.9
102.0	101.2	116.4	99.2	102.8	100.0	100.7	103.7	102.7	93.3
98.8	104.1	115.7	98.0	100.5	89.8	91.7	102.6	99.9	97.4
102.2	101.8	102.5	99.0	100.1	97.7	94.2	99.7	101.2	99.5
101.7	98.8	108.4	99.8	101.2	98.5	109.0	118.1	97.0	98.1
99.6	91.0	110.5	95.6	98.9	98.1	93.7	100.9	95.6	96.7
93.3	100.3	95.4	99.1	99.6	100.0	101.8	99.7	102.0	96.5
98.2	102.3	99.6	99.3	99.9	93.7	118.6	112.0	101.1	
92.2	100.7	100.2	100.2	100.6	94.8	114.2	107.6	104.6	
99.6	101.8	100.4	95.6	101.4	96.9	105.3	111.4	106.0	
98.3	100.1	96.6	98.4	101.4	94.0	119.1	110.9	111.4	
100.0	99.6	97.2	95.9	100.6	98.0	105.2	102.5	109.3	
102.1	99.7	105.0	93.7	105.0	98.0	110.6	109.7	107.8	
100.2	100.3	124.5	92.2	101.6	94.5	98.5	88.9	98.4	
97.7	101.6	101.6	101.2	101.8	93.7	108.0	111.0	108.0	
101.9	95.9	100.7	95.4	104.5	102.7	117.0	108.6	105.8	
98.3	102.9	101.0	102.1	103.6	97.9	99.6	102.0	97.4	

7-3　市区居民消费价格指数（2012 年，以上年价格为 100）
CONSUMER PRICE INDEX OF URBAN RESIDENTS（2012, PRECEDING YEAR=100）

指　标	Item	2012
居民消费价格指数	**Residents Consumer Price Index**	102.5
服务项目价格指数	Price index of Service	103.0
消费品价格指数	Price index of Consumer Goods	102.3
食　品	Food	104.9
#粮　食	Grain	105.3
肉禽及其制品	Meat and Poultry	103.0
水产品	Aquatic Products	107.0
鲜　菜	Fresh Vegetables	106.2
烟酒及用品	Tobacco and Liquor and Articles	103.3
烟　草	Tobacco	100.8
酒	Liquor	109.7
衣　着	Clothing	101.6
服　装	Garments	101.4
衣着材料	Clothing Material	108.3
鞋袜帽	Shoes,Socks and Caps	102.1
衣着加工服务	Clothing Making Services	100.7
家庭设备用品及服务	Household Appliances and Services	107.2
耐用消费品	Durable Consumer Goods	101.5
室内装饰品	Interior Decorations	100.4
床上用品	Bed Articles	120.7
家庭日用杂品	Daily Use Household Articles	104.4
家庭服务及加工维修服务	Household Services,Processing and Repairing Services	118.9
医疗保健及个人用品	Health Care and Personal Articles	99.6
医疗保健	Medicine and Healthcare	98.9
个人用品及服务	Individual Articals and Services	100.9
交通和通讯	Transportation and Communication	99.4
交　通	Transportation	100.2
通　信	Communication	97.3
娱乐教育文化用品及服务	Recreational,Educational and Cultural Goods and Services	101.0
文娱用耐用消费品及服务	Durable Consumer Goods for Recreational Use and Services	92.6
教　育	Education	102.2
文化娱乐用品	Cultural and Recreational Articles	100.8
旅游及外出	Tour and External Business	103.0
居　住	Housing	102.5
建房及装修材料	Building Materials	96.2
租　房	Rent	103.6
自有住房	Housing	104.8
水、电、燃料	Water,Electricity and Fuels	101.0

7-4 市区商品零售价格指数（2012 年，以上年价格为 100）
RETAIL PRICE INDEX OF URBAN COMMODITIES（2012, PRECEDING YEAR=100）

指 标	Item	2012
商品零售价格指数	**Retail Price Index of commodities**	101.7
食 品	Food	105.1
#粮 食	Grain	105.3
淀粉及制品	Starches and Related Product	106.3
干豆类及豆制品	Bean and Its Products	103.4
油 脂	Oil or Fat	101.6
肉禽及其制品	Meat, Poultry and Related Product	103.3
蛋	Eggs	99.8
水产品	Aquatic Products	107.8
菜	Vegetables	105.5
#鲜 菜	Fresh Vegetables	106.2
调味品	Flavoring	107.7
#糖	Carbohydrate	101.6
干鲜瓜果	Dried and Fresh Fruits and Melons	97.3
糕点饼干面包	Cake，Biscuit and Brad	104.1
奶及奶制品	Milk and Its Products	102.7
在外用膳食品	Out Ward Dinner	108.4
其它食品	Others Foods	103.8
饮料烟酒	Beverages,Tobacco and Liquor	103.3
服装鞋帽	Clothing,Shoes and Hats	105.6
纺织品	Textiles	131.5
家用电器及音像器材	Household Appliances and Acoutic and Visual Equipment	97.9
文化办公用品	Cultural Stationery	97.9
日用品	Articles for Daily Use	103.6
体育娱乐用品	Sports and Entertainment Articles	102.1
交通、通信用品	Tansportation and Telecommunication Facilities	96.0
家 具	Furniture	102.0
化妆品	Cosmetics	102.9
金银珠宝	Jewellery	99.6
中西药品及医疗保健用品	Chinese and Western Medicine and Medical care Articles	98.3
书报杂志及电子出版物	Newspaper, Magazine & Electronic Publication	101.0
燃 料	Fuels	102.0
建筑材料及五金电料	Construction Materials & Hardware Materials	97.4

7-5　市区分月主要农副产品价格（2012 年）
MAIN AGRICULTURAL AND SIDELINE PRODUCTS IN URBAN AREA BY MONTH（2012）

品　种	Name	规格等级	Specification and Grade	1 月 Jan.	2 月 Feb.
粳　米	Polished Rice	特　一	Special First Grade	5.30	5.38
植物油	Vegetable Oil	豆　油	Soybean Oil	11.00	10.92
猪　肉	Pork	去骨后腿肉	Thigh Meat without Bone	29.08	28.68
鸡	Chicken	活草鸡	Live Chicken	23.41	22.62
鲜　蛋	Fresh Eggs	新鲜完整	Fresh and Whole	8.85	7.45
鲢　鱼	Silver Carp	1.0千克以上	Above 1.0 Kilogram	13.42	14.76
鲫　鱼	Crucian	活200克左右	Live and Weight about 200 Gram	15.29	15.01
虾	Shrimps	活河虾	Live Shimps	124.04	138.91
大白菜	Chinese Cabbage	一　等	First Grade	1.93	2.36
油　菜	Rape	一　等	First Grade	3.30	4.89
芹　菜	Celery	一　等	First Grade	7.77	8.70
黄　瓜	Cucumber	一　等	First Grade	8.26	8.26
西红柿	Tomato	一　等	First Grade	8.50	8.56
萝　卜	Radish	一　等	First Grade	2.55	2.98
青　椒	Green Pepper	一　等	First Grade	12.36	12.10
生　姜	Ginger	一　等	First Grade	6.88	7.03
豆　芽	Bean Sprout	一　等	First Grade	4.21	3.92
苹　果	Apples	一　级	First Grade	9.50	9.84
梨	Pears	一　级	First Grade	5.98	6.01
香　蕉	Bananas	一　级	First Grade	7.11	6.99

单位：元/千克（yuan/kg）

3月 Mar.	4月 Apr.	5月 May	6月 June	7月 July	8月 Aug.	9月 Sept.	10月 Oct.	11月 Nov.	12月 Dec.
5.51	5.59	5.51	5.46	5.46	5.55	5.62	5.58	5.56	5.57
10.88	11.09	11.13	11.89	11.98	11.98	11.98	11.82	11.65	11.75
27.43	25.75	25.33	24.86	24.69	24.95	24.93	24.90	24.94	25.63
21.29	21.23	21.21	21.27	21.80	21.90	22.12	22.38	22.73	22.78
7.21	7.28	7.21	8.63	8.30	9.59	10.58	9.40	9.29	9.84
15.39	16.09	16.93	17.04	16.07	15.26	14.73	14.00	14.07	13.93
15.81	16.64	19.01	19.41	19.21	18.85	17.74	16.97	16.83	16.82
140.97	133.71	77.51	80.78	111.07	130.00	129.83	130.00	130.11	130.31
2.77	3.02	3.51	2.73	3.10	4.29	3.98	3.19	2.45	2.06
5.10	3.62	4.88	4.61	5.43	7.02	6.23	3.60	2.79	3.45
9.00	6.67	7.33	6.42	6.77	8.43	9.28	7.69	6.29	6.61
7.89	6.78	5.54	4.26	5.16	6.60	6.07	4.87	5.59	6.88
8.99	8.68	7.16	4.83	5.02	6.84	7.34	7.03	7.04	7.33
3.37	3.30	3.70	3.02	3.23	3.60	3.73	3.06	2.38	2.53
12.56	11.99	8.77	6.95	6.89	6.79	6.79	6.49	6.37	7.08
7.07	7.09	7.01	7.10	7.04	6.54	6.20	6.16	6.90	7.32
3.90	3.90	3.90	3.90	3.89	3.90	3.96	3.96	3.96	3.96
9.76	9.76	9.63	9.81	10.00	10.21	10.23	10.23	10.29	10.63
5.99	6.00	5.74	5.56	5.83	6.20	5.34	5.30	5.16	5.27
6.86	6.88	6.33	5.60	5.56	5.37	5.04	4.98	5.00	5.14

8

CHAPTER 8

人民生活

PEOPLE' S LIVELIHOOD

常州统计年鉴

8 人民生活
PEOPLE'S LIVELIHOOD

2012 年主要统计指标
MAJOR STATISTICAL INDICATORS OF 2012

城市居民人均可支配收入	Per Capita Disposable Income of Urban Residents	33857元	（yuan）
比上年增长	Over the Previous Year	12.6%	
城市居民人均消费性支出	Per Capita Consuming Expenditures of Urban Residents	20519元	（yuan）
比上年增长	Over the Previous Year	8.6%	
农民人均纯收入	Per Capita Net Income of Rural Residents	16737元	（yuan）
比上年增长	Over the Previous Year	12.8%	
农村居民人均生活消费支出	Living Expenditure of Rural Residents （yuan）	12027元	（yuan）
比上年增长	Over the Previous Year	7.3%	

8-1 市区居民家庭基本情况（1984-2012 年）
BASIC INDICATORS OF URBAN HOUSEHOLDS（1984-2012）

年 份 Year	调查户数（户） Households Surveyed (household)	户均家庭人口（人） Number of Persons Per Household (person)	户均就业人口（人） Number of Employed Persons Per Household (person)	每一就业者负担人口（人） Persons Supported by Each Employee (person)	人均可支配收入（元） Per Capita Disposable Income (yuan)	人均现住房屋使用面积（平方米） Per Capita Subsidiary Usable Floor Space (sq.m)	恩格尔系数（%） Engel Coefficient (%)	基尼系数 Gini Coefficient
1984	100	3.58	2.37	1.51	701	10.06	56.8	
1985	100	3.33	2.07	1.61	889	11.59	56.1	0.1476
1986	100	3.29	2.02	1.63	1089	12.07	54.0	0.1358
1987	100	3.21	1.88	1.71	1236	12.49	54.0	0.1463
1988	100	3.17	1.92	1.65	1417	12.12	53.0	0.1487
1989	100	3.12	1.87	1.66	1559	12.99	59.0	0.1339
1990	100	3.06	1.81	1.69	1769	13.22	61.6	0.1439
1991	100	2.98	1.67	1.78	1996	13.51	61.0	0.1250
1992	100	2.91	1.72	1.69	2509	14.03	59.0	0.1414
1993	100	3.02	1.75	1.73	3195	13.70	56.0	0.1776
1994	100	3.13	1.88	1.66	4617	15.60	55.0	0.1488
1995	100	3.04	1.73	1.76	5632	15.04	54.9	0.1365
1996	100	3.00	1.67	1.80	6743	15.65	50.0	0.1337
1997	100	3.01	1.46	2.06	6853	15.25	46.0	0.1793
1998	100	2.96	1.49	1.99	7107	15.55	52.0	0.2088
1999	100	2.97	1.50	1.98	7874	15.87	44.0	0.2187
2000	200	2.93	1.53	1.91	8540	15.19	40.1	0.2461
2001	200	2.91	1.48	1.96	9406	16.23	36.9	0.2525
2002	200	2.89	1.56	1.85	9933	17.44	36.8	0.2804
2003	300	2.86	1.47	1.95	11303	20.35	36.2	0.2786
2004	300	2.85	1.46	1.95	12867	20.65	37.2	0.3142
2005	300	2.89	1.51	1.91	14589	21.04	35.9	0.2934
2006	300	2.83	1.49	1.90	16649	21.49	35.7	0.3317
2007	300	2.80	1.46	1.92	19089	21.77	35.0	0.3232
2008	300	2.85	1.47	1.94	21592	24.38	33.8	0.3090
2009	300	2.81	1.46	1.92	23751	24.69	33.7	0.3060
2010	300	2.80	1.48	1.89	26269	24.91	32.7	0.3190
2011	300	2.73	1.31	2.08	29829	26.11	35.8	0.2990
2012	300	2.69	1.32	2.04	33587	26.50	36.1	0.3010

注：“每一就业者负担人口”包括就业者本人,下同。
Note：“Persons Supported by Each Employee” includes the employee himself,the same below.

8-2 市区居民家庭人均消费支出情况（1984-2012 年）
PER CAPITA LIVING EXPENDITURE OF URBAN HOUSEHOLDS（1984-2012）

单位：元（yuan）

年份 Year	人均消费支出 Per Capita Living Expenditure	其中 of which 食品 Food	衣着 Clothing	设备用品及服务 Facilities, Articles and Services	医疗保健 Medicine and Medical Services	交通与通讯 Transport, Post and Communication Services	文教娱乐服务 Recreation, Education and Cultural Services	居住 Residence	杂项商品及服务 Miscellaneous Commodities and Services
1984	595	338	90	33	9	17	42	44	22
1985	746	419	112	46	11	19	54	56	28
1986	918	499	136	63	15	24	71	74	36
1987	1059	576	137	74	18	30	89	93	43
1988	1359	715	178	93	23	46	122	123	59
1989	1469	860	154	87	24	48	117	117	63
1990	1498	922	167	75	22	44	101	112	54
1991	1705	1046	210	83	28	49	110	123	56
1992	2000	1170	254	169	28	25	132	138	83
1993	2456	1377	308	199	36	50	195	205	87
1994	3503	1910	400	218	65	109	328	343	131
1995	4426	2429	462	253	61	208	431	379	203
1996	4946	2469	633	293	113	234	437	435	331
1997	5442	2506	620	379	145	265	510	764	253
1998	5282	2722	368	417	196	240	525	591	225
1999	6107	2658	398	461	514	305	610	850	312
2000	6759	2710	536	708	411	396	826	746	425
2001	7526	2777	495	958	513	728	722	867	466
2002	7973	2933	587	553	644	661	1394	876	326
2003	8944	3240	689	579	791	1052	1411	816	365
2004	9878	3673	680	856	676	1181	1387	1042	384
2005	10718	3848	1041	696	815	1309	1481	1063	464
2006	12503	4467	1072	911	782	1616	1637	1541	476
2007	13789	4824	1193	750	1005	2586	1657	1289	486
2008	14967	5056	1510	1027	1284	1970	2020	1519	581
2009	15961	5379	1615	987	1055	2831	2327	1078	690
2010	17124	5603	1629	1136	1108	2928	2574	1408	737
2011	18893	6760	1754	1299	1409	2957	2962	1250	502
2012	20519	7406	1993	1383	1449	3253	3107	1317	613

8-3 主要年份市区居民家庭收支情况
INCOME AND EXPENSE CONDITION OF URBAN HOUSEHOLDS IN MAIN YEARS

指标	Item	1990	1995	2000	2005	2010	2012
调查户数（户）	**Number of Household Surveyed （household）**	**100**	**100**	**200**	**300**	**300**	**300**
户均家庭人口（人）	**Average Household Size （person）**	3.06	3.04	2.93	2.89	2.80	2.69
有收入者人数	Number of People with Income	2.24	2.34	2.22	2.19	2.18	2.09
#离退休人数	Number of Retired People	0.43	0.60	0.69	0.62	0.66	0.66
无收入者人数	Number of People without Income	0.82	0.70	0.70	0.70	0.62	0.60
人均家庭总收入（元）	**Per Capita Family Income （yuan）**	**1782**	**5636**	**8577**	**15820**	**29008**	**36638**
#可支配收入	Disposable Income	1769	5632	8540	14589	26269	33587
最低收入户（占10%）	Lowest Income （Make up 10%）	1075	3868	2901	5089	9238	11724
低收入户（占10%）	Low Income （Make up 10%）	1295	3991	4984	7434	13599	18246
中等偏下收入户（占20%）	Medium-Low Income （Make up 20%）	1524	4619	6428	9910	17408	23132
中等收入户（占20%）	Medium Income （Make up 20%）	1722	5219	7901	12620	21942	29901
中等偏上收入户（占20%）	Medium-High Income （Make up 20%）	2026	6285	10448	16097	29650	39963
高收入户（占10%）	High Income （Make up 10%）	2290	7290	13254	21405	40129	52526
最高收入户（占10%）	Highest Income （Make up 10%）	2964	8575	17430	39873	73396	80735
人均家庭总支出（元）	**Per Capita Family Expenditure （yuan）**	**1590**	**4785**	**8453**	**16551**	**25048**	**29541**
#消费性支出	Expenditure for Consumption	1498	4426	6759	10718	17124	20519
最低收入户（占10%）	Lowest Income （Make up 10%）	1058	3645	2829	5049	8879	9442
低收入户（占10%）	Low Income （Make up 10%）	957	3798	4886	6315	11536	15531
中等偏下收入户（占20%）	Medium-Low Income （Make up 20%）	1278	3711	5453	8455	13587	16137
中等收入户（占20%）	Medium Income （Make up 20%）	1544	4427	6546	10124	13981	21948
中等偏上收入户（占20%）	Medium-High Income （Make up 20%）	1716	5030	7455	10635	19019	22542
高收入户（占10%）	High Income （Make up 10%）	1928	4911	8381	14234	22546	26161
最高收入户（占10%）	Highest Income （Make up 10%）	2264	5330	14292	26323	41018	38046
购房与建房支出	Expenditure on Housing Purchas and Construction				3140	2454	2108
人均借贷支出（元）	**Per Capita Debit and Credit Expenditures （yuan）**	**375**	**1496**	**2871**	**5803**	**11573**	**15120**
#存入储蓄款	Deposit Money in Bank	316	1447	2532	4199	10682	13848
购买有价证券	Buy Valuable Negotiable Securities	7	1	10	0.2	50.9	

8-4　市区居民家庭人口分组（2012 年）
POPULATION OF URBAN HOUSEHOLDS（2012）

指　标	Item	总平均 Average	最低收入组（占10%） Lowest Income Households（Make up 10%）
调查户数（户）	**Number of Household Surveyed （household）**	**300**	**30**
家庭人口	**Household Population （person）**	**2.69**	**2.87**
有收入者人数	Number of Persons with Income	2.09	1.77
就业人数	Number of Persons Employed	1.32	1.03
国有经济单位职工	Workers and Staff of State Capital Involved Enterprises	0.26	0.03
城镇集体经济单位职工	Workers and Staff of Township Collective Capital Involved Enterprises	0.04	0.10
其他各种经济类型单位职工	Workers and Staff of Other Ownership Enterprises	0.53	0.33
个体经营者	Self-employed Individuals	0.12	0.17
个体被雇者	Employed Individuals	0.25	0.30
离退休再就业者	Reemployed Retirees	0.07	
其他就业者	Other Employment	0.06	0.10
离退休人数	Number of Retired Persons	0.66	0.40
其他有收入者人数	Number of Other People with Income	0.11	0.33
无收入者人数	Number of Persons without Income	0.60	1.10
平均每一就业者负担人数	**Number of Persons Supported by Each Employee**	**2.04**	**2.79**
期末家庭人口	**Household Population at Year-end**	**2.69**	**2.87**
附:非家庭人口在家用餐人次	Number of Non-family Members who frequently have dinner in the Family	12.84	2.50

单位：人（person）

按收入水平分组 Grouped by Level of Income							
其中 of which	低收入组（占10%）	中等偏下组（占20%）	中等收入组（占20%）	中等偏上组（占20%）	高收入组（占10%）	最高收入组（占10%）	其中 of which
#更低收入组（占5%） Poor Households（Make up 5%）	Low Income Households（Make up 10%）	Lower Middle Income Households（Make up 20%）	Middle Income Households（Make up 20%）	Upper Middle Income Households（Make up 20%）	High Income Households（Make up 10%）	Highest Income Households（Make up 10%）	#更高收入组（占5%） Higher Income Households（Make up 5%）
15	**30**	**60**	**60**	**60**	**30**	**30**	**15**
3.07	**3.17**	**2.90**	**2.63**	**2.48**	**2.30**	**2.50**	**2.47**
1.80	2.20	2.25	2.12	2.10	1.90	2.10	2.07
1.13	1.33	1.52	1.12	1.23	1.40	1.70	1.80
	0.07	0.20	0.32	0.33	0.20	0.60	0.33
	0.10	0.05		0.03		0.03	0.07
0.33	0.80	0.52	0.47	0.45	0.80	0.47	0.60
0.07	0.10	0.12	0.10	0.07	0.07	0.27	0.33
0.53	0.20	0.43	0.15	0.22	0.13	0.23	0.33
		0.03	0.05	0.13	0.20	0.07	0.07
0.20	0.07	0.17	0.03			0.03	0.07
0.40	0.53	0.65	0.97	0.85	0.50	0.20	
0.27	0.33	0.08	0.03	0.02		0.20	0.27
1.27	0.97	0.65	0.52	0.38	0.40	0.40	0.40
2.72	**2.38**	**1.91**	**2.35**	**2.02**	**1.64**	**1.47**	**1.37**
3.07	**3.17**	**2.90**	**2.63**	**2.48**	**2.30**	**2.50**	**2.47**
4.07	2.60	3.57	21.67	21.17	14.10	16.43	15.53

8-5　市区居民家庭人均收支情况（2012 年）
PER CAPITA INCOME OF URBAN RESIDENTS AND EXPENDITURE CONDITION（2012）

指　标	Item	总平均 Average	最低收入组（占10%）Lowest Income Households（Make up 10%）
期初手存现金	**Cash on Hand at Beginning of Year**	**764.95**	**736.58**
家庭总收入	**Total Family Income**	**36637.99**	**13503.58**
#可支配收入	Including: Disposable Income	33587.03	11724.29
工薪收入	Income from Wages and Salaries	23608.99	5555.17
工资及补贴收入	Wages and Subsidies Income	23245.88	4816.27
其他劳动收入	Other Labor Income	363.11	738.90
经营净收入	Operating Net Income	2600.51	1225.15
财产性收入	Property Income	775.04	371.35
利息收入	Interest Income	203.61	64.10
股息与红利收入	Divident and Bonus Income	10.80	
保险收益	Insurance Yield	1.24	
其它投资收入	Other Investment Income	16.62	
出租房屋收入	Housing Rent Income	540.20	286.15
其它财产性收入	Other Property Income	2.56	21.10
转移性收入	Transfer Income	9653.46	6351.91
养老金或离退休金	Pension or Retirement Pay	8150.30	4161.60
社会救济收入	Income from Social Relief	161.73	923.37
辞退金	Dismissal Compensation	5.98	
赔偿收入	Compensation income	22.72	
保险收入	Insurance Income	31.85	
#失业保险金	Including: Unemployment Insurance Money	8.01	
赡养收入	Income from Support	273.85	649.60
捐赠收入	Income from Donation	610.55	221.21
提取住房公积金	Withdraw Public Accumulation Fund for Housing Construction		
记帐补贴	Charge Account Subsidy	199.12	186.81
其他转移性收入	Other Transfer Income	197.36	209.31
出售财物收入	**Income from Property Sold**	**14.98**	**0.44**
借贷收入	**Debit and Credit Income**	**7962.49**	**6317.58**
提取储蓄存款	Withdraw Savings Deposits	7067.47	6280.22
借入款	Loan	128.20	37.36
收回借出款	Recover Loan	2.48	
收回储蓄性保险本	Recover Savings Insurance Capital	26.67	
住房贷款	Bank Loan for Housing Purchasing	731.48	
其它贷款	Other Loans	4.96	
其它借贷收入	Other Loan Income	1.24	

单位：元（yuan）

按收入水平分组 Grouped by Level of Income							
其中 of which # 更低收入组（占5%） Poor Households（Make up 5%）	低收入组（占10%） Low Income Households（Make up 10%）	中等偏下组（占20%） Lower Middle Income Households（Make up 20%）	中等收入组（占20%） Middle Income Households（Make up 20%）	中等偏上组（占20%） Upper Middle Income Households（Make up 20%）	高收入组（占10%） High Income Households（Make up 10%）	最高收入组（占10%） Highest Income Households（Make up 10%）	其中 of which # 更高收入组（占5%） Higher Income Households（Make up 5%）
656.07	**563.50**	**797.23**	**832.98**	**814.44**	**736.20**	**775.16**	**796.12**
10862.66	**20083.10**	**25190.24**	**32455.98**	**43361.80**	**58519.29**	**86547.63**	**98191.78**
9313.16	18246.31	23131.53	29900.90	39963.35	52525.62	80735.20	93159.78
5636.31	12791.60	15493.49	19350.21	28117.74	43903.74	58132.22	66901.86
5395.00	12324.87	15353.64	19116.26	27886.05	42905.59	57991.78	66654.27
241.30	466.73	139.85	233.95	231.69	998.15	140.44	247.60
1988.89	1386.25	1677.20	2051.37	1579.98	4708.17	9199.39	15588.69
19.96	629.70	362.39	615.81	769.33	525.37	3066.34	3378.87
19.96	59.37	61.31	277.02	211.90	225.27	701.73	831.88
		0.65			91.57	22.38	
						13.99	
			4.49			177.64	368.21
	570.34	300.42	333.36	557.43	208.53	2150.60	2178.79
			0.94				
3217.50	5275.54	7657.16	10438.60	12894.75	9382.02	16149.68	12322.35
1485.04	4188.52	6920.14	9211.44	10947.14	7954.92	13431.44	10161.63
1007.96	263.63	61.24	7.95	65.24			
				32.33			
						256.32	434.89
	20.82		75.94	1.88		160.32	187.34
						90.38	187.34
247.83	194.62	37.95	30.51	674.41	312.66	104.91	
215.22	316.39	398.18	623.78	794.67	700.93	1481.99	987.20
193.48	153.15	201.79	195.99	216.44	197.54	242.90	255.57
67.98	138.42	37.87	292.99	162.64	215.98	471.80	295.72
		2.48	**4.63**	**1.49**	**2.22**	**147.02**	**293.87**
1482.61	**4357.16**	**3703.21**	**7320.09**	**9200.37**	**5355.98**	**26355.52**	**31920.75**
1419.57	4357.16	3327.68	7294.66	6718.99	5102.58	22676.77	31920.75
63.04		375.53		254.75			
						27.98	
				14.34	253.40		
				2212.29		3636.79	
			25.43				
						13.98	

8-5 续表 continued

指　标	Item	总平均 Average	最低收入组（占10%） Lowest Income Households（Make up 10%）
家庭总支出	**Total Expenditures of Households**	**29540.50**	**15976.29**
消费支出	Consumption Expenditure	20519.00	9442.31
#服务性消费支出	Expenditure on Service	5719.91	2442.31
购房与建房支出	Expenditure on Housing Purchas and Construction	2107.66	3956.04
购　房	Housing Purchase	2107.66	3956.04
转移性支出	Transfer Expenditure	3811.94	870.12
交纳的个人收入税	Personal Income Tax	148.40	
捐赠支出	Expenditure on Donation	2527.59	777.22
购买彩票	Lottery Purchase	12.26	
赡养支出	Expenditure on Support	776.80	73.63
#在外就学子女费用	Expenditure on Children Study Outside	470.03	
各种非储蓄性保险支出	Non-savings Insurance Expenditure	309.81	17.43
#车辆保险支出	Expenditure on Automobile Insurance	265.48	
其他转移性支出	Other Transfer Expenditure	37.08	1.84
社会保障支出	Expenditure on Social Security	2703.44	1592.48
个人交纳的养老基金	Pension Fund Paid by Individual	1150.25	1192.84
个人交纳的住房公积金	Public Accumulation Fund for Housing Construction Paid by Individual	1049.79	52.21
个人交纳的医疗基金	Medical Treatment Fund Paid by Individual	383.19	296.25
个人交纳的失业基金	Unemployment Fund Paid by Individual	78.54	35.79
其他社会保障支出	Other Expenditure on Social Security	41.67	15.38
借贷支出	**Debit and Credit expenditure**	**15119.54**	**3913.96**
存入储蓄款	Savings Deposits	13847.88	3848.02
借出款	Lending	0.62	
归还借款	Return Loan	26.97	11.54
储蓄性保险支出	Expenditure on Savings Insurance	231.05	21.43
购买有价证券	Valuable Securities Purchasing		
其它投资支出	Other Investment Expenditures	1.09	
归还住房贷款	Return Loan for Housing Purchase	992.74	32.97
归还汽车贷款	Car Loan Repayment	18.57	
其他借贷支出	Other Debit and Credit Expenditure	0.62	
期末手存现金	**Cash on Hand at Year-end**	**722.55**	**667.94**

单位：元（yuan）

按收入水平分组				Grouped by Level of Income			
其中 of which #更低收入组（占5%） Poor Households（Make up 5%）	低收入组（占10%） Low Income Households（Make up 10%）	中等偏下组（占20%） Lower Middle Income Households（Make up 20%）	中等收入组（占20%） Middle Income Households（Make up 20%）	中等偏上组（占20%） Upper Middle Income Households（Make up 20%）	高收入组（占10%） High Income Households（Make up 10%）	最高收入组（占10%） Highest Income Households（Make up 10%）	其中 of which #更高收入组（占5%） Higher Income Households（Make up 5%）
10013.45	**19088.68**	**19935.80**	**28868.31**	**34414.15**	**37129.91**	**66229.08**	**67293.54**
7935.82	15531.15	16136.64	21947.51	22541.81	26160.89	38046.08	38554.43
1990.99	3527.07	3887.04	5860.88	6303.44	8656.33	12404.34	11987.27
				4022.35		10350.86	8117.90
				4022.35		10350.86	8117.90
721.61	1675.62	1856.67	4381.32	4435.24	5350.03	10745.22	12923.91
	2.62	24.99	135.46	203.83	388.23	474.57	291.04
617.83	1284.58	1247.60	3028.89	3212.33	3010.27	6334.35	7151.58
	27.06	0.70	37.47	0.68	0.13	16.32	27.98
69.57	239.58	390.04	731.87	609.85	1501.77	2959.09	4009.66
		187.36	512.11	188.18	933.52	2352.72	3406.62
31.61	115.99	183.32	411.76	380.59	378.74	788.88	1155.79
	83.26	169.40	294.51	332.72	359.85	765.10	1144.04
2.61	5.78	10.03	35.87	27.95	70.89	172.02	287.86
1356.02	1681.02	1831.94	2223.62	2978.18	5407.91	5094.96	4485.39
838.88	953.60	961.07	956.71	1075.68	1818.48	1664.18	1721.02
65.24	391.30	394.76	802.98	1431.62	2789.36	2603.61	1915.18
391.86	300.79	371.86	399.53	332.61	551.56	520.32	516.13
29.60	30.67	71.33	53.39	100.83	183.48	110.52	64.84
30.43	4.65	32.92	11.02	37.45	65.02	196.34	268.22
2309.13	**5264.47**	**9050.60**	**11006.46**	**18234.34**	**26748.84**	**46759.58**	**63070.54**
2297.17	4457.07	8134.82	9631.12	16974.68	25241.78	42962.18	58694.47
			3.18				
11.96	62.45	54.51	4.45		26.16	41.96	
	71.56	409.36	141.80	141.46	291.51	619.05	222.81
	9.16						
	664.23	451.91	1129.41	1116.19	1189.38	3136.39	4153.26
			95.23				
			1.27	2.01			
678.76	**656.56**	**704.14**	**740.17**	**716.41**	**776.92**	**840.68**	**848.40**

8-6　市区居民家庭人均消费支出情况（2012 年）
PER CAPITA LIVING EXPENDITURES OF URBAN HOUSEHOLDS（2012）

指　标	Item	总平均 Average	最低收入组（占10%） Lowest Income Households（Make up 10%）
消费支出	**Consumption Expenditures**	**20519.00**	**9442.31**
#服务性消费支出	Expenditure on Service	5719.91	2442.31
食　品	**Food**	**7405.65**	**4074.48**
粮油类	Grain and Edible Oil	676.13	578.57
粮　食	Grain	414.65	348.78
淀粉及薯类	Starches and Tubers	58.34	47.69
干豆类及豆制品	Beans and Bean Products	95.18	82.47
油脂类	Oil and Fat	107.96	99.62
肉禽蛋水产品类	Meat, Poultry, Eggs and Aquatic Products	1994.58	1346.84
肉　类	Meat	939.88	643.36
禽　类	Poultry	342.01	243.14
蛋　类	Eggs	114.78	99.33
水产品类	Aquantic Products	597.91	360.99
蔬菜类	Vegetables	771.61	650.09
鲜　菜	Fresh Vegetables	713.36	608.39
干　菜	Dried Vegetables	34.11	20.46
菜制品	Vegetables Product	24.13	21.24
调味品	Condiments	72.93	53.03
糖烟酒饮料类	Sugar, Cigarette, Wine and Beverage	896.62	306.94
糖　类	Sugar	56.59	26.45
烟草类	Tobacco	544.44	176.53
酒　类	Liquor	186.44	54.82
饮　料	Beverages	109.16	49.14
干鲜瓜果类	Dried and Fresh Melons and Fruits	621.80	227.33
鲜　果	Fresh Fruits	348.40	121.43
鲜　瓜	Fresh Melons	65.21	25.94
其它干鲜瓜果类及制品	Other Dried and Fresh Melons and Fruits and Products	208.20	79.96
糕点、奶及奶制品	Cake, Milk and Dairy Products	461.04	257.76
糕　点	Cake	164.25	61.68
奶及奶制品	Milk and Dairy Products	296.78	196.07
其他食品	Other Food	119.61	46.19
饮食服务	Catering service	1791.32	607.73
食品加工服务费	Service Fee of Food Processing	13.10	12.57
在外饮食	Eating outside	1778.22	595.17
衣　着	**Clothing**	**1992.66**	**557.74**
服　装	Garments	1543.77	413.23
衣着材料	Clothing Materials	28.78	4.62
鞋　类	Footware	352.95	119.12

单位：元（yuan）

按收入水平分组				Grouped by Level of Income			
其中 of which #更低收入组（占5%） Poor Households（Make up 5%）	低收入组（占10%） Low Income Households（Make up 10%）	中等偏下组（占20%） Lower Middle Income Households（Make up 20%）	中等收入组（占20%） Middle Income Households（Make up 20%）	中等偏上组（占20%） Upper Middle Income Households（Make up 20%）	高收入组（占10%） High Income Households（Make up 10%）	最高收入组（占10%） Highest Income Households（Make up 10%）	其中 of which #更高收入组（占5%） Higher Income Households（Make up 5%）
7935.82	**15531.15**	**16136.64**	**21947.51**	**22541.81**	**26160.89**	**38046.08**	**38554.43**
1990.99	3527.07	3887.04	5860.88	6303.44	8656.33	12404.34	11987.27
3787.68	**6232.66**	**6535.02**	**7556.89**	**8003.77**	**8060.75**	**12951.70**	**12566.93**
562.24	645.92	596.21	758.69	717.63	604.49	833.82	641.11
340.81	401.27	394.09	469.44	411.02	353.66	516.23	418.06
49.10	48.39	43.72	67.48	77.84	55.73	61.00	54.82
72.51	87.26	82.03	110.88	107.07	98.31	89.69	60.20
99.82	109.00	76.37	110.89	121.71	96.78	166.90	108.03
1244.26	1825.66	1951.22	2099.49	2237.30	2067.11	2331.47	2043.53
600.20	880.67	935.46	982.19	1041.69	1003.83	1033.16	1015.46
234.94	335.69	317.97	352.25	401.61	333.56	394.05	306.50
103.91	101.11	106.18	131.07	124.42	108.20	123.78	91.64
305.22	508.18	591.61	633.97	669.58	621.52	780.48	629.94
631.34	706.69	742.64	762.21	858.67	767.96	923.33	738.23
595.29	651.73	687.82	700.95	793.96	720.71	840.03	684.94
12.17	20.78	28.60	38.12	44.42	23.82	62.82	33.66
23.87	34.17	26.23	23.13	20.28	23.42	20.49	19.63
53.91	71.16	60.32	88.67	81.19	66.40	84.90	62.94
342.79	893.27	668.62	1207.81	763.56	710.43	1970.32	2607.44
31.16	57.40	44.73	87.36	57.37	42.92	66.53	80.24
194.47	627.81	420.35	713.90	480.43	446.00	1053.17	1401.29
58.25	99.56	124.49	276.22	123.13	127.01	611.90	821.69
58.91	108.51	79.05	130.33	102.62	94.50	238.72	304.21
226.43	519.40	537.34	599.86	681.13	628.98	1373.43	1368.91
128.56	294.31	278.08	325.83	363.38	408.10	826.98	666.29
30.18	60.25	62.23	72.25	67.90	57.45	115.89	133.88
67.69	164.84	197.04	201.78	249.85	163.42	430.55	568.74
196.09	427.68	323.58	503.82	563.67	497.88	734.43	610.06
57.29	149.92	100.80	196.03	194.92	213.32	274.30	244.45
138.80	277.76	222.78	307.79	368.75	284.56	460.13	365.61
44.17	42.85	139.78	122.45	122.11	162.18	212.69	215.27
486.45	1100.04	1515.30	1413.90	1978.52	2555.32	4487.30	4279.44
4.51	16.21	7.49	16.10	18.99	10.65	6.24	0.52
481.93	1083.83	1507.81	1397.81	1959.53	2544.67	4481.06	4278.92
573.31	**838.49**	**1551.00**	**1729.34**	**2316.68**	**3587.39**	**4588.45**	**4602.44**
397.45	581.39	1175.05	1291.26	1790.17	2868.41	3752.84	3678.45
6.27	47.05	50.61	26.72	13.34	37.05	12.49	11.68
145.67	178.93	275.57	353.85	407.83	579.13	704.81	804.68

8-6 续表 continued

指　标	Item	总平均 Average	最低收入组（占10%）Lowest Income Households (Make up 10%)
其他衣着用品	Other Clothing Supplies	55.94	15.67
衣着加工服务费	Clothing Processing and Service Fees	11.23	5.09
家庭设备用品及服务	**Household Facilities, Articles and Service**	**1382.51**	**528.82**
耐用消费品	Durable Consumer Goods	508.72	234.13
室内装饰品	Room Decorations	36.98	
床上用品	Bed Articles	132.46	14.89
家庭日用杂品	Household Articles for Daily Use	530.17	255.17
家具材料	Furniture Materials	1.24	0.03
家庭服务	Household Services	172.94	24.60
医疗保健	**Medicine and Medical Services**	**1449.05**	**1695.88**
医疗器具	Medical Appliance	9.47	51.98
保健器具	Health Care Articles	22.04	21.54
药品费	Medcial Expenses	631.56	759.55
滋补保健品	Tonics	295.62	119.66
医疗费	Health Care Service	481.95	739.99
其　他	Others	8.41	3.18
交通和通讯	**Transportation and Communications**	**3252.69**	**752.40**
交　通	Traffic	2424.07	310.11
家庭交通工具	Family Traffic Facility	1089.02	104.95
车辆用燃料及零配件	Vehicles Applied Fuel and Fittings	786.32	88.56
交通工具服务支出	Expenditure on Vehicles Service	302.57	39.51
交通费	Traffic Fare	246.16	77.09
通　信	Post and Telecommunication	828.62	442.29
通信工具	Telecommunication Facilities	180.49	55.66
通信服务	Communication Service	648.13	386.63
教育文化娱乐服务	**Entertainment and Culture and Education Service**	**3106.72**	**1060.44**
文化娱乐用品	Stationery and Recreational Articles	672.73	288.59
文化娱乐服务	Cultural and Recreational Service	1561.42	203.85
教　育	Education	872.58	567.99
居　住	**Residence**	**1316.82**	**638.49**
住　房	Residential Housing	318.63	65.66
水电燃料及其他	Water, Electricity and Others	839.79	549.15
居住服务费	Residence Service Expenses	158.41	23.68
杂项商品和服务	**Miscellaneous Commodities and Service**	**612.90**	**134.06**
杂项商品	Miscellaneous Commodities	364.05	65.94
服　务	Service	248.84	68.12

单位：元（yuan）

按收入水平分组 Grouped by Level of Income：其中 of which #更低收入组（占5%） Poor Households（Make up 5%）	低收入组（占10%） Low Income Households（Make up 10%）	中等偏下组（占20%） Lower Middle Income Households（Make up 20%）	中等收入组（占20%） Middle Income Households（Make up 20%）	中等偏上组（占20%） Upper Middle Income Households（Make up 20%）	高收入组（占10%） High Income Households（Make up 10%）	最高收入组（占10%） Highest Income Households（Make up 10%）	其中 of which #更高收入组（占5%） Higher Income Households（Make up 5%）
15.94	27.65	38.21	46.89	92.36	86.13	97.80	89.56
7.98	3.48	11.55	10.62	13.00	16.67	20.51	18.07
400.37	**949.98**	**1320.75**	**1539.74**	**1247.62**	**1981.59**	**2488.05**	**2061.79**
154.26	452.88	481.79	714.29	434.85	765.60	422.59	258.06
	92.71	74.92	20.03	18.63	16.30	19.18	0.67
6.37	53.90	145.45	155.59	126.10	169.96	280.00	491.39
226.11	326.19	483.01	558.56	618.60	614.11	926.54	825.82
		0.36	2.61	0.53		6.29	
13.63	24.29	135.20	88.66	48.91	415.61	833.44	485.85
838.17	**1054.70**	**830.94**	**1739.97**	**1479.88**	**1653.62**	**2169.15**	**2301.94**
		3.97	7.83	2.45	6.54	2.21	
	0.46	16.90	15.16	28.12	44.24	42.28	22.09
433.93	519.63	423.08	742.08	677.03	554.67	844.72	610.81
65.66	209.52	180.98	391.54	414.83	304.08	431.25	337.48
337.80	314.36	200.67	575.77	344.71	736.45	836.15	1313.23
0.77	10.73	5.35	7.60	12.75	7.64	12.54	18.32
670.29	**3289.98**	**2316.96**	**4109.02**	**3753.63**	**3277.10**	**5590.60**	**7134.32**
185.04	2447.95	1679.03	3267.41	2914.75	2144.15	4223.26	5957.39
87.61	1693.11	756.38	1890.64	1214.49	76.08	1355.40	2745.01
8.26	426.54	513.52	795.83	1053.17	1232.57	1733.10	1655.32
18.09	187.00	239.16	336.40	301.01	418.55	744.00	1009.66
71.08	141.30	169.97	244.54	346.07	416.94	390.76	547.39
485.25	842.03	637.92	841.61	838.88	1132.95	1367.34	1176.94
61.63	53.75	92.84	200.55	216.82	357.46	402.98	281.14
423.62	788.27	545.08	641.06	622.05	775.49	964.36	895.8
959.91	**1141.16**	**2061.43**	**3330.41**	**3617.83**	**5495.66**	**6654.05**	**5786.17**
147.03	247.79	549.04	618.90	594.98	1490.13	1425.06	1416.23
129.31	392.30	889.43	1937.05	1958.02	2407.44	3853.95	2448.17
683.56	501.07	622.96	774.46	1064.83	1598.09	1375.04	1921.77
575.96	**1378.90**	**1007.00**	**1469.15**	**1510.20**	**1244.01**	**2151.56**	**2249.5**
32.61	523.06	147.51	403.96	478.61	10.73	568.71	894.62
526.96	782.05	741.67	882.35	824.64	1067.16	1208.75	1084.97
16.39	73.79	117.81	182.84	206.95	166.12	374.11	269.91
130.13	**645.30**	**513.55**	**472.99**	**612.20**	**860.79**	**1452.51**	**1851.34**
83.33	317.83	371.01	309.30	376.97	401.27	843.30	1195.56
46.80	327.48	142.54	163.69	235.22	459.52	609.20	655.78

8-7　市区居民家庭不同收入水平收支情况（2012 年）
INCOME AND EXPENDITURE CONDITIONS OF DIFFERENT INCOME LEVELS OF URBAN HOUSEHOLDS（2012）

指　标	Item	合　计 Total	按人均每月可支配收入分组 200以下 Below 200	200 ~ 400	400 ~ 600
调查户数（户）	**Number of Households Surveyed （household）**	**300.00**	**0.75**	**0.58**	**3.92**
平均每户家庭人口数（人）	**Average Household Size （person）**	**2.69**			**2.60**
就业人口数	Number of Persons Employed	1.32		0.71	0.36
#国有集体职工人数	Number of staff and Workers in Stateowned and Collective-owned Units	0.26			
期初手存现金（元）	**Cash on Hand at Beginning of Year （yuan）**	**764.95**			**673.49**
家庭总收入（元）	**Total Family Income （yuan）**	**36637.99**	**664.24**	**8290.00**	**7828.72**
#可支配收入	Disposable Income	33587.03	346.59	3412.67	6209.56
#工薪收入	Income from Wagers and Salaries	23608.99		3173.33	1472.49
经营净收入	Operating Net Income	2600.51		2970.00	1436.10
财产性收入	Income from Property	775.04	268.24		54.63
转移性收入	Transfer Income	9653.46	396.00	2146.67	4865.50
借贷收入（元）	**Debit and Credit Income （yuan）**	**7962.49**	**2117.65**	**3933.33**	**1834.15**
家庭总支出（元）	**Total Family Expenditure （yuan）**	**29540.50**	**9082.05**	**11246.13**	**8759.60**
消费性支出	Consumption Expenditure	20519.00	9082.05	5435.46	7065.52
食　品	Foodstuff	7405.65	6346.74	2653.93	3166.34
#粮油类	Grain and Edible Oil	676.13	801.81	533.87	675.16
肉禽蛋水产品类	Meat, Poultry and Aquatic Products	1994.58	1059.78	963.00	980.04
蔬菜类	Vegetables	771.61	1155.54	523.41	687.79
调味品	Condiments	72.93	124.09	43.67	67.89
糖烟酒饮料类	Sugar, Cigarette, Wine and Beverage	896.62	360.35	104.33	130.12
干鲜瓜果类	Reserved or Fresh Fruits	621.80	367.07	242.40	150.75
糕点、奶及奶制品	Cakes, Milk and Milk Products	461.04	272.69	136.84	113.25
其他食品	Other Foods	119.61	7.76	21.08	10.19
饮食服务	Catering service	1791.32	2197.62	85.33	351.16
#食品加工服务费	Service Fee of Food Processing	13.10			
在外饮食	Eating outside	1778.22	2197.62	85.33	351.16
衣　　着	Clothing	1992.66	470.05	514.67	440.09
#服　　装	Garments	1543.77	436.24	388.00	409.75

Per Capita Monthly Disposable Income by Group								
600 ~ 800	800 ~ 1000	1000 ~ 1500	1500 ~ 2000	2000 ~ 2500	2500 ~ 3000	3000 ~ 4000	4000 ~ 5000	5000以上 Over 5000
5.75	**10.92**	**39.42**	**60.58**	**54.25**	**34.17**	**42.25**	**18.75**	**28.08**
2.25	**3.55**	**3.00**	**2.88**	**2.76**	**2.58**	**2.50**	**2.16**	**2.50**
1.35	1.30	1.33	1.47	1.36	1.26	1.22	1.14	1.47
0.03	0.08	0.16	0.17	0.27	0.34	0.34	0.37	0.46
587.46	**680.27**	**706.45**	**747.54**	**791.40**	**871.88**	**700.29**	**868.86**	**804.24**
10431.67	**12437.94**	**17452.31**	**23052.19**	**29126.22**	**36151.31**	**44783.55**	**57721.89**	**119133.39**
8675.81	10508.96	15332.26	20901.26	26660.71	32616.32	40858.74	53500.86	113925.17
6031.78	8008.05	11272.67	15124.23	17712.01	22735.10	26482.00	33703.66	85265.73
2828.93	1077.79	1028.40	1578.64	1862.08	923.40	2347.95	2702.40	12675.82
64.93	264.97	473.73	361.94	325.84	676.62	933.57	1026.99	3527.83
1506.03	3087.14	4677.50	5987.39	9226.28	11816.20	15020.03	20288.84	17664.01
2707.25	**1729.66**	**6788.48**	**5536.60**	**7822.29**	**8707.40**	**6250.24**	**26009.28**	**11895.08**
11316.82	**11885.38**	**20745.29**	**21565.29**	**28064.56**	**32824.94**	**34598.90**	**59575.88**	**54348.43**
9007.56	8796.16	13755.92	17535.99	18844.74	23909.98	25141.30	30834.21	37523.72
4094.57	4248.49	5870.40	6315.20	6918.98	8491.95	8932.91	9070.22	12405.15
465.33	494.22	567.20	626.11	646.59	806.35	822.19	771.09	766.55
1303.56	1401.97	1599.12	1903.99	1968.20	2364.55	2513.70	2306.85	2221.66
586.07	576.96	609.73	722.13	756.67	895.60	957.25	899.80	852.91
49.49	54.77	59.71	63.74	69.83	106.02	85.74	77.23	79.61
538.95	430.35	817.49	721.56	861.51	1040.36	789.38	1000.14	1933.50
334.86	251.21	410.74	509.18	546.96	722.95	816.42	658.76	1335.43
309.85	271.04	513.95	328.04	465.18	584.15	544.49	534.11	571.79
49.01	74.58	68.63	117.72	95.33	134.72	151.65	166.09	232.90
457.46	693.39	1223.84	1322.73	1508.72	1837.25	2252.10	2656.16	4410.81
12.46	12.24	5.82	9.84	14.86	25.00	17.81	21.32	6.43
445.00	681.16	1218.02	1312.89	1493.86	1812.25	2234.29	2634.85	4404.39
761.58	807.55	1122.25	1437.92	1736.51	2313.14	2617.35	3367.10	4477.34
580.87	576.20	822.00	1031.92	1335.39	1762.37	2097.60	2722.07	3653.50

8-7 续表 continued

指 标	Item	合 计 Total	按人均每月可支配收入分组 200以下 Below 200	200～400	400～600
衣着材料	Clothing Materials	28.78			
鞋　类	Footwear	352.95		126.67	16.59
其它衣着用品	Other Clothing Items	55.94	33.81		13.27
衣着加工服务费	Tailoring and Laundering Service Fees	11.23			0.49
家庭设备用品及服务	Household Facilities, Articles and Services	1382.51	119.51	49.13	495.19
耐用消费品	Durable Consumption Goods	508.72		6.67	
室内装饰品	Indoor Decoration	36.98			
床上用品	Bedding	132.46	19.06		197.85
家庭日用杂品	Home Supplies	530.17	100.45	42.47	283.19
家具材料	Furniture Material	1.24			
家庭服务	Household Services	172.94			14.15
医疗保健	Medical Care	1449.05	1289.36	280.20	1121.96
医疗器具	Medical Appliance	9.47			
保健器具	Health Care Articles	22.04			
药品费	Medcial Expenses	631.56	1172.33	280.20	668.63
滋补保健品	Tonics	295.62	117.04		1.76
医疗费	Health Care Service	481.95			451.39
其　他	Others	8.41			0.20
交通和通讯	Transportation and Communications	3252.69	165.81	118.20	417.35
交　通	Transportation	2424.07	28.24	6.53	139.61
通　信	Communications	828.62	137.58	111.67	277.74
教育文化娱乐服务	Recreation Education and Cultural Services	3106.72	21.18	1058.67	744.64
文化娱乐用品	Stationery and Recreational Articles	672.73	4.24		35.28
文化娱乐服务	Cultural and Recreational Service	1561.42	16.94	1058.67	69.27
教　育	Education	872.58			640.10
居　住	Residence	1316.82	573.76	720.00	628.05
住　房	Residential Housing	318.63			48.78
水电燃料及其他	Water, Electricity and Others	839.79	573.76	720.00	520.74
居住服务费	Residence Service Expenses	158.41			58.54
杂项商品和服务	Miscellaneous Commodities and Services	612.90	95.65	40.67	51.89
杂项商品	Miscellaneous Commodities	364.05	44.12	34.67	14.72
服　务	Services	248.84	51.53	6.00	37.17
借贷支出（元）	**Debit and Credit Expenditure （yuan）**	**15119.54**			**1126.83**
期末手存现金（元）	**Cash on Hand At Year-end （yuan）**	**722.55**			**914.52**

Per Capita Monthly Disposable Income by Group								
600 ~ 800	800 ~ 1000	1000 ~ 1500	1500 ~ 2000	2000 ~ 2500	2500 ~ 3000	3000 ~ 4000	4000 ~ 5000	5000以上 Over 5000
2.32	22.91	32.94	42.55	29.63	34.39	16.87	15.43	18.86
168.69	169.21	224.67	301.87	319.71	434.42	402.08	551.47	684.66
8.08	29.36	34.58	53.56	38.41	67.69	83.97	66.65	107.67
1.62	9.88	8.07	8.02	13.38	14.27	16.84	11.48	12.65
1061.36	457.43	914.02	1204.82	1232.44	1758.73	1930.73	1934.09	2099.89
836.58	46.43	305.41	415.78	486.69	834.29	1031.58	325.13	341.98
	0.08	1.46	103.23	8.09	86.50	7.31	14.14	29.83
12.17	56.30	54.45	128.89	167.83	161.77	111.22	156.48	238.49
202.05	290.59	447.11	475.79	502.31	566.05	637.93	658.37	852.83
			0.36	2.81	0.62	0.26		6.41
10.55	64.03	105.58	80.76	64.71	109.50	142.43	779.98	630.35
567.41	697.35	997.61	1215.29	1312.48	1607.16	1610.81	2619.58	2665.55
		38.93	4.08	6.83	0.18	2.32		13.64
	3.53	26.67	5.46	25.92	38.70	31.94	18.82	33.31
200.85	416.77	495.95	555.35	559.94	515.67	857.50	1170.61	904.01
84.90	70.09	168.57	189.22	489.21	416.41	320.69	377.38	368.78
281.22	206.10	255.57	456.28	220.02	618.99	388.15	1047.29	1343.32
0.43	0.86	11.92	4.89	10.55	17.21	10.20	5.48	2.49
820.69	839.62	1642.78	3400.06	2743.46	4501.34	3874.64	5219.95	5583.80
172.52	375.56	886.92	2714.90	1976.51	3605.47	3015.89	4058.54	4124.75
648.17	464.06	755.87	685.15	766.95	895.87	858.75	1161.41	1459.05
953.86	966.60	1689.58	2392.89	2813.60	3360.59	3880.46	6577.10	6533.18
201.86	179.77	400.54	475.75	609.53	577.78	846.52	1326.97	1729.11
207.65	154.31	563.65	1291.09	1323.10	1969.88	1838.55	4053.50	3398.30
544.35	632.52	725.39	626.05	880.97	812.93	1195.39	1196.63	1405.76
612.24	607.61	1052.97	1237.62	1238.58	1359.77	1566.94	1337.43	2348.42
57.97	37.93	236.65	378.70	286.48	331.92	399.86		
544.04	554.64	701.31	729.24	797.15	892.29	990.47	1075.13	1268.31
10.23	15.04	115.01	129.68	154.94	135.55	176.62	146.13	448.21
135.86	171.51	466.31	332.20	848.69	517.31	727.45	708.74	1410.39
93.54	90.22	207.45	172.45	590.11	297.58	476.26	303.33	861.68
42.32	81.30	258.86	159.75	258.59	219.73	251.20	405.41	548.71
2004.71	**2473.04**	**3501.95**	**7103.09**	**8833.66**	**11665.34**	**16904.35**	**24196.13**	**76728.41**
656.58	**459.79**	**545.72**	**727.15**	**758.13**	**739.95**	**749.42**	**931.15**	**855.60**

8-8　主要年份市区居民主要消费品人均消费量
PER CAPITA CONSUMPTION ON MAJOR CONSUMER GOODS OF URBAN RESIDENTS IN MAIN YEARS

指　标	Item	1995	2000	2005	2010	2012
大　米（千克）	Rice（kg）	82.61	55.59	50.51	43.62	47.58
食用植物油（千克）	Edible Vegetable Oil（kg）	7.69	7.58	8.88	6.23	7.18
猪　肉（千克）	Pork（kg）	23.82	18.17	20.60	18.03	24.73
牛　肉（千克）	Beef（kg）	0.58	0.98	0.88	1.74	2.43
羊　肉（千克）	Mutton（kg）	0.19	0.19	0.15	0.18	0.49
鸡（千克）	Chieken（kg）	6.33	5.32	5.31	5.57	7.86
鸭（千克）	Duck（kg）	0.34	0.40	1.75	1.35	2.48
鲜　蛋（千克）	Eggs（kg）	22.32	11.34	9.87	9.63	10.41
鱼（千克）	Aquantic Products（kg）	3.27	5.18	11.01	11.82	13.93
虾（千克）	Shrimp（kg）	1.60	3.37	3.86	3.11	4.22
鲜　菜（千克）	Fresh Vegetables（kg）	123.73	114.10	107.53	113.68	123.52
白　酒（千克）	Liquor（kg）	1.43	1.51	1.02	1.08	1.11
果　酒（千克）	Wine（kg）	0.25	0.11	0.27	0.35	0.20
啤　酒（千克）	Beer（kg）	6.70	5.77	6.07	3.20	3.48
碳酸饮料（千克）	Carbonated Drinks（kg）	1.52	1.55	2.38	0.96	0.81
糕　点（千克）	Cakes（kg）	3.03	3.08	4.94	7.33	12.05
茶　叶（千克）	Tea（kg）	0.20	0.23	0.16	0.17	0.26
水　果（千克）	Fruits（kg）	13.66	22.14	55.71	51.86	35.62
鲜乳品及酸奶（千克）	Fresh Milk and Yogurt（kg）	4.36	21.51	31.64	26.78	30.29
生活用水（立方米）	Household Water Consumption（cubic meters）	34.27	38.83	33.96	37.23	55.74
生活用电（千瓦时）	Household Power Consumption（kwh）	230.85	339.66	549.52	702.34	874.17
液化石油气（千卡）	Liquified Petroleum Gas（kc）	38.25	26.76	17.45	8.06	7.42
管道煤气（立方米）	Pipeline Gas（cubic meters）	22.92	57.77	37.92	45.12	64.57

8-9 市区每百户居民家庭年末耐用消费品拥有量（2007-2012 年）
NUMBER OF DURABLE CONSUMER GOODS OWNED PER 100 URBAN HOUSEHOLDS AT YEAR-END（2007-2012）

指 标	Item	2007	2008	2009	2010	2011	2012
摩托车（辆）	Motorcycle （unit）	45.85	23.33	22.33	21.67	10.00	10.33
助力车（辆）	Scooter （unit）	56.81	64.00	70.00	74.67	66.33	70.33
家用汽车（辆）	Family Car （unit）	7.97	13.00	16.00	19.67	27.67	31.33
洗衣机（台）	Washing Machine （unit）	100.33	102.33	103.33	103.67	101.67	101.67
电冰箱（台,含冰柜）	Refrigerator （unit，Include Freezer）	95.68	101.00	102.67	104.00	98.00	99.67
彩色电视机（台）	Color TV Set （unit）	172.09	189.33	191.00	195.33	188.00	191.33
家用电脑（台）	Family Computer （unit）	62.46	71.67	75.00	82.67	95.00	100.67
组合音响（套）	Hi-Fi Stereo Component System （unit）	34.22	37.67	38.67	39.33	32.67	32.67
摄像机（架）	Pickup Camera （unit）	3.65	6.00	7.00	7.33	11.33	11.00
照相机（架）	Camera （unit）	48.50	60.33	61.00	65.00	55.00	58.00
钢琴（架）	Piano （set）	2.33	4.00	4.67	5.67	3.67	3.67
其他中高档乐器（件）	Other Medium and High Class Music Instruments （unit）	2.99	7.67	7.67	8.00	3.33	3.67
微波炉（台）	Microwave Oven （unit）	91.03	94.33	96.00	96.67	93.67	93.33
空调器（台）	Air Conditioner （unit）	153.82	186.67	192.67	199.00	213.67	220.00
淋浴热水器（台）	Shower Heater （unit）	89.37	95.67	98.33	101.33	99.67	100.67
消毒碗柜（台）	Disinfectant Cupboard （unit）	5.32	12.00	12.33	12.67	7.67	7.00
洗碗机（台）	Dishwasher （unit）	0.66	0.67	0.67	0.67	0.67	0.67
健身器材（套）	Healthy Equipment （unit）	4.98	6.33	6.33	6.67	5.00	5.67
普通电话（部）	Telephone （set）	97.67	92.00	91.67	91.67	82.00	83.00
移动电话（部）	Mobile Telephone （set）	181.40	195.00	204.33	211.00	192.00	194.67

注：2007年起移动电话中包含小灵通，2007年以前小灵通包含在普通电话中。
Note： The Little Smart has been included in the mobile telephone since the year of 2007, and it was included in the ordinary telephone before 2007.

8-10　农民家庭基本情况（1985-2012 年）
BASIC CONDITIONS OF RURAL HOUSEHOLDS（1985-2012）

年 份 Year	调查户数（户） Households Surveyed (household)	农民人均纯收入（元） Per Capita Net Income of Rural Residents（yuan）	农民人均生活消费支出（元） Per Capita Living Expenditure of Rural Residents（yuan）	每户整半劳动力（人） Number of Able-bodied and Semi-able-Bodied Laboerers Per Household（yuan）	每一劳动力负担人口（人） Number of Persons Supported by Each Laborer（person）	人　均住房面积（平方米） Per Capita Living Space（sq.m）	户均住房面　积（平方米） Living Space Per Household（sq.m）	恩格尔系　数（%） Engel Coefficient（%）
1985	340	618	563	2.74	1.55	21.03	89.49	49.7
1986	340	777	697	2.74	1.55	22.33	93.08	44.8
1987	340	855	782	2.76	1.51	23.89	99.42	44.3
1988	340	1108	1161	2.78	1.47	25.72	105.24	42.1
1989	340	1301	1305	2.75	1.42	29.74	116.26	49.0
1990	340	1401	1231	2.74	1.43	31.66	123.92	49.5
1991	320	1318	1205	2.71	1.44	32.69	127.39	53.1
1992	320	1588	1442	2.70	1.41	33.46	127.04	50.0
1993	280	2041	1762	2.36	1.37	32.66	120.73	45.8
1994	280	2707	2259	2.74	1.35	33.78	124.99	49.7
1995	280	3397	2952	2.54	1.32	35.90	129.48	49.9
1996	300	4172	3598	2.51	1.39	38.81	135.59	45.5
1997	300	4216	3754	2.50	1.38	37.27	128.82	49.6
1998	280	4289	3045	2.42	1.41	36.97	126.62	46.6
1999	280	4313	3316	2.37	1.44	42.04	143.83	41.0
2000	300	4430	3243	2.30	1.44	49.27	162.75	43.1
2001	300	4719	3277	2.40	1.38	48.18	159.17	43.9
2002	410	5138	3698	2.42	1.40	54.20	182.30	40.4
2003	410	5550	3953	2.43	1.38	55.90	185.70	40.1
2004	410	6235	4793	2.42	1.38	55.70	186.40	42.0
2005	510	7002	5712	2.37	1.42	56.20	186.80	39.8
2006	510	8001	6518	2.41	1.38	58.27	193.54	37.7
2007	510	9033	7400	2.39	1.38	57.70	190.20	38.0
2008	380	10171	8128	2.37	1.37	58.73	191.50	37.7
2009	380	11198	8843	2.39	1.37	59.48	192.21	36.2
2010	380	12637	9924	2.39	1.34	58.40	187.49	35.1
2011	520	14838	11208	2.42	1.45	61.52	190.17	35.5
2012	520	16737	12027	2.38	1.37	60.31	185.56	36.1

注：“每一劳动力负担人口”包括就业者本人,下同。
Note：“Persons Supported by Each Laborer” includes the laborer himself, the same below.

8-11 分地区农民家庭基本情况（2012 年）
BASIC CONDITIONS OF RURAL HOUSEHOLDS BY REGION（2012）

指 标	Item	全 市 Whole Municipality	其 中 of which 溧阳市 Liyang City	金坛市 Jintan City
调查户数（户）	**Number of Households Surveyed （household）**	**520**	**150**	**120**
调查人数（人）	**Number of Residents Surveyed （person）**			
常住人口	Number of Permanent Residents in the Households Surveyed	1601	438	320
户均常住人口	Average Number of Permanent Residents Per household	3.08	2.92	2.67
户均整、半劳动力	Average Number of Able-bodied and Semi-able-bodied Laborers Per Household	2.38	2.27	2.30
户均非农业劳动力	Average Number of Non-agricultual Laborers Per Household	1.87	1.37	1.36
平均每一劳动力负担人数	Average Number of Persons Supported by a Laborer	1.32	1.28	1.17
人均总收入（元）	**Per Capita Total Income（yuan）**	**19860**	**19650**	**21134**
#纯收入	Per Capita Net Income	16737	15261	15608
工资性收入	Wage Income	11100	8832	10424
家庭经营收入	Household Business Income	3504	5265	3338
转移性收入	Transfer Income	1183	791	935
财产性收入	Property Income	950	373	911
人均总支出（元）	**Per Capita Total Expenditure （yuan）**	**16574**	**17741**	**20603**
家庭经营费用支出	Household Business Expenditure	2617	3633	5136
购置生产用固定资产支出	Expenditure On Productive Fixed Assets	61	29	296
税费支出	Expenditure for Taxes	1		3
生活消费支出	Living Expenditure	12027	12957	12401
#食品支出	Food	4337	4599	4348
食品消费品支出	Food Consumption Goods	3576	3530	3733
食品消费服务性支出	Food Consumption Services	762	1070	615
衣 着	Clothing	885	1173	724
居 住	Residence	1401	1247	1147

8-11　续表　continued

指　标	Item	全　市 Whole Municipality	其　中 of which 溧阳市 Liyang City	金坛市 Jintan City
家庭设备、用品及服务	Household Facilities, Articles and Services	846	826	1095
医疗保健	Medicine and Medicinal Services	913	818	1166
交通和通信	Transportation and Communications	1530	1686	1484
文教娱乐用品及服务	Cultural, Education and Recreation Articles and Services	1840	2365	2252
其它商品和服务	Other Commodities and Services	275	241	185
财产性支出	Property Expenditure	12	16	1
转移性支出	Transfer Expenditure	1855	1107	2761
期末人均手存现金（元）	**Per Capita Cash in Hand at Year-end （yuan）**	**1467**	**893**	**2985**
期末人均存款（元）	**Per Capita Savings Deposits at Year-end （yuan）**	**20289**	**16906**	**28817**
农民家庭住房情况	**Housing Conditions of Rural Residential Buildings**			
户均使用面积（平方米）	Average Floor Space of Residential Buildings Per Household（sq.m）	185.56	145.36	133.30
住房价值（元/人）	Value of Residential Buildings（yuan/person）	49915	35420	19494
人均使用住房面积（平方米）	Per Capita Floor Space of Residential Buildings（sq.m）	60.31	49.78	50.00
#钢筋混泥土结构面积	Reinforced Concrete Structure	44.59	45.95	39.00
砖木结构面积	Brick and Wood Structure	15.71	4.42	11.00
农民家庭居住条件	Living Conditions of Peasant Households			
使用水冲式厕所户数的比重（%）	Proportion of Households with Dry latrines （%）	92.5	88.0	98.0
使用空调户数的比重（%）	Proportion of Households with Air Conditioning （%）	86.9	88.0	87.0
使用燃气户数的比重（%）	Proportion of Households with Gas（%）	83.5	69.3	83.0
饮用自来水户数的比重（%）	Proportion of Households with Tap Water（%）	95.8	93.3	100.0
通水泥或柏油路面户数的比重（%）	Proportion of Households Nearby Roads Paved with Cement or Asphalt （%）	88.7	86.7	94.0

8-12 分地区农民家庭主要消费品人均消费量（2012 年）
PER CAPITA CONSUMPTION OF MAJOR CONSUMER GOODS OF RURAL HOUSEHOLDS BY REGION（2012）

单位：千克（kg）

指标	Item	全市 Whole Municipality	其中 of which 溧阳市 Liyang City	金坛市 Jintan City
粮食	Grain	141.32	113.98	144.00
#谷物	Corn	139.19	113.55	140.00
#小麦	Wheat	8.62	4.30	14.00
稻谷	Rice	129.21	109.11	123.00
薯类	Tubers	0.67	0.13	2.19
豆类	Beans	1.36	0.29	2.22
油脂类	Edible Oil	7.61	9.07	3.12
#植物油	Vegetable Oil	7.48	8.86	3.09
豆制品	Bean Products	5.89	4.07	8.80
蔬菜及菜制品	Vegetables &Related Products	108.67	78.57	127.00
鲜菜	Fresh Vegetables	105.33	77.15	121.30
干菜	Dried Food	0.63	0.28	2.08
鲜菌	Fresh Mushroom	1.32	0.43	1.20
瓜类	Melons	8.88	13.42	6.80
水果类	Fruits	15.69	14.23	13.30
肉禽及其制品	Meats，Poultry and Related Products	32.82	34.19	40.70
#猪肉	Pork	17.83	17.77	19.56
牛肉	Beef	0.98	0.72	0.78
羊肉	Mutton	0.22	0.37	0.17
家禽	Poultry	7.44	12.24	8.28
蛋类及蛋制品	Eggs & Related Products	8.26	9.52	9.24
奶和奶制品	Milk & Related Products	7.97	6.08	10.50
水产品	Aquatic Products	16.38	10.30	38.80
食糖	Sugar	1.92	0.71	4.74
酒	Liquor	12.89	12.78	16.24
#白酒	Liquor	4.28	7.51	7.18
啤酒	Beer	6.58	5.05	8.20

8-13 每百户农民家庭年末耐用消费品拥有量（2012 年）
NUMBER OF DURABLE CONSUMER GOODS OWNED PER 100 RURAL HOUSEHOLDS AT YEAR-END（2012）

指 标	Item	全 市 Whole Municipality	其中 of which 溧阳市 Liyang City	金坛市 Jintan City
自行车（辆）	Bicycle（unit）	217.46	105.00	190.00
摩托车（辆）	Motorcycle（coach）	58.34	45.00	42.00
家用汽车（辆）	Famliy Car（unit）	17.50	7.00	2.00
电 话（部）	Telephone Set（unit）	90.36	99.00	109.00
移动电话（部）	Mobile Telephone Sets（unit）	240.30	173.00	219.00
电视机（台）	TV Set（unit）	215.60	129.00	157.00
#彩 电	Color TV Set	215.60	129.00	157.00
摄像机（台）	Pickup Camera（unit）	0.96	1.00	2.00
影碟机（架）	Video Disc Player（unit）	31.50	17.00	24.00
照相机（架）	Camera（unit）	22.31	7.00	23.00
洗衣机（台）	Washing Machine（unit）	133.50	91.00	100.00
电冰箱（台）	Refrigerator（unit）	134.20	95.00	99.00
抽排油烟机（台）	Smoke Absorber（unit）	99.80	43.00	77.00
微波炉（台）	Microwave Oven（unit）	80.77	60.00	70.00
吸尘器（台）	Dust Catcher（unit）	10.50	9.00	11.00
淋浴热水器（台）	Shower Heater（unit）	135.20	97.00	96.00
家用电脑（台）	Computer（unit）	71.50	41.00	43.00
空调器（台）	Air Conditioner（unit）	1740.00	103.00	98.00

注：全市农村住户抽样调查样本数为520户，其中溧阳市150户、金坛市100户。

Note：The sample number of rural residential household investigation in the whole year totalled 520 households,including 150 households from Liyang and 100 households from Jintan.

9

CHAPTER 9

固定资产投资

INVESTMENT IN FIXED ASSETS

常州统计年鉴

9 固定资产投资
INVESTMENT IN FIXED ASSETS

2012 年主要统计指标
MAJOR STATISTICAL INDICATORS OF 2012

全社会固定资产投资完成额	Total Investment in Fixed Assets	2760.14 亿元	(100 million yuan)
比上年增长	Over the Previous Year	18.0%	
在建项目个数	Number of projects under Construction	4427 个	(unit)
比上年增长	Over the Previous Year	12.3%	
民间投资	Nongovernmental Investment	1973.08 亿元	(100 million yuan)
比上年增长	Over the Previous Year	15.7%	
公共基础设施投资	Public Infrastructure Investment	402.06 亿元	(100 million yuan)
比上年增长	Over the Previous Year	35.9%	
工业投资	Transformation and Renovation Investment	1525.98 亿元	(100 million yuan)
比上年增长	Over the Previous Year	18.0%	
第三产业投资	Investment in Tertiary Industry	1220.36 亿元	(100 million yuan)
比上年增长	Over the Previous Year	18.1%	
房地产开发投资	Real Estate Investment	597.01 亿元	(100 million yuan)
比上年增长	Over the Previous Year	5.5%	

9-1　历年全社会固定资产投资完成额
TOTAL INVESTMENT IN FIXED ASSETS OVER THE YEARS

单位：万元（10000 yuan）

年 份 Year	全 市 Whole Municipality	其中 of which 市 区 Urban Area	年 份 Year	全 市 Whole Municipality	其中 of which 市 区 Urban Area
1949	31	24	1981	24198	30321
1950	129	105	1982	36336	46289
1951	148	94	1983	31428	43426
1952	456	257	1984	60334	53083
1953	494	394	1985	104735	93054
1954	557	431	1986	161834	127213
1955	829	659	1987	201796	156071
1956	1323	1032	1988	259486	201601
1957	964	654	1989	212533	163734
1958	6490	5657	1990	227093	170921
1959	8246	7390	1991	309921	237860
1960	11184	10223	1992	443866	355392
1961	3189	2975	1993	879129	706406
1962	1198	913	1994	964621	777442
1963	1070	825	1995	1150612	852333
1964	1714	1454	1996	1242072	922999
1965	1279	1060	1997	1319585	1009095
1966	1537	1238	1998	1401110	1066040
1967	793	578	1999	1448908	1117208
1968	749	555	2000	1634262	1268963
1969	1397	1037	2001	1906854	1509623
1970	2398	1823	2002	2500118	1977105
1971	3411	3075	2003	4465944	3583446
1972	4944	4219	2004	5886129	4730966
1973	5900	4832	2005	7698021	6097516
1974	3994	3486	2006	9515629	7386948
1975	3490	3119	2007	12039417	9327048
1976	3528	3194	2008	14481662	11028826
1977	3093	2634	2009	17047690	13340391
1978	8852	7553	2010	21035519	16489817
1979	13203	11327	2011	23389418	18211797
1980	23699	26313	2012	27601436	21660862

9-2 固定资产投资完成额（1985-2012 年）
REALIZED INVESTMENT IN FIXED ASSETS（1985-2012）

单位：万元（10000 yuan）

年 份 Year	全社会固定资产投资总额 Total Investment in Fixed Assets	其中 of which 第一产业 Primary Industry	第二产业 Secondary Industry	其中 of which 工业投资 Industrial Investment	第三产业投资 Investment in Tertiary Industry	公共基础设施投资 Public Infrastructure Investment	民间投资 Civil Investment
1985	104735	952	62475	61503	41308		
1986	161834	3732	98907	98383	59195		
1987	201796	1499	142569	135828	57728		
1988	259486	1244	190533	189871	67709		
1989	212533	2932	170954	170860	38647		
1990	227093	4642	160225	159955	62226	17820	95088
1991	309921	2789	256344	225608	50788	24629	94167
1992	443866	3176	332873	331741	107817	34729	76327
1993	879129	1309	528769	499487	349051	91302	199902
1994	964621	4889	509772	453869	449960	140547	262832
1995	1150612	9776	559360	548978	581476	153314	295241
1996	1242072	6088	604167	597020	631817	278333	375196
1997	1319585	19848	568241	559112	731496	308134	475233
1998	1401110	34000	536977	526974	830133	453150	479621
1999	1448908	55225	528263	520078	865420	547041	753172
2000	1634262	49771	604813	593913	979678	532296	888199
2001	1906854	53626	837711	830062	1015517	628214	1078742
2002	2500118	29619	1252088	1237465	1218411	699987	1445567
2003	4465944	20138	2591293	2508342	1854513	1262439	2666795
2004	5886129	5643	3451340	3425615	2429146	1597078	3533558
2005	7698021	11902	4648555	4597843	3037564	2042125	4798730
2006	9515629	20219	5653538	5629015	3841872	1857842	6307633
2007	12039417	6455	6870313	6808672	5162649	2284530	7987997
2008	14481662	29965	8391957	8315442	6059740	2428248	9626044
2009	17047690	39949	9788147	9710508	7219594	3555953	11469166
2010	21035519	73876	11865093	11804077	9096550	3403292	14816856
2011	23389418	100341	12958199	12934251	10330878	2958588	17051330
2012	27601436	58109	15339739	15259792	12203588	4020574	19730820

注：公共基础设施投资指电力、燃气、水的生产和供应业；交通运输、仓储和邮政业；电信、广播电视和卫星传输服务业；水利、环境和公共设施管理业；教育、卫生、社会保障和社会福利业；文化、体育、娱乐等行业的投资。

Note：Public infrastructure investment refers to the investment in production and supply of electricity, gas and water; transportation, storage and postal industries; telecommunications, radio and television and satellite transmission services; water conservancy, environment and public facility management industries; education, health, social security and social welfare; and culture, sports, entertainment industries and so on.

9-3　分地区全社会固定资产投资完成额（2012 年）
TOTAL INVESTMENT IN FIXED ASSETS BY REGION（2012）

指　标	Item	全　市 Whole Municipality	市　区 Urban Area
投资总额	**Total Investment**	**27601436**	**21660862**
按建设性质分	**Grouped by Type of Construction**		
新　建	New Construction	9186300	6595602
扩　建	Expansion	7191174	5485299
改　建	Reconstruction	3484359	2522158
其　它	Others	7739603	7057803
按构成分	**Grouped by Composition**		
建筑工程	Construction	13102997	10073690
安装工程	Installation	1551414	1134626
设备工器具购置	Purchase of Equipment and Investment	9138642	7033481
其他费用	Others	3808383	3419065
按经济类型分	**Grouped by Economic Types**		
国有及国有控股企业	State-owned and State Holding Enterprises	3790415	3407445
非国有投资	Non State-owned Investment	23811021	18253417
民间投资	Civil Investment	19730820	14431645
外商及港澳台商投资	Foreign Merchants & Hong Kong, Macao and Taiwan	4080201	3821772
按登记注册类型分	**Grouped by Registration Status**		
内　资	Domestically-Funded	23457750	17775605
国　有	State-owned	3658794	3353702
集　体	Collective-owned	1097927	955493
股份合作	Share-holding Cooperative	21896	21896
集体联营	State-owned Joint Operation	12700	12700
国有独资公司	State-funded Corporations	127221	52743
其它有限责任公司	Other Limited Liability Corporations	7286508	5347028
股份有限公司	Share-holding Corporations Ltd.	466330	365142
私　营	Private	10403455	7341937
其　他	Others	382919	324964
港澳台商投资	Investment from Hong Kong, Macao and Taiwan	2442080	2306885
外商投资	Enterprises withForeign Investment	1638121	1514887
个体经营	Individual	63485	63485
个体户	Self-employed Individuals	52387	52387

单位：万元（10000 yuan）

其 中 of which						
武进区 wujin District	新北区 Xinbei District	天宁区 Tianning District	钟楼区 Zhonglou District	戚墅堰区 Qishuyan District	溧阳市 Liyang City	金坛市 Jintan City
8448528	**5975217**	**2795646**	**2695496**	**697065**	**3740515**	**2200059**
2934029	1567743	558849	677119	106658	1437659	1153039
2722852	1435477	683450	384322	102870	1074977	630898
1102495	406279	340922	463656	71326	836534	125667
1689152	2565718	1212425	1170399	416211	391345	290455
3658422	2157174	1766431	1693598	302376	1825107	1204200
292121	212406	202421	214025	37458	354081	62707
3359487	2555867	280870	477428	300912	1283761	821400
1138498	1049770	545924	310445	56319	277566	111752
1201893	825918	329025	65137	38814	168610	214360
7246635	5149299	2466621	2630359	658251	3571905	1985699
6063748	3673033	1958802	2174526	552338	3474509	1824666
1182887	1476266	507819	455833	105913	97396	161033
7264721	4479534	2282130	2202212	591152	3643119	2039026
1184819	816185	326175	64137	38814	92732	212360
416553	134225	255068	135595	14052	108103	34331
14666		2400	4830			
	4950		7750			
17074	9733	2850			74478	
2146406	1694427	380239	1030414	92544	1815753	123727
77528	56519	181606	36819	6470	37123	64065
3279080	1724285	1131742	848864	357966	1490154	1571364
128595	39210	2050	73803	81306	24776	33179
709328	646672	413021	373039	86799	35991	99204
473559	829594	94798	82794	19114	61405	61829
920	19417	5697	37451			
920	8319	5697	37451			

9-3 续表 continued

指 标	Item	全 市 Whole Municipality	市 区 Urban Area
按产业分	**Grouped by Industries**		
第一产业	Primary Industry	58109	22408
第二产业	Secondary Industry	15339739	10891983
#工　业	Industry	15259792	10812036
第三产业	Tertiary Industry	12203588	1074647
按国民经济行业分	**Grouped by Sector**		
农林牧渔业	Farming,Forestry,Animal Husbandry and Fishery	58109	22408
采矿业	Mining	97861	
制造业	Manufacturing	1471034	10539713
电力、热力、燃气及水的生产和供应业	Production and Supply of Electricity, Heat, Gas and Water Industry	451797	272323
建筑业	Construction	79947	79947
批发和零售业	Wholesale and Retail Trade	574847	475180
交通运输、仓储和邮政业	Transportation , Storage and Post	656014	523650
住宿和餐饮业	Accommodation and Catering Services	402868	288827
信息传输、软件和信息技术服务业	Information Transmission, Software and IT Services Industry	184551	182479
金融业	Banking	81503	75263
房地产业	Real Estate Industry	6794857	6106718
租赁和商务服务业	Rent and Business Services	371817	261415
科学研究和技术服务	Scientific Researches and Technical Services	200517	185651
水利、环境和公共设施管理业	Water Conservancy, Environment and Public Facilities Management	1806284	1617124
居民服务、修理和其他服务业	Residential Services, Repairing and other Services Industry	154107	146447
教　育	Education	226289	197384
卫生和社会工作	Health and Social Work	217084	206700
文化、体育和娱乐业	Culture, Sports and Entertainment	347430	332066
公共管理、社会保障和社会组织	Public Administration, Social Security and Social Organizations	185420	147567

其 中 of which					溧阳市 Liyang City	金坛市 Jintan City
武进区 wujin District	新北区 Xinbei District	天宁区 Tianning District	钟楼区 Zhonglou District	戚墅堰区 Qishuyan District		
19508	2900				5775	29926
5149670	3701398	353852	592137	369910	2859950	1587806
5149670	3701398	353852	531655	350445	2859950	1587806
3279350	2270919	2441794	2103359	327155	874790	582327
19508	2900				5775	29926
					87700	10161
5131590	3649586	340577	528345	339615	2634161	1536260
18080	51812	13275	3310	10830	138089	41385
			60482	19465		
80761	24219	158312	238195	23693	69110	30557
140665	77242	45680	23289	21875	37070	95294
38110	8679	154780	83569	3689	94904	19137
	26980	18555	10090			2072
		61313	13950		6240	
1814977	1597356	1503675	1237688	249936	382435	305704
32579	64960	47185	107175	9516	60533	49869
72258		66450	36434	10509	14866	
837038	325269	53279	153427	1308	149117	40043
41972	924	46316	57235		2860	4800
40251	65834	22155	61804	1440	27005	1900
65199	10376	45874	34464	4300	5500	4884
82073	11911	178327	31757		6030	9334
33467	57169	39893	14282	889	19120	18733

9-4 分地区工业各行业固定资产投资完成额（2012 年）
INVESTMENTS IN FIXED ASSETS OF INDUSTRIAL TRADES BY REGION（2012）

单位：万元（10000 yuan）

行业	Sector	全市 Whole Municipality	市区 Urban Area	溧阳市 Liyang City	金坛市 Jintan City
农副食品加工业	Food Processing	68029	11830	23018	33181
食品制造业	Food Production	72511	42366	19515	10630
酒、饮料和精制茶制造业	Beverages and Refined Tea Manufacturing	20604	14174	3430	3000
纺织业	Textile Industry	471621	355246	66007	50368
纺织服装、服饰业	Textile and clothing Industry	144508	36812	48316	59380
皮革、毛皮、羽毛及其制品和制鞋业	Leather, Fur, Feathers and Their Products, and Footwear Industry	41584	10965	2823	27796
木材加工及木、竹、藤、棕、草制品业	Timber Processing, Bamboo, Cane, Palm Fiber and Straw Products	116385	107985	8400	
家具制造业	Furniture Manufacturing	23423	16163	7260	
造纸及纸制品业	Papermaking and Paper Products	151221	55117	10290	85814
印刷和记录媒介复制业	Printing and Recorded Media Duplication Industry	84488	50863	29525	4100
文教、工美、体育和娱乐用品制造业	Cultural & Educational, Arts & Crafts, Sports & Entertainment Articles Manufacturing	49892	27365	19796	2731
石油加工、炼焦及核燃料加工业	Petroleum Processing, Coking and Nuclear Fuel Processing	10857	4310		6547
化学原料及化学制品制造业	Raw Chemical Materials and Chemica Products	1210860	859676	265942	85242
医药制造业	Medical and Pharmaceutical Products	324248	253930	37159	33159
化学纤维制造业	Chemical Fiber	207368	172313	28977	6078
橡胶和塑料制品业	Rubber and Plastic Products Industry	395650	252194	40479	102977
非金属矿物制品业	Nonmetal Mineral Products	787363	361020	312589	113754
黑色金属冶炼及压延加工业	Smelting and Pressing of Ferrous Metals	562635	400968	125317	36350
有色金属冶炼及压延加工业	Smelting and Pressing of Nonferrous Metals	196382	93053	55940	47389
金属制品业	Metal Products	685156	440352	154143	90661
通用设备制造业	General Equipment Manufacturing	1634790	993356	364169	277265
专用设备制造业	For Special Purposes Equipment Manufacturing	1477574	1008040	397352	72182
汽车制造业	Automotive Industry	560734	485546	60247	14941
铁路、船舶、航空航天和其他运输设备制造	Railways, Shipping, Aerospace and other Transportation Equipment Manufacturing	322726	302577	19649	500
电气机械及器材制造业	Electric Equipment and Machinery	2194685	1654234	337859	202592
计算机、通信和其他电子设备制造	Computer, Communications and other Electronic Equipment Manufacturing	1372464	1160866	125216	86382
仪器仪表制造业	Instrumentation Manufacturing	659917	578112	47268	34537
其他制造业	Other Manufacturings	262943	215188	9755	38000
废弃资源综合利用业	Comprehensive Utilization of Waste Resources Industry	26331	18050	690	7591
金属制品、机械和设备修理业	Metal Products, Machinery & Equipment Repairing Industry	23185	7042	13030	3113
电力、热力生产和供应业	Production and Supply of Electricity & Heat Industry	358519	215578	120756	22185
燃气生产和供应业	Production and Supply of Gas Industry	31468	24028	7440	
水的生产和供应业	Production and Supply of water Industry	61810	32717	9893	19200

9-5 分地区全社会新增固定资产（2012 年）
TOTAL NEWLY INCREASED FIXED ASSETS BY REGION（2012）

单位：万元（10000 yuan）

行 业	Sector	全 市 Whole Municipality	市 区 Urban Area	溧阳市 Liyang City	金坛市 Jintan City
总 计	**Total**	**19428125**	**15439939**	**2577298**	**1410888**
按建设性质分	**Grouped by Type of Construction**				
新 建	New Construction	5498223	3858810	901731	737682
扩 建	Expansion	5800677	4607306	777124	416247
改 建	Reconstruction	2786789	1887027	806415	93347
其 它	Others	5342436	5086796	92028	163612
按经济类型分	**Grouped by Economic Types**				
国有及国有控股企业	State-owned and State Holding Enterprises	2214862	2138047	40523	36292
非国有投资	Non State-owned Investment	17213263	13301892	2536775	1374596
民间投资	Civil Investment	14622404	10919089	2443513	1259802
外商及港澳台商投资	Foreign Merchants & Hong Kong, Macao and aiwan	2590859	2382803	93262	114794
按登记注册类型分	**Grouped by Registration Status**				
内 资	Domestically-Funded	16763017	12982887	2484036	1296094
国 有	State-owned	2174409	2098994	39123	36292
集 体	Collective-owned	847747	798952	43179	5616
股份合作	Share-holding Cooperative	22223	22223		
集体联营	Collective-owned Joint Operation	2760	2760		
国有独资公司	State-funded Corporations	38053	38053		
其它有限责任公司	Other Limited Liability Corporations	5714014	4055812	1636029	22173
股份有限公司	Share-holding Corporations Ltd.	388420	293401	20164	74855
私 营	Private	7299919	5440320	733241	1126358
其 他	Others	275472	232372	12300	30800
港澳台商投资	Investment from Hong Kong, Macao and Taiwan	1245149	1120384	29338	95427
外商投资	Enterprises with Foreign Investment	1345710	1262419	63924	19367
个体经营	Individual	74249	74249		
个体户	Self-employed Individuals	46249	46249		

9-5 续表　Continued　　　　单位：万元（10000 yuan）

行　业	Sector	全　市 Whole Municipality	市　区 Urban Area	溧阳市 Liyang City	金坛市 Jintan City
按产业分	**Grouped by Industries**				
第一产业	Primary Industry	44523	24183	4140	16200
第二产业	Secondary Industry	11190773	7877333	2195600	1117840
#工　业	Industry	11120184	7806744	2195600	1117840
第三产业	Tertiary Industry	8192829	7538423	377558	276848
按国民经济行业分	**Grouped by Sector**				
农林牧渔业	Farming,Forestry,Animal Husbandry and Fishery	**44523**	24183	4140	16200
采矿业	Mining	19161		9000	10161
制造业	Manufacturing	10761271	7514197	2171350	1075724
电力、热力、燃气及水的生产和供应业	Production and Supply of Electricity, Heat, Gas and Water Industry	339752	292547	15250	31955
建筑业	Construction	70589	70589		
批发和零售业	Wholesale and Retail Trade	485392	404442	59550	21400
交通运输、仓储和邮政业	Transportation , Storage and Post	539252	477732	22720	38800
住宿和餐饮业	Accommodation and Catering Services	315253	268697	46556	
信息传输、软件和信息技术服务业	Information Transmission, Software and IT Services Industry	190604	190604		
金融业	Banking	79505	74995	4510	
房地产业	Real Estate Industry	4264645	4000545	79618	184482
租赁和商务服务业	Rent and Business Services	190637	147857	42780	
科学研究和技术服务	Scientific Researches and Technical Services	70072	65724	4348	
水利、环境和公共设施管理业	Water Conservancy, Environment and Public Facilities Management	1074294	972670	85024	16600
居民服务、修理和其他服务业	Residential Services, Repairing and other Services Industry	108377	100717	2860	4800
教　育	Education	192841	189219	3322	300
卫生和社会工作	Health and Social Work	100656	93536	4120	3000
文化、体育和娱乐业	Culture, Sports and Entertainment	420062	414532	5530	
公共管理、社会保障和社会组织	Public Administration, Social Security and Social Organizations	161239	137153	16620	7466

9-6 分地区工业各行业新增固定资产（2012 年）
NEW FIXED ASSETS OF INDUSTRIAL SECTORS BY REGION （2012）

单位：万元（10000 yuan）

行业	Sector	全市 Whole Municipality	市区 Urban Area	溧阳市 Liyang City	金坛市 Jintan City
农副食品加工业	Food Processing	53307	11830	16178	25299
食品制造业	Food Production	34255	10040	13585	10630
酒、饮料和精制茶制造业	Beverages and Refined Tea Manufacturing	19988	14158	3430	2400
纺织业	Textile Industry	404153	312093	67487	24573
纺织服装、服饰业	Textile and clothing Industry	102999	27155	35495	40349
皮革、毛皮、羽毛及其制品和制鞋业	Leather, Fur, Feathers and Their Products, and Footwear Industry	39040	10217	2823	26000
木材加工及木、竹、藤、棕、草制品业	Timber Processing, Bamboo, Cane, Palm Fiber and Straw Products	102635	95845	6790	
家具制造业	Furniture Manufacturing	17818	10558	7260	
造纸及纸制品业	Papermaking and Paper Products	145490	56387	9290	79813
印刷和记录媒介复制业	Printing and Recorded Media Duplication Industry	78114	44989	29525	3600
文教、工美、体育和娱乐用品制造业	Cultural & Educational, Arts & Crafts, Sports & Entertainment Articles Manufacturing	47501	22895	21956	2650
石油加工、炼焦及核燃料加工业	Petroleum Processing, Coking and Nuclear Fuel Processing	9795	3545		6250
化学原料及化学制品制造业	Raw Chemical Materials and Chemica Products	951069	671857	213886	65326
医药制造业	Medical and Pharmaceutical Products	197904	151179	28425	18300
化学纤维制造业	Chemical Fiber	146157	115304	24775	6078
橡胶和塑料制品业	Rubber and Plastic Products Industry	346629	239422	39729	67478
非金属矿物制品业	Nonmetal Mineral Products	511647	279460	193099	39088
黑色金属冶炼及压延加工业	Smelting and Pressing of Ferrous Metals	509043	385430	94224	29389
有色金属冶炼及压延加工业	Smelting and Pressing of Nonferrous Metals	174102	78263	53940	41899
金属制品业	Metal Products	508221	339854	135078	33289
通用设备制造业	General Equipment Manufacturing	1392522	817085	352574	222863
专用设备制造业	For Special Purposes Equipment Manufacturing	1140601	757423	328172	55006
汽车制造业	Automotive Industry	355384	307042	34207	14135
铁路、船舶、航空航天和其他运输设备制造	Railways, Shipping, Aerospace and other Transportation Equipment Manufacturing	297724	276745	20479	500
电气机械及器材制造业	Electric Equipment and Machinery	1511798	1062959	299478	149361
计算机、通信和其他电子设备制造	Computer, Communications and other Electronic Equipment Manufacturing	1033432	908127	73005	52300
仪器仪表制造业	Instrumentation Manufacturing	429137	364893	47385	16859
其他制造业	Other Manufacturings	153595	110240	5355	38000
废弃资源综合利用业	Comprehensive Utilization of Waste Resources Industry	18909	13930	690	4289
金属制品、机械和设备修理业	Metal Products, Machinery & Equipment Repairing Industry	28302	15272	13030	
电力、热力生产和供应业	Production and Supply of Electricity & Heat Industry	223728	201773		21955
燃气生产和供应业	Production and Supply of Gas Industry	66045	60105	5940	
水的生产和供应业	Production and Supply of water Industry	49979	30669	9310	10000

9-7　分地区全社会固定资产投资效果（2012 年）
EFFECT OF INVESTMENT IN FIXED ASSETS BY REGION （2012）

指　标	Item	全　市 Whole Municipality	市　区 Urban Area	溧阳市 Liyang City	金坛市 Jintan City
施工项目数（个）	Projects under Construction （unit）	4427	3166	924	337
# 本年新开工	Beginning Projects in this Year	3668	2736	692	240
本年建成投产项目数（个）	Number of Projects Completed （unit）	3678	2772	694	212
项目建成投产率（%）	Rate of Projects Completed and Put into Use （%）	83.1	87.6	75.1	62.9
计划总投资（万元）	Plan of General Investment （10000 yuan）	69497516	55959700	8141687	5396129
本年完成投资（万元）	Completed Investment Value this year （10000 yuan）	27601436	21660862	3740515	2200059
建设周期（年）	Construction Cycle （year）	2.5	2.6	2.2	2.5
本年新增固定资产（万元）	Newly Increased Fixed Assets this year （10000 yuan）	19428125	15439939	2577298	1410888
固定资产交付使用率（%）	Rate of Fixed Assets Put into Use （%）	70.4	71.3	68.9	64.1
本年施工房屋面积（万平方米）	Floor Space of Buildings under Construction this year （10000 sq.km）	7358.72	6090.06	752.33	516.33
# 住　宅	Residential Buildings	3401.13	2881.39	311.03	208.71
本年竣工房屋面积（万平方米）	Floor Space of Buildings Completed this year （10000 sq.km）	2686.16	2184.78	349.91	151.47
# 住　宅	Residential Buildings	775.73	714.67	24.27	36.79
房屋竣工率（%）	Rate of Buildings Completed （%）	36.5	35.9	46.5	29.3

9-8 分地区全社会固定资产投资资金来源（2012 年）
FUND RESOURCES OF FIXED ASSETS INVESTMENT BY REGION （2012）

单位：万元（10000 yuan）

指 标	Itemr	全 市 Whole Municipality	市 区 Urban Area	溧阳市 Liyang City	金坛市 Jintan City
资金来源总计	**Total Capital Sources**	**31533663**	**24853587**	**4272619**	**2407457**
上年末结余资金	Balance of Last Year	2296551	2049883	138068	108600
本年资金来源	Total Funds of This Year	29237112	22803704	4134551	2298857
国家预算内资金	State Budgetary Appropriation	509807	453328	26180	30299
国内贷款	Domestic Loans	3641888	2073366	1392183	176339
利用外资	Foreign Investment	915343	866887	32756	15700
# 外商直接投资	Foreign Direct Investment	674652	628816	32756	13080
自筹资金	Fundraising	18681522	14599114	2232012	1850396
其他资金来源	Other Fund Resources	5488552	4811009	451420	226123
附：本年各项应付款	**Accounts Payable of This Year**	**4585955**	**3983908**	**451869**	**150178**
# 工程款	Funds of Projects	1823884	1410333	315112	98439

9-9 分地区房地产开发投资资金来源（2012 年）
FUNDING SOURCES FOR REAL ESTATE DEVELOPMENT & INVESTMENT BY REGION （2012）

单位：万元（10000 yuan）

指 标	Item	全 市 Whole Municipality	市 区 Urban Area	溧阳市 Liyang City	金坛市 Jintan City
资金来源总计	**Total Capital Sources**	**10207395**	**8859170**	**853677**	**494548**
上年末结余资金	Balance of Last Year	2163580	1917912	138068	107600
本年资金来源	Total Funds of This Year	8043815	6941258	715609	386948
国内贷款	Domestic Loans	1320440	1021439	169551	129450
利用外资	Foreign Investment	15683	13083	2600	
# 外商直接投资	Foreign Direct Investment	14208	11608	2600	
自筹资金	Fundraising	2097986	1969075	96151	32760
其他资金来源	Other Fund Resources	4609706	3937661	447307	224738
附：本年各项应付款	**Accounts Payable of This Year**	**1683408**	**1321562**	**238562**	**123284**
# 工程款	Funds of Projects	913002	715644	118610	78478

9-10　房地产开发主要指标（1990-2012 年）
MAJOR INDICATORS OF REAL ESTATE DEVELOPMENT（1990-2012）

单位：万元、万平方米（10000 yuan、10000 sq.m）

年 份 Year	房地产开发投资额 Investment in Real Estate Development	商品房屋施工面积 Construction Area of Commodity Housing	其中 of which 住 宅 Residence	商品房屋竣工面积 Completion Area of Commodity Housing	其中 of which 住 宅 Residence	商品房屋销售面积 Sales Area of Commodity Housing	其中 of which 住 宅 Residence
1990	9384	34.15	30.86	19.38	16.78		
1991	18274	61.87	54.58	28.53	23.51	16.91	
1992	34620	125.50	107.98	40.27	34.59	24.32	
1993	106860	206.39	175.07	99.08	82.86	44.95	
1994	157903	316.28	175.64	144.78	113.07	61.19	
1995	184684	258.48	181.05	120.28	101.41	70.74	61.20
1996	153586	248.16	163.46	134.28	104.96	80.78	72.65
1997	187827	241.81	161.21	121.65	88.20	93.16	85.64
1998	223200	315.52	234.31	132.77	104.08	103.61	93.67
1999	255026	346.92	288.73	169.31	143.19	135.36	123.15
2000	299834	407.39	343.75	204.02	160.96	149.26	133.59
2001	321709	487.47	398.14	192.98	169.51	172.85	162.39
2002	410169	526.05	439.66	268.79	226.74	248.61	223.82
2003	527754	645.00	489.23	249.17	190.56	205.91	170.48
2004	978955	991.33	744.99	250.33	187.75	236.56	196.68
2005	1142730	1246.07	953.78	520.72	397.84	422.53	363.29
2006	1710416	1706.26	1350.55	397.78	297.58	479.12	407.89
2007	2250453	2190.26	1700.02	616.25	486.21	579.49	514.52
2008	3089162	2577.34	1844.19	685.14	541.65	504.49	425.53
2009	3062037	2748.89	1995.22	749.81	547.12	922.64	802.50
2010	4469606	3208.11	2192.84	732.50	486.98	915.75	775.14
2011	5659063	3926.82	2712.48	682.22	472.38	661.12	537.94
2012	5970105	4314.38	3047.37	927.33	642.5	756.81	664.99

9-11 分地区房地产开发投资完成额（2012 年）
TOTAL INVESTMENT IN REAL ESTATE DEVELOPMENT BY REGION （2012）

单位：万元（10000 yuan）

指 标	Item	全 市 Whole Municipality	市 区 Urban Area	溧阳市 Liyang City	金坛市 Jintan City
投资完成额	**Total Investment**	**5970105**	**5317445**	**376235**	**276425**
按构成分	**Grouped by Composition**				
建筑工程	Construction	3794875	3270867	295025	228983
安装工程	Installation	386664	360104	19617	6943
设备工器具购置	Purchase of Equipment and Investment	157670	152769	2001	2900
其他费用	Others	1630896	1533705	59592	37599
按工程用途分	**Grouped by Use of funds**				
住 宅	Residential Buildings	4161126	3674417	282356	204353
#90 平方米以下	under 90 square meters	785175	732895	37388	14892
144 平方米以上	upon 144 square meters	1280675	1153822	65428	61425
办公楼	Office Buildings	218204	213429	2900	1875
商业营业用房	Buildings for Business Use	893703	770451	80682	42570
其 他	Others	697072	659148	10297	27627
按登记注册类型分	**Grouped by Registration Status**				
内 资	Domestically-Funded	4247841	3626902	366850	254089
国 有	State-owned	317284	219070		98214
集 体	Collective-owned	76753	48650	28103	
国有独资公司	State-funded Corporations	91552	17074	74478	
其它有限责任公司	Other Limited Liability Corporations	1852240	1797337	42000	12835
股份有限公司	Share-holding Corporations Ltd.	114495	102479	11900	116
私营独资	Private	72240	51140	21100	
私营合伙	Private Partnership			27795	
私营有限责任公司	Private Limited Liability Company			149530	142924
其 他	Others	100477	88601	11876	
港澳台商投资	Investment from Hong Kong, Macao and Taiwan	1499745	1486827	9385	3533
外商投资	Enterprises with Foreign Investment	222519	203716		18803

9-12　分地区房地产开发企业经营情况（2012 年）
MANAGEMENT OF REAL ESTATE DEVELOPMENT ENTERPRISES BY REGION （2012）

行　业	Sector	全　市 Whole Municipality	市　区 Urban Area	溧阳市 Liyang City	金坛市 Jintan City
开发企业个数（个）	**Number of Development Enterprises （unit）**	**422**	**319**	**48**	**55**
内　资	Domestically-Funded	348	259	40	49
国　有	State-owned	12	10		2
集　体	Collective-owned	2	1	1	
股份合作	Share-holding Cooperative	1	1		
国有独资公司	Share-Owned Companies	2	1	1	
其他有限责任公司	Limited liability Corpora-tion	117	103	10	4
股份有限公司	Share-holding Corporations Ltd.	11	9	1	1
私营独资	Private	6	4	2	
私营合伙	Private Partnership			1	
私营有限责任公司	Private Limited Liability Corporation	186	122	22	42
私营股份有限公司	Private Company Limited by Shares	4	3	1	
其　他	Others	6	5	1	
港澳台商投资	Investment from Hong Kong, Macao and Taiwan	52	42	7	3
外商投资	Enterprises withForeign Investment	22	18	1	3
平均从业人员（人）	**Average Number of Employed Persons （person）**	**11759**	**9381**	**1221**	**1157**
土地开发及购置	**Land Area （sq.m）**				
待开发土地面积（平方米）	Land Space Needed to Development（sq.m）	4386694	3778654	303650	304390
本年购置土地面积（平方米）	Land Space Purchases of This Year（sq.m）	2418544	2296731	104312	17501
本年土地成交款（万元）	Total Value of Land Purchased（10000 yuan）	872187	828562	33860	9765
经营情况（万元）	**Management Condition （10000 yuan）**				
实收资本	Paid-up Capital	5924586	5515656	252291	156639
资产总计	Total Assets	26566989	23166761	2035531	1364698
累计折旧	Accumulated Depreciation of Fixed Assets	190726	155289	21078	14359
#本年折旧	Depreciation of This Year	59800	52847	4200	2753
负债总计	Total Liabilities	19081312	16215214	1696640	1169458
所有者权益	Owner's Equity	7485678	6951547	338890	195240
主营业务收入	Operating Income	6080391	5342667	463962	273763
土地转让收入	Income from Land Transferred	39278	39278		
商品房屋销售收入	Income from Commercial Houses Sold	5982310	5253337	456494	272479
房屋出租收入	Housing Rental Income	26349	24142	1690	518
其他收入	Other Incomes	32453	25910	5777	766
主营业务成本	Operational Cost	4554205	3972909	373198	208098
销售费用	Sales Expenses	156382	135379	12156	8846
主营业务税金及附加	Business Tax and Extra Charges	500907	443110	37513	20284
主营业务利润	Major Business Profits	1025279	926647	53251	45381
其他业务利润	Other Business Profits	3510	-2898	2933	3474
管理费用	Management Expenses finance Charge	242235	199204	24996	18034
财务费用	finance Charge	77320	68957	6922	1441
投资收益	Income from Investment	32239	30428	-192	2003
营业利润	Operating Surpius	566500	537929	10736	17835
营业外收入	Nonbusiness Income	11771	8866	898	2007
营业外支出	Nonbusiness Expenditure	22535	19539	1940	1056
利润总额	Total Profits	566349	536973	9477	19899

9-13 房地产开发企业房屋建设情况（2012 年）
CONSTRUCTION OF BUILDINGS DEVELOPED BY REAL ESTATE COMPANIES（2012）

指 标	Item	施工面积（万平方米） Floor Space under Construction (10000 sq.m)	其中 of which #本年新开工 Floor Space Started This Year	竣工面积（万平方米） Floor Space Completed (10000 sq.m)	竣工价值（万元） Value Completed (10000 yuan)
总 计	**Total**	**4314.38**	**1100.18**	**927.33**	**2845239**
#溧阳市	Liyang City	375.38	93.09	24.50	59533
金坛市	Jintan City	282.65	91.50	49.88	104530
按经济成份分	**By Economic Sector**				
国 有	State-owned	233.63	97.78	26.52	91016
集 体	Collective-owned	36.77	10.55		
其 它	Others	4043.97	991.85	900.81	2754223
按用途分	**By Use**				
住 宅	Residential Buildings	3047.37	804.30	642.50	1929315
#90 平方米以下	under 90 square meters	551.29	82.00	143.78	430503
144 平方米以上	upon 144 square meters	772.77	208.70	95.07	302275
#别墅、高档公寓	Villas, Top Grade Apartments	304.75	125.56	22.63	113482
办公楼	Office Buildings	171.77	21.63	38.37	132518
商业营业用房	Buildings for Business Use	562.96	134.40	136.06	483870
其 他	Others	532.28	139.86	110.40	299536

9-14 市区房地产开发企业房屋建设情况（2012 年）
CONSTRUCTION OF BUILDINGS DEVELOPED BY REAL ESTATE COMPANIES IN URBAN AREA （2012）

指 标	Item	施工面积（万平方米） Floor Space under Construction (10000 sq.m)	其中 of which #本年新开工 Floor Space Started This Year	竣工面积（万平方米） Floor Space Completed (10000 sq.m)	竣工价值（万元） Value Completed (10000 yuan)
总 计	**Total**	**3656.35**	**915.59**	**852.95**	**2681176**
按经济成份分	**By Economic Sector**				
国 有	State-owned	164.60	33.88	26.52	91016
集 体	Collective-owned	7.43	5.74		
其 它	Others	3484.32	875.97	826.44	2590160
按用途分	**By Use**				
住 宅	Residential Buildings	2528.50	644.50	582.31	1794420
#90 平方米以下	under 90 square meters	502.65	73.89	137.99	419739
144 平方米以上	upon 144 square meters	671.60	180.90	85.64	280833
#别墅、高档公寓	Villas, Top Grade Apartments	297.59	123.07	22.25	112368
办公楼	Office Buildings	168.31	20.46	37.55	131243
商业营业用房	Buildings for Business Use	469.24	123.10	130.41	471380
其 他	Others	490.30	127.54	102.68	284133

9-15　房地产开发企业商品房销售和出租情况（2012 年）
SOLD AND LEASEDCOMMODITY HOUSES OF REAL ESTATE DEVELOPMENT COMPANIES（2012）

指　标	Item	销售面积（万平方米）Actually Sales（10000sq.m）	其中 of which 现房 Existing house	期房 Future marketable housing	待售面积（万平方米）Needed to sales（10000sq.m）
总　计	**Total**	**756.81**	**92.57**	**664.24**	**248.01**
# 溧阳市	Liyang City	46.64	1.38	45.25	13.16
金坛市	Jintan City	50.84	9.23	41.61	48.92
按经济成份分	**By Economic Sector**				
国　有	State-owned	15.15	2.53	12.63	11.59
集　体	Collective-owned	2.19	0.11	2.08	0.01
其　它	Others	739.46	89.94	649.52	236.41
按用途分	**By Use**				
住　宅	Residential Buildings	664.99	60.96	604.02	89.72
#90 平方米以下	under 90 square meters	118.00	16.31	101.69	14.45
144 平方米以上	upon 144 square meters	133.35	10.50	122.85	37.94
# 别墅、高档公寓	Villas, Top Grade Apartments	58.59	5.20	53.40	10.50
办公楼	Office Buildings	16.76	4.18	12.59	16.14
商业营业用房	Buildings for Business Use	56.76	15.56	41.20	82.26
其　他	Others	18.30	11.88	6.42	59.89

9-15 续表　Continued

指　标	Item	销售额（万元）Total Actually（10000 yuan）	其中 of which 现房 Existing house	期房 Future marketable housing	出租面积（万平方米）Rent（10000sq.m）
总　计	**Total**	**5153089**	**501253**	**4651836**	**27.60**
# 溧阳市	Liyang City	392463	15854	376609	5.51
金坛市	Jintan City	266134	39637	226497	3.62
按经济成份分	**By Economic Sector**				
国　有	State-owned	63868	7255	56613	
集　体	Collective-owned	11620	539	11081	
其　它	Others	5077601	493459	4584142	27.60
按用途分	**By Use**				
住　宅	Residential Buildings	4333133	330815	4002318	
#90 平方米以下	under 90 square meters	679038	66617	612421	
144 平方米以上	upon 144 square meters	1114245	70294	1043951	
# 别墅、高档公寓	Villas, Top Grade Apartments	559400	80142	479258	
办公楼	Office Buildings	112607	21155	91452	0.86
商业营业用房	Buildings for Business Use	646218	115225	530993	22.02
其　他	Others	61131	34058	27073	4.71

9-16 市区房地产开发企业商品房销售和出租情况（2012 年）
COMMODITY HOUSES OF REAL ESTATE DEVELOPMENT COMPANIESSOLD AND LEASED IN URBAN AREA（2012）

指标	Item	销售面积（万平方米）Actually Sales（10000sq.m）	其中 of which 现房 Existing house	期房 Future marketable housing	待售面积（万平方米）Needed to sales（10000sq.m）
总计	**Total**	**659.34**	**81.96**	**577.37**	**185.94**
按经济成份分	**By Economic Sector**				
国有	State-owned	12.63	0.39	12.24	4.28
集体	Collective-owned	2.19	0.11	2.08	0.01
其它	Others	644.52	81.47	563.05	181.64
按用途分	**By Use**				
住宅	Residential Buildings	583.06	54.55	528.52	65.59
#90 平方米以下	under 90 square meters	113.63	15.74	97.89	13.27
144 平方米以上	upon 144 square meters	112.74	7.48	105.27	27.92
# 别墅、高档公寓	Villas, Top Grade Apartments	56.72	4.72	52.00	7.38
办公楼	Office Buildings	16.69	4.10	12.59	13.77
商业营业用房	Buildings for Business Use	44.40	13.02	31.39	54.62
其他	Others	15.18	10.30	4.88	51.95

9-16 续表 Continued

指标	Item	销售额（万元）Total Actually（10000 yuan）	其中 of which 现房 Existing house	期房 Future marketable housing	出租面积（万平方米）Rent（10000sq.m）
总计	**Total**	**4494492**	**445762**	**4048730**	**18.47**
按经济成份分	**By Economic Sector**				
国有	State-owned	56599	1903	54696	
集体	Collective-owned	11620	539	11081	
其它	Others	4426273	443320	3982953	18.47
按用途分	**By Use**				
住宅	Residential Buildings	3810981	297338	3513643	
#90 平方米以下	under 90 square meters	649980	64915	585065	
144 平方米以上	upon 144 square meters	965325	47347	917978	
# 别墅、高档公寓	Villas, Top Grade Apartments	535879	75276	460603	
办公楼	Office Buildings	112446	20994	91452	0.86
商业营业用房	Buildings for Business Use	522118	98329	423789	12.89
其他	Others	48947	29101	19846	4.71

10

CHAPTER 10

农业

AGRICULTURE

常州统计年鉴

10 农 业 AGRICULTURE

2012 年主要统计指标
MAJOR STATISTICAL INDICATORS OF 2012

年底乡村实有从业人员	Number of Persons Employed In Rural Area at Year-end	129.93 万人	（10000 persons）
比上年增长	Over the Previous Year	-2.2%	
农林牧渔业总产值	Total Output value of Farming,Forestry,Animal Husbandry and Fishing	219.58 亿元	（100 million yuan）
比上年增长	Over the Previous Year	12.8%	
粮食总产量	Total Output of Grain	114.80 万吨	（10000 tons）
比上年增长	Over the Previous Year	-0.4%	
油料总产量	Total Output of Oil-Bearing	3.77 万吨	（10000 tons）
比上年增长	Over the Previous Year	17.6%	

10-1 分地区农林牧渔业总产值（1978-2012年）
GROSS OUTPUT VALUE OF FARMING, FORESTRY, ANIMAL HUSBANDARY AND FISHERY BY REGION（1978-2012）

按现价计算 At Current Prices

单位：亿元（100 million yuan）

年 份 Year	全 市 Whole Municipality	其中 of which 市 区 Urban Area	溧阳市 Liyang City	金坛市 Jintan City
1978	6.96	3.75	1.96	1.25
1979	8.13	4.00	2.15	1.89
1980	8.12	3.89	2.54	1.69
1981	8.14	3.99	2.48	1.67
1982	9.66	4.75	2.85	2.06
1983	10.08	5.04	2.95	2.09
1984	13.71	6.97	4.08	2.66
1985	15.10	8.08	4.27	2.75
1986	17.42	9.63	4.39	3.40
1987	19.17	10.19	5.00	3.98
1988	25.01	13.07	6.79	5.16
1989	26.87	14.40	6.76	5.70
1990	29.06	15.48	7.52	6.06
1991	27.78	16.22	6.46	5.10
1992	35.22	19.59	8.03	7.60
1993	45.95	26.05	10.65	9.25
1994	63.64	34.30	16.43	12.91
1995	74.74	39.34	20.02	15.39
1996	87.28	44.98	24.13	18.16
1997	82.16	43.64	21.45	17.07
1998	84.01	43.96	22.15	17.90
1999	83.67	42.77	22.37	18.54
2000	85.88	43.81	22.06	20.01
2001	89.37	44.94	23.21	21.22
2002	92.67	45.89	24.53	22.25
2003	90.63	42.62	24.52	23.50
2004	99.42	46.03	27.16	26.23
2005	104.10	47.90	28.64	27.55
2006	101.99	46.65	27.74	27.60
2007	108.87	49.16	30.41	29.30
2008	149.77	69.60	45.11	35.06
2009	160.77	73.91	49.59	37.27
2010	174.08	78.39	54.57	41.12
2011	194.68	86.69	62.02	45.97
2012	219.58	97.99	69.75	51.84

注:2006年至2008年数据依据普查数据作相应调整。

Note: The data from year 2006 to year 2008 was adjusted in accordance with the records of general survey.

10-2 主要年份年末耕地面积
YEAR-END AREA UNDER CULTIVATION IN MAIN YEARS

单位：千公顷（1000 hectares）

年份 Year	全市 Whole Municipality	其中 of which 市区 Urban Area	溧阳市 Liyang City	金坛市 Jintan City
1949	232.64	109.47	73.15	50.01
1952	235.41	108.91	75.53	50.97
1957	231.09	106.19	75.25	49.89
1962	217.05	98.03	72.94	46.08
1965	218.25	103.29	68.86	46.10
1970	209.59	100.90	65.61	43.08
1975	212.21	103.31	65.55	43.36
1978	210.15	100.84	65.36	43.95
1979	209.67	100.47	65.29	43.92
1980	209.13	100.24	65.23	43.66
1981	208.91	100.13	65.16	43.61
1982	206.73	98.09	65.06	43.57
1983	207.14	98.61	64.99	43.54
1984	206.79	98.38	64.93	43.49
1985	206.57	98.25	64.87	43.45
1986	206.16	98.08	64.68	43.40
1987	206.05	98.04	64.65	43.36
1988	205.31	97.38	64.63	43.31
1989	204.97	97.19	64.50	43.28
1990	204.54	97.01	64.34	43.19
1991	204.27	96.86	64.26	43.15
1992	203.60	96.59	63.94	43.07
1993	203.23	96.42	63.80	43.01
1994	202.42	95.81	63.68	42.93
1995	200.88	94.80	63.44	42.64
1996	205.35	90.16	68.99	46.19
1997	204.99	80.57	68.87	46.23
1998	204.70	80.29	68.87	46.25
1999	204.81	89.31	69.19	46.32
2000	204.25	88.75	69.15	46.35
2001	202.63	87.03	69.23	46.37
2002	199.97	84.93	68.91	46.13
2003	197.67	82.78	68.64	46.25
2004	178.09	66.14	66.89	45.06
2005	176.32	64.27	66.83	45.22
2006	161.81	60.58	62.24	38.99
2007	161.09	59.89	62.34	38.86
2008	161.09	59.32	62.60	39.17
2009	148.13	60.37	55.83	31.93
2010	150.39	59.25	57.64	33.50
2011	150.00	58.60	57.59	33.81
2012	149.71	58.37	57.59	33.75

注：2012年末耕地面积为初步统计数据。
Note：The arable land calculated in the end of 2012 was based on the preliminary statistics.

10-3　主要年份粮食总产量
TOTAL OUTPUT OF GRAIN IN MAIN YEARS

单位：万吨（10000 tons）

年 份 Year	全 市 Whole Municipality	其中 of which 市 区 Urban Area	溧阳市 Liyang City	金坛市 Jintan City
1949	57.89	34.54	11.86	11.48
1952	78.41	42.77	19.87	15.77
1957	71.52	37.60	18.34	15.57
1962	74.80	44.49	15.45	14.86
1965	116.93	65.31	29.20	22.43
1970	114.48	61.81	29.11	23.56
1975	121.23	68.96	30.90	21.37
1978	150.25	81.96	40.03	28.26
1979	154.07	81.35	43.61	29.11
1980	139.42	75.25	37.38	26.79
1981	132.79	71.57	37.23	23.98
1982	157.60	84.85	43.84	28.91
1983	164.73	85.76	48.47	30.49
1984	177.75	91.79	53.12	32.84
1985	153.34	80.46	44.50	28.39
1986	162.13	85.82	45.09	31.22
1987	151.45	81.42	42.92	29.80
1988	157.63	85.37	41.56	30.70
1989	160.60	85.87	43.17	31.55
1990	164.50	89.07	41.98	33.46
1991	138.39	77.55	35.15	25.70
1992	158.62	88.06	40.53	30.02
1993	154.24	82.17	40.52	31.56
1994	144.79	77.74	37.07	29.98
1995	159.57	81.30	43.55	34.72
1996	166.37	83.73	46.03	36.61
1997	170.77	85.47	48.39	36.92
1998	153.28	72.02	47.82	33.43
1999	154.83	76.13	46.00	32.70
2000	136.22	66.11	41.87	28.24
2001	126.14	57.32	41.89	26.94
2002	122.86	53.78	42.96	26.11
2003	103.54	42.49	38.53	22.52
2004	106.08	41.43	40.96	23.69
2005	98.06	39.28	36.61	22.17
2006	95.25	36.30	36.87	22.08
2007	94.84	31.91	40.96	21.97
2008	113.35	36.84	49.41	27.10
2009	114.18	36.37	49.78	28.03
2010	115.16	34.22	52.72	28.22
2011	115.19	32.34	54.47	28.38
2012	114.80	32.02	54.52	28.26

注：2006、2007年数据依据第二次农业普查数据作相应调整。
Note：Data of year 2006 and 2007 are adjusted in accordance with the data of the second agricultural census.

10-4 主要年份棉花总产量
TOTAL OUTPUT OF COTTON IN MAIN YEARS

单位：吨（ton）

年 份 Year	全 市 Whole Municipality	其 中 of which 市 区 Urban Area	溧阳市 Liyang City	金坛市 Jintan City
1949	261	195		66
1952	390	301		89
1957	50	4		46
1962	1		1	
1965	112	42	19	51
1970	34	27		7
1975	503		1	502
1978	2045		366	1679
1979	3274		482	2792
1980	5509		1831	3678
1981	10495	104	3366	7025
1982	11615	594	3457	7564
1983	11973	914	2937	8122
1984	12860	1198	3729	7933
1985	7240	559	2444	4237
1986	3464	227	1591	1646
1987	2954	252	1518	1184
1988	3325	215	1819	1291
1989	2259	125	1273	861
1990	2255	78	1193	984
1991	1956	86	1170	700
1992	2840	74	2031	735
1993	1828	27	1497	304
1994	1050		913	137
1995	1276		1086	190
1996	936		758	181
1997	1114		924	190
1998	1150		902	248
1999	589		388	201
2000	764		544	220
2001	708		348	360
2002	637		406	231
2003	305		182	123
2004	368		236	132
2005	298		185	113
2006	303		241	62
2007	283		204	79
2008	484		406	78
2009	454		332	120
2010	506		451	55
2011	491		457	34
2012	493		470	23

注：2006、2007年数依据第二次农业普查数据作相应调整。
Note: Data of year 2006 and 2007 are adjusted in accordance with the data of the second agricultural census.

10-5　主要年份油料总产量
TOTAL OUTPUT OF OIL-BEARING CROPS IN MAIN YEARS

单位：吨（ton）

年 份 Year	全 市 Whole Municipality	其 中 of which 市 区 Urban Area	溧阳市 Liyang City	金坛市 Jintan City
1949	4455	1250	1244	1961
1952	5027	936	3538	553
1957	4146	550	3130	466
1962	2154	233	1414	507
1965	2493	118	1795	580
1970	7195	2969	2209	2017
1975	10586	4962	3382	2242
1978	13515	4713	6046	2756
1979	14894	5028	7040	2826
1980	17724	5747	9473	2504
1981	27590	9895	12578	5117
1982	52438	13308	31780	7350
1983	38895	10578	22205	6112
1984	38175	10080	22780	5315
1985	69961	13383	43870	12708
1986	55603	12017	32795	10791
1987	57063	11526	35544	9993
1988	46657	10347	27518	8792
1989	54054	10341	33295	10418
1990	63899	11710	38899	13290
1991	53931	10879	31126	11926
1992	68040	10594	42774	14672
1993	61498	10114	26942	24442
1994	51683	10610	29530	11543
1995	72786	12068	41895	18823
1996	70526	12793	38632	19101
1997	66204	11240	37689	17275
1998	35932	5154	21286	9492
1999	72421	9981	42509	19931
2000	91629	17412	53102	21115
2001	86994	15027	52238	19729
2002	73015	10270	45111	17634
2003	72586	8954	47360	16272
2004	85537	8725	59109	17703
2005	85960	8489	60469	17002
2006	76904	7074	56485	13345
2007	51326	4868	35198	11260
2008	52575	4316	38703	9556
2009	51608	4513	36561	10534
2010	40035	3922	26411	9702
2011	32048	3138	20710	8200
2012	37684	3228	25847	8609

注：2006、2007年数据依据第二次农业普查数据作相应调整。
Note：Data of year 2006 and 2007 are adjusted in accordance with the data of the second agricultural census.

10-6 主要年份人均占有主要农产品产量
PER CAPTIA OUTPUT OF MAJOR FARM PRODUCTS IN MAIN YEARS

单位：千克 / 人（kg/person）

年 份 Year	粮 食 Grain	油 料 Oil-bearing Crops	蚕 茧 Silkworm Cocoons	茶 叶 Tea	水 果 Fruit	猪 肉 Pork	水产品 Aquatic Products
1952	427.68	2.74	1.30	0.01	1.30		4.06
1957	351.09	2.04	0.68	0.01	1.60		4.96
1965	485.63	1.04	0.40	0.14	0.86		4.26
1970	429.06	2.70	1.08	0.36	0.94		3.76
1975	425.84	3.72	0.87	0.47	0.85		4.48
1978	516.31	4.64	0.61	0.47	1.01		4.49
1980	471.14	5.99	0.76	0.54	1.93	23.64	4.85
1985	499.71	22.80	1.78	0.89	2.79	19.64	9.22
1986	523.43	17.95	2.04	0.96	2.96	19.17	12.01
1987	492.13	18.22	2.05	1.09	3.42	19.32	13.00
1988	497.16	14.12	2.38	1.20	3.93	19.86	15.73
1989	499.29	16.81	2.77	1.17	3.38	20.13	13.81
1990	506.40	19.67	2.69	1.15	2.98	21.55	16.36
1991	423.38	16.50	2.64	1.03	2.95	22.44	11.44
1992	482.75	20.71	2.88	1.13	3.07	23.77	15.69
1993	468.36	18.67	3.38	1.24	4.17	23.98	21.14
1994	436.85	15.59	3.54	1.20	6.08	25.31	24.27
1995	478.25	21.82	3.01	0.76	6.81	26.97	27.15
1996	492.88	20.89	1.47	0.72	6.49	25.94	29.16
1997	503.41	19.52	1.51	0.80	6.32	17.47	27.57
1998	450.83	10.60	1.43	0.79	7.10	18.32	31.11
1999	455.78	21.32	1.28	0.81	7.92	17.56	32.16
2000	398.90	26.83	1.41	0.79	8.68	18.83	32.51
2001	369.40	25.47	1.53	0.77	10.55	19.83	33.80
2002	357.92	21.27	1.47	0.78	10.79	19.51	35.08
2003	299.06	20.97	1.30	0.78	17.30	21.30	36.02
2004	303.99	24.51	1.26	0.76	17.41	19.16	36.48
2005	278.88	24.45	0.81	0.79	19.13	18.46	37.03
2006	268.56	21.68	0.92	0.82	16.88	19.05	37.13
2007	265.37	14.36	0.68	0.93	20.69	16.52	37.83
2008	315.96	14.66	0.46	1.06	27.14	17.78	39.63
2009	317.33	14.34	0.20	1.09	23.12	17.40	39.13
2010	319.17	11.10	0.19	0.96	27.60	16.57	41.00
2011	317.45	8.83	0.14	0.95	25.61	16.74	45.31
2012	314.71	10.33	0.13	0.96	32.19	18.24	49.67

注：2006、2007年数依据第二次农业普查数据作相应调整。
Note: Data of year 2006 and 2007 are adjusted in accordance with the data of the second agricultural census.

10-7 主要年份农村经济主要指标
MAJOR ECONOMIC INDICATORS OF AGRICULTURE IN MAIN YEARS

指 标	Item	1985	1990	1995	2000	2005	2010	2012
农业机械总动力（万千瓦）	Total Power of Agricultural Machinery （10000 kw）	105.65	116.92	137.19	167.67	162.03	150.22	158.54
农林牧渔业总产值（亿元）	Total Output Value of Farming,Forestry, Animal Husbandry and Fishery （100 million yuan）	13.35	29.06	74.74	85.88	104.10	174.08	219.58
# 农业产值	Value of Farming	9.30	15.95	44.65	51.37	50.14	95.03	120.82
林业产值	Value of Forestry	0.14	0.17	0.51	0.88	1.24	1.26	1.55
牧业产值	Value of Animal Hubandry	3.10	8.28	17.52	12.97	18.74	27.41	34.25
渔业产值	Value of Fishery	0.81	2.60	12.06	20.66	29.01	42.37	52.40
粮食产量（万吨）	Total Output of Grain （10000 tons）	153.34	164.50	159.57	136.22	98.06	115.16	114.80
棉花产量（吨）	Total Output of Cotton （ton）	7240	2255	1276	764	298	506	493
油料产量（吨）	Total Output of Oil-bearing Grops （ton）	69961	63899	72786	91629	85960	40035	37684
水产品产量（吨）	Output of Aquatic Products （ton）	26848	53149	90571	111188	130198	147938	181240
蚕茧产量（吨）	Output of Silkworm Cocoons （ton）	5476	8726	10055	4815	2843	671	469
水果产量（吨）	Output of Fruits （ton）	8551	9670	22716	29639	67275	99565	117431
茶叶产量（吨）	Output of Tea （ton）	2727	3730	2550	2680	2762	3464	3502

10-8 主要年份农村经济主要指标增长速度
GROWTH RATE OF MAJOR INDICATORS OF AGRICULTURAL ECONOMY IN MAIN YEARS

单位：%

指 标	Item	2012年比下列各年增长 Growth Rate of 2012 over Following Years						
		1985	1990	1995	2000	2005	2010	2011
农业机械总动力	Total Power of Agricultural Machinery	50.1	35.6	15.6	-5.4	-2.2	5.5	2.1
农林牧渔业总产值	Total Output Value of Farming,Forestry, Animal Husbandry and Fishery	15.5倍	6.6倍	1.9倍	1.6倍	1.1倍	26.1	12.8
# 农业产值	Value of Farming	12.0倍	6.6倍	1.7倍	1.4倍	1.4倍	27.1	12.1
林业产值	Value of Forestry	10.1倍	8.1倍	2.0倍	76.0	25.0	23.0	4.7
牧业产值	Value of Animal Hubandry	10.0倍	3.1倍	95.5	1.6倍	82.7	25.0	6.4
渔业产值	Value of Fishery	63.7倍	19.2倍	3.3倍	1.5倍	80.6	23.7	17.6
粮食产量	Total Output of Grain	-25.1	-30.2	-28.1	-15.7	17.1	-0.3	-0.3
油料产量	Total Output of Oil-bearing Grops	-46.1	-41.0	-48.2	-58.9	-56.2	-5.9	17.6
水产品产量	Output of Aquatic Products	5.8倍	2.4倍	1.0倍	63.0	39.2	22.5	10.2
蚕茧产量	Output of Silkworm Cocoons	-91.4	-94.6	-95.3	-90.3	-83.5	-30.1	-13.8
水果产量	Output of Fruits	12.7倍	11.1倍	4.2倍	3.0倍	74.6	17.9	26.4
茶叶产量	Output of Tea	28.4	-6.1	37.3	30.7	26.8	1.1	1.5

10-9 主要年份农村基本情况
FUNDAMENTAL CONDITION OF VILLAGE IN MAIN YEARS

指 标	Item	1990	1995	2000	2005	2010	2012
农村基层组织（个）	**Village Units （unit）**						
镇政府	Town Governments	32	73	70	73	39	37
村民委员会	Number of Villagers' Committees	1933	1924	1909	1101	811	776
村民小组	Villager Group	21557	21638	21485	17999	17147	16510
乡村户数、人口数	**Households and Rural Population**						
总户数（万户）	Number of Households （10000 households）	74.68	76.80	80.41	79.98	78.72	76.17
总人口（万人）	Rural Population（10000 persons）	242.34	239.14	236.86	235.30	237.55	230.98
乡村实有从业人员（万人）	**Number of Rural Laborers （10000 persons）**	**135.80**	**136.31**	**128.67**	**126.86**	**133.95**	**129.93**
按性别分	Grouped by Sex						
男劳动力	Male	70.50	70.77	66.66	66.02	70.55	68.55
女劳动力	Female	65.30	65.54	62.01	60.84	63.40	61.38
按行业分	**Grouped by Sector**						
农林牧渔业	Farming, Forestry, Animal Husbandry and Fishery	65.45	54.65	51.03	32.21	27.39	25.36
# 种植业	Planting	59.15	47.29	43.98	26.11	21.84	19.90
工 业	Industry	37.58	42.88	36.98	48.35	58.20	57.61
建筑业	Construction	11.22	12.86	13.54	15.89	16.66	17.28
交通运输、仓储、邮电通信业	Transport, Storage, Post and Telecommunications	4.18	5.23	5.27	5.91	5.44	5.36
批发零售贸易餐饮业	Wholesale and Retail Trade, Catering Service	2.71	3.92	5.67	7.91	7.13	6.78
金融保险业	Banking and Insurance	0.10	0.11	0.17	0.49	0.76	0.83
房地产、社会服务业	Real Estate and Social Services	0.49	0.39	0.72	1.42	1.69	1.49
卫生、体育和社会福利业	Health Care, Sporting and Social Welfare	0.41	0.41	0.39	0.42	0.56	0.60
教育、文化艺术和广电业	Culture, Education and Arts, Radio, Film and Television	0.60	0.47	0.38	0.48	0.60	0.62
科研和综合技术服务业	Scientific Research and Polytechnical Services	0.08	0.07	0.14	0.16	0.24	0.21
乡经济组织管理业	Rural Economic Management	0.74	0.94	0.87	0.58	0.45	0.32
其他行业	Others	12.24	14.38	13.51	13.04	14.83	13.47

注：本表按当年口径统计，2012 年以后，交通运输、仓储、邮电通信业指交通运输、仓储和邮政业；批发零售贸易餐饮业指批发和零售业。
Notes:The table is in line with the current statistical caliber. Starting from 2012, the transportation, storage, and post and telecommunications industries refer to the transportation, storage and postal industries; and the wholesale & retail trade and catering services sectors refer to the wholesale & retail trade sector.

10-10　分地区农业现代化情况（2012 年）
STATISTICS ON AGRICULTURAL MODERNIZATION BY REGION（2012）

指 标	Item	全 市 Whole Municipality	武进区 Wujin District
农业机械情况	**Statistics on Agricultural Machinery**		
机耕地面积（千公顷）	Area Ploughed by Tractors （1000 hectares）	158.28	22.88
#占耕地面积（%）	Percentage of Coverage Area under Cultivation （%）	105.72	55.79
机播面积（千公顷）	Seeded Area by Tractors （1000 hectares）	130.16	22.88
机械植保面积（千公顷）	Plant Protection Area by Tractors （1000 hectares）	161.72	22.65
机收面积（千公顷）	Harvest Area by Tractors （1000 hectares）	146.20	22.65
机械脱粒粮食（万吨）	Amount of Shelling by Thresher （10000 tons）	104.86	34.00
农村电气化情况	**Electrization in Rural Area**		
农村用电量（万千瓦小时）	Electricity Consumed in Rural Area （10000 kwh）	1573506	816710
农村化学化情况	**Chemification Conditions of Village**		
化肥施用量（折纯量，吨）	Consumption of Chemical Fertilizer （ton）	63379	8056
#氮　肥	Nitrogenous Fertilizer	37605	4615
磷　肥	Phosphate Fertilizer	2268	435
钾　肥	Potash Fertilizer	1021	174
复合肥	Compound Fertilizer	22485	2832
农药使用量（吨）	Consumption of Agricultural Chemical Pesticide （ton）	3459	772
农用薄膜使用量（吨）	Consumption of Agricultural Film （ton）	2739	853
#地膜使用量（吨）	Consumption of Mulching Film （ton）	1112	336
地膜覆盖面积（公顷）	Area of Coverage of Mulching Film （hectare）	6646	1180
农用柴油（吨）	Agricultural Diesel Oil （ton）	26199	9458
通汽车村数（个）	**Number of Villages with Traffic Service （unit）**	**776**	**246**
自来水受益村数（个）	**Number of Villages with Access to Tap Water （unit）**	**776**	**246**

其　中　of　which					
新北区 Xinbei District	天宁区 Tianning District	钟楼区 Zhonglou District	戚墅堰区 Qishuyan District	溧阳市 Liyang City	金坛市 Jintan City
19.93				77.62	37.84
123.88				134.78	112.10
9.13				64.93	33.22
18.47				77.62	42.98
19.93				67.476	36.144
0.15				44.01	26.70
13756	33054	96645	15142	415506	182693
9761	6		89	22961	22506
6890	5		54	14932	11109
350			12	1445	26
421			11	372	43
2100	1		12	6212	11328
445			2	1390	850
220	3		6	972	685
120	1		2	447	206
392	26		28	4205	815
2511			24	9231	4975
115	**34**	**41**	**9**	**175**	**156**
115	**34**	**41**	**9**	**175**	**156**

10-11　分地区农村基本情况（2012 年底）
FUNDAMENTAL CONDITION OF VILLAGE BY REGION（END OF 2012）

指 标	Item	全 市 Whole Municipality	武进区 Wujin District
农村基层组织情况（个）	**Village Units （unit）**		
镇政府	Town Governments	37	14
村民委员会	Number of Villagers' Committees	776	246
村民小组	Villager Group	16510	6579
乡村户数、人口	**Households and Rural Population**		
乡村总户数（万户）	Number of Households （10000 households）	76.17	24.35
乡村总人口（万人）	Rural Population （10000 persons）	230.98	75.66
乡村实有从业人员数（万人）	**Number of Rural Laborers （10000 persons）**	**129.93**	**43.91**
按性别分	**Grouped by Sex**		
男劳动力	Male	68.55	22.8
女劳动力	Female	61.38	21.11
按行业分	**Grouped by Sector**		
农林牧渔业	Farming, Forestry, Animal Husbandry and Fishery	25.36	8.98
# 种植业	Planting	19.90	7.46
工　业	Industry	57.61	22.17
建筑业	Construction	17.28	2.26
交通运输、仓储和邮政业	Transport,Storage and Post	5.36	1.68
信息传输、软件和信息技术服务业	Information Transmission, Software and IT Services Industry	0.54	0.12
批发和零售业	Wholesale and Retail Trade	6.78	1.99
住宿和餐饮业	Accommodation and Catering Services	2.64	0.62
金融保险业	Banking and Insurance	0.83	0.15
房地产、社会服务业	Real Estate and Social Services	1.49	0.75
卫生、体育和社会福利业	Health Care, Sporting and Social Welfare	0.60	0.14
教育、文化艺术和广电业	Culture, Education and Arts,Radio, Film and Television	0.62	0.19
科研和综合技术服务业	Scientific Research and Polytechnical Services	0.21	0.04
乡经济组织管理业	Rural Economic Management	0.32	0.07
其他行业	Others	10.29	4.75

其　中　of　which					
新北区 Xinbei District	天宁区 Tianning District	钟楼区 Zhonglou District	戚墅堰区 Qishuyan District	溧阳市 Liyang City	金坛市 Jintan City
6				10	7
115	34	41	9	175	156
2512	180	509	219	4932	1579
10.58	2.32	3.65	1.00	20.10	14.17
37.00	7.70	10.52	2.99	60.83	36.28
20.67	**5.33**	**5.70**	**2.00**	**31.99**	**20.33**
10.86	2.73	2.93	1.07	16.74	11.42
9.81	2.60	2.77	0.93	15.25	8.91
2.42	0.05	0.02	0.11	8.37	5.41
2.15	0.04		0.07	6.09	4.09
11.25	4.15	3.11	1.26	8.62	7.05
1.31	0.11	0.11	0.12	8.99	4.38
0.70	0.14	0.16	0.04	1.77	0.87
0.11	0.06	0.06	0.01	0.05	0.13
1.13	0.30	0.57	0.12	1.76	0.91
0.40	0.24	0.14	0.08	0.71	0.45
0.13	0.06	0.06	0.05	0.33	0.05
0.14	0.08	0.06	0.09	0.21	0.16
0.11	0.04	0.08	0.01	0.14	0.08
0.15	0.03	0.05	0.01	0.12	0.07
0.01	0.01	0.01		0.09	0.05
0.05	0.02	0.05	0.01	0.07	0.05
2.76	0.04	1.22	0.09	0.76	0.67

10-12　分地区农林牧渔业总产值（2012 年）
OUTPUT VALUE OF FARMING, FORESTRY, ANIMAL HUSBANDRY AND FISHERY BY REGION（2012）

指　标	Item	全　市 Whole Municipality	武进区 Wujin District
总　计	**Total**	**2195768**	**741072**
农业产值	**Output Value of Farming**	**1208173**	**456997**
谷物及其他作物	Grain and Other Crop	362647	52245
蔬菜园艺作物	Vegetable and Horticultural Crop	613538	332333
水果、坚果、饮料和香料作物	Fruit, Nut, Beverage and Aromatic Crop	231482	72419
林业产值	**Output Value of Forestry**	**15503**	**1561**
林木培养和种植	Forest Cultivation and Planting	7741	1505
林产品	Forest Products	1364	
竹木采运	Bamboo and Wood Cuttingand Transportation	6398	56
牧业产值	**Output Value of Animal Husbandry**	**342447**	**119207**
牲　畜	Livestock	14046	2824
家　禽	Poultry	201759	69439
猪的饲养	Pig Breeding	121310	46139
捕　猎	Hunting	168	
其它畜牧业	Others	5164	805
渔业产值	**Output Value of Fishery**	**523982**	**120796**
内陆水域产品	Lnland Waters Aquatic Products	523982	120796
#养　殖	Artificial Culture	456254	86175
#贝　类	Shellfish	4366	344
其　他	Others	6559	2072
农林牧渔服务业	**Services**	**105663**	**42511**

单位：万元（10000 yuan）

其中 of which					
新北区 Xinbei District	天宁区 Tianning District	钟楼区 Zhonglou District	戚墅堰区 Qishuyan District	溧阳市 Liyang City	金坛市 Jintan City
232925	**1091**	**4200**	**523**	**697525**	**518432**
143900	**959**		**523**	**380759**	**225035**
42013			286	178081	90022
95960	959		237	84386	99663
5927				118108	35028
1290				**9396**	**3256**
1032				3091	2113
26				624	714
232				5681	429
41728		**4200**		**67533**	**109779**
1088		4200		3798	2136
17926				35724	78670
21570				26251	27350
					168
1144				1760	1455
35918	**132**			**214727**	**152409**
35918	132			214727	152409
31849				208499	129731
1317				1097	1608
1430				162	2895
10089				**25110**	**27953**

10-13 农林牧渔业增加值（2012 年）
VALUE ADDED OF FARMING, FORESTRY, ANIMAL HUSBANDARY AND FISHERY（2012）

指 标	Item	总产值（万元）Gross Output Value（10000 yuan）	其中 of which 中间消耗 Depreciation	增加值 Value-Added	增加值率（%）Value-adding Rate（%）
总 计	**Total**	**2195768**	**932095**	**1263673**	**57.5**
农 业	Farming	1208173	426012	782161	64.7
林 业	Forestry	15503	7686	7817	50.4
牧 业	Animal Husbandry	342447	219267	123180	36.0
渔 业	Fishery	523982	242032	281950	53.8
农林牧渔服务业	Services	105663	37098	68565	64.9

10-14 分地区农林牧渔业增加值（2012 年）
VALUE ADDED OF FARMING, FORESTRY, ANIMAL HUSBANDARY AND FISHERY BY REGION（2012）

单位：万元（10000 yuan）

地 区	Region	增加值 Value-Added	其中 of which 农 业 Farming	林 业 Forestry	牧 业 Animal Husbandry	渔 业 Fishery	农林牧渔服务业 Services
全 市	**Whole Municipality**	**1263673**	**782161**	**7817**	**123180**	**281950**	**68565**
市 区	Urban Area	597001	404792	1781	65356	91161	33911
武进区	Wujin District	460709	311111	1003	48812	71442	28341
新北区	New District	134091	92851	778	15201	19691	5570
天宁区	Tianning District	618	590			28	
钟楼区	Zhonglou District	1343			1343		
戚墅堰区	Qishuyan District	240	240				
溧阳市	Liyang City	390237	236089	3711	22282	110557	17598
金坛市	Jintan City	276435	141280	2325	35542	80232	17056

10-15 分地区农业机械拥有情况（2012 年底）
POSSESSION OF AGRICULTURAL MACHINERY BY REGION（END OF 2012）

指 标	Item	全 市 Whole Municipality	其中 of which 武进区 Wujin District	新北区 Xinbei District	溧阳市 Liyang City	金坛市 Jintan City
农业机械总动力（万千瓦）	**Total Power of Agricultural Machinery（10000 kw）**	**158.54**	**54.43**	**10.28**	**52.64**	**41.18**
拖拉机及配套机械	**Tractors and Subsidiary Machinery**					
大中型拖拉机（台）	Large and Medium Tractors（unit）	2780	1095	335	815	535
#轮式拖拉机	Roller Tractors	2780	1095	335	815	535
小型拖拉机（台）	Mini-tractors（unit）	20285	5123	1625	8150	5387
种植业机械	**Machinery of Farm Production**					
机引犁（台）	Trailed Tractor Plow（unit）	13404	3816	698	6162	2728
农用排灌动力机械（台）	Machinery for Agricultural Drainage and Irrigation（unit）	26401	5657	1052	13570	6122
机动喷雾（粉）机（台）	Motorized Duster（unit）	16899	3671	1534	6650	5044
联合收割机（台）	Combined Harvesters（unit）	1901	917	179	437	368
机动脱粒机（台）	Threshing and Drying Machine（unit）	41414	26535	2977	2232	9670
农副产品加工机械	**Machinery of Agricultural and Sideline Products Processing**					
农副产品加工动力（台）	Machinery of Agricultural and Sideline Products Processing（unit）	13476	2271	869	4332	6004
#柴油机	Diesel Engines	2460	372	219	736	1133
电动机	Motor	10469	1899	650	3049	4871
农副产品加工作业机械（台）	Operation Machinery of Agricultural and Sideline Products Processing（unit）	10228	2271	869	3806	3282
畜牧业机械	**Machinery of Livestock Husbandry**					
饲料粉碎机（台）	Fodder Grinder（unit）	2898	1111	820	395	572
林果机械（台）	**Forestry and Fruit Industry Machinery（unit）**	**139**	**43**		**28**	**68**
渔业机械（台）	**Machinery of Fishery（unit）**	**59516**	**20683**	**1746**	**27376**	**9711**
农田基本建设机械（台）	**Machinery of Farmland Fundamental Construction（unit）**	**5821**	**357**	**163**	**4819**	**482**

10-16 分地区农村经济收益分配（2012 年）
RURAL ECONOMIC PROFIT DISTRIBUTION BY REGION（2012）

指 标	Item	全 市 Whole Municipality	武进区 Wujin District
经济总收入	**Total Economic Income**	**90118136**	**37294434**
农 业	Agriculture	1024060	379074
# 种植业	Planting	986177	379065
林 业	Forestry	38726	1488
牧 业	Animal Husbandry	404927	126879
渔 业	Fishery	596737	162384
工 业	Industry	78337691	34372612
建筑业	Construction	3219600	598338
运输业	Transportation	673514	311671
贸易餐饮业	Trade and Catering Services	2003046	710044
服务业	Services	1009577	275089
其 他	Other Income	2810258	356856
经济总费用	**Total Economic Expenses**	**75802480**	**32621943**
# 生产费用	Production Expenses	63084362	28422771
管理费用	Management Expenses	7770841	2927560
经济净收入	**Net Economic Income**	**14315656**	**4672491**
投资收益	**Profit from Investment**	**39370**	**1994**
农民外出劳务收入	**Labor Service Income of Farmers from Outside**	**530201**	**98301**
可分配收入总额	**Total Disposable Income**	**14885228**	**4772785**
国家税金	State Tax	2868961	1144544
上交有关部门	Turn Over to Relevant Departments	990148	561144
外来投资分利	Bonus of Investment from Outside	477541	66103
外来人员带走劳务收入	Labor Service Payment to Persons from Outside	1684884	579082
企业各项留利	Reserved by Enterprises	4811350	887109
乡村集体所得	Earnings of Town and Township Collective	276541	135509
农民经营所得	Farmers' Eargings	3775802	1399294
农民从集体再分配收入	**Redistributed Earnings to Farmers from Collectives**	**282195**	**191813**
农民所得	**Farmers' Earnings**	**4057998**	**1591107**
每人平均（元）	Per Capita （yuan）	17450	17900

单位：万元（10000 yuan）

其中 of which					
新北区 Xinbei District	天宁区 Tianning District	钟楼区 Zhonglou District	戚墅堰区 Qishuyan District	溧阳市 Liyang City	金坛市 Jintan City
18243507	**979586**	**5370028**	**2256728**	**17950298**	**8023555**
51748	510		1226	303817	287684
46898	330		927	285191	273766
3847			10	13478	19903
32185			144	97835	147884
16625			411	186092	231224
15392038	458690	5160057	2180346	14733765	6040184
82651	55263	1	14351	1888039	580957
57606	990	4803	6488	145037	146919
567887	98560	148515	29046	157670	291325
66613	82210	7152	11539	360026	206948
1972306	283363	49500	13167	64539	70526
15456654	**880650**	**3238919**	**1887071**	**15032745**	**6684497**
12671090	597620	2817846	1252948	12775011	4547076
1374717	253120	421055	268306	1897953	628130
2786853	**98936**	**2131109**	**369657**	**2917553**	**1339058**
10534	**2256**	**1800**	**681**	**20045**	**2061**
115981	**1456**	**1501**	**5272**	**116845**	**190845**
2913368	**102648**	**2134410**	**375610**	**3054443**	**1531963**
563754	19578	75455	134990	597173	333468
101859	17463	2800	15026	206625	85230
75589	2560	4002	3613	269684	55990
515397	25104		35218	364372	165710
934195	18543	1967140	122718	604054	277591
74817	3900	1500	32500	21106	7210
647758	15500	83513	31545	991429	606763
34027	**4985**	**552**	**4371**	**42694**	**3754**
681784	**20485**	**84065**	**35916**	**1034123**	**610517**
17168	14632	17340	18706	17380	16829

10-17 分地区农作物播种面积（2012 年）
SOWN AREA OF FARM CROPS BY REGION（2012）

单位：千公顷（1000 hectares）

指 标	Item	全 市 Whole Municipality	其 中 of which 武进区 Wujin District	新北区 Xinbei District	天宁区 Tianning District	戚墅堰区 Qishuyan District	溧阳市 Liyang City	金坛市 Jintan City
农作物总播种面积	**Total Sown Area**	**226.37**	**47.72**	**26.51**	**0.11**	**0.28**	**95.03**	**56.73**
粮食作物	**Grain Crops**	**155.65**	**24.40**	**21.04**		**0.13**	**70.67**	**39.41**
夏收粮食	Summer Grain	63.80	10.44	10.27			26.46	16.63
谷 物	Cereal	62.01	10.21	10.17			25.46	16.17
小 麦	Wheat	61.53	10.14	9.92			25.46	16.01
元 麦	Hullless Barley	0.30	0.06	0.24				
大 麦	Barley	0.18	0.01	0.01				0.16
秋收粮食	Autumn Grain	91.85	13.96	10.77		0.13	44.21	22.78
谷 物	Autumn Cereal	84.83	12.73	9.78		0.13	41.64	20.55
#稻 谷	Rice	82.89	12.68	9.70		0.13	40.28	20.10
单季晚稻	Single Harvest Late Rice	82.89	12.68	9.70		0.13	40.28	20.10
其他谷物	Other cereals	0.04		0.04				
玉 米	Corn	1.90	0.05	0.04			1.36	0.45
豆 类	Beans	4.63	0.88	0.74			1.52	1.49
#大 豆	Soybeans	4.15	0.86	0.72			1.21	1.36
薯 类	Tubers	2.39	0.35	0.35		0.03	1.05	0.74
油 料	**Oil-bearing Crops**	**17.23**	**0.89**	**0.71**		**0.03**	**11.52**	**4.08**
#油菜籽	Rapeseeds	15.67	0.78	0.63			10.60	3.63
棉 花	**Cotton**	**0.57**					**0.55**	**0.02**
麻 类	**Fiber Crops**	**0.01**						**0.01**
糖 料	**Sugar Crops**	**0.08**		**0.01**			**0.06**	**0.01**
药 材	**Crude Drugs**	**0.11**				**0.12**	**0.03**	**0.08**
蔬 菜	**Vegetable**	**27.42**	**9.64**	**3.45**	**0.11**		**8.43**	**5.68**
瓜果类	**Melon Crops**	**3.54**	**0.72**	**0.18**			**2.07**	**0.57**
其他农作物	**Other Farm Crops**	**21.76**	**12.07**	**1.12**			**1.70**	**6.87**
#青饲料	Green Fodder	1.87	0.26	0.10			0.84	0.67
绿 肥	Green Manure	1.26	0.04				0.64	0.58

10-18 分地区农产品总产量（2012 年）
TOTAL YIELD OF FARM CROPS BY REGION（2012）

单位：吨（ton）

指标	Item	全市 Whole Municipality	其中 of which 武进区 Wujin District	新北区 Xinbei District	戚墅堰区 Qishuyan District	溧阳市 Liyang City	金坛市 Jintan City
粮食作物	**Grain Crops**	**1147972**	**174442**	**144584**	**1086**	**545243**	**282617**
夏收粮食	Summer Grain	317928	47909	49101		138467	82451
谷　物	Cereal	313875	47404	48925		136116	81430
小　麦	Wheat	312160	47142	48179		136117	80722
元　麦	Hullless Barley	963	245	718			
大　麦	Barley	753	17	28			708
秋收粮食	Autumn Grain	830044	126533	95483	1086	406775	200167
谷　物	Cereal	801580	121959	92184	1086	393384	192967
#稻　谷	Rice	787958	121655	91530	1086	383139	190548
玉　米	Corn	13332	304	364		10245	2419
豆　类	Beans	13613	2861	1762		5500	3490
#大　豆	Soybeans	12222	2797	1730		4546	3149
薯　类	Tubers	14851	1713	1537		7892	3709
油　料	**Oil-bearing Crops**	**37684**	**1784**	**1387**	**57**	**25847**	**8609**
#油菜籽	Rapeseeds	34417	1580	1244	57	23804	7732
棉　花	**Cotton**	**493**				**470**	**23**
麻　类	**Fiber Crops**	**28**					**28**
糖　料	**Sugar Crops**	**5051**		**700**		**4320**	**31**

10-19　分地区农产品单产（2012 年）
YIELD OF FARM CROPS PER HECTARE BY REGION（2012）

单位：公斤 / 公顷（kg/hectare）

指 标	Item	全 市 Whole Municipality	其中 of which 武进区 Wujin District	新北区 Xinbei District	戚墅堰区 Qishuyan District	溧阳市 Liyang City	金坛市 Jintan City
粮食作物	**Grain Crops**	**7375**	**7149**	**6872**	**8354**	**7715**	**7171**
夏收粮食	Summer Grain	4983	4589	4781		5233	4958
谷 物	Cereal	5062	4643	4811		5346	5036
小 麦	Wheat	5073	4649	4857		5346	5042
元 麦	Hullless Barley	3210	4083	2992			
大 麦	Barley	4183	1275	2100			4425
秋收粮食	Autumn Grain	9037	9064	8866	8354	9201	8787
谷 物	Cereal	9449	9580	9426	8354	9447	9390
#稻 谷	Rice	9506	9594	9436	8354	9512	9480
玉 米	Corn	7017	6079	9106		7533	5376
豆 类	Beans	2940	3252	2380		3619	2342
#大 豆	Soybeans	2945	3252	2403		3757	2315
薯 类	Tubers	6214	4894	6148		7516	5013
油 料	**Oil-bearing Crops**	**2187**	**2004**	**1954**	**1900**	**2244**	**2110**
# 油菜籽	Rapeseeds	2196	2026	1975	190	2246	2130
棉 花	**Cotton**	**865**				**855**	**1150**
麻 类	**Fiber Crops**	**2800**					**2800**
糖 料	**Sugar Crops**	**63138**		**70000**		**72000**	**3100**

10-20 分地区畜牧业生产情况（2012 年）
STATISTICS ON LIVESTOCK HUSBANDRY BY REGION（2012）

指标	Item	全市 Whole Municipality	其中 of which 武进区 Wujin District	新北区 Xinbei District	钟楼区 Zhonglou District	溧阳市 Liyang City	金坛市 Jintan City
当年出栏数	**Slaughtered Livestock of the Year**						
牛（头）	Cattle and Buffaloes（head）	800		300		100	400
猪（万头）	Hogs（10000 heads）	88.58	32.31	15.00		18.74	22.53
羊（万只）	Sheep and Goats（10000 heads）	10.88	0.65	0.90		5.78	3.55
家禽（万只）	Poultry（10000 heads）	4941.33	1945.64	305.00		627.00	2063.69
年末存栏数	**Livestock Being Raised at Year-end**						
牛（头）	Cattle and Buffaloes（head）	6300	3100		2100	900	200
猪（万头）	Hogs（10000 heads）	49.40	18.12	6.80		7.60	16.80
羊（万只）	Sheep and Goats（10000 heads）	5.74	0.23	0.30		1.48	3.73
# 山羊	Goats	5.74	0.23	0.30		1.48	3.73
家禽（万只）	Poultry（10000 heads）	1261.46	429.70	91.60		256.00	484.16
产量	**Output**						
肉类（吨）	Meat（ton）	143203	53887	19100		24481	45735
#猪牛羊肉	Pork,Beef and Mutton	68167	22715	15200		13715	16537
牛肉	Beef	342				19	305
猪肉	Pork	66540	22617	15105		13118	15700
羊肉	Mutton	1303	98	95		578	532
禽肉	Poultry	74534	31130	3900		10405	29099
牛奶（吨）	Cow Milk（ton）	24005	9843	1250	12000	912	
蜂蜜（吨）	Honey（ton）	164	106			54	4
禽蛋（吨）	Poultry Eggs（ton）	33565	5697	4100		13572	10196

10-21　分地区林业、蚕茧、茶叶、水果生产情况（2012 年）
STATISTICS ON FORESTRY, SILKWORM COCOONS, TEA AND FRUITS BY REGION（2012）

指　标	Item	全　市 Whole Municipality	其中 of which 武进区 Wujin District	新北区 Xinbei District	戚墅堰区 Qishuyan District	溧阳市 Liyang City	金坛市 Jintan City
林　业	**Forestry**						
当年造林面积（公顷）	Forestation Area at Current Year（hectare）	4479	1091	1346		1202	840
木材产量（立方米）	Output of Timber（cu.m）	3699	75	17		2919	688
蚕　桑	**Silkworm Cocoons and Mulberry**						
年末桑园面积（公顷）	Mulberry Field Area at Year-en（hectare）	1033				667	367
蚕茧产量（吨）	Output of Silkworm Cocoons（ton）	469				246	223
茶　叶	**Tea**						
年末茶园面积（公顷）	Tea Field Area at Year-end（hectare）	7895	257			4885	2753
茶叶产量（吨）	Output of Tea（ton）	3502	107			1990	1405
# 红毛茶	Black Tea	8				3	5
绿毛茶	Green Tea	3493	107			1987	1399
其它茶	Other Tea	1					1
水　果	**Fruits**						
年末果园面积（公顷）	Area of Orchards at Year-end（hectare）	11892	4278	387		5729	1499
# 桃　园	Peaches	2050	1010	36		717	287
板栗园	Chinese chestnuts	4047				3913	133
梨　园	Pears	1186	592	109	7	291	187
葡萄园	Grapes	3021	2083	131	10	157	640
水果产量（吨）	Output of Fruits（ton）	117431	67976	7383	392	21890	19790
# 桃	Peaches	27226	17587	779		4060	4800
板　栗	Chinese chestnuts	3280				2730	550
梨	Pears	22155	11444	2476	140	5795	2300
葡　萄	Grapes	46983	34438	2263	252	2170	7860

10-22 分地区淡水产品生产情况（2012 年）
STATISTICS ON FRESHWATER AQUATIC PRODUCTS BY REGION（2012）

指标	Item	全市 Whole Municipality	其中 of which 武进区 Wujin District	新北区 Xinbei District	天宁区 Tianning District	钟楼区 Tianning District	戚墅堰区 Qishuyan District	溧阳市 Liyang City	金坛市 Jintan City
淡水产品产量（吨）	**Output of Freshwater Aquatic Products（ton）**	**181240**	**60503**	**8369**	**100**	**112**	**100**	**67400**	**44656**
#鱼　类	Fish	131733	51479	7992	100	112	35	50584	21431
#青　鱼	Mackerel	8025	5708	790	5	9	1	1170	342
草　鱼	Grass Carp	20404	7018	2198	10	24	11	8155	2988
鲢　鱼	Silver Carp	20768	7580	2186	20	17	8	5447	5510
鲫　鱼	Crucian	27811	5144	1260	15	21	5	16156	5210
鳊　鱼	Bream	29590	18949	741	30	23	3	6565	3279
鳜　鱼	Mandarin Fish	1208	310	28				250	620
甲壳类	Crustacean	38268	4369	114				14172	19613
#河　蟹	River Crabs	27430	3567	38				9336	14489
青　虾	Shrimps	10578	788	22				4720	5048
鳖	Soft-shelled Turtle	1054	336	70				160	488
珍　珠	Pearl	26000						4000	22000
淡水养殖面积（公顷）	**Freshwater Raise Areas（hectares）**	**39277**	**8333**	**1167**	**14**	**12**	**25**	**13726**	**16000**
#特种养殖	Special Species Breeding	26022	3472	240				10285	12025
#池　塘	Pond	34093	7487	967	14	12		13072	12541
湖　泊	Lake	3024	724					654	1646
水　库	Reservoir	533							533
河　沟	Brook	1627	122	200			25		1280

10-23 分镇、街道基本情况（2012 年）
BASIC STATISTICS ON TOWNS AND SUBDISTRICTS（2012）

镇、街道	Towhs and Subdistricts	总户数（户）Total Households（Household）	总人口（人）Total Population（person）	从业人员（人）Employment（person）	年底耕地面积（公顷）Cultivated Area Year-end（hectare）	农业机械总动力（千瓦）Total Agricultural Machinery Power（kw）	地区生产总值（万元）Gross Domestic Product（10000 yuan）
武进区	**Wujin District**						
湖塘镇	Hutang Town	95203	270377	123859	94	2068	1819337
牛塘镇	Niutang Town	25395	81529	39905	543	5891	894066
洛阳镇	Luoyang Town	27339	88346	55560	1761	23828	814299
遥观镇	Yaoguan Town	36204	107238	59933	704	9108	1168907
横林镇	Henglin Town	28850	93108	49271	912	17387	868215
横山桥镇	Hengshanqiao Town	29138	86186	55320	1238	27448	1082933
郑陆镇	Zhenlu Town	40691	117220	41737	2759	38687	904937
雪堰镇	Xueyan Town	35125	98661	42850	3310	74069	693397
前黄镇	Qianhuang Town	26090	83941	37392	3521	84452	565482
礼嘉镇	Lijia Town	16350	58480	31250	2269	47560	659042
邹区镇	Zhouqu Town	32244	93164	45886	2415	56740	1015314
嘉泽镇	Jiaze Town	29024	86861	52116	4587	41226	531149
湟里镇	Huangli Town	28217	75961	40235	3525	36402	923888
奔牛镇	Benniu Town	20154	66156	32877	2514	24153	448309
新北区	**Xinbei District**						
龙虎塘街道	Longhutang Subdistrict	8725	36239	27043	61	90	646129
春江镇	Chunjiang Town	42879	154705	63323	4352	25229	2063214
新桥镇	Xinqiao Town	8046	30321	12219	647	9846	283222
薛家镇	Xuejia Town	13436	46821	22455	450	7800	640500
罗溪镇	Luoxi Town	15259	52453	25115	2045	20233	490800
西夏墅镇	Xixiashu Town	16910	56065	20560	2515	18140	282500
孟河镇	Menghe Town	23555	92360	44723	3748	18756	521017
三井街道	Sanjin Town	10315	43007	34007			1058000
天宁区	**Tianning District**						
雕庄街道	Diaozhuang Subdistrict	11217	35014	25296		64	1502769
青龙街道	Qinlong Subdistrict	11923	40120	28048	280	276	733895

其中 of which 第一产业 Primary Industry	第二产业 Secondary Industry	第三产业 Tertiary Industry	乡镇企业营业收入总额（万元） Total Business Income of Township Enterprises（10000 yuan）	其中 of which #乡镇企业净利润总额 Total Net Profit of Township Enterprises	出口产品交货额 Transaction Volume of Exported Products	粮食总产量（吨） Total Output of Grain（ton）	乡镇财政收入（万元） Fiscal Revenue of Town and Township（10000 yuan）	储蓄存款余额（万元） Balance of Savings Deposits（10000 yuan）	农民人均纯收入（元） Per Capita Net Income of Rural Resident（yuan）
1614	905924	911799	3578037	105102	51967	129	266158	1760503	19056
12731	553165	328170	3142216	59639	26041	653	58200	289688	18049
17058	582869	214372	2555322	114601	22413	8885	49527	276025	18765
4238	897563	267106	4350100	293871	104501	4454	120687	193381	18417
5573	527547	335095	2772178	85643	94461	5201	63342	507977	17809
10594	620156	452183	2874855	120744	19588	7659	57619	303349	18573
61296	452519	391122	1871986	80983	28241	19489	75279	320163	16958
32953	320930	339514	1492752	58510	10630	26176	70472	294635	18262
58085	229888	277509	1279840	39594	10489	38916	32648	289455	17598
21624	384631	252787	1800553	85520	43556	19681	43100	232500	17905
20371	391614	603329	1474430	50788	21029	3567	69002	333971	17402
75049	151565	304535	451179	8867	2651	131	25624	287733	18018
45564	500569	377755	2500116	64225	10907	1057	41496	125920	18168
16901	195799	235609	917729	14265	3251.1	26237	37178	38321	17551
194	400892	245043	4950323	86443	307237		52405	72841	19000
51611	1690360	321243	9606123	271132	112711	46068	159357	48225	17511
5677	186745	90800	825985	61805	104320	6533	63452	67214	19203
5400	514500	120600	2603000	73819	44824	4891	108575	134000	18978
17000	343600	130200	1472942	55143	6650	18270	37388	102142	17150
7500	205000	70000	851163	32677	12206	24796	45412	145000	14698
34070	335921	151026	1370681	909652	6602.01	44795	48262	319430	16298
	593000	465000	2946156	164857	80700		178822	161645	20100
	774922	727847	7975900	158936	35273.34		116985	30234	14160
618	499290	233987	3052450	94108	46600		162139	59560	14682

10-23　续表　Continued

镇、街道	Towns and Subdistricts	总户数（户） Total Households (Household)	总人口（人） Total Population (person)	从业人员（人） Employment (person)	年底耕地面积（公顷） Cultivated Area Year-end (hectare)	农业机械总动力（千瓦） Total Agricultural Machinery Power (kw)	地区生产总值（万元） Gross Domestic Product (10000 yuan)
钟楼区	**Zhonglou District**						
新闸镇	Xinzha Town	8090	31620	19879			849195
五星街道	Wuxing Subdistrict	21076	69795	45627			399736
永红街道	Yonghong Subdistrict	8915	37152	18222			288120
北港街道	Beigang Subdistrict	6550	19490	10769			20502
西林街道	Xilin Subdistrict	8436	23001	14473		11135	211782
戚墅堰区	**Qishuyan District**						
丁堰镇	Dingyan Town	5379	26473	17427	132	1950	234695
潞城镇	Lucheng Town	7239	30127	19789	268	364	382643
溧阳市	**Liyang City**						
溧城镇	Licheng Town	112307	333785	173568	5606	24816	2479889
埭头镇	Litou Town	9244	27664	19230	2006	22605	244572
上黄镇	Shanghuang Town	8876	26248	13243	2122	320	208629
戴埠镇	Daibu Town	19464	52188	31620	3684	24000	227001
天目湖镇	Tianmuhu Town	23059	73211	34618	5705	41811	333207
别桥镇	Bieqiao Town	23794	70052	44678	6554	60157	275963
上兴镇	Shangxing Town	27004	79525	37725	9722	63380	408100
竹箦镇	Zhuze Town	21483	62577	32614	6762	45260	205005
南渡镇	Nandu Town	25730	75892	39719	6784	58260	288972
社渚镇	Shezhu Town	23170	72578	40082	7866	61238	419556
金坛市	**Jintan City**						
金城镇	Jincheng Town	69128	187708	149478	6669	101856	1118300
直溪镇	zhixi Town	23280	58787	40992	4285	45851	381047
朱林镇	Zhulin Town	14560	37799	26153	3410	31628	183509
薛埠镇	Xuebu Town	26040	67623	47160	6494	86327	291600
指前镇	Zhiqian Town	15098	41469	24836	3051	36392	135200
儒林镇	Rulin Town	13465	34406	17137	1580	42500	182600
尧塘镇	Yaoyang Town	22079	57877	42563	3429	55000	266000
开发区	Development Zone	25790	67445	50535	2343	12266	884000

其中 of which			乡镇企业营业收入总额（万元）Total Business Income of Township Enterprises (10000 yuan)	其中 of which		粮食总产量（吨）Total Output of Grain (ton)	乡镇财政收入（万元）Fiscal Revenue of Town and Township (10000 yuan)	储蓄存款余额（万元）Balance of Savings Deposits (10000 yuan)	农民人均纯收入（元）Per Capita Net Income of Rural Resident (yuan)
第一产业 Primary Industry	第二产业 Secondary Industry	第三产业 Tertiary Industry		#乡镇企业净利润总额 Total Net Profit of Township Enterprises	出口产品交货额 Transaction Volume of Exported Products				
	748974	100221	3661000	188161	15928		59723	1548	17423
	231726	168010	1557936	45823	27499.9		70726	123182	16767
	133145	154975	588202	55102	17680		42057		16650
	12078	8424	405701	15421			105343	41056	16651
	133522	78260	752655	19773	3387		25481	70394	15782
182	183279	51234	840346	69690	25700	221	53143	15561	15704
131	288626	93886	1340557	83553	13400	826	72549	13715	13502
51198	1703414	725277	13176244	513874	50201	49481	196881	251390	20448
12215	200182	32175	659622	29909		18441	30607	56049	18713
35430	95683	77516	374974	18159	1013	15516	19947	59600	20644
28185	107815	91001	820173	6345	1416	28306	27084	40200	16474
32434	170627	130146	845632	52153	10194	33068	51752	160800	18606
43178	137488	95297	546781	22674	15836	56703	18647	50942	15346
38433	248457	121210	1015711	123471	15688	103461	33205	78388	15813
31735	100280	72990	421094	18988	1886	61852	26766	96822	16068
32075	144654	112243	455695	34177	6466	71688	32348	35685	16965
42106	228643	148807	831770	109354	1701	105559	30128	141994	15754
66600	556500	495200	1308536	90753	26177	62970	117644	1725308	19928
35598	212549	132900	825137	106935	26000	48422	21776	118275	18508
25909	124100	33500	448074	59024	4297	34901	12063	74500	16640
42200	118700	130700	387281	42469	2788	44878	80652	84520	18210
30300	74400	30500	311850	36283	2550	33692	15969	55290	16529
30000	95900	56700	300753	27988	2400	13262	17906	56300	17202
33200	193800	39000	610000	1800	17250	25037	29389	124330	18268
7929	632269	243802	2764628	184408	37655	19455	196906	36304	16545

11

CHAPTER 11

工 业

INDUSTRY

常州统计年鉴

11 工 业
INDUSTRY

2012年主要统计指标
MAJOR STATISTICAL INDICATORS OF 2012

规模以上工业总产值	Total Output Value of Industry above Designated Size	8970.3 亿元	(100 million yuan)
规模以上工业主营业务收入	Main Business Income of Industrial above Designated Size	9097.95 亿元	(100 million yuan)
规模以上工业实现利税	Profits and Taxes of Industry above Designated Size	730.3 亿元	(100 million yuan)
规模以上工业实现利润	Profit of Industry above Designated Size	443.77 亿元	(100 million yuan)
规模以上工业总资产	Total Industrial Assets above Designated Size	6754.38 亿元	(100 million yuan)

11-1 历年工业生产发展指数
INDICES OF GROSS INDUSTRIAL OUTPUT OVER THE YEARS

按可比价计算 1949=100　　Calculated by comparable price: 1949=100

年 份 Year	全 市 Whole Municipality	其中 of which #市 区 Urban Area	年 份 Year	全 市 Whole Municipality	其中 of which #市 区 Urban Area
1949	100.0	100.0	1981	4887.2	4765.6
1950	145.5	148.1	1982	5206.0	5023.9
1951	181.0	184.8	1983	5916.3	5712.2
1952	231.0	235.1	1984	7092.8	6745.8
1953	281.9	288.4	1985	9357.8	8807.2
1954	293.3	297.0	1986	10410.6	9688.6
1955	260.0	260.4	1987	12618.2	11457.3
1956	337.0	334.2	1988	15683.8	13769.0
1957	325.0	315.8	1989	16677.0	14582.2
1958	585.6	589.7	1990	18500.8	16280.5
1959	756.8	749.3	1991	21422.5	18847.3
1960	824.6	825.9	1992	27496.4	24117.3
1961	496.2	497.0	1993	38501.3	32980.7
1962	387.5	379.6	1994	47311.0	39967.6
1963	383.8	373.3	1995	53542.2	45391.8
1964	483.5	472.8	1996	64109.9	52915.2
1965	614.8	603.8	1997	63557.5	54208.9
1966	737.3	729.0	1998	61998.0	52938.4
1967	567.9	539.7	1999	69415.3	59018.4
1968	659.3	642.4	2000	76647.0	64689.3
1969	872.2	872.6	2001	86446.1	72835.6
1970	1161.9	1163.6	2002	102096.2	86752.5
1971	1431.8	1411.5	2003	130391.2	111681.7
1972	1667.0	1645.5	2004	146677.1	126836.9
1973	1963.5	1923.5	2005	178762.5	151521.9
1974	2047.4	2021.0	2006	219517.7	191379.5
1975	2305.4	2276.4	2007	266849.7	232001.2
1976	2531.8	2495.3	2008	292010.9	251498.2
1977	2890.9	2836.1	2009	358518.1	312735.6
1978	3208.7	3146.5	2010	329998.3	287947.2
1979	3632.7	3565.9	2011	305683.3	266768.9
1980	4409.7	4287.7	2012	341570.1	300176.0

11-2 规模以上工业企业主要经济指标（1982-2012 年）
MAJOR ECONOMIC INDICATORS OF INDUSTRIAL ENTERPRISES ABOVE DESIGNATED SIZE （1982-2012）

单位：亿元（100 million yuan）

年 份 Year	主营业务收入 Main Business Income of Industrial	利税总额 Total Profits and Taxes	利润总额 Total Profits	固定资产原价 Original Value of Fixed Assets	年 份 Year	主营业务收入 Main Business Income of Industrial	利税总额 Total Profits and Taxes	利润总额 Total Profits	固定资产原价 Original Value of Fixed Assets
1982	45.72	8.53	5.47	20.96	1998	635.22	35.98	8.25	343.40
1983	51.14	9.69	6.47	24.64	1999	718.07	46.05	16.31	378.43
1984	57.68	10.75	7.08	27.87	2000	836.10	59.64	25.44	395.90
1985	75.01	14.14	9.26	33.41	2001	944.65	68.25	31.25	323.00
1986	82.63	12.93	8.10	40.16	2002	1135.55	86.03	45.89	508.89
1987	103.18	14.33	9.07	49.73	2003	1510.77	114.41	65.62	584.71
1988	136.36	17.02	10.48	58.09	2004	2064.71	136.24	82.49	697.26
1989	151.55	15.44	7.99	68.26	2005	2459.56	161.84	96.23	796.70
1990	160.85	13.21	5.26	80.42	2006	3243.79	228.91	142.26	992.68
1991	199.51	11.81	2.58	95.17	2007	4171.08	301.73	188.78	1198.27
1992	264.13	17.80	6.46	115.28	2008	5089.94	371.12	221.44	1370.82
1993	399.13	24.64	9.63	145.96	2009	5868.05	450.07	276.77	1576.26
1994	429.87	25.63	6.22	193.91	2010	7274.88	620.18	413.47	2219.00
1995	542.82	34.65	11.83	252.19	2011	8212.53	713.30	468.43	2485.28
1996	562.96	32.28	8.76	282.65	2012	9097.95	730.30	443.77	3353.34
1997	558.17	31.29	7.69	314.77					

注：1978-1997年规模以上工业口径为乡及乡以上全部独立核算工业企业，1998至2010年为全部国有企业及年销售收入500万元以上工业企业，2012 年为主营业务收入 2000 万元以上的法人工业企业。

Note：During year 1978 and 1997, the scaled industrial caliber involved industrial enterprises with wholly independent accounting;All the "state-owned companies and the industrial enterprises with annual main business income of 5 million yuan and above" cited from 1998 to 2010 has been altered to "corporate industrial enterprises with annual main business income of 20 million yuan and above".

11-3 规模以上工业企业单位数、工业总产值（1998-2012 年）
THE NUMBER AND GROSS OUTPUT VALUE OF INDUSTRIAL ENTERPRISES ABOVE DESIGNATED SIZE （1998-2012）

年 份 Year	企业单位数 （个） Number of Enterprises (unit)	工业总产值 （万元） Gross Industrial Output Value (10000 yuan)	按地区分 Grouped by Region			
			市 区 Urban Area	其 中 of which #武进区 Wujin District	溧阳市 Liyang City	金坛市 Jintan City
1998	2016	6934265	3200874	2584387	683278	465727
1999	2054	7699337	6384288	2894976	772913	542136
2000	2059	8746325	7307378	3238846	871781	567166
2001	2185	10012488	8380690	3730814	990805	640993
2002	2474	11670167	9737547	4025683	1170019	762601
2003	2804	15272769	12705644	5560192	1504701	1062424
2004	4707	21272032	17734014.9	8344588	2062119	1475899
2005	3593	25041903	20323885	9350753	2790052	1927966
2006	4223	32937718	26651563	12775644	3665369	2620786
2007	4768	42539096	33985939	16307805	4950478	3602679
2008	5030	52001203	41229707	20510878	6288701	4482795
2009	6493	59829073	48011691	23980866	7283391	4533991
2010	6375	73960851	58731617	29548158	9326507	5902727
2011	3638	82707703	64466417	32237118	11372284	6869002
2012	3869	89702986	70432514	35590244	13556800	5713673

注：2010年及以前规模以上工业企业为全部国有企业及年销售收入500万元以上工业企业，2011年起规模以上工业企业调整为主营业务收入2000万元以上企业。

Note:Before 2010,industrial enterprises above Designated Size refers to enterprise with main business income above 5 million yuan;Form 2011,industrial enterprises above Designated Sise Refers to enterprise With main business income above 20 million yuan.

按轻重工业分 Grouped by Light and Heavy IndustryGrouped by Light		按经济类型分 Grouped by Economic type			按企业规模分 Grouped by Size of Enterprises		
轻工业 Light Industry	重工业 Heavy Industry	#国有工业 State-owned	集体工业 Collective owned	其他工业 Other Industries	大型企业 Large	中型企业 Medium-sized	小型企业 Small
2804344	4129922	1188513	2091252	3654500	1431178	1808339	3694748
3129671	4569666	1168296	2168551	4362490	1772567	1680778	4245992
3398700	5347625	1014739	1753500	5978086	1826100	1818832	5101393
3936827	6075661	914054	1595517	7502917	2831899	2096893	5083696
4720707	6949460	804912	992787	9872468	3331394	2436048	5902725
5564940	9707829	696256	755597	13820916	2575835	5418160	7278774
7374271	13897762	494034	894936	19883062	1512383	6976498	12783152
7441957	17599946	701147	769236	23571520	3874604	7368895	13798404
9087163	23850555	555090	1030039	31352589	4899288	10188471	17849959
10315119	32223977	712690	1206437	40619969	6157127	13680857	22701112
12069457	39931746	942058	994995	50064150	8427722	16507572	27065909
13102615	46726458	639506	267577	58921990	12657601	19059066	28112406
15965600	57995251	916713	145710	72898428	17429595	23014060	33517196
15478418	67229285	1007972	57972	81641759	29159406	22308844	30915652
19618121	70084865	1398170	56849	88247967	32166130	21069320	35847962

11-4 规模以上工业企业主要经济指标（2012 年）
MAJOR ECONOMIC INDICATORS OF INDUSTRIAL ENTERPRISES ABOVE DESIGNATED SIZE （2012）

指 标	Item	企 业 单位数（个）Number of Enterpr-ises (unit)	其中 of which #亏损企业 Loss-incurring Enter-prises	工 业 总产值 Gross Industrial Output Value
总 计	**Total**	**3869**	**547**	**89702986**
按地区分	**Grouped by Region**			
市 区	Urban Area	3152	376	70432514
武进区	Wujin District	1731	172	35590244
新北区	Xinbei District	853	143	17825180
天宁区	Tianning District	227	28	7048373
钟楼区	Zhonglou District	244	17	7200292
戚墅堰区	Qishuyan District	97	16	2768426
溧阳市	Liyang City	349	75	13556800
金坛市	Jintan City	368	96	5713673
按登记注册类型分	**Grouped by Registration Status**			
内 资	Domestic Investment	3071	365	62222609
国 有	State-owned	22	3	1398170
集 体	Collective-owned	7	1	56849
股份合作	Share-holding Cooperative	18	1	787974
有限责任公司	Limited Liability Corporations	124	27	5059993
股份有限公司	Share-holding Corporations Ltd.	23		1756986
私营及其他	Private and others	2877	333	53162637
港澳台商投资	Investment from Hong Kong, Macao and Taiwan	318	58	9503514
合资经营	Joint-Venture	166	32	4033359
合作经营	Cooperative	11	3	211344
独资经营	Sole Investment	133	21	4405602
股份有限公司	Share-holding Corporations Ltd.	8	2	853208
外商投资	Foreign Investment	480	124	17976864
中外合资经营	Joint Ventures	204	40	9861398
中外合作经营	Cooperative Enterprises	20	3	339374
外商独资	Sole Foreign Investment	252	79	7523192
股份有限公司	Share-holding Corporations Ltd.	4	2	252900
按轻重工业分	**Grouped by Light and Heavy Industry**			
轻工业	Light Industry	1209	183	19618121
重工业	Heavy Industry	2660	364	70084865
按企业规模分	**Grouped by Size of Enterprises**			
大 型	Large-sized	93	5	32166130
中 型	Medium-sized	488	57	21069320
小 型	Small-sized	3210	463	35847962
微 型	Micro-sized	78	22	619574

单位：万元（10000 yuan）

工业销售产值 Value of Industrial Products Sales	流动资产合计 Current Assets	其中 of which #应收帐款净额 Net Account Income	存货 Existing Stock	其中 of which #产成品 Manufac-tured Products	固定资产合计 Total Fixed Assets	固定资产原价合计 Total Original Value of Fixed Assets	累计折旧 Accumula-tive Deprecia-tion	资产总计 Total Assets
88796982	**41875942**	**12329527**	**9331803**	**3696509**	**18484017**	**33533391**	**15960549**	**67543796**
69817051	33976401	10237362	7915339	3193554	14359289	27906943	14152443	54215460
35137235	17222862	4589805	4082936	1607867	7044046	11731174	4978650	27174763
17519190	10264492	3468798	2457692	1029956	4399294	11069447	6885416	16092430
7024697	2584255	737927	453388	206389	977943	1618495	739564	4396718
7386407	2557895	896845	545032	246712	1155114	2314741	1152393	4083037
2749522	1346896	543988	376292	102631	782893	1173085	396420	2468512
13428959	4998619	1362243	880489	290617	2679580	3473524	1073272	8571898
5550972	2900923	729922	535974	212337	1445148	2152924	734834	4756438
61571714	29179969	8232872	6358283	2535923	11780741	20751358	9516348	46507147
1405906	959767	357934	280609	60483	672613	1285417	593456	1802589
54795	25724	10574	3695	1253	11531	23222	11691	44748
779392	270017	67698	95804	49862	92784	243662	154865	404664
4930276	2291656	654420	576985	260940	1453077	3020770	1623764	4247249
1682093	1923993	382736	307503	130013	714367	1292147	529274	3336763
52719252	23708812	6759510	5093688	2033373	8836370	14886140	6603298	36671134
9344032	4766112	1419298	1066354	425436	2330808	4934394	2657349	7744905
3977501	2021183	689831	493265	187257	1038162	1638874	637078	3422157
209070	74141	15245	12450	4167	27620	50314	22750	107888
4329287	2239408	598265	508569	204654	1023357	2801304	1795187	3496964
828175	431381	115957	52071	29358	241668	443901	202333	717896
17881235	7929861	2677357	1907165	735150	4372469	7847639	3786852	13291744
9831545	3410834	977960	978147	402016	1917715	3321052	1625214	5677754
332608	106814	30800	31125	13152	134669	216395	83376	267850
7458275	4223956	1616456	881016	309301	2267814	4237117	2057457	7007465
258807	188258	52141	16878	10681	52270	73076	20806	338675
19428451	9137122	2653639	2095276	889491	3799858	6880538	3247554	15035347
69368531	32738820	9675888	7236527	2807018	14684159	26652853	12712995	52508450
32017454	14937009	3554749	2991973	1105117	7105724	12968139	6157617	24809295
20851746	11230774	3325755	2874793	1207959	5255935	9961133	4991467	18406456
35321155	15404599	5358991	3417203	1361084	6068524	10488507	4748992	23896968
606626	303560	90032	47833	22349	53835	115613	62472	431077

11-4 续表 Continued

指标	Item	负债总计 Total Liabilities	其中 of which 流动负债合计 Total Current Liabilities	非流动负债合计 Total Non-current Liabilities	所有者权益 Owner's Equity
总 计	**Total**	**41207911**	**37112387**	**3708909**	**26320652**
按地区分	**Grouped by Region**				
市 区	Urban Area	32033466	29104587	2571277	22166967
武进区	Wujin District	16417936	15426303	713564	10753270
新北区	Xinbei District	9498649	8291901	1189208	6582312
天宁区	Tianning District	2356245	2077646	269793	2040473
钟楼区	Zhonglou District	2425805	2172758	199880	1657232
戚墅堰区	Qishuyan District	1334832	1135979	198832	1133680
溧阳市	Liyang City	5917027	5536378	352160	2654870
金坛市	Jintan City	3257417	2471422	785472	1498815
按登记注册类型分	**Grouped by Registration Status**				
内 资	Domestic Investment	28935238	26149917	2428288	17566131
国 有	State-owned	1223182	1061409	161773	579408
集 体	Collective-owned	24980	20140	4496	19768
股份合作	Share-holding Cooperative	156972	155101	1855	247691
有限责任公司	Limited Liability Corporations	2693305	2306121	386324	1553918
股份有限公司	Share-holding Corporations Ltd.	1526443	815519	710925	1810320
私营及其他	Private and others	23310357	21791627	1162917	13355026
港澳台商投资	Investment from Hong Kong, Macao and Taiwan	4456382	3977986	453288	3279068
合资经营	Joint-Venture	1984558	1719588	262048	1431809
合作经营	Cooperative	79675	78468	1103	28213
独资经营	Sole Investment	1956491	1797879	136532	1536808
股份有限公司	Share-holding Corporations Ltd.	435658	382052	53606	282238
外商投资	Foreign Investment	7816291	6984483	827332	5475453
中外合资经营	Joint Ventures	3595323	3474009	120484	2082431
中外合作经营	Cooperative Enterprises	154776	135011	19765	113074
外商独资	Sole Foreign Investment	3893951	3205747	684560	3113513
股份有限公司	Share-holding Corporations Ltd.	172240	169717	2524	166435
按轻重工业分	**Grouped by Light and Heavy Industry**				
轻工业	Light Industry	8883656	8170435	699772	6151483
重工业	Heavy Industry	32324255	28941952	3009137	20169170
按企业规模分	**Grouped by Size of Enterprises**				
大 型	Large-sized	15333388	13397186	1631482	9475907
中 型	Medium-sized	10643224	9679138	939541	7763233
小 型	Small-sized	14950379	13769992	1128561	8937762
微 型	Micro-sized	280920	266072	9325	143751

单位：万元（10000 yuan）

主营业务收入 Main Business Income	销售费用 Cost of Sales	管理费用 Cost of Management	财务费用 Finance Charge	营业利润 Business Profit	实现利税总额 Total Profits and Taxes	其中 of which: 利润总额 Total Profits	其中 of which: 主营业务税金及附加 Main Business Tax and Surcharges	其中 of which: 应交增值税 Value Added Tax Payable	亏损企业亏损总额 Amount of Loss in Loss-incurring Enterprises	应付职工薪酬 Remuneration Payable to Employees
90979451	**1576856**	**3369248**	**1276724**	**4903602**	**7303013**	**4437735**	**299413**	**2549522**	**513275**	**4915633**
71568551	1278924	2817164	925786	3763312	5622398	3417935	235655	1957194	355090	4177467
36301306	487081	1272458	526459	2079389	2803273	1681400	104719	1011598	103561	2265305
17662239	415575	838405	231473	632669	1227659	664976	67364	491285	220180	1090850
7222403	205983	298165	74374	390214	614724	413800	28234	172292	13752	375113
7471973	118754	275340	54186	402417	619546	392690	24700	202155	13243	287107
2910631	51530	132796	39294	258624	357197	265069	10638	79864	4354	159094
13643186	167178	287649	242225	826090	1098493	673922	38367	384915	31284	372020
5767714	130754	264436	108712	314199	582122	345877	25391	207413	126901	366146
63454054	966825	2281621	934369	3527986	5123817	3196900	207822	1709754	219102	3199483
1389547	22685	85857	37442	77926	152054	93989	6508	51557	2301	99490
58495	1760	4888	249	2110	5412	3295	152	1965	161	5068
783150	9874	15709	5550	30999	69390	32272	1801	35317	898	56618
5038741	97526	190822	71114	202553	377423	227029	16526	133203	60007	287999
1815560	71337	108097	26114	146228	221376	166179	6070	49128		140055
54368560	763641	1876248	793901	3068170	4298163	2674137	176765	1438584	155734	2610253
9546229	179372	389584	116228	609167	942105	626636	32980	281924	53357	700550
4001151	103452	193583	71725	270572	436625	280030	20225	136279	31376	394970
214280	2799	8064	2719	7129	14356	7496	461	6399	717	9047
4501966	63449	160144	34113	308511	451854	313701	10992	126686	10485	248462
828832	9671	27793	7671	22954	39271	25410	1301	12560	10779	48071
17979169	430659	698043	226127	766450	1237090	614199	58612	557844	240816	1015600
9872734	196139	261218	132433	490334	668874	336285	27805	302476	41367	366337
337807	7604	17098	5902	18080	29665	18229	1234	10197	252	21170
7503409	226219	410583	84362	222579	494462	224449	29524	236365	198973	615374
265220	697	9145	3429	35457	44090	35235	48	8806	225	12719
19632446	492359	851732	268380	931253	1721405	983378	89030	648538	74156	1658910
71347006	1084496	2517516	1008343	3972350	5581608	3454357	210384	1900984	439120	3256724
33552834	412324	953270	451701	1969512	2387628	1397841	88547	901186	162657	1916612
21358579	577750	996375	340065	1335712	2240122	1415014	92496	729385	138015	1423066
35466540	580727	1403849	478688	1585591	2648791	1612273	116613	906900	206048	1562263
601499	6055	15755	6269	12788	26471	12608	1758	12051	6556	13692

11-5 规模以上工业企业分行业主要经济指标（2012 年）
MAJOR ECONOMIC INDICATORS OF INDUSTRIAL ENTERPRISES ABOVE DESIGNATED SIZE BY SECTOR（2012）

指 标	Item	企 业单位数（个）Number of Enterpr-ises（unit）	其中 of which #亏损企业 Loss-incurring Enterprises	工 业总产值 Gross Industrial Output Value
黑色金属矿采选业	Ferrous Metal Mining Industry	1		5348
非金属矿采选业	Nonmetal Minerals Mining and Dressing	4	2	23058
农副食品加工业	Food Processing	15	5	224247
食品制造业	Food Production	14	4	210902
酒、饮料和精制茶制造业	Beverages and Refined Tea Manufacturing	4	2	95619
纺织业	Textile Industry	358	43	4550288
纺织服装、服饰业	Textile and clothing Industry	141	23	2363717
皮革、毛皮、羽毛及其制品和制鞋业	Leather, Fur, Feathers and Their Products, and Footwear Industry	38	10	435080
木材加工及木、竹、藤、棕、草制品业	Timber Processing, Bamboo, Cane, Palm Fiber and Straw Products	59	2	745897
家具制造业	Furniture Manufacturing	6	2	47768
造纸及纸制品业	Papermaking and Paper Products	49	7	411370
印刷和记录媒介复制业	Printing and Recorded Media Duplication Industry	35	6	256239
文教、工美、体育和娱乐用品制造业	Cultural & Educational, Arts & Crafts, Sports & Entertainment Articles Manufacturing	74	10	1007935
石油加工、炼焦及核燃料加工业	Petroleum Processing, Coking and Nuclear Fuel Processing	13	1	272824
化学原料及化学制品制造业	Raw Chemical Materials and Chemica Products	414	58	13586534
医药制造业	Medical and Pharmaceutical Products	63	8	1149539
化学纤维制造业	Chemical Fiber	46	13	431682
橡胶和塑料制品业	Rubber and Plastic Products Industry	122	13	955804
非金属矿物制品业	Nonmetal Mineral Products	165	21	3014510
黑色金属冶炼及压延加工业	Smelting and Pressing of Ferrous Metals	169	36	14984731
有色金属冶炼及压延加工业	Smelting and Pressing of Nonferrous Metals	72	14	2314655
金属制品业	Metal Products	228	27	4234089
通用设备制造业	General Equipment Manufacturing	383	61	4148095
专用设备制造业	For Special Purposes Equipment Manufacturing	308	34	5491026
汽车制造业	Automotive Industry	141	10	2003006
铁路、船舶、航空航天和其他运输设备制造	Railways, Shipping, Aerospace and other Transportation Equipment Manufacturing	96	8	2923596
电气机械及器材制造业	Electric Equipment and Machinery	495	76	16037602
计算机、通信和其他电子设备制造	Computer, Communications and other Electronic Equipment Manufacturing	226	34	4603022
仪器仪表制造业	Instrumentation Manufacturing	92	9	1923507
其他制造业	Other Manufacturing	4	2	44659
废弃资源综合利用业	Comprehensive Utilization of Waste Resources Industry	3		72026
金属制品、机械和设备修理业	Metal Products, Machinery & Equipment Repairing Industry	1	1	10181
电力、热力生产和供应业	Production and Supply of Electricity & Heat Industry	19	3	857150
燃气生产和供应业	Production and Supply of Gas Industry	4		187487
水的生产和供应业	Production and Supply of water Industry	7	2	79794

单位：万元（10000 yuan）

工业销售产值 Value of Industrial Products Sales	流动资产合计 Current Assets	其中 of which: #应收帐款净额 Net Account Income	存货 Existing Stock	其中 of which: #产成品 Manufac-tured Products	固定资产合计 Total Fixed Assets	固定资产原价合计 Total Original Value of Fixed Assets	累计折旧 Accumula-tive Deprecia-tion	资产总计 Total Assets
4476	2295	50	1218	1067	5406	4764	411	8851
23058	19032	9119	455	355	4362	5579	1273	39347
224668	79682	13394	26803	7550	53743	66271	16950	147557
207026	113042	24922	24614	10065	93322	168632	75748	265203
101281	37988	2417	23438	1607	38869	66408	35235	78420
4501324	1781978	495545	509990	254483	650682	1189209	565279	3033746
2357118	744614	230065	204128	72154	299797	565868	274133	1180666
424236	128626	25237	31364	10866	35934	57583	23045	174491
736268	255841	51483	99006	30791	52000	80763	30434	336814
46870	64628	1488	2910	457	6882	9401	2519	138923
401314	322021	74543	56970	19975	74961	122259	51030	441412
254460	170274	64403	31017	13510	68936	128516	63568	268148
989384	460988	145152	120526	42732	205031	303628	120464	764393
265426	133442	28447	31585	8318	27561	38674	14769	187828
13514615	5659212	1685594	1058837	472301	2342615	7226232	4993730	9207618
1117255	816908	187691	155465	75799	239164	385696	161086	1196731
423058	244457	90082	55875	30713	83637	160062	74972	374010
943209	524727	215959	122221	52180	196567	346365	167868	827341
3013206	1969263	580234	275490	82264	921037	1498348	598895	3439517
15009052	4573031	523035	1118430	464146	3050764	4224510	1469965	8266187
2279047	658305	157458	231285	49215	256474	384325	138504	1033921
4227591	1948065	636182	466114	215105	610577	1070898	496361	2819574
4040519	2790745	805742	588138	230628	1102513	1753083	700021	4228498
5416037	3547731	1145450	1203080	436470	1349393	2746931	1463734	5404306
2004372	1053881	392137	206576	93171	483674	772749	319956	1730990
2890950	1946924	651458	599986	172543	738996	1225675	507741	2964915
15841657	7704085	2696633	1265994	553494	2490086	4356415	1964133	11176853
4435350	2403187	899447	479011	197284	1246233	1819166	614289	3946329
1865062	1164354	373314	272180	91271	497338	784006	284772	1872034
44234	9100	3840	1089	350	3146	2985	614	12370
69119	36362	11692	7190	4108	25538	32385	6847	68969
10687	7627	1677	3716	1448	5394	3802	1159	13026
851708	251844	82768	28940		791411	1321994	536630	1145531
187487	136879	13803	5576	88	123803	158242	38178	291739
75860	114805	9066	22587		308176	451965	146235	457541

11-5 续表 Continued

指 标	Item	负债总计 Total Liabilities	其中 of which 流动负债合计 Total Current Liabilities	非流动负债合计 Total Non-current Liabilities	所有者权益 Owner's Equity
黑色金属矿采选业	Ferrous Metal Mining Industry	7911	7911		939
非金属矿采选业	Nonmetal Minerals Mining and Dressing	28648	28648		10699
农副食品加工业	Food Processing	102632	96386	6247	44925
食品制造业	Food Production	178344	175963	2365	86860
酒、饮料和精制茶制造业	Beverages and Refined Tea Manufacturing	44392	36198	8194	34028
纺织业	Textile Industry	1851381	1668266	180046	1182165
纺织服装、服饰业	Textile and clothing Industry	668281	643829	21804	512384
皮革、毛皮、羽毛及其制品和制鞋业	Leather, Fur, Feathers and Their Products, and Footwear Industry	129183	124000	4607	45308
木材加工及木、竹、藤、棕、草制品业	Timber Processing, Bamboo, Cane, Palm Fiber and Straw Products	237913	237820		98901
家具制造业	Furniture Manufacturing	115938	93938	22000	22986
造纸及纸制品业	Papermaking and Paper Products	296007	242164	53435	145405
印刷和记录媒介复制业	Printing and Recorded Media Duplication Industry	208184	191963	15673	59964
文教、工美、体育和娱乐用品制造业	Cultural & Educational, Arts & Crafts, Sports & Entertainment Articles Manufacturing	475431	456178	17937	288962
石油加工、炼焦及核燃料加工业	Petroleum Processing, Coking and Nuclear Fuel Processing	136460	133001	3459	51369
化学原料及化学制品制造业	Raw Chemical Materials and Chemica Products	5674635	5088489	572822	3520717
医药制造业	Medical and Pharmaceutical Products	585007	565710	18217	611724
化学纤维制造业	Chemical Fiber	233037	217642	15394	140973
橡胶和塑料制品业	Rubber and Plastic Products Industry	466185	434362	30347	361155
非金属矿物制品业	Nonmetal Mineral Products	2351299	2242382	105600	1089908
黑色金属冶炼及压延加工业	Smelting and Pressing of Ferrous Metals	5592569	5300810	18205	2673618
有色金属冶炼及压延加工业	Smelting and Pressing of Nonferrous Metals	619657	599279	20101	414174
金属制品业	Metal Products	1910460	1775056	78773	908606
通用设备制造业	General Equipment Manufacturing	2683517	2031354	650996	1544954
专用设备制造业	For Special Purposes Equipment Manufacturing	3058478	2704737	349471	2345778
汽车制造业	Automotive Industry	994177	889432	104561	736813
铁路、船舶、航空航天和其他运输设备制造	Railways, Shipping, Aerospace and other Transportation Equipment Manufacturing	1844134	1711978	129094	1120781
电气机械及器材制造业	Electric Equipment and Machinery	6305927	5644932	647538	4870826
计算机、通信和其他电子设备制造	Computer, Communications and other Electronic Equipment Manufacturing	2125722	1935651	184677	1816942
仪器仪表制造业	Instrumentation Manufacturing	996052	921860	73791	875966
其他制造业	Other Manufacturing	8418	8418		3953
废弃资源综合利用业	Comprehensive Utilization of Waste Resources Industry	60641	55641	5000	8328
金属制品、机械和设备修理业	Metal Products, Machinery & Equipment Repairing Industry	12820	12723	98	206
电力、热力生产和供应业	Production and Supply of Electricity & Heat Industry	659055	395000	264055	486476
燃气生产和供应业	Production and Supply of Gas Industry	220476	203878	16598	71264
水的生产和供应业	Production and Supply of water Industry	324942	236791	87807	132600

单位：万元（10000 yuan）

主营业务收入 Main Business Income	销售费用 Cost of Sales	管理费用 Cost of Management	财务费用 Finance Charge	营业利润 Business Profit	实现利税总额 Total Profits and Taxes	其中 of which 利润总额 Total Profits	主营业务税金及附加 Main Business Tax and Surcharges	应交增值税 Value Added Tax Payable	亏损企业亏损总额 Amount of Loss in Loss-incurring Enterprises	应付职工薪酬 Remuneration Payable to Employees
4476		400	28	-188	143	30	10	103		207
22889		6807	801	-901	1436	-922	842	1516	1050	1314
231675	4031	5213	3042	-299	6815	3824	107	2884	1205	6029
216640	22270	13599	9491	9732	23914	9752	4245	9917	1056	9615
81911	13185	5680	209	2069	15798	2986	7807	5005	281	11024
4596245	54959	153740	69107	190343	352231	203780	18024	130295	11353	237146
2428566	58889	106586	20980	121528	194591	126765	9036	58584	7070	313403
442193	5963	13295	2805	24487	44021	24752	2264	17005	649	54885
739631	29930	25775	5791	41507	71527	41488	4745	25294	1886	34804
46852	2131	3148	2508	724	2074	718	375	981	280	4045
399731	7812	14648	13548	6323	25670	12886	1226	11558	3105	17632
253921	5095	13171	7303	9592	18637	10505	1004	7129	2441	22383
1016375	19820	40093	16656	39375	73046	41402	3517	28060	5321	73610
265525	3739	3721	4371	4282	7000	4285	393	2322	593	6740
13774630	206057	391159	175838	510188	886872	527861	31097	327291	77544	541216
1098794	111187	98986	14586	102955	173634	108621	7347	57667	2670	93422
421759	6755	16128	9854	14834	28868	16382	1403	11084	2691	26403
964038	24396	49679	11118	37215	62269	34554	2865	24850	5462	60372
3036215	55860	116625	99371	202450	403749	247078	15619	138633	9933	141951
16292176	41135	229205	229977	967379	726007	365837	22570	335759	12128	421015
2349783	10786	38432	17115	107812	198093	114569	5514	75753	18939	75475
4240046	76962	139819	61036	276850	376282	242361	14682	117723	12968	225519
4064864	93355	220743	81743	222373	355828	229500	15115	109136	25714	297444
5434970	159230	299491	62885	353929	569765	354437	20006	193375	35079	355824
1984249	41582	117733	20350	109476	188133	111655	8345	67620	17198	138514
2880361	46817	216056	41437	209394	349293	227663	20450	101084	13872	216313
16082852	312470	583692	172946	718066	1182406	741955	48476	390160	162403	828432
4508510	94971	258147	46594	273865	449059	276904	15657	155822	55642	487420
1851015	54960	140368	24190	189832	277910	191116	9050	77631	18766	146564
44124	563	1166	335	2412	5850	2125	161	3565	359	1878
78936	627	3728	3422	843	5227	829	344	4053		3324
10623	543	1219	300	-937	-609	-921	84	228	921	1867
849476	19	18115	34860	105940	166939	113610	5783	47505	3320	36886
187312	3806	12724	4903	38980	45059	38418	750	5891		8964
78086	6951	10159	7224	11174	15479	10933	504	4042	1377	13995

11-6 规模以上民营工业企业主要经济指标（2012 年）
MAJOR ECONOMIC INDICATORS OF PRIVATE INDUSTRIAL ENTERPRISES ABOVE DESIGNATED SIZE（2012）

指 标	Item	企业单位数（个）Number of Enterpr-ises（unit）	其中 of which #亏损企业 Loss-incurring Enterprises	工业总产值 Gross Industrial Output Value	工业销售产值 Value of Industrial Products Sales
总 计	**Total**	**3016**	**359**	**58779940**	**58160432**
按地区分	**Grouped by Region**				
市 区	Urban Area	2459	231	45904315	45531923
武进区	Wujin District	1484	115	29341782	29017843
新北区	Xinbei District	569	74	7757901	7565650
天宁区	Tianning District	150	15	3260814	3262608
钟楼区	Zhonglou District	179	13	4514428	4651395
戚墅堰区	Qishuyan District	77	14	1029389	1034427
溧阳市	Liyang City	295	63	8815355	8710804
金坛市	Jintan City	262	65	4060270	3917704
按轻重工业分	**Grouped by Light and Heavy Industry**				
轻工业	Light Industry	900	110	12770710	12698761
重工业	Heavy Industry	2116	249	46009229	45461670
按企业规模分	**Grouped by Size of Enterprises**				
大 型	Large-sized	49	1	20499695	20475903
中 型	Medium-sized	295	29	11839654	11696797
小 型	Small-sized	2609	314	25910136	25466780
微 型	Micro-sized	63	15	530455	520953
按工业行业分	**Grouped by Sector**				
黑色金属矿采选业	Ferrous Metal Mining Industry	1		5348	4476
非金属矿采选业	Nonmetal Minerals Mining and Dressing	3	2	20606	20606
农副食品加工业	Food Processing	14	5	181022	182842
食品制造业	Food Production	9	2	59310	59065
酒、饮料和精制茶制造业	Beverages and Refined Tea Manufacturing	2	1	42697	42440
纺织业	Textile Industry	293	31	3328176	3309674
纺织服装、服饰业	Textile and clothing Industry	67	12	1112092	1114091
皮革、毛皮、羽毛及其制品和制鞋业	Leather, Fur, Feathers and Their Products, and Footwear Industry	25	8	223650	216863

单位：万元（10000 yuan）

流动资产合计 Current Assets	其中 of which #应收帐款净额 Net Account Income	存货 Existing Stock	其中 of which #产成品 Manufac-tured Products	固定资产合计 Total Fixed Assets	固定资产原价合计 Total Original Value of Fixed Assets	累计折旧 Accumula-tive Deprecia-tion	资产总计 Total Assets
26717121	**7443312**	**5734377**	**2300296**	**10073285**	**17644192**	**8183828**	**41463935**
20646734	5774470	4754283	1924423	7592364	14154643	7057868	31854943
13706042	3469669	3324168	1295276	5295868	9055523	4028144	21304217
4068556	1330722	878918	409970	1260963	3209851	2062266	5936628
1154944	373134	187004	78180	398621	603068	275922	1892385
1246947	429072	242233	90336	521324	1082290	599868	1995786
470244	171874	121960	50660	115588	203911	91668	725927
4031018	1159012	584559	209328	1495375	2058456	649535	6336894
2039369	509831	395535	166545	985546	1431093	476425	3272098
5531135	1646582	1318718	555995	2036621	3977858	2046685	8819695
21185986	5796730	4415659	1744301	8036664	13666334	6137143	32644240
9519559	1607442	1931125	714782	3822748	7255710	3604487	14974803
6077994	1773660	1410807	616815	2670433	4550613	2094283	10000866
10929500	4007391	2357501	952929	3556307	5786475	2457052	16241566
190068	54820	34945	15770	23798	51394	28006	246700
2295	50	1218	1067	5406	4764	411	8851
18208	8473	455	355	3625	4114	545	37786
67108	11342	22561	6603	44756	55225	14461	123884
30578	6034	10060	6620	11794	18633	7174	49053
15843	340	9298	252	21652	35617	20872	37658
1012855	307756	338892	159208	448362	792652	360748	1642063
296955	112341	87782	24827	175153	328975	159357	555136
55995	13352	23024	7960	22677	35233	13790	85249

11-6 续表 1 Continued 1

指 标	Item	企业单位数（个）Number of Enterpr-ises (unit)	其中 of which #亏损企业 Loss-incurring Enterprises	工业总产值 Gross Industrial Output Value	工业销售产值 Value of Industrial Products Sales
木材加工及木、竹、藤、棕、草制品业	Timber Processing, Bamboo, Cane, Palm Fiber and Straw Products	55	2	613406	604448
家具制造业	Furniture Manufacturing	4		40065	39159
造纸及纸制品业	Papermaking and Paper Products	42	5	315574	305636
印刷和记录媒介复制业	Printing and Recorded Media Duplication Industry	29	3	209382	208808
文教、工美、体育和娱乐用品制造业	Cultural & Educational, Arts & Crafts, Sports & Entertainment Articles Manufacturing	51	7	574494	555934
石油加工、炼焦及核燃料加工业	Petroleum Processing, Coking and Nuclear Fuel Processing	10		148851	138270
化学原料及化学制品制造业	Raw Chemical Materials and Chemica Products	332	32	9136240	9081535
医药制造业	Medical and Pharmaceutical Products	46	4	758636	718342
化学纤维制造业	Chemical Fiber	42	13	311100	303344
橡胶和塑料制品业	Rubber and Plastic Products Industry	98	6	720503	713754
非金属矿物制品业	Nonmetal Mineral Products	141	18	2552715	2557253
黑色金属冶炼及压延加工业	Smelting and Pressing of Ferrous Metals	159	35	10796200	10821202
有色金属冶炼及压延加工业	Smelting and Pressing of Nonferrous Metals	65	10	2072607	2050887
金属制品业	Metal Products	189	19	3459592	3436025
通用设备制造业	General Equipment Manufacturing	309	42	3053227	2972622
专用设备制造业	For Special Purposes Equipment Manufacturing	236	19	3221763	3176434
汽车制造业	Automotive Industry	112	6	1240613	1208836
铁路、船舶、航空航天和其他运输设备制造	Railways, Shipping, Aerospace and other Transportation Equipment Manufacturing	71	3	1762889	1732067
电气机械及器材制造业	Electric Equipment and Machinery	382	53	9809479	9703169
计算机、通信和其他电子设备制造	Computer, Communications and other Electronic Equipment Manufacturing	141	13	1577056	1502944
仪器仪表制造业	Instrumentation Manufacturing	72	5	1166734	1122840
其他制造业	Other Manufacturing	3	1	40762	40337
废弃资源综合利用业	Comprehensive Utilization of Waste Resources Industry	3		72026	69119
金属制品、机械和设备修理业	Metal Products, Machinery & Equipment Repairing Industry	1	1	10181	10687
电力、热力生产和供应业	Production and Supply of Electricity & Heat Industry	5	1	103810	98819
燃气生产和供应业	Production and Supply of Gas Industry	1		19815	19815
水的生产和供应业	Production and Supply of water Industry	3		19320	18092

单位：万元（10000 yuan）

流动资产合计 Current Assets	其中 of which			固定资产合计 Total Fixed Assets	固定资产原价合计 Total Original Value of Fixed Assets	累计折旧 Accumula-tive Deprecia-tion	资产总计 Total Assets
	#应收帐款净额 Net Account Income	存货 Existing Stock	其中 of which #产成品 Manufac-tured Products				
220412	45402	93135	27000	42370	67772	27073	288977
61957	2891	2042	315	4134	5661	1527	126745
255140	58585	48503	14675	43856	71649	30869	327391
139639	58361	26307	11713	55732	96826	45082	213433
219728	80321	60117	17381	112734	169742	67947	389636
47159	13076	18897	4564	23302	29167	9206	92498
3794893	1100585	668641	308280	1217288	3716167	2601116	5931810
540512	128718	100072	48841	130179	214169	91975	759351
174930	64680	46694	26694	54880	106612	53178	257407
404273	167692	78953	35143	114859	193586	95775	613826
1663676	503625	225107	65129	748263	1261042	514587	2923517
4035402	446167	913614	398966	2099636	3147977	1175359	6768523
514817	111621	195439	38201	149721	228758	89514	760261
1439719	511206	324398	143714	406645	695354	315978	2062280
2143159	597303	406285	153808	651510	1072921	474551	3063460
1648033	578012	474327	160680	580619	953871	399681	2470743
684520	244699	120990	55858	256322	386035	149864	1078543
1127913	335582	312234	102584	289886	533172	261004	1507152
4383668	1376465	762602	326349	1398026	2035321	730592	6352921
859495	308876	207358	93942	507042	666567	187395	1485260
707198	205360	132857	53737	297716	494818	206900	1116407
7837	3691	832	185	2135	2723	588	10097
36362	11692	7190	4108	25538	32385	6847	68969
7627	1677	3716	1448	5394	3802	1159	13026
59442	16876	6331		62776	108586	49967	129531
30246	5508	4418	88	48981	55969	10727	84915
9529	4953	29		10317	18328	8011	27578

11-6 续表 2 Continued 2

指 标	Item	负债总计 Total Liabilities	其中 of which 流动负债合计 Total Current Liabilities	非流动负债合计 Total Non-current Liabilities	所有者权益 Owner's Equity	主营业务收入 Main Business Income
总 计	**Total**	**26005178**	**23795331**	**1852816**	**15452979**	**59969738**
按地区分	**Grouped by Region**					
市 区	Urban Area	19450600	18258031	864446	12398772	47005067
武进区	Wujin District	13349385	12653165	418257	7951276	30177164
新北区	Xinbei District	3596862	3349958	230764	2337752	7641425
天宁区	Tianning District	1006810	914000	86120	885575	3371042
钟楼区	Zhonglou District	1230063	1077626	125126	765723	4644431
戚墅堰区	Qishuyan District	267481	263282	4178	458446	1171004
溧阳市	Liyang City	4282269	3930000	323780	2054624	8909047
金坛市	Jintan City	2272310	1607300	664590	999583	4055625
按轻重工业分	**Grouped by Light and Heavy Industry**					
轻工业	Light Industry	5614741	5260804	344266	3204745	12781106
重工业	Heavy Industry	20390438	18534526	1508550	12248233	47188632
按企业规模分	**Grouped by Size of Enterprises**					
大 型	Large-sized	9361518	8197716	864014	5613284	21944064
中 型	Medium-sized	5727731	5265029	440150	4273135	12041537
小 型	Small-sized	10746480	10171829	545328	5495714	25471672
微 型	Micro-sized	169450	160757	3325	70845	512465
按工业行业分	**Grouped by Sector**					
黑色金属矿采选业	Ferrous Metal Mining Industry	7911	7911		939	4476
非金属矿采选业	Nonmetal Minerals Mining and Dressing	28104	28104		9682	20444
农副食品加工业	Food Processing	90408	90403	5	33476	181126
食品制造业	Food Production	24778	23127	1635	24275	54241
酒、饮料和精制茶制造业	Beverages and Refined Tea Manufacturing	17434	17434		20224	31997
纺织业	Textile Industry	1113978	1041752	69443	527885	3364515
纺织服装、服饰业	Textile and clothing Industry	337882	334319	3216	217254	1165914
皮革、毛皮、羽毛及其制品和制鞋业	Leather, Fur, Feathers and Their Products, and Footwear Industry	64247	59693	3978	21002	224885

单位：万元（10000 yuan）

销售费用 Cost of Sales	管理费用 Cost of Management	财务费用 Finance Charge	营业利润 Business Profit	实现利税总额 Total Profits and Taxes	其中 of which 利润总额 Total Profits	主营业务税金及附加 Main Business Tax and Surcharges	应交增值税 Value Added Tax Payable	亏损企业亏损总额 Amount of Loss in Loss-incurring Enterprises	应付职工薪酬 Remuneration Payable to Employees
861662	**2075826**	**859101**	**3324476**	**4735995**	**2944151**	**192068**	**1590505**	**213824**	**2938015**
637713	1668113	627762	2556601	3528141	2160406	145446	1214355	95448	2416308
354379	955393	458437	1620165	2096653	1216688	84059	792269	51485	1683760
154401	369952	96045	409683	622470	413041	25917	180994	26451	377661
64537	152359	34148	163032	273432	177657	15497	79992	4729	160412
45141	130581	35824	267731	409768	258920	15877	134971	8808	145272
19255	59827	3310	95991	125819	94101	4097	26128	3976	49203
139268	230356	164752	524251	785084	512864	30769	240517	22964	279011
84681	177357	66587	243625	422770	270881	15853	135633	95412	242695
231235	502921	184530	468907	943056	506544	49303	386952	27598	921088
630427	1572905	674571	2855569	3792939	2437607	142765	1203553	186226	2016927
231508	553274	304102	1403424	1538010	949273	54277	534460	43801	990103
234874	519656	200933	750202	1226285	799088	50644	374898	57838	798066
390997	990701	349754	1157227	1945922	1182559	85678	670123	109486	1139936
4283	12195	4313	13623	25778	13231	1469	11023	2698	9910
	400	28	-188	143	30	10	103		207
	6735	801	-1010	793	-1026	451	1369	1050	1134
2649	4515	3064	-3307	3257	897	107	2253	1205	4738
1600	2806	1379	2410	4144	2547	279	1318	98	3313
6935	2806	155	-1081	6462	-186	3795	2853	256	4413
38387	105249	43750	110221	225176	121237	12476	91356	7712	162843
25205	52688	11056	38483	74366	48170	3540	22506	1136	127292
2914	7405	2062	10381	18510	10649	1028	6833	588	28920

11-6 续表 3 Continued 3

指标	Item	负债总计 Total Liabilities	其中 of which		所有者权益 Owner's Equity	主营业务收入 Main Business Income
			流动负债合计 Total Current Liabilities	非流动负债合计 Total Non-current Liabilities		
木材加工及木、竹、藤、棕、草制品业	Timber Processing, Bamboo, Cane, Palm Fiber and Straw Products	200713	200620		88264	606811
家具制造业	Furniture Manufacturing	114516	92516	22000	12229	39207
造纸及纸制品业	Papermaking and Paper Products	241165	200813	40342	86226	301099
印刷和记录媒介复制业	Printing and Recorded Media Duplication Industry	173428	157295	15584	40005	208598
文教、工美、体育和娱乐用品制造业	Cultural & Educational, Arts & Crafts, Sports & Entertainment Articles Manufacturing	268772	253623	13833	120864	569560
石油加工、炼焦及核燃料加工业	Petroleum Processing, Coking and Nuclear Fuel Processing	66207	62748	3459	26292	138598
化学原料及化学制品制造业	Raw Chemical Materials and Chemica Products	3601557	3378299	210089	2323778	9254677
医药制造业	Medical and Pharmaceutical Products	358607	348146	9382	400745	709785
化学纤维制造业	Chemical Fiber	181135	178376	2759	76271	300251
橡胶和塑料制品业	Rubber and Plastic Products Industry	355253	341301	12475	258573	723442
非金属矿物制品业	Nonmetal Mineral Products	2052469	1951089	98062	872738	2576810
黑色金属冶炼及压延加工业	Smelting and Pressing of Ferrous Metals	4427409	4142671	11183	2341115	12109608
有色金属冶炼及压延加工业	Smelting and Pressing of Nonferrous Metals	484734	468647	15810	275439	2113294
金属制品业	Metal Products	1423084	1333033	53367	638687	3469826
通用设备制造业	General Equipment Manufacturing	2108594	1525390	582086	954840	2980031
专用设备制造业	For Special Purposes Equipment Manufacturing	1596475	1450492	141742	874217	3176446
汽车制造业	Automotive Industry	567156	515811	51344	511387	1200938
铁路、船舶、航空航天和其他运输设备制造	Railways, Shipping, Aerospace and other Transportation Equipment Manufacturing	943610	857132	83416	563542	1724036
电气机械及器材制造业	Electric Equipment and Machinery	3354306	3063441	281615	2998515	9837758
计算机、通信和其他电子设备制造	Computer, Communications and other Electronic Equipment Manufacturing	939376	849467	86541	545884	1490691
仪器仪表制造业	Instrumentation Manufacturing	610030	590735	18895	506362	1125487
其他制造业	Other Manufacturing	6980	6980		3116	40337
废弃资源综合利用业	Comprehensive Utilization of Waste Resources Industry	60641	55641	5000	8328	78936
金属制品、机械和设备修理业	Metal Products, Machinery & Equipment Repairing Industry	12820	12723	98	206	10623
电力、热力生产和供应业	Production and Supply of Electricity & Heat Industry	77957	77677	280	51575	95282
燃气生产和供应业	Production and Supply of Gas Industry	73299	65829	7470	11616	19815
水的生产和供应业	Production and Supply of water Industry	20148	12094	7710	7431	20194

单位：万元（10000 yuan）

销售费用 Cost of Sales	管理费用 Cost of Management	财务费用 Finance Charge	营业利润 Business Profit	实现利税总额 Total Profits and Taxes	其中 of which: 利润总额 Total Profits	其中 of which: 主营业务税金及附加 Main Business Tax and Surcharges	其中 of which: 应交增值税 Value Added Tax Payable	亏损企业亏损总额 Amount of Loss in Loss-incurring Enterprises	应付职工薪酬 Remuneration Payable to Employees
21662	18047	4444	32436	55752	32497	3117	20138	1886	26087
1731	2658	2222	943	2077	998	375	704		2996
4262	10754	11414	1476	17892	8607	1021	8264	1560	13808
3950	8920	5704	10979	18039	11494	791	5754	391	14658
11211	23680	8439	14487	32914	15072	1882	15960	1875	36990
1393	2491	1047	1713	2998	1700	134	1164		5627
143680	268471	111731	416625	692838	417356	24863	250619	24499	419009
24864	57683	11000	54062	90663	58502	3264	28898	1432	58140
3148	11030	7084	9019	18971	9322	875	8775	2691	21575
15172	35822	8634	31701	49622	31125	2247	16249	1517	42019
39813	90869	87822	163306	331252	198646	13354	116903	7572	108070
33716	205158	167323	699854	482075	246854	18221	215159	11678	370007
6136	26401	12940	122686	192754	129317	4804	56375	2453	64161
56890	101145	51471	252410	333748	217457	12288	104003	8762	176385
59552	152472	70962	188112	293359	193732	11114	87253	11176	203292
69207	167491	36211	242757	360689	239405	13772	107512	7677	197614
27839	65295	14958	63124	115137	68090	5186	41347	4777	80397
26709	125823	22841	203163	274836	203877	12399	58477	1237	99748
165061	320068	104780	515944	776109	530127	28556	216920	59573	428906
33255	105913	28464	22385	81066	26053	6767	48084	46741	144199
31040	76245	17321	106949	153992	106932	4249	42811	1687	78226
562	944	279	2759	6204	2479	161	3565	5	1570
627	3728	3422	843	5227	829	344	4053		3324
543	1219	300	-937	-609	-921	84	228	921	1867
2	5152	4627	8675	11471	9379	386	1665	1672	5171
214	4862	1129	988	1552	789	82	682		511
1735	883	241	2112	2519	2118	47	354		801

11-7 规模以上三资工业企业主要经济指标（2012 年）
MAJOR ECONOMIC INDICATORS OF FOREIGN-FUNDED ENTERPRISES ABOVE DESIGNATED SIZE（2012）

指 标	Item	企 业 单位数（个） Number of Enterpr-ises (unit)	其中 of which #亏损企业 Loss-incurring Enterprises	工 业 总产值 Gross Industrial Output Value	工业销售产值 Value of Industrial Products Sales
总 计	**Total**	**798**	**182**	**27480377**	**27225267**
按地区分	**Grouped by Region**				
市 区	Urban Area	652	142	21540358	21306655
武进区	Wujin District	242	57	6180152	6051753
新北区	Xinbei District	271	67	9239338	9147672
天宁区	Tianning District	71	12	3499902	3461031
钟楼区	Zhonglou District	54	4	1847772	1880101
戚墅堰区	Qishuyan District	14	2	773194	766098
溧阳市	Liyang City	46	11	4528784	4525863
金坛市	Jintan City	100	29	1411236	1392749
按轻重工业分	**Grouped by Light and Heavy Industry**				
轻工业	Light Industry	298	70	6564213	6454058
重工业	Heavy Industry	500	112	20916165	20771209
按企业规模分	**Grouped by Size of Enterprises**				
大 型	Large-sized	35	4	10003719	9912374
中 型	Medium-sized	176	26	8376297	8315536
小 型	Small-sized	572	145	9011242	8911684
微 型	Micro-sized	15	7	89120	85674
按工业行业分	**Grouped by Sector**				
农副食品加工业	Food Processing	1		43225	41825
食品制造业	Food Production	4	2	118770	115376
酒、饮料和精制茶制造业	Beverages and Refined Tea Manufacturing	2	1	52922	58841
纺织业	Textile Industry	64	12	1123241	1096003
纺织服装、服饰业	Textile and clothing Industry	72	11	1233704	1225139
皮革、毛皮、羽毛及其制品和制鞋业	Leather, Fur, Feathers and Their Products, and Footwear Industry	13	2	211430	207373

单位：万元（10000 yuan）

流动资产合计 Current Assets	其中 of which #应收帐款净额 Net Account Income	存货 Existing Stock	其中 of which #产成品 Manufac-tured Products	固定资产合计 Total Fixed Assets	固定资产原价合计 Total Original Value of Fixed Assets	累计折旧 Accumula-tive Deprecia-tion	资产总计 Total Assets
12695973	**4096655**	**2973520**	**1160586**	**6703276**	**12782033**	**6444201**	**21036650**
11142052	3725292	2587069	1044700	5302481	11061206	5920767	17892534
3481683	1113133	742617	302964	1715600	2624988	932421	5794627
5635001	1989901	1417007	549683	2696894	6892523	4299455	8985138
1024576	270965	214337	107502	499483	831374	357343	1635502
706806	234043	147821	67041	317378	553516	243969	1096366
293986	117249	65287	17509	73125	158805	87579	380900
796484	167414	253772	74161	1049363	1204146	344482	1898599
757437	203949	132678	41726	351432	516681	178952	1245518
3119010	922447	727596	309203	1626272	2650018	1079800	5214962
9576963	3174208	2245923	851383	5077005	10132015	5364402	15821688
4087723	1472995	710269	264854	2505413	4214639	1888345	7061437
4490466	1371844	1291551	524041	2205054	4698942	2580769	7234175
4004292	1216605	958811	365113	1962772	3804234	1940621	6556661
113492	35212	12889	6579	30037	64219	34466	184377
12574	2052	4242	947	8987	11046	2489	23674
74382	13842	13006	2677	74779	141054	66377	197828
22145	2077	14140	1355	17217	30791	14363	40762
477213	121285	140519	81477	163365	291639	135902	709762
426008	117597	116346	47327	117600	224623	109551	596364
72631	11885	8341	2907	13256	22350	9255	89242

11-7 续表 1 Continued 1

指 标	Item	企 业 单位数（个）Number of Enterpr-ises (unit)	其中 of which #亏损企业 Loss-incurring Enterprises	工 业 总产值 Gross Industrial Output Value	工业销售产值 Value of Industrial Products Sales
木材加工及木、竹、藤、棕、草制品业	Timber Processing, Bamboo, Cane, Palm Fiber and Straw Products	4		132491	131821
家具制造业	Furniture Manufacturing	2	2	7703	7712
造纸及纸制品业	Papermaking and Paper Products	7	2	95796	95678
印刷和记录媒介复制业	Printing and Recorded Media Duplication Industry	4	2	30741	29782
文教、工美、体育和娱乐用品制造业	Cultural & Educational, Arts & Crafts, Sports & Entertainment Articles Manufacturing	23	3	433441	433450
石油加工、炼焦及核燃料加工业	Petroleum Processing, Coking and Nuclear Fuel Processing	3	1	123973	127156
化学原料及化学制品制造业	Raw Chemical Materials and Chemica Products	76	26	4167198	4163982
医药制造业	Medical and Pharmaceutical Products	16	4	320389	329790
化学纤维制造业	Chemical Fiber	4		120582	119714
橡胶和塑料制品业	Rubber and Plastic Products Industry	24	7	235301	229455
非金属矿物制品业	Nonmetal Mineral Products	20	2	325553	329078
黑色金属冶炼及压延加工业	Smelting and Pressing of Ferrous Metals	10	1	4188532	4187850
有色金属冶炼及压延加工业	Smelting and Pressing of Nonferrous Metals	6	4	191037	180600
金属制品业	Metal Products	37	8	684523	699453
通用设备制造业	General Equipment Manufacturing	70	19	718356	692320
专用设备制造业	For Special Purposes Equipment Manufacturing	66	15	1851446	1842823
汽车制造业	Automotive Industry	27	3	660246	686349
铁路、船舶、航空航天和其他运输设备制造	Railways, Shipping, Aerospace and other Transportation Equipment Manufacturing	19	5	487031	491111
电气机械及器材制造业	Electric Equipment and Machinery	108	23	5892581	5781957
计算机、通信和其他电子设备制造	Computer, Communications and other Electronic Equipment Manufacturing	84	21	2969338	2877510
仪器仪表制造业	Instrumentation Manufacturing	20	4	756772	742222
其他制造业	Other Manufacturing	1	1	3898	3898
电力、热力生产和供应业	Production and Supply of Electricity & Heat Industry	6	1	80553	80101
燃气生产和供应业	Production and Supply of Gas Industry	3		167671	167671
水的生产和供应业	Production and Supply of water Industry	2		51936	49229

单位：万元（10000 yuan）

流动资产合计 Current Assets	其中 of which # 应收帐款净额 Net Account Income	存货 Existing Stock	其中 of which # 产成品 Manufac-tured Products	固定资产合计 Total Fixed Assets	固定资产原价合计 Total Original Value of Fixed Assets	累计折旧 Accumula-tive Deprecia-tion	资产总计 Total Assets
35429	6081	5872	3792	9630	12991	3361	47837
2672	-1403	868	142	2748	3741	993	12178
66881	15958	8467	5300	31105	50611	20160	114021
23437	5299	3273	1395	6927	17966	11039	39184
241260	64831	60409	25351	92297	133886	52517	374757
86283	15371	12688	3754	4260	9508	5564	95330
1746192	569182	377531	158376	971816	3256574	2312178	2982201
223096	55810	45231	20651	97437	148202	57916	356066
69528	25402	9181	4019	28756	53451	21794	116603
120454	48267	43268	17037	81708	152779	72093	213515
181682	55433	29138	7595	84369	122499	45676	277331
537629	76868	204816	65180	951127	1076533	294606	1497664
133511	41555	33635	9329	104684	150694	46186	259845
437171	110738	102124	45652	191848	349875	166798	665836
421148	145062	115961	41580	296768	391029	140430	777574
1568871	441231	623975	224317	637530	1417375	827553	2360393
294411	125411	72831	26243	200192	275427	85937	530184
247410	71220	78612	32300	126883	223535	98225	401871
3065424	1201090	428286	203198	1005976	2086151	1093191	4445832
1463205	559680	254073	90989	729255	1140061	424291	2357188
457156	167954	139323	37534	199622	289189	77873	755627
1263	149	257	165	1011	262	27	2274
35801	14546	3724		106641	207657	102805	148927
106633	8295	1158		74822	102273	27451	206824
44474	3888	22225		270661	388265	117604	339961

11-7 续表 2 Continued 2

指标	Item	负债总计 Total Liabilities	其中 of which 流动负债合计 Total Current Liabilities	非流动负债合计 Total Non-current Liabilities	所有者权益 Owner's Equity	主营业务收入 Main Business Income
总 计	**Total**	**12272673**	**10962469**	**1280621**	**8754521**	**27525398**
按地区分	**Grouped by Region**					
市 区	Urban Area	10073779	8843941	1200359	7809299	21530254
武进区	Wujin District	3001408	2705994	295307	2793219	6061503
新北区	Xinbei District	5214481	4437808	775273	3761203	9213409
天宁区	Tianning District	976870	893046	81709	658632	3553756
钟楼区	Zhonglou District	667176	604323	36997	429189	1914576
戚墅堰区	Qishuyan District	213845	202771	11074	167056	787011
溧阳市	Liyang City	1393458	1384577	8880	505141	4536684
金坛市	Jintan City	805436	733951	71382	440081	1458460
按轻重工业分	**Grouped by Light and Heavy Industry**					
轻工业	Light Industry	2825665	2576175	245712	2389296	6556201
重工业	Heavy Industry	9447008	8386294	1034908	6365225	20969197
按企业规模分	**Grouped by Size of Enterprises**					
大 型	Large-sized	4554928	4027675	522321	2506510	9945590
中 型	Medium-sized	4126093	3779012	345088	3108082	8422892
小 型	Small-sized	3480182	3050468	407212	3067023	9067883
微 型	Micro-sized	111471	105315	6000	72906	89034
按工业行业分	**Grouped by Sector**					
农副食品加工业	Food Processing	12225	5983	6242	11449	50549
食品制造业	Food Production	140822	140092	729	57006	125480
酒、饮料和精制茶制造业	Beverages and Refined Tea Manufacturing	26958	18765	8194	13803	49914
纺织业	Textile Industry	444909	430174	14449	264853	1120807
纺织服装、服饰业	Textile and clothing Industry	324870	303982	18588	271493	1244614
皮革、毛皮、羽毛及其制品和制鞋业	Leather, Fur, Feathers and Their Products, and Footwear Industry	64936	64307	629	24306	217309

单位：万元（10000 yuan）

销售费用 Cost of Sales	管理费用 Cost of Management	财务费用 Finance Charge	营业利润 Business Profit	实现利税总额 Total Profits and Taxes	其中 of which 利润总额 Total Profits	主营业务税金及附加 Main Business Tax and Surcharges	应交增值税 Value Added Tax Payable	亏损企业亏损总额 Amount of Loss in Loss-incurring Enterprises	应付职工薪酬 Remuneration Payable to Employees
610031	**1087627**	**342355**	**1375616**	**2179195**	**1240835**	**91592**	**839768**	**294174**	**1716151**
555046	969553	239683	1035023	1769615	1045346	76588	644002	256651	1523017
131683	313525	67197	458018	703180	463506	20584	217171	52076	577871
241719	437136	116237	176941	504531	190666	36916	275435	192003	662730
123793	116057	33686	178282	275518	179942	10831	84633	7759	185071
32515	86602	14338	105354	160080	102777	6321	50982	4435	74107
25336	16232	8225	116428	126306	108455	1936	15782	379	23237
23703	41580	67323	282995	272135	133363	6386	132031	7750	78724
31283	76495	35349	57598	137446	62127	8618	63734	29773	114410
233167	310687	79199	406587	701521	413933	37295	250091	44950	700996
376864	776940	263156	969029	1477674	826902	54296	589677	249223	1015155
133977	293996	117182	470543	666676	324338	27443	314839	118855	776372
306094	411726	117254	549553	921083	560961	37665	320883	78111	546137
168187	378346	105963	356356	590743	356159	26195	203017	93350	389859
1772	3560	1956	-836	694	-623	289	1028	3857	3782
1382	698	-22	3009	3557	2927		630		1291
9355	10293	8056	6840	18180	6722	3813	7645	959	6139
6251	2874	54	3149	9336	3172	4012	2152	24	6612
14581	35348	21476	52158	89494	48185	4767	36516	3641	60888
33231	49262	9837	76857	111238	72407	5246	33529	5934	182638
3049	5891	744	14106	25511	14103	1236	10172	61	25966

11-7 续表 3 Continued 3

指 标	Item	负债总计 Total Liabilities	其中 of which 流动负债合计 Total Current Liabilities	非流动负债合计 Total Non-current Liabilities	所有者权益 Owner's Equity	主营业务收入 Main Business Income
木材加工及木、竹、藤、棕、草制品业	Timber Processing, Bamboo, Cane, Palm Fiber and Straw Products	37200	37200		10637	132820
家具制造业	Furniture Manufacturing	1421	1421		10757	7645
造纸及纸制品业	Papermaking and Paper Products	54842	41351	13093	59179	98632
印刷和记录媒介复制业	Printing and Recorded Media Duplication Industry	29189	29099	89	9995	29396
文教、工美、体育和娱乐用品制造业	Cultural & Educational, Arts & Crafts, Sports & Entertainment Articles Manufacturing	206659	202555	4104	168097	446815
石油加工、炼焦及核燃料加工业	Petroleum Processing, Coking and Nuclear Fuel Processing	70253	70253		25077	126927
化学原料及化学制品制造业	Raw Chemical Materials and Chemica Products	1891046	1604824	286066	1085365	4240639
医药制造业	Medical and Pharmaceutical Products	209802	202939	6862	146264	322886
化学纤维制造业	Chemical Fiber	51901	39266	12635	64702	121508
橡胶和塑料制品业	Rubber and Plastic Products Industry	110933	93061	17872	102582	240596
非金属矿物制品业	Nonmetal Mineral Products	108798	107178	1620	168533	332249
黑色金属冶炼及压延加工业	Smelting and Pressing of Ferrous Metals	1165161	1158139	7022	332503	4182569
有色金属冶炼及压延加工业	Smelting and Pressing of Nonferrous Metals	123935	120623	3312	135910	189937
金属制品业	Metal Products	437273	395103	22223	228563	679359
通用设备制造业	General Equipment Manufacturing	407068	351099	55919	370506	713922
专用设备制造业	For Special Purposes Equipment Manufacturing	1193186	1023566	169592	1167206	1853162
汽车制造业	Automotive Industry	323299	312755	10360	206885	681713
铁路、船舶、航空航天和其他运输设备制造	Railways, Shipping, Aerospace and other Transportation Equipment Manufacturing	199778	194184	5594	202093	479733
电气机械及器材制造业	Electric Equipment and Machinery	2661870	2301111	356552	1783962	5899324
计算机、通信和其他电子设备制造	Computer, Communications and other Electronic Equipment Manufacturing	1133495	1033333	98137	1220028	2911970
仪器仪表制造业	Instrumentation Manufacturing	386022	331126	54896	369605	725528
其他制造业	Other Manufacturing	1437	1437		837	3788
电力、热力生产和供应业	Production and Supply of Electricity & Heat Industry	76582	50465	26117	72345	80108
燃气生产和供应业	Production and Supply of Gas Industry	147177	138048	9128	59647	167497
水的生产和供应业	Production and Supply of water Industry	229628	159031	70597	110333	48005

单位：万元（10000 yuan）

销售费用 Cost of Sales	管理费用 Cost of Management	财务费用 Finance Charge	营业利润 Business Profit	实现利税总额 Total Profits and Taxes	其中 of which 利润总额 Total Profits	主营业务税金及附加 Main Business Tax and Surcharges	应交增值税 Value Added Tax Payable	亏损企业亏损总额 Amount of Loss in Loss-incurring Enterprises	应付职工薪酬 Remuneration Payable to Employees
8268	7728	1348	9070	15775	8991	1628	5156		8718
400	489	286	-219	-3	-280		277	280	1049
3550	3893	2134	4847	7779	4279	205	3294	1545	3824
832	2024	1560	-2027	-896	-1628	116	615	1820	5214
8609	16414	8217	24888	40133	26331	1635	12100	3445	36620
2345	1230	3324	2569	4002	2585	259	1158	593	1113
56858	106626	56329	85802	169152	95940	5004	67584	53046	111194
74854	33023	4104	29544	58856	30864	3202	24791	1239	24147
3608	5098	2770	5815	9897	7060	528	2309		4828
9224	13857	2484	5514	12647	3429	617	8601	3945	18353
13069	18202	3393	32406	50745	33565	1709	15471	1450	22190
7420	24047	62654	267526	243932	118983	4348	120601	450	51008
3831	11481	3886	-15134	4459	-15068	494	19033	16486	10464
15857	31003	9816	24538	39594	24310	2094	11674	4206	35242
19500	51674	12181	26725	52963	27465	3871	20810	14538	70021
76979	112288	22159	99719	180505	97164	5332	76063	27403	127912
13631	50129	6517	43409	68260	39910	2871	25479	10926	54182
14160	28843	2044	-139	35328	7028	5586	22700	12635	46963
128701	242425	61367	189972	376961	196438	18389	160825	102831	370075
48636	139967	17343	244060	356809	243520	8495	104280	8901	338373
23921	64124	6869	82883	123918	84184	4800	34820	17079	68338
	222	57	-347	-354	-354			354	308
17	4612	1976	9701	14163	10783	271	3109	384	3222
3593	7862	3774	37992	43506	37629	668	5209		8453
4323	6002	5620	10383	13751	10192	395	3165		10805

11-8　大中型工业企业主要经济指标（2012 年）
MAJOR ECONOMIC INDICATORS OF LARGE AND MEDIUM-SIZED ENTERPRISES（2012）

指　标	Item	企　业单位数（个）Number of Enterpr-ises（unit）	其中 of which #亏损企业 Loss-incurring Enterprises	工　业总产值 Gross Industrial Output Value	工业销售产值 Value of Industrial Products Sales
总　计	**Total**	**581**	**62**	**53235450**	**52869200**
按地区分	**Grouped by Region**				
市　区	Urban Area	453	44	41359182	41141913
#武进区	Wujin District	233	19	24112587	23985993
溧阳市	Liyang City	58	7	8569498	8540223
金坛市	Jintan City	70	11	3306770	3187065
按登记注册类型分	**Grouped by Registration Status**				
内　资	Domestic Investment	370	32	34855435	34641291
国　有	State-owned	9		838627	830225
集　体	Collective-owned	1		8768	8791
股份合作	Share-holding Cooperative	3		700937	694338
有限责任公司	Limited Liability Corporations	34	9	3890717	3774889
股份有限公司	Share-holding Corporations Ltd.	17		1703846	1627789
私营及其他	Private and others	306	23	27712541	27705258
港澳台商投资	Investment from Hong Kong, Macao and Taiwan	91	8	6415042	6293703
合资经营	Joint-Venture	51	6	2769900	2727117
合作经营	Cooperative	1		70030	70030
独资经营	Sole Investment	33	1	2798706	2742486
股份有限公司	Share-holding Corporations Ltd.	6	1	776407	754071
外商投资	Foreign Investment	120	22	11964974	11934207
中外合资经营	Joint Ventures	51	6	6666886	6679369
中外合作经营	Cooperative Enterprises	3		53806	54025
外商独资	Sole Foreign Investment	65	16	5011556	4961767
股份有限公司	Share-holding Corporations Ltd.	1		232725	239045
按轻重工业分	**Grouped by Light and Heavy Industry**				
轻工业	Light Industry	207	29	10990798	10945162
重工业	Heavy Industry	374	33	42244652	41924038
按企业规模分	**Grouped by Size of Enterprises**				
大　型	Large-sized	93	5	32166130	32017454
中　型	Medium-sized	488	57	21069320	20851746

单位：万元（10000 yuan）

流动资产合计 Current Assets	其中 of which：# 应收帐款净额 Net Account Income	存货 Existing Stock	其中 of which：# 产成品 Manufac-tured Products	固定资产合计 Total Fixed Assets	固定资产原价合计 Total Original Value of Fixed Assets	累计折旧 Accumula-tive Deprecia-tion	资产总计 Total Assets
26167783	**6880504**	**5866766**	**2313076**	**12361659**	**22929272**	**11149084**	**43215751**
21228669	5841296	4897386	1981417	9418965	18939912	9854362	34464394
11238817	2414689	2577930	993519	5079520	8643316	3738261	18240037
3022050	686447	646335	202702	1869854	2402611	776551	5493415
1917064	352761	323045	128957	1072839	1586748	518171	3257942
17589594	4035666	3864946	1524181	7651191	14015691	6679970	28920139
653664	288949	207543	34200	304720	650795	325095	1072261
6049	3965	1389	40	2198	5434	3235	8434
223001	49943	76931	43645	72853	200718	131372	325218
1713635	436109	458518	211163	1113968	2518887	1450359	3212105
1888551	369194	299545	124859	704037	1280641	525757	3286474
13104693	2887506	2821021	1110274	5453416	9359217	4244152	21015647
3118653	929383	745581	292132	1715989	3461435	1777308	5290047
1354172	441527	342439	1169 79	805029	1269735	489583	2422478
32188	2851	3569	167	7350	9939	2589	39904
1360237	387665	357369	149914	694133	1791341	1104092	2213251
372055	97340	42204	25073	209478	390420	181044	614414
5459536	1915455	1256239	496763	2994479	5452146	2691806	9005565
2270361	604553	734856	297022	1538513	2482105	1141314	4001034
37775	11382	12650	4918	16325	20007	5072	62441
2976882	1250293	494824	185139	1401849	2899579	1532758	4636885
174519	49228	13910	9683	37792	50454	12662	305206
5590633	1451726	1210043	497006	2439220	4666888	2332942	9546767
20577150	5428778	4656723	1816070	9922438	18262384	8816142	33668984
14937009	3554749	2991973	1105117	7105724	12968139	6157617	24809295
11230774	3325755	2874793	1207959	5255935	9961133	4991467	18406456

11-8 续表 Continued

指标	Item	负债总计 Total Liabilities	其中 of which 流动负债合计 Total Current Liabilities	非流动负债合计 Total Non-current Liabilities	所有者权益 Owner's Equity	主营业务收入 Main Business Income
总 计	**Total**	**25976612**	**23076323**	**2571023**	**17239139**	**54911413**
按地区分	**Grouped by Region**					
市 区	Urban Area	19884445	17881471	1701729	14579950	42810728
#武进区	Wujin District	10745381	9977152	493494	7494657	25238712
溧阳市	Liyang City	3775799	3617429	130350	1717616	8735340
金坛市	Jintan City	2316368	1577424	738944	941574	3365345
按登记注册类型分	**Grouped by Registration Status**					
内 资	Domestic Investment	17295591	15269637	1703614	11624548	36542931
国 有	State-owned	757679	698099	59580	314582	823809
集 体	Collective-owned	4041	3962	79	4394	10209
股份合作	Share-holding Cooperative	118440	118440		206777	695425
有限责任公司	Limited Liability Corporations	2008142	1709525	297949	1203963	3909308
股份有限公司	Share-holding Corporations Ltd.	1509619	799494	710125	1776855	1759702
私营及其他	Private and others	12897671	11940116	635883	8117976	29344478
港澳台商投资	Investment from Hong Kong, Macao and Taiwan	3047463	2696337	347357	2242584	6406920
合资经营	Joint-Venture	1471548	1241369	227554	950931	2741658
合作经营	Cooperative	33281	33281		6623	73638
独资经营	Sole Investment	1157860	1081666	75048	1055391	2836897
股份有限公司	Share-holding Corporations Ltd.	384775	340021	44754	229639	754728
外商投资	Foreign Investment	5633558	5110350	520052	3372007	11961562
中外合资经营	Joint Ventures	2580295	2503752	76209	1420738	6670458
中外合作经营	Cooperative Enterprises	24022	23817	205	38418	53773
外商独资	Sole Foreign Investment	2875845	2429386	443639	1761041	4991873
股份有限公司	Share-holding Corporations Ltd.	153396	153396		151810	245458
按轻重工业分	**Grouped by Light and Heavy Industry**					
轻工业	Light Industry	5353224	4860424	485388	4193543	11101065
重工业	Heavy Industry	20623388	18215900	2085635	13045596	43810348
按企业规模分	**Grouped by Size of Enterprises**					
大 型	Large-sized	15333388	13397186	1631482	9475907	33552834
中 型	Medium-sized	10643224	9679138	939541	7763233	21358579

单位：万元（10000 yuan）

销售费用 Cost of Sales	管理费用 Cost of Management	财务费用 Finance Charge	营业利润 Business Profit	实现利税总额 Total Profits and Taxes	其中 of which: 利润总额 Total Profits	其中 of which: 主营业务税金及附加 Main Business Tax and Surcharges	其中 of which: 应交增值税 Value Added Tax Payable	亏损企业亏损总额 Amount of Loss in Loss-incurring Enterprises	应付职工薪酬 Remuneration Payable to Employees
990074	**1949645**	**791767**	**3305223**	**4627750**	**2812854**	**181043**	**1630571**	**300672**	**3339678**
789449	1612336	542685	2528101	3534915	2169419	135869	1227873	192957	2870708
290506	774991	350797	1639038	2008126	1221186	65612	721328	34854	1611340
127944	171662	163135	622451	751645	463097	27654	260539	3345	230628
72681	165647	85946	154672	341191	180338	17519	142159	104370	238343
550002	1243923	557331	2285127	3039992	1927555	115934	994848	103705	2017169
15719	63061	19803	23892	67589	38547	3199	25843		80211
8	2860	19	-376	1208	12	50	1146		1686
8708	10489	4386	30692	66674	31958	1524	33193		49107
65689	133808	56208	153698	293204	173718	12358	107128	49641	229691
69832	102835	26366	141804	213971	161485	5786	46700		136048
390047	930870	450550	1935417	2397345	1521835	93017	780839	54064	1520426
126045	263151	75688	460081	698745	474219	22567	201904	30631	562904
80107	136388	54167	203575	328331	211982	14845	101449	19862	325235
992	1081	1091	2189	3504	2162	83	1258		2689
36679	102294	14144	233458	331148	236896	6468	87784	273	190495
8268	23389	6286	20859	35762	23179	1171	11412	10495	44485
314026	442571	158747	560015	889013	411080	42541	433819	166336	759605
163161	169445	96480	375071	485918	223308	21374	239706	22339	269725
2803	5177	1175	1965	3695	2029	205	1456		5982
148034	261583	58189	149976	358261	152972	20962	184288	143997	473818
28	6366	2903	33004	41140	32771		8369		10080
320983	483515	152311	597478	1108705	642130	57890	408586	32644	1193068
669091	1466130	639456	2707746	3519046	2170724	123153	1221985	268028	2146610
412324	953270	451701	1969512	2387628	1397841	88547	901186	162657	1916612
577750	996375	340065	1335712	2240122	1415014	92496	729385	138015	1423066

11-9 规模以上工业企业主要经济分析指标（2012 年）
MAJOR ECONOMIC ANALYTICAL INDICATORS OF INDUSTRIAL ENTERPRISES ABOVE DESIGNATED SIZE（2012）

指 标	Item	工业产品销售率（%） Sales Ratio of Industrial products	工业成本费用利润率（%） Ratio of Profits to Industrial Cost
总 计	**Total**	**98.99**	**5.15**
按地区分	**Grouped by Region**		
市 区	Urban Area	99.13	5.03
武进区	Wujin District	98.73	4.90
新北区	Xinbei District	98.28	3.91
天宁区	Tianning District	99.66	6.01
钟楼区	Zhonglou District	102.58	5.57
戚墅堰区	Qishuyan District	99.32	9.97
溧阳市	Liyang City	99.06	5.26
金坛市	Jintan City	97.15	6.36
按登记注册类型分	**Grouped by Registration Status**		
内 资	Domestic Investment	98.95	5.33
国 有	State-owned	100.55	7.16
集 体	Collective-owned	96.39	5.80
股份合作	Share-holding Cooperative	98.91	4.30
有限责任公司	Limited Liability Corporations	97.44	4.68
股份有限公司	Share-holding Corporations Ltd.	95.74	9.59
私营及其他	Private and others	99.17	5.21
港澳台商投资	Investment from Hong Kong, Macao and Taiwan	98.32	7.00
合资经营	Joint-Venture	98.62	7.48
合作经营	Cooperative	98.92	3.62
独资经营	Sole Investment	98.27	7.48
股份有限公司	Share-holding Corporations Ltd.	97.07	3.14
外商投资	Foreign Investment	99.47	3.57
中外合资经营	Joint Ventures	99.70	3.59
中外合作经营	Cooperative Enterprises	98.01	5.71
外商独资	Sole Foreign Investment	99.14	3.08
股份有限公司	Share-holding Corporations Ltd.	102.34	15.34
按轻重工业分	**Grouped by Light and Heavy Industry**		
轻工业	Light Industry	99.03	5.26
重工业	Heavy Industry	98.98	5.12
按企业规模分	**Grouped by Size of Enterprises**		
大 型	Large-sized	99.54	4.40
中 型	Medium-sized	98.97	7.08
小 型	Small-sized	98.53	4.77
微 型	Micro-sized	97.91	2.15

每百元固定资产原值实现利税（元） Profits and Taxes of Original Value of Fixed Assets Per One Hundred Yuan（yuan）	其中 of which	平均每一从业人员（元） Per Person Employed（yuan）		
	#利润 Profits	实现利税 Profits and Taxes	占有固定资产原值 Original Value of Fixed Assets	实现工业总产值 Gross Industrial Output Value Achieved
21.78	**13.23**	**86178**	**395706**	**1058528**
20.15	12.25	81792	405978	1024620
23.90	14.33	71653	299853	909699
11.09	6.01	71115	641220	1032560
37.98	25.57	116231	306023	1332698
26.77	16.96	133898	500268	1556147
30.45	22.60	146506	481147	1135485
31.62	19.40	144269	456190	1780463
27.04	16.07	69393	256643	681107
24.69	15.41	88291	357575	1072182
11.83	7.31	123170	1041245	1132580
23.31	14.19	50065	214819	525890
28.48	13.24	86564	303969	983001
12.49	7.52	82830	662944	1110476
17.13	12.86	99281	579490	787957
28.87	17.96	87534	303162	1082676
19.09	12.70	76816	402335	774886
26.64	17.09	72634	272632	670963
28.53	14.90	78878	276451	1161231
16.13	11.20	89116	552482	868886
8.85	5.72	39244	443591	852611
15.76	7.83	85641	543273	1244496
20.14	10.13	112934	560733	1665017
13.71	8.42	72177	526508	825726
11.67	5.30	62662	536962	953401
60.33	48.22	199952	331410	1146939
25.02	14.29	58368	233301	665199
20.94	12.96	101023	482396	1268481
18.41	10.78	95422	518276	1285529
22.49	14.21	91251	405767	858259
25.25	15.37	75737	299898	1025001
22.90	10.91	133088	581259	3115004

11-10 规模以上工业企业分行业主要经济分析指标（2012 年）
MAJOR ECONOMIC ANALYTICAL INDICATORS OF INDUSTRIAL ENTERPRISES ABOVE DESIGNATED SIZE BY SECTOR（2012）

指 标	Item	工业产品销售率（%）Sales Ratio of Industrial products	工业成本费用利润率（%）Ratio of Profits to Industrial Cost
黑色金属矿采选业	Ferrous Metal Mining Industry	83.69	0.65
非金属矿采选业	Nonmetal Minerals Mining and Dressing	100.00	-4.02
农副食品加工业	Food Processing	100.19	1.66
食品制造业	Food Production	98.16	4.80
酒、饮料和精制茶制造业	Beverages and Refined Tea Manufacturing	105.92	4.16
纺织业	Textile Industry	98.92	4.59
纺织服装、服饰业	Textile and clothing Industry	99.72	5.50
皮革、毛皮、羽毛及其制品和制鞋业	Leather, Fur, Feathers and Their Products, and Footwear Industry	97.51	5.96
木材加工及木、竹、藤、棕、草制品业	Timber Processing, Bamboo, Cane, Palm Fiber and Straw Products	98.71	5.98
家具制造业	Furniture Manufacturing	98.12	1.56
造纸及纸制品业	Papermaking and Paper Products	97.56	3.28
印刷和记录媒介复制业	Printing and Recorded Media Duplication Industry	99.31	4.30
文教、工美、体育和娱乐用品制造业	Cultural & Educational, Arts & Crafts, Sports & Entertainment Articles Manufacturing	98.16	4.25
石油加工、炼焦及核燃料加工业	Petroleum Processing, Coking and Nuclear Fuel Processing	97.29	1.64
化学原料及化学制品制造业	Raw Chemical Materials and Chemica Products	99.47	3.98
医药制造业	Medical and Pharmaceutical Products	97.19	10.93
化学纤维制造业	Chemical Fiber	98.00	4.02
橡胶和塑料制品业	Rubber and Plastic Products Industry	98.68	3.73
非金属矿物制品业	Nonmetal Mineral Products	99.96	8.70
黑色金属冶炼及压延加工业	Smelting and Pressing of Ferrous Metals	100.16	2.38
有色金属冶炼及压延加工业	Smelting and Pressing of Nonferrous Metals	98.46	5.07
金属制品业	Metal Products	99.85	6.11
通用设备制造业	General Equipment Manufacturing	97.41	5.96
专用设备制造业	For Special Purposes Equipment Manufacturing	98.63	6.99
汽车制造业	Automotive Industry	100.07	5.98
铁路、船舶、航空航天和其他运输设备制造	Railways, Shipping, Aerospace and other Transportation Equipment Manufacturing	98.88	8.46
电气机械及器材制造业	Electric Equipment and Machinery	98.78	4.84
计算机、通信和其他电子设备制造	Computer, Communications and other Electronic Equipment Manufacturing	96.36	6.55
仪器仪表制造业	Instrumentation Manufacturing	96.96	11.49
其他制造业	Other Manufacturing	99.05	5.11
废弃资源综合利用业	Comprehensive Utilization of Waste Resources Industry	95.96	1.06
金属制品、机械和设备修理业	Metal Products, Machinery & Equipment Repairing Industry	104.97	-7.97
电力、热力生产和供应业	Production and Supply of Electricity & Heat Industry	99.37	15.18
燃气生产和供应业	Production and Supply of Gas Industry	100.00	22.14
水的生产和供应业	Production and Supply of water Industry	95.07	13.05

每百元固定资产原值实现利税（元） Profits and Taxes of Original Value of Fixed Assets Per One Hundred Yuan（yuan）	其中 of which #利润 Profits	平均每一从业人员（元）Per Person Employed（yuan） 实现利税 Profits and Taxes	占有固定资产原值 Original Value of Fixed Assets	实现工业总产值 Gross Industrial Output Value Achieved
3.00	0.63	21985	732938	822785
25.73	-16.52	46456	180560	746227
10.28	5.77	46484	452056	1529653
14.18	5.78	116937	824608	1031306
23.79	4.50	70905	298062	429168
29.62	17.14	72334	244216	934447
34.39	22.40	32239	93752	391616
76.45	42.98	36840	48191	364114
88.56	51.37	105653	119295	1101768
22.06	7.64	30954	140319	712954
21.00	10.54	54409	259133	871915
14.50	8.17	35931	247766	494003
24.06	13.64	44516	185038	614258
18.10	11.08	61402	339247	2393192
12.27	7.30	118376	964526	1813472
45.02	28.16	112167	249157	742596
18.04	10.23	54009	299461	807638
17.98	9.98	46449	258365	712967
26.95	16.49	155503	577087	1161034
17.19	8.66	126304	734940	2606902
51.54	29.81	176255	341957	2059485
35.14	22.63	85009	241934	956554
20.30	13.09	56879	280229	663069
20.74	12.90	91723	442212	883967
24.35	14.45	71539	293843	761657
28.50	18.57	102909	361109	861351
27.14	17.03	90810	334579	1231710
24.68	15.22	49195	199293	504269
35.45	24.38	117863	332502	815771
196.02	71.19	154359	78747	1178338
16.14	2.56	98062	607600	1351323
-16.02	-24.24	-19585	122248	327350
12.63	8.59	471447	3733393	2420644
28.47	24.28	522724	1835748	2175019
3.42	2.42	90307	2636903	465545

11-11 规模以上民营工业企业主要经济分析指标（2012 年）
MAJOR ECONOMIC ANALYTICAL INDICATORS OF PRIVATE INDUSTRIAL ENTERPRISES ABOVE DESIGNATED SIZE（2012）

指 标	Item	工业产品销售率（%）Sales Ratio of Industrial products	工业成本费用利润率（%）Ratio of Profits to Industrial Cost
总 计	**Total**	**98.95**	**5.19**
按地区分	**Grouped by Region**		
市 区	Urban Area	99.19	4.86
武进区	Wujin District	98.90	4.25
新北区	Xinbei District	97.52	5.73
天宁区	Tianning District	100.06	5.55
钟楼区	Zhonglou District	103.03	5.94
戚墅堰区	Qishuyan District	100.49	8.74
溧阳市	Liyang City	98.81	6.11
金坛市	Jintan City	96.49	7.13
按轻重工业分	**Grouped by Light and Heavy Industry**		
轻工业	Light Industry	99.44	4.12
重工业	Heavy Industry	98.81	5.49
按企业规模分	**Grouped by Size of Enterprises**		
大 型	Large-sized	99.88	4.59
中 型	Medium-sized	98.79	7.10
小 型	Small-sized	98.29	4.88
微 型	Micro-sized	98.21	2.66
按工业行业分	**Grouped by Sector**		
黑色金属矿采选业	Ferrous Metal Mining Industry	83.69	0.65
非金属矿采选业	Nonmetal Minerals Mining and Dressing	100.00	-4.89
农副食品加工业	Food Processing	101.01	0.49
食品制造业	Food Production	99.59	4.94
酒、饮料和精制茶制造业	Beverages and Refined Tea Manufacturing	99.40	-0.63
纺织业	Textile Industry	99.44	3.73
纺织服装、服饰业	Textile and clothing Industry	100.18	4.26
皮革、毛皮、羽毛及其制品和制鞋业	Leather, Fur, Feathers and Their Products, and Footwear Industry	96.97	4.98

每百元固定资产原值实现利税（元） Profits and Taxes of Original Value of Fixed Assets Per One Hundred Yuan（yuan）	其中 of which	平均每一从业人员（元） Per Person Employed（yuan）		
	#利润 Profits	实现利税 Profits and Taxes	占有固定资产原值 Original Value of Fixed Assets	实现工业总产值 Gross Industrial Output Value Achieved
26.84	**16.69**	**86340**	**321665**	**1071596**
24.93	15.26	81504	326990	1060447
23.15	13.44	72515	313194	1014813
19.39	12.87	77687	400605	968225
45.34	29.46	99527	219513	1186916
37.86	23.92	156981	414623	1729467
61.70	46.15	125305	203078	1025186
38.14	24.92	134464	352560	1509840
29.54	18.93	73828	249911	709044
23.71	12.73	56073	236517	759325
27.75	17.84	99724	359317	1209680
21.20	13.08	117771	555597	1569739
26.95	17.56	83403	309498	805243
33.63	20.44	72182	214644	961112
50.16	25.74	195730	390235	4027750
3.00	0.63	21985	732938	822785
19.27	-24.95	29700	154097	771760
5.90	1.62	26225	444649	1457503
22.24	13.67	49566	222884	709450
18.14	-0.52	55232	304421	364932
28.41	15.30	65008	228839	960845
22.61	14.64	25326	112037	378739
52.53	30.22	29469	56095	356074

11-11 续表 Continued

指 标	Item	工业产品销售率（%）Sales Ratio of Industrial products	工业成本费用利润率（%）Ratio of Profits to Industrial Cost
木材加工及木、竹、藤、棕、草制品业	Timber Processing, Bamboo, Cane, Palm Fiber and Straw Products	98.54	5.69
家具制造业	Furniture Manufacturing	97.74	2.63
造纸及纸制品业	Papermaking and Paper Products	96.85	2.88
印刷和记录媒介复制业	Printing and Recorded Media Duplication Industry	99.73	5.82
文教、工美、体育和娱乐用品制造业	Cultural & Educational, Arts & Crafts, Sports & Entertainment Articles Manufacturing	96.77	2.72
石油加工、炼焦及核燃料加工业	Petroleum Processing, Coking and Nuclear Fuel Processing	92.89	1.24
化学原料及化学制品制造业	Raw Chemical Materials and Chemica Products	99.40	4.74
医药制造业	Medical and Pharmaceutical Products	94.69	8.93
化学纤维制造业	Chemical Fiber	97.51	3.19
橡胶和塑料制品业	Rubber and Plastic Products Industry	99.06	4.50
非金属矿物制品业	Nonmetal Mineral Products	100.18	8.21
黑色金属冶炼及压延加工业	Smelting and Pressing of Ferrous Metals	100.23	2.15
有色金属冶炼及压延加工业	Smelting and Pressing of Nonferrous Metals	98.95	6.45
金属制品业	Metal Products	99.32	6.76
通用设备制造业	General Equipment Manufacturing	97.36	6.90
专用设备制造业	For Special Purposes Equipment Manufacturing	98.59	8.17
汽车制造业	Automotive Industry	97.44	6.01
铁路、船舶、航空航天和其他运输设备制造	Railways, Shipping, Aerospace and other Transportation Equipment Manufacturing	98.25	13.22
电气机械及器材制造业	Electric Equipment and Machinery	98.92	5.71
计算机、通信和其他电子设备制造	Computer, Communications and other Electronic Equipment Manufacturing	95.30	1.78
仪器仪表制造业	Instrumentation Manufacturing	96.24	10.48
其他制造业	Other Manufacturing	98.96	6.62
废弃资源综合利用业	Comprehensive Utilization of Waste Resources Industry	95.96	1.06
金属制品、机械和设备修理业	Metal Products, Machinery & Equipment Repairing Industry	104.97	-7.97
电力、热力生产和供应业	Production and Supply of Electricity & Heat Industry	95.19	10.77
燃气生产和供应业	Production and Supply of Gas Industry	100.00	3.88
水的生产和供应业	Production and Supply of water Industry	93.65	11.74

每百元固定资产原值实现利税（元）Profits and Taxes of Original Value of Fixed Assets Per One Hundred Yuan (yuan)	其中 of which	平均每一从业人员（元） Per Person Employed (yuan)		
	#利润 Profits	实现利税 Profits and Taxes	占有固定资产原值 Original Value of Fixed Assets	实现工业总产值 Gross Industrial Output Value Achieved
82.26	47.95	103590	125923	1139736
36.69	17.63	51158	139426	986825
24.97	12.01	47941	191984	845589
18.63	11.87	46818	251299	543426
19.39	8.88	37620	194013	656640
10.28	5.83	31199	303504	1548916
18.64	11.23	122006	654405	1608861
42.33	27.32	87378	206408	731145
17.79	8.74	41649	234054	682986
25.63	16.08	49214	191992	714572
26.27	15.75	157942	601269	1217143
15.31	7.84	96577	630655	2162874
84.26	56.53	202899	240798	2181692
48.00	31.27	90927	189444	942540
27.34	18.06	62961	230270	655283
37.81	25.10	87652	231803	782931
29.83	17.64	65411	219313	704813
51.55	38.24	150167	291319	963222
38.13	26.05	94531	247905	1194806
12.16	3.91	26964	221709	524549
31.12	21.61	104628	336199	792726
227.87	91.04	217698	95537	1430228
16.14	2.56	98062	607600	1351323
-16.02	-24.24	-19585	122248	327350
10.56	8.64	140056	1325838	1267516
2.77	1.41	129367	4664067	1651283
13.74	11.56	289563	2106690	2220644

11-12 规模以上三资工业企业主要经济分析指标（2012 年）
MAJOR ECONOMIC ANALYTICAL INDICATORS OF FOREIGN-FUNDED INDUSTRIAL ENTERPRISES ABOVE DESIGNATED SIZE（2012）

指 标	Item	工业产品销售率（%）Sales Ratio of Industrial products	工业成本费用利润率（%）Ratio of Profits to Industrial Cost
总 计	**Total**	**99.07**	**4.74**
按地区分	**Grouped by Region**		
市 区	Urban Area	98.92	5.10
武进区	Wujin District	97.92	8.28
新北区	Xinbei District	99.01	2.11
天宁区	Tianning District	98.89	5.29
钟楼区	Zhonglou District	101.75	5.69
戚墅堰区	Qishuyan District	99.08	16.12
溧阳市	Liyang City	99.94	3.14
金坛市	Jintan City	98.69	4.43
按轻重工业分	**Grouped by Light and Heavy Industry**		
轻工业	Light Industry	98.32	6.73
重工业	Heavy Industry	99.31	4.13
按企业规模分	**Grouped by Size of Enterprises**		
大 型	Large-sized	99.09	3.43
中 型	Medium-sized	99.27	7.11
小 型	Small-sized	98.90	4.09
微 型	Micro-sized	96.13	-0.70
按工业行业分	**Grouped by Sector**		
农副食品加工业	Food Processing	96.76	6.16
食品制造业	Food Production	97.14	5.83
酒、饮料和精制茶制造业	Beverages and Refined Tea Manufacturing	111.19	7.53
纺织业	Textile Industry	97.58	4.49
纺织服装、服饰业	Textile and clothing Industry	99.31	6.23
皮革、毛皮、羽毛及其制品和制鞋业	Leather, Fur, Feathers and Their Products, and Footwear Industry	98.08	6.99

每百元固定资产原值实现利税（元） Profits and Taxes of Original Value of Fixed Assets Per One Hundred Yuan (yuan)	其中 of which	平均每一从业人员（元） Per Person Employed (yuan)		
	#利润 Profits	实现利税 Profits and Taxes	占有固定资产原值 Original Value of Fixed Assets	实现工业总产值 Gross Industrial Output Value Achieved
17.05	**9.71**	**81589**	**478558**	**1028862**
16.00	9.45	77981	487432	949216
26.79	17.66	69407	259099	610012
7.32	2.77	57898	790962	1060274
33.14	21.64	125509	378724	1594343
28.92	18.57	137396	475080	1585934
79.54	68.29	259249	325954	1587016
22.60	11.08	181738	804158	3024432
26.60	12.02	54557	205089	560170
26.47	15.62	57628	217693	539235
14.58	8.16	101654	697015	1438892
15.82	7.70	65576	414561	983988
19.60	11.94	103262	526793	939057
15.53	9.36	78183	503479	1192610
1.08	-0.97	10321	955634	1326183
32.21	26.50	158813	493125	1929701
12.89	4.77	153290	1189329	1001437
30.32	10.30	88237	291030	500204
30.69	16.52	71889	234267	902274
49.52	32.23	36817	74344	408322
114.14	63.10	45009	39432	373024

11-12 续表 Continued

指 标	Item	工业产品销售率（%）Sales Ratio of Industrial products	工业成本费用利润率（%）Ratio of Profits to Industrial Cost
木材加工及木、竹、藤、棕、草制品业	Timber Processing, Bamboo, Cane, Palm Fiber and Straw Products	99.49	7.36
家具制造业	Furniture Manufacturing	100.11	-3.44
造纸及纸制品业	Papermaking and Paper Products	99.88	4.58
印刷和记录媒介复制业	Printing and Recorded Media Duplication Industry	96.88	-5.20
文教、工美、体育和娱乐用品制造业	Cultural & Educational, Arts & Crafts, Sports & Entertainment Articles Manufacturing	100.00	6.26
石油加工、炼焦及核燃料加工业	Petroleum Processing, Coking and Nuclear Fuel Processing	102.57	2.08
化学原料及化学制品制造业	Raw Chemical Materials and Chemica Products	99.92	2.30
医药制造业	Medical and Pharmaceutical Products	102.93	10.56
化学纤维制造业	Chemical Fiber	99.28	6.13
橡胶和塑料制品业	Rubber and Plastic Products Industry	97.52	1.46
非金属矿物制品业	Nonmetal Mineral Products	101.08	11.21
黑色金属冶炼及压延加工业	Smelting and Pressing of Ferrous Metals	99.98	3.04
有色金属冶炼及压延加工业	Smelting and Pressing of Nonferrous Metals	94.54	-7.27
金属制品业	Metal Products	102.18	3.72
通用设备制造业	General Equipment Manufacturing	96.38	4.05
专用设备制造业	For Special Purposes Equipment Manufacturing	99.53	5.56
汽车制造业	Automotive Industry	103.95	6.27
铁路、船舶、航空航天和其他运输设备制造	Railways, Shipping, Aerospace and other Transportation Equipment Manufacturing	100.84	1.48
电气机械及器材制造业	Electric Equipment and Machinery	98.12	3.45
计算机、通信和其他电子设备制造	Computer, Communications and other Electronic Equipment Manufacturing	96.91	9.14
仪器仪表制造业	Instrumentation Manufacturing	98.08	13.09
其他制造业	Other Manufacturing	100.00	-8.56
电力、热力生产和供应业	Production and Supply of Electricity & Heat Industry	94.79	18.86
燃气生产和供应业	Production and Supply of Gas Industry	100.00	3.88
水的生产和供应业	Production and Supply of water Industry	93.65	11.74

每百元固定资产原值实现利税（元）Profits and Taxes of Original Value of Fixed Assets Per One Hundred Yuan (yuan)	其中 of which	平均每一从业人员（元） Per Person Employed (yuan)		
	#利润 Profits	实现利税 Profits and Taxes	占有固定资产原值 Original Value of Fixed Assets	实现工业总产值 Gross Industrial Output Value Achieved
121.43	69.21	113651	93594	954545
-0.08	-7.48	-117	141693	291773
15.37	8.45	78889	513291	971559
-4.99	-9.06	-10140	203239	347747
29.98	19.67	52392	174786	565850
42.09	27.19	223553	531145	6925872
5.19	2.95	101788	1959667	2507641
39.71	20.83	147768	372086	804391
18.52	13.21	125275	676589	1526356
8.28	2.24	38059	459762	708098
41.43	27.40	153077	369529	982061
22.66	11.05	322448	1423044	5536724
2.96	-10.00	27680	935408	1185826
11.32	6.95	61904	547021	1070236
13.54	7.02	47078	347582	638539
12.74	6.86	103169	810114	1058211
24.78	14.49	84522	341043	817541
15.80	3.14	48189	304917	664344
18.07	9.42	82938	458989	1296469
31.30	21.36	59020	188577	491157
42.85	29.11	139847	326361	854048
-135.35	-135.35	-37681	27840	414628
6.82	5.19	269770	3955373	1534337
42.54	36.79	586340	1378338	2259720
3.54	2.62	130717	3690731	493683

11-13 大中型工业企业主要经济分析指标（2012 年）
MAIN ECONOMIC ANALYTICAL INDICATORS OF LARGE AND MEDIUM-SIZED INDUSTRIAL ENTERPRISES（2012）

指 标	Item	工业产品销售率（%） Sales Ratio of Industrial products	工业成本费用利润率（%） Ratio of Profits to Industrial Cost
总 计	**Total**	**99.31**	**5.43**
按地区分	**Grouped by Region**		
市 区	Urban Area	99.47	5.36
#武进区	Wujin District	99.48	5.15
溧阳市	Liyang City	99.66	5.71
金坛市	Jintan City	96.38	5.64
按登记注册类型分	**Grouped by Registration Status**		
内 资	Domestic Investment	99.39	5.60
国 有	State-owned	99.00	4.84
集 体	Collective-owned	100.27	0.10
股份合作	Share-holding Cooperative	99.06	4.82
有限责任公司	Limited Liability Corporations	97.02	4.61
股份有限公司	Share-holding Corporations Ltd.	95.54	9.61
私 营	Private	99.97	5.54
港澳台商投资	Investment from Hong Kong, Macao and Taiwan	98.11	7.96
合资经营	Joint-Venture	98.46	8.31
合作经营	Cooperative	100.00	3.03
独资经营	Sole Investment	97.99	9.11
股份有限公司	Share-holding Corporations Ltd.	97.12	3.15
外商投资	Foreign Investment	99.74	3.61
中外合资经营	Joint Ventures	100.19	3.55
中外合作经营	Cooperative Enterprises	100.41	3.91
外商独资	Sole Foreign Investment	99.01	3.17
股份有限公司	Share-holding Corporations Ltd.	102.72	15.42
按轻重工业分	**Grouped by Light and Heavy Industry**		
轻工业	Light Industry	99.58	6.10
重工业	Heavy Industry	99.24	5.26
按企业规模分	**Grouped by Size of Enterprises**		
大 型	Large-sized	99.54	4.40
中 型	Medium-sized	98.97	7.08

每百元固定资产原值实现利税（元） Profits and Taxes of Original Value of Fixed Assets Per One Hundred Yuan（yuan）	其中 of which	平均每一从业人员（元） Per Person Employed（yuan）		
	#利润 Profits	实现利税 Profits and Taxes	占有固定资产原值 Original Value of Fixed Assets	实现工业总产值 Gross Industrial Output Value Achieved
20.18	**12.27**	**93357**	**462558**	**1073932**
18.66	11.45	87473	468676	1023451
23.23	14.13	84752	364788	1017662
31.28	19.27	180207	576028	2054543
21.50	11.37	68401	318107	662932
21.69	13.75	99724	459769	1143393
10.39	5.92	69230	666594	858985
22.23	0.21	25702	115606	186547
33.22	15.92	105648	318044	1110659
11.64	6.90	86132	739957	1142950
16.71	12.61	99079	592999	788964
25.61	16.26	103040	402268	1191112
20.19	13.70	75348	373257	691753
25.86	16.70	73928	285899	623683
35.25	21.75	77862	220867	1556216
18.49	13.22	86288	466775	729266
9.16	5.94	37656	411099	817529
16.31	7.54	90597	555616	1219323
19.58	9.00	123511	630905	1694598
18.47	10.14	28958	156797	421680
12.36	5.28	64308	520477	899579
81.54	64.95	228553	280301	1292916
23.76	13.76	59773	251602	592537
19.27	11.89	113437	588693	1361769
18.41	10.78	95422	518276	1285529
22.49	14.21	91251	405767	858259

11-14 规模以上工业企业资本金构成（2012 年）
CAPITAL CONDITION OF INDUSTRIAL ENTERPRISES ABOVE DESIGNATED SIZE（2012）

指 标	Item	实收资本合计 Total Paid-up Capital
总 计	**Total**	**13673976**
按地区分	**Grouped by Region**	
市 区	Urban Area	10398865
武进区	Wujin District	4841712
新北区	Xinbei District	3602867
天宁区	Tianning District	755723
钟楼区	Zhonglou District	593081
戚墅堰区	Qishuyan District	605482
溧阳市	Liyang City	1481720
金坛市	Jintan City	1793391
按登记注册类型分	**Grouped by Registration Status**	
内 资	Domestic Investment	8241182
国 有	State-owned	436777
集 体	Collective-owned	5196
股份合作	Share-holding Cooperative	60585
有限责任公司	Limited Liability Corporations	733259
股份有限公司	Share-holding Corporations Ltd.	443061
私 营	Private	6562304
港澳台商投资	Investment from Hong Kong, Macao and Taiwan	1910628
合资经营	Joint-Venture	749076
合作经营	Cooperative	20985
独资经营	Sole Investment	986368
股份有限公司	Share-holding Corporations Ltd.	154199
外商投资	Foreign Investment	3522167
中外合资经营	Joint Ventures	1077564
中外合作经营	Cooperative Enterprises	67466
外商独资	Sole Foreign Investment	2331086
股份有限公司	Share-holding Corporations Ltd.	46051
按轻重工业分	**Grouped by Light and Heavy Industry**	
轻工业	Light Industry	3349547
重工业	Heavy Industry	10324429
按企业规模分	**Grouped by Size of Enterprises**	
大 型	Large-sized	3361784
中 型	Medium-sized	3644754
小 型	Small-sized	6548726
微 型	Micro-sized	118712

单位：万元（10000 yuan）

国家资本 National Capital	法人资本 Capital of Legal Person	集体资本 Collective-owned Capital	个人资本 Individual Capital	港澳台资本 Captial of Hongkong, Macao and Taiwan	外商资本 Foreign Capital
529660	**296369**	**3886293**	**4840716**	**1389508**	**2729431**
490821	280395	2943075	2966748	1199367	2516461
51045	214543	1488838	1897092	634622	555573
77361	25454	800936	580547	429942	1688628
80226	28112	184375	226216	76430	160364
114189	2997	197454	177442	41249	57750
168000	9289	271471	85451	17124	54146
28400	1778	534290	679802	130977	106472
10439	14196	408928	1194166	59163	106498
471005	263154	2762357	4599785	73006	69875
106590	500	329688			
	4108		1088		
	572	26189	32951	275	598
205028	1435	420159	102089	1568	2979
131629	16157	142098	139000		12177
27759	240381	1844223	4324657	71163	54121
17109	21324	479704	90651	1130236	171604
17109	20472	298640	76785	258582	77489
		6882	6719	7384	
	852	118245	7148	788654	71469
		55937		75616	22646
41546	11891	644232	150280	186265	2487952
17635	9756	519045	82640	97679	350808
20730	2135	18512	13672	3315	9103
3181		84175	53968	85272	2104490
		22500			23551
117529	255068	1084850	731943	605587	554570
412131	41301	2801443	4108773	783921	2174861
284744	29701	1233428	741013	319228	753669
142425	28915	1215621	892783	570291	792719
98350	237752	1411184	3151115	473837	1176487
4140		26060	55806	26151	6556

11-15 规模以上工业企业分行业资本金构成（2012 年）
CAPITAL COMPOSITION OF INDUSTRIAL ENTERPRISES ABOVE DESIGNATED SIZE BY SECTOR（2012）

指 标	Item	实收资本合计 Total Paid-up Capital
黑色金属矿采选业	Ferrous Metal Mining Industry	1000
非金属矿采选业	Nonmetal Minerals Mining and Dressing	10178
农副食品加工业	Food Processing	37846
食品制造业	Food Production	67317
酒、饮料和精制茶制造业	Beverages and Refined Tea Manufacturing	30804
纺织业	Textile Industry	494463
纺织服装、服饰业	Textile and clothing Industry	209975
皮革、毛皮、羽毛及其制品和制鞋业	Leather, Fur, Feathers and Their Products, and Footwear Industry	44128
木材加工及木、竹、藤、棕、草制品业	Timber Processing, Bamboo, Cane, Palm Fiber and Straw Products	48408
家具制造业	Furniture Manufacturing	20620
造纸及纸制品业	Papermaking and Paper Products	121039
印刷和记录媒介复制业	Printing and Recorded Media Duplication Industry	40999
文教、工美、体育和娱乐用品制造业	Cultural & Educational, Arts & Crafts, Sports & Entertainment Articles Manufacturing	167548
石油加工、炼焦及核燃料加工业	Petroleum Processing, Coking and Nuclear Fuel Processing	319514
化学原料及化学制品制造业	Raw Chemical Materials and Chemica Products	1802747
医药制造业	Medical and Pharmaceutical Products	181435
化学纤维制造业	Chemical Fiber	258927
橡胶和塑料制品业	Rubber and Plastic Products Industry	191336
非金属矿物制品业	Nonmetal Mineral Products	709886
黑色金属冶炼及压延加工业	Smelting and Pressing of Ferrous Metals	1596295
有色金属冶炼及压延加工业	Smelting and Pressing of Nonferrous Metals	240752
金属制品业	Metal Products	514239
通用设备制造业	General Equipment Manufacturing	825794
专用设备制造业	For Special Purposes Equipment Manufacturing	1301420
汽车制造业	Automotive Industry	392936
铁路、船舶、航空航天和其他运输设备制造	Railways, Shipping, Aerospace and other Transportation Equipment Manufacturing	587326
电气机械及器材制造业	Electric Equipment and Machinery	2090164
计算机、通信和其他电子设备制造	Computer, Communications and other Electronic Equipment Manufacturing	912161
仪器仪表制造业	Instrumentation Manufacturing	320963
其他制造业	Other Manufacturing	3900
废弃资源综合利用业	Comprehensive Utilization of Waste Resources Industry	6158
金属制品、机械和设备修理业	Metal Products, Machinery & Equipment Repairing Industry	2135
电力、热力生产和供应业	Production and Supply of Electricity & Heat Industry	311233
燃气生产和供应业	Production and Supply of Gas Industry	33315.5
水的生产和供应业	Production and Supply of water Industry	64579

单位：万元（10000 yuan）

国家资本 National Capital	法人资本 Capital of Legal Person	集体资本 Collective-owned Capital	个人资本 Individual Capital	港澳台资本 Captial of Hongkong, Macao and Taiwan	外商资本 Foreign Capital
			1000		
	78	10100			
123	35	3080	27778	6831	
		20200	12416	8147	26554
		28268	800		1736
54846	17980	114794	168149	86533	52162
40	8639	87738	34440	43807	35310
4043	96	3742	14473	11590	10184
		5050	39900	45	3413
			11044		9576
		57108	16027	25136	22768
3193		13872	18164	5770	
	7318	29042	48855	21945	60389
		896	14970	1249	14836
38624	5761	724811	413645	337342	280565
	3000	50544	82927	16576	28387
	200000	14141	35743	7988	1055
2094	13965	65098	49230	16427	44521
4321	143	212070	413540	1365	78447
	100	165124	1373488	43968	13616
5240	300	45482	71765	246	117719
2000		108784	227049	79525	96882
60187	1370	202876	313750	31263	216347
71723	3900	418502	290841	94961	421493
15300	497	142739	119540	18402	96458
172500	1860	180792	116134	16908	99132
901	23186	669283	617234	121569	657991
9885	4200	187267	157274	340684	212852
58	400	63647	143054	17666	96138
			2681		1219
6000			158		
		2092	43		
25993	1292	245539	4605	16027	17778
8300		13116			11900
44290	2250	500		17539	

11-16 规模以上工业主要产品产量（2012 年）
OUTPUT OF INDUSTRIAL ENTERPRISES ABOVE DESIGNATED SIZE（2012）

产品名称	Name of Products	全 市 Whole Municipality	其中 of which #市 区 Urban Area
原 盐（吨）	Crude Salt（ton）	3258984	
大 米（吨）	Grain（ton）	340	
饲 料（吨）	Feedign Stuff（ton）	460415	71958
精制食用植物油（吨）	Purified Edible Vegetable Oil（ton）	2200	2200
饮料酒（千升）	Drinks（kilolitre）	296507	155807
#啤 酒	Beer	296507	155807
纱（万吨）	Yarn（10000 tons）	16	13
#棉 纱	Cotton Yarn	12	10
布（万米）	Cloth（10000 m）	107437	99200
#棉 布	Cotton Cloth	80369	80019
#牛仔布	Jean	4569	4569
印染布（万米）	Printing and Dyeing Cloth（10000 m）	46847	46847
服 装（万件）	Garment（10000 units）	45454	27720
复合木地板（万平方米）	Laminate Flooring（10000m^2）	8222	8222
纸制品（吨）	Paper Products（ton）	74523	65724
润滑油（吨）	Lubricants（ton）	105700	105700
硫 酸（折100%,吨）	Sulfuric Acid（100%, ton）	246800	246800
盐 酸（含量31%以上,吨）	Hydrochloric Acid（content above 31%, ton）	113750	29072
烧 碱（折100%,吨）	Caustic Soda（100%, ton）	250019	82582
化学农药原药（折有效成份100%，吨）	Chemical pesticide（Converted into effective components 100%,ton）	49557	41628

11-16 续表 1 Continued 1

产品名称	Name of Products	全 市 Whole Municipality	其中 of which #市 区 Urban Area
涂 料（吨）	Coating （ton）	222307	214995
初级形态的塑料（吨）	Primary-form Plastic （ton）	1548053	1525112
单晶硅（吨）	Monocrystalline silicon （ton）	378946	
多晶硅（吨）	Polysilicon （ton）	59380	59380
化学药品原药（吨）	Chemical Pesticide （ton）	9290	9188
化学纤维（吨）	Chemical Fiber （ton）	113902	70553
水泥熟料（万吨）	Cement Clinker （10000 tons）	1590	
水 泥（万吨）	Cement （10000 tons）	2662	67
钢化玻璃（平方米）	Tempered Glass （square meter）	437446	437446
生 铁（万吨）	Pig Iron （10000 tons）	974	749
粗 钢（万吨）	Raw Steel （10000 tons）	1130	901
钢 材（万吨）	Rolled-Steel （10000 tons）	1327	967
铁合金（万吨）	Ferroalloy （10000 tons）	11	11
金属集装箱（万立方米）	Metal Container （10000 m^3）	1124	1124
金属切削机床（台）	Metal-Cutting Machine Tool （unit）	2553	603
滚动轴承（万套）	Rolling Axle Bearing （10000 units）	34552	19749
电动手提式工具（台）	Portable Electric Tools （unit）	5653323	5098420
衡 器（秤,台）	Weighing Apparatus （unit）	306397	306397
减速机（台）	Reducer （unit）	571963	571963
挖掘机（台）	Mechanical Excavator （unit）	7645	7645
装载机（台）	Shovel Loader （unit）	3861	3861
金属冶炼设备（吨）	Melting Equipment （ton）	13624	13624

11-16 续表 2 Continued 2

产品名称	Name of Products	全 市 Whole Municipality	其 中 of which #市 区 Urban Area
金属轧制设备（吨）	Metal Rolling Equipment （ton）	29912	29912
大中型拖拉机（台）	Large and Medium Size Tractor （unit）	69639	69639
小型拖拉机（台）	Mini-tractors （unit）	72626	72626
汽 车（辆）	Motor Vehicles （City Buses,unit）	1011	1011
铁路机车（辆）	Locomotive （unit）	84	84
民用钢质船舶（载重吨）	Civil Steel Ship （deadweight tons） （DWT）	7024	
摩托车整车（万辆）	Finished Motorcycle （10000 units）	21	21
两轮脚踏自行车（万辆）	Bicycles （10000 units）	200	200
电动自行车（万辆）	Electric Bicycle （10000 units）	56	56
交流电动机（千瓦）	AC Machine （ kw）	578440	578440
变压器（兆伏安）	Transformer （MVA）	144511	86269
通信电缆（对千米）	Telecommunications Cable （pair,km）	40160	40160
电力电缆（千米）	Electric Cable （1000 m）	649441	429530
光 缆（芯千米）	Fiber Optic Cable （core km）	2558513	2558513
原电池（折R20标准万只）	Primary battery （converted into R20 standard unit）	38873	26414
太阳能电池（兆瓦）	Solar Cell （megawatt）	3164	2406
房间空气调节器（台）	Air Conditioners （unit）	75097	75097
GPS接收机（台）	GPS Receiver （unit）	68951	68951
彩色电视机（台）	Color TV Sets （unit）	242905	242905
激光视盘机（台）	Video-CD Players （unit）	442042	442042
半导体分立器件（万只）	Semiconduction Separating Part （10000 units）	2558865	2558865
光学仪器（台）	Optical Instruments （unit）	189523	189523
发电量（万千瓦时）	Power Generation （10000 kwh）	1589275	1424112

12

CHAPTER 12

常州统计年鉴

建筑业

CONSTRUCTION

12 建 筑 业 CONSTRUCTION

2012年主要统计指标
MAJOR STATISTICAL INDICATORS OF 2012

年底建筑业企业数（含劳务企业）	Number of Construction Enterprises (Including Labor Services Enterprises)	687个	(unit)
#施工总承包企业数	Number of Construction Contracting Enterprises	594个	(unit)
建筑业企业总产值（含劳务企业）	Construction Enterprises Output Value (Including Labor Service Enterprises)	1071.66亿元	(100 million yuan)
比上年增长	Over the Previous Year	19.1%	
房屋建筑施工面积	Floor Space of Buildings Under Construction	8765.07万平方米	(10000 sq.m)
比上年增长	Over the Previous Year	14.5%	
房屋建筑竣工面积	Floor Space of Buildings Completed	3067.89万平方米	(10000 sq.m)
比上年增长	Over the Previous Year	8.3%	
直接从事生产经营活动的平均人数	Average Number of Persons Directly Engaged in Production and Business Activities	407728人	(person)
比上年增长	Over the Previous Year	13.0%	

12-1 分地区建筑业企业生产情况（2012 年）
STATISTICS ON CONSTRUCTION ENTERPRISES BY REGION（2012）

指 标	Item	全 市 Whole Municipality	其中 of which 市 区 Urban Area	溧阳市 Liyang City	金坛市 JintanCity
企业个数（不含劳务企业，个）	Number of Enterprises （Excluding Labor Enterprises, unit）	594	437	89	68
建筑业总产值（万元）	Gross Output Value of Construction （10000 yuan）	10501993	4388208	4321172	1792614
# 装饰装修产值	Output of Decoration and Fitment	914913	692024	167594	55296
在外省完成的产值	Output Achieved out of Jiangsu Province	2862844	505809	1694946	662089
按构成分	**Grouped by Composition**				
建筑工程	Construction Projects	9371814	4219025	3383168	1769622
安装工程	Installation Projects	1038009	142094	875326	20589
其它产值	Other Output Value	92170	27088	62679	2403
竣工产值（万元）	Output Value of Buildings Completed （10000 yuan）	8484608	3239224	3764924	1480460
房屋建筑施工面积（万平方米）	Floor Space of Buildings Under Construction （10000 sq.m）	8765.07	4002.61	3181.55	1580.91
房屋建筑竣工面积（万平方米）	Floor Space of Buildings Completed （10000 sq.m）	3067.89	1264.54	1159.24	644.10
# 住 宅	Residential Buildings	1854.62	791.38	666.79	396.45
自有施工机械设备年末净值（万元）	Net Value of Existing Machinery and Equipment at Year-end （10000yuan）	335320	175153	117030	43137
自有机械设备年底总台数（台）	Number of Machinery and Equipment at Year-end （unit）	93686	32253	48946	12487
自有施工机械设备年底总功率（千瓦）	Total Power of Existing Machinery and Equipment （kw）	2293269	1382156	720113	191000
平均从业人员（人）	Average Number of Staff of Calculating Labor Productivity （person）	434114	213938	153499	66677
直接从事生产经营活动的平均人数（人）	Average Number of Persons Directly Engaged in Production and Business Activities （person）	407728	174474	134573	98681

12-2 分行业建筑业企业生产情况（2012年）
STATISTICS ON CONSTRUCTION ENTERPRISES BY SECTOR（2012）

指标	Item	合计 Total	房屋和土木工程建筑业 Building and Civil Engineering	建筑安装业 Installation	建筑装饰业 Decoration	其他建筑业 Others
企业个数（不含劳务企业，个）	Number of Enterprises（Excluding Labor Enterprises, unit）	594	324	76	136	58
建筑业总产值（万元）	Gross Output Value of Construction（10000 yuan）	10501993	8392229	1240212	752162	117390
#装饰装修产值	Output of Decoration and Fitment	914913	209094	40793	663645	1382
在外省完成的产值	Output Achieved out of Jiangsu Province	2862844	1890422	745445	198325	28652
按构成分	**Grouped by Composition**					
建筑工程	Construction Projects	9371814	8112930	436050	731423	91411
安装工程	Installation Projects	1038009	203614	796530	14801	23065
其它产值	Other Output Value	92170	75686	7633	5938	2914
竣工产值（万元）	Output Value of Buildings Completed（10000 yuan）	8484608	6709660	1116724	559295	98929
房屋建筑施工面积（万平方米）	Floor Space of Buildings Under Construction（10000 sq.m）	8765.07	8564.99	200.08		
房屋建筑竣工面积（万平方米）	Floor Space of Buildings Completed（10000 sq.m）	3067.89	2993.28	74.61		
#住宅	Residential Buildings	1854.62	1840.67	13.95		
自有施工机械设备年末净值（万元）	Net Value of Existing Machinery and Equipment at Year-end（10000yuan）	335320	276549	36641	12543	9586
自有机械设备年底总台数（台）	Number of Machinery and Equipment at Year-end（unit）	93686	66825	18972	6362	1527
自有施工机械设备年底总功率（千瓦）	Total Power of Existing Machinery and Equipment（kw）	2293269	1958733	237946	57353	39237
平均从业人员（人）	Average Number of Staff of Calculating Labor Productivity（person）	434114	344396	53968	30867	4883
直接从事生产经营活动的平均人数（人）	Average Number of Persons Directly Engaged in Production and Business Activities（person）	407728	334784	42367	26484	4093

12-3 分登记注册类型建筑业企业生产情况（2012 年）
STATISTICS ON CONSTRUCTION ENTERPRISES BY REGISTER STATUS（2012）

指 标	Item	合 计 Total	内资企业 Domestic Funded Enterprises
企业个数（不含劳务企业，个）	Number of Enterprises （Excluding Labor Enterprises, unit）	594	586
建筑业总产值（万元）	Gross Output Value of Construction （10000 yuan）	10501993	10463747
# 装饰装修产值	Output of Decoration and Fitment	914913	896747
在外省完成的产值	Output Achieved out of Jiangsu Province	2862844	2850265
按构成分	**Grouped by Composition**		
建筑工程	Construction Projects	9371814	9338784
安装工程	Installation Projects	1038009	1033603
其它产值	Other Output Value	92170	91360
竣工产值（万元）	Output Value of Buildings Completed （10000 yuan）	8484608	8456693
房屋建筑施工面积（万平方米）	Floor Space of Buildings Under Construction （10000 sq.m）	8765.07	8757.27
房屋建筑竣工面积（万平方米）	Floor Space of Buildings Completed （10000 sq.m）	3067.89	3065.09
# 住 宅	Residential Buildings	1854.62	1851.82
自有施工机械设备年末净值（万元）	Net Value of Existing Machinery and Equipment at Year-end（10000 yuan）	335320	333621
自有机械设备年底总台数（台）	Number of Machinery and Equipment at Year-end （unit）	93686	93320
自有施工机械设备年底总功率（千瓦）	Total Power of Existing Machinery and Equipment （kw）	2293269	2292418
平均从业人员（人）	Average Number of Staff of Calculating Labor Productivity （person）	434114	406294
直接从事生产经营活动的平均人数（人）	Average Number of Persons Directly Engaged in Production and Business Activities（person）	407728	432467

其中 of which					港澳台投资企业 Enterprises With Investment From HongKong, Macao and Taiwan
国有企业 State-owned Enterprises	集体企业 Collective-owned Enterprises	有限责任公司 Limited Liability Corporations	股份有限公司 Share-holding Corporations Ltd	私营企业 Private Enterprises	
4	3	68	4	507	8
47449	21581	1245516	137999	9011203	38246
	118	81653	610	814366	18167
1647		148437	105186	2594995	12579
47449	21581	1158916	135937	7974902	33030
		85417	890	947296	4406
		1183	1172	89005	810
51750	25251	1054235	152971	7172486	27915
		1258.69	168.53	7330.05	7.80
		443.35	61.90	2559.84	2.80
		274.55	34.75	1542.52	2.80
1440	225	24026	5328	302602	1698
96	116	9340	474	83294	366
6713	2846	329932	26910	1926017	851
1283	501	53078	5326	346106	1434
1580	660	75916	6027	348284	1647

12-4 分资质等级建筑业企业生产情况（2012 年）
STATISTICS ON CONSTRUCTION ENTERPRISES BY GRADE（2012）

指 标	Item	总 计 Total
企业个数（不含劳务企业，个）	Number of Enterprises（Excluding Labor Enterprises, unit）	594
建筑业总产值（万元）	Gross Output Value of Construction（10000 yuan）	10501993
# 装饰装修产值	Output of Decoration and Fitment	914913
在外省完成的产值	Output Achieved out of Jiangsu Province	2862844
按构成分	**Grouped by Composition**	
建筑工程	Construction Projects	9371814
安装工程	Installation Projects	1038009
其它产值	Other Output Value	92170
竣工产值（万元）	Output Value of Buildings Completed（10000 yuan）	8484608
房屋建筑施工面积（万平方米）	Floor Space of Buildings Under Construction（10000 sq.m）	8765.07
房屋建筑竣工面积（万平方米）	Floor Space of Buildings Completed（10000 sq.m）	3067.89
# 住 宅	Residential Buildings	1854.62
自有施工机械设备年末净值（万元）	Net Value of Existing Machinery and Equipment at Year-end（10000 yuan）	335320
自有机械设备年底总台数（台）	Number of Machinery and Equipment at Year-end（unit）	93686
自有施工机械设备年底总功率（千瓦）	Total Power of Existing Machinery and Equipment（kw）	2293269
平均从业人员（人）	Average Number of Staff of Calculating Labor Productivity（person）	434114
直接从事生产经营活动的平均人数（人）	Average Number of Persons Directly Engaged in Production and Business Activities（person）	407728

施工总承包 Contracted Construction	其中 of which 一级 First Grade	二级 Second Grade	三级及以下 Under Third Grade	专业承包 Professional Contracting	其中 of which 一级 First Grade	二级 Second Grade	三级及以下 Under Third Grade
282	37	106	139	312	32	83	197
9068772	4682242	3071221	1315309	1433221	640456	379691	413074
199749	151569	35515	12665	715165	469074	156103	89987
2400669	1557057	685042	158570	462175	279325	77742	105108
8202258	3907053	3015401	1279804	1169557	556581	298935	314040
795918	731683	42387	21848	242091	82465	73940	85686
70596	43506	13434	13657	21574	1410	6816	13348
7514301	3967169	2529765	1017367	970307	420286	270045	279977
8681.42	4516.58	3120.37	1044.48	83.65		20.45	63.20
3003.11	1459.97	1149.95	393.20	64.77		16.81	47.96
1828.31	824.91	781.90	221.49	26.32			26.32
282668	97487	103001	82180	52651	11859	16886	23907
73988	28089	35199	10700	19698	5395	7185	7118
1993654	646246	919178	428230	299615	145904	47407	106304
310154	130676	128355	51123	97574	25359	13111	59104
369056	161457	143073	64526	65058	33006	14240	17812

12-5　分地区建筑业企业财务状况（2012 年）
FINANCIAL CONDITIONS OF CONSTRUCTION ENTERPRISES BY REGION（2012）

单位：万元（10000 yuan）

指　标	Item	全　市 Whole Municipality	其中 of which 市　区 Urban Area	溧阳市 Liyang City	金坛市 JintanCity
年末资产负债	**Asset and Liabilities at Year-end**				
年初存货	Opening Stock	1426682	965890	232047	228745
流动资产	Current Assets	6669896	4723621	1218757	727518
固定资产	Fixed Assets	743072	426260	219985	96827
固定资产原价	Original Value of Fixed Assets	923649	577603	243269	102778
累计折旧	Accumulative Total Depreciation	367473	245666	79382	42425
# 本年折旧	Depreciation Within the Year	65159	42664	17042	5454
在建工程	Projects Under Construction	146771	71668	43959	31144
资产合计	Total Assets	7876971	5404174	1523184	949613
流动负债	Liquid Liabilities	4417441	3154198	751045	512198
长期负债	Long-term Liabilities	59295	48701	7283	3311
负债合计	Total Liabilities	4919203	3568533	796262	554409
所有者权益	Owners' Equity	2957769	1835642	726922	395205
损益及分配	**Expenditure,Income and Distribution**				
营业收入	Business Income	9364877	4549181	3636064	1179632
营业税金及附加	Business Tax and Surcharges	312353	148742	122675	40936
其他业务利润	Other Business Profit	4602	3965	379	258
管理费用	Management and Financial Expenditures	245528	166620	55333	23576
财务费用	Financial Costs	90512	63142	19239	8131
营业利润	Operating Surplus	404147	204603	139854	59689
利润总额	Total Profits	406758	208248	139109	59401
补充资料	**Supplementary Material**				
应付职工薪酬	Remuneration Payable to Employees	1619138	668630	747563	202946
应收工程款	Project Fund Payable	2198080	1528249	381085	288746
# 竣工工程款	Completed Project Fund	1156855	731531	199375	225948

注：本表统计范围不含劳务企业。
Note：The statistical rang of this table doesn't including Labour Service Enterprises.

12-6 分行业建筑业企业财务状况（2012 年）
FINANCIAL CONDITIONS OF CONSTRUCTION ENTERPRISES BY SECTOR（2012）

单位：万元（10000 yuan）

指 标	Item	合 计 Total	房屋和土木工程建筑业 Building and Civil Engineering	建 筑 安装业 Installation	建 筑 装饰业 Decoration	其 他 建筑业 Others
年末资产负债	**Asset and Liabilities at Year-end**					
年初存货	Opening Stock	1426682	1237186	69472	98386	21638
流动资产	Current Assets	6669896	5335960	520066	708004	105866
固定资产	Fixed Assets	743072	607501	61966	49192	24413
固定资产原价	Original Value of Fixed Assets	923649	742212	81414	66907	33117
累计折旧	Accumulative Total Depreciation	367473	301929	24857	29375	11312
# 本年折旧	Depreciation Within the Year	65159	50881	5729	6823	1726
在建工程	Projects Under Construction	146771	135029	1219	10155	368
资产合计	Total Assets	7876971	6299832	629460	810884	136796
流动负债	Liquid Liabilities	4417441	3484362	363975	514847	54257
长期负债	Long-term Liabilities	59295	42889	4227	11917	264
负债合计	Total Liabilities	4919203	3949586	369858	539072	60686
所有者权益	Owners' Equity	2957769	2350245	259601	271812	76111
损益及分配	**Expenditure,Income and Distribution**					
营业收入	Business Income	9364877	7318548	1080926	846850	118554
营业税金及附加	Business Tax and Surcharges	312353	250293	32719	25357	3984
其他业务利润	Other Business Profit	4602	3133	662	238	570
管理费用	Management and Financial Expenditures	245528	158767	27914	51043	7804
财务费用	Financial Costs	90512	81659	3806	4762	286
营业利润	Operating Surplus	404147	311651	43525	40907	8064
利润总额	Total Profits	406758	310227	43560	44181	8790
补充资料	**Supplementary Material**					
应付职工薪酬	Remuneration Payable to Employees	1619138	1281630	233874	85721	17914
应收工程款	Project Fund Payable	2198080	1691777	191402	285385	29516
# 竣工工程款	Completed Project Fund	1156855	916867	100115	124949	14925

注：本表统计范围不含劳务企业。
Note: The statistical rang of this table doesn't including Labour Service Enterprises.

12-7 分登记注册类型建筑业企业财务状况（2012 年）
FINANCIAL CONDITIONS OF CONSTRUCTION ENTERPRISES BY REGISTER STATUS（2012）

指 标	Item	合 计 Total	内资企业 Domestic Funded Enterprises
年末资产负债	**Asset and Liabilities at Year-end**		
年初存货	Opening Stock	1426682	1420703
流动资产	Current Assets	6669896	6623242
固定资产	Fixed Assets	743072	733822
固定资产原价	Original Value of Fixed Assets	923649	912927
累计折旧	Accumulative Total Depreciation	367473	364419
# 本年折旧	Depreciation Within the Year	65159	64527
在建工程	Projects Under Construction	146771	145190
资产合计	Total Assets	7876971	7816278
流动负债	Liquid Liabilities	4417441	4385372
长期负债	Long-term Liabilities	59295	59283
负债合计	Total Liabilities	4919203	4887121
所有者权益	Owners' Equity	2957769	2929157
损益及分配	**Expenditure,Income and Distribution**		
营业收入	Business Income	9364877	9326699
营业税金及附加	Business Tax and Surcharges	312353	311394
其他业务利润	Other Business Profit	4602	4602
管理费用	Management and Financial Expenditures	245528	243484
财务费用	Financial Costs	90512	89891
营业利润	Operating Surplus	404147	400549
利润总额	Total Profits	406758	403236
补充资料	**Supplementary Material**		
应付职工薪酬	Remuneration Payable to Employees	1619138	1614131
应收工程款	Project Fund Payable	2198080	2187333
# 竣工工程款	Completed Project Fund	1156855	1149252

单位：万元（10000 yuan）

其中 of which					港澳台投资企业 Enterprises With Investment From HongKong, Macao and Taiwan
国有企业 State-owned Enterprises	集体企业 Collective-owned Enterprises	有限责任公司 Limited Liability Corporations	股份有限公司 Share-holding Corporations Ltd	私营企业 Private Enterprises	
7764	329	250141	21204	1141265	5979
30857	20535	1523745	51938	4996167	46654
4037	1593	104814	25314	598065	9250
5135	3423	129937	12512	761920	10723
1098	1866	51976	6330	303149	3054
117	132	12019	1070	51189	632
	36	25536	19132	100486	1581
104550	23190	1680521	78475	5929542	60693
44579	12569	882831	44103	3401289	32069
		5580		53703	13
44579	12569	1216950	44103	3568919	32082
59971	10621	463571	34372	2360623	28611
43818	22664	1332652	144101	7783465	38178
1491	406	39085	6036	264375	959
		1235	447	2921	
1260	1684	55583	2135	182822	2044
54		10771	1104	78015	621
2602	2288	52782	4325	338551	3598
2602	2172	57579	4499	336384	3522
4753	3833	205492	14051	1386003	5007
9692	2960	371730	14996	1787955	10747
2805	297	127449	5215	1013487	7603

12-8 分资质等级建筑业企业财务状况（2012 年）
FINANCIAL CONDITIONS OF CONSTRUCTION ENTERPRISES BY GRADE（2012）

指 标	Item	总 计 Total
年末资产负债	**Asset and Liabilities at Year-end**	
年初存货	Opening Stock	1426682
流动资产	Current Assets	6669896
固定资产	Fixed Assets	743072
固定资产原价	Original Value of Fixed Assets	923649
累计折旧	Accumulative Total Depreciation	367473
# 本年折旧	Depreciation Within the Year	65159
在建工程	Projects Under Construction	146771
资产合计	Total Assets	7876971
流动负债	Liquid Liabilities	4417441
长期负债	Long-term Liabilities	59295
负债合计	Total Liabilities	4919203
所有者权益	Owners' Equity	2957769
损益及分配	**Expenditure,Income and Distribution**	
营业收入	Business Income	9364877
营业税金及附加	Business Tax and Surcharges	312353
其他业务利润	Other Business Profit	4602
管理费用	Management and Financial Expenditures	245528
财务费用	Financial Costs	90512
营业利润	Operating Surplus	404147
利润总额	Total Profits	406758
补充资料	**Supplementary Material**	
应付职工薪酬	Remuneration Payable to Employees	1619138
应收工程款	Project Fund Payable	2198080
# 竣工工程款	Completed Project Fund	1156855

注：本表统计范围不含劳务企业。
Note：The statistical rang of this table doesn't including Labour Service Enterprises.

单位：万元（10000 yuan）

施工总承包 Contracted Construction	其中 of which 一级 First Grade	二级 Second Grade	三级及以下 Under Third Grade	专业承包 Professional Contracting	其中 of which 一级 First Grade	二级 Second Grade	三级及以下 Under Third Grade
1174911	410720	578479	185713	251771	92034	68261	91477
5183974	1831414	1920681	1431880	1485922	539309	455256	491357
588371	173610	219318	195443	154701	34858	56519	63324
716163	261547	268401	186215	207486	59443	76778	71266
280662	114896	105178	60588	86812	33498	27041	26273
46705	16048	16779	13878	18454	4294	6628	7532
120604	14194	45306	61104	26167	8450	3125	14592
6112082	2128872	2290049	1693161	1764889	628337	557538	579015
3452985	1358693	1397060	697232	964456	439080	288952	236423
40187	7706	24506	7975	19109	10039	4630	4440
3886524	1397460	1484591	1004474	1032679	449127	319726	263826
2225558	731412	805459	688688	732211	179210	237812	315190
7800860	3790674	2795049	1215136	1564018	616557	524270	423191
263591	123299	98666	41626	48762	20865	14459	13438
2828	1386	913	529	1775	680	783	312
151206	52274	59361	39572	94322	21890	49942	22490
80666	32383	33264	15019	9846	5208	3316	1322
305763	135378	101483	68903	98384	27649	38919	31816
303390	134332	99872	69186	103368	27104	43261	33004
1436560	705683	533173	197704	182578	85403	50053	47122
1649868	638324	589519	422025	548212	204309	175191	168712
884170	358203	314946	211021	272685	99633	69180	103871

13

CHAPTER 13

交通运输　邮电通信

TRANSPORTATION,POST AND TELCOMMUNICATIONS

13 交通运输 邮电通信 TRANSPORTATION, POST AND TELECOMMUNICATIONS

2012 年主要统计指标 MAJOR STATISTICAL INDICATORS OF 2012

客运量	Passenger Traffic	17257 万人	(10000 persons)
比上年增长	Over the Previous Year	8.9%	
货运量	Freight Traffic	17154 万吨	(10000 tons)
比上年增长	Over the Previous Year	9.7%	
邮电业务收入	Revenue from Post & Telecommunication Services	65.93 亿元	(100 million yuan)
比上年增长	Over the Previous Year	10.0%	
年底本地网电话用户数	Number of Telephone Subscribers of Local Telephone Net	161.61 万户	(10000 households)
比上年增长	Over the Previous Year	1.8%	
年底移动电话用户	Number of Mobile Phones Subscribers at Year-End	519.35 万户	(10000 households)
比上年增长	Over the Previous Year	-5.3%	
年底互联网用户	Number of Internet Subscribers	127.87 户	(10000 households)
比上年增长	Over the Previous Year	22.2%	

13-1 主要年份客、货运量
TOTAL PASSENGER AND FREIGHT TRAFFIC IN MAIN YEARS

年份 Year	客运量（万人）Passenger Traffic (10000 persons)	其中 of which 铁路 Railways	民航 Civil Aviation	公路 Highways	水路 Waterways	货运量（万吨）Freight Traffic (10000 tons)	其中 of which 铁路 Railways	民航 Civil Aviation	公路 Highways	水路 Waterways
1949	192	41		41	110	96	2		17	78
1952	273	68		83	122	139	7		38	95
1957	535	69		170	296	168	13		24	131
1962	867	165		295	407	289	25		68	196
1965	712	110		438	164	405	20		111	274
1970	1005	125		618	262	498	28		131	339
1975	1837	180		1194	463	1072	47		319	706
1980	3071	245		2465	361	1839	51		621	1167
1981	3701	261		2917	523	1842	54		641	1147
1982	4074	282		3396	396	1926	59		679	1188
1983	4199	353		3563	283	2299	109		938	1251
1984	4373	429		3732	212	2880	117		1510	1253
1985	4373	488		3760	125	4351	128		2330	1893
1986	4389	511	1	3773	104	4836	135	0.02	2369	2332
1987	4958	544	2	4333	79	4612	132	0.05	2627	1853
1988	5259	647	3	4534	75	4983	126	0.06	3051	1806
1989	4877	395	3	4431	48	4812	131	0.06	3061	1620
1990	5048	585	3	4428	32	4375	126	0.06	2943	1306
1991	5361	579	3	4740	39	5998	136	0.05	4246	1616
1992	5372	639	5	4706	23	6266	162	0.12	3833	2271
1993	5492	700	6	4766	19	5987	158	0.10	3707	2121
1994	5336	697	10	4620	9	6173	162	0.20	3802	2209
1995	7270	734	7	6522	6	5804	187	0.10	3551	2065
1996	7099	570	12	6513	4	5917	127	0.15	3843	1947
1997	7687	490	27	7168	2	5246	193	0.45	3375	1677
1998	8042	492	23	7526	1	5167	193	0.50	3340	1634
1999	9216	550	22	8643	1	4909	222	0.50	3299	1388
2000	10196	557	19	9620	1	4696	223	0.60	3335	1137
2001	10507	566	13	9928		4830	240	0.30	3445	1144
2002	11216	603	15	10598		5140	246	0.30	3783	1111
2003	11413	577	16	10820		5437	254	0.30	4040	1143
2004	12679	682	24	11973		5648	361	0.40	4334	952
2005	15235	715	15	14505		6032	296	0.47	4950	786
2006	16719	741	20	15958		6855	298	0.42	5692	865
2007	19096	745	21	18330		8083	396	0.54	6710	976
2008	21018	818	34	20166		8729	258	0.54	7490	980
2009	24778	840	23	23837	78	11206	232	0.53	9839	1134
2010	29361	874	27	28380	80	13109	219	0.55	11600	1290
2011	15845	981	36	14733	95	15644	195	0.68	13936	1512
2012	17257	1100	43	16030	84	17154	190	0.91	15344	1619

注：公路、水路客、货运量2011年以前年份数据为全社会口径，2011年起为营业性口径。

Note: The statistical coverage of passenger and cargo by land and river throughput before 2011 refers to the whole society, which has been altered to business statistical data from 2011.

13-2 主要年份客、货运周转量
PASSENGER TRAFFIC AND FREIGHT TRAFFIC IN MAIN YEARS

年份 Year	客运周转量（万人公里） Passenger-kilometers (10000 persons-km)	其中 of which 公路 Highways	水路 Waterways	货运周转量（万吨公里） Freight Ton-kilometers (10000 tons-km)	其中 of which 公路 Highways	水路 Waterways
1949	4327	610	3717	6037	40	5997
1952	5681	1235	4446	7559	84	7475
1957	10032	3153	6879	7997	68	7929
1962	20259	9859	10400	13965	1004	12961
1965	13336	9723	3613	19800	1660	18140
1970	22934	17776	5158	28970	3272	25698
1975	40465	33385	7080	73230	12065	61165
1980	68882	62748	6134	144838	27546	117292
1981	79911	70592	9319	151476	30279	121197
1982	90280	82680	7600	166308	32469	133839
1983	94294	88286	6008	209359	36518	172841
1984	107560	102404	5156	223855	47519	176336
1985	125797	121910	3887	220817	63970	156847
1986	136856	133160	3696	245502	70345	175157
1987	152028	148706	3322	262000	81134	180866
1988	164462	161268	3194	273096	99083	174013
1989	162072	159840	2232	265580	108727	156853
1990	168514	166596	1918	246937	111072	135865
1991	193806	191781	2025	287995	128732	159263
1992	223327	222135	1192	376867	133152	243715
1993	226534	225580	954	377914	154140	223774
1994	191495	190916	579	380862	154382	226480
1995	310456	309924	532	354690	139846	214844
1996	316737	316392	345	344144	138748	205396
1997	324783	324585	198	319055	142140	176915
1998	321356	321172	184	307452	135819	171633
1999	395343	395174	169	327542	148289	179253
2000	440379	440154	225	273472	145475	127997
2001	454239	454239		279312	150555	128757
2002	474890	474890		274835	151418	123417
2003	479180	479180		291913	164781	127132
2004	579976	579976		299376	187981	111395
2005	640944	640944		312269	220159	92110
2006	765984	765984		379974	267524	112450
2007	888260	888260		461815	328558	133257
2008	992311	992311		505902	369226	136676
2009	1286371	1286051	320	774413	596587	177826
2010	1541228	1540900	328	898400	698600	199800
2011	897763	897373	390	1098169	858887	239282
2012	976796	976342	454	1212857	948211	264646

13-3　主要年份公路总里程
TOTAL LENGTH OF HIGHWAYS IN MAIN YEARS

单位：公里（km）

年　份 Year	公路总里程 Total Length of Highways	其中 of which 高速公路 Expressway	一级公路 First Class	二级公路 Second Class	三级公路 Third Class	四级公路 Fourth Class	等外公路 Substandard Highways
1949	179			45	17	116	1
1952	220			45	17	117	41
1957	312			60	53	138	61
1962	405			60	65	184	96
1965	442			60	69	217	96
1970	531			60	83	262	126
1975	659			60	101	351	147
1980	838			73	101	499	165
1981	862			73	101	523	165
1982	907			88	104	546	169
1983	940			90	97	590	163
1984	1020			95	130	628	167
1985	1044			102	140	635	167
1986	1106			134	155	650	167
1987	1183			155	201	660	167
1988	1215			162	232	654	167
1989	1215		5	185	233	628	164
1990	1215		5	192	263	613	142
1991	1226		5	230	308	615	68
1992	1227		5	236	337	588	61
1993	1228		5	249	348	573	53
1994	1230		5	299	362	511	53
1995	1241		41	311	348	500	41
1996	1296	43	33	338	346	483	53
1997	1313	43	77	319	342	479	53
1998	1344	43	122	315	339	472	53
1999	1384	43	140	313	374	471	43
2000	1384	43	144	321	362	471	43
2001	5165	43	200	457	910	2262	1293
2002	5232	43	250	467	926	2254	1292
2003	5404	60	297	532	987	2294	1234
2004	5999	117	336	736	1033	2694	1083
2005	5444	117	406	886	1266	1816	953
2006	5546	117	459	908	1247	2278	537
2007	6732	221	558	1095	1572	2763	523
2008	7185	221	809	1130	1229	3547	249
2009	7479	221	794	1167	1227	3849	221
2010	8348	221	855	1170	1282	4768	52
2011	8446	247	882	1179	1301	4784	52
2012	8677	268	918	1215	1312	4912	52

13-4 分地区客、货运量（2012 年）
TOTAL PASSENGER AND FREIGHT TRAFFIC BY REGION （2012）

指 标	Item	全 市 Whole Municipality	市 区 Urban Area	溧阳市 Liyang City	金坛市 Jintan City
客运量（万人）	**Passenger Traffic （10000 Persons）**	**17257**	**12396**	**2881**	**1980**
铁 路	Railway	1100	1100		
公 路	Highway	16030	11253	2797	1980
民 航	Civil Aviation	43	43		
水 路	Waterway	84		84	
旅客周转量（万人公里）	**Passenger-kilometers （10000 persons-km）**	**976796**	**681165**	**175170**	**120461**
公 路	Highway	976342	681165	175170	120007
水 路	Waterway	454			454
货运量（万吨）	**Freight Traffic （10000 tons）**	**17154**	**11707**	**3195**	**2252**
铁 路	Railway	190	190		
公 路	Highway	15344	11057	2804	1483
水 路	Waterway	1619	459	391	769
民 航	Civil Aviation	1	1		
货运周转量（万吨公里）	**Freight Ton-kilometers （10000 tons-km）**	**1212857**	**761130**	**235227**	**216500**
公 路	Highway	948211	683875	171854	92542
水 路	Waterway	264646	77315	63373	123958

13-5 交通系统分地区客、货运量（2012 年）
PASSENGER AND FREIGHT TRAFFIC OF COMMUNICATIONS SYSTEM BY REGION （2012）

指 标	Item	全 市 Whole Municipality	市 区 Urban Area	溧阳市 Liyang City	金坛市 Jintan City
客运量（万人）	**Passenger Traffic （10000 Persons）**	**4976**	**2459**	**1560**	**957**
铁 路	Railway	1100	1100		
公 路	Highway	3768	1251	1560	957
民 航	Aviation	108	108		
旅客周转量（万人公里）	**Passenger-kilometers （10000 persons-km）**	**283885**	**169171**	**65675**	**49039**
公 路	Highway	283885	169171	65675	49039
货运量（万吨）	**Freight Tranfic （10000 tons）**	**12012**	**11322**	**10**	**680**
铁 路	Railway	190	190		
公 路	Highway	114	61	10	43
水 路	Waterway	650	13		637
民 航	Aviation	11058	11058		
货运周转量（万吨公里）	**Freight Ton-kilometers （10000 tons-km）**	**119981**	**3707**	**1995**	**114279**
公 路	Highway	9131	1030	1995	6106
水 路	Waterway	110850	2677		108173

13-6 公路和内河航道里程数（2012 年）
TOTAL LENGTH OF HIGHWAYS AND NAVIGABLE INLAND WATERWAYS （2012）

单位：公里（km）

指 标	Item	全 市 Whole Municipality	市 区 Urban Area	溧阳市 Liyang City	金坛市 Jintan City
公路总里程	**Total Length of Highways**	**8677**	**4147**	**2509**	**2021**
# 高速公路	Expressway	268	150	55	62
一级公路	First Class	918	683	103	131
二级公路	Second Class	1215	593	304	318
三级公路	Third Class	1312	763	384	165
四级公路	Fourth Class	4912	1957	1662	1293
航道里程	**Length of Navigable Inland Waterways**	**1088**	**533**	**296**	**259**
# 通机动船里程	Length of Navigation of Motor Vessels	857	376	281	200

13-7 分地区全社会港口吞吐量（2012 年）
THE WHOLE-SOCIETY PORTS THROUGHPUT BY REGIONS （2012）

指 标	Item	全 市 Whole Municipality	市 区 Urban Area	其中 of which #长江港 Changzhou Yangtze River Port	溧阳市 Liyang City	金坛市 Jintan City
码头泊位个数（个）	**Number of Berths（unit）**	**804**	**407**	**30**	**322**	**75**
货物吞吐量（万吨）	**Cargo at Ports Throughput（10 000 tons）**	**8997**	**4422**	**2667**	**3287**	**1288**
#外 贸	Freight Trade	391	391	391		
按进出港分	Divided by Arrive at/Leave Port					
出 港	Leave Port	4829	1419	972	2525	885
#外 贸	Foreign Trade	121	121	121		
进 港	Arrive at Port	4168	3003	1695	762	403
#外 贸	Foreign Trade	270	270	270		
集装箱吞吐量	**International Containes**					
箱 数（万标箱）	Containers （10000 TEU）	14	14	14		
重 量（万吨）	Weight （10000 tons）	208	208	208		
#货 物	Freight	179	179	179		

13-8 机动车辆数（2012 年）
NUMBER OF MOTOR VEHICLES （2012）

单位：辆（unit）

指 标	Item	合 计 Total	其中 of which 私 人 Private
民用汽车	**Civil Vehicles**	**659312**	**523417**
客 车	Passenger Vehicles	587238	499302
#大 型	Large-scale	5756	21
中 型	Medium-sized	6442	2399
小 型	Compact car	561720	484852
微 型	Minicar	13320	12030
#轿 车	Sedan	425405	373800
货 车	Freight Trucks	68084	23373
#重 型	Heavy-duty	20316	4366
中 型	Medium-sized	16407	2848
轻 型	Pick-up Truck	31114	15981
微 型	Minicar	247	178
其他汽车	Other Motorcar	3990	742
摩托车	**Motorcycle**	**291603**	**289891**
#普通摩托车	Ordinary Motorcycle	288206	286498
轻便摩托车	Scooter	3397	3393
挂 车	**Trailer**	**3562**	**524**
其他机动车	**Other Motor Vehicles**	**24**	**4**
附：机动车驾驶员人数（人）	**Number of Drivers of Motor Vehicles（person）**	**1135310**	
#汽车驾驶员人数	NumberofDriverofVehicles	975880	

13-9 历年邮电业务主要指标
MAJOR INDICATORS OF POST AND TELECOMMUNICATIONS OVER THE YEARS

年 份 Year	邮电局所数（个）Number of Post and Telecommun-ications Offices（unit）	邮路单程长度（公里）Lengh of Postal Routs（one way,km）	邮电业务总量（万元）Business Volume of Post and Telecommunications（10000 yuan）	市话交换机容量（门）Capacity of Urban Telephones Exchanges（line）
1952	261		235	1620
1953	282		266	1640
1954	263		266	1650
1955	213		259	1670
1956	210		284	1670
1957	201		302	1670
1958	249	4190	372	1830
1959	194	3999	525	2730
1960	204	3642	619	3030
1961	203	3012	600	3030
1962	189	2740	514	3020
1963	193	3776	513	3120
1964	194	6237	537	3180
1965	171	7579	567	3280
1966	171	7953	593	3280
1967	173	8330	531	3280
1968	173	8330	503	3280
1969	170	9311	589	3180
1970	241	8937	662	3180
1971	244	8452	669	3180
1972	238	9496	747	3250
1973	203	9629	792	4100
1974	204	10043	884	4250
1975	207	10217	928	4250
1976	207	10427	964	4250
1977	208	10076	1031	5250
1978	209	10029	1127	6250
1979	210	9948	1202	6420
1980	206	10108	1368	7420
1981	212	4554	1470	7850

13-9 续表 Continued

年 份 Year	邮电局所数 （个） Number of Post and Telecommun-ications Offices （unit）	邮路单程长度 （公里） Lengh of Postal Routs （one way,km）	邮电业务总量 （万元） Business Volume of Post and Telecommunications （10000 yuan）	市话交换机容量 （门） Capacity of Urban Telephones Exchanges （line）
1982	215	2854	1561	7400
1983	212	2762	1743	7400
1984	217	2788	1920	12350
1985	218	3078	2454	17200
1986	215	2065	2780	17200
1987	211	2233	3442	17200
1988	210	1892	4776	23000
1989	204	1889	6026	32000
1990	196	1881	7477	40500
1991	193	1715	10315	44000
1992	181	1790	16184	67500
1993	167	2226	27740	121300
1994	166	2516	43122	144000
1995	220	2502	56746	160000
1996	223	2419	77169	402000
1997	233	5509	107951	539609
1998	297	5776	131919	560375
1999	255	6297	175449	539108
2000	248	9401	284105	606730
2001	263	9799	192078	675348
2002	263	9799	247394	1142675
2003	375	9947	281939	1342600
2004	250	10129	318161	1332400
2005	250	10129	348747	1311800
2006	166	9045	391996	1712600
2007	166	10161	451700	2918700
2008	160	8995	505176	2975000
2009	190	7903	538059	2884424
2010	167	3740	574083	2844144
2011	151	4269	594741	3099600
2012	150	4269	644801	3658000

注：1、从 2006 年起邮电局所数不包括电信网点数字 ;1952-2000 年邮电业务总量按 1990 年价格计算 , 2001 年起按 2000 年价格计算。
2、年末邮路单程长度不包括速递邮路单程长度。

Note：1、The number of post stations and offices excludes the number of telecommunication network offices since the year of 2006.The total business volumes of post and telecommunication from 1952 to 2000 have been calculated by the price of 1990, The figures from the year of 2001 have been calculated according to the price in 2000.
2、The one-way postal length by the end of year does not include the one-way length of postal express.

13-10 分地区邮政电信情况（2012 年）
POSTS AND TELECOMMUNCIATIONS BY REGION（2012）

指 标	Item	全 市 Whole Municipality	其中 of which 市 区 Urban Area	溧阳市 Liyang City	金坛市 Jintan City
年末邮政机构数（个）	**Number of Network Points of Post**	**150**	**86**	**27**	**37**
# 邮政局	Post Offices	3	1	1	1
邮政支局	Post Branches	126	82	26	18
自办所	Self-Run Post Services	21	3		18
年末邮路单程长度（公里）	**Lengh of Postal Routes（single way,km）**	**4269**	**3446**	**260**	**563**
农村投递线路（公里）	**Rural Delivery Routes（km）**	**13658**	**8404**	**2493**	**2761**
年末电话交换机总容量（万门）	**Total Capacity of Urban and Rural Telephone Exchanges（10000 lines）**	**365.80**	**284.30**	**43.18**	**38.29**
邮电业务收入（亿元）	**Total Business Volume of Post & Telecommunications（100 mitlion yuan）**	**65.93**	**52.24**	**7.81**	**5.88**
邮政业务收入	Total Business Volume of Post Services	6.73	4.98	0.93	0.82
通信业务收入	Total Business Volume of Communications Services	59.2	47.26	6.88	5.06
主要业务量	**Major Business Volume**				
函 件（万件）	Number of Letters（10000 pcs）	10774.89	9560.38	666.68	547.83
特快专递（万件）	Pieces of Express Mail Services（10000 pcs）	566.61	498.61	31.17	36.83
包 件（万件）	Pieces of Courier Services（10000 pcs）	7.83	6.75	0.72	0.36
汇 票（万件）	Number of Bill of Exchange（10000 pcs）	85.17	55.65	11.60	17.933
集邮业务（万枚）	Business Volume of Philately（10000 pcs）	624.69	512.89	46.76	65.04
年末本地网电话用户数（万户）	**Number of Telephone Subscribers of Local Telephone Net（10000 households）**	**161.61**	**118.05**	**23.50**	**20.06**
城市电话用户	Urban Telephone Subscribers	87.98	68.60	10.41	8.97
# 住 宅	Residential Telephone Subscribers	63.57	47.75	7.89	7.93
农村电话用户	Rural Telephone Subscribers	55.94	31.76	14.10	10.08
# 住 宅	Residential Telephone Subscribers	24.54	7.26	10.76	6.52
无线市话用户	Wireless Urban Telephone Subscribers	5.20	3.34	0.49	1.37
年末移动电话用户数（万户）	**Number of Mobile Telephone Subscribers（10000 households）**	**519.35**	**395.03**	**71.09**	**53.23**
年末互联网用户（万户）	**Number of Internet Subscribers（10000 households）**	**127.87**	**102.65**	**14.02**	**11.20**
# 宽带网用户	Widebband Network Subscribers	117.37	92.71	13.74	10.92

注：1、年末电话交换机总容量不包括无线市话，宽带网用户中含无线上网用户。
2、年末邮路单程长度不包括速递邮路单程长度。

Note：1、Total capacity of urban and rural telephone exchanges doesn’t including wireless urban telephone,internet subscribers include wireless internet subscribers.
2、The one-way postal length by the end of year does not include the one-way length of postal express.

14
CHAPTER 14

贸易　住宿餐饮业

TRADE,ACCOMMODATION AND CATERING TRADE

14 贸易 住宿餐饮业
TRADE, ACCOMMODATION AND CATERING TRADE

2012 年主要统计指标
MAJOR STATISTICAL INDICATORS OF 2012

社会消费品零售总额	Total Retail of Consumer Goods	1413.33 亿元	(100 million yuan)
比上年增长	Over the Previous Year	14.3%	
限额以上批发零售贸易企业商品销售总额	Total Sales of Wholesale and Retail Trade above Designated Size	1981.80 亿元	(100 million yuan)
比上年增长	Over the Previous Year	15.8%	
超亿元商品交易市场成交额	Transaction Value of Trade Market of Goods	1890.88 亿元	(100 million yuan)
比上年增长	Over the Previous Year	16.5%	

14-1 历年分地区社会消费品零售总额
TOTAL RETAIL SALES OF CUNSUMER GOODS BY REGION OVER THE YEARS

单位：万元（10000 yuan）

年 份	全 市	其 中 of which			年 份	全 市	其 中 of which		
		市 区	溧阳市	金坛市			市 区	溧阳市	金坛市
Year	Whole Municipality	Urban Area	Liyang City	Jintan City	Year	Whole Municipality	Urban Area	Liyang City	Jintan City
1949	8102	5816	1389	897	1981	79614	48181	17532	13901
1950	9594	7076	1576	942	1982	89417	53600	20312	15505
1951	11884	8727	1869	1288	1983	108328	65763	22645	19920
1952	12572	8833	2215	1524	1984	129310	81806	25874	21630
1953	14109	9664	2685	1760	1985	181736	119591	35557	26588
1954	14814	10163	2813	1838	1986	202929	133243	39765	29921
1955	13435	9007	2773	1655	1987	248014	165286	46660	36068
1956	14622	9869	2927	1826	1988	323678	213641	61009	49028
1957	14603	10067	2725	1811	1989	363259	242555	63731	56973
1958	17975	12581	3279	2115	1990	381931	262148	66529	53254
1959	19734	14172	3220	2342	1991	436920	300243	76502	60175
1960	22434	16325	3589	2520	1992	558904	402730	97255	58919
1961	18873	13966	2794	2113	1993	782257	547972	132046	102239
1962	20377	14290	3541	2546	1994	1002394	673218	191109	138067
1963	18044	12217	3569	2258	1995	1317764	849886	285210	182668
1964	19142	12326	4055	2761	1996	1575902	1016554	330375	228973
1965	21379	13042	4857	3480	1997	1679581	1110655	334340	234586
1966	22577	13729	5002	3846	1998	1739300	1143964	341290	254046
1967	23951	14451	5329	4171	1999	1844235	1208355	364403	271477
1968	21685	12506	5356	3823	2000	2023126	1338778	391687	292661
1969	21764	11629	5945	4190	2001	2226101	1480205	425803	320093
1970	26295	14902	6897	4496	2002	2488005	1659780	469821	358404
1971	26512	14514	7461	4537	2003	2806470	1907533	494016	404921
1972	30343	17743	7551	5049	2004	3240528	2193610	581878	465040
1973	31821	17804	8376	5641	2005	4449415	3292101	652950	504364
1974	34606	20093	8639	5874	2006	5178307	3840209	753775	584323
1975	38450	23473	8692	6285	2007	6144075	4581050	881159	681866
1976	40233	24572	8951	6710	2008	7640631	5740836	1072741	827054
1977	44298	27330	9594	7374	2009	8915444	6745496	1218920	951028
1978	48236	28813	10881	8542	2010	10543943	7906496	1475388	1162058
1979	58116	34682	13371	10063	2011	12361038	9262314	1732009	1366715
1980	72740	42012	17880	12848	2012	14133300	10583451	1982562	1567287

注：2005 年至 2008 年数据已按照第二次经济普查结果重新进行了修订。
Note: The statistic data from year 2005 to year 2008 was adjusted in accordance with the second economic survey.

14-2 分地区社会消费品零售总额（2012 年）
TOTAL RETAIL SALES OF CONSUMER GOODS BY REGION（2012）

单位：万元（10000 yuan）

指 标	Item	全 市 Whole Municipality	其中 of which 市 区 Urban Area	溧阳市 Liyang City	金坛市 Jintan City
总 计	**Total**	**14133300**	**10583451**	**1982562**	**1567287**
按销售地区分	**Grouped by Sales Region**				
城 镇	Urban and Town	13193677	10482593	1283866	1427218
乡 村	Countryside	939623	100858	698697	140069
按行业分	**Grouped by Sector**				
批发零售贸易业	Wholesale,Retail Sales	12931579	9724997	1799549	1407032
住宿餐饮业	Accommodation Catering Trade	1201721	858454	183013	160255

14-3 分地区批发零售贸易业商品销售总额（2012 年）
TOTAL COMMODITIES SALES VOLUME OF WHOLESALE AND RETAIL TRADES BY REGION（2012）

单位：万元（10000 yuan）

指 标	Item	全 市 Whole Municipality	其中 of which 市 区 Urban Area	溧阳市 Liyang City	金坛市 Jintan City
总 计	**Total**	**51546999**	**45567709**	**3201335**	**2777956**
限额以上企业	Enterprises above Designated Size	19818007	18718274	504485	595248
批 发	Wholesale	14529127	14006618	138433	384076
零 售	Retail	5288880	4711656	366052	211172
限额以下企业及个体（含大个体）	Enterprises below Designated Size and Self-employed Households（including large self-employed households）	31728992	26849435	2696850	2182707
批 发	Wholesale	22859930	21220056	780634	859239
零 售	Retail	8869062	5629379	1916215	1323468

14-4 分地区住宿餐饮业营业额（2012 年）
SALES TURNOVER OF ACCOMMODATION & CATERING TRADE GROUPED BY REGION（2012）

单位：万元（10000 yuan）

指 标	Item	全 市 Whole Municipality	其中 of which 市 区 Urban Area	溧阳市 Liyang City	金坛市 Jintan City
总 计	**Total**	**1794065**	**1298406**	**303398**	**192261**
限额以上企业	Enterprises above Designated Size	531867	435271	72292	24304
批 发	Accommodation	191630	117896	61228	12505
零 售	Catering	340237	317374	11064	11799
限额以下企业及个体（含大个体）	Enterprises below Designated Size and Self-employed Households（including large self-employed households）	1262198	863135	231106	167957
批 发	Accommodation	254642	165092	70955	18595
零 售	Catering	1007556	698044	160151	149361

14-5 限额以上批发和零售业基本情况（2012 年）
BASIC CONDITIONS ENTERPRISES ABOVE DESIGNATED SIZE IN WHOLESALE AND RETAIL TRADES（2012）

指 标	Item	法人企业数（个）Number of Corporations (unit)	零售营业面积（平方米）Floor Space Of Retail Business (sq.m)	从业人员（人）Persons Engaged (Person)
总 计	**Total**	**1126**	**1667542**	**51297**
市 区	Urban Area	981	1433002	43834
溧阳市	Liyang City	50	147878	3358
金坛市	Jintan City	95	86662	4105
批发贸易业	**Wholesale Trade**	**753**	**49564**	**18011**
#国有控股	State-owned and State Share Holding	12	5030	1008
按地区分	**Grouped by Region**			
市 区	Urban Area	693	46220	15503
溧阳市	Liyang City	14	970	394
金坛市	Jintan City	46	2374	2114
按登记注册类型分	**Group by Registration Status**			
内 资	Domestic Investment	742	49148	17120
国 有	State-owned	7	5000	941
集 体	Collective-owned	1		7
股份合作	Share-holding Cooperative	1		134
有限责任公司	Limited Liability Corporations	48	9613	1158
股份有限公司	Share-holding Cooperative Ltd.	3	140	1472
私 营	Private	678	34395	13387
其 他	Others	4		21
港澳台商投资	Hong Kong,Macao and Taiwan Funded	9	416	881
外商投资	Foreign Investment	2		10
按主要行业分	**Group by Sector**			
农、林、牧产品批发	Wholesale of Products of Agriculture, Forestry and Animal Husbandry	26	6612	568
食品、饮料及烟草制品批发	Wholesale of Food,Beverages and Tobaccos	26	4787	1672
纺织、服装及家庭用品批发	Specialized Retail of Textile, Garments and Commodity	71	2190	3220
文化、体育用品及器材批发	Specialized Retail of Stationers Goods, Sports Goods and Apparatus	6		67
医药及医疗器材批发	Wholesale of Medicine and Medical Appliance	10	20	2339
矿产品、建材及化工产品批发	Wholesale of Mineral Product, Building Material and Chemical Product	506	20580	6597
机械设备、五金产品及电子产品批发	Wholesale of Machinery, Hardware,Transport, Electric and Electronic Equipment	74	14663	2984
贸易经纪与代理	Trade Broker and Agent	10		266
其他批发	Others	24	712	298
零售贸易业	**Retail Trade**	**373**	**1617978**	**33286**
#国有控股	State-owned and State Share Holding	11	36662	861
按地区分	**Grouped by Region**			
市 区	Urban Area	288	1386782	28331

14-5 续表 Continued

指 标	Item	法人企业数（个） Number of Corporations (unit)	零售营业面积（平方米） Floor Space Of Retail Business (sq.m)	从业人员（人） Persons Engaged (Person)
溧阳市	Liyang City	36	146908	2964
金坛市	Jintan City	49	84288	1991
按登记注册类型分组	**Group by Registration Status**			
内 资	Domestic Investment	358	1405932	28596
国 有	State-owned	3	20285	363
集 体	Collective-owned	3	5720	31
股份合作	Share-holding Cooperative	2	550	29
有限责任公司	Limited Liability Corporations	47	361021	6083
股份有限公司	Share-holding Cooperative Ltd.	4	85084	1113
私 营	Private	295	927928	20859
其 他	Others	4	5344	118
港澳台商投资	Hong Kong,Macao and Taiwan Funded	8	109615	2687
外商投资	Foreign Investment	7	102431	2003
按主要行业分组	**Group by Sector**			
综合零售	Comprehensive Retail	52	748068	13709
食品、饮料及烟草制品专门零售	Speicalized Retail of Food, Beverage and Tobacco	25	15368	894
纺织、服装及日用品专门零售	Specialized Retail of Textile, Garments and Commodity	12	5132	502
文化、体育用品及器材专门零售	Specialized Retail of Stationers Goods, Sports Goods and Apparatus	41	47603	1473
医药及医疗器材专门零售	Specialized Retail of Medicine and Medical aapplиance	17	44701	2844
汽车、摩托车、燃料及零配件专门零售	Specialized Retail of Automobile, Motorcycle, Fuel and Fittings	157	554016	10239
家用电器及电子产品专门零售	Specialized Retail of Household Appliance and Electronic Products	43	177862	2962
五金、家具及室内装修材料专门零售	Specialized Retail of Hardware, Furniture and Interior Decoration Materials	14	13348	307
货摊、无店铺及其他零售业	Stall，Retail without Shops and Other Retail	12	11880	356
按经营方式分组	**Group by Means of Operation**			
独立商店	Independent Store	308	1206020	23318
连锁商店总店	Head Office of Chain Store	13	182876	4344
连锁商店分店	Branch Store of Chain Store	20	185678	4443
其 他	Others	32	43404	1181
按零售业态分组	**Group by Retail Size**			
食杂店	Traditional Grocery Stores	1	180	24
便利店	Convenience Stores	3	3484	403
超 市	Supermarket	11	36092	1760
大型超市	Large Supermarket	19	334702	7654
百货店	Composite Store	21	375990	4053
专业店	Specialized Store	205	463119	10522
专卖店	Speciality Store	104	388792	8308
家居建材店	Home Building Materials Stores	1	5913	99
厂家直销中心	Factory Outlet Centers	6	8106	378
网上商店	Online stores	2	1600	85

14-6 限额以上批发零售贸易业商品购进、销售、库存总额（2012 年）
TOTAL PURCHASES，SALES AND INVENTORY OF WHOLESALE AND RETAIL TRADE ABOVE DESIGNATED SIZE （2012）

单位：万元（10000 yuan）

指 标	Item	购进总额 Total Purchases	销售额 Total Sales	其中 of which 批发额 Wholesale	零售额 Retail Sales	年末库存总额 Inventory (year-end)
总 计	**Total**	**18118102**	**19818007**	**14742856**	**5075152**	**1184770**
市 区	Urban Area	17141750	18718274	14214019	4504254	1081188
溧阳市	Liyang City	456638	504485	144619	359867	48749
金坛市	Jintan City	519715	595248	384218	211031	54834
批发贸易业	**Wholesale Trade**	**13495044**	**14529127**	**14417189**	**111939**	**613964**
#国有控股	State-owned and State Share Holding	922127	1158611	1157581	1030	92230
按地区分	**Grouped by Region**					
市 区	Urban Area	13000991	14006618	13898813	107805	562112
溧阳市	Liyang City	130995	138433	136845	1588	20568
金坛市	Jintan City	363058	384076	381530	2546	31284
按登记注册类型分组	**Group by Registration Status**					
内 资	Domestic Investment	13123322	14055503	13943635	111868	599977
国 有	State-owned	498742	652589	651618	971	52900
集 体	Collective-owned	84288	85813	85813		3537
股份合作	Share-holding Cooperative	392957	399904	399904		8200
有限责任公司	Limited Liability Corporations	1996264	2143018	2106367	36651	94070
股份有限公司	Share-holding Cooperative Ltd.	280062	294026	291875	2151	6663
私 营	Private	9847778	10454432	10382338	72095	426973
其 他	Others	23231	25721	25721		7634
港澳台商投资	Hong Kong,Macao and Taiwan Funded	193963	277077	277005	71	4436
外商投资	Foreign Investment	177758	196548	196548		9551
按主要行业分组	**Group by Sector**					
农、林、牧产品批发	Wholesale of Products of Agriculture, Forestry and Animal Husbandry	287583	289273	278247	11025	48607
食品、饮料及烟草制品批发	Wholesale of Food,Beverages and Tobaccos	680052	859222	849548	9674	52076
纺织、服装及家庭用品批发	Specialized Retail of Textile, Garments and Commodity	1299455	1378529	1346395	32134	45618
文化、体育用品及器材批发	Specialized Retail of Stationers Goods, Sports Goods and Apparatus	46147	49506	49506		2250
医药及医疗器材批发	Wholesale of Medicine and Medical Appliance	229847	239047	236972	2074	15763
矿产品、建材及化工产品批发	Wholesale of Mineral Product, Building Material and Chemical Product	9189601	9727419	9683863	43556	369390
机械设备、五金产品及电子产品批发	Wholesale of Machine Hardware,Transport, Electric and Electronic Equipment	1034937	1186354	1173897	12457	65368
贸易经纪与代理	Trade Broker and Agent	268869	286507	286507		2850
其他批发	Others	458554	513273	512253	1019	12041
零售贸易业	**Retail Trade**	**4623058**	**5288880**	**325667**	**4963213**	**570806**
#国有控股	State-owned and State Share Holding	273427	331206	110289	220917	27362
按地区分	**Grouped by Region**					
市 区	Urban Area	4140758	4711656	315206	4396449	519076

14-6 续表 Continued

单位：万元（10000 yuan）

指 标	Item	购进总额 Total Purchases	销售额 Total Sales	其 中 of which 批发额 Wholesale	零售额 Retail Sales	年末库存总额 Inventory (year-end)
溧阳市	Liyang City	325643	366052	7773	358279	28181
金坛市	Jintan City	156657	211172	2688	208484	23549
按登记注册类型分组	**Group by Registration Status**					
内 资	Domestic Investment	4201455	4868667	325381	4543287	539593
国 有	State-owned	44509	51690	691	50999	10912
集 体	Collective-owned	3503	4023		4023	251
股份合作	Share-holding Cooperative	4527	4669	706	3963	335
有限责任公司	Limited Liability Corporations	851308	994381	133773	860608	104744
股份有限公司	Share-holding Cooperative Ltd.	303325	479980	113732	366248	24189
私 营	Private	2984196	3322478	73827	3248651	398063
其 他	Others	10085	11448	2652	8796	1099
港澳台商投资	Hong Kong,Macao and Taiwan Funded	216050	226144	91	226053	11620
外商投资	Foreign Investment	205554	194069	196	193873	19593
按主要行业分组	**Group by Sector**					
综合零售	Comprehensive Retail	843571	1190904	5848	1185056	191998
食品、饮料及烟草制品专门零售	Speicalized Retail of Food, Beverage and Tobacco	77541	86993	3039	83954	11203
纺织、服装及日用品专门零售	Specialized Retail of Textile, Garments and Commodity	29354	32390	3029	29361	6835
文化、体育用品及器材专门零售	Specialized Retail of Stationers Goods, Sports Goods and Apparatus	245849	272101	38767	233333	58994
医药及医疗器材专门零售	Specialized Retail of Medicine and Medical aappliance	574575	648483	227848	420635	51275
汽车、摩托车、燃料及零配件专门零售	Specialized Retail of Automobile, Motorcycle, Fueland Fittings	2464692	2627522	37685	2589837	217224
家用电器及电子产品专门零售	Specialized Retail of Household Appliance and Electronic Products	317510	356785	3249	353536	26855
五金、家具及室内装修材料专门零售	Specialized Retail of Hardware, Furniture and Interior Decoration Materials	27034	30276	5002	25274	3282
货摊、无店铺及其他零售业	Stall，Retail without Shops and Other Retail	42933	43425	1200	42226	3141
按经营方式分组	**Group by Means of Operation**					
独立商店	Independent Store	3787022	4307261	189842	4117419	468835
连锁商店总店	Head Office of Chain Store	240727	289421	801	288620	34400
连锁商店分店	Branch Store of Chain Store	406116	483462	99527	383935	38389
其 他	Others	189193	208737	35498	173239	29182
按零售业态分组	**Group by Retail Size**					
食杂店	Traditional Grocery Stores	1437	1397		1397	40
便利店	Convenience Stores	9976	12101		12101	943
超 市	Supermarket	98759	109362		109362	7685
大型超市	Large Supermarket	447241	521070	747	520323	56136
百货店	Composite Store	296848	559386	5101	554285	128030
专业店	Specialized Store	1367948	1515464	53179	1462285	161649
专卖店	Speciality Store	2192814	2311808	156359	2155449	201827
家居建材店	Home Building Materials Stores	975	1079		1079	420
厂家直销中心	Factory Outlet Centers	201116	250860	109999	140860	13840
网上商店	Online stores	5944	6354	282	6073	236

14-7 市区限额以上批发零售贸易业商品购进、销售、库存总额（2012 年）

TOTAL PURCHASES, SALES AND INVENTORY OF WHOLESALE AND RETAIL TRADE ABOVE DESIGNATED SIZE IN URBAN AREA（2012）

单位：万元（10000 yuan）

指标	Item	购进总额 Total Purchases	销售额 Total Sales	其中 of which 批发额 Wholesale	零售额 Retail Sales	年末库存总额 Inventory (year-end)
总 计	**Total**	**17141750**	**18718274**	**14214019**	**4504254**	**1081188**
批发贸易业	**Wholesale Trade**	**13000991**	**14006618**	**13898813**	**107805**	**562112**
#国有控股	State-owned and State Share Holding	884156	1123629	1122599	1030	69057
按登记注册类型分组	**Group by Registration Status**					
内 资	Domestic Investment	12635609	13539187	13431453	107734	548271
国 有	State-owned	460771	617607	616636	971	29727
集 体	Collective-owned	84288	85813	85813		3537
股份合作	Share-holding Cooperative	392957	399904	399904		8200
有限责任公司	Limited Liability Corporations	1993631	2140274	2103623	36651	93956
股份有限公司	Share-holding Cooperative Ltd.	237365	239881	239804	77	4125
私 营	Private	9443365	10029987	9959952	70035	401093
其 他	Others	23231	25721	25721		7634
港澳台商投资	Hong Kong,Macao and Taiwan Funded	187624	270883	270812	71	4290
外商投资	Foreign Investment	177758	196548	196548		9551
按主要行业分组	**Group by Sector**					
农、林、牧产品批发	Wholesale of Products of Agriculture, Forestry and Animal Husbandry	184499	190309	179285	11024	20115
食品、饮料及烟草制品批发	Wholesale of Food,Beverages and Tobaccos	675077	853809	845387	8422	49464
纺织、服装及家庭用品批发	Specialized Retail of Textile, Garments and Commodity	1273617	1351855	1319721	32134	44779
文化、体育用品及器材批发	Specialized Retail of Stationers Goods, Sports Goods and Apparatus	46147	49506	49506		2250
医药及医疗器材批发	Wholesale of Medicine and Medical Appliance	174148	170969	170969		12757
矿产品、建材及化工产品批发	Wholesale of Mineral Product, Building Material and Chemical Product	8996900	9523312	9479761	43551	356703
机械设备、五金产品及电子产品批发	Wholesale of Machinery, Hardware,Transport, Electric and Electronic Equipment	1006633	1157694	1145520	12174	63609
贸易经纪与代理	Trade Broker and Agent	263870	281516	281516		2826
其他批发	Others	380100	427648	427148	500	9610
零售贸易业	**Retail Trade**	**4140758**	**4711656**	**315206**	**4396449**	**519076**
#国有控股	State-owned and State Share Holding	262613	319776	110289	209488	24051
按登记注册类型分组	**Group by Registration Status**					
内 资	Domestic Investment	3785232	4360223	314920	4045303	490042
国 有	State-owned	42951	50138	691	49447	10905
股份合作	Share-holding Cooperative	3906	3891		3891	144

14-7 续表 Continued　　　　单位：万元（10000 yuan）

指 标	Item	购进总额 Total Purchases	销售额 Total Sales	其中 of which 批发额 Wholesale	零售额 Retail Sales	年末库存总额 Inventory (year-end)
有限责任公司	Limited Liability Corporations	795596	930779	133773	797006	92049
股份有限公司	Share-holding Cooperative Ltd.	299580	475914	113732	362182	22663
私 营	Private	2637256	2893640	64072	2829568	363708
其 他	Others	5943	5861	2652	3209	572
港澳台商投资	Hong Kong,Macao and Taiwan Funded	166417	172924	91	172833	11329
外商投资	Foreign Investment	189110	178509	196	178313	17705
按主要行业分组	**Group by Sector**					
综合零售	Comprehensive Retail	681223	949451	5143	944308	182429
食品、饮料及烟草制品专门零售	Speicalized Retail of Food, Beverage and Tobacco	71583	81033	1808	79225	9867
纺织、服装及日用品专门零售	Specialized Retail of Textile, Garments and Commodity	28482	31388	3029	28359	6707
文化、体育用品及器材专门零售	Specialized Retail of Stationers Goods, Sports Goods and Apparatus	227008	252180	38005	214174	51681
医药及医疗器材专门零售	Specialized Retail of Medicine and Medical aappliance	556643	623134	227848	395287	47884
汽车、摩托车、燃料及零配件专门零售	Specialized Retail of Automobile, Motorcycle, Fuel and Fittings	2243804	2399462	33298	2366165	193641
家用电器及电子产品专门零售	Specialized Retail of Household Appliance and Electronic Products	296397	334857	1782	333075	23080
五金、家具及室内装修材料专门零售	Specialized Retail of Hardware, Furniture and Interior Decoration Materials	21933	24986	3902	21084	2958
货摊、无店铺及其他零售业	Stall，Retail without Shops and Other Retail	13686	15165	392	14773	828
按经营方式分组	**Group by Means of Operation**					
独立商店	Independent Store	3399732	3844000	183220	3660779	428415
连锁商店总店	Head Office of Chain Store	222169	262970	801	262169	31429
连锁商店分店	Branch Store of Chain Store	343238	411644	96147	315497	30572
其 他	Others	175619	193041	35038	158004	28660
按零售业态分组	**Group by Retail Size**					
食杂店	Traditional Grocery Stores	1437	1397		1397	40
便利店	Convenience Stores	9976	12101		12101	943
超 市	Supermarket	60105	67200		67200	6463
大型超市	Large Supermarket	403358	414340	747	413593	49082
百货店	Composite Store	217036	466824	4396	462429	126737
专业店	Specialized Store	1130235	1272791	51163	1221628	132541
专卖店	Speciality Store	2112409	2220922	149131	2071791	189736
家居建材店	Home Building Materials Stores	975	1079		1079	420
厂家直销中心	Factory Outlet Centers	199283	248648	109488	139160	12878
网上商店	Online stores	5944	6354	282	6073	236

14-8　限额以上批发零售贸易企业主要财务指标（2012 年）
MAIN FINANCIAL INDICATORS OF WHOLESALE AND RETAIL ENTERPRISES ABOVE DESIGNATED SIZE（2012）

指　标	Item	流动资产合　计 Total Circulating Funds	固定资产原　价 Original Value of Fixed Assets	资产总计 Total Assets	负债总计 Total Liabilities
总　计	**Total**	**6285606**	**794719**	**7699011**	**6026251**
市　区	Urban Area	5902539	675575	7077390	5572916
溧阳市	Liyang City	152190	74337	281582	194893
金坛市	Jintan City	230877	44807	340039	258442
批发贸易业	**Wholesale Trade**	**4463417**	**285619**	**5085356**	**3945633**
# 国有控股	State-owned and State Share Holding	443437	49263	489896	176768
按地区分	**Grouped by Region**				
市　区	Urban Area	4232235	260746	4770665	3694382
溧阳市	Liyang City	69544	11537	87631	68532
金坛市	Jintan City	161638	13336	227061	182720
按登记注册类型分组	**Group by Registration Status**				
内　资	Domestic Investment	4258453	276100	4864564	3787429
国　有	State-owned	356440	47243	395843	105240
集　体	Collective-owned	4613	4	4614	3297
股份合作	Share-holding Cooperative	60439	5709	70475	65167
有限责任公司	Limited Liability Corporations	519057	42722	612188	505220
股份有限公司	Share-holding Cooperative Ltd.	92221	401	132652	120027
私　营	Private	3220655	180007	3643755	2986323
其　他	Others	5028	13	5037	2156
港澳台商投资	Hong Kong,Macao and Taiwan Funded	140819	7133	155173	93042
外商投资	Foreign Investment	64145	2386	65619	65163
按主要行业分组	**Group by Sector**				
农、林、牧产品批发	Wholesale of Products of Agriculture, Forestry and Animal Husbandry	125785	14171	153389	113417
食品、饮料及烟草制品批发	Wholesale of Food,Beverages and Tobaccos	393925	46582	441967	141014
纺织、服装及家庭用品批发	Specialized Retail of Textile, Garments and Commodity	417211	26595	459045	379942
文化、体育用品及器材批发	Specialized Retail of Stationers Goods, Sports Goods and Apparatus	12493	466	17102	12941
医药及医疗器材批发	Wholesale of Medicine and Medical Appliance	275406	14067	411672	349615
矿产品、建材及化工产品批发	Wholesale of Mineral Product, Building Material and Chemical Product	2636913	148599	2932231	2391702
机械设备、五金产品及电子产品批发	Wholesale of Machinery, Hardware,Transport, Electric and Electronic Equipment	358036	24212	405896	343009
贸易经纪与代理	Trade Broker and Agent	119361	8982	133708	122822
其他批发	Others	124287	1944	130347	91172
零售贸易业	**Retail Trade**	**1822189**	**509100**	**2613655**	**2080618**
# 国有控股	State-owned and State Holding Majority Shares	155035	20553	179869	148966
按地区分	**Grouped by Region**				
市　区	Urban Area	1670304	414828	2306726	1878534
溧阳市	Liyang City	82646	62800	193951	126361
金坛市	Jintan City	69239	31471	112978	75723

单位：万元（10000 yuan）

所有者权益 Creditors Equity	实收资本 Total Capital Hold	其中 of which #国家资本 State Capital	营业收入 Business Revenues	其中 of which #主营业务收入 Major Business Revenues	主营业务成本 Major Business Cost	主营业务税金及附加 Major Business Taxes and Extra Charges	营业利润 Profits from Bus iness	利润总额 Total Profits	本年应交增值税 Value Added Tax Payable	本年应交所得税 Income tax payable	应付职工薪酬 Remuneration Payable to Employees
1672760	**1127606**	**21893**	**17154326**	**17063089**	**15960602**	**53155**	**257768**	**240853**	**181509**	**56746**	**226015**
1504475	972603	18707	16140344	16058484	15046565	48347	248279	227447	156690	52110	198570
86689	74751	3000	476162	470257	423913	2842	6182	7663	12674	3227	13252
81597	80253	185	537821	534348	490123	1967	3307	5744	12146	1409	14193
1139723	**732433**	**18344**	**12622517**	**12585660**	**11889397**	**38599**	**223984**	**198652**	**129370**	**37863**	**92279**
313129	24422	9343	963272	961916	812573	28064	93844	97352	21578	21667	8708
1076283	674061	15158	12147400	12111112	11445706	36639	222336	193095	112471	36848	83779
19099	15058	3000	125874	125683	120761	954	-2561	-896	7309	165	1386
44341	43314	185	349244	348864	322930	1006	4209	6453	9590	849	7114
1077136	666544	18344	12210464	12173617	11530665	37470	202727	177490	121581	34909	82274
290604	6802	6773	550995	550673	420016	27955	83987	87305	20794	20510	8108
1317	1027		73345	73345	66010	8	2168	48	68	5	25
5308	362		343899	342210	335264	100	2770	2761	749	114	569
106968	85896	2571	1872916	1871590	1790925	2272	27891	28482	17747	2770	6860
12625	20000		162384	162362	147027	208	6757	6663	1747	6	4667
657433	549902	9000	9182839	9149351	8748813	6919	79264	52350	80407	11488	61964
2881	2555		24086	24086	22610	9	-111	-119	69	16	81
62131	61353		233069	233058	191501	1122	11078	10982	7715	2882	9918
456	4536		178985	178985	167231	8	10179	10181	74	72	87
39972	29696	3216	296937	296837	289684	569	-78	2746	497	715	2271
300953	13760	2557	747740	747299	603609	28239	88707	90134	23166	21548	9903
79103	49032	500	1270374	1255387	1182766	613	18851	5013	9635	2861	17655
4161	2215		45884	45884	41592	67	1392	268	106	83	317
62057	63910		207474	207452	184406	372	3261	3155	2614	273	7971
540529	502392	12070	8264422	8243499	7912934	3643	92197	70778	47955	6688	30059
62887	39752	1	1067830	1067471	979953	1481	17356	17815	12902	4541	19793
10887	10599		272416	272389	263986	122	-512	-135	160	203	1986
39175	21078		449441	449441	430467	3493	2810	8878	32335	951	2325
533037	**395173**	**3549**	**4531809**	**4477430**	**4071205**	**14556**	**33784**	**42201**	**52140**	**18883**	**133736**
30902	19779	1830	272053	270439	254039	300	1606	2883	1400	274	5602
428192	298541	3549	3992944	3947372	3600860	11708	25943	34352	44219	15262	114791
67590	59694		350288	344574	303152	1888	8744	8559	5365	3062	11865
37255	36938		188577	185484	167193	960	-902	-709	2556	560	7080

14-8 续表 Continued

指 标	Item	流动资产合计 Total Circulating Funds	固定资产原价 Original Value of Fixed Assets	资产总计 Total Assets	负债总计 Total Liabilities
按登记注册类型分组	**Group by Registration Status**				
内 资	Domestic Investment	1758818	416682	2433129	1908004
国 有	State-owned	12891	11698	20376	13286
集 体	Collective-owned	2052	43	2080	1878
股份合作	Share-holding Cooperative	914	987	5943	4997
有限责任公司	Limited Liability Corporations	379104	55867	447901	378449
股份有限公司	Share-holding Cooperative Ltd.	150780	60065	239115	125012
私 营	Private	1208787	282833	1709924	1378696
其 他	Others	4290	5189	7790	5686
港澳台商投资	Hong Kong,Macao and Taiwan Funded	39063	65540	126583	101763
外商投资	Foreign Investment	24308	26878	53943	70851
按主要行业分组	**Group by Sector**				
综合零售	Comprehensive Retail	531111	271896	882365	726536
食品、饮料及烟草制品专门零售	Speicalized Retail of Food, Beverage and Tobacco	22922	3569	26412	16411
纺织、服装及日用品专门零售	Specialized Retail of Textile, Garments and Commodity	11884	1568	13489	9753
文化、体育用品及器材专门零售	Specialized Retail of Stationers Goods, Sports Goods and Apparatus	106255	26253	127176	76226
医药及医疗器材专门零售	Specialized Retail of Medicine and Medical Appliance	255592	15202	296042	208560
汽车、摩托车、燃料及零配件专门零售	Specialized Retail of Automobile, Motorcycle, Fuel and Fittings	749942	156938	1085934	916880
家用电器及电子产品专门零售	Specialized Retail of Household Appliance and Electronic Products	122381	25455	150837	105299
五金、家具及室内装修材料专门零售	Specialized Retail of Hardware, Furniture and Interior Decoration Materials	8102	5376	11753	9673
货摊、无店铺及其他零售业	Stall，Retail without Shops and Other Retail	14001	2844	19647	11281
按经营方式分组	**Group by Means of Operation**				
独立商店	Independent Store	1421670	438167	2132091	1695911
连锁商店总店	Head Office of Chain Store	111872	16874	128250	100313
连锁商店分店	Branch Store of Chain Store	191629	37912	229941	207976
其 他	Others	97018	16147	123373	76418
按零售业态分组	**Group by Retail Size**				
食杂店	Traditional Grocery Stores	342	35	353	276
便利店	Convenience Stores	4830	2327	10147	7805
超 市	Supermarket	28993	14548	42221	36473
大型超市	Large Supermarket	138939	98666	236761	237413
百货店	Composite Store	361105	156667	596299	445453
专业店	Specialized Store	443399	116465	625538	472627
专卖店	Speciality Store	703556	114767	948227	747771
家居建材店	Home Building Materials Stores	595	125	1383	1456
厂家直销中心	Factory Outlet Centers	137645	5276	148770	128982
网上商店	Online stores	2784	223	3956	2362

单位：万元（10000 yuan）

所有者权益 Creditors Equity	实收资本 Total Capital Hold	其中 of which #国家资本 State Capital	营业收入 Business Revenues	其中 of which #主营业务收入 Major Business Revenues	主营业务成本 Major Business Cost	主营业务税金及附加 Major Business Taxes and Extra Charges	营业利润 Profits from Business	利润总额 Total Profits	本年应交增值税 Value Added Tax Payable	本年应交所得税 Income Tax Payable	应付职工薪酬 Remuneration Payable to Employees
525125	315019	3549	4212969	4170553	3804139	12644	41562	47053	47132	18136	117455
7090	1500	1500	31183	30585	24938	83	913	1332	557	73	2201
202	162		3438	3438	3221	2	31	6	16	2	95
946	850		4155	3990	3800	13	1	1	104	3	94
69452	59564	330	874226	862863	767362	4135	13853	15442	10328	5146	25727
114103	14006	1719	420275	413258	370655	1385	25535	26203	6772	5097	7470
331228	236953		2869892	2846635	2625333	6994	1666	4600	29180	7814	81379
2104	1985		9800	9784	8829	32	-436	-532	176	1	489
24820	49840		202567	196220	171123	993	-4248	-2548	2917	706	9668
-16908	30314		116273	110656	95943	919	-3530	-2303	2090	42	6613
155830	148523		1033188	993317	843244	7704	19158	25565	21388	10265	50178
10001	7794		52634	52622	45395	134	723	402	794	221	2577
3736	2769		25399	25357	21278	59	-96	-114	451	65	1438
50951	13171	1500	225520	224663	193773	2749	10135	11284	3515	2339	6842
87482	32005	1719	559249	557076	519234	874	13438	14777	5315	2335	12794
169054	154616		2273049	2265840	2133982	2059	-9810	-9888	15322	2187	46080
45537	27117		298163	294050	255050	824	-34	349	4723	1339	11440
2080	1180		24436	24397	22480	35	82	27	196	54	929
8366	7999	330	40170	40109	36769	119	188	-201	437	78	1459
436179	336306	3549	3736293	3697221	3380769	11903	28238	32904	41396	15301	101587
27937	11464		241203	239341	197866	972	3642	4434	5272	1578	14121
21965	25345		382998	373178	340241	1109	-172	2772	3873	1365	13314
46956	22058		171314	167689	152329	573	2077	2092	1599	639	4714
77	50		1194	1194	1135	1	7	6	10	1	61
2342	2287		10401	10401	8229	33	-750	-244	286	100	1195
5749	5228		94574	94574	80588	307	-269	918	1907	378	6110
-652	64336		435948	417425	361701	2208	-3858	745	7245	2149	23506
150847	76960		500224	478875	399393	5177	24451	24557	12128	7741	19900
152912	98451	1830	1293113	1283740	1161933	4259	6144	7337	14449	5317	41268
200456	128946	1719	1974154	1969569	1845405	2325	8167	8778	15487	3083	38427
-74	100		922	922	734	1	126	126	6		200
19787	17308		215818	215268	207236	182	23	514	599	98	2503
1594	1508		5460	5460	4849	63	-258	-536	23	15	567

14-9 市区限额以上批发零售贸易企业主要财务指标（2012 年） MAIN FINANCIAL INDICATORS OF WHOLESALE AND RETAIL ENTERPRISES ABOVE DESIGNATED SIZE IN URBAN AREA（2012）

指 标	Item	流动资产合计 Total Circulating Funds	固定资产原价 Original Value of Fixed Assets	资产总计 Total Assets	负债总计 Total Liabilities
总 计	**Total**	**5902539**	**675575**	**7077390**	**5572916**
#国有控股	State-owned and State Share Holding	565349	56965	620251	284394
批发贸易业	**Wholesale Trade**	**4232235**	**260746**	**4770665**	**3694382**
#国有控股	State-owned and State Share Holding	414996	38968	446117	139126
按登记注册类型分组	**Group by Registration Status**				
内 资	Domestic Investment	4028151	251262	4550769	3536600
国 有	State-owned	327999	36949	352064	67598
集 体	Collective-owned	4613	4	4614	3297
股份合作	Share-holding Cooperative	60439	5709	70475	65167
有限责任公司	Limited Liability Corporations	518405	42674	611461	504801
股份有限公司	Share-holding Cooperative Ltd.	12548	114	12582	7582
私 营	Private	3099119	165800	3494537	2885999
其 他	Others	5028	13	5037	2156
港澳台商投资	Hong Kong,Macao and Taiwan Funded	139939	7099	154276	92619
外商投资	Foreign Investment	64145	2386	65619	65163
按主要行业分组	**Group by Sector**				
农、林、牧产品批发	Wholesale of Products of Agriculture, Forestry and Animal Husbandry	82778	2935	87054	71612
食品、饮料及烟草制品批发	Wholesale of Food,Beverages and Tobaccos	389640	44199	435587	134816
纺织、服装及家庭用品批发	Specialized Retail of Textile, Garments and Commodity	411176	26422	452788	375897
文化、体育用品及器材批发	Specialized Retail of Stationers Goods, Sports Goods and Apparatus	12493	466	17102	12941
医药及医疗器材批发	Wholesale of Medicine and Medical Appliance	187310	12798	281997	228207
矿产品、建材及化工产品批发	Wholesale of Mineral Product, Building Material and Chemical Product	2568516	139851	2848249	2332941
机械设备、五金产品及电子产品批发	Wholesale of Machinery, Hardware,Transport, Electric and Electronic Equipment	351249	23381	398558	336877
贸易经纪与代理	Trade Broker and Agent	117949	8842	132225	122010
其他批发	Others	111125	1853	117104	79081
零售贸易业	**Retail Trade**	**1670304**	**414828**	**2306726**	**1878534**
#国有控股	State-owned and State Share Holding	150353	17997	174134	145268
按登记注册类型分组	**Group by Registration Status**				
内 资	Domestic Investment	1615770	353011	2190739	1743065
国 有	State-owned	12891	11698	20376	13286

单位：万元（10000 yuan）

所有者权益 Creditors Equity	实收资本 Total Capital Hold	其中 of which # 国家资本 State Capital	营业收入 Business Revenues	其中 of which # 主营业务收入 Major Business Revenues	主营业务成本 Major Business Cost	主营业务税金及附加 Major Business Taxes and Extra Charges	营业利润 Profits from Business	利润总额 Total Profits	本年应交增值税 Value Added Tax Payable	本年应交所得税 Income Tax Payable	应付职工薪酬 Remuneration Payable to Employees
1504475	**972603**	**18707**	**16140344**	**16058484**	**15046565**	**48347**	**248279**	**227447**	**156690**	**52110**	**198570**
335858	41015	7988	1191512	1188897	1026274	28328	96978	99422	22960	21941	12938
1076283	**674061**	**15158**	**12147400**	**12111112**	**11445706**	**36639**	**222336**	**193095**	**112471**	**36848**	**83779**
306992	21237	6158	928195	926934	778466	28064	95979	97284	21578	21667	8171
1014170	608309	15158	11741394	11705117	11092691	35510	201153	171995	104682	33911	73906
284466	3617	3588	515918	515691	385909	27955	86123	87238	20794	20510	7571
1317	1027		73345	73345	66010	8	2168	48	68	5	25
5308	362		343899	342210	335264	100	2770	2761	749	114	569
106660	85596	2571	1870173	1868847	1788306	2272	27888	28473	17747	2768	6814
4999	5000		116027	116027	110999	9	3928	3946	89	6	80
608538	510152	9000	8797946	8764911	8383593	5158	78388	49647	65167	10491	58766
2881	2555		24086	24086	22610	9	-111	-119	69	16	81
61657	61217		227022	227011	185784	1122	11004	10920	7715	2866	9786
456	4536		178985	178985	167231	8	10179	10181	74	72	87
15442	11151	31	198198	198193	195183	401	-368	287	69	148	1569
300771	13644	2557	743113	742673	599801	28230	88626	90060	23083	21529	9744
76890	47896	500	1243876	1228889	1157505	612	18527	4696	9630	2825	17260
4161	2215		45884	45884	41592	67	1392	268	106	83	317
53790	47410		148627	148627	136755	160	606	610	836	252	3214
515309	484297	12070	8083996	8063527	7744993	3230	91683	69964	45127	6405	28320
61681	39142	1	1042335	1041975	955909	1448	17154	17693	10960	4511	19299
10216	9879		267458	267431	259363	121	-495	-129	157	203	1889
38023	18428		373913	373913	354605	2370	5212	9646	22503	892	2170
428192	**298541**	**3549**	**3992944**	**3947372**	**3600860**	**11708**	**25943**	**34352**	**44219**	**15262**	**114791**
28866	19779	1830	263318	261964	247808	264	999	2138	1382	274	4767
447675	247410	3549	3735932	3700564	3385635	10259	31432	36923	40127	14678	101869
7090	1500	1500	31183	30585	24938	83	913	1332	557	73	2201

14-9 续表 Continued

指 标	Item	流动资产合计 Total Circulating Funds	固定资产原价 Original Value of Fixed Assets	资产总计 Total Assets	负债总计 Total Liabilities
股份合作	Share-holding Cooperative	650	940	5663	4787
有限责任公司	Limited Liability Corporations	352872	51295	416165	358787
股份有限公司	Share-holding Cooperative Ltd.	149334	58522	236730	123278
私 营	Private	1098016	226010	1507106	1239609
其 他	Others	2007	4545	4700	3318
港澳台商投资	Hong Kong,Macao and Taiwan Funded	33326	36233	66220	67969
外商投资	Foreign Investment	21209	25585	49767	67500
按主要行业分组	**Group by Sector**				
综合零售	Comprehensive Retail	476475	201949	706233	615869
食品、饮料及烟草制品专门零售	Speicalized Retail of Food, Beverage and Tobacco	19384	2897	21487	13488
纺织、服装及日用品专门零售	Specialized Retail of Textile, Garments and Commodity	11059	1225	12530	9634
文化、体育用品及器材专门零售	Specialized Retail of Stationers Goods, Sports Goods and Apparatus	96514	22791	115578	66940
医药及医疗器材专门零售	Specialized Retail of Medicine and Medical Appliance	245283	14320	284890	202891
汽车、摩托车、燃料及零配件专门零售	Specialized Retail of Automobile, Motorcycle, Fuel and Fittings	697490	139262	1008148	857624
家用电器及电子产品专门零售	Specialized Retail of Household Appliance and Electronic Products	113106	24758	141002	99836
五金、家具及室内装修材料专门零售	Specialized Retail of Hardware, Furniture and Interior Decoration Materials	5564	5126	9168	7436
货摊、无店铺及其他零售业	Stall，Retail without Shops and Other Retail	5430	2500	7691	4815
按经营方式分组	**Group by Means of Operation**				
独立商店	Independent Store	1297120	354136	1862526	1523105
连锁商店总店	Head Office of Chain Store	102231	15126	116805	94157
连锁商店分店	Branch Store of Chain Store	177039	31476	210383	190508
其 他	Others	93915	14090	117013	70763
按零售业态分组	**Group by Retail Size**				
食杂店	Traditional Grocery Stores	342	35	353	276
便利店	Convenience Stores	4830	2327	10147	7805
超 市	Supermarket	21990	10344	32211	27665
大型超市	Large Supermarket	109640	76542	176605	203842
百货店	Composite Store	342772	113049	490333	377165
专业店	Specialized Store	370916	98239	525169	400590
专卖店	Speciality Store	679862	109379	920062	730438
家居建材店	Home Building Materials Stores	595	125	1383	1456
厂家直销中心	Factory Outlet Centers	136573	4565	146507	126935
网上商店	Online stores	2784	223	3956	2362

单位：万元（10000 yuan）

所有者权益 Creditors Equity	实收资本 Total Capital Hold	其中 of which #国家资本 State Capital	营业收入 Business Revenues	其中 of which #主营业务收入 Major Business Revenues	主营业务成本 Major Business Cost	主营业务税金及附加 Major Business Taxes and Extra Charges	营业利润 Profits from Business	利润总额 Total Profits	本年应交增值税 Value Added Tax Payable	本年应交所得税 Income Tax Payable	应付职工薪酬 Remuneration Payable to Employees
876	800		3491	3326	3185	12	-3	-3	97	2	68
57377	55164	330	796393	785096	702102	3961	9627	11090	9120	3985	22919
113452	14006	1719	416657	409833	368086	1351	25349	25975	6766	5097	7084
267497	174956		2483199	2466715	2282945	4837	-4246	-1171	23553	5520	69309
1381	985		5009	5009	4379	15	-208	-300	34	1	288
-1749	21317		155028	150441	131462	663	-2060	-346	2432	543	7075
-17734	29814		101984	96368	83763	786	-3429	-2226	1661	41	5848
90363	83761		818001	785731	667555	5470	13071	19475	16271	8079	40785
7998	6528		46855	46843	40938	99	296	305	738	187	2210
2896	2189		24406	24364	20410	58	94	47	442	65	1386
48638	12822	1500	208827	208229	180696	2515	9696	10599	3389	2334	5573
81999	28835	1719	536907	535287	503518	758	11347	12681	4377	1769	10940
150524	137161		2047896	2040961	1922285	1900	-8520	-8629	14182	1452	41429
41166	23367		278881	274886	237368	805	-23	280	4564	1301	10815
1732	1080		19106	19068	17579	27	13	-41	129	32	791
2876	2799	330	12065	12005	10510	77	-31	-364	127	43	863
339421	245547	3549	3298917	3265715	2994463	9517	24551	29278	35259	13002	87744
22647	8359		218576	216715	180917	858	1557	2324	4365	1013	12549
19874	23240		317884	310870	286043	765	-2269	644	3029	613	10139
46250	21394		157566	154073	139438	568	2104	2106	1566	633	4361
77	50		1194	1194	1135	1	7	6	10	1	61
2342	2287		10401	10401	8229	33	-750	-244	286	100	1195
4546	3349		56920	56920	48587	148	-315	862	1159	210	3953
-27237	41336		339744	325996	284488	1360	-8196	-3653	4930	1026	19229
113168	37076		418894	400372	332919	3950	22748	22921	10074	6845	16941
124579	74880	1830	1050488	1042158	937846	3924	5915	6979	12871	4598	34390
189624	121197	1719	1895150	1890728	1776314	2077	6890	7377	14271	2368	35852
-74	100		922	922	734	1	126	126	6		200
19572	16758		213770	213220	205758	151	-224	514	590	98	2404
1594	1508		5460	5460	4849	63	-258	-536	23	15	567

14-10 限额以上住宿餐饮企业主要情况（2012 年）
MAIN CONDITION OF ACCOMMODATION AND CATERING BUSINESS ABOVE DESIGNATED SIZE（2012）

指 标	Item	法人企业数（个）Number of Enterprises (unit)	年末餐饮营业面积（平方米）Operation Area of Catering At Year-end (sq.m)	从业人员（人）Persons Engaged (Person)
总 计	**Total**	**147**	**522337**	**35118**
市 区	Urban Area	103	386122	28297
溧阳市	Liyang City	25	85655	4763
金坛市	Jintan City	19	50560	2058
# 国有控股	State-owned and State Share Holding	6	11959	463
按登记注册类型分组	**Group by Registration Status**			
内 资	Domestic Investment	139	461150	29808
国 有	State-owned	5	11439	417
集 体	Collective-owned	2	500	118
股份合作	Cooperative	1	660	40
有限责任公司	Limited Liability Corporations	12	52440	3614
私 营	Private	118	394773	25579
其 他	Others	1	1338	40
港澳台商投资	Hong Kong,Macao and Taiwan Funded	5	51108	3974
外商投资	Foreign Investment	3	10079	1336
住宿业	**Accommodation Trade**	**63**	**202345**	**11243**
# 国有控股	State-owned and State Share Holding	6	11959	463
按登记注册类型分组	**Group by Registration Status**			
内 资	Domestic Investment	59	180887	10029
国 有	State-owned	5	11439	417
集 体	Collective-owned	1		62
有限责任公司	Limited Liability Corporations	6	30477	1569
私 营	Private	47	138971	7981
港澳台商投资	Hong Kong,Macao and Taiwan Funded	2	19458	965
外商投资	Foreign Investment	2	2000	249

营业收入（万元）Operational Revenues（10000 yuan）	其中 of which				床位数（张）Number of Beds（bed）	餐位数（位）Catering Seats Available（Seat）
	客房收入 Room Rate Revenues	餐费收入 Catering Revenues	商品销售收入 Commodity Sales Revenues	其他收入 Other Revenues		
531867	**96598**	**409724**	**4712**	**20832**	**21690**	**89672**
435271	69621	348874	2362	14413	14777	67911
72292	22216	43714	1808	4554	5563	15496
24304	4761	17136	541	1865	1350	6265
8521	2730	4170	1175	446	1115	2180
437038	80253	334630	4203	17952	19128	80601
8021	2517	3941	1175	388	1018	2000
1314	1002	210	23	80	350	30
342	60	282			64	300
62378	17627	41596	188	2967	3519	9175
364302	59047	287921	2818	14517	14177	68696
681		681				400
67992	11778	54645	1	1568	1801	5559
26837	4568	20449	508	1312	761	3512
191630	**70807**	**102350**	**3662**	**14811**	**15943**	**34903**
8521	2730	4170	1175	446	1115	2180
159954	59537	84024	3474	12919	14327	30850
8021	2517	3941	1175	388	1018	2000
853	853				200	
26396	8842	14905	180	2470	1809	4108
124684	47325	65179	2119	10061	11300	24742
27054	9257	16698	1	1098	1306	3203
4622	2013	1628	187	794	310	850

14-10 续表 Continued

指标	Item	法人企业数（个）Number ofEnterprises（unit）	年末餐饮营业面积（平方米）OperationArea ofCateringAt Year-end（sq.m）	从业人员（人）Persons Engaged（Person）
按星级饭店分组	**Restaurants Grouped By Star Level**			
一 星	One-star	1	980	90
二 星	Two-star	2	1885	71
三 星	Three-star	15	35919	1200
四 星	Four-star	16	56243	4333
五 星	Five-star	6	32223	2662
其 他	Others	23	75095	2887
餐饮业	**Catering Trade**	**84**	**319992**	**23875**
按登记注册类型分组	**Group by Registration Status**			
内 资	Domestic Investment	80	280263	19779
集 体	Collective-owned	1	500	56
股份合作	Cooperative	1	660	40
有限责任公司	Limited Liability Corporations	6	21963	2045
私 营	Private	71	255802	17598
其 他	Others	1	1338	40
港澳台商投资	Hong Kong,Macao and Taiwan Funded	3	31650	3009
外商投资	Foreign Investment	1	8079	1087
按主要行业分组	**Group by Sector**			
正 餐	Dinner	77	218625	11882
快 餐	Fast Food	5	99042	11720
饮料及冷饮服务	Beverage and Cold Drinks		1235	62
其他餐饮业	Other	2	1090	211
按经营方式分组	**Group by Means of Operation**			
独立商店	Independent Store	76	211879	11477
连锁商店总店	Head Office of Chain Store	3	97035	11298
连锁商店分店	Branch Store of Chain Store	3	9188	729
其 他	Others	2	1890	371

营业收入（万元）Operational Revenues（10000 yuan）	其　　中　　of　　which				床位数（张）Number of Beds（bed）	餐位数（位）Catering Seats Available（Seat）
	客房收入 Room Rate Revenues	餐费收入 Catering Revenues	商品销售收入 Commodity Sales Revenues	其他收入 Other Revenues		
2009	662	137		1210	270	128
749	249	456	42	2	247	400
15829	6601	8336	151	742	3106	6136
70156	27316	34443	803	7594	4743	12474
60543	18972	36415	1382	3774	2723	7525
42343	17007	22563	1284	1489	4854	8240
340237	**25792**	**307374**	**1050**	**6021**	**5747**	**54769**
277084	20716	250606	729	5033	4801	49751
461	149	210	23	80	150	30
342	60	282			64	300
35982	8785	26691	8	498	1710	5067
239618	11721	222742	699	4456	2877	43954
681		681				400
40937	2521	37947		469	495	2356
22216	2555	18821	321	519	451	2662
185968	25792	153179	977	6021	5747	46116
146286		146286				7840
2392		2319	73			485
5591		5591				328
179777	24172	148793	1038	5774	5352	43767
138112		138112				7450
14450	1314	12876	12	247	322	2720
7899	306	7594			73	832

14-11　市区限额以上住宿餐饮企业主要情况（2012 年）
MAIN CONDITION OF ACCOMMODATION AND CATERING TRADE ABOVE DESIGNATED SIZE WITHIN CITY（2012）

指　标	Item	法人企业数（个）Number ofEnterprises (unit)	年末餐饮营业面积（平方米）OperationArea ofCateringAt Year-end (sq.m)	从业人员（人）Persons Engaged (Person)
总　计	**Total**	**103**	**386122**	**28297**
#国有控股	State-owned and State Share Holding	3	6439	291
按登记注册类型分组	**Group by Registration Status**			
内　资	Domestic Investment	98	334225	23531
国　有	State-owned	3	6439	291
集　体	Collective-owned	1		62
股份合作	Share-holding Cooperative	1	660	40
有限责任公司	Limited Liability Corporations	10	46620	3173
私　营	Private	82	279168	19925
其　他	Others	1	1338	40
港澳台商投资	Hong Kong,Macao and Taiwan Funded	4	45108	3839
外商投资	Foreign Investment	1	6789	927
住宿业	**Accommodation Trade**	**34**	**103483**	**6337**
#国有控股	State-owned and State Share Holding	3	6439	291
按登记注册类型分组	**Group by Registration Status**			
内　资	Domestic Investment	31	83525	5227
国　有	State-owned	3	6439	291
集　体	Collective-owned	1		62
有限责任公司	Limited Liability Corporations	4	24957	1178
私　营	Private	23	52129	3696
港澳台商投资	Hong Kong,Macao and Taiwan Funded	2	19458	965
外商投资	Foreign Investment	1	500	145

营业收入（万元） Operational Revenues (10000 yuan)	其中 of which 客房收入 Room Rate Revenues	餐费收入 Catering Revenues	商品销售收入 Commodity Sales Revenues	其他收入 Other Revenues	床位数（张） Number of Beds (bed)	餐位数（位） Catering Seats Available (Seat)
435271	**69621**	**348874**	**2362**	**14413**	**14777**	**67911**
6480	1898	3060	1175	348	762	1420
350055	53816	282683	1875	11681	12432	60590
6480	1898	3060	1175	348	762	1420
853	853				200	
342	60	282			64	300
56648	16175	37737	160	2576	3200	7973
285050	34831	240923	540	8757	8206	50497
681		681				400
66379	11631	53323	1	1423	1726	4959
18837	4174	12868	486	1309	619	2362
117896	**44836**	**60875**	**1665**	**10520**	**9587**	**18351**
6480	1898	3060	1175	348	762	1420
87494	33961	43403	1499	8631	8113	14948
6480	1898	3060	1175	348	762	1420
853	853				200	
20966	7389	11338	160	2079	1490	3078
59194	23821	29005	164	6205	5661	10450
27054	9257	16698	1	1098	1306	3203
3348	1619	774	165	790	168	200

14-11 续表 Continued

指 标	Item	法人企业数（个）Number of Enterprises（unit）	年末餐饮营业面积（平方米）Operation Area of Catering At Year-end（sq.m）	从业人员（人）Persons Engaged（Person）
按星级饭店分组	**Restaurants Grouped By Star Level**			
一 星	One-star	1	980	90
三 星	Three-star	9	23074	710
四 星	Four-star	7	23406	2342
五 星	Five-star	2	16258	1270
其 他	Others	15	39765	1925
餐饮业	**Catering Trade**	**69**	**282639**	**21960**
按登记注册类型分组	**Group by Registration Status**			
内 资	Domestic Investment	67	250700	18304
股份合作	Cooperative	1	660	40
有限责任公司	Limited Liability Corporations	6	21663	1995
私 营	Private	59	227039	16229
其 他	Others	1	1338	40
港澳台商投资	Hong Kong,Macao and Taiwan Funded	2	25650	2874
外商投资	Foreign Investment		6289	782
按主要行业分组	**Group by Sector**			
正 餐	Dinner	64	183162	10294
快 餐	Fast Food	4	97252	11415
饮料及冷饮服务	Beverage and Cold Drinks		1235	62
其他餐饮业	Other	1	990	189
按经营方式分组	**Group by Means of Operation**			
独立商店	Independent Store	62	176316	9867
连锁商店总店	Head Office of Chain Store	3	97035	11298
连锁商店分店	Branch Store of Chain Store	2	7398	424
其 他	Others	2	1890	371

营业收入（万元）Operational Revenues（10000 yuan）	其 中 of which				床位数（张）Number of Beds（bed）	餐位数（位）Catering Seats Available（Seat）
	客房收入 Room Rate Revenues	餐费收入 Catering Revenues	商品销售收入 Commodity Sales Revenues	其他收入 Other Revenues		
2009	662	137		1210	270	128
10675	4602	5332	151	589	1672	3156
40173	14966	19668	211	5328	2578	6332
31639	11031	18474	39	2096	1208	3875
33400	13575	17264	1264	1296	3859	4860
317374	**24785**	**287999**	**697**	**3893**	**5190**	**49560**
262561	19855	239280	376	3050	4319	45642
342	60	282			64	300
35681	8785	26399		498	1710	4895
225856	11010	211918	376	2552	2545	40047
681		681				400
39325	2375	36625		325	420	1756
15489	2555	12094	321	519	451	2162
170005	24785	140703	624	3893	5190	41415
139559		139559				7340
2392		2319	73			485
5418		5418				320
163641	23165	136145	685	3646	4795	39058
138112		138112				7450
7722	1314	6149	12	247	322	2220
7899	306	7594			73	832

14-12 限额以上住宿餐饮企业财务指标（2012 年）
FINANCIAL INDEX OF ACCOMMODATION AND CATERING TRADE ABOVE DESIGNATED SIZE（2012）

指标	Item	流动资产合计 Total Circulating Funds	固定资产原价 Original Value of Fixed Assets	资产总计 Total Assets	负债总计 Total Liabilities
总 计	**Total**	**233784**	**383185**	**613577**	**532382**
市 区	Urban Area	167634	282325	440873	390879
溧阳市	Liyang City	40258	70407	103456	82830
金坛市	Jintan City	25892	30453	69248	58673
# 国有控股	State-owned and State Holding	9455	17071	18038	5518
按登记注册类型分组	**Group by Registration Status**				
内 资	Domestic Investment	222347	355478	577702	499146
国 有	State-owned	9356	17021	17925	5276
集 体	Collective-owned	1052	860	1581	2397
股份合作	Cooperative	104	211	216	152
有限责任公司	Limited Liability Corporations	30141	72852	102799	89975
私 营	Private	181597	264456	455062	401301
其 他	Others	98	78	118	47
港澳台商投资	Hong Kong,Macao and Taiwan Funded	10168	11087	22179	21407
外商投资	Foreign Investment	1268	16620	13696	11829
住宿业	**Accommodation Trade**	**109154**	**278444**	**349368**	**319343**
# 国有控股	State-owned and State Holding	9455	17071	18038	5518
按登记注册类型分组	**Group by Registration Status**				
内 资	Domestic Investment	99816	253435	325103	292897
国 有	State-owned	9356	17021	17925	5276
集 体	Collective-owned	567	699	1038	1162
有限责任公司	Limited Liability Corporations	21245	51915	67483	55056
私 营	Private	68648	183801	238657	231404
港澳台商投资	Hong Kong,Macao and Taiwan Funded	8537	9010	12196	14811
外商投资	Foreign Investment	802	16000	12069	11636

单位：万元（10000 yuan）

所有者权益 Creditors Equity	实收资本 Total CapitalHold	其中 of which #国家资本 State Capital	营业收入 Business Revenues	其中 of which #主营业务收入 Major Business Revenues	主营业务成本 Major Business Cost	主营业务税金及附加 Major Business Taxes and Extra Charges	营业利润 Profits from Business	利润总额 Total Profits	本年应交所得税 Income Tax Payable	应付职工薪酬 Remuneration Payable to Employees
81194	**159734**	**8263**	**470560**	**468275**	**194137**	**24761**	**-3480**	**-5809**	**4114**	**96157**
49994	110660	4934	375939	374329	161793	19420	-665	-1236	3470	77056
20626	25779	3309	70918	70415	22458	3913	1095	-751	541	12697
10575	23295	20	23703	23532	9886	1429	-3910	-3822	103	6404
12519	4822	4822	8521	8480	3313	388	-225	-194	14	1610
78556	143875	5182	411488	409391	167545	21923	-4050	-6459	3736	83612
12649	4802	4802	8021	7981	3112	363	-81	-47	14	1404
-815	30		1314	1314	254	74	-49	-51		342
65	20		342	342	283	19	12	12	7	98
12825	54864	20	47188	47188	19889	2632	-6209	-5979	110	10763
53762	84129	360	353941	351885	143636	18798	2263	-409	3603	70890
71	30		681	681	372	38	14	14	3	115
772	6745		49332	49332	21893	2306	825	910	212	10933
1867	9114	3081	9741	9553	4699	532	-255	-260	166	1612
30024	**101248**	**7903**	**164315**	**163355**	**56199**	**9070**	**-8927**	**-11376**	**764**	**33449**
12519	4822	4822	8521	8480	3313	388	-225	-194	14	1610
32206	91859	4822	143714	142942	50100	7931	-8591	-11051	663	30418
12649	4802	4802	8021	7981	3112	363	-81	-47	14	1404
-123	10		853	853	9	49	-2	-2		194
12427	47474	20	19164	19163	9053	1076	-5060	-4866	37	4993
7253	39573		115677	114945	37926	6444	-3448	-6137	612	23827
-2614	781		16441	16441	3381	920	584	600	101	1994
433	8608	3081	4160	3971	2718	219	-920	-925		1037

14-12 续表 Continued

指 标	Item	流动资产合计 Total Circulating Funds	固定资产原价 Original Value of Fixed Assets	资产总计 Total Assets	负债总计 Total Liabilities
按星级饭店分组	**Restaurants Grouped By Star Level**				
一 星	One-star	3093	2108	3965	3217
二 星	Two-star	280	45	474	292
三 星	Three-star	24312	34455	60093	54121
四 星	Four-star	22779	114596	97219	85291
五 星	Five-star	35907	101703	133859	130100
其 他	Others	22784	25538	53757	46323
餐饮业	**Catering Trade**	**124629**	**104741**	**264209**	**213039**
按登记注册类型分组	**Group by Registration Status**				
内 资	Domestic Investment	122532	102043	252599	206249
集 体	Collective-owned	485	161	543	1235
股份合作	Cooperative	104	211	216	152
有限责任公司	Limited Liability Corporations	8896	20937	35317	34919
私 营	Private	112949	80656	216405	169897
其 他	Others	98	78	118	47
港澳台商投资	Hong Kong,Macao and Taiwan Funded	1631	2077	9983	6597
外商投资	Foreign Investment	466	620	1627	193
按主要行业分组	**Group by Sector**				
正 餐	Dinner	82294	86613	184136	167901
快 餐	Fast Food	41796	17001	74209	41019
其他餐饮业	Others	540	1127	5864	4118
按经营方式分组	**Group by Means of Operation**				
独立商店	Independent Store	79966	84278	178966	162232
连锁商店总店	Head Office of Chain Store	41270	16985	74123	42860
连锁商店分店	Branch Store of Chain Store	2257	1258	4097	1332
其 他	Others	1137	2219	7023	6616

单位：万元（10000 yuan）

所有者权益 Creditors Equity	实收资本 Total Capital Hold	其中 of which #国家资本 State Capital	营业收入 Business Revenues	其中 of which #主营业务收入 Major Business Revenues	主营业务成本 Major Business Cost	主营业务税金及附加 Major Business Taxes and Extra Charges	营业利润 Profits from Business	利润总额 Total Profits	本年应交所得税 Income Tax Payable	应付职工薪酬 Remuneration Payable to Employees
748	1000		2009	2009	382	62	667	24	5	276
182	182		749	749	683	45	-70	14	1	177
5972	10302	3772	15730	15682	6132	929	-546	-629	58	3873
11929	50015	3081	61889	61528	21977	3471	-1115	-1068	259	10425
3759	30608		50003	49567	12894	2730	-2680	-4491	282	9841
7434	9140	1050	33934	33821	14132	1833	-5185	-5226	158	8857
51170	**58486**	**360**	**306245**	**304920**	**137939**	**15691**	**5447**	**5567**	**3350**	**62708**
46350	52016	360	267774	266449	117445	13993	4541	4592	3073	53194
-692	20		461	461	245	25	-47	-49		148
65	20		342	342	283	19	12	12	7	98
398	7390		28025	28025	10836	1556	-1149	-1113	73	5770
46509	44556	360	238265	236939	105710	12355	5711	5728	2991	47063
71	30		681	681	372	38	14	14	3	115
3386	5964		32890	32890	18512	1386	241	310	111	8939
1434	506		5582	5582	1981	313	665	665	166	575
16235	42380	360	159249	157935	71382	8854	-5508	-5627	448	34302
33189	15556		141677	141677	62828	6540	10877	11135	2887	27696
1746	550		5319	5308	3729	297	78	60	15	710
16734	41930	360	150100	149989	67644	8418	-4884	-5112	455	32095
31263	14800		138112	136897	61713	6270	10144	10484	2713	27643
2766	1106		10135	10135	3787	561	364	385	167	1691
408	650		7899	7899	4795	442	-177	-191	15	1280

14-13 市区限额以上住宿餐饮企业财务指标（2012 年）
FINANCIAL INDEX OF ACCOMMODATION AND CATERING TRADE ABOVE DESIGNATED SIZE WITHIN CITY（2012）

指 标	Item	流动资产合 计 Total Circulating Funds	固定资产原 价 Original Value of Fixed Assets	资产总计 Total Assets	负债总计 Total Liabilities
总 计	**Total**	**167634**	**282325**	**440873**	**390879**
#国有控股	State-owned and State Share Holding	8749	12583	14599	5041
按登记注册类型分组	**Group by Registration Status**				
内 资	Domestic Investment	157224	260314	410126	362301
国 有	State-owned	8749	12583	14599	5041
集 体	Collective-owned	567	699	1038	1162
股份合作	Cooperative	104	211	216	152
有限责任公司	Limited Liability Corporations	15176	67624	65721	61026
私 营	Private	132530	179118	328434	294874
其 他	Others	98	78	118	47
港澳台商投资	Hong Kong,Macao and Taiwan Funded	9791	10551	21228	20204
外商投资	Foreign Investment	619	11460	9519	8374
住宿业	**Accommodation Trade**	**52109**	**193097**	**204087**	**201933**
#国有控股	State-owned and State Share Holding	8749	12583	14599	5041
按登记注册类型分组	**Group by Registration Status**				
内 资	Domestic Investment	42953	172628	182372	178749
国 有	State-owned	8749	12583	14599	5041
集 体	Collective-owned	567	699	1038	1162
有限责任公司	Limited Liability Corporations	6280	46687	30404	26107
私 营	Private	27356	112659	136331	146438
港澳台商投资	Hong Kong,Macao and Taiwan Funded	8537	9010	12196	14811
外商投资	Foreign Investment	619	11460	9519	8374

单位：万元（10000 yuan）

所有者权益 Creditors Equity	实收资本 Total CapitalHold	其中 of which #国家资本 State Capital	营业收入 Business Revenues	其中 of which #主营业务收入 Major Business Revenues	主营业务成本 Major Business Cost	主营业务税金及附加 Major Business Taxes and Extra Charges	营业利润 Profits from Business	利润总额 Total Profits	本年应交所得税 Income Tax Payable	应付职工薪酬 Remuneration Payable to Employees
49994	**110660**	**4934**	**375939**	**374329**	**161793**	**19420**	**-665**	**-1236**	**3470**	**77056**
9557	1493	1493	6480	6480	2730	280	-92	-59	11	1083
47825	96894	1853	325334	323912	138346	17050	-780	-1434	3258	65841
9557	1493	1493	6480	6480	2730	280	-92	-59	11	1083
-123	10		853	853	9	49	-2	-2		194
65	20		342	342	283	19	12	12	7	98
4695	38964		41959	41959	18033	2341	-3080	-3045	110	9190
33560	56377	360	275017	273595	116920	14323	2368	1646	3128	55160
71	30		681	681	372	38	14	14	3	115
1024	6659		47719	47719	21200	2216	820	907	212	10495
1145	7108	3081	2886	2698	2247	153	-704	-709		721
2154	**57590**	**4574**	**91111**	**90747**	**33244**	**5036**	**-6538**	**-7249**	**350**	**19473**
9557	1493	1493	6480	6480	2730	280	-92	-59	11	1083
3623	49701	1493	71783	71607	27616	3963	-6418	-7141	249	16758
9557	1493	1493	6480	6480	2730	280	-92	-59	11	1083
-123	10		853	853	9	49	-2	-2		194
4297	31574		13934	13934	7197	786	-1931	-1932	37	3420
-10107	16624		50515	50340	17680	2849	-4392	-5148	201	12061
-2614	781		16441	16441	3381	920	584	600	101	1994
1145	7108	3081	2886	2698	2247	153	-704	-709		721

14-13 续表 Continued

指 标	Item	流动资产合计 Total Circulating Funds	固定资产原价 Original Value of Fixed Assets	资产总计 Total Assets	负债总计 Total Liabilities
按星级饭店分组	**Restaurants Grouped By Star Level**				
一 星	One-star	3093	2108	3965	3217
三 星	Three-star	7051	27138	36477	36661
四 星	Four-star	10897	91686	70062	61292
五 星	Five-star	10548	49820	45378	59937
其 他	Others	20519	22344	48206	40826
餐饮业	**Catering Trade**	**115525**	**89228**	**236786**	**188946**
按登记注册类型分组	**Group by Registration Status**				
内 资	Domestic Investment	114271	87686	227754	183553
股份合作	Cooperative	104	211	216	152
有限责任公司	Limited Liability Corporations	8896	20937	35317	34919
私 营	Private	105174	66460	192103	148436
其 他	Others	98	78	118	47
港澳台商投资	Hong Kong,Macao and Taiwan Funded	1254	1541	9032	5394
按主要行业分组	**Group by Sector**				
正 餐	Dinner	73716	71758	158413	144016
快 餐	Fast Food	41329	16380	72582	40826
其他餐饮业	Other	480	1089	5791	4104
按经营方式分组	**Group by Means of Operation**				
独立商店	Independent Store	71328	69385	153170	138332
连锁商店总店	Head Office of Chain Store	41270	16985	74123	42860
连锁商店分店	Branch Store of Chain Store	1791	638	2470	1138
其 他	Others	1137	2219	7023	6616

单位：万元（10000 yuan）

所有者权益 Creditors Equity	实收资本 Total Capital Hold	其中 of which #国家资本 State Capital	营业收入 Business Revenues	其中 of which #主营业务收入 Major Business Revenues	主营业务成本 Major Business Cost	主营业务税金及附加 Major Business Taxes and Extra Charges	营业利润 Profits from Business	利润总额 Total Profits	本年应交所得税 Income tax payable	应付职工薪酬 Remuneration Payable to Employees
748	1000		2009	2009	382	62	667	24	5	276
-184	3719	463	10584	10584	4139	648	-430	-425	52	2506
8771	42113	3081	31963	31602	13787	1800	-1481	-1377	60	6590
-14559	2728		21299	21299	4155	1189	-1119	-1316	101	3645
13437	8030	1030	25255	25252	10780	1338	-4175	-4156	132	6456
47840	**53070**	**360**	**284828**	**283582**	**128549**	**14383**	**5873**	**6014**	**3120**	**57583**
44202	47193	360	253551	252305	110730	13087	5637	5707	3009	49083
65	20		342	342	283	19	12	12	7	98
398	7390		28025	28025	10836	1556	-1149	-1113	73	5770
43668	39753	360	224502	223256	99240	11474	6760	6794	2927	43100
71	30		681	681	372	38	14	14	3	115
3638	5877		31278	31278	17819	1297	236	307	111	8501
14397	37520	360	143586	142340	64066	7868	-4415	-4514	385	29803
31755	15050		136096	136096	60847	6228	10212	10470	2721	27121
1687	500		5147	5147	3637	288	76	58	15	660
14837	37020	360	134264	134233	60236	7423	-3793	-4000	391	27545
31263	14800		138112	136897	61713	6270	10144	10484	2713	27643
1332	600		4553	4553	1806	249	-301	-280	1	1115
408	650		7899	7899	4795	442	-177	-191	15	1280

14-14 亿元商品交易市场基本情况（2012 年）
MARKETS WITH TRANSACTION VOLUME OVER 100 MILLION YUAN（2012）

指 标	Item	市场个数（个）Number of Markets（unit）	市场摊位总量（个）Number of Market Booth（unit）	摊位出租率（%）Occupancy Rate（%）	市场营业面积（平方米）Operation Area（sq.m）	商品成交总额（万元）Transaction Volume（10000 yuan）
总 计	**Total**	**59**	**41547**	**88.9**	**5252187**	**18908818**
按经营环境分	**By Operation Environment**					
露天式	Outdoor	6	2153	100.0	725276	2411507
封闭式	Close	43	32364	87.8	3484891	12655835
其 他	Other	10	7030	90.4	1042020	3841476
按经营方式分	**By Operation Method**					
批 发	Wholesale	33	26110	86.8	4064389	16352336
零 售	Retail	26	15437	92.3	1187798	2556482
按市场类别分	**By Market Type**					
综合市场	**Comprehensive Market**	**18**	**10560**	**91.0**	**755727**	**2179142**
生产资料综合市场	Production Materials Market	1	820	82.9	3000	43714
工业消费品综合市场	Industrial Consumable Market	2	2159	100.0	383360	871534
农产品综合市场	Farm and Side-line Products	13	6215	87.4	70408	406502
其他综合市场	Others	2	1366	98.2	298959	857392
专业市场	**Professional Market**	**41**	**30987**	**88.1**	**4496460**	**16729676**
生产资料市场	Markets of Means of Production	12	8395	80.5	1298450	6881404
农业生产用具市场	Agricultural Appliances Market	1	460	100.0	45860	53560
木材市场	Timber	2	3191	100.0	282300	560753
建材市场	Building Materials Market	3	725	100.0	430196	415159
化工材料及制品市场	Chemical Materials and Related Products Market	2	1592	61.4	221000	2866500
金属材料市场	Metal Materials Market	3	2007	51.2	312594	2975419
机械设备市场	Mechanical Equipment Market	1	420	90.0	6500	10012

14-14 续表 Continued

指 标	Item	市场个数（个）Number of Markets (unit)	市场摊位总量（个）Number of Market Booth (unit)	摊位出租率（%）Occupancy Rate (%)	市场营业面积（平方米）Operation Area (sq.m)	商品成交总额（万元）Transaction Volume (10000 yuan)
农产品市场	Agricultural Products Market	2	2198	100.0	432764	2072464
水产品市场	Aquatic Products Market	1	100	100.0	6780	30375
棉麻土畜、烟叶市场	Cotton Gunny Specialty Livestock and Tobacco Market	1	2098	100.0	425984	2042089
食品、饮料及烟酒市场	Foodstuff, Beverage, Cigarette & Wine	5	4370	76.9	541820	2649632
食品饮料市场	Food and Beverage Market	2	1220	46.8	19000	156010
茶叶市场	Tea Market	1	420	95.2	39960	23005
其他食品、饮料及烟酒市场	Others	2	2730	87.5	482860	2470617
纺织、服装、鞋帽市场	Textile, Garment, Shoes and Hat	2	3352	100.0	90000	310739
日用品及文化用品市场	Daily Necessities and Cultural Arti cles Market	3	2558	97.8	27448	146054
小商品市场	Small Commodities Market	2	2063	100.0	19448	129477
其他日用品及文化用品市场	Other Daily Products and Stationery Market	1	495	88.5	8000	16578
电器、通讯器材、电子设备市场	Appliance communication Equipment and Electronic Device Market	1	426	55.2	10000	10913
计算机及辅助设备市场	Computer and Component Market	1	426	55.2	10000	10913
家具、五金及装饰材料市场	Furniture,Hardware and Decorative Material Market	12	6438	94.1	1060978	1932491
家具市场	Furniture Market	4	1865	82.7	366515	230773
装饰材料市场	Decorative Materials Market	3	1032	100.0	225556	494568
灯具市场	Lighting Fixtures Market	3	2233	100.0	358147	760559
五金材料市场	Hardware Materials Market	2	1308	95.7	110760	446590
汽车、摩托车及零配件市场	Automobile,Motorcycle and Parts & Material Market	3	1650	75.1	575000	1569880
汽车市场	Automobile Market	2	860	99.9	515000	1226380
机动车零配件市场	Auto Parts Market	1	790	48.1	60000	343500
花、鸟、鱼、虫市场	Flowers, Birds, Fish and Insects Market	1	1600	100.0	460000	1156100
花卉市场	Flowers	1	1600	100.0	460000	1156100

15

CHAPTER 15

个体　私营经济

INDIVIDUAL AND PRIVATE ECONOMY

15 个体　私营经济 INDIVIDUAL AND PRIVATE ECONOMY

2012年主要统计指标 MAJOR STATISTICAL INDICATORS OF 2012

年底私营个体经济单位数	Number of Individual and Private Economy at Year-end	26.29万户	(10000 units)
比上年增长	Over the Previous Year	6.9%	
年底私营个体企业注册资金	Registered Capital of Individual and Private Economy at Year-end	2590.06亿元	(100 million yuan)
比上年增长	Over the Previous Year	15.6%	
年底私营个体企业从业人数	Number of Employees in Individual and Private Enterprises at Year-end	165.39万人	(10000 persons)
比上年增长	Over the Previous Year	6.1%	

15-1 个体、私营经济主要指标（2008-2012 年）
MAIN INDICATORS OF THE INDIVIDUAL AND PRIVATE ECONOMIES（2008-2012）

指 标	Item	2008	2009	2010	2011	2012
个体工商业户数（户）	**The Number of Individual Industrial and Commercial Households （Unit）**	**127837**	**143339**	**157532**	**170755**	**182669**
第一产业	Primary Industry	604	747	902	1091	1508
第二产业	Secondary Industry	13671	15003	17512	19315	20734
第三产业	Tertiary Industry	113562	127589	139118	150349	160420
个体工商业从业人数（人）	**The Number of Individual Industrial and Commercial Practitioners （people）**	**238031**	**268869**	**320352**	**331195**	**351981**
第一产业	Primary Industry	1403	1683	2156	2515	3599
第二产业	Secondary Industry	40917	47522	67329	62088	64805
第三产业	Tertiary Industry	195711	219664	250867	266592	283567
私营企业户数（户）	**The Number of Private Enterprises （Unit）**	**56828**	**59659**	**67203**	**75216**	**80216**
第一产业	Primary Industry	456	455	538	655	768
第二产业	Secondary Industry	30630	31337	34060	36638	38121
第三产业	Tertiary Industry	25742	27867	32605	37923	41327
私营企业从业人员（人）	**The Number of Private Enterprises' Employees （people）**	**1069125**	**1109882**	**1201563**	**1227556**	**1301874**
第一产业	Primary Industry	6818	5847	7568	8667	9627
第二产业	Secondary Industry	801639	835374	875657	873611	916815
第三产业	Tertiary Industry	260668	268661	318338	345278	375432
私营企业注册资金（万元）	**Registered Capital of Private Enterprises （10000 yuan）**	**10003083**	**12022022**	**16287776**	**21700710**	**25040852**
第一产业	Primary Industry	89319	121979	168834	201584	247979
第二产业	Secondary Industry	6003500	6919112	8478498	10534812	12033309
第三产业	Tertiary Industry	3910263	4980932	7640444	10964314	12759564

15-2 分地区个体、私营经济主要指标（2012 年）
MAIN INDICATORS OF THE INDIVIDUAL AND PRIVATE ECONOMIES BY REGIONS（2012）

指　标	Item	全　市 Whole Municipality	其中 of which 市　区 Urban Area	溧阳市 Liyang City	金坛市 Jintan City
个体工商业户数（户）	**The Number of Individual Industrial and Commercial Households（Unit）**	**182669**	**139654**	**26117**	**16898**
按产业分	Grouped By Industry				
第一产业	Primary Industry	1508	653	672	183
第二产业	Secondary Industry	20734	16004	2471	2259
第三产业	Tertiary Industry	160420	122993	22972	14455
按城乡分	Grouped By City and Village				
城　镇	Urban and Town	173929	139051	21852	13026
农　村	Countryside	8740	603	4265	3872
个体工商业从业人数（人）	**The Number of Individual Industrial and Commercial Practitioners（people）**	**351981**	**264571**	**53188**	**34222**
按产业分	Grouped By Industry				
第一产业	Primary Industry	3599	1460	1576	563
第二产业	Secondary Industry	64805	47798	9080	7927
第三产业	Tertiary Industry	283567	215307	42529	25731
按城乡分	Grouped By City and Village				
城　镇	Urban and Town	335090	263394	44521	27175
农　村	Countryside	16891	1177	8667	7047
私营企业户数（户）	**The Number of Private Enterprises（Unit）**	**80216**	**68303**	**6076**	**5837**
按产业分	Grouped By Industry				
第一产业	Primary Industry	768	253	322	193
第二产业	Secondary Industry	38121	31912	2724	3485
第三产业	Tertiary Industry	41327	36138	3030	2159
按城乡分	Grouped By City and Village				
城　镇	Urban and Town	77322	67904	4544	4874
农　村	Countryside	2894	399	1532	963
私营企业从业人员（人）	**The Number of Private Enterprises' Employees（people）**	**1301874**	**953832**	**194694**	**153348**
按产业分	Grouped By Industry				
第一产业	Primary Industry	9627	3138	3898	2591
第二产业	Secondary Industry	916815	655265	152946	108604
第三产业	Tertiary Industry	375432	295429	37850	42153
按城乡分	Grouped By City and Village				
城　镇	Urban and Town	1203014	940845	138447	123722
农　村	Countryside	98860	12987	56247	29626
私营企业注册资金（万元）	**Registered Capital of Private Enterprises（10000 yuan）**	**25040852**	**18847749**	**4159776**	**2033327**
按产业分	Grouped By Industry				
第一产业	Primary Industry	247979	76841	117010	54128
第二产业	Secondary Industry	12033309	8571992	2353968	1107349
第三产业	Tertiary Industry	12759564	10198916	1688798	871850
按城乡分	Grouped By City and Village				
城　镇	Urban and Town	23378325	18637880	2933739	1806706
农　村	Countryside	1662528	209869	1226037	226621

16

CHAPTER 16

对外经济　旅游

FOREIGN ECONOMY AND TOURISM

16 对外经济　旅游
FOREIGN ECONOMY AND TOURISM

2012 年主要统计指标
MAJOR STATISTICAL INDICATORS OF 2012

进出口总额	Total Imports and Exports	290.46 亿美元	(USD 100 million)
比上年增长	Over the Previous Year	1.4%	
出口总额	Total Exports	199.62 亿美元	(USD 100 million)
比上年增长	Over the Previous Year	3.1%	
新签外资项目数	The number of new foreign investment projects signed	298 个	(unit)
比上年增长	Over the Previous Year	-3.2%	
协议（合同）外资金额	Amount of Foreign Capital in the Newly Signed Agreements	47.49 亿美元	(USD 100 million)
比上年增长	Over the Previous Year	2.5%	
实际到帐注册外资	Foreign Capital Actually Utilized	33.61 亿美元	(USD 100 million)
比上年增长	Over the Previous Year	10.1%	
国家及省级开发区	Number of State and Provincial Development Zones	10 个	(unit)
# 国家级开发区	State Development Zone	2 个	(unit)
接待国际旅游者人数	Number of International Tourists	45.57 万人次	(10000 persons-times)
比上年增长	Over the Previous Year	10.3%	

16-1 主要年份对外经济指标
MAJOR INDICATORS OF FOREIGN TRADE AND ECONOMIC COOPERATION IN MAJOR YEARS

单位：万美元（USD 10000）

年 份 Year	进出口总额 Total Import and Export	其中 of which 进口 Import	出口 Export	协议（合同）外资金额 Amount of Foreign Capital in the Signed Agreements	实际利用外资金额 Amount of Foreign Capital Actually Utilized	新签对外承包劳务合同额 Amount of Newly Signed Foreign Contracted Labor Contract	对外承包劳务营业额 Business Value of Foreign Contracted Labor
1982						110	9
1985	128		128	3617	1455	581	567
1990	6153	1180	4973	1751	666	433	73
1991	11520	2279	9241	9002	2384	1432	599
1992	20188	2516	17672	36897	8557	3842	1619
1993	38847	6047	32800	62412	14440	3076	1408
1994	64564	8101	56463	52882	27772	2859	1843
1995	99315	22371	76944	88728	32858	4568	3817
1996	135493	35261	100232	99906	51764	7448	6623
1997	168431	45457	122974	107417	56639	7321	6849
1998	159380	28345	131035	82327	55681	8630	7544
1999	192723	65056	127667	90158	62569	9424	8309
2000	282208	96174	186034	100285	70006	12480	9409
2001	325884	109306	216577	117625	62192	10275	7644
2002	391831	126244	265587	122132	56102	13997	9837
2003	525126	172170	352956	205376	85522	16189	12371
2004	690551	218920	471631	218671	58000	20432	14594
2005	833364	220936	612428	285100	73120	26010	20561
2006	1044213	255109	789104	329575	125145	40695	26479
2007	1322596	338192	984404	440087	183481	51694	32618
2008	1762893	438540	1324353	340952	204002	52231	37175
2009	1507929	421284	1086645	422114	226129	52280	41082
2010	2227750	671944	1555806	474203	267000	57685	46913
2011	2863464	927380	1936084	463196	305238	58005	49505
2012	2904567	908397	1996170	474925	336073	59870	53985

注：1、从 1999 年起进出口为海关数。
2、从 2001 年起新签对外承包劳务合同额、营业额为经贸部口径。
3、从 2002 年起协议合同外资金额、实际利用外资金额为新口径，即协议注册外资额、实际到帐注册外资。
4、从 2004 年起实际利用外资金额为有验资报告的实际到帐注册外资数。

Note：1.The indices of import and export are the statistical figures of the customs since 1999.
2.Since the year of 2001, the amount of newly signed foreign contracted labor contracts and the business value of foreign contracted labor belong to the statistical figures of the Ministry of Foreign Trade and Cooperation.
3.The amount of foreign capital in signed agreements and contracts and foreign capital actually utilized are based on new statistical specifications since 2002,Namely the actual paid up amount of contracted foreign capital and registered foreign capital.
4.The amount of foreign capital actually utilized since 2004 has been included in capital verification report.

16-2 分地区对外经济主要指标（2012 年）
MAJOR INDICATORS OF FOREIGN TRADE AND ECONOMIC COOPERATION BY REGION（2012）

指 标	Item	全 市 Whole Municipality	其 中 of which		
			市 区 Urban Area	溧阳市 Liyang City	金坛市 Jintan City
进出口总额（万美元）	**Total Import and Export （USD 10000）**	**2904567**	**2631277**	**112941**	**160349**
对外贸易公司	Foreign Trade Corporation	243800	237258	4131	2411
自营生产企业	Self-supporting Manufacturing Enterprises	1303308	1223991	37666	41651
三资企业	Three Types of Foreign-funded Enterprises	1357455	1188984	58588	109883
出 口	**Export**	**1996170**	**1774142**	**85532**	**136496**
对外贸易公司	Foreign Trade Corporation	216686	211501	2794	2391
自营生产企业	Self-supporting Manufacturing Enterprises	829301	762652	31169	35480
三资企业	Three Types of Foreign-funded Enterprises	950182	812943	42094	95145
进 口	**Import**	**908397**	**857137**	**27408**	**23852**
对外贸易公司	Foreign Trade Corporation	27114	25757	1337	20
自营生产企业	Self-supporting Manufacturing Enterprises	474007	461339	6497	6171
三资企业	Three Types of Foreign-funded Enterprises	407273	376041	16494	14738
新签外商直接投资项目（个）	**Newly Signed Foreign Capital Project （unit）**	**298**	**218**	**39**	**41**
港、澳、台商投资企业	Enterprises with Investment from Hongkong, Macao and Taiwan	145	88	28	29
外商投资企业	Enterprises with Foreign Investment	153	130	11	12

16-2　续表　Continued

指　标	Item	全　市 Whole Municipality	其　中　of　which 市　区 Urban Area	溧阳市 Liyang City	金坛市 Jintan City
协议（合同）外资（万美元）	**Amount of Foreign Capital in the Newly Signed Agreements （USD 10000）**	**474923**	**334090**	**71265**	**69568**
港、澳、台商投资企业	Enterprises with Investment from Hongkong, Macao and Taiwan	313155	205576	46975	60604
外商投资企业	Enterprises with Foreign Investment	161768	128514	24290	8964
实际到帐注册外资（万美元）	**Foreign Capital Actually Utilized （USD 10000）**	**336073**			
期末实有外商投资企业数（个）	**Number of Foreign-funded Enterprises at Year-end（unit）**	**2780**			
新签对外承包工程和劳务合作	**Newly Signed Foreign Contracted Projects and Labor Cooperation**				
项目个数（个）	Number of Project （unit）	498	472	24	2
合同金额（万美元）	Amount of Contracts （USD 10000）	59870	36123	8137	15610
营业额（万美元）	Business Value （USD 10000）	53985	26455	6536	20994
派出人数（人）	Number of Persons Sent Abroad （person）	2715	472	331	1912
期末在外人数（人）	Number of Persons Abroad （person）	3755	914	1272	1569
新批海外投资企业	**Newly Approved Enterprises with Overseas Investment**				
本年新签海外投资企业（个）	Accumulated Number of Enterprises with Overseas Investment under Operation （unit）	51	39	3	9
本年海外投资开业企业（个）	Number of Newly Contracted overseas Investment Enterprises（unit）	40	31	2	7

注：1、从 2001 年起新签对外承包工程和劳务合作指标为经贸部口径。
　　2、从 2002 年起新签协议外资和实际利用外资为新口径，即协议注册外资额、实际到帐注册外资。
　　3、从 2004 年起实际利用外资金额为有验资报告的实际到帐注册外资数。

Notes：1.The newly signed Contracted Projects Overseas and Labor Cooperation Indicators from the year of 2001 come from the statistical data of the Ministry of Foreign Trade and Economic Cooperation.
2. The amount of foreign capital in signed agreements and contracts and foreign capital actually utilized are based on new statistical specifications since 2002,Namely the actual paid up amount of contracted foreign capital and registered foreign capital.
3.The amount of foreign capital actually utilized since 2004 has been included in capital verification report.

16-3 按贸易方式和产品类别分的外贸进出口商品总额（2008-2012 年）
TOTAL VALUE OF IMPORTS AND EXPORTS BY TRADE AND DIFFERENT PRODUCTS（2008-2012）

单位：万美元（USD 10000）

指标	Items	2008	2009	2010	2011	2012
进口总额	**Total Value of Imports**	**438540**	**421284**	**671944**	**927380**	**908397**
# 高新技术产品	High and New Technological Products	34525	25310	102608	149083	220825
按贸易方式分	**Grouped by Trade**					
# 一般贸易	Original Trade	238199	274993	428833	592868	518042
来料加工装配贸易	Processing and Assembling Trade Provided with Raw Material	12959	13860	12729	10927	10157
进料加工贸易	Raw Material Input Processing Trade	130344	101016	151752	194032	170020
外商投资企业投资设备	Goods as Invested for Import Equipments	41830	17235	33606	76196	34372
按产品类别分	**Grouped by Different Products**					
# 化工产品	Chemicals and Related Products	112292	81495	119721	161721	151547
纺织服装	Textile Materials and Products	26786	23240	36626	52904	52898
机电产品	Electrical and Mechanical Products	168704	182595	315480	425225	389193
出口总额	**Total Value of Exports**	**1324353**	**1086645**	**1555806**	**1936084**	**1996170**
# 高新技术产品	High and New Technological Products	198794	158996	368401	410518	397422
按贸易方式分	**Grouped by Trade**					
# 一般贸易	Original Trade	949515	768604	1091793	1376255	1389861
来料加工装配贸易	Processing and Assembling Trade Provided with Raw Material	23893	23050	24555	22715	21017
进料加工贸易	Raw Material Input Processing Trade	350863	291921	434304	529221	457499
按产品类别分	**Grouped by Different Products**					
# 化工产品	Chemicals and Related Products	110416	99953	136707	179065	173724
纺织服装	Textile Materials and Products	253957	242653	304682	375169	354448
机电产品	Electrical and Mechanical Products	721909	558068	870062	1033688	1054890

16-4　分国别或地区进出口总额（2012 年）
TOTAL IMPORTS AND EXPORTS BY COUNTRY OR REGION（2012）

单位：万美元（USD 10000）

国别或地区	Region	进出口总额 Total Import and Export	其中 of which 出口 Export	进口 Import
总　计	**Total**	**2904567**	**1996170**	**908397**
亚　洲	**Asia**	**1363428**	**877335**	**486093**
#香　港	Hongkong	195729	192213	3516
日　本	Japan	318621	183089	135531
韩　国	Korea,Rep.	125525	51138	74387
台　湾	Taiwan	83206	27251	55954
非　洲	**Africa**	**85159**	**69985**	**15174**
欧　洲	**Europe**	**655576**	**459716**	**195860**
#英　国	United Kindom	46972	42940	4032
德　国	Germany	199569	88669	110900
法　国	France	34719	28038	6681
俄罗斯	Russia	48696	47815	881
拉丁美洲	**Latin America**	**193393**	**127129**	**66264**
北美洲	**North America**	**477211**	**409466**	**67745**
#美　国	United States	434422	373421	61000
大洋洲	**Oceania**	**129033**	**51941**	**77093**
#澳大利亚	Australia	123771	46852	76918

16-5 外商直接投资情况（2012 年）
FOREIGN INVESTMENT CONDITIONS（2012）

指　标	Item	新签项目个数（个）Number of Newly Signed Agreements（unit）	协议外资金额（万美元）Amount of Contractual Foreign Captial（USD 10000）	实际到帐注册外资（万美元）Actual Foreign Investment（USD 10000）
总　计	**Total**	**298**	**474923**	**336073**
按企业登记注册类型分	**Grouped by Type of Registration**			
合资经营企业	Joint Venture	76	49888	56178
合作经营企业	Cooperative	3	3757	1938
独资经营企业	Sole Investment	219	420309	276137
股份有限公司	Share-holding Corporations Ltd.		971	1820
按国民经济行业分	**Grouped by Sector**			
农、林、牧、渔业	Farming,Forestry,Animal Husbandry and Fishery	10	7980	12789
采矿业	Mining		176	176
制造业	Manufacturing	168	333722	209511
# 农副食品加工业	Food Processing	1	1400	220
食品制造业	Food Production		100	100
纺织业	Textile Industry	1	2690	4154
纺织服装、鞋、帽制造业	Textile, Garments, Shoes and Hat Processing	2	3076	2647
皮革、毛皮、羽毛（绒）及其制品业	Leather, Furs, Down and Related Products		160	198
家具制造业	Furniture Manufacturing	1	561	644
造纸及纸制品业	Papermaking and Paper Products	2	2145	2335
文教体育用品制造业	Cultural, Educational and Sports Goods	2	6190	1793
石油加工、炼焦及核燃料加工业	Petroleum Processing, Coking and Nuclear Fuel Processing		-159	
化学原料及化学制品制造业	Raw Chemical Materials and Chemica Products	8	35818	24461
医药制造业	Medical and Pharmaceutical Products	2	6421	1407
化学纤维制造业	Chemical Fiber		-26	
橡胶制品业	Rubber Products	1	190	583

16-5 续表 1 Continued 1

指 标	Item	新签项目个数（个）Number of Newly Signed Agreements (unit)	协议外资金额（万美元）Amount of Contractual Foreign Captial (USD 10000)	实际到帐注册外资（万美元）Actual Foreign Investment (USD 10000)
塑料制品业	Plastic Products	3	6244	5086
非金属矿物制品业	Nonmetal Mineral Products	8	10514	3503
有色金属冶炼及压延加工业	Smelting and Pressing of Nonferrous Metals	2	4078	6567
金属制品业	Metal Products	8	8940	7571
通用设备制造业	General Equipment Manufacturing	52	99560	55923
专用设备制造业	For Special Purposes Equipment Manufacturing	21	39581	27720
交通运输设备制造业	Transport Equipment Manufacturing	16	37647	14157
电气机械及器材制造业	Electric Equipment and Machinery	18	29929	34777
通信设备、计算机及其他电子设备制造业	Communication, Computer and Other Electronic Equipment	16	34552	7088
仪器仪表及文化、办公用机械制造业	Instruments, Meters, Cultural and Office Machinery	3	3231	3416
工艺品及其他制造业	Artcraft and Other Manufacturing	1	877	408
电力、燃气及水的生产和供应业	Production and Supply of Electricity, Gas and Water		-91	424
建筑业	Construction	4	1472	61
交通运输、仓储和邮政业	Transportation , Storage and Post	1	3610	6117
信息传输、计算机服务和软件业	Information Transformation, Computer Service and Software	9	245	340
批发和零售业	Wholesale and Retail Trade	43	33499	25143
住宿和餐饮业	Accommodation and Catering Services	5	-49	166
金融业	Banking	1	1250	50
房地产业	Real Estate Industry	10	49848	68833
租赁和商务服务业	Rent and Business Services	13	28123	7094
科学研究、技术服务和地质勘查业	Scientific Research and Technology Service and Geologic Examination	26	-1081	1667
水利、环境和公共设施管理业	Water Conservancy, Environment and Public Facilities Management	4	3671	1498
卫生、社会保障和社会福利业	Hygiene, Social Security and Social Welfare	1	1050	
文化、体育和娱乐业	Culture, Sports and Entertainment	3	11500	2006

16-5 续表 2 Continued 2

指 标 Item		新签项目个数（个）Number of Newly Signed Agreements（unit）	协议外资金额（万美元）Amount of Contractual Foreign Captial（USD 10000）	实际到帐注册外资（万美元）Actual Foreign Investment（USD 10000）
按投资国别、地区分	**Grouped by Country and Region**	**298**	**474923**	**336077**
亚 洲	**Asia**	**202**	**358235**	**266335**
#香 港	Hongkong	116	270223	199457
台 湾	Taiwan	28	35530	4206
新加坡	Singapore	7	4655	22601
日 本	Japan	35	32133	29462
韩 国	Korea	4	3	637
非 洲	**Africa**	**3**	**1651**	**6695**
#塞舌尔	Seychelle	1	671	5626
南 非	South-Africa	1	880	
欧 洲	**Europe**	**27**	**22586**	**23606**
#英 国	United Kindom	1	470	1005
德 国	Germany	10	6908	4191
法 国	France	2	1356	3111
荷 兰	Netherlands	2	5456	9226
意大利	Italy	2	353	95
西班牙	Spain	1	126	840
芬 兰	Finland	1	2800	61
瑞 典	Sweden	1	2780	560
瑞 士	Switzerland	2	1684	1161
拉丁美洲	**Latin America**	**4**	**10225**	**8215**
#阿根廷	Argentina	1	2680	
开曼群岛	CaymanIslands		622	1000
智 利	Chile	1	2250	850
英属维尔京群岛	British West Indies	2	4667	5245
北美洲	**North America**	**49**	**45338**	**15939**
#加拿大	Canada	15	23409	5699
美 国	United States	34	21929	10240
大洋洲	**Oceania**	**10**	**16541**	**3470**
#澳大利亚	Australia	6	12242	2025
新西兰	New Zealand	2	4362	682

16-6 分国别人境过夜旅游者人数（2012 年）
THE NUMBER OF INBOUND OVERNIGHT TOURISTS BY COUNTRY （2012）

单位：人次（person-time）

指 标	Item	全 市 Whole Municipality	其 中 of which 市 区 Urban Area	溧阳市 Liyang City	金坛市 Jintan City
总 计	**Total**	**398670**	**381007**	**10285**	**7378**
日 本	Japan	101531	97549	1988	1994
韩 国	Korea	21888	20747	508	633
印度尼西亚	Indonesia	2185	1967	129	89
马来西亚	Malaysia	6255	5393	711	151
菲律宾	Philippines	2907	2810	86	11
新加坡	Singapore	9114	8487	303	324
泰 国	Thailand	4230	4085	109	36
印 度	India	7303	6932	142	229
英 国	United Kindom	10760	10292	184	284
法 国	France	8885	7991	734	160
德 国	Germany	56133	54319	1040	774
意大利	Italy	8407	8163	99	145
瑞 士	Switzerland	7254	7092	134	28
瑞 典	Sweden	2497	2435	56	6
俄罗斯	Russia	4076	3983	65	28
西班牙	Spain	2570	2361	125	84
美 国	United States	50482	49121	723	638
加拿大	Canada	11816	11313	352	151
澳大利亚	Australia	11297	11025	105	167
新西兰	New Zealand	766	721	39	6

16-7 分地区旅游人数和收入（2012 年）
NUMBER OF TOURISTS AND ERANINGS FROM TOURISM BY REGION（2012）

指 标	Item	全 市 Whole Municipality	其 中 of which 市 区 Urban Area	溧阳市 Liyang City	金坛市 Jintan City
旅游总人数（万人次）	**Number of Tourists （10000 persons-times）**	**4003.84**	**2360.29**	**1067.70**	**575.85**
国内旅游人数	Number of Dometic Tourists	3958.27	2316.75	1066.52	575.00
入境旅游人数	Number of International Tourists	45.57	43.54	1.18	0.85
旅游总收入	**Total Earnings from Tourism**	**520.34**	**352.84**	**108.72**	**58.78**
国内旅游收入（亿元）	Domestic Tourism （100 million yuan）	490.37	324.21	107.85	58.31
旅游创汇（万美元）	International Tourism （USD 10000）	47440	45319	1370	751
旅游景区（点）	**Scenic Spots**				
接待游客（万人次）	Number of Tourists （10000 persons-times）	8133	5788	1579	766
营业收入（万元）	Business Income （10000 yuan）	305397	179219	117412	8766

16-8 分地区国际旅游人数和收入（2012 年）
TOTAL NUMBER OF INTERNATIONAL TOURISTS AND ERANINGS FROM INTERNATIONAL TOURISM BY REGION（2012）

指 标	Item	全 市 Whole Municipality	其 中 of which 市 区 Urban Area	溧阳市 Liyang City	金坛市 Jintan City
国际旅游接待人数（人次）	**Number of International Tourists （person-time）**	**455706**	**435408**	**11845**	**8453**
外国人	Foreigners	398670	381007	10285	7378
香 港	Hongkong	20539	19434	635	470
澳 门	Macao	862	779	22	61
台 湾	Taiwan	35635	34188	903	544
国际旅游接待天数（人天）	**Number of International Tourists （person-day）**	**2489142**	**2380927**	**70553**	**37662**
外国人	Foreigners	1936123	1843823	59982	32318
香 港	Hongkong	159002	153032	3384	2586
澳 门	Macao	2352	2210	125	17
台 湾	Taiwan	391665	381863	7061	2741
旅游创汇（万美元）	**Foreign Exchange Earings of Tourism （USD 10000）**	**47440**	**45319**	**1370**	**751**

16-9 主要旅游区（点）情况（2012 年）
MAIN SCENIC SPOTS（2012）

名 称 Name	接待人数（万人次）Persons Reception (10000 persons-times)	营业收入（万元）Business Income (10000 yuan)	地 址 Address	联系电话 Contact Telephone Number	邮政编码 Post Code
中华恐龙园 China Dinosaur Park	473.43	55532	常州新区长江东路1号 No. 1 East Changjing Rd. New District, Changzhou	85106668	213022
天宁禅寺 Tianning Temple	45.57	2652	常州延陵东路636号 No. 636 East Yanling Rd., Changzhou	88111447	213003
亚细亚影视城 Asia Flim Town	160.78	2796	常州怀德中路21号 No.21 Middle Huaide Rd., Changzhou	86608965	213003
红梅公园 Red Plum Park	729.60	2490	常州罗汉路1号 No. 1 Luohan Rd., Changzhou	88108020	213003
东坡公园 Dongpo Park	41.37	18	常州延陵东路水门桥堍 Shuimen Bridge, East Yanling Rd., Changzhou	88815005	213003
瞿秋白纪念馆 Qu Qiubai Memorial	50.59		常州延陵西路102号 No.102 West Yanling Rd. ,Changzhou	86636909	213003
张太雷纪念馆 Zhang Tailei Memorial	18.45		常州清凉路子和里3号 No. 3 Ziheli Qingliang Rd., Changzhou	88813757	213003
青枫公园 Qingfeng Park	287.28	129	常州钟楼区星港大道 Xinggang Boulevard, Zhonglou District, Changzhou	88156617	213200
春秋淹城遗址旅游区 Tourist Resort of Yancheng Remains of Spring and Autumn Period	392.80	35459	常州市武进区武宜南路588号 No.588 South Wuyi Road, Wujin District, Changzhou	86318622	213161
太湖湾旅游度假区 Taihu Lake Bay Tourism Resort	295.19	38535	武进雪堰镇太湖湾 Taihu Lake Bay, Xueyan Town, Wujin	86543001	213179
环球动漫嬉戏谷 Global Animation Joyland	224.52	30565	常州市武进区雪堰镇太北路1号 1 North Taibei Road, Xueyan Town, Wujin District, Changzhou	88888821	213179
中华孝道园 China Filial Piety Park	10.40	181	常州市武进区雪堰镇环湖路101号 101 Huanhu Road, Xueyan Town, Wujin District, Changzhou	86692018	213179
武进横山风景旅游区 Wujin Hengshan Scenic Spot	81.14	147	武进区横山桥镇 Hengshanqiao Town,Wujin District	88605967	213119
武进艺林园 Wujin Horticulture Garden	33.54	983	武进区夏溪镇厚余街 Huoyu St., Xiaxi Town, Wujin District	83681109	213146
溧阳天目湖旅游度假区 Liyang Tianmu Lake Tourism and Vacation Zone	742.31	91580	溧阳市天目湖镇 Tianmu Lake Town, Liyang City	87980388	213333
溧阳南山竹海旅游度假区 Liyang South Mount and Bamboo Sea Tourism Vacation Zone	224.03	8102	溧阳市横涧镇 Hengjian Town, Liyang City	87935088	213333
天目湖御水温泉景区 Tianmu Lake Yushui Hot Spring	92.05	12026	溧阳市戴埠镇李家园村 Lijiayuan Village, Daibu Town, Liyang	87935681	213300
金坛茅山风景名胜区 Jintan Maoshan Scenic Spot	166.79	2531	金坛市茅东林场西侧 West of Maodong Forestry Center, Jintan City	82669388	213200
金坛华罗庚公园 Jintan Hua Luogeng Park	187.75		金坛市市府路38号 No. 38 Shifu Rd., Jintan City	82822957	213200
金坛城南风景区 Jintan Chengnan Scenic Spot	94.59	254	金坛市金城镇 Jincheng Town, Jintan City	82823427	213200

16-10 旅游涉外饭店、宾馆情况（2012 年底）
FOREIGN-CONCERNED HOTEL AND RESTAURANT CONDITIONS（END OF 2012）

名 称 Name	星级标准 Standard		地 址 Address	联系电话 Contact Telephone Number	客房数（间） Number of Guest Room（room）	客房出租率（%） Room Occupancy Rate（%）
常州大酒店	五星	Five-star	常州市延陵西路65号	88109988	216	56.19
常州富都大酒店有限公司	五星	Five-star	新区通江大道398号	85168888	378	60.79
江苏天目湖宾馆有限公司	五星	Five-star	溧阳市天目湖旅游度假区	87168888	171	54.40
溧阳宾馆有限公司	五星	Five-star	溧阳市西大街118号	87222777	267	64.66
溧阳市天目湖国际饭店有限公司	五星	Five-star	溧阳市天目湖旅游度假区	87989999	80	57.86
江苏润澳花园大酒店集团有限公司	五星	Five-star	金坛市东环二路1088号	82799999	130	64.89
常州市和平假日大饭店有限公司	四星	Four-star	常州市和平南路151号	88163388	171	77.06
常州阳光国际大酒店有限公司	四星	Four-star	常州市怀德中路45号	86606888	333	53.42
常州市明都大饭店管理有限公司	四星	Four-star	常州市和平北路39号	88118888	236	69.06
江苏中天凤凰集团有限公司中天凤凰大酒店	四星	Four-star	常州市新区通江大道555号	86187888	211	71.80
溧阳市天目湖华天度假村有限公司	四星	Four-star	溧阳市天目湖旅游度假区	87980999	203	50.53
溧阳市天目湖静泊山庄有限公司	四星	Four-star	溧阳天目湖旅游度假区内	87169999	159	53.68
溧阳假日酒店有限公司	四星	Four-star	溧阳罗湾路99号	87199999	146	61.33
常州万豪花都国际大酒店	四星	Four-star	常州晋陵北路168号	88222222	184	55.66
奥体明都国际饭店	四星	Four-star	新北区龙锦路1261号	85608888	202	78.57
涵田度假村酒店	四星	Four-star	溧阳市戴埠镇	87178888	396	68.16
常州九洲环宇商务广场管理有限公司	四星	Four-star	关河东路38号	85228820	110	70.22
常州香树湾花园酒店有限公司	四星	Four-star	新北区汉江路2号	85118900	121	76.21
常州电力燃料有限公司海阳大酒店	四星	Four-star	通江大道371号	88516778	142	74.05
金坛颐丰大酒店有限公司	四星	Four-star	金坛市丹阳门中路188号	82796666	66	75.56
常州锦江国际大酒店有限公司	四星	Four-star	新北区通江中路769号	85198888	261	67.41
金坛市九九宾馆有限公司	四星	Four-star	金坛市横街16-18号	82838899	81	85.56
金坛樱花大酒店有限公司	四星	Four-star	金坛西门大街88号	82396666	110	66.31
常州金色南都国际大酒店有限公司	四星	Four-star	武进区湖塘环府路58号	86319588	70	85.67
常州德泰恒大酒店	四星	Four-star	常州小河沿1号	85221688	115	70.03
溧阳市公路运输有限公司皇廷国际大酒店	四星	Four-star	溧阳市燕山中路9号	83106888	145	61.40
常州湟里金鼎国际大酒店有限公司	四星	Four-star	武进区湟里镇金鼎路8号	83349898	147	56.80
西太湖明都国际会议中心	四星	Four-star	经济开发区禾香路118号	89852888	124	54.77
开元大酒店	四星	Four-star	太湖湾旅游度假区竺山路8号	83599999	193	41.33
溧阳市扬子国际大酒店	四星	Four-star	溧阳市溧城镇安顺路9号	87928888	118	64.28
常州新都大酒店	四星	Four-star	北环路17号	85577888	126	68.24
常州九龙云天酒店管理有限公司	四星	Four-star	钟楼区中吴大道1803号	86992888	163	61.15
常州宾馆有限公司	三星	Three-star	钟楼区长生巷7号	86188888	150	42.85
常州市武进区新苑宾馆有限公司	三星	Three-star	武进湖塘环府路	86312888	97	65.90

16-10 续表　Continued

名 称 Name	星级标准 Standard		地 址 Address	联系电话 Contact Telephone Number	客房数（间） Number of Guest Room（room）	客房出租率（%） Room Occupancy Rate（%）
新锦江假日酒店	三星	Three-star	常州市新丰街14号	88101710	188	69.25
国瑞宾馆	三星	Three-star	武进横山桥镇	88603888	152	48.76
武进兰新大饭店	三星	Three-star	武进湖塘新常漕路12号	86569888	99	44.37
溧阳市江南大酒店	三星	Three-star	溧阳市平陵中路268号	87217987	102	59.83
溧阳市望湖岭山庄	三星	Three-star	溧阳市天目湖旅游度假区	87982785	50	41.51
溧阳市天目水庐宾馆	三星	Three-star	溧阳市天目湖旅游度假区	87981798	67	50.72
武进金龙大酒店	三星	Three-star	武进湖塘人民路1号	86550978	86	70.79
溧阳虹枫美食休闲度假村	三星	Three-star	溧阳天目湖旅游度假区内	87167718	243	47.54
宫苑宾馆	三星	Three-star	常州市延陵西路85号	86602606	106	66.35
溧阳云海宾馆	三星	Three-star	溧阳燕山路33号	87179666	92	66.69
常州馨雅楼宾馆	三星	Three-star	戚机厂工房1区1号	85052122	116	66.13
常瑞宾馆	三星	Three-star	常州市浦南路8号	86183888	131	57.11
椿庭楼宾馆	三星	Three-star	常州市局前街27号	88152222	125	50.58
常州锦海城市大酒店	三星	Three-star	常州市会馆浜路11号	86856577	82	68.88
金坛市九龙宾馆	三星	Three-star	金坛市东环二路39号	82399000	68	78.46
常州苏南枫泽山庄大酒店	三星	Three-star	武进夏溪章庄	88368077	75	43.32
武进区郑陆舜杰明都大酒店	三星	Three-star	武进区郑陆镇焦溪常焦路2号	81231777	54	55.94
溧阳市天目湖假日花园酒店	三星	Three-star	天目湖旅游度假区	87176766	88	54.13
溧阳市翠谷庄园	三星	Three-star	溧阳市戴埠镇南山竹海大道旁	87933888	60	48.76
溧阳市李家园大酒店	三星	Three-star	溧阳市戴埠镇	87938777	53	60.43
溧阳辉煌温泉度假酒店	三星	Three-star	溧阳市溧城镇平陵西路352号	87668888	158	48.46
常州锦湖酒店	三星	Three-star	常武中路89号	86309888	137	49.31
星港中信国际商务酒店	三星	Three-star	钟楼区星港路88号	88891888	77	74.05
大成假日酒店	三星	Three-star	天宁区关河东路44号	85220000	168	64.10
竺山湖小镇酒店	三星	Three-star	太湖湾旅游度假区竺山路	83591000	137	49.31
艺林园森林酒店	三星	Three-star	嘉泽厚余艺林园内	83680008	44	61.29
溧阳市交通大酒店	二星	Two-star	溧阳市西大街142号	87225188	79	63.20
溧阳市翠竹园宾馆	二星	Two-star	溧阳市天目湖旅游度假区	87980358	125	55.00
金坛市凯利大酒店	二星	Two-star	金坛市丹阳门北路2号	82851000	50	60.08
溧阳天目湖大酒店	二星	Two-star	溧阳天目湖镇	87980396	51	49.45
武进假日酒店	准评星	Units Qualified for Star Levels	武进区延政中路33号	86313888	280	49.44
维景国际大酒店	准评星	Units Qualified for Star Levels	新北区河海东路56号	82088888	266	60.02
凯纳豪生大酒店	准评星	Units Qualified for Star Levels	钟楼区通江南路8号	88808888	343	61.35
万达喜来登	准评星	Units Qualified for Star Levels	新北区通江中路88-1号	81588888	247	59.48
常州金陵江南大饭店	准评星	Units Qualified for Star Levels	新北区通江路466号	85119988	205	69.88

16-11 开发区建设情况（2012 年）
CONSTRUCTION OF THE DEVELOPMENT ZONES（2012）

指 标	Item	合 计 Total	常州高新技术产业开发区 Changzhou High and New Technology Industries Development Zone	江苏省武进高新技术产业园区 Wujin Hi-tech Industrial Zone Jiangsu
本年全社会固定资产投资（亿元）	Total Investment in Fixed Assets at This Year（100 million yuan）	1573.92	597.52	209.02
本年批准外商投资企业（个）	Approved Foreign-funded Enterprises in Current Year （unit）	219	80	33
本年新签协议注册外资（万美元）	Accumulated Contractual Foreign Capital of Approved Enterprises at This Year （USD 10000）	374240	145860	49524
本年实际到帐注册外资（万美元）	Accumulated Actual Foreign Investment at This Year （USD 10000）	279651	84612	54575
本年建成外商投资企业投产开业（个）	Foreign-funded Enterprises Completed in Current Year Starting Operation （unit）	86	22	16
业务总收入（亿元）	Total Business Income （100 million yuan）	11332.76	4038.90	1974.21
#工业产品销售收入	Sales Revenue from Industrial Products	7869.15	2366.80	1406.00
公共财政预算收入（亿元）	Public Finance Budget Revenue （100 million Yuan）	234.42	82.66	41.59

注：各开发区包括进区企业。
Note: All development zones include the enterprises settled down in the zone.

江苏省武进经济开发区 Wujin Economic Development Zone Jiangsu	江苏省金坛经济开发区 Jintan Economic Development Zone, Jiangsu	江苏省溧阳经济开发区 Liyang Economic Development Zone, Jiangsu	江苏省常州天宁经济开发区 Tianning Economic Development Zone, Changzhou, Jiangsu	江苏省常州钟楼经济开发区 Zhonglou Economic Development Zone, Changzhou, Jiangsu	江苏省常州戚墅堰经济开发区 Qishuyan Economic Development Zone, Changzhou, Jiangsu	天目湖旅游度假区 Tianmu Lake Tourist Resort
79.50	125.51	151.62	164.38	170.67	48.79	26.92
20	28	26	8	13	9	2
22026	53863	54658	7674	22007	17185	1443
22426	18865	32961	10931	19567	5083	1771
19	10	6	3	5	5	
421.29	751.41	1650.31	1228.06	827.36	321.58	119.64
340.61	644.01	1337.57	773.36	697.20	228.19	75.41
7.06	16.56	28.56	33.91	14.45	6.71	2.92

17

CHAPTER 17

能源消费

CONSUMPTION OF ENERGY

常州统计年鉴

17 能源消费
CONSUMPTION OF ENERGY

2012 年主要统计指标
MAJOR STATISTICAL INDICATORS OF 2012

全社会用电量	Total Electriccity Consumed	351.51亿千瓦时	(100 million kw.h)
比上年增长	Over the Previous Year	6.0%	
工业用电量	Industrial Electricity Consumption	277.88亿千瓦时	(100 million kw.h)
比上年增长	Over the Previous Year	4.0%	
城乡居民生活用电量	Electricity Consumption by Urban and Rural Residents	32.20亿千瓦时	(100 million kw.h)
比上年增长	Over the Previous Year	14.8%	
规模以上工业企业生产综合能源消费量	Production of the Comprehensive energy Consumption of Industrial Enterprises above Designated Size	1544.75万吨	(10000 tons)
比上年增长	Over the Previous Year	3.9%	

17-1 全社会用电量（1980-2012 年）
TOTAL ELECTRICITY CONSUMPTION（1980-2012）

单位：万千瓦时（10000 kw.h）

年 份 Year	全社会用电量 Total Electricity Consumption	其中 of which # 农林牧渔水利业 Farming, Forestry, Animal Husbandry, Fishery and Water Conservancy	工 业 Industry	交通运输、邮电通信业 Transportation, Post and Telecommuni-cations Services	城乡居民生活 Electricity Consumption by of Urban and Rural Residents
1980	134387	27134	102715	459	4079
1981	144076	33226	105738	375	4737
1982	155004	35467	113498	293	5746
1983	166728	41084	119095	321	6228
1984	180092	45608	126691	291	7502
1985	195387	54628	131151	287	9321
1986	226192	27971	183961	778	7059
1987	253060	28737	207018	340	9549
1988	268665	31616	214548	921	12346
1989	270752	32965	213121	1322	14256
1990	293370	38930	223449	1709	17283
1991	330885	42703	250208	3915	18973
1992	378832	47382	286052	2024	25103
1993	424120	51949	310357	2627	33968
1994	483755	57671	342772	3287	46000
1995	522521	60136	362325	3726	57620
1996	557030	63478	381807	4248	62910
1997	586748	71269	391600	5735	68439
1998	601148	72676	391733	6975	77286
1999	641191	79090	421049	7435	78497
2000	743453	87042	492989	7924	97199
2001	813527	96264	542864	8812	108352
2002	988809	112040	686011	10134	110380
2003	1269745	142175	915670	12391	118145
2004	1522392	164706	1107854	15586	128541
2005	1826605	34748	1452046	36287	149200
2006	2126844	23952	1749992	16396	172817
2007	2306172	17285	1908046	12272	186762
2008	2373291	17634	1920858	15038	213800
2009	2554100	18246	2054113	15913	229934
2010	2911875	21420	2318221	23790	275163
2011	3316562	22438	2672080	32690	280418
2012	3515102	23255	2778770	35876	321920

注：本表按当年口径统计, 1986年行业用电分类按调整口径统计, 1991年以前交通运输、邮电通信业仅指交通运输业，2006年以后的交通运输、邮电通信业指交通运输、仓储和邮政业。

Notes：This form is in compliance with the specification of this year. The statistic data of the electricity consumption by sectors in 1986 was based upon the regulatory specification. The transportation, post and telecommunications had only indicated the transportation before 1991, After 2006, transportation, post and telecommunications refers to transportation, storage and postal industry.

17-2 全社会分月用电量（2012 年）
TOTAL ELECTRICITY CONSUMPTION BY MONTH（2012）

单位：万千瓦时 （10000 kw.h）

月份 Month		全社会用电量 Total Electricity Consumption	其中 of witch	
			#工业 Industry	城乡居民生活用电 Electricity Consumption by of Urban and Rural Residents
总计	**Total**	**3515102**	**2778770**	**321920**
第一季度	First Quarter	793300	606721	85723
1		222457	169843	23201
2		263485	195171	29966
3		307358	241707	32556
第二季度	Second Quarter	862919	706962	68136
4		280541	221708	27502
5		290967	242081	21820
6		291411	243173	18814
第三季度	Third Quarter	959648	738723	96842
7		341780	278519	22734
8		331653	250699	35461
9		286215	209505	38647
第四季度	Fourth Quarter	899235	726364	71219
10		280427	221151	27227
11		291434	239813	19562
12		327374	265400	24430

17-3 分地区全社会用电量（2012 年）
TOTAL ELECTRICITY CONSUMPTION BY REGION（2012）

单位：万千瓦时（10000 kw.h）

指 标	Item	全 市 Whole Municipality	其 中 of witch 市 区 Urban Area	溧阳市 Liyang City	金坛市 Jintan City
总 计	**Total**	**3515102**	**2541410**	**595701**	**377991**
农林牧渔业	Farming,Forestry,Animal Husbandry and Fishery	23255	10673	5071	7511
农 业	Agriculture	2819	1435	558	826
林 业	Forestry	627	415	126	86
畜牧业	Animal Husbandry	4134	1589	424	2121
渔 业	Fishery	7175	1941	2642	2592
农、林、牧、渔服务业	Farming,Forestry, Animal Husbandry and Fishery	8500	5293	1321	1886
#排 灌	Irrigation and Drainage	6078	3710	1103	1265
工 业	Industry	2778770	1961658	505405	311707
采矿业	Mining				
制造业	Manufacturing	2541925	1794096	472033	275796
食品、饮料和烟草制造业	Production of Food ,Beverages and Tobacco	18321	11075	4496	2750
纺织业	Textiles	262441	238768	12562	11111
服装鞋帽、皮革羽绒及其制品业	Garments, leather Down and Related Products	26896	16454	2731	7711
木材加工及制品和家具制品业	Timber Processing and products, and Furniture Manufacturing	29972	27956	1878	138
造纸及纸制品业	Papermaking and Paper Production	8967	6983	1121	863
印刷业和记录媒介的复制	Printing and Record Duplicating	5437	4583	277	577
文体用品制造业	Culture and Sports Goods	3018	2877	14	127
石油加工、炼焦及核燃料加工业	Petroleum Processing, Coking and Nuclear Fuel Processing	862	845	17	
化学原料及化学制品制造业	Raw Chemical Materials and Chemica Production	205769	118160	11806	75803
医药制造业	Medical and Pharmaceutical Production	22922	15264	3014	4644
化学纤维制造业	Chemical Fiber	21296	15649	2585	3062
橡胶和塑料制品业	Rubber and Plastic Production	140216	125772	5582	8862
非金属矿物制品业	Nonmetal Mineral Production	333988	55035	205208	73745
黑色金属冶炼及压延加工业	Smelting and Pressing of Ferrous Metals	548815	425212	100623	22980
有色金属冶炼及压延加工业	Smelting and Pressing of Nonferrous Metals	40876	30362	1583	8931

17-3 续表 continued　　单位：万千瓦时（10000 kwh）

指 标	Item	全 市 Whole Municipality	其 中 of witch 市 区 Urban Area	溧阳市 Liyang City	金坛市 Jintan City
金属制品业	Metal Products	225422	159711	57180	8531
通用及专用设备制造业	Universal & Special Equipments Manufacturing	319007	241961	43953	33093
交通运输、电气、电子设备制造业	Electronic and Transportation Equipment	289892	267711	16574	5607
工艺品及其他制造业	Other Industry	35009	27384	539	7086
废弃资源和废旧材料回收加工业	Waste Resources and Materials Recycling and Processing	2799	2334	290	175
电力、燃气及水的生产和供应业	Production and Supply of Electric Power, Gas and Water	236845	167562	33372	35911
电力、热力的生产和供应业	Production and Supply of Electric Power and Thermal Power	203402	145346	30775	27281
燃气生产和供应业	Production and Supply of Gas	7918	1190	318	6410
自来水生产和供应业	Production and Supply of Running Water	25525	21026	2279	2220
建筑业	Construction	32457	24094	5771	2592
交通运输、仓储和邮政业	Communication and Transportation, Storage and Post Industry	35876	33623	1215	1038
商业、住宿和餐饮业	Commerce, Accommodation and Catering Industry	122375	95123	17578	9674
信息传输、计算机服务和软件业	Information transmission, computer service and software	16025	12144	2437	1444
金融、房地产、租赁和商务、居民服务和其他服务业	Finance, Real Estate, Renting and Business, Residents Services and Other Services	79684	70467	5542	3675
卫生、社会保障和社会福利事业	Health Care,Social Security and Social Welfare	16982	13760	1611	1611
教育、文化体育和娱乐业	Education,Culture,Sports and recreation	35912	31551	2411	1950
科学研究、技术服务和地质堪查业	Scientific Research,Polytechnical Services and Geological Exploration	2195	1940	113	142
公共管理和社会组织、国际组织	Public Administration and Social or International Organizations	19352	15590	2297	1465
水利、环境和公共设施管理业	Water, Environment and Public Facilities	30299	27211	1814	1274
城乡居民生活用电	Electricity Consumption by Urban and Rural Residents	321920	243576	44436	33908
农 村	Villiage	182663	135393	27735	19535
城 市	City	139257	108183	16701	14373

17-4　规模以上工业企业分行业生产综合能源消费量（2012 年）
COMPREHENSIVE ENERGY CONSUMPTION IN PRODUCTION OF ABOVE-SCALE INDUSTRIAL ENTERPRISES BY SECTOR（2012）

指　标	Item	企业单位数（个）Number of Enterpr-ises (unit)	综合能源消费量（吨标准煤）Comprehensive Energy Consumption (tce)
总　计	**Total**	**3580**	**15447510**
按地区分	**Grouped by Region**		
市　区	Urban Area	2920	10213782
#武进区	Wujin District	1611	6538859
溧阳市	Liyang City	311	4425828
金坛市	Jintan City	349	807900
按行业分	**Grouped by Sector**		
非金属矿采选业	Nonmetal Minerals Mining and Dressing	3	135537
农副食品加工业	Food Processing	13	9330
食品制造业	Food Production	12	18944
酒、饮料和精制茶制造业	Beverages and Refined Tea Manufacturing	4	15711
纺织业	Textile Industry	356	600655
纺织服装、服饰业	Textile and clothing Industry	146	96782
皮革、毛皮、羽毛及其制品和制鞋业	Leather, Fur, Feathers and Their Products, and Footwear Industry	20	8769
木材加工及木、竹、藤、棕、草制品业	Timber Processing, Bamboo, Cane, Palm Fiber and Straw Products	59	18831
家具制造业	Furniture Manufacturing	6	855
造纸及纸制品业	Papermaking and Paper Products	40	28545
印刷和记录媒介复制业	Printing and Recorded Media Duplication Industry	25	7483
文教、工美、体育和娱乐用品制造业	Cultural & Educational, Arts & Crafts, Sports & Entertainment Articles Manufacturing	29	17926
石油加工、炼焦及核燃料加工业	Petroleum Processing, Coking and Nuclear Fuel Processing	13	4746
化学原料及化学制品制造业	Raw Chemical Materials and Chemical Products	389	1004874
医药制造业	Medical and Pharmaceutical Products	58	109733
化学纤维制造业	Chemical Fiber	45	48686
橡胶和塑料制品业	Rubber and Plastic Products Industry	129	61742
非金属矿物制品业	Nonmetal Mineral Products	153	2350489
黑色金属冶炼及压延加工业	Smelting and Pressing of Ferrous Metals	165	7327486
有色金属冶炼及压延加工业	Smelting and Pressing of Nonferrous Metals	68	90742
金属制品业	Metal Products	212	199350
通用设备制造业	General Equipment Manufacturing	363	173074
专用设备制造业	For Special Purposes Equipment Manufacturing	287	167710
汽车制造业	Automotive Industry	115	48912
铁路、船舶、航空航天和其他运输设备制造	Railways, Shipping, Aerospace and other Transportation Equipment Manufacturing	90	85910
电气机械及器材制造业	Electric Equipment and Machinery	465	390220
计算机、通信和其他电子设备制造	Computer, Communications and other Electronic Equipment Manufacturing	193	142812
仪器仪表制造业	Instrumentation Manufacturing	84	37158
其他制造业	Other Manufacturing	5	19375
废弃资源综合利用业	Comprehensive Utilization of Waste Resources Industry	4	1179
金属制品、机械和设备修理业	Metal Products, Machinery & Equipment Repairing Industry	1	391
电力、热力生产和供应业	Production and Supply of Electricity & Heat Industry	19	2203647
燃气生产和供应业	Production and Supply of Gas Industry	3	1094
水的生产和供应业	Production and Supply of water Industry	6	18816

17-5 年耗能5000吨标煤及以上工业企业生产综合能源消费量（2012年）
COMPREHENSIVE ENERGY CONSUMPTION IN PRODUTTION OF INDUSTRIAL ENTERPRISES WITH ANNUAL CONSUMPTION OF 5000 TCE AND ABOVE（2012）

指 标	Item	企业单位数（个）Number of Enterpr-ises (unit)	综合能源消费量（吨标准煤）Comprehensive Energy Consumption (tce)
总 计	**Total**	**190**	**13534953**
按地区分	**Grouped by Region**		
市 区	Urban Area	133	8684246
#武进区	Wujin District	54	5702660
溧阳市	Liyang City	40	4225922
金坛市	Jintan City	17	624784
按行业分	**Grouped by Sector**		
非金属矿采选业	Nonmetal Minerals Mining and Dressing	1	135016
食品制造业	Food Production	1	5364
酒、饮料和精制茶制造业	Beverages and Refined Tea Manufacturing	2	15446
纺织业	Textile Industry	32	302987
纺织服装、服饰业	Textile and clothing Industry	5	44969
造纸及纸制品业	Papermaking and Paper Products	1	6461
化学原料及化学制品制造业	Raw Chemical Materials and Chemical Products	33	709554
医药制造业	Medical and Pharmaceutical Products	5	57181
化学纤维制造业	Chemical Fiber	1	5927
橡胶和塑料制品业	Rubber and Plastic Products Industry	1	5432
非金属矿物制品业	Nonmetal Mineral Products	15	2243224
黑色金属冶炼及压延加工业	Smelting and Pressing of Ferrous Metals	30	7203566
有色金属冶炼及压延加工业	Smelting and Pressing of Nonferrous Metals	3	37643
金属制品业	Metal Products	4	75183
通用设备制造业	General Equipment Manufacturing	4	42335
专用设备制造业	For Special Purposes Equipment Manufacturing	6	63440
汽车制造业	Automotive Industry	2	16249
铁路、船舶、航空航天和其他运输设备制造	Railways, Shipping, Aerospace and other Transportation Equipment Manufacturing	2	36716
电气机械及器材制造业	Electric Equipment and Machinery	17	217700
计算机、通信和其他电子设备制造	Computer, Communications and other Electronic Equipment Manufacturing	5	70689
仪器仪表制造业	Instrumentation Manufacturing	1	8087
其他制造业	Other Manufacturing	1	19071
电力、热力生产和供应业	Production and Supply of Electricity & Heat Industry	17	2201759
水的生产和供应业	Production and Supply of water Industry	1	10950

17-6 规模以上工业企业分行业主要能源品种消费量（2012 年）
ENERGY CONSUMPTION OF MAIN VARIETIES OF ABOVE-SCALE INDUSTRIAL ENTERPRISES BY SECTOR（2012）

指 标	Item	原 煤 （吨） Raw Coal (ton)
总 计	**Total**	**10335489**
按地区分	**Grouped by Region**	
市 区	Urban Area	6701801
#武进区	Wujin District	1709379
溧阳市	Liyang City	2950559
金坛市	Jintan City	683128
按行业分	**Grouped by Sector**	
非金属矿采选业	Nonmetal Minerals Mining and Dressing	
农副食品加工业	Food Processing	5405
食品制造业	Food Production	
酒、饮料和精制茶制造业	Beverages and Refined Tea Manufacturing	11054
纺织业	Textile Industry	69442
纺织服装、服饰业	Textile and clothing Industry	28180
皮革、毛皮、羽毛及其制品和制鞋业	Leather, Fur, Feathers and Their Products,and Footwear Industry	3737
木材加工及木、竹、藤、棕、草制品业	Timber Processing, Bamboo, Cane, Palm Fiber and Straw Products	3670
造纸及纸制品业	Papermaking and Paper Products	11963
印刷和记录媒介复制业	Printing and Recorded Media Duplication Industry	4568
文教、工美、体育和娱乐用品制造业	Cultural & Educational, Arts & Crafts, Sports & Entertainment Articles Manufacturing	4005
石油加工、炼焦及核燃料加工业	Petroleum Processing, Coking and Nuclear Fuel Processing	1612
化学原料及化学制品制造业	Raw Chemical Materials and Chemical Products	493922
医药制造业	Medical and Pharmaceutical Products	55432
化学纤维制造业	Chemical Fiber	14495
橡胶和塑料制品业	Rubber and Plastic Products Industry	14156
非金属矿物制品业	Nonmetal Mineral Products	2789226
黑色金属冶炼及压延加工业	Smelting and Pressing of Ferrous Metals	788586
有色金属冶炼及压延加工业	Smelting and Pressing of Nonferrous Metals	12663
金属制品业	Metal Products	102714
通用设备制造业	General Equipment Manufacturing	12066
专用设备制造业	For Special Purposes Equipment Manufacturing	36066
汽车制造业	Automotive Industry	280
铁路、船舶、航空航天和其他运输设备制造	Railways, Shipping, Aerospace and other Transportation Equipment Manufacturing	2220
电气机械及器材制造业	Electric Equipment and Machinery	32530
计算机、通信和其他电子设备制造	Computer, Communications and other Electronic Equipment Manufacturing	10972
仪器仪表制造业	Instrumentation Manufacturing	7811
其他制造业	Other Manufacturing	
废弃资源综合利用	Comprehensive Utilization of Waste Resources Industry	
金属制品、机械和设备修理业	Metal Products, Machinery & Equipment Repairing Industry	
电力、热力生产和供应业	Production and Supply of Electricity & Heat Industry	5818713
燃气生产和供应业	Production and Supply of Gas Industry	
水的生产和供应业	Production and Supply of water Industry	

洗精煤（吨）Fien Coal (ton)	焦炭（吨）Coke (ton)	天然气（万立方米）Natural Gas (10000 cubicmeters)	汽油（吨）Gasoline (ton)	煤油（吨）Kerosene (ton)	柴油（吨）Diesel Oil (ton)	燃料油（吨）Fuel Oil (ton)	液化石油气（吨）LPG (ton)	热力（百万千焦）Heat (1million kilojoule)
2809174	**3833303**	**106566**	**42592**	**2359**	**67828**	**1587**	**4561**	**25531710**
1124944	3526356	100442	38770	2077	59546	1587	4492	21167889
1124891	3510672	14909	9159	320	21081	153	935	6362081
1684040	302914	3088	953	202	4337		6	483304
190	4032	3036	2870	81	3945		63	3880517
								3265515
		28	118		18			22560
		232	1027		57	483	1	256389
			142		86			142091
108		2560	1650		1066		256	9172637
		1481	1167		718		62	831096
			792		78		5	25143
		65	101		618	714		242939
			360		186			
		24	99		82		302	73530
		149	43		366			
190		3556	5290	165	3787			7282341
		303	2262		680			844586
		169	86	3	121		27	3895
		467	1338		475		5	80372
	2899	4443	1216	1	23963	220	1	131720
2807876	3787267	4473	471	2	3945	87	112	2101812
	2375	2955	1244	16	365			38610
	2579	1519	2048	40	3665		212	13247
687	26523	571	5335	342	5604	75	8	38596
228	2831	2170	3655	6	2886		111	11681
	60	587	1115	1	633		38	146217
	243	495	1796	1685	10835	5	3242	268679
	8218	5958	8439	85	5293	3	141	535747
		1897	1159	1	902		3	2307
85	275	140	860	12	519		32	
					115			
		4	45					
	34		13					
		72319	56		175			
		2	114					
			120		37			

17-7 年耗能 5000 吨标煤及以上工业企业主要能源品种消费量（2012 年） ENERGY CONSUMPTION OF MAIN VARIETIES OF INDUSTRIAL ENTERPRISES WITH ANNUAL CONSUMPTION OF 5000 TCE AND ABOVE（2012）

指 标	Item	原 煤（吨）Raw Coal（ton）
总 计	**Total**	**9853794**
按地区分	**Grouped by Region**	
市 区	Urban Area	6403731
#武进区	Wujin District	1484113
溧阳市	Liyang City	2843344
金坛市	Jintan City	606719
按行业分	**Grouped by Sector**	
非金属矿采选业	Nonmetal Minerals Mining and Dressing	
食品制造业	Food Production	
酒、饮料和精制茶制造业	Beverages and Refined Tea Manufacturing	11054
纺织业	Textile Industry	12856
纺织服装、服饰业	Textile and clothing Industry	9781
造纸及纸制品业	Papermaking and Paper Products	
化学原料及化学制品制造业	Raw Chemical Materials and Chemical Products	347949
医药制造业	Medical and Pharmaceutical Products	31963
橡胶和塑料制品业	Rubber and Plastic Products Industry	
非金属矿物制品业	Nonmetal Mineral Products	2771131
黑色金属冶炼及压延加工业	Smelting and Pressing of Ferrous Metals	724864
有色金属冶炼及压延加工业	Smelting and Pressing of Nonferrous Metals	
金属制品业	Metal Products	76201
通用设备制造业	General Equipment Manufacturing	540
专用设备制造业	For Special Purposes Equipment Manufacturing	25918
汽车制造业	Automotive Industry	
铁路、船舶、航空航天和其他运输设备制造	Railways, Shipping, Aerospace and other Transportation Equipment Manufacturing	15
电气机械及器材制造业	Electric Equipment and Machinery	22186
计算机、通信和其他电子设备制造	Computer, Communications and other Electronic Equipment Manufacturing	4287
仪器仪表制造业	Instrumentation Manufacturing	2566
其他制造业	Other Manufacturing	
电力、热力生产和供应业	Production and Supply of Electricity & Heat Industry	5812482
水的生产和供应业	Production and Supply of water Industry	

洗精煤（吨） Fien Coal (ton)	焦 炭（吨） Coke (ton)	天然气（万立方米） Natural Gas (10000 cubicmeters)	汽 油（吨） Gasoline (ton)	煤 油（吨） Kerosene (ton)	柴 油（吨） Diesel Oil (ton)	液化石油气（吨） LPG (ton)	热 力（百万千焦） Heat (1million kilojoule)
2807876	**3801252**	**95361**	**5516**	**318**	**18005**	**1658**	**19813652**
1124523	3505185	90400	4792	128	16441	1658	16111708
1124523	3493234	9175	586		3838	195	4180867
1683353	296068	2537	357	190	1162		357835
		2425	367		403		3344109
							3265515
		198	29				83206
			142		86		139115
		905	395		188	89	6418514
		998	179		129		571491
			12		30		142049
		2233	2532		644		5825614
			135		270		529653
		159					
		4008	29		260		54258
2807876	3780408	3722	249		3322	96	2101812
		1982			130		
		231	463		438		
	12608	44	331	119	1830		23993
	2806	1402	3	1	575	77	
		533	20		23		81099
	66		285	118	8922	1396	235716
	5365	4924	451	80	860		341617
		1685	100				
		19					
					115		
		72319	56		152		
			106		32		

18

CHAPTER 18

财政 金融 保险

PUBLIC FINANCE, BANKING AND INSURANCE

18 财政　金融　保险
PUBLIC FINANCE, BANKING AND INSURANCE

2012 年主要统计指标
MAJOR STATISTICAL INDICATORS OF 2012

公共财政预算收入	Public Finance Budget Revenue	378.99亿元	(100 million yuan)
比上年增长	Over the Previous Year	8.0%	
公共财政预算支出	Public Finance Budget Expenditure	391.22亿元	(100 million yuan)
比上年增长	Over the Previous Year	8.1%	
年底金融机构本外币存款余额	Balance of Domestic and Foreign Currency Deposits in Financial Institutions at Year-end	5789.88亿元	(100 million yuan)
比上年增长	Over the Previous Year	15.1%	
年底金融机构人民币存款余额	RMB Deposits Balance of Banking Institutions at Year-end	5604.90亿元	(100 million yuan)
比上年增长	Over the Previous Year	14.3%	
年底城乡居民本外币储蓄存款余额	Balance of Domestic and Foreign Currency Savings Deposits of Urban and Rural Residents at Year-end	2489.97亿元	(100 million yuan)
比上年增长	Over the Previous Year	14.7%	
年底城乡居民人民币储蓄存款余额	RMB Urban and Rural Saving Deposits Balance at Year-end	2473.27亿元	(100 million yuan)
比上年增长	Over the Previous Year	14.6%	
年底金融机构本外币贷款余额	Balance of Domestic and Foreign Currency Loans in Financial Institutions at Year-end	4018.21亿元	(100 million yuan)
比上年增长	Over the Previous Year	14.6%	
年底金融机构人民币贷款余额	RMB Loans Balance of Banking Institutions at Year-end	3832.80亿元	(100 million yuan)
比上年增长	Over the Previous Year	12.5%	

18-1 历年财政总收入、财政支出
TOTAL FINANCIAL REVENUE AND FINANCIAL EXPENDITURE OVER THE YEARS

单位：万元（10000 yuan）

年 份	财政总收入	其中 of which	财政支出	其中 of which	年 份	财政总收入	其中 of which	财政支出	其中 of which
		#市 区		#市 区			#市 区		#市 区
Year	Financial Revenue	Urban Area	Financial Expenditure	Urban Area	Year	Financial Revenue	Urban Area	Financial Expenditure	Urban Area
1949	1209	861	17	17	1981	72163	67767	10615	7837
1950	2664	1974	207	93	1982	70139	65046	13109	9805
1951	3885	3074	357	254	1983	73628	67892	16885	12799
1952	5155	4129	741	538	1984	80543	77320	21601	16794
1953	6258	4886	854	591	1985	100364	92691	25231	19660
1954	6956	5500	1033	750	1986	103337	94451	31333	24513
1955	6338	5084	957	678	1987	109850	99516	32565	25238
1956	7146	5900	1431	993	1988	115680	103528	38331	29560
1957	7813	6602	2025	1557	1989	126680	113446	47647	36535
1958	18880	17106	7633	6408	1990	130953	116644	51082	38698
1959	18662	17008	3048	2065	1991	117190	103734	55849	41716
1960	18853	17106	2766	1563	1992	136516	119384	59228	43719
1961	11878	10729	2041	1279	1993	198857	171003	99387	74698
1962	8694	7503	1915	1341	1994	246778	210378	114387	86228
1963	9551	8280	1977	1441	1995	285043	239948	133252	101585
1964	13225	11873	2306	1634	1996	343032	289773	153820	116570
1965	16044	14639	2533	1832	1997	401779	337700	193880	150801
1966	20250	18886	2674	1880	1998	450937	376665	224114	176498
1967	12603	11205	2574	1793	1999	492092	415554	257172	202273
1968	13793	12354	2411	1641	2000	602271	507742	325043	259763
1969	21562	20027	4376	3419	2001	753317	633537	414753	331521
1970	31837	29958	3917	2706	2002	1029032	866120	610099	495583
1971	33681	31894	6148	4888	2003	1361047	1136921	847597	690368
1972	37363	35414	6843	5382	2004	1447666	1181910	1048820	1181910
1973	43564	40973	6180	4860	2005	2204491	1821223	1402776	1126903
1974	44651	42029	6162	4394	2006	2772705	2269853	1710373	1341912
1975	49437	46665	5470	3992	2007	4143811	3399957	2743954	2192203
1976	52558	49769	6359	4561	2008	5426800	4536087	3844112	3178717
1977	57904	54827	6843	4970	2009	6817200	5737600	5208061	4297952
1978	62128	58560	9259	6583	2010	8416700	7101100	6382050	5291309
1979	62364	58983	13585	8481	2011	9777913	8102756	7430767	6050417
1980	66960	63122	11603	8293	2012	11170283	9305089	8849217	7263458

注：2002年7月起财政收入包括行政性收费收入、基金收入。
Note: The financial revenue includes the incomes from administrative charge and funds since July 2002.

18-2 分地区公共财政预算收入、支出（1997-2012 年）
PUBLIC FINANCE BUDGETARY REVENUE AND EXPENDITURE BY REGION （1997-2012）

单位：万元（10000 yuan）

年份 Year	公共财政预算收入 Public Finance Budget Revenue	其中 of which 市区 Urban Area	溧阳市 Liyang City	金坛市 Jintan City	年份 Year	公共财政预算支出 Public Finance Budget Expenditure	其中 of which 市区 Urban Area	溧阳市 Liyang City	金坛市 Jintan City
1997	189210	157949	17173	14088	1997	186742	144839	23756	18147
1998	222536	185568	19889	17079	1998	219440	172644	26428	20368
1999	251712	210724	21946	19042	1999	254124	199993	30822	23309
2000	322524	270430	28035	24059	2000	318283	254115	36046	28122
2001	420961	351387	36968	32606	2001	411581	329178	45098	37305
2002	461972	386364	40399	35209	2002	518223	418456	53993	45774
2003	566729	473538	52977	40214	2003	630490	514181	67521	48788
2004	673407	556044	68201	49162	2004	756627	611906	87767	56954
2005	949905	791432	91088	67385	2005	978458	797957	109280	71221
2006	1188818	984472	118008	86338	2006	1176965	945667	135700	95598
2007	1580688	1305365	162588	112735	2007	1546367	1250226	175098	121043
2008	1851888	1527880	196188	127820	2008	1866796	1510855	218523	137418
2009	2158888	1786378	231688	140822	2009	2187465	1715610	284866	186989
2010	2861788	2391480	290028	180280	2010	2814401	2258104	334681	221616
2011	3508800	2906762	371280	230758	2011	3618123	2877736	443228	297159
2012	3789900	3153808	404988	231104	2012	3912183	3136649	458353	317181

18-3　分地区金融机构存、贷款余额（1990-2012 年）
DEPOSIT AND LOAN BALANCE OF FINANCIAL INSTITUTIONS BY REGION（1990-2012 年）

单位:亿元（100 million yuan）

年 份 Year	存款余额 Deposits Balance	其中 of which 市 区 Urban Area	溧阳市 Liyang City	金坛市 Jintan City	年 份 Year	贷款余额 Loans Balance	其中 of which 市 区 Urban Area	溧阳市 Liyang City	金坛市 Jintan City
1990	59.37	46.24	7.50	5.63	1990	74.24	58.52	8.98	6.74
1991	81.35	64.79	9.64	6.92	1991	93.10	73.94	10.95	8.21
1992	104.84	83.34	12.83	8.67	1992	112.46	89.96	13.27	9.23
1993	127.73	101.60	17.06	9.07	1993	132.16	105.84	15.81	10.51
1994	192.71	158.68	21.74	12.29	1994	180.48	148.54	19.31	12.63
1995	257.61	205.93	32.12	19.56	1995	211.88	170.12	25.43	16.33
1996	308.89	251.34	35.73	21.82	1996	237.04	192.43	26.71	17.90
1997	403.16	329.26	44.15	29.75	1997	304.83	242.25	36.05	26.53
1998	479.80	387.49	56.17	36.14	1998	342.13	272.79	39.93	29.41
1999	560.03	454.81	62.86	42.36	1999	369.06	298.86	40.39	29.80
2000	629.36	511.00	69.00	49.36	2000	389.26	324.19	39.52	25.55
2001	735.25	596.55	79.78	58.92	2001	444.54	376.32	40.08	28.14
2002	904.71	738.30	95.75	70.66	2002	559.85	476.15	46.97	36.69
2003	1170.56	964.37	117.88	88.31	2003	799.14	683.11	66.72	49.31
2004	1362.22	1129.93	134.10	98.19	2004	956.38	835.85	70.05	50.48
2005	1649.61	1375.25	159.62	114.74	2005	1113.25	966.84	87.90	58.51
2006	1974.05	1644.73	190.81	138.51	2006	1348.60	1164.62	108.67	75.31
2007	2263.84	1893.65	216.59	153.58	2007	1590.11	1349.12	140.68	100.30
2008	2819.42	2348.91	281.79	188.72	2008	1851.69	1550.76	181.86	119.09
2009	3765.91	3141.89	382.84	241.18	2009	2513.97	2100.23	256.02	157.71
2010	4550.47	3800.47	454.64	295.37	2010	3011.67	2518.92	299.11	193.64
2011	4902.15	4024.70	541.80	335.65	2011	3406.35	2817.27	361.26	227.81
2012	5604.90	4558.74	645.20	400.96	2012	3832.80	3109.26	436.64	286.90

18-4 历年分地区城乡居民储蓄存款余额
URBAN AND RURAL SAVINGS DEPOSITS BALANCE OVER THE YEARS BY REGION

单位：万元（10000 yuan）

年份 Year	全市 Whole Municipality	其中 of which			年份 Year	全市 Whole Municipality	其中 of which		
		市区 Urban Area	溧阳市 Liyang City	金坛市 Jintan City			市区 Urban Area	溧阳市 Liyang City	金坛市 Jintan City
1949	8	8			1981	20123	15454	2623	2046
1950	59	57	2		1982	26767	20211	3767	2789
1951	280	239	28	13	1983	36154	26686	5139	4329
1952	598	544	37	17	1984	48512	34826	7328	6358
1953	734	664	43	27	1985	67304	48969	10596	7739
1954	913	782	69	62	1986	92511	67526	13841	11144
1955	970	833	73	64	1987	134174	96557	21849	15768
1956	1256	1070	124	62	1988	157915	117394	22716	17805
1957	1666	1329	250	87	1989	230962	170915	34123	25924
1958	1580	1400	119	61	1990	342914	254479	52128	36307
1959	2267	1945	137	185	1991	462939	348651	67370	47425
1960	2333	2013	165	155	1992	568704	429591	83516	56210
1961	2281	1951	148	182	1993	673404	496160	115022	62206
1962	1594	1410	99	85	1994	909347	675495	153622	80232
1963	1968	1719	151	98	1995	1286526	969196	207815	109515
1964	2662	2311	204	147	1996	1726519	1321397	259967	142439
1965	2829	2453	232	144	1997	2246590	1733748	302559	210283
1966	3144	2737	283	124	1998	2841400	2324026	414700	269400
1967	2974	2658	189	127	1999	3326100	2522385	479400	324400
1968	2981	2477	302	202	2000	3555700	2681100	511000	363600
1969	2503	2059	263	181	2001	4126500	3099500	596000	430900
1970	2566	2197	208	161	2002	4999400	3798700	697100	503600
1971	3236	2621	388	227	2003	6229200	4783000	832900	613200
1972	3577	2975	336	266	2004	7243600	5609100	946100	688400
1973	4313	3520	478	315	2005	8653900	6718200	1137300	798400
1974	4530	3803	412	315	2006	10140100	7903800	1310600	925700
1975	4960	4148	464	348	2007	10921400	8514000	1397400	1010000
1976	5137	4317	455	365	2008	14312100	11181700	1855300	1275100
1977	5928	4942	551	435	2009	17562400	13727400	2303800	1531200
1978	7182	6008	652	522	2010	20092400	15672600	2629800	1790000
1979	12032	9256	1403	1373	2011	21573900	16740000	2865800	1968100
1980	16337	12704	1960	1673	2012	24732700	19111400	3325400	2295900

18-5 分地区财政总收入（2012 年）
TOTAL FINANCIAL REVENUE BY REGION (2012)

单位：万元（10000 yuan）

指 标	Item	全 市 Whole Municipality	其中 of which 市 区 Urban Area	溧阳市 Liyang City	金坛市 Jintan City
总 计	**Total**	**11170283**	**9305089**	**1129570**	**735624**
中央收入	Revenue of Central Government	2463805	2035929	266405	161471
增值税（75%）	Value-added Tax （75%）	1517849	1248840	157260	111749
消费税	Consumption Tax	37458	32844	4288	326
企业所得税（60%）	Corporate Income Tax （60%）	609997	504341	72870	32786
个人所得税（60%）	Individual Income Tax （60%）	298501	249904	31987	16610
公共财政预算收入	Public Finance Budget Revenue	3789900	3153808	404988	231104
税收收入	Tax Revenue	3038930	2497641	344245	197044
#增值税（25%）	Value-added Tax （25%）	515654	423590	54095	37969
营业税	Operation Tax	838113	684923	102384	50806
企业所得税（40%）	Enterprise's Income Tax （40%）	406665	336227	48580	21858
个人所得税（40%）	Individual Income Tax （40%）	199001	166603	21324	11074
资源税	Resources Tax	11827		7777	4050
城市维护建设税	Tax on Urban Construction and Maintenance	204639	167825	22633	14181
房产税	Tax on Real Estates	114087	93791	12360	7936
印花税	Stamp Tax	52276	42474	6597	3205
城镇土地使用税	Tax on Use of Urban Land	136393	116168	13323	6902
土地增值税	Land Value Added Tax	213733	180856	22390	10487
车船税	Vehicle and Vessel Usage Tax	21715	18103	2136	1476
耕地占用税	Tax on the Occupancy of Cultivated Land	45491	34167	2598	8726
契 税	Contract Tax	279336	232914	28048	18374
非税收入	Non-tax Revenue	750970	656167	60743	34060
专项收入	pecial Revenue	108874	86279	14856	7739
行政性收费收入	Income From Administrative Fees	214456	184410	19800	10246
罚没收入	Fine and Confiscatory Revenue	62375	47728	9791	4856
国有资本经营收入	Revenue from State-owned Assets	29272	20892		8380
财政基金收入	Fund Revenue	4916578	4115352	458177	343049

18-6 分地区财政支出（2012 年）
FINANCIAL EXPENDITURE BY REGION （2012）

单位：万元（10000 yuan）

指 标	Item	全 市 Whole Municipality	其中 of which 市 区 Urban Area	溧阳市 Liyang City	金坛市 Jintan City
总 计	**Total**	**8849217**	**7263458**	**918904**	**666855**
公共财政预算支出	Public Finance Budget Expenditure	3912183	3136649	458353	317181
#一般公共服务	General Public Services	425611	327918	54089	43604
国 防	National Defense	34848	31376	3048	424
公共安全	Public Security	228551	185298	24444	18809
教 育	Education	661143	482237	107607	71299
科学技术	Science and Technology	189317	163938	15108	10271
文化体育与传媒	Culture, Sports and Media	100242	89529	6085	4628
社会保障和就业	Social Security and Employment	416641	335147	50875	30619
医疗卫生	Medical Treatment and Health	227850	170859	34696	22295
节能环保	Energy saving and Environmental Protection	151345	107076	20376	23893
城乡社区事务	Urban and Rural Community Affairs	646342	605458	27675	13209
农林水事务	Agriculture, Forestry and Water Affairs	286138	177622	69466	39050
交通运输	Traffic and Transportation	112651	93789	14298	4564
资源勘探电力信息等事务	Resource Exploration and Power Information	80661	68484	6994	5183
商业服务业等事务	Business and Services	72582	63300	3752	5530
金融监管等事务	Financial Regulation	8565	5380	2644	541
国土资源气象等事务	Land, Resources and Weather	19047	12167	5784	1096
住房保障支出	Housing Security Expenditure	107665	80765	7045	19855
粮油物资储备管理事务	Food, Oil and Material Reserves Management	3283	1560	1034	689
其 他	Others	139701	134746	3333	1622
财政基金支出	Fund Expenditure	4937034	4126809	460551	349674

18-7 五区财政收支（2012 年）
FINANCIAL REVENUE AND EXPENDITURE OF FIVE DISTRICTS（2012）

单位：万元（10000 yuan）

指 标	Item	武进区 wujin District	新北区 Xinbei District	天宁区 Tianning District	钟楼区 Zhonglou District	戚墅堰区 Qishuyan District
财政收入	**Financial Revenue**	**3381359**	**1923299**	**686532**	**546801**	**199655**
中央收入	Revenue of Central Government	827878	579634	270919	186061	95549
公共财政预算收入	Public Finance Budget Revenue	1170475	826645	400728	334965	95853
税收收入	Tax Revenue	950664	662622	342276	276131	82030
# 增值税	Value-added Tax	171635	127345	55176	37112	23254
营业税	Operation Tax	232274	150511	128346	115550	15085
企业所得税	Enterprise's Income Tax	148057	83569	52573	35139	13220
个人所得税	Individual Income Tax	66064	45303	20219	16303	4177
城市维护建设税	Tax on Urban Construction and Maintenance	56307	48808	23499	17998	7401
房产税	Tax on Real Estates	33974	25956	12424	12809	3187
印花税	Stamp Tax	17553	12666	4801	3878	1178
契 税	Contract Tax	100446	59949	18	5	1
非税收入	Non-tax Revenue	219811	164023	58452	58834	13823
财政基金收入	Fund Revenue	1383006	517020	14885	25775	8253
财政支出	**Financial Expenditure**	**2500587**	**995790**	**199534**	**207807**	**65172**
公共财政预算支出	Public Finance Budget Revenue	1119153	483431	189164	185741	57875
# 一般公共服务	General Public Services	100871	48922	32630	25416	10374
国 防	National Defense	12912	1	1399	207	463
公共安全	Public Security	43641	12307	10686	4856	2993
教 育	Education	183343	80646	35550	32296	10469
科学技术	Science and Technology	64966	46666	7882	16105	1753
文化体育与传媒	Culture, Sports and Media	22599	5911	5912	767	230
社会保障和就业	Social Security and Employment	61000	86555	30420	24782	10128
医疗卫生	Medical Treatment and Health	50648	34862	9428	9224	2500
环境保护	Environmental Protection	27606	26491	2044	7233	303
城乡社区事务	Urban and Rural Community Affairs	363045	87210	19391	51657	11865
农林水事务	Agriculture, Forestry and Water Affairs	102451	23488	26543	5599	2608
交通运输	Traffic and Transportation	18014	2			2
商业服务业等事务	Business and Services	24044	4766	1681	1147	552
住房保障支出	Housing Security Expenditure	19326	0	4165	4801	1916
其 他	Others	24687	25604	1433	1651	1719
财政基金支出	Fund Expenditure	1381434	512359	10370	22066	7297

18-8 分地区金融机构信贷收支情况（2012 年）
CREDIT FUNDS BALANCE OF FINANCIAL INSTITUTIONS GROUPED BY REGION（2012）

单位：亿元（100 million yuan）

指 标	Item	全 市 Whole Municipality	其中 of which 市 区 Urban Ared	溧阳市 Liyang City	金坛市 Jintan City
金融机构存贷款余额（本外币）	**Balance of Deposits and Loans in Financial Institutions（Domestic and Foreign Currency）**				
各项存款余额	Balance of Deposits	5789.88	4717.59	653.94	418.35
# 个人存款	Svings Deposits	2547.27	1975.25	336.92	235.10
# 储蓄存款	Savings Deposits	2489.97	1925.68	333.52	230.77
各项贷款余额	Balance of Loans	4018.21	3262.88	455.50	299.83
金融机构存贷款余额（人民币）	**Balance of Deposits and Loans in Financial Institutions（RMB）**				
各项存款余额	Balance of Deposits	5604.90	4558.74	645.20	400.96
# 企业存款	Deposits of Enterprises	2931.00	2471.68	296.61	162.71
个人存款	Svings Deposits	2529.86	1960.06	335.89	233.91
# 储蓄存款	Savings Deposits	2473.27	1911.14	332.54	229.59
各项贷款余额	Balance of Loans	3832.80	3109.26	436.64	286.90
短期贷款	Short-term Loans	2095.36	1661.94	275.40	158.02
# 个人贷款及透支	Personal Loan and Overdraft	211.74	141.30	46.22	24.22
# 个人消费贷款	Personal Consumption and Overdraft	28.72	24.08	2.32	2.32
单位贷款及透支	Unit Loan and Overdraft	1698.15	1371.14	209.62	117.39
# 经营贷款	Operating Loans	1669.86	1347.07	206.25	116.54
固定资产贷款	Fixed Asset Loans	28.30	24.08	3.37	0.85
银团贷款	Syndicated Loans	4.73	3.43		1.30
贸易融资	Trade Financing	180.74	146.07	19.56	15.11
中长期贷款	Medium-term and Long-term Loans	1618.67	1339.34	153.53	125.80
# 个人贷款及透支	Personal Loan and Overdraft	641.51	533.57	60.69	47.25
# 个人消费贷款	Personal Consumption and Overdraft	545.88	456.86	48.60	40.42
单位贷款及透支	Unit Loan and Overdraft	904.58	747.71	87.44	69.43
# 经营贷款	Operating Loans	138.59	108.46	12.18	17.95
固定资产贷款	Fixed Asset Loans	765.98	639.24	75.26	51.48
银团贷款	Syndicated Loans	63.34	48.82	5.40	9.12

18-9　分地区金融机构外汇信贷收支情况（2012 年）
CREDIT FUNDS BALANCE IN FOREIGN CURRENCIES OF FINANCIAL INSTITUTIONS GROUPED BY REGION（2012）

单位：万美元（USD 10000）

项　目	Item	全　市 Whole Municipality	其中 of which 市　区 Urban Area	溧阳市 Liyang City	金坛市 Jintan City
金融机构外币存款余额	**Deposits Balance in Foreign Currencies of Banking Institutions**	**294305**	**252725**	**13911**	**27669**
# 企业存款	Deposits of Enterprises	264812	226763	12271	25778
个人存款	Svings Deposits	27694	24169	1640	1885
# 储蓄存款	Savings Deposits	26572	23129	1565	1878
金融机构外币贷款余额	**Loans Balance in Foreign Currencies of Banking Institutions**	**294988**	**244414**	**30000**	**20574**
短期贷款	Short-term Loans	290280	239893	29851	20536
中长期贷款	Medium-term and Long-term Loans	3584	3546		38
贸易融资	Export and Import Trade Financing	279413	229026	29851	20536

18-10　证券交易情况（2012 年）
TRADING SUMMARY FOR SECURITIES（2012）

单位：亿元（100 million yuan）

项　目	Item	全　市 Whole Municipality
证券交易总额（亿元）	Total Transaction Volume of Securities（100 million yuan）	3493.76
A 股	A Shares	3331.56
B 股	B Shares	6.63
基　金	Funds	52.72
债　券	Bonds	102.85
资金帐户总数（万户）	Total Capital Accounts（10000 households）	62.55

18-11 分地区保险业务情况（2012 年）
BASIC STATISTICS ON INSURANCE BY REGION（2012）

单位：万元（10000 yuan）

指标	Item	全市 Whole Municipality	其中 of which		
			市区 Urban Area	溧阳市 Liyang City	金坛市 Jintan City
财产险	**Property Insurance**				
承保金额	Insurance Value	128207865	113387966	9454074	5365825
企业财产险	Enterprise Property Insurance	33294189	28728863	2955966	1609360
机动车辆险	Motor Vehicle Insurance	31246963	25591263	3499660	2156040
货物运输险	Freight Transport Insurance	9454338	8820898	340356	293084
工程险	Project Liability Insurance	1143132	1041393	60586	41153
家庭财产险	Family Property Insurance	1922690	1492008	394151	36531
责任险	Liability Insurance	28151120	26518355	703778	928987
其它险	Other Insurance	22995433	21195186	1499577	300670
保费收入	Premium Income	338066	278723	35804	23539
企业财产险	Enterprise Property Insurance	29758	25563	2356	1839
机动车辆险	Motor Vehicle Insurance	270320	224342	27496	18482
货物运输险	Freight Transport Insurance	5178	4013	935	230
工程险	Project Liability Insurance	1622	1479	111	32
家庭财产险	Family Property Insurance	1548	1116	410	22
责任险	Liability Insurance	11124	9424	979	721
其它险	Other Insurance	18516	12786	3517	2213
赔付支出	Indemnity Experditur	189717	157233	18437	14047
企业财产险	Enterprise Property Insurance	14472	12516	1047	909
机动车辆险	Motor Vehicle Insurance	162597	135404	15352	11841
货物运输险	Freight Transport Insurance	2052	1792	102	158
工程险	Project Liability Insurance	388	324	55	9
家庭财产险	Family Property Insurance	384	254	106	24
责任险	Liability Insurance	5196	4097	590	509
其它险	Other Insurance	4628	2846	1185	597
人寿险	**Life Insurance**				
保费收入	Premium Income	756321	642598	60235	53488
意外伤害险	Personal and Accident Insurance	15410	12486	1859	1065
健康险	Health Insurance	12769	11445	578	746
人寿险	Life Insurance	728142	618667	57798	51677
赔付支出	Indemnity Experditur	22006	18920	1491	1595
意外伤害险	Personal and Accident Insurance	4112	3383	430	299
健康险	Health Insurance	7080	6340	331	409
人寿险	Life Insurance	10814	9197	730	887

18-12 分地区企业职工基本养老保险情况（2012 年）
BASIC CONDITIONS OF PENSION INSURANCE OF ENTERPRISES' STAFF AND WORKERS GROUPED BY REGION（2012）

指 标	Item	全 市 Whole Municipality	其 中 of which 市 区 Urban Area	溧阳市 Liyang City	金坛市 Jintan City
参保单位数（个）	Number of Units Covered by Insurance （unit）	44924	38341	3975	2608
参保职工人数（人）	Number of Employees Covered by Insurance （person）	1211287	950629	144196	116462
领取养老保险金人数（人）	Number of People Receiving Pension Insurance （person）	365274	292804	45390	27080
基金总收入（万元）	General Fund Revenue （10000 yuan）	987718	769806	104885	113027
#基本养老保险费	Basic Pension Insurance Premiums	933725	726508	96084	111133
基金总支出（万元）	General Fund Expenditure （1000 yuan）	730420	610173	70220	50027
#基本养老金	Basic Pension	692932	579355	66517	47060

18-13 分地区城乡居民社会养老保险情况（2012 年）
BASIC CONDITIONS OF THE URBAN AND RURAL SOCIAL PENSION INSURANCE GROUPED BY REGION（2012）

指 标	Item	全 市 Whole Municipality	其 中 of which 市 区 Urban Area	溧阳市 Liyang City	金坛市 Jintan City
参保缴费人数（万人）	Number of People with Pension Insurance （10000 persons）	45.82	18.65	14.03	13.14
领取养老金人数（人）	Number of Pensioners （person）	443162	231845	125616	85701
基金总收入（万元）	General Fund Revenue （10000 yuan）	114830	70854	22954	21022
基金总支出（万元）	General Fund Expenditure （10000 yuan）	91856	62485	17310	12061

18-14 分地区基本医疗保险情况（2012 年）
BASIC CONDITIONS OF MEDICAL INSURANCE GROUPED BY REGION（2012）

指 标	Item	全 市 Whole Municipality	其 中 of which 市 区 Urban Area	溧阳市 Liyang City	金坛市 Jintan City
参保人数（人）	Number of Persons Coverd by Insurance （person）	1628638	1318970	171477	138191
在职职工	Employed Staff and Workers	1239355	1000025	129843	109487
退休人员	Retirees	389283	318945	41634	28704
基金总收入（万元）	General Fund Revenue （10000 yuan）	366732	307733	29664	29335
#统筹账户	Pool Account	217071	181495	16019	19557
基金总支出（万元）	General Fund Expenditure （10000 yuan）	291335	242132	27165	22038
#统筹账户	Pool Account	169170	140336	14764	14070

18-15 分地区失业保险情况（2012 年）
BASIC CONDITIONS OF UNEMPLOYMENT INSURANCE GROUPED BY REGION（2012）

指 标	Item	全 市 Whole Municipality	其 中 of which 市 区 Urban Area	溧阳市 Liyang City	金坛市 Jintan City
参保人数（人）	Number of People Covered by Insurance（person）	959814	762942	108488	88384
领取失业保险金人数（人）	Number of People Receiving Unemployment Insurance（person）	41567	35479	2167	3921
基金总收入（万元）	General Fund Revenue（10000 yuan）	88993	76366	6765	5863
基金总支出（万元）	General Fund Expenditure（10000 yuan）	39810	30247	4529	5033

18-16 分地区工伤保险情况（2012 年）
BASIC CONDITIONS OF WORK-RELATED INJURY INSURANCE GROUPED BY REGION（2012）

指 标	Item	全 市 Whole Municipality	其 中 of which 市 区 Urban Area	溧阳市 Liyang City	金坛市 Jintan City
参保人数（人）	Number of People Covered by Insurance（person）	1009123	796422	92889	119812
基金总收入（万元）	General Fund Revenue（10000 yuan）	25320	18147	3002	4171
基金总支出（万元）	General Fund Expenditure（10000 yuan）	30288	22002	4073	4213
当年享受工伤保险待遇人次（人次）	Number of People Receiving Work-Related Injury Insurance（person-time）	7915	4986	1842	1087

18-17 分地区生育保险情况（2012 年）
BASIC CONDITIONS OF MATERNITY INSURANCE GROUPED BY REGION（2012）

指 标	Item	全 市 Whole Municipality	其 中 of which 市 区 Urban Area	溧阳市 Liyang City	金坛市 Jintan City
参保人数（人）	Number of People Covered by Insurance（person）	886309	745190	61686	79433
基金总收入（万元）	General Fund Revenue（10000 yuan）	21153	18011	1376	1766
基金总支出（万元）	General Fund Expenditure（10000 yuan）	14785	13704	428	653
当年享受生育保险待遇人次（人次）	Number of People Receiving Maternity Insurance（person-time）	15418	13187	1446	785

19

CHAPTER 19

城市建设 环境保护

URBAN CONSTRUCTION AND ENVIRONMENTAL PROTECTION

19 城市建设　环境保护 URBAN CONSTRUCTION AND ENVIRONMENTAL PROTECTION

2012 年主要统计指标 MAJOR STATISTICAL INDICATORS OF 2012

城区人口密度	Urban Population Density	3665 人 / 平方公里	(person/sq.km)
城区实有道路面积	Area of Existing Road in Urban District	3451 万平方米	(10000 sq.m)
城区人均公园绿地面积	Per Capita Green Area of Parks in Urban District	12.49 平方米	(sq.m)
城区出租车营运数量	Number of Taxi in Operation in Urban Area	2542 辆	(coach)
城区燃气普及率	Gas Penetration Rate in Urban District	99.7%	

19-1　市区城市公用事业基本情况（1978-2012 年）
BASIC STATISTICS ON URBAN PUBLIC UTILITIES（1978-2012）

年　份 Year	建成区面积（平方公里） Developed Area（sq.km）	年末实有铺装道路长度（公里） Length of Roads at Year-end（km）	年末实有铺装道路面积（万平方米） Area of Paved Roads at Year-end（10000 sq.m）	城市下水道总长度（公里） Total Length of Urban Sewerage Drain（km）	园林绿地面积（公顷） Parkes,Gardens and Green Areas（hectare）	其中 of which # 公园绿地面积（公顷） Green Space of Park（hectare）
1978	24.44	98	83	140	145	54
1979	26.80	102	86	145	150	55
1980	27.85	105	89	150	161	56
1981	28.98	109	90	155	171	59
1982	29.58	119	93	161	174	61
1983	31.00	124	103	190	177	64
1984	32.52	127	108	195	272	68
1985	34.30	121	104	225	275	71
1986	35.10	198	154	231	283	76
1987	35.90	320	263	284	294	80
1988	37.20	326	273	289	310	99
1989	37.80	332	279	229	322	107
1990	39.00	336	296	231	343	121
1991	39.60	354	312	238	364	137
1992	41.10	355	314	260	389	147
1993	54.80	415	359	271	920	223
1994	57.40	449	432	312	947	233
1995	60.60	483	450	698	1067	283
1996	65.00	559	606	714	1105	301
1997	67.00	593	662	736	1188	357
1998	68.14	648	713	818	1300	412
1999	68.14	671	777	894	1378	440
2000	68.95	697	868	929	1441	458
2001	70.95	821	1024	1040	1509	500
2002	90.50	2497	2907	1544	4779	1101
2003	92.28	3828	3563	2414	4813	1193
2004	98.50	3548	3772	2775	5213	1433
2005	104.31	3584	3954	2918	5529	1568
2006	107.58	1349	2158	2366	4037	1333
2007	112.50	1551	2247	2918	6057	1389
2008	120.51	1565	2606	3223	6468	1450
2009	133.90	1656	2809	3458	6773	1561
2010	153.05	1753	3023	3627	7222	1632
2011	173.15	1811	3230	3807	7535	1704
2012	183.24	1892	3451	4214	7914	1759

注：1、本表数据按当年行政区划统计；从1995年起，供水总量中不包括单位自备水量。
2、由于建设局统计口径发生变化，2006年起均为城区口径，同时公共绿地面积调整为公园绿地面积。
3、自2010年起年末实有公共汽车营运车辆统计口径调整为市区口径。

Note：1、The data in the tabal were calculated according to the administrative division of that year;Since 1995,the total volume of water supply excludes the volume oh self-prepared water supply by units.
2、Due to the change of statistic coverage of municipal construction authorities, the data were calculated as per statistic coverage of urban area since the year of 2006, meanwhile, public green area was adjusted as green area of park.
3、Since 2010, the actual number of buses in operation by the end of year has been calculated as per statistical coverage of urban areas.

供水总量（万立方米） Total Annual Volume of Water Supply（10000 m^3）	年末实有公共汽车营运车辆（辆） Number of Operating Public Transport Vehicles at Year-end（coach）	全年公共汽车客运总数（万人次） Total Number of Annual Passengers Despatched by Public Transport Vehicles（10000 persons/time）	年末实有出租汽车营运车辆（辆） Number of Operating Taxies at Year-end（coach）	管道燃气供气总量（万立方米） Total Pipe Natural Gas Supply（10000 m^3）	液化气供气总量（吨） Total Liquefied of Gas Supply（ton）
20578	117	7184			
20876	133	9706			
21219	147	10862		109	
21385	157	11023		143	
21881	167	10907		115	
22911	182	10171		224	
24332	205	10119		333	
25759	227	11271		515	
26611	217	11082	92	996	2386
26878	209	10762	116	1058	2798
27050	211	10519	131	1157	4161
24871	208	10290	136	1415	3757
25994	232	9482	137	1601	5469
26066	244	9632	146	1655	10556
28353	254	10201	290	1654	22877
26240	283	9129	356	1667	20802
25789	297	8354	419	1729	22940
11257	307	8704	592	1783	24662
11491	348	8768	1029	2624	28995
14870	371	9199	1209	3224	28923
15310	1415	11490	1173	3533	33405
15291	1423	12624	1564	3846	35443
16631	1572	14616	1443	4256	38827
20123	1703	14865	1442	4502	43835
31431	1651	14195	1442	5058	92852
30517	1804	15523	1442	5898	87464
30965	2065	18089	1642	5694	77510
32384	2105	21829	1842	8030	80800
20940	1608	18940	1842	14892	42115
23636	1779	25973	2142	26943	37025
23220	1788	33150	2142	31298	26656
23633	1934	35583	2142	33444	23532
21981	2518	38948	2542	48099	11037
21664	2600	40717	2542	52355	8182
21801	2590	41190	2542	55209	7043

19-2　主要年份市区城市设施水平
URBAN CIVIL FACILITIES IN MAIN YEARS

指　标	Item	2000	2005	2010	2012
人均日生活用水量（升）	Per Capita Daily Consumption of Tap Water for Rrsidential Use （liter）	224.2	181.6	238.7	226.8
自来水普及率（%）	Percentage of Population with Access to Tap Water （%）	100.0	92.7	100.0	100.0
每万人拥有公交车辆（标台）	Average Public Service Vehicles per 10000 Persons （coach）	15.6	9.0	13.1	14.6
燃气普及率（%）	Percentage of Population with Access to Fuel Gas （%）	99.8	92.0	99.0	99.7
人均拥有道路面积（平方米）	Per Capita Area of Roads （sq.m）	10.7	17.9	22.9	24.5
污水处理率（%）	Rate of Sewerage Disposal（%）	69.0	86.8	89.8	93.8
人均公园绿地面积（平方米）	Per Capita Green Area of Parks （sq.m）	5.6	7.1	12.4	12.5
建成区绿化覆盖率（%）	Rate of the Green Space in Constructed Areas （%）	31.7	38.8	42.2	42.2
生活垃圾无害化处理率（%）	Rate of No Harm Disposal of Living Garbage （%）	50.5	92.1	100.0	100.0

19-3　分地区城市建设用地情况（2012 年）
LAND USE OF URBAN CONSTRUCTION BY REGION（2012）

单位：平方公里　（sq.km）

指　标	Item	市　区 Urban Area	溧阳市 Liyang City	金坛市 Jintan City
建成区面积	Area of Constructed Regions	183.24	24.45	22.00
城市建设用地面积	Floor space of Urban Constructed Area	174.60	24.37	22.00
居住用地	Residential Area	51.44	7.78	7.09
公共管理与公共服务用地	Public Management & Public Service Sites	9.89	2.51	2.43
商业服务业设施用地	Business Services Facilities	8.10	2.12	5.26
工业用地	Industrial Area	44.09	6.43	0.45
物流仓储用地	Logistics & Warehousing Space	3.57	0.61	1.41
交通设施用地	Transportation Facilities	22.45	2.24	2.31
公用设施用地	Communal Facilities	5.97	1.01	0.93
绿　地	Green Area	29.09	1.67	2.12

19-4 分地区城市市政设施情况（2012 年）
URBAN CIVIL FACILITIES BY REGION（2012）

指 标	Item	市 区 Urban Area	溧阳市 Liyang City	金坛市 Jintan City
实有道路长度（公里）	Length of Roads （km）	1892	221	224
实有道路面积（万平方米）	Area of Roads （10000 sq.m）	3451	374	292
桥梁数（座）	Number of Bridges （unit）	1029	55	46
排水管道长度（公里）	Length of Sewage Pipelines （km）	4214	269	310
污水日处理能力（万立方米）	Capacity of Sewage Disposal （10000 m^3）	107	5	7
防洪堤长度（公里）	Length of Anti-Flood Diker （km）	2030		9
路灯盏数（千盏）	Street Lamps （1000 sets）	173	10	20

19-5 分地区城市园林绿化情况（2012 年）
URBAN PARKS, GARDENS AND GREEN AREAS BY REGION（2012）

指 标	Item	市 区 Urban Area	溧阳市 Liyang City	金坛市 Jintan City
园林绿地面积（公顷）	Parkes,Gardens and Green Areas （hectare）	7914	1181	925
公园绿地面积（公顷）	Green Space of Park （hectare）	1759	191	212
建成区绿化覆盖面积（公顷）	Green Space in Constucted Areas （hectare）	7735	1013	903
人均公园绿地面积（平方米）	Per Capita Green Area of Park （sq.m）	12.5	9.4	12.1
建成区绿地率（%）	Rate of the Green Space in Constructed Areas （%）	38.6	38.5	37.1
建成区绿化覆盖率（%）	Rate of the Green Space in Constructed Areas （%）	42.2	41.4	41.1
城市公园个数（个）	Urban Parks （unit）	26	6	5
公园面积（公顷）	Park Area （hectare）	553	135	128

19-6　分地区城市公共汽车、出租汽车情况（2012 年）
URBAN PUBLIC SERVICE VEHICLES AND TAXIES BY REGION（2012）

指　标	Item	市　区 Urban Area	溧阳市 Liyang City	金坛市 Jintan City
公共汽车	**Public Service Vehicles**			
年底营运车辆数（辆）	Number in Operation at Year-end （coach）	2590	165	66
年底营运线路条数（条）	Number of Operating Routes at Year-end （line）	197	19	9
年底营运线路网长度（公里）	Length of Operating Route Net at Year-end （km）	3457	232	272
客运总量（万人次）	Total volume of travellers （10000 Persons/times）	41190	2280	868.7
每万人拥有公交车辆（标台）	Average Public Service Vehicles per 10000 Persons （coach）	14.6	3.8	6.4
出租汽车	**Taxies**			
营运车辆（辆）	Operation Vehicles （coach）	2542	359	279

19-7　分地区城市自来水情况（2012 年）
URBAN TAP WATER CONDITION BY REGION（2012）

指　标	Item	市　区 Urban Area	溧阳市 Liyang City	金坛市 Jintan City
自来水综合生产能力（万立方米 / 日）	General Production Capacity of Water Treatment Plant （10000 m^3 /day）	167.5	10.0	5.0
供水管道长度（公里）	Length of Water Supply Piplines （km）	11393	610	988
供水总量（万立方米）	Total Water Supply （10000 m^3）	21801	2447	2618
# 生产用水量	Water for Production	6625	940	838
生活用水量	Water for Livelihood	11662	1167	1140
用水人口（万人）	Population with Access to Tap Water （10000 persons）	140.87	20.23	17.50
人均日生活用水量（升）	Per Capita Daily Comsumption of Tap Water for Livelihood （litre）	226.82	158.04	178.50
自来水普及率（%）	Percentage of Population with Access to Tap Water （%）	100.0	100.0	100.0

19-8 分地区城市燃气情况（2012 年）
URBAN GAS SUPPLY BY REGION（2012）

指 标	Item	市 区 Urban Area	溧阳市 Liyang City	金坛市 Jintan City
天然气	**Natural Gas**			
燃气管道长度（公里）	Length of natural gas pipelines（km）	4339	443	443
供气总量（万立方米）	Total Gas Supply（10000 m^3）	55209	5900	10712
#家庭用量	Consumption for Residential Use	11251	765	623
用气户数（户）	Total Number of Residents with Access to Gas（household）	502372	41768	50792
#家庭用户	Households Consumers	486194	41200	50400
用气人口（万人）	Total Population with Access to Gas（10000 persons）	136.95	15.00	12.50
天然气汽车加气站（座）	Natural Gas Filling Stations for Automobiles（unit）	10	2	1
液化石油气	**Liquefied Petroleum Gas**			
供气总量（吨）	Total Gas Supply（ton）	7043	3856	6549
#家庭用量	Consumption for Residential Use	1776	2312	2788
用气户数（户）	Total Number of Residents with Access to Gas（household）	13683	14988	32520
#家庭用户	Households Consumers	12348	14668	24500
用气人口（万人）	Total Population with Access to Gas（10000 persons）	3.50	5.09	5.00
燃气普及率（%）	**Percentage of Population with Access to Fuel Gas（%）**	**99.7**	**99.3**	**100.0**

19-9 分地区城市环境卫生情况（2012 年）
URBAN ENVIRONMENT SANITATION BY REGION（2012）

指 标	Item	市 区 Urban Area	溧阳市 Liyang City	金坛市 Jintan City
实际清扫面积（万平方米）	Actually Cleaned Area（10000 sq.m）	2543	256	391
生活垃圾清运量（万吨）	Volume of Residential Garbage Disposal（10000 tons）	58.08	6.18	5.91
粪便清运量（万吨）	Clearing of Excrement and Urine（10000 tons）	0.64	0.10	1.04
公共厕所（座）	Public Lavatories（unit）	796	56	74
环卫机械数（台）	Environmental Sanitation Equipment（unit）	276	63	161

19-10　市区城市生态自然环境情况（2007-2012 年）
URBAN ECOLOGICAL NATURAL ENVIRONMENT（2007-2012）

指　标	Item	2007	2008	2009	2010	2012
园林绿化	**Parks,Gardens and Green Areas**					
园林绿地面积（公顷）	Parkes,Gardens and Green Areas（hectare）	6468	6773	7222	7535	7914
公园绿地面积（公顷）	Green Space of Park （hectare）	1450	1561	1632	1704	1759
建成区绿化覆盖面积（公顷）	Green Space in Constucted Areas（hectare）	5076	5640	6451	7302	7735
建成区绿化覆盖率（%）	Rate of Green Space in Constructed Areas（%）	42.1	42.1	42.2	42.2	42.2
人均公园绿地面积（平方米）	Per Capita Green Area of Park（sq.m）	12.12	12.20	12.35	12.41	12.49
城市公园个数（个）	Urban Parks（unit）	21	24	25	25	26
公园面积（公顷）	Park Area（hectare）	465	489	520	520	553
水、空气和噪声情况	**Water, Air and Noise**					
城市集中式饮用水源地水质达标率（%）	Rate up to the Standards of Water Quality for Urban Potable Water Sources（%）	100.0	100.0	100.0	100.0	100.0
空气污染指数小于100天数占全年天数的比例（%）	Proportion of Days with Air Pollution Index less than 100 to Whole Year（%）	86.1	91.5	91.5	92.1	92.1
区域环境噪声平均值（分贝）	Average Value of Noise in Whole Area（dB）	55.0	54.7	54.4	54.7	53.9
交通干线噪声平均值（分贝）	Average Value of Noise Along Main Traffic Artery（dB）	67.0	67.8	67.4	67.3	67.5
生活垃圾无害化处理	**Harmless Disposal of Household Garbage**					
垃圾清运量（万吨）	Wastes Transported（10000 Tons）	46.64	49.16	51.99	54.95	58.08
垃圾无害化处理量（万吨）	Volume of Garbage Disposal（10000 ton）	46.64	49.16	51.99	54.95	58.08
生活垃圾无害化处理率（%）	Rate of Harmless Disposal of Household Garbage（%）	100.0	100.0	100.0	100.0	100.0

19-11 环境保护情况（1986-2012 年）
ENVIRONMENTAL PROTECTION（1986-2012）

年 份 Year	工业废水排放总量（万吨） Total Volume of Industrial Wastewater Discharged（10000 tons）	工业废水中 COD 排放总量（吨） Total Volume of COD in Industrial Wastewater Discharged（ton）	工业废气中二氧化硫排放总量（吨） Total Volume of Sulphur Dioxide Emission in Industrial Waste Gas（ton）	工业废气中烟尘排放总量（吨） Total Volume of Soot Emission in Industrial Waste Gas（ton）	工业废气中粉尘排放总量（吨） Total Volume of Dust Emission in Industrial Waste Gas（ton）
1986	20681	64856	42527	49395	32500
1987	22647	51396	41072	38406	27800
1988	22386	43617	46968	37395	33700
1989	20546	35879	56252	56307	32700
1990	20439	30508	56099	55662	43400
1991	21455	28797	73472	62014	25700
1992	18697	31121	75671	57791	19200
1993	12070	27998	45906	26704	19000
1994	10931	22308	55355	28196	31300
1995	11489	22865	55971	25282	34300
1996	10523	15979	57236	28991	65900
1997	11193	26763	74320	35814	104600
1998	10183	17436	51476	26563	30300
1999	16455	19873	47409	33895	48700
2000	14728	16436	39042	30798	41200
2001	27086	29903	48242	17590	46400
2002	23912	29289	45133	19329	41447
2003	24071	30015	45722	15375	43986
2004	23082	43018	62958	28086	54602
2005	32519	51579	86215	35804	61091
2006	27300	36215	82930	31465	59396
2007	31875	30944	72243	29496	52085
2008	32601	28273	66656	25392	14904
2009	35942	26354	62255	24917	11299
2010	37715	24827	48000	19582	10784
2011	17371	9416	43734	38563	
2012	14630	8158	35984	27589	

注：从2011年起工业废气中烟尘、粉尘排放总量合并成烟（粉）尘排放量。

Note： The Total Dust and Powder Emissions in Industrial Emissions was combined as Smoke（Powder）Dust Emissions starting from 2011.

19-12　分地区环境保护情况（2012 年）
ENVIRONMENTAL PROTECTION BY REGION（2012）

指　标	Item	全　市 Whole Municipality	其　中　of　which 市　区 Urban Area	溧阳市 Liyang City	金坛市 Jintan City
废水排放	**Wastewater Discharged**				
工业废水排放总量（万吨）	Total Volume of Industrial Wastewater Discharged（10000 tons）	14630	11321	2078	1231
废水中化学需氧量排放量（吨）	Volume of Chemical Oxygen Demand in Wastwater Discharged（ton）	8158	6231	1249	679
废水中氨氮排放量（吨）	Ammonia Emissions from Wastewater（ton）	398.42	271.75	89.21	37.46
废气排放	**Waste Gas**				
工业废气排放总量（万标立方米）	Total Volume of Industrial Waste Gas Emission（10000 Nm^3）	29737152	23684857	3737743	2314552
二氧化硫排放量（吨）	Volume of Sulphur Dioxide Emission（ton）	35984	24371	9147	2467
氮氧化物排放量（吨）	Nitrogen Oxides（ton）	81708	47640	27238	6830
烟（粉）排放量（吨）	Smoke（Powder）Dust Emissions（ton）	27589	16718	6971	3900
工业固体废物	**Industrail Solid Wastes**				
工业固体废物产生量（万吨）	Volume of Industrial Solid Wastes Produced（10000 tons）	584.13	483.96	84.76	15.41
工业固体废物综合利用量（万吨）	Volume of Industrial Solid Wastes Utilized（10000 tons）	571.12	470.95	84.76	15.41
工业固体废物处置量（万吨）	Volume of Industrial Solid Wastes Treated（10000 tons）	13.01	13.01	0.00	0.00
工业固体废物综合利用率（%）	Percentage of Industrial Solid Wastes Utilized（%）	97.8	97.3	100.00	100.00
环境建设	**Environmental Construction**				
自然保护区覆盖率（%）	Coverage Rate of Nature Reserves（%）	1.56	0.00	4.45	1.00

20

CHAPTER 20

科技 教育 文化

SCIENCE,TECHNOLOGY, EDUCATION AND CULTURE

20 科技 教育 文化
SCINECE & TECHNOLOGY EDUCATION AND CULTURE

2012 年主要统计指标
MAJOR STATISTICAL INDICATORS OF 2012

普通高等学校数	Number of Institutions of Higher Education	9 所	(unit)
普通高等学校在校学生数	Students Enrollment of Institutions of Higher Education	12.46 万人	(10000 persons)
普通中学数	Regular Secondary Schools	162 所	(unit)
普通中学在校学生数	Student Enrollment of Regular Secondary Schools	16.91 万人	(10000 persons)
小学学校数	Primary Schools	187 所	(unit)
小学学校在校学生数	Student Enrollment of Primary Schools	23.43 万人	(10000 persons)
年底公共图书馆	Number of Public Libraries	4 个	(unit)
电视台数	Number of Television Stations	4 座	(unit)
广播电台数	Number of Broadcasting Stations	4 座	(unit)

20-1　科研开发基本情况（2008-2012 年）
BASIC STATISTICS OF SCIENCE RESEARCH DEVELOPMENT（2008-2012）

指　标	Item	2008	2009	2010	2011	2012
机构数（个）	**Number of Institutes（unit）**	**19**	**19**	**18**	**17**	**17**
从业人数（人）	**Number of Employed Persons（person）**	**2982**	**2970**	**3375**	**3741**	**3170**
# 从事科技活动人数	Number of Personnel Engaged in Science and Technology	1237	1335	1338	1496	1208
从事 R&D 人员数	Number of Personnel Engaged in R&D	529	969	914	964	1002
课题活动人数	Number of Persons Engaged in Subject Activity	588	612	864	893	887
经费收入总额（万元）	**Total Funds Income（10000 yuan）**	**176534**	**194707**	**292888**	**301408**	**291966**
# 政府资金	Government Funds	2262	3881	2119	3316	8432
技术性收入	Technological Income	5978	7538	8449	11809	8912
经营收入	Operating Income	161701	175634	270125	279966	272142
经费支出总额（万元）	**Total Expenditure（10000 yuan）**	**106906**	**153210**	**190045**	**237057**	**191865**
#R&D 经费支出	Expenditure on Research and Development	5255	13688	17853	24310	19197
# 购置科研仪器设备	Purchasing Scientific Research Instruments and Equipments	1282	1439	1956	4715	3605
发表科技论文（篇）	**Number of Published Scientific and Technological Thesis（piece）**	**114**	**126**	**128**	**197**	**226**

20-2 国家级、省级科技计划数（2012 年）
NUMBER OF SCIENTIFIC AND TECHNOLOGICAL PLANS AT STATE LEVEL OR PROVINCE LEVEL（2012）

计划名称	Name of Plan	合计（项）Total (Unit)	其中 of which 国家级 State Level	省级 Province Level	总投资（亿元）Total Investment (100 million yuan)	上级拨款（万元）Higher Organizations Appropriations (10000 yuan)	其中 of which 国家 State	省 Province
国家863计划	National 863 Plan	4	4			3433	3433	
国家科技支撑计划	National Science & Technology Pillar Program	4	4			1650	1650	
科技型中小企业技术创新基金	Technology Innovation Funds for Scientific and Technical Type Small and Medium Enterprises	66	66			4516	4516	
国家农业科技成果转化资金	National Agricultural Scientific and Technological Achievements Transformation Funds	4	4			468	468	
国家重大科技专项	Major National Science and Technology Projects	2	2			3037	3037	
国家国际科技合作	National and International Scientific and Technological Cooperation	6	6		2	2900	2900	
国家火炬计划	National Torch Plan	29	29					
国家重点新产品计划	National Key New Product Plan	12	12					
省科技支撑计划（工业）	Provincial Scientific and Technological Support Plan （Industry）	22		22	1.35	2040		2040
省科技支撑计划（农业）	Provincial Scientific and Technological Support Plan （Agriculture）	3		3	0.08	100		100
省科技支撑计划（社会发展）	Provincial Scientific and Technological Support Plan （Social Development）	8		8	0.38	230		230
省科技支撑计划（重要技术标准）	Provincial Scientific and Technological Support Plan （Key Technology Standards）	3		3		300		300
省工程技术研究中心	Provincial Engineering and Technology Reaearch Center	49		49				
省国际科技合作计划	International Scientific and Technologic Cooperation Plan	8		8	0.20	300		300
省基础研究计划	Provincial Fundamental Research Plan	30		30		440		440
省科技成果转化专项资金	Special Fund for Scientific and Technological Achievements Transfer	15		15	11.26	13500		13500
省知识产权战略推进计划	Provincial Promotion Plan of Intellectual Property Rights Strategy	5		5	0.20	180		180
省专利实施计划	Provincial Patent Implementation Plan	2		2		29		29
省软科学研究	Provincial Soft Science Research	3		3		9		9
省科技创新资金	Provincial Science & Technology Innovation Capital	22		22		550		550
省企业重大研发机构	Provincial Major Enterprise R&D Institutions	4		4	1.24	1800		1800
省产学研联合创新资金	Provincial Industry-University Joint Innovation Fund	19		19	0.39	620		620
省科技公共服务平台	Provincial Science & Technology Public Service Platform	7		7	1.37	1722		1722
省企业院士工作站	Provincial Enterprise Academician Workstations	1		1	0.10	200		200
省科技创新团队项目	Provincial Technology Innovation Team Projects	2		2		600		600

注：本表项目数和上级拨款为当年新上项目数及新上项目的上级拨款总额。

Note: The number of projects and appropriation from higher authorities in this table shall be the number of new projects and total appropriations of the current year.

20-3　市级科技计划项目情况（2012 年）
SCIENTIFIC AND TECHNOLOGICAL PLAN AT CITY LEVEL（2012）

单位：万元（10000 yuan）

项目名称	Name of Project	项数（项）Number of Project（unit）	科技拨款 Scientific and Technological appropriations
农业科技	Agricultural Science and Technology	45	670
工业科技	Industrial Science and Technology	155	2545
社会发展科技	Social Development Science and Technology	118	1319
软课题	Research Task	54	141

注：本表未包括指导性计划。
Note： This table doesn't include guidance plans.

20-4　科技进步获奖情况（2012 年）
STATISTICS ON PRIZE OF ADVANCE OF SCIENCE AND TECHNOLOGY（2012）

单位：项（unit）

奖励级别	Prize Grade	合　计 Total	其　中　of　which 一等奖 First Prize	二等奖 Second Prize	三等奖 Third Prize
国家级	State Level	5		5	
省　级	Provincial Level	11		5	6
市　级	City Level	79	9	23	47

20-5　分地区专利申请及授权情况（2012 年）
STATISTICS ON PATENT APPLICATIONS EXAMINED AND GRANTED BY REGION（2012）

单位：项（unit）

指　标	Item	合　计 Total	其　中　of　which 市　区 Urban Area	溧阳市 Liyang City	金坛市 Jintan City
专利申请量	**Number of Patent Applications Examined**	**39391**	**31742**	**4337**	**3312**
发明专利	Patent for Invention	10123	8403	978	742
实用新型专利	Practical New-type Patent	14668	13210	898	560
外观专利	Appearance Patent	14600	10129	2461	2010
专利授权量	**Number of Patent Authorizations Granted**	**15379**	**11737**	**3033**	**609**
发明专利	Patent for Invention	1188	1069	78	41
实用新型专利	Practical New-type Patent	9162	8224	538	400
外观专利	Appearance Patent	5029	2444	2417	168

20-6 分地区政府科技拨款数（2012 年）
GOVERNMENT APPROPRIATION OF SCIENCE AND TECHNOLOGY BY REGION（2012）

单位：万元（10000 yuan）

指标	Item	全市 Whole Municipality	其中 of which 市区 Urban Area	溧阳市 Liyang City	金坛市 Jintan City
总 计	**Total**	**218584**	**196429**	**15108**	**7047**
科学技术管理事务	Scientific & Technical Management Affairs	2320	1589	496	235
基础研究	Basic Research	150	140		10
应用研究	Applied Research	802	613	189	
技术研究与开发	Technology Research and Development	55632	38956	10913	5763
科技条件与服务	Scientific & Technical Conditions and Service	3062	2469	213	380
社会科学	Social Science				
科学技术普及	Science & Technology Popularization	1646	1249	263	134
科技交流与合作	Science and Technology Exchange and Cooperation	1984	1984		
科技重大专项	Special science and Technology Major	43000	43000		
其他科学技术支出	Other Expenditure For Science & Technology	109988	106429	3034	525

20-7 分地区高新技术企业情况（2012 年）
STATISTICS ON HIGH AND NEW TECHNOLOGY ENTERPRISES BY REGION（2012）

指标	Item	全市 Whole Municipality	其中 of which 市区 Urban Area	溧阳市 Liyang City	金坛市 Jintan City
年末高新技术企业数（家）	Number of High and New Technology Enterprises at Year-end （unit）	797	710	41	46
# 当年确认数	Confirmed Number at Current Year	208	187	9	12
企业总产值（亿元）	Gross Output Value of Enterprises （100 million yuan ）	2091.15	1773.20	185.39	132.56
新技术产品产值（亿元）	Output Value of New Technological Products （100 million yuan ）	934.76	782.06	89.50	63.20
出口创汇总额（亿美元）	Total Exports （USD 100 million）	69.44	58.28	4.37	6.79
利税总额（亿元）	Total Amount of Pre-tax （100 million yuan ）	199.42	179.70	16.45	3.27
研究与开发经费（亿元）	Research and Development Funds （100 million yuan ）	85.18	71.51	8.91	4.76
职工总数（万人）	Number of staff and workers （10000 persons）	21.58	18.76	1.32	1.50

20-8　分地区高新技术产品情况（2012 年）
STATISTICS ON HIGH AND NEW TECHNOLOGICAL PRODUCTS BY REGION（2012）

指 标	Item	全 市 Whole Municipality	其中 of which 市 区 Urban Area	溧阳市 Liyang City	金坛市 Jintan City
省级高新技术产品累计数（只）	Accumulated Number of High and New Technological Products at Provincial Level （unit）	2803	2425	281	97
当年经省确认的高新技术产品数（只）	Number of High and New Technological Products Confirmed by the Province at This Year （unit）	819	675	107	37

20-9　技术（市场）贸易情况（2012 年）
STATISTICS ON TECHNOLOGY （MARKET） TRADE（2012）

指 标	Item	全 市 Whole Municipality
网上登记技术合同（项）	Number of Online Registered Technology Contracts （unit）	1856
网上登记技术合同成交金额（万元）	Business Volume of Online Registered Technology Contracts （10000 yuan）	222300

20-10　科技企业孵化器、加速器情况（2012 年）
STATISTICS ON SCIENTIFIC AND TECHNOLOGICAL ENTERPRISE INCUBATORS AND ACCELERATORS（2012）

指 标	Item	全 市 Whole Municipality	其中 of which 市 区 Urban Area	溧阳市 Liyang City	金坛市 Jintan City
孵化器个数（个）	Number of Incubators and Accelerators（unit）	64	58	4	2
#省级以上	Provincial Level and Above	34	30	2	2
场地面积（万平方米）	Site Area （10000 square meters）	501	446	39	16
#省级以上	Provincial Level and Above	330	290	24	16
本年在孵企业数（家）	Number of Entered Enterprises（unit）	4260	3895	218	147
#省级以上	Provincial Level and Above	2995	2678	170	147
在孵企业总收入（万元）	Gross Income of Entered Enterprises（10000 yuan）	1228076	1154779	66797	6500
#省级以上	Provincial Level and Above	791855	723937	61418	6500
在孵企业从业人员数（人）	Persons Employed in Entered Enterprises（person）	47054	39493	6556	1005
累计毕业企业数（家）	Accumulated Number of Incubated Enterprises （unit）	901	817	57	27
#当年毕业企业数	Number of Incubated Enterprises at Current Year	189	176	6	7

20-11 分地区规模以上工业企业科技活动情况（2012 年）
SCIENTIFIC AND TECHNOLOGICAL ACTIVITIES OF ABOVE-SCALE INDUSTRIAL ENTERPRISES BY REGION（2012）

指 标	Item	全 市 Whole Municipality	其中 of which 市 区 Urban Area	溧阳市 Liyang City	金坛市 Jintan City
企业基本情况	**Statistics on Industrial Enterprises**				
有 R&D 活动企业数（个）	Number of Enterprises Having R&D Activities（unit）	1143	939	133	71
有 R&D 活动企业所占比重（%）	Percentage of Enterprises Having R&D Activities to Total Number of Enterprises（%）	30.5	30.8	39.6	19.8
R&D 活动情况	**Statistics on R&D Activities**				
R&D 人员（人）	Total Number of R&D Personnel（person）	44198	36705	5227	2266
R&D 经费内部支出（万元）	Intramural Expenditure on R&D（10000 yuan）	949118	731329	128506	89284
R&D 项目数（项）	Total Number of R&D Projects（unit）	4171	3331	493	347
企业办科技机构情况	**Scientific and Technological Institutions Run by Enterprises**				
企业办科技机构数（个）	Number of Scientific and Technological Institutions Run by Enterprises（unit）	1364	1061	161	142
机构科技活动人员（人）	Number of Scientific and Technological Personnel in Technological Institutions（person）	42023	35488	4289	2246
# 博士生	Ph.D. Owners	546	372	118	56
硕士生	Master's Degree Owners	2805	2327	286	192
新产品开发及生产情况	**Statitstics on New Product Development and Production**				
新产品开发项目数（个）	Number of New Products（unit）	5339	4379	580	380
新产品开发经费支出（万元）	Expenditure on New Product Development（10000 yuan）	1299301	1039369	156249	103683
新产品产值（万元）	Output Value of New Products（10000 yuan）	15042992	12671791	1685798	685403
新产品销售收入（万元）	Sales Income of New Products（10000 yuan）	14753350	12419800	1703761	629790
# 新产品出口	Export	2852618	2655903	62096	134620
专利情况	**Statistics on Patent**				
专利申请数（件）	Patent Applications（piece）	8852	7607	758	487
# 发明专利	Inventions	2629	2008	380	241
有效发明专利数（件）	Number of Patents In Force（piece）	3613	3047	370	196
技术改造和技术获取情况	**Technical Innovation and Technology Acquisition**				
引进技术经费支出（万元）	The Introduction of Technology Expenditures（10000 yuan）	32476	29027	2178	1272
消化吸收经费支出（万元）	Digestion and Absorption of Expenditures（10,000 yuan）	15443	9504	4821	1118
购买国内技术经费支出（万元）	Expenditure on Purchasing Domestic Technology（10000 yuan）	19482	9267	9258	957
技术改造经费支出（万元）	Appropriation Expenditure on Technical Inovation（10000 yuan）	1767608	1556279	144441	66889

20-12　分地区大中型工业企业科技活动情况（2012 年）
SCIENTIFIC AND TECHNOLOGICAL ACTIVITIES OF LARGE AND MEDIUM INDUSTRIAL ENTERPRISES BY REGION（2012）

指　标	Item	全　市 Whole Municipality	其中 of which 市　区 Urban Area	溧阳市 Liyang City	金坛市 Jintan City
企业基本情况	**Statistics on Industrial Enterprises**				
有 R&D 活动企业数（个）	Number of Enterprises Having R&D Activities（unit）	408	340	40	28
有 R&D 活动企业所占比重（%）	Percentage of Enterprises Having R&D Activities to Total Number of Enterprises（%）	70.3	75.1	70.2	40.0
R&D 活动情况	**Statistics on R&D Activities**				
R&D 人员（人）	Total Number of R&D Personnel（person）	28856	24575	2854	1427
R&D 经费内部支出（万元）	Intramural Expenditure on R&D（10000 yuan）	657440	508707	82192	66541
R&D 项目数（项）	Total Number of R&D Projects（unit）	2102	1721	210	171
企业办科技机构情况	**Scientific and Technological Institutions Run by Enterprises**				
企业办科技机构数（个）	Number of Scientific and Technological Institutions Run by Enterprises（unit）	632	492	62	78
机构科技活动人员（人）	Number of Scientific and Technological Personnel In Technological Institutions（person）	28226	24516	2349	1361
# 博士生	Ph.D. Owners	306	226	50	30
硕士生	Master's Degree Owners	1914	1654	144	116
新产品开发及生产情况	**Statitstics on New Product Development and Production**				
新产品开发项目数（个）	Number of New Products（unit）	2721	2241	304	176
新产品开发经费支出（万元）	Expenditure on New Product Development（10000 yuan）	915479	734495	108161	72823
新产品产值（万元）	Output Value of New Products（10000 yuan）	11656761	10022590	1051488	582683
新产品销售收入（万元）	Sales Income of New Products（10000 yuan）	11348554	9733502	1079488	535563
# 新产品出口	Export	2346147	2180653	55082	110412
专利情况	**Statistics on Patent**				
专利申请数（件）	Patent Applications（piece）	4039	3545	234	260
# 发明专利	Inventions	1179	921	120	138
有效发明专利数（件）	Number of Patents In Force（piece）	1711	1432	146	133
技术改造和技术获取情况	**Technical Innovation and Technology Acquisition**				
引进技术经费支出（万元）	The Introduction of Technology Expenditures（10000 yuan）	24937	21759	2178	1000
消化吸收经费支出（万元）	Digestion and Absorption of Expenditures（10,000 yuan）	9119	5915	2240	964
购买国内技术经费支出（万元）	Expenditure on Purchasing Domestic Technology（10000 yuan）	11394	3781	6733	880
技术改造经费支出（万元）	Appropriation Expenditure on Technical Inovation（10000 yuan）	1163366	1007331	99255	56779

20-13 历年各类学校数
NUMBER OF SCHOOLS BY TYPE OVER THE YEARS

单位：所（unit）

年份 Year	合计 Total	其中 of which			
		# 普通高等院校 Institutions of Higher Education	普通中等专业学校 Specialized Secondary Schools	普通中学 Regular Secondary Schools	小学 Primary Schools
1949	1666		3	54	1607
1950	1865		4	52	1807
1951	1983		5	54	1923
1952	2076		5	55	2015
1953	2033		3	55	1974
1954	2017		2	58	1956
1955	2003		2	59	1941
1956	2281		3	66	2211
1957	2138		2	68	2067
1958	2862	4	9	110	2465
1959	2921	3	9	116	2634
1960	2651	3	10	123	2367
1961	2436	2	6	116	2217
1962	2391		2	117	2245
1963	2348		2	116	2199
1964	3181		2	115	2974
1965	3726		2	103	3322
1966	3252		5	117	2855
1967	3038		5	120	2636
1968	2907		5	129	2467
1969	2615		4	183	2380
1970	2649		4	192	2445
1971	2712		5	308	2390
1972	2736		6	333	2390
1973	2769		6	300	2457
1974	2638		7	345	2281
1975	2641		8	427	2201
1976	2691		7	635	2043
1977	2612		7	632	1967
1978	2477		8	509	1952
1979	2466		10	478	1968
1980	2490		13	360	2104

20-13　续表　Continued　　单位：所（unit）

年 份 Year	合 计 Total	其中 of which #普通高等院校 Institutions of Higher Education	普通中等专业学校 Specialized Secondary Schools	普通中学 Regular Secondary Schools	小 学 Primary Schools
1981	2386	2	12	266	2093
1982	2400	2	11	282	2092
1983	2369	2	11	278	2061
1984	2294	2	14	282	1974
1985	2253	3	14	275	1933
1986	2212	3	15	270	1895
1987	2176	3	16	266	1862
1988	2136	3	16	260	1830
1989	2072	3	16	248	1776
1990	2021	3	16	235	1736
1991	1955	3	17	219	1678
1992	1822	3	16	212	1550
1993	1758	3	16	205	1497
1994	1633	3	16	199	1374
1995	1597	3	17	201	1332
1996	1448	3	17	193	1189
1997	1228	3	17	184	978
1998	1018	3	17	178	771
1999	927	3	17	176	683
2000	816	3	14	174	581
2001	736	5	12	177	498
2002	681	8	8	177	450
2003	550	8	8	174	327
2004	528	9	8	173	307
2005	499	9	7	172	284
2006	468	9	8	172	252
2007	446	9	8	169	234
2008	430	9	8	168	221
2009	408	9	8	166	206
2010	388	9	12	163	190
2011	384	9	13	162	186
2012	382	9	12	162	187

20-14 历年在校学生数 NUMBER OF STUDENTS OVER THE YEARS

单位：人（person）

年 份 Year	合 计 Total	其中 of which # 普通高等院校 Institutions of Higher Education	普通中等专业学校 Specialized Secondary Schools	普通中学 Regular Secondary Schools	小 学 Primary Schools
1949	154997		586	13223	140949
1950	158060		855	12568	144402
1951	186276		1404	16334	168353
1952	260160		1919	25587	221884
1953	270719		923	28973	230248
1954	264525		740	31813	231904
1955	284551		726	34113	249646
1956	311969		1243	30826	279829
1957	321017		1010	44123	275815
1958	416767	1069	2099	53013	338334
1959	436537	855	2991	59030	351695
1960	475975	1004	4614	65497	380691
1961	424200	1037	3487	61509	347389
1962	361579		1406	50482	306269
1963	353245		571	47779	301894
1964	412149		213	50043	355244
1965	447588		468	5225	372321
1966	464351		1027	74009	382302
1967	441394		1113	69817	364815
1968	450651		890	60215	360821
1969	500982		479	95506	403911
1970	446826			90659	352914
1971	497600			102324	391535
1972	558081		625	134911	419129
1973	549911		1220	124534	422645
1974	574459		1785	128937	442630
1975	601646		1725	159492	439205
1976	614776		464	193235	419580
1977	645041		1203	261068	381334
1978	598917	434	1980	215461	379391
1979	561234	542	2962	185704	369719
1980	539645	481	3064	173164	360399

20-14　续表　Continued　　单位：人（person）

年 份 Year	合 计 Total	其中 of which # 普通高等院校 Institutions of Higher Education	普通中等专业学校 Specialized Secondary Schools	普通中学 Regular Secondary Schools	小 学 Primary Schools
1981	513322	1312	3686	161621	343001
1982	492065	1036	3878	158452	324956
1983	486181	1240	5100	161380	312593
1984	487492	2059	6655	155577	314954
1985	491522	3161	9717	148865	319954
1986	493492	4044	12462	150555	313588
1987	483933	4578	13657	150979	301508
1988	476768	4839	14024	147573	296839
1989	468608	5079	14777	146394	289683
1990	461007	5085	15715	149037	277043
1991	453827	5190	15616	153409	262497
1992	452175	5469	16799	157068	253370
1993	460296	8897	20868	153547	255823
1994	478422	10908	26562	155908	261261
1995	501879	11644	33885	158586	271583
1996	526262	12182	42918	157074	289272
1997	542890	13156	49260	149390	305431
1998	550361	14251	52981	146903	312446
1999	561141	15120	53704	159995	309019
2000	571011	20013	49925	182332	300091
2001	584831	26668	49267	203570	287717
2002	603213	35159	52535	221258	273755
2003	622271	53059	50887	229845	263522
2004	642190	73862	51821	228206	255632
2005	648778	95396	48848	220718	244589
2006	648373	107742	46247	215938	234874
2007	643540	119131	39477	211346	229781
2008	630821	123174	36448	205966	224181
2009	614813	125468	34523	199351	216791
2010	603938	122802	36029	188436	221533
2011	600423	123947	38231	177639	229035
2012	596907	124637	40527	169063	234305

20-15 教育事业基本情况（2012 年）
BASIC STATISTICS ON EDUCATION（2012）

单位：人（person）

指标	Item	学校数（所）Number of Schools（Unit）	毕业生数 Number of Graduates	招生数 Number of New Students Enrollment	在校学生数 Number of Students Enrollment	毕业班学生数 Number of Students in Graduate Class	教职工数 Number of Staff and Teachers	其中 of which # 专任教师 Number of Full-time Teachers
总　计	**Total**	**382**	**149775**	**160396**	**596907**	**139095**	**42593**	**34833**
按地区分	**Grouped by Region**							
市　区	Urban Area	244	114934	128851	467262	105829	30612	24738
溧阳市	Liyang City	80	21852	19422	78628	20563	6872	5681
金坛市	Jintan City	58	12989	12123	51017	12703	5109	4414
按学校类型分	**Grouped by Type of School**							
普通高等学校	Institutions of Higher Education	9	37087	40118	124637	38086	7735	5249
普通中等专业学校	Specilized Secondary Schools	12	5501	13253	40527	6693	3191	2565
技工学校	Technical Schools	7	9675	10096	26435		1264	717
职业中学	Vocational Schools		2291		1201	1201		
普通中学	Regular Secondary Schools	162	59015	55676	169063	56952	17357	13944
高　中	Senior Secondary Schools	36	21929	18803	59856	20963		4772
初　中	Junior Secondary Schools	126	37086	36873	109207	35989		9172
小　学	Primary Schools	187	36122	41132	234305	36163	12906	12257
特殊教育学校	Special Education Schools	5	84	121	739		140	101

20-16 市区教育事业基本情况（2012 年）
BASIC STATISTICS ON EDUCATION OF URBAN AREA（2012）

单位：人（person）

指标	Item	学校数（所）Number of Schools（Unit）	毕业生数 Number of Graduates	招生数 Number of New Students Enrollment	在校学生数 Number of Students Enrollment	毕业班学生数 Number of Students in Graduate Class	教职工数 Number of Staff and Teachers	其中 of which # 专任教师 Number of Full-time Teachers
总　计	**Total**	**244**	**114934**	**128851**	**467262**	**105829**	**30612**	**24738**
普通高等学校	Institutions of Higher Education	9	36750	39756	123949	37760	7735	5249
普通中等专业学校	Specilized Secondary Schools	9	4190	9357	29338	3940	2333	1844
技工学校	Technical Schools	6	9553	9844	25719		1212	679
职业中学	Vocational Schools							
普通中学	Regular Secondary Schools	100	38637	38845	115507	38012	10808	8756
高 中	Senior Secondary Schools	24	13918	12082	37871	13099		2943
初 中	Junior Secondary Schools	76	24719	26763	77636	24913		5813
小 学	Primary Schools	117	25726	30940	172145	26117	8405	8119
特殊教育学校	Special Education Schools	3	78	109	604		119	91

20-17 成人教育基本情况（2012 年）
BASIC STATISTICS ON ADULT EDUCATION（2012）

单位：人（person）

指 标	Item	学校数（所）Number of Schools (Unit)	毕业生数 Number of Graduates	招生数 Number of New Students Enrollment	在校学生数 Number of Students Enrollment	毕业班学生数 Number of Students in Graduate Class	教职工数 Number of Staff and Teachers	其中 of which #专任教师 Number of Full-time Teachers
总 计	**Total**	**268**	**1019594**	**14585**	**927777**	**12432**	**6247**	**5033**
按地区分	**Grouped by Region**							
市 区	Urban Area	180	764294	14585	817548	12432	4842	3850
溧阳市	Liyang City	46	148100		16316		566	451
金坛市	Jintan City	42	107200		93913		839	732
按学校类型分	**Grouped by Type of School**							
成人高等学校	Institutions of Higher Education for Adults	1	22344	14585	31034	12432	554	422
成人中等专业学校	Specialized Secondary Schools for Adults	2			136		16	11
成人中学	Secondary School for Adults	1	49		31		12	9
职业技术培训学校	Technical Training School for Adults	264	997201		896576		5665	4591

20-18 市区成人教育基本情况（2012 年）
BASIC STATISTICS ON URBAN ADULT EDUCATION（2012）

单位：人（person）

指 标	Item	学校数（所）Number of Schools (Unit)	毕业生数 Number of Graduates	招生数 Number of New Students Enrollment	在校学生数 Number of Students Enrollment	毕业班学生数 Number of Students in Graduate Class	教职工数 Number of Staff and Teachers	其中 of which #专任教师 Number of Full-time Teachers
总 计	**Total**	**180**	**764294**	**14585**	**817548**	**12432**	**4842**	**3850**
成人高等学校	Institutions of Higher Education of Adults	1	22344	14585	31034	12432	554	422
成人中等专业学校	Specialized Secondary Schools for Adults	1						
职业技术培训学校	Technical Training School for Adults	178	741950		786514		4288	3428

20-19 分地区中小学专任教师学历和职称情况（2012 年）
EDUCATIONAL BACKGROUNDS AND PROFESSIONAL TITLES OF FULL-TIME TEACHERS IN MIDDLE SCHOOL AND PRIMARY SCHOOLS BY REGION（2012）

单位：人（person）

指标	Item	全市 Whole Munici pality	其中 of which		
			市区 Urban Area	溧阳市 Liyang City	金坛市 Jintan City
总计	**Total**	**26201**	**16875**	**5208**	**4118**
高中	**Senior Secondary School**	**4772**	**2943**	**1035**	**794**
按学历分	Grouped by Educational Background				
研究生毕业	Postgraduate	434	238	85	111
本科毕业	Graduate	4288	2665	947	676
专科毕业	Junior College	49	39	3	7
高中阶段毕业	Senior Secondary School	1	1		
按职称分	Grouped by Professional Titles				
中学高级	Senior Teacher	1574	1048	271	255
中学一级	Teacher 1st Grade	1979	1249	398	332
中学二级	Teacher 2nd Grade	1130	572	352	206
中学三级	Teacher 3rd Grade	4	3		1
未定职级	Unspecified Position Level	85	71	14	
初中	**Junior Secondary School**	**9172**	**5813**	**1845**	**1514**
按学历分	Grouped by Educational Background				
研究生毕业	Postgraduate	214	155	37	22
本科毕业	Graduate	8231	5196	1707	1328
专科毕业	Junior College	694	440	98	156
高中阶段毕业	Senior Secondary School	32	21	3	8
高中阶段毕业以下	Under Senior Secondary School	1	1		
按职称分	Grouped by Professional Titles				
中学高级	Senior Teacher	2561	1646	463	452
中学一级	Teacher 1st Grade	4280	2610	929	741
中学二级	Teacher 2nd Grade	2031	1337	400	293
中学三级	Teacher 3rd Grade	36	11	16	10
未定职级	Unspecified Position Level	264	209	37	18
小学	**Primary School**	**12257**	**8119**	**2328**	**1810**
按学历分	Grouped by Educational Background				
研究生毕业	Postgraduate	114	97	12	5
本科毕业	Graduate	9272	5957	1837	1478
专科毕业	Junior College	2386	1738	366	282
高中阶段毕业	Senior Secondary School	484	326	113	45
高中阶段毕业以下	Under Senior Secondary School	1	1		
按职称分	Grouped by Professional Titles				
中学高级、	Senior Teacher of Secondary School	1976	1226	376	374
小学高级	Senior Teacher of Primary School	7098	4570	1496	1032
小学一级	Teacher 1st Grade	2541	1766	426	349
小学二级	Teacher 2nd Grade	116	93	2	21
小学三级	Teacher 3rd Grade				
未定职级	Unspecified Position Level	526	464	28	34

20-20　普通高校基本情况（2012 年）
BASIC CONDITIONS OF INSTITUTIONS OF HIGHER EDUCATION（2012）

单位：人（person）

学校名称	Name of Institutions	招生数 Number of New Students Enrollment	在校学生数 Number of Students Enrollment	毕业班学生数 Number of Students in Graduate Class	教职工数 Number of Staff and Teachers	其中 of which #专任教师 Number of Full-time Teachers
总　计	**Total**	**40118**	**124637**	**38086**	**7735**	**5249**
常州大学	Changzhou University	3611	13492	3265	1197	807
江苏技术师范学院	Jiangsu Teacher's College of Technology	3287	11891	2628	1130	804
常州工学院	Changzhou Institute of Technology	2425	8324	1766	1085	720
常州信息职业技术学院	Changzhou Vocational Technological College of Information	3790	10725	3282	635	475
常州纺织服装职业技术学院	Changzhou Technical College of Textile and Garment	3339	9809	3213	630	446
常州轻工职业技术学院	Changzhou Vocational Technological College of Light Industry	3416	9828	3156	574	395
常州工程职业技术学院	Changzhou Vocational Technological College of Engineering	3466	9666	2887	713	479
常州机电职业技术学院	Changzhou Vocational Technological College of Electromechanical	3439	9899	3269	662	423
建东职业技术学院（民办）	Jiandong College （Private）	1783	4599	1673	264	158
河海大学常州校区	Hohai University Changzhou Branch	1518	5885	1508	599	333
常州大学怀德学院	Changzhou University Huaide College	1498	6032	1733	246	209
常州工学院延陵学院	Yanlin Campus of Changzhou Instutute of Technology	1175	6169	1911		
江苏技术师范学院东方学院	Dongfang Campus of Jiangsu Teachers University of Technology	1151	5188	1605		
江苏城市职业学院常州办学点	Changzhou Campus of The City Vocational College Of Jiangsu	519	1615	701		
江苏城市职业学院武进办学点	Wujin Campus of The City Vocational College Of Jiangsu	763	2114	912		
江苏城市职业学院金坛办学点	Jintan Campus of The City Vocational College Of Jiangsu	129	252	123		
江苏城市职业学院溧阳办学点	Liyang Campus of The City Vocational College Of Jiangsu	233	436	203		
江苏联合职业技术学院常州分院	Changzhou Campuses of Jiangsu Union Technical Institute	4342	8346	4118		
江苏教育学院常州学前教育分院	Changzhou Pre-school Campus of Jiangsu Institute of Education	234	367	133		

20-21 中等专业学校基本情况（2012 年）
BASIC CONDITIONS OF SPECIALIZED SECONDARY SCHOOLS（2012）

单位：人（person）

学校名称	Name of Institutions	招生数 Number of New Students Enrollment	在校学生数 Number of Students Enrollment	毕业班学生数 Number of Students in Graduate Class	教职工数 Number of Staff and Teachers	其中 of which #专任教师 Number of Full-time Teachers
总　计	**Total**	**13253**	**40527**	**6693**	**3191**	**2565**
江苏省常州建设高等职业技术学校	Jiangsu Changzhou Higher Vocational School of Construction	1394	4464	378	386	285
常州铁道高等职业技术学校	Changzhou Railway Vocational Technical School	732	2220	326	203	140
常州卫生高等职业技术学校	Changzhou Senior Vocational School of Health	852	2690	168	182	132
常州艺术高等职业学校	Changzhou Art Vocational College of Jiangsu Province	425	1497	19	134	101
常州刘国钧高等职业技术学校	Changzhou Liu Guojun Higher Vocational School	1169	3510	287	327	278
常州旅游商贸高等职业技术学校	Changzhou Tourism and Commerce Vocational Technology Academy	1214	4008	525	340	286
常州市体育运动学校	Changzhou Sports School	122	284	106	36	34
常州职业中等专业学校	Changzhou Vocational Secondary School	125	521	255		
常州幼儿师范学校	Kindergarten Normal School	622	1752	327	144	106
江苏省武进中等专业学校	Jiangsu Wujin Vocational Secondary School	1954	5819	1549	581	482
江苏省溧阳中等专业学校	Jiangsu Liyang Vocational Secondary School	1518	4807	1814	363	292
江苏省溧阳市天目湖中等专业学校	Tianmuhu Specialized Secondary School, Liyang, Jiangsu	868	1885		205	178
江苏省金坛中等专业学校	Jiangsu Jintan Vocational Secondary School	1079	3212	939	290	251
常州市广播电视大学	Changzhou Radio and TV University	107	565			
江苏省城市职业学院武进办学点	Jiangsu City Vocational Institute Wujin Campus	641	2008			
江苏省城市职业学院溧阳办学点	Jiangsu City Vocational Institute Liyang Campus	259	803			
江苏省城市职业学院金坛办学点	Jiangsu City Vocational Institute Jintan Campus	172	482			

20-22　技工学校基本情况（2012 年）
BASIC CONDITIONS OF TECHNICAL SCHOOLS（2012）

单位：人（person）

学校名称	Name of School	招生数 Number of New Students Enrollment	在校学生数 Number of Students Enrollment	其中 of which #高级班 Senior Classes	毕业生数 Number of Students in Graduate Class	教职工数 Staff and Teachers
总　计	**Total**	**10096**	**26435**	**10542**	**9675**	**1264**
江苏省常州技师学院	Changzhou Technician College Jiangsu Province（Main Campus）	4747	12525	4564	5109	624
常州交通技师学院	Changzhou Communication College of Technician	1413	3871	917	1223	130
常州冶金技师学院	Changzhou Metallurgy College of Technician	568	2319	681	1200	89
常州航空技工学校	Changzhou Aviation Technical School	686	1543	170	508	62
常州市工贸技工学校	Changzhou Industry and Trade Technical School	862	1369	1274		98
常州市武进技工学校	Changzhou Wujin Technical School	1568	4092	2492	1513	209
金坛市技工学校	Jintan Technical School	252	716	444	122	52

20-23　中小学师资配备情况（2012 年）
TEACHERS IN MIDDLE SCHOOLS AND PRIMARY SCHOOLS（2012）

指　标	Item	班级数（个） Number of Classes（unit）	学生数（人） Number of Students（person）	教师数（人） Number of Teachers（person）	每班教师数（人/班） Number of Teachers Per Class（persons/class）	每一教师负担学生数（人） Student-Teacher Ratio（person）
小　学	Primary Schools	5301	234305	12257	2.31	19.12
#市　区	Urban Area	3797	172145	8119	2.14	21.20
初　中	Junior Secondary Schools	2554	109207	9172	3.59	11.91
#市　区	Urban Area	1722	77636	5813	3.38	13.36
高　中	Senior Secondary Schools	1254	59856	4772	3.81	12.54
#市　区	Urban Area	796	37871	2943	3.70	12.87

20-24 分地区幼儿教育基本情况（2012 年）
BASIC STATISTICS ON INFANT EDUCATION BY REGION（2012）

单位：人（person）

指 标	Item	全 市 Whole Municipality	其 中 of which 市 区 Urban Area	溧阳市 Liyang City	金坛市 Jintan City
学校数（所）	Number of Schools （unit）	232	138	63	31
毕业生数	Number of Graduates of Kindergartens	35526	25141	6475	3910
招生数	Number of New Students Enrollment	40328	30430	5653	4245
在校学生数	Number of Students Enrollment	107853	77029	18720	12104
教职工数	Number of Staff & Teachers	9405	6812	1668	925
# 专任教师	Full-time Teachers	6030	4410	1042	578

20-25 分地区升学率、入学率（2012 年）
PERCENTAGE OF GRADUATES AND ENROLLMENT RATE BY REGION（2012）

单位：%

指 标	Item	全 市 Whole Municipality	其 中 of which 市 区 Urban Area	溧阳市 Liyang City	金坛市 Jintan City
小学入学率	Enrollemnt Rate in Primary Schools	100.0	100.0	100.0	100.0
小学升学率	Percentage of Graduates in Primary Schools	102.1	104.0	97.0	97.6
初中入学率	Enrollemnt Rate in Junior Secondary Schools	100.0	100.0	100.0	100.0
初中升学率	Percentage of Graduates in Junior Secondary Schools	99.94	99.96	99.91	99.91

20-26　分地区每一专任教师负担学生数（2012 年）
STUDENT-TEACHER OF FULL-TIME RATIO BY REGION（2012）

单位：人（person）

指　标	Item	全　市 Whole Municipality	其　中 of which 市　区 Urban Area	溧阳市 Liyang City	金坛市 Jintan City
总　计	**Total**	**17.16**	**18.93**	**13.83**	**11.57**
普通高等学校	Institutions of Higher Education	23.74	23.61		
普通中等职技校	Regular Secondary Vocation & Technical School	20.77	21.82	18.50	15.26
普通中学	Regular Secondary Schools	12.12	13.19	11.10	9.35
小　学	Primary Schools	19.12	21.20	16.08	13.66

20-27　分地区每万人拥有在校学生数（2012 年）
NUMBER OF STUDENTS ENROLLMENT PER 10000 PERSONS BY REGION（2012）

单位：人（person）

指　标	Item	全　市 Whole Municipality	其　中 of which 市　区 Urban Area	溧阳市 Liyang City	金坛市 Jintan City
总　计	**Total**	**1642.97**	**2037.99**	**997.49**	**924.35**
普通高等学校	Institutions of Higher Education	343.49	541.31	5.54	4.57
普通中等职技校	Regular Secondary Vocation & Technical School	187.85	240.44	110.45	79.96
普通中学	Regular Secondary Schools	465.92	504.44	406.08	391.39
小　学	Primary Schools	645.72	751.79	475.41	448.43

20-28 分地区文化事业机构数（2012 年底）
NUMBER OF INSTITUTIONS OF CULTURE BY REGION（END OF 2012）

单位：个（unit）

指 标	Item	全 市 Whole Municipality	其中 of which 市 区 Urban Area	溧阳市 Liyang City	金坛市 Jintan City
艺术事业	**Art**				
艺术表演团体	Art Performance Troupes	11	9	1	1
艺术表演场所	Art Performance Places	7	5	1	1
图书馆	**Libraries**	**4**	**2**	**1**	**1**
群众文化事业	**Mass Cultural**				
博物馆	Museums	19	17	1	1
群众艺术馆、文化馆	Mass Art Centers and Cultural Centers	8	6	1	1
文化站（文化部门）	Cultural Stations （Cultural Department）	59	41	10	8
教育事业	**Education**	**1**	**1**		
其他文化事业	**Others**	**9**	**6**		**3**

20-29 分地区文化事业人员数（2012 年底）
NUMBER OF PERSONS ENGAGED IN CULTURE BY REGION（END OF 2012）

单位：人（person）

指 标	Item	全 市 Whole Municipality	其中 of which 市 区 Urban Area	溧阳市 Liyang City	金坛市 Jintan City
艺术事业	**Art**				
艺术表演团体	Art Performance Troupes	331	253	48	30
艺术表演场所	Art Performance Places	468	433		35
图书馆	**Libraries**	**136**	**105**	**19**	**12**
群众文化事业	**Mass Cultural**				
博物馆	Museums	267	211	18	38
群众艺术馆、文化馆	Mass Art Centers and Cultural Centers	106	78	16	12
文化站（文化部门）	Cultural Stations （Cultural Department）	247	183	41	23
教育事业	**Education**	**132**	**132**		
其他文化事业	**Others**	**27**	**23**		**4**

20-30 分地区博物馆、图书馆基本情况（2012 年）
BASIC STATISTICS ON MUSEUMS AND LIBRARIES BY REGION（2012）

指 标	Item	全 市 Whole Municipality	其中 of which 市 区 Urban Area	溧阳市 Liyang City	金坛市 Jintan City
博物馆	**Museums**				
文物藏品（件）	Number of Collections （piece）	209806	189962	11760	8084
# 一级品	Grade One	72	58	3	11
参观人次（千人次）	Number of Visitors （1000 person-times）	1623	1108	360	155
图书馆	**Libraries**				
总藏量（千册、千件）	Total Collections （1000 volumes）	3754	3170	333	251
# 图 书	Books Published	2080	1596	295	189
# 古 籍	Ancient Books	118	116	1	1
报 刊	Newspapers and Magazines	267	225	8	34
图书流通人次（千人次）	Number of Books Circulation（1000 persons-times）	1881	1560	200	121

20-31 分地区艺术事业基本情况（2012 年）
BASIC STATISTICS ON ART BY REGION（2012）

指 标	Item	全 市 Whole Municipality	其中 of which 市 区 Urban Area	溧阳市 Liyang City	金坛市 Jintan City
艺术表演场所	**Art Performance Places**				
座席数（个）	Number of Seats （unit）	8173	6499	1230	444
演（映）出场次（场）	Number of Performance （time）	34877	30152		4725
# 电影放映场次	Number of Films Projection	34072	29347		4725
观众人次（千人次）	Number of Spectators （1000 persons-times）	1332	1234		98
# 电影放映	Films Projection	1173	1075		
艺术表演团体	**Art Performance Troupes**				
新排上演节目（个）	Newly Staged Shows （unit）	3	2	1	
# 本团创作首演剧目	First Performance Drama created by the Troupe	3	2	1	
国内演出场次（场）	Number of Domestic Performance （time）	3630	3138	140	352
国内观众人次（千人次）	Number of Domestic Spectators （1000 persons-times）	1800	1278	170	352

20-32 广播电视事业基本情况（2012 年）
BASIC STATISTICS ON BROADCASTING AND TELEVISION（2012）

指 标	Item	全 市 Whole Municipality	其中 of which # 市 区 Urban Area
广 播	Broadcasting		
广播电台数（座）	Number of Broadcasting Stations （unit）	4	2
对内广播节目套数（套）	Number of Home Broadcasting Programs （set）	7	5
广播全年自办播出时间（小时）	Broadcasting Hours of the Whole Year （hour）	44208	34310
广播全年自制节目时间（小时）	Broadcasting Self-made Program Hours of the Whole Year （hour）	35258	28315
中、短波发射台（座）	Number of Broadcasting Transmitting Stations with Medium and Short Wave（unit）	1	1
广播人口综合覆盖率（%）	Listener Rating （%）	100	100
电 视	Television		
电视台数（座）	Number of Television Station （unit）	4	2
自办电视节目套数（套）	Number of Television Programs （set）	8	5
电视节目全年自办播出时间（小时）	Broadcasting Hours of Television Program of the Whole Year （hour）	56285	44368
电视全年自制节目时间（小时）	Time of Self-made Television Program of the Whole Year （hour）	30313	24106
电视发射台数（座）	Number of Television Transmitting Stations （unit）	4	2
电视综合覆盖率（%）	Televiewer Rating （%）	100	100
有线广播电视	Wire Broadcasting and Television		
模拟有线广播电视传输节目（套）	Number of Modeling Cable Radio & TV Programs （set）	8	8
数字有线广播电视传输节目套数（套）	Number of Digital Cable TV Programmes（set）	170	170
# 标清广播电视传输节目套数	Number of SDTV Programmes	159	159
高清广播电视传输节目套数	Number of HDTV Programmes	11	11
有线电视用户数（万户）	Number of Subscribers of Wire Television （10000 households）	132.20	84.37
# 数字整体平移用户	Number of Overall Translated Digital Subscribers	108.96	84.37

20-33 分地区广播电视从业人员数（2012 年底）
NUMBER OF PERSONNEL ENGAGED IN BROADCASTING AND TELEVISION（END OF 2012）

单位：人（person）

指 标	Item	全 市 Whole Municipality	其 中 of which 市 区 Urban Area	溧阳市 Liyang City	金坛市 Jintan City
总 计	**Total**	**4934**	**3881**	**456**	**597**
行政管理人员	Administration Staff	1591	1354	20	217
专业人员	Professional Technical Personnel	1618	1106	194	318
编辑、记者	Editor and Reporter	368	260	50	58
播音员、主持人	Announcer and host	85	54	15	16
工程技术人员	Engineering and Technical Personnel	671	476	110	85
艺术人员	Artistic Personnel	172	170	2	
经营人员	Operating Personnel	106	92		14
其他人员	Others	1725	1421	242	62

21

CHAPTER 21

卫生 体育

HEALTH AND SPORTS

21 卫生　体育
HEALTH AND SPORTS

2012 年主要统计指标
MAJOR STATISTICAL INDICATORS OF 2012

年底全社会卫生事业机构数	Health Care Institutions （Year-end）	1128个	（unit）
年底卫生机构床位数	Beds of health Care Institutions （Year-end）	20497张	（bed）
年底医院（含妇保院）数	Number of Hospitals （Including Those of Women's and Children's Hospitals） By The End of The Year	46个	（unit）
年底医院（含妇保院）床位数	Number of Hospital Beds （Including Those of Women's and Children's Hospitals） By The End of The Year	14742张	（bed）
年底全社会卫生技术人员数	Medical Technial Personnel （Year-end）	25274人	（person）
#执业（助理）医师数	Practicing （Assistant） Doctors	10094人	（person）
等级裁判员发展人数	Number of Certified Referees	330人	（person）
等级运动员发展人数	Number of Certified Athletes	244人	（person）

21-1 历年卫生事业基本情况
BASIC STATISTICS ON PUBLIC HEALTH OVER THE YEARS

年份 Year	机构数（个） Institutions (unit)	其中 of which #医院（含妇保院）、卫生院 Hospitals (include Women-Children Health Care Hospitals) and Health Care Centers	床位数（张） Beds (bed)	其中 of which #医院（含妇保院）、卫生院 Hospitals (include Women-Children Health Care Hospitals) and Health Care Centers	卫生技术人员（人） Medical Technical Personnel (person)	其中 of which #医生 Doctors
1949	13	6	325	291	1450	1270
1950	19	6	376	371	1559	1315
1951	92	5	649	447	1752	1431
1952	249	5	970	675	2072	1625
1953	272	7	1296	1078	2378	1622
1954	296	7	1392	1049	2594	1641
1955	321	7	1930	1138	2877	1714
1956	359	8	2147	1222	2834	1963
1957	374	8	2171	1229	3020	2007
1958	440	105	3273	2449	3138	2036
1959	693	107	3824	2633	3884	2127
1960	926	133	4254	3350	4141	2118
1961	665	147	3929	3096	4381	2445
1962	531	94	3047	2277	4179	2577
1963	633	95	3489	2696	4362	2821
1964	509	89	3586	2828	4190	2653
1965	540	89	3975	3168	4245	2677
1966	444	146	4125	3199	3950	2467
1967	403	146	3024	2877	3944	2360
1968	337	152	3860	3164	3893	2265
1969	294	151	4166	3299	3656	2027
1970	426	147	5378	3767	3570	2083
1971	475	150	5893	4379	3868	2290
1972	466	150	6276	4631	4517	2332
1973	552	152	7063	5497	4916	2278
1974	527	154	8045	6021	5272	2389
1975	566	155	7802	5743	6027	2368
1976	621	156	8477	6368	6454	2668
1977	663	156	7401	5896	6973	2633
1978	684	158	8222	6982	7499	3021
1979	772	159	8371	7313	8194	3110
1980	803	159	8422	7337	8615	3238

21-1 续表 Continued

年 份 Year	机构数（个） Institutions (unit)	其中 of which #医院（含妇保院）、卫生院 Hospitals (include Women-Children Health Care Hospitals) and Health Care Centers	床位数（张） Beds (bed)	其 中 of which #医院（含妇保院）、卫生院 Hospitals (include Women-Children Health Care Hospitals) and Health Care Centers	卫生技术人员（人） Medical Technical Personnel (person)	其中 of which #医 生 Doctors
1981	814	161	9553	7864	9178	3749
1982	823	162	9474	7775	9711	4039
1983	802	160	9773	7937	9759	4198
1984	827	161	9282	7839	10061	4384
1985	831	162	9405	7993	10458	4437
1986	841	162	9883	8505	10957	4586
1987	859	163	10054	8734	11397	4570
1988	913	163	9996	8979	12098	5268
1989	881	163	10253	9313	12539	5923
1990	890	163	10460	9495	12942	6144
1991	880	163	10454	9538	13470	6345
1992	873	159	10607	9693	13695	6511
1993	855	160	11190	9992	13971	6411
1994	855	161	11138	10000	14580	6973
1995	855	161	11566	10339	14963	7073
1996	855	162	11268	10893	15538	7520
1997	833	161	11273	10843	16031	7567
1998	833	161	11223	10813	16405	7685
1999	824	161	11213	10803	16495	7680
2000	782	117	11143	10730	16731	7779
2001	769	114	11393	11030	16743	7737
2002	620	111	11842	11613	15242	6424
2003	625	111	12135	11687	15597	6592
2004	611	109	12352	11932	15707	6586
2005	1269	113	12474	11734	17859	8356
2006	1180	116	13247	12207	18414	8570
2007	1173	111	14696	14100	18091	8323
2008	1261	99	15113	14242	19795	8725
2009	1089	100	16170	15278	20244	9512
2010	1103	93	16701	15263	21921	9962
2011	1101	94	16936	15589	22877	10376
2012	1128	109	20497	19140	25274	10943

注：1、2002年起卫生技术人员包含领取医师执业证书和注册护士证书的人数以及药师（士）、技师（士）、其他卫技人员；
2、2005年起机构数的统计口径调整为含村级卫生室；
3、2008年起，规范城市社区和乡村卫生机构统计口径后，卫生院机构数有所减少。

Note: 1. Since year 2002, the medical technical personnel has been including Physician Practice Certificate holders, Registered Nurse Certificate holders, pharmacists, technicians and other medical technical personnel.
2. Since year 2005, the statistics of institution numbers has been including village health stations.
3. Since year 2008, the scope of statistics of health service institutions in urban communities and villages has been regulated, which caused the reduction of health service institutions.

21-2 分地区卫生事业机构数（2012 年底）
NUMBER OF HEALTH SERVICE INSTITUTIONS BY REGION（END OF 2012）

单位：个（unit）

指 标	Item	全 市 Whole Municipality	其中 of which 市 区 Urban Area	溧阳市 Liyang City	金坛市 Jintan City
总 计	**Total**	**1128**	**731**	**220**	**177**
医 院	Hospitals	44	27	11	6
非营利性医院	Non-profitmaking Hospitals	29	21	4	4
#综合医院	Polyclinics	26	14	9	3
中医医院	Hospitals for Maternity and Child Care	5	2	2	1
儿童医院	Children's Hospitals	1	1		
营利性医院	profitmaking Hospitals	15	6	7	2
卫生院、社区卫生服务中心（站）	Health Center and Community Health Service Center（Station）	209	161	20	28
门诊部	Outpatient Department	22	19		3
疗养院	Sanatoriums	1	1		
急救中心	First-aid Center	2	1		1
采供血机构	Flood Extraction and Supply Organizations	3	1	1	1
妇幼保健院（所、站）	Maternity and Child Care Centers（Office, Station）	8	6	1	1
专科疾病防治院（所、站）	Specialized Disease Prevention and Cure Hospitals（Office,Station）	2	1	1	
疾病预防控制中心（防疫站）	Disease Prevention and Control Centers（Epidemic Prevention Station）	8	6	1	1
卫生监督所	Sanitation Supervise Offices	8	6	1	1
医学科学研究机构	Institutions of Medical Sciences Research	2	2		
医学在职培训机构	On-the-job Training Institute of The Hospital	4	2	1	1
其他卫生机构	Other Health Institutions	3	3		
诊所、卫生保健所、医务室机构	Clinics, Health Care Centers and Medical Institutions	347	275	44	28
村卫生室	Village Health Station	464	219	139	106

21-3 分地区卫生机构床位和人员数（2012 年底）
HEALTH INSTITUTIONS, BEDS AND PERSONS ENGAGED BY REGION（END OF 2012）

指标	Item	全市 Whole Municipality	其中 of which 市区 Urban Area	溧阳市 Liyang City	金坛市 Jintan City
床位数（张）	**Number of Beds（bed）**	**20497**	**15859**	**2591**	**2047**
#医院（含妇保院）床位	Number of Hospital Beds（Including Those of Women's and Children's Hospitals）	14742	11568	1660	1514
卫生院床位	Number of Rural Township Hospital Beds	4428	3198	882	348
人员数（人）	**Personnel（person）**	**30771**	**23013**	**4622**	**3136**
卫生技术人员	Medical Technical Personnel	25274	19278	3521	2475
#执业（助理）医师	Practicing（Assistant）Doctors	10094	7404	1617	1073
注册护士	Certified Junior Nurses	10192	8042	1262	888
药剂师（士）	Pharmacists	1358	1025	170	163
技　师（士）	Technicians	1240	912	184	144
其他卫生技术人员	Other Medical Technical Personnel	2390	1895	288	207
其他技术人员	Other Technical Personnel	1197	923	119	155
管理人员	Managerial Personnel	1166	1025	106	35
工勤技能人员	Personnel with Professional Qualification Serving at Government and State-owned Enterprises	2135	1425	517	193

21-4　分地区乡卫生院运营情况（2012 年）
STATISTICS ON HOSPITALS AT AND ABOVE COUNTY LEVEL BY REGION（2012）

指标	Item	全市 Whole Municipality	其中 of which 市区 Urban Area	溧阳市 Liyang City	金坛市 Jintan City
机构数（个）	Number of Medical Institution （unit）	63	34	18	11
诊疗人次（万人次）	Number of Persons Diagnosed and Treated （10000 persons-times）	632.90	445.14	79.64	108.12
#门诊人次	Number of Outpatients	571.87	394.89	74.32	102.66
急诊人次	Number of Persons Received Emergency Treatment	42.86	35.03	3.11	4.72
健康检查（万人）	Health Examination （10000 persons）	35.25	20.58	11.33	3.34
出院人数（人）	Number of Patients Left Hospitals （person）	96191	56450	29743	9998

21-5　分地区医院运营情况（2012 年）
STATISTICS ON HOSPITALS OPERATION BY REGION（2012）

指标	Item	全市 Whole Municipality	其中 of which 市区 Urban Area	溧阳市 Liyang City	金坛市 Jintan City
医院（妇保院）（个）	Hospitals （Including Those of Womens' and Children's Hospitals）	46	28	12	6
诊疗人次（万人次）	Number of Persons Diagnosed and Treated （10000 persons-times）	1113.76	908.16	117.82	87.78
#门诊人次	Number of Outpatients	863.25	702.00	98.65	62.60
急诊人次	Number of Persons Received Emergency Treatment	162.16	139.05	14.03	9.08
健康检查（万人）	Health Examination （10000 persons）	59.37	42.99	7.50	8.88
出院人数（人）	Number of Patients Left Hospitals （person）	420660	329675	51911	39074
年末实有医院（含妇保院）床位数（张）	Number of Beds of Hospitals （include Women-Children Health Care Hospitals） by the End of Year （Bed）	14712	11538	1660	1514
病床周转次数（次）	Number of Turnover of Hospital Beds （time）	38	38	37	27
病床工作日（日）	Number of Days Per Bed in Use （day）	372	383	330	380
病床使用率（%）	Untilization Rate of Beds （%）	101.72	104.59	90.15	103.94
出院者平均住院日（日）	Average of Hospitalization Period （day）	10	10	9	14

21-6 分地区妇幼保健发展情况（2012 年）
STATISTICS ON HEALTH CARE FOR WOMEN AND CHILDREN BY REGION（2012）

指 标	Item	全 市 Whole Municipality	其中 of which 市 区 Urban Area	溧阳市 Liyang City	金坛市 Jintan City
婴儿死亡率（男，‰）	Death Rate of Infant（Boy，‰）	2.54	2.90	1.50	2.28
婴儿死亡率（女，‰）	Death Rate of Infant（Girl，‰）	2.58	2.94	2.30	1.00
5岁以下儿童死亡率（男，‰）	Death Rate of Child under 5 Years Old（Boy，‰）	4.14	4.80	2.50	3.19
5岁以下儿童死亡率（女，‰）	Death Rate of Child under 6 Years Old（Girl，‰）	4.23	4.24	4.02	4.51
围产儿死亡率（‰）	Death Rate of Perinatal Infant（‰）	5.07	5.80	2.40	3.94
新生儿疾病筛查率（%）	Rate of Selected Examination of Newborn Diseases（%）	97.31	97.48	96.96	96.97
新生儿出生缺陷发生率（‰）	Incidence of Congenital Anomalies of Newborn（‰）	5.83	6.77	2.54	4.15
7岁以下儿童保健管理率（%）	Rate of Health Care for Children under 7 Years Old（%）	98.87	98.62	99.13	99.77
5岁以下儿童中重度营养不良患病率（%）	Morbidity Rate of Moderate and Serious Malnutri-tion of Children under 5 Years（%）	0.29	0.15	0.35	0.31
孕产妇死亡率（1/10万）	Death Rate of Pregnant Women and Lying-in Women（1/100 thousand）	2.75	4.05		
妇女病普查率（%）	Rate of General Survey of Women's Disease（%）	95.11	93.65	95.70	99.09
孕产妇保健管理率（%）	System Management Rate of Pregnant Women and Lying-in Women（%）	99.77	99.96	99.03	100
住院分娩率（%）	Hospitalized Parturition Rate（%）	100	100	100	100
婚前医学检查率（%）	Antenuptial Medical Examination Ratio（%）	94.91	95.65	92.96	93.96
托幼机构卫生保健合格率（%）	Qualification Rate of Health-care in Nursery（%）	100	100	100	100

21-7 分地区体育事业情况（2012 年）
STATISTICS ON SPORTS CAUSE BY REGION（2012）

指 标	Item	全 市 Whole Municipality	其中 of which 市 区 Urban Area	溧阳市 Liyang City	金坛市 Jintan City
运动会	**Sports Meets**				
举办县级以上运动会次数（含单项）（次）	Number of Sports Meets Held at and above County Level（Including Individual Events）（time）	158	126	19	13
参加县级以上运动会人数（含单项）（人）	Number of Athletes Participating Sports Meets at and above County Level（Including Individual Events）（person）	42712	33956	5646	3110
等级运动员发展人数（人）	**Number of Athletes Developed in Grades（person）**	**244**	**218**	**11**	**15**
#女 性	Female	112	99	9	4
等级裁判员发展人数（人）	**Number of Referees Developed in Grades（person）**	**330**	**292**	**22**	**16**
#女 性	Female	128	120	6	2
公共体育运动场地	**Public Stadiums and Gymnasiums**				
体育场地个数（个）	Number of Stadiums and Gymnasiums（unit）	25	19	2	4
体育场	Stadiums	8	6	1	1
体育馆	Gymnasiums	10	8	0	2
室内外游泳池	Indoor and Outdoor Swimming Pools	7	5	1	1

注：等级运动员发展人数中不含三级运动员。
Note： The number of sportspersons with grade under development excludes those third grades.

21-8 参加体育竞赛获奖数（2012 年）
NUMBER OF PRIZES WON IN SPORTS GAMES（2012）

单位：枚（unit）

指 标	Item	金 牌 Gold Medals	银 牌 Silver Medals	铜 牌 Bronze Medals
总 计	**Total**	**131.5**	**127**	**110**
参加国际比赛获奖数	Number of Prizes Won in International Sports Games	6	6	1
参加全国比赛获奖数	Number of Prizes Won in National Sports Games	37	56	32
参加全省比赛获奖数	Number of Prizes Won in Provinical Sports Games	88.5	65	77

22

CHAPTER 22

民政 司法 其他

CIVIL ADMINISTRATION JUDICATURE AND OTHERS

常州统计年鉴

22 民政 司法 其他
CIVIL ADMINISTRATION JUDICATURE AND OTHERS

2012年主要统计指标
MAJOR STATISTICAL INDICATORS OF 2012

社会福利院数	Socail Welfare Institutions	3个	(unit)
精神病福利院数	Psychotics Welfare Institutions	1个	(unit)
老年福利机构数	Aged People's Homes	178个	(unit)
社会福利院床位数	Beds of Socail Welfare Institutions	1216张	(bed)
精神病福利院床位数	Beds of Psychotics Welfare Institutions	828张	(bed)
老年福利机构床位数	Beds of Aged People's Homes	24678张	(bed)
律师事务所	Lawyer Offices	91个	(unit)
专职律师数	Full-time Lawyers	986人	(person)
公证处数	Notary Public Offices	5个	(unit)
办理公证件数	Notarized Documents	38324件	(case)
人民调解委员会数	People's Mediation Committees	1541个	(unit)
调解民间纠纷数	Civil Disputes Mediated	27771件	(case)

22-1　分地区社会福利事业情况（2012 年底）
BASIC STATISTICS ON SOCIAL WELFARE BY REGION（END OF 2012）

指标	Item	全市 Whole Municipality	其中 of which 市区 Urban Area	溧阳市 Liyang City	金坛市 Jintan City
社会福利院	**Social Welfare Homes**				
院数（个）	Number of Homes（unit）	3	2		1
年底职工人数（人）	Number of Staff and Workers at Year-end（person）	144	139		5
年底床位数（张）	Number of Beds at Year-end（bed）	1216	806		410
年底在院人数（人）	Number of Persons Housed at Year-end（person）	673	625		48
#老　人	Elders	439	391		48
精神病福利院	**Mental Homes**				
院　数（个）	Number of Homes（unit）	1	1		
年底职工人数（人）	Number of Staff and Workers at Year-end（person）	233	233		
年底床位数（张）	Number of Beds at Year-end（bed）	828	828		
年底在院人数（人）	Number of Persons Housed at Year-end（person）	828	828		
老年福利机构	**Elderly Welfare Unit**				
单位数（个）	Number of Unit（unit）	178	125	21	32
年底职工人数（人）	Number of Staff and Workers at Year-end（person）	1560	996	255	309
年底床位数（张）	Number of Beds at Year-end（bed）	24678	16789	4585	3304
年底在院人数（人）	Number of Persons Housed at Year-end（person）	17442	11069	3402	2971
#老　人	Elders	17323	10989	3402	2932

注：老年福利机构床位数包括城镇各类养老机构（含公办和民办）、农村五保供养服务机构、以老年人为主的综合性社会福利机构、老年人社区日间照料机构、光荣院、农村老年人互助幸福院中的养老床位数之和。

Note:Note: The number of beds of social welfare institutions for the aged is the total number of beds of all kinds of institutions for the aged（including public and private ones）in cities and towns, institutions of the Five-guarantees System in rural areas, elderly-based comprehensive social welfare agencies, community day-care institutions for the aged, Guangrong Homes, and mutual-aid Xingfu Homes for the aged.

22-2　分地区集体社会福利企业情况（2012 年）
STATISTICS ON COLLECTIVE SOCIAL WELFARE ENTERPRISES BY REGION（2012）

指标	Item	全市 Whole Municipality	其中 of which 市区 Urban Area	溧阳市 Liyang City	金坛市 Jintan City
单位数（个）	Number of Units（unit）	268	177	35	56
职工人数（人）	Number of Staff & Workers（person）	26986	17113	5149	4724
销售收入（亿元）	Sales Income（100 million yuan）	217.5	199.0	4.7	13.8
利润总额（亿元）	Total Profits（100 million yuan）	12.35	8.05	4.30	

22-3 分地区居民最低生活保障情况（2012 年底）
STATISTICS ON LOWEST COST-OF-LIVING WELFARE FOR RESIDENTS BY REGION（END OF 2012）

指标	Item	全市 Whole Municipality	其中 of which 市区 Urban Area	溧阳市 Liyang City	金坛市 Jintan City
城镇居民最低生活保障人数（人）	Number of Urban Residents Receiving Lowest Cost-of-living Welfare（person）	18287	15391	1405	1491
#在职人员	Persons Employed	739	714	1	24
老年人	Elderly	3377	2815	245	317
城镇居民最低生活保障家庭数（户）	Number of Urban Households Receiving Lowest Cost-of-living Welfare（Household）	10035	8425	738	872
农村居民最低生活保障人数（人）	Number of Rural Residents Receiving Lowest Cost-of-living Welfare（person）	34239	13893	11159	9187
农村居民最低生活保障家庭数（户）	Number of Rural Households Receiving Lowest Cost-of-living Welfare（Household）	18593	7493	5721	5379

22-4 分地区优抚对象享受优待抚恤情况（2012 年底）
STATISTICS ON PERSONS RECEIVING PERIODICAL COMPENSATION AND SUBSIDIES BY REGION（END OF 2012 ）

单位：人（person）

指标	Item	全市 Whole Municipality	其中 of which 市区 Urban Area	溧阳市 Liyang City	金坛市 Jintan City
抚恤、补助优抚对象人数	Number of People Subject to Pension, Subsidy and Special Care	20947	8596	6826	5525
优抚对象定期抚恤人数	Number of Persons Receiving Periodical Compen-sation	593	246	159	188
烈士家属	Family Members of Martyrs	278	130	84	64
牺牲军人家属	Family Members of Sacrificed Servicemen	98	43	16	39
病故军人家属	Family Members of Deceased Servicemen	217	73	59	85
优抚对象定期补助人数	Number of Persons Receiving Periodical Subsidies	18006	7129	5967	4910
#在乡复员军人	Servicemen Demobilized before Nov. 1,1954 in Rural Area	2683	725	939	1019

22-5 分地区城镇社区服务和农村服务网络（2012 年底）
URBAN COMMUNITY SERVICES AND RURAL SERVICE NETWORK BY REGION（END OF 2012）

指 标	Item	全 市 Whole Municipality	其中 of which 市 区 Urban Area	溧阳市 Liyang City	金坛市 Jintan City
城镇社区服务	**Urban Community Service**				
城镇社区服务设施数（个）	Number of Urban Community Service Facilities（unit）	1360	758	277	325
从业人员数（人）	Number of Persons Engaged（person）	6729	2368	3325	1036
#安置下岗人员	Laid-off Persons Arrangement	1374	295	517	562
便民利民服务网点（个）	Number of Convenient Service Points for Civilian（unit）	3235	1059	277	1899
社区服务志愿者组织（个）	Number of Volunteers Organizations of Urban Community Service（unit）	5034	4361	435	238
社区服务志愿者人数（人）	Number of Persons Supported by Urban Community Service（person）	203014	183063	4951	15000
建立农村社会保障网络的乡镇数（个）	**Number of Towns and Townships Established Rural Social Security Network（unit）**	**37**	**20**	**10**	**7**

22-6 分地区婚姻登记情况（2012 年）
BASIC STATISTICS ON MARRIAGE REGISTRATION BY REGION（2012）

指 标	Item	全 市 Whole Municipality	其中 of which 市 区 Urban Area	溧阳市 Liyang City	金坛市 Jintan City
结婚登记数（对）	Marriage Legally Registered（couple）	37719	23094	8931	5694
初 婚（人）	First Marriages（person）	62703	38428	14938	9337
再 婚（人）	Remarriages（person）	12735	7760	2924	2051
离婚登记数（对）	Legally Registered Divorces（couple）	8678	5464	1994	1220

22-7 律师、公证、调解工作情况（2012 年）
STATISTICS ON LAWYERS, NOTARIZATION AND MEDIATION（2012）

指 标	Item	全 市 Whole Municipality	其中 of which: #市 区 Urban Area
律师工作	**Lawyers**		
律师事务所（个）	Number of Law Offices（unit）	91	35
取得律师资格（人）	Persons with Lawyer's Qualification（person）	1011	496
专职律师	Full-time Lawyers	986	476
兼职律师	Part-time Lawyers	25	20
聘请担任常年法律顾问单位（个）	Number of Units with Permanent Legal advisors（unit）	5429	2691
民事诉讼代理（件）	Agent of Civil Cases（case）	18062	7827
刑事诉讼辩护及代理（件）	Defender and Agent of Criminal Cases（case）	2585	1312
行政诉讼代理（件）	Agent of Administrative Action（case）	315	147
非诉讼法律事务（件）	Agent of Non-litigious Legal Affairs（case）	2413	1755
法律咨询（件）	Agent of Legal Advisory services（case）	12208	3142
代写法律事务文书（件）	Agent of Legal Documents Written on Behalf of Clients（case）	1896	704
公证工作	**Notarization**		
公证处（个）	Number of Notary Offices（unit）	5	3
公证人员（人）	Notarial Personnel（person）	74	59
#公证员（一、二、三、四级）	Notaries（Grade1, 2,3,4）	31	23
公证员助理	Assistant Notaries	21	16
办理公证件数（件）	Number of Notarial Documents Issued（case）	38324	32265
国内民事	Domestic Civil Relations	11444	9987
国内经济	Domestic Economic Affairs	14716	12512
涉外及港澳台公证	Foreign-related and Hongkong,Macao and Taiwan Notarization	12164	9766
人民调解工作	**People's Mediation**		
专职司法助理员（名）	Number of Full-time Judical assistants（person）	361	290
人民调解委员会（个）	Number of People's Mediation Committees（unit）	1541	919
调解人员数（人）	Number of Mediators（person）	5887	3163
调解民间纠纷数（件）	Number of Civil Disputes Mediated（case）	27771	20016

22-8 国内公证文书分类情况（2008-2012 年）
DOMESTIC NOTARIAL DOCUMENT BY TYPE（2008-2012）

单位：件（unit）

指 标	Item	2008	2009	2010	2011	2012
总 计	**Total**	**27560**	**21295**	**23722**	**22346**	**26160**
经济公证	Notarized Documents on Economic Affairs	3957	6818	7459	5718	14716
# 购 销	Purchases and Sales of products	2		2	12	20
拍 卖	Auctions	2				
贷 款	Loans	145	37	29	49	1194
招标、投标	Bidding	257	291	357	507	908
劳务合同	Labor Contracts	2				5
建筑工程承包	Construction Project Contracts					
农林牧渔业承包	Farming,Forestry,Animal Husbandry,Sideline Production and Fishery Contracts			1		
财产租赁	Property Leases	3				
企业租赁	Enterprises Leases					
其他经济合同	Other Business Contracts	647	934	421	347	304
法人（代表人）资格	Legal Person（agent）Identification	16	14	25	48	23
法人委托书	Legal Person Trust deeds	1279	1918	2066	1807	10236
民事公证	Notarized Documents on Civil Relations	12321	14477	16263	16628	11444
# 继承权	Rights of Inheritance	2578	3577	3210	2990	3544
遗 嘱	Testaments	334	362	250	260	151
产 权	Property Rights					20
亲属关系	Kinship Confirmation	38	59	108	221	210
房屋买卖	Purchases and Sales of House	189	231	220	318	153
房屋租赁	House Leases	5	15	3	23	
遗赠抚养协议	Donations and Family Fostering	3	12	2	3	2
委托书	Trust Deeds	4087	5114	1725	1031	
赠与书	Presentaton Documents	814	550	6902	6924	460
声明书	Declarations	918	959	623	942	3475
现场监督	Field Supervision	501	39	664	606	66

22-9 涉外及涉港澳台公证文书分类情况（2008-2012 年）
FOREIGN AND HONG KONG, MACAO AND TAIWAN NOTARIAL DOCUMENT BY TYPE（2008-2012）

单位：件（unit）

指标	Item	2008	2009	2010	2011	2012
总 计	**Total**	**11282**	**11485**	**12802**	**11686**	**11680**
出 生	Births	1635	2075	1745	1481	1469
学 历	Schooling	1129	1066	1187	903	297
经 历	Personal Histories	86	115	119	125	67
生存、居住	Survial and Residence	24	17	362	391	8
死 亡	Deaths	28	18	13	112	22
收养子女	Children Adoption	1				
亲属关系	Family Relationship	975	1006	1237	964	1161
婚姻状况	Marriages	463	441	796	689	261
委托书	Trust Deeds	159	201	220	331	184
声明书	Declarations	221	179	233	193	378
受、未受刑事处分	Criminal Records and Uncriminal Records	1448	1253	2153	1263	1907
文本相符	Confirmation of Copies & Photo-Offest Copies to Originals	2608	2156	2486	2217	4257
其 他	Others	1105	2958	2251	3017	1674

22-10 调解民事纠纷分类情况（2008-2012 年）
STATISTICS ON CIVIL DISPUTES MEDIATED BY TYPE（2008-2012）

单位：件（unit）

指标	Item	2008	2009	2010	2011	2012
总 计	**Total**	**24116**	**20783**	**21831**	**16230**	**15001**
婚 姻	Marriages	4053	3409	3370	3465	3347
房屋宅基地	Housing And Housing Sites	1210	344	466	621	470
生产经营	Business	239	1480	854	225	140
邻 里	Neighbor Disputes	5146	4227	3887	4114	4236
损害赔偿	Compensation for Damages	768	3087	3468	4084	3723
其 他	Others	12700	8236	9786	3721	3085

22-11 分地区道路、船舶交通事故及火灾情况（2012 年）
STATISTICS ON HIGHWAYS,WATERWAY TRAFFIC ACCIDENTS AND FIRES BY REGION（2012）

指 标	Item	全 市 Whole Munici pality	其中 of which 市 区 Urban Area	溧阳市 Liyang City	金坛市 Jintan City
道路交通事故	**Road Accidents**				
发生起数（起）	Number of Traffic Accident（case）	1293	862	302	129
死亡人数（人）	Number of Death（person）	264	194	40	30
受伤人数（人）	Number of Injuries（person）	1351	829	383	139
损失折款（万元）	Losses Coverted into Cash（10000 yuan）	304	140	105	59
船舶交通事故	**Waterway Accidents**				
发生起数（起）	Number of Traffic Accident（case）	31	31		
损失折款（万元）	Losses Coverted into Cash（10000 yuan）	71	71		
火灾事故	**Fires**				
发生起数（起）	Number of Traffic Accident（case）	394	303	59	32
死亡人数（人）	Number of Death（person）	10	5	5	
受伤人数（人）	Number of Injuries（person）	2		2	
损失折款（万元）	Losses Coverted into Cash（10000 yuan）	286	237	41	8

22-12 主要年份住房公积金情况 STATEMENT OF PUBLIC ACCUMULATION FUND FOR HOUSING CONSTRUCTION IN MAIN YEARS

年 份 Year	缴存人数（人） Number of Paypable Persons (person)	缴存比例（%） Payment proportion（%）	人均月缴存额（元） Per capita monthly payment amount (yuan)	缴存金额（万元） Payment Amount (10000 yuan)	提取金额（万元） Withdrawed Amount (10000 yuan)	缴存余额（万元） Payment Balance (10000 yuan)
1992	278000	10	14	2929	103	2825
1995	323230	10	37	8775	854	23229
2000	334997	12-14	121	39759	11750	134776
2001	316781	14-16	142	49727	18076	168577
2002	321151	14-16	192	59676	28973	210625
2003	311722	16-24	264	80298	34153	259442
2004	303994	20-24	330	106998	45344	325051
2005	313772	20-24	384	132568	46627	410992
2006	322824	20-24	437	163392	83478	500853
2007	344071	20-24	510	196771	113598	584026
2008	373059	20-24	587	250796	125442	709381
2009	370396	20-24	616	275505	189093	795793
2010	430171	20-24	627	323831	204934	914690
2011	485392	20-24	732	405620	216913	1103397
2012	530158	20-24	831	528639	293277	1338758

22-12 续表 Continued

年 份 Year	个人贷款发放户数（户） Number of Household with loan (houshold)	个人贷款发放金额（万元） Amount of Loans (10000 yuan)	个人贷款回收金额（万元） Individual Loan Repayment Amount (10000 yuan)	个人贷款逾期率（%） Overdue Rate of Loans（%）	提取廉租房补充资金总额（万元） Accumulated Amount of Withdrawn Supplementory Financing to Low Rent Houses (10000 yuan)
1992					
1995	5	15			
2000	4241	26742	6940	0.050	
2001	4242	32886	11603	0.050	5003
2002	6510	65839	20259	0.050	6669
2003	6869	85740	32594	0.030	8505
2004	7213	111401	57474	0.020	9503
2005	8472	150552	64320	0.010	10694
2006	12071	212077	84107	0.004	12410
2007	12647	225062	101970	0.0004	14349
2008	10132	184035	100529	0.0007	18510
2009	12350	264884	140548	0	23000
2010	10185	239414	143443	0	27541
2011	11272	286306	144702	0	35856
2012	15051	409421	174069	0.0001	55385

22-13　分地区住房公积金情况（2012 年）
CONDITION OF PUBLIC ACCUMULATION FUND FOR HOUSING CONSTRUCTION （HOUSING FUND） BY REGION（2012）

指　标	Item	全 市 Whole Municipality	其中 of which 市 区 Urban Area	溧阳市 Liyang City	金坛市 Jintan City
住房公积金缴存	**Payment of Housing Fund**				
应缴单位（个）	Work Unit Payable （Unit）	14045	12226	966	853
当年新开户单位（个）	New Account-opening Unit （Unit）	2986	2540	286	160
缴存人数（人）	Number of Paypable Persons （person）	530158	448736	45625	35797
当年新开户人数（人）	Number of New Account-opening Persons （person）	104515	91126	8020	5369
缴存金额（万元）	Payment Amount （10000 yuan）	528639	449147	44830	34662
缴存余额（万元）	Payment Balance （10000 yuan）	1338758	1117501	126363	94894
累计缴存金额（万元）	Accumulated Payment Amount （10000 yuan）	2770228	2365638	222388	182202
住房公积金提取	**Withdrawal of Housing Fund**				
提取人数（人）	Number of Person Withdrawed Fund （person）	140116	121978	9713	8425
#转帐还贷提取	Withdrawal for Transfer Account and Repay Loan	86028	73365	6966	5697
提取金额（万元）	Withdrawed Amount （10000 yuan）	293277	249924	25355	17999
#转帐还贷提取	Withdrawal for Transfer Account and Repay Loan	155388	132641	13087	9660
累计提取金额（万元）	Accumulated Withdrawed Amount （10000 yuan）	1431469	1248137	96024	87308
住房公积金个人贷款	**Housing fund for Individual Loan**				
贷款户数（户）	Number of Household with loan （household）	15051	13280	920	851
贷款金额（万元）	Amount of Loans （10000 yuan）	409421	359832	28126	21464
平均贷款年数（年）	Average Loan Term （year）	16	16	15	14
平均贷款金额（万元）	Average Loan Amount （10000 yuan）	27.20	27.10	30.57	25.22
贷款余额（万元）	Balance of Loans （10000 yuan）	1239272	1051595	103243	84434
贷款逾期率（%）	Overdue Rate of Loans （%）	0.0001	0.0001	0.0000	0.0000
累计贷款金额（万元）	Accumulated Amount of Loans （10000 yuan）	2314150	1954751	190034	169364
住房公积金运用	**Application of Housing Fund**				
廉租房补充资金（万元）	Supplementary Fund of Bargain Tenement （10000 yuan）	19529	16104	1574	1850
资金使用率（%）	Fund Utility Rate （%）	92.57	94.10	81.70	88.98
个人贷款比率（%）	Individual Loan Ratio （%）	92.57	94.10	81.70	88.98

附　录

APPENDIX

附录 1　全国经济社会发展主要指标（2012 年）
MAJOR INDEX IN THE DEVELOPING OF SOCIETY AND ECONOMY IN CHINA（2012）

指标	Item	2012	比上年增减（%）Increase/Decrease over the previous year（%）
年末总人口（万人）	Total Population By the End of the Year（10000 persons）	135404	0.5
就业人员（万人）	Employed Persons	76704	0.4
#城　镇	Urban	37102	3.3
农民工总量（万人）	Total Number of Peasant Workers（10000 persons）	26261	3.9
#外出农民工	Migrant Workers from Rural Areas	16336	3.0
年末城镇登记失业率（%）	Registred Unemployment rate by the end of the Year（%）	4.1	"平 equal"
国内生产总值（亿元）	GDP（100 million yuan）	519322	7.8
第一产业	Primary Industry	52377	4.5
第二产业	Secondary Industry	235319	8.1
工　业	Industry	199860	7.9
建筑业	Construction	35459	9.3
第三产业	Tertiary Industry	231626	8.1
全社会固定资产投资总额（亿元）	Total Investment in Fixed Assets（100 million yuan）	374676	20.3
#固定资产投资总额	Investment in Fixed Assets	364835	20.6
第一产业	Primary Industry	9004	32.2
第二产业	Secondary Industry	158672	20.2
第三产业	Tertiary Industry	197159	20.6
#农　户	Peasant household	9841	8.3
#房地产开发	Real Estate Development	71804	16.2
货物运输总量（亿吨）	Total Freight Traffic（100 million tons）	412	11.5
货物周转量（亿吨公里）	Total Volume of Cargo Transported（100 million tons kilometers）	173145	8.7
旅客运输总量（亿人）	Total Passenger Traffic（100 million persons）	379	7.6
旅客周转量（亿人公里）	Total Volume of Passenger Transported（100 million persons kilometers）	33369	7.7
邮电业务总量（亿元）	Business Volume of Post and Telecommunications（100 million yuan）	15022	13
电话普及率（部/百人）	Popularized Rate of Telephone（set/100 persons）	103.2	8.3部（sets）

附录1　续表　　　　Appendix 1 Continued

指　标	Item	2012	比上年增减（%）Increase/Decrease over the previous year（%）
互联网普及率（%）	Internet Penetration Rate（%）	42.1	3.8个百分点 percentage points
社会消费品零售总额（亿元）	Total Volume of Social Consumption Retail Sale（100 million yuan）	210307	14.3
按消费形态分	Group by Consumption Patterns		
商品零售额	Retail Sales	186859	14.4
餐饮收入额	Revenue of Restaurant and Catering	23448	13.6
居民消费价格指数（上年=100）	Consumption Price Index of Residents（preceding year=100）	102.6	2.6个百分点 percentage points
进出口总额（亿美元）	Gross Value of Export and Import（USD 100 million）	38668	6.2
出　口	Export	20489	7.9
进　口	Import	18178	4.3
实际外商直接投资（亿美元）	Actual Foreign Direct Investment（USD 100 million）	1117	-3.7
金融机构本外币存款余额（亿元）	Total Deposit of Financiai Departments（100 million yuan）	943102	14.1
#住户存款	Household Deposit	410201	16.6
#人民币余额	Balance of RMB	406192	16.7
金融机构本外币贷款余额（亿元）	Total Loans of Financial Departments（100 million yuan）	672875	15.6
公共财政收入（亿元）	Gross Finance Revenue（100 million yuan）	117210	12.8
财政支出（亿元）	Finance Expenditure（100 million yuan）	125712	15.1
城镇居民人均可支配收入（元）	Per Capita Disposable Income of Urban Residents（yuan）	24565	12.6
农民人均纯收入（元）	Per Capita Net Income of Rural Residents（yuan）	7917	13.5
城镇居民家庭恩格尔系数（%）	Engel Coefficient of Urban Households（%）	36.2	-0.1个百分点 percentage points
农村居民家庭恩格尔系数（%）	Engel Coefficient of Rural Households（%）	39.3	-1.1个百分点 percentage points
普通高等学校本专科在校学生（万人）	Students in Regular Institutions of Higher Education（10000 persons）	2391.3	3.6
科学研究与试验发展（R&D）经费支出（亿元）	Appropriation Expenditure on Science Research and Development（100 million yuan）	10240	17.9
申请专利件数（万件）	Number of Patent Applications Examined（10000 units）	205.1	25.6

附录 2　全国主要工农业产品产量（2012 年）
OUTPUT OF MAJOR INDUSTRIAL AND AGRICULTURAL PRODUCTS（2012）

产品名称	Name of Products	2012	比上年增减（%） Increase/Decrease over the previous year （%）
农产品产量（万吨）	**Output of Agricultural Products （10000 tons）**		
粮　食	Grain	58957	3.2
夏　粮	Summer Grain	12995	2.8
早　稻	Early Season Rice	3329	1.6
秋　粮	Autumn Grain	42633	3.5
油　料	Oil-bearing Crops	3476	5.1
棉　花	Cotton	684	3.8
糖　料	Sugar Crops	13493	7.8
烤　烟	Tabacco	320	11.5
茶　叶	Tea	180	11.2
肉类总产量	Total Output of Meat	8384	5.4
水产品产量	Total Output of Aquatic Products	5906	5.4
工业产品产量	**Output Of Industrial Products**		
纱（万吨）	Yarn （10000 tons）	2984	9.8
布（亿米）	Cloth （100 million meters）	840.8	3.3
化　纤（万吨）	Chemical Fibre （10000 tons）	3800	12.1
成品糖（万吨）	Finished Sugar （10000 tons）	1406.8	18.5
卷　烟（亿支）	Cigarette （100 million pieces）	25160.9	2.8
彩色电视机（万台）	Colour TV （10000 units）	12823.3	4.8
家用电冰箱（万台）	Household Refrigerator （10000 units）	8427	-3.1
房间空调器（万台）	Household Air-conditioner （10000 units）	13281.1	-4.5
一次能源生产总量（亿吨标准煤）	Total Output of Primary Energy （100 million tons of SCE）	33.3	4.8
原　煤（亿吨）	Coal （100 million tons）	36.5	3.8
原　油（亿吨）	Crude Oil （100 million tons）	2.07	2.3
天然气（亿立方米）	Natural Gas （100 million cu.m）	1072.2	4.4
发电量（亿千瓦时）	Electricity （100 million kw.h）	49377.7	4.8
粗　钢（万吨）	Steel （10000 tons）	71716	4.7
钢　材（万吨）	Steel Products （10000 tons）	95317.6	7.6
十种有色金属（万吨）	10 Kinds of Nonferrous Metals （10000 tons）	3672.2	6.9
# 精炼铜（铜）	Refined Copper （copper）	574	9.5
电解铝	Electrolytic Aluminum	1985.8	12.3
氧化铝（万吨）	Alumina （10000 tons）	3769.6	10.3
水　泥（亿吨）	Cement （100 million tons）	22.1	5.3
硫　酸（万吨）	Sulfuric Acid （10000 tons）	7686.3	2.7
纯　碱（万吨）	Soda Ash （10000 tons）	2408.8	5.0
烧　碱（万吨）	Caustic Soda （10000 tons）	2696.1	9.0
乙　烯（万吨）	Ethene （10000 tons）	1486.8	-2.7
化　肥（折100%,万吨）	Chemical Fertilizer （10000 tons）	7296	10.1
发电设备（万千瓦）	Electricity Generation Equiments （10000 kw）	13005.6	-9.7
汽　车（万辆）	Motor Vehicles （10000 coaches）	1927.7	4.7
# 轿　车	Cars	1077.1	6.4
大中型拖拉机（万台）	Tractors （10000 units）	46.3	15.3
集成电路（亿块）	Integrated Citcuit （100 million pcs）	823.1	14.4
程控交换机（万线）	Distance Exchange and Transmitting Machine （10000 lines）	2826.3	-6.8
移动通信手持机（万部）	Mobile Telephone （10000 units）	118154.3	4.3
微型电子计算机（万部）	Micro-computers （10000 units）	35411	10.5

附录3 江苏省经济社会发展主要指标（2012年）
MAJOR INDEX IN THE DEVELOPING OF SOCIETY AND ECONOMY IN JIANGSU PROVINCE（2012）

指 标	Item	2012	比上年增减（%） Increase/Decrease over the previous year （%）
常住人口（万人）	permanent population（10000 persons）	7920.0	0.3
就业人口（万人）	Employed Persons（10000 persons）	4759.53	0.02
年末城镇登记失业率（%）	Registred Unemployment rate by the end of the Year （%）	3.14	-0.08个百分点 percentage points
地区生产总值（亿元）	GDP （100 million yuan）	54058.2	10.1
第一产业	Primary Industry	3418.3	4.6
第二产业	Secondary Industry	27121.9	11.0
第三产业	Tertiary Industry	23518.0	9.7
规模以上工业增加值（亿元）	Added Value of Industry （100million yuan）	26606.14	12.6
#国有及国有控股企业	State-owned and State Share-holding Enterprises	5087.8	7.9
集体企业	Collective Enterprises	217.8	6.0
股份制企业	Joint-share Enterprises	12880.3	16.7
外商及港澳台投资企业	Enterprises with Investment from Foreign, Hong Kong, Macao and Taiwan.	10134.3	7.9
工业企业实现利税总额（亿元）	Pre-tax Profit realized By Industrial Enterprises （100 million yuan）	11214.2	9.1
工业企业实现利润总额（亿元）	Gross Profit realized By Industrial Enterprises （100 million yuan）	6881.8	5.8
工业产品销售率（%）	Sales Rate of Industrial Products （%）	98.32	-0.4个百分点 percentage points
建筑业总产值（亿元）	Gross Output Value of Construction	17927.2	18.5
固定资产投资总额（亿元）	Investment in Fixed Assets （100 million yuan）	31707.2	20.5
第一产业	Primary Industry	204.2	31.6
第二产业	Secondary Industry	16646.4	19.5
第三产业	Tertiary Industry	14856.5	21.5
#房地产开发	Real Estate Development	6206.1	11.5

附录 3 续表 Appendix 3 Continued

指 标	Item	2012	比上年增减（%）Increase/Decrease over the previous year（%）
货物周转量（亿吨公里）	Total Volume of Cargo Transported（100 million tons kilometers）	8474.6	12.8
旅客周转量（亿人公里）	Total Volume of Passenger Transported（100 million persons kilometers）	1949.8	9.7
电话普及率（部/百人）	Popularized Rate of Telephone （set/100 persons）	125	10部（sets）
社会消费品零售总额（亿元）	Total Volume of Social Consumption Retail Sale （100 million yuan）	18331.30	14.7
居民消费价格指数（上年=100）	Consumption Price Index of Residents （preceding year=100）	102.6	2.6个百分点 percentage points
商品零售价格指数（上年=100）	Retail Price Index （preceding year=100）	102.1	2.1个百分点 percentage points
进出口总额（亿美元）	Gross Value of Export and Import （USD 100 million）	5480.9	1.5
出 口	Export	3285.4	5.1
进 口	Import	2195.6	3.3
协议（合同）外资金额（亿美元）	Amount of Foreign Capital in the Newly Signed Agreements（USD 100 million）	571.4	-4.1
实际到帐注册外资（亿美元）	Foreign Capital Actually Utilized （USD 100 million）	357.6	11.3
金融机构人民币存款余额（亿元）	RMB Deposits Balance of Financial Departments（100 million yuan）	75481.5	14.8
#单位存款	Deposits of Enterprises	42152.6	13.0
城乡居民储蓄存款	Urban and Rural Savings Deposits	30057.2	16.0
金融机构人民币贷款余额（亿元）	RMB Loans Balance of Financial Departments （100 million yuan）	54412.3	13.7
公共财政预算收入（亿元）	Public Finance Budget Revenue（100 million yuan）	5860.7	13.8
公共财政预算支出（亿元）	Public Finance Budget Expenditure（100 million yuan）	6996.6	12.5
城镇居民人均可支配收入（元）	Per Capita Disposable income of Urban Residents （yuan）	29677	12.7
农民人均纯收入（元）	Per Capita Net Income of Rural Residents （yuan）	12202	12.9
城镇居民家庭恩格尔系数（%）	Engel Coefficient of Urban Households （%）	35.4	-0.7个百分点 percentage points
农村居民家庭恩格尔系数（%）	Engel Coefficient of Rural Households （%）	37.4	1.1个百分点 percentage points
普通高校在校学生（万人）	Students in Ordinary High Schools （10000 persons）	167.12	0.7
科学研究与试验发展（R&D）经费支出（亿元）	Appropriation Expenditure on Science Research and Development（100 million yuan）	1230	14.7
专利授权件数（万件）	Number of Patent Authorizations Granted（10000 units）	27	35.1
报纸出版量（亿份）	Total Volume of Newspaper Issued （100 million copies）	29.4	3.5

附录 4 江苏省主要工农业产品产量（2012 年）
OUTPUT OF MAJOR INDUSTRIAL AND AGRICULTURAL PRODUCTS IN JIANGSU PROVINCE（2012）

产品名称	Name of Products	2012	比上年增减（%） Increase/Decrease over the previous year（%）
农产品产量（万吨）	**Output of Agricultural Products （10000 tons）**		
粮 食	Grain	3372.5	2.0
棉 花	Cotton	22.0	-10.7
油 料	Oil-bearing Crops	147.0	2.0
#油菜籽	Rapeseeds	109.1	3.7
花 生	Peanut	36.0	-2.6
蚕 茧	Silkworm Cocoons	6.8	-3.4
茶 叶	Tea	1.5	6.9
水 果	Fruits	800.2	5.8
肉 类	Meat	386.0	5.6
禽 蛋	Poultry Eggs	197.2	1.2
牛 奶	Cow Milk	61.3	3.6
水产品	Aquatic Products	493.7	3.7
工业产品产量	**Output Of Industrial Products**		
纱（万吨）	Yarn （10000 tons）	449.5	6.8
布（亿米）	Cloth （100 million meters）	80.3	7.4
化 纤（万吨）	Chemical Fibre （10000 tons）	1276.9	10.2
卷 烟（亿支）	Cigarette （100 million piece）	1006.2	1.5
彩色电视机（万部）	Colour TV （10000 sets）	1431.9	-17.9
家用电冰箱（万台）	Household Refrigerator （10000 units）	1103.2	-8.5
房间空调器（万台）	Household Air-conditioner （10000 units）	496.0	-6.2
发电量（亿千瓦·时）	Electricity （100 Million kw·h）	3928.4	4.7
粗 钢（万吨）	Crude Steel （10000 tons）	7419.7	8.0
钢 材（万吨）	Steel Products （10000 tons）	10989.2	9.8
十种有色金属（万吨）	10 Kinds of Nonferrous Metals （10000 tons）	57.7	7.4
水 泥（万吨）	Cement （10000 tons）	16775.5	10.1
硫 酸（万吨）	Sulfuric Acid （10000 tons）	397.3	-14.1
纯 碱（万吨）	Soda Ash （10000 tons）	338.3	6.0
乙 烯（万吨）	Ethene （10000 tons）	132.5	-13.9
化 肥（折100%,万吨）	Chemical Fertilizer （10000 tons）	270.6	10.1
汽 车（万辆）	Motor Vehicles （10000 coach）	88.7	6.5
#轿 车	Cars	45.5	18.7
发电设备（万千瓦）	Electricity Generation Equiments （10000 kw）	596.4	11.7
集成电路（亿块）	Integrated Citcuit （100 million pcs）	292.6	14.5
程控交换机（万线）	Distance Exchange and Transmitting Machine （10000 lines）	4.6	-24.1
微型电子计算机（万部）	Micro-computers （10000 units）	8862.1	2.0
移动通讯基站设备（信道）	Mobile Communication Devices （Channels）	1825456	-54.3

附录 5　江苏省市、县主要经济指标（2012 年）
MAJOR ECONOMY INDICATORS OF CITIES AND COUNTIES OF JIANGSU PROVINCE（2012）

指　标	Item	南京市 Nanjing City	溧水县 Lishui County	高淳县 Gaochun County
年末总人口（万人）	Year-end Population （10000 persons）	638.48	41.88	43.26
年末常住人口（万人）	Year-end permanent population（10000 persons）	816.1	41.86	41.91
土地面积（平方公里）	Area of Land （sq.km）	6587	1064	790
地区生产总值（亿元）	Gross Domestic Products （100 million yuan）	7201.57	369.38	365.27
第一产业	Primary Industry	185.06	29.33	30.29
第二产业	Secondary Industry	3170.78	222.11	193.31
#工　业	Industry	2748.46	188.41	154.37
第三产业	Tertiary Industry	3845.73	117.94	141.67
人均地区生产总值（元）	Per Capita GDP （yuan）	88525	88167	87139
固定资产投资完成额（亿元）	Investment in Fixed Assets（100 million yuan）	4558.49	350.11	302.01
公共财政预算收入（亿元）	Public Finance Budget Revenue（100 million yuan）	733.02	29.20	22.00
#税收收入	Tax Revenue	602.79	23.36	17.62
公共财政预算支出（亿元）	Public Finance Budget Expenditure（100 million yuan）	769.66	34.97	31.73
年底金融机构存款余额（亿元）	Balance of Deposits of Financial Institutions at Year-end（100 million yuan）	16131.41	210.12	176.88
#城乡居民储蓄	Savings Deposits of Residents	4465.37	111.20	100.58
年底金融机构贷款余额（亿元）	Balance of Loans of Financial Institutions at Year-end（100 million yuan）	12314.41	160.84	156.79
规模以上工业企业主要指标	**Major Economic Indicators of Industrial Enterprises Above Designated Size**			
工业总产值（亿元）	Gross Industrial Output Value （100 million yuan）	11437.80	621.67	611.48
主营业务收入（亿元）	Main Business Income （100 million yuan）	11283.26	620.81	636.15
利润总额（亿元）	Total Profits （100 million yuan）	604.44	66.27	49.93
利税总额（亿元）	Total Pre-tax Profits （100 million yuan）	1372.78	97.45	79.50
工业用电量（亿千瓦时）	Industrial Electricity Consumption （100 million kw.h）	265.64	10.36	3.21
社会消费品零售总额（亿元）	Total Retail Sales of Consumer Goods （100 million yuan）	3103.82	103.18	120.07
进出口总额（亿美元）	Total Imports （USD 100 million）	552.35	3.37	3.38
#出　口	Exports	319.16	3.17	3.12
实际到帐注册外资（亿美元）	Foreign Capital Actually Utilized （USD 100 million）	41.30	1.51	0.81
城镇居民人均可支配收入（元）	Per Capita Disposable Income of Urban Residents（yuan）	35092	31602	33032
城镇居民人均消费支出（元）	Per Capita Consuming Expenditures of Urban Residents（yuan）	22446	18295	19061
农民人均纯收入（元）	Per Capita Net Income of Rural Residents（yuan）	14786	14356	14816
农民人均生活消费支出（元）	Per Capita Living Expenditure of Rural Residents （yuan）	11114	10780	10945

注：城市居民人均可支配收入、城市居民人均消费性支出数据为全市口径。
Note：The data of per capita disposable income and per capita nonproductive expenditure of urban residents is subject to the municipal caliber.

附录 5 续表 1

指 标	Item	无锡市 Wuxi City	江阴市 Jiangyin City	宜兴市 Yixing City
年末总人口（万人）	Year-end Population （10000 persons）	470.07	121.26	107.73
年末常住人口（万人）	Year-end permanent population（10000 persons）	646.55	162.43	124.80
土地面积（平方公里）	Area of Land （sq.km）	4627	987	1997
地区生产总值（亿元）	Gross Domestic Products （100 million yuan）	7568.15	2535.38	1085.98
第一产业	Primary Industry	137.22	47.69	47.68
第二产业	Secondary Industry	4012.03	1443.91	581.22
#工 业	Industry	3717.88	1393.27	497.48
第三产业	Tertiary Industry	3418.90	1043.78	457.08
人均地区生产总值（元）	Per Capita GDP （yuan）	117357	156471	87168
固定资产投资完成额（亿元）	Investment in Fixed Assets（100 million yuan）	3618.07	834.28	480.56
公共财政预算收入（亿元）	Public Finance Budget Revenue（100 million yuan）	658.03	167.19	78.38
#税收收入	Tax Revenue	540.01	139.24	66.66
公共财政预算支出（亿元）	Public Finance Budget Expenditure（100 million yuan）	648.61	154.00	82.52
年底金融机构存款余额（亿元）	Balance of Deposits of Financial Institutions at Year-end（100 million yuan）	10293.40	2347.59	1490.35
#城乡居民储蓄	Savings Deposits of Residents	3731.83	792.49	648.64
年底金融机构贷款余额（亿元）	Balance of Loans of Financial Institutions at Year-end（100 million yuan）	7467.03	1811.65	1115.57
规模以上工业企业主要指标	**Major Economic Indicators of Industrial Enterprises Above Designated Size**			
工业总产值（亿元）	Gross Industrial Output Value （100 million yuan）	14446.85	5915.23	2694.80
主营业务收入（亿元）	Main Business Income （100 million yuan）	14191.69	5786.94	2665.89
利润总额（亿元）	Total Profits （100 million yuan）	878.69	385.29	135.97
利税总额（亿元）	Total Pre-tax Profits （100 million yuan）	1261.48	565.88	195.25
工业用电量（亿千瓦时）	Industrial Electricity Consumption （100 million kw.h）	464.51	205.88	70.66
社会消费品零售总额（亿元）	Total Retail Sales of Consumer Goods （100 million yuan）	2443.24	515.48	371.28
进出口总额（亿美元）	Total Imports （USD 100 million）	707.72	192.65	49.59
#出 口	Exports	413.13	105.15	31.89
实际到帐注册外资（亿美元）	Foreign Capital Actually Utilized （USD 100 million）	40.10	7.98	4.70
城镇居民人均可支配收入（元）	Per Capita Disposable Income of Urban Residents（yuan）	35663	39437	33210
城镇居民人均消费支出（元）	Per Capita Consuming Expenditures of Urban Residents（yuan）	23000	26643	19133
农民人均纯收入（元）	Per Capita Net Income of Rural Residents（yuan）	18509	19660	16862
农民人均生活消费支出（元）	Per Capita Living Expenditure of Rural Residents （yuan）	12795	11991	12523

注：城市居民人均可支配收入、城市居民人均消费性支出数据为全市口径。
Note：The data of per capita disposable income and per capita nonproductive expenditure of urban residents is subject to the municipal caliber.

Appendix 5　Continued 1

徐州市 Xuzhou City	丰 县 Feng County	沛 县 Pei County	睢宁县 Shuining County	新沂市 Xiyi City	邳州市 Pizhou City	常州市 Changzhou City	溧阳市 Liyang City	金坛市 Jintan City
990.53	116.62	128.67	137.36	107.15	179.86	364.77	78.99	55.31
856.41	94.93	111.31	102.49	90.83	143.36	468.68	76.03	55.84
11259	1446	1349	1767	1571	2088	4372	1535	976
4016.58	228.73	431.30	302.45	350.16	513.49	3969.87	559.20	373.81
382.46	46.39	67.91	57.18	47.91	79.32	126.37	39.02	27.64
1968.52	103.82	203.81	132.34	149.44	223.64	2100.76	306.58	197.80
1666.62	73.42	165.73	105.68	127.13	183.79	1900.55	278.79	169.83
1665.60	78.52	159.58	112.93	152.81	210.53	1742.74	213.60	148.37
46877	24021	38633	29427	38443	35736	85039	73768	67129
2685.89	127.33	292.32	153.22	270.64	393.88	2621.56	373.24	219.93
366.76	24.92	38.96	25.56	32.85	42.12	378.99	40.50	23.11
284.14	20.34	31.73	20.56	26.32	33.26	303.89	34.42	19.70
530.05	47.26	61.81	48.62	52.83	68.22	391.22	45.84	31.72
3364.47	174.42	292.91	215.60	180.01	251.48	5604.90	645.20	400.96
1794.72	129.26	191.81	152.56	124.10	167.76	2473.27	332.54	229.59
2047.23	96.64	108.77	117.23	157.13	188.92	3832.80	436.64	286.90
8882.29	328.83	1001.24	559.86	878.41	1502.86	8970.30	1355.68	571.37
8837.26	319.38	996.88	543.52	907.75	1485.78	9097.95	1364.32	576.77
743.38	27.25	75.27	60.00	67.64	163.27	443.77	67.39	34.59
1319.96	48.11	138.07	85.26	112.41	251.71	730.30	109.85	58.21
246.08	9.61	21.32	13.10	28.03	18.31	277.88	50.54	31.17
1312.50	68.58	124.42	85.22	83.06	114.06	1413.33	198.26	156.73
83.27	1.71	3.76	7.22	4.30	14.43	290.46	11.29	16.03
62.88	1.71	3.69	4.89	2.51	14.02	199.62	8.55	13.65
17.00	0.69	1.70	1.29	1.85	1.80	33.61	4.05	2.51
21716	16186	19227	16447	17617	20542	33326	29852	31738
13730	11768	13062	11051	15210	11301	20918	19741	21009
10762	9783	11351	9541	9808	11282	16737	15261	15608
6742	7095	8558	5616	6481	5866	12027	12957	12401

附录 5 续表 2

指 标	Item	苏州市 Suzhou City	常熟市 Changshu City	张家港市 Zhangjiagang City
年末总人口（万人）	Year-end Population （10000 persons）	647.81	106.78	91.02
年末常住人口（万人）	Year-end permanent population（10000 persons）	1054.91	150.71	124.18
土地面积（平方公里）	Area of Land （sq.km）	8488	1276	990
地区生产总值（亿元）	Gross Domestic Products （100 million yuan）	12011.65	1870.19	2050.58
第一产业	Primary Industry	195.08	37.02	27.53
第二产业	Secondary Industry	6502.25	996.95	1175.51
#工 业	Industry	6055.10	952.62	1129.98
第三产业	Tertiary Industry	5314.32	836.22	847.54
人均地区生产总值（元）	Per Capita GDP （yuan）	114029	123882	164441
固定资产投资完成额（亿元）	Investment in Fixed Assets（100 million yuan）	5142.51	602.12	691.07
公共财政预算收入（亿元）	Public Finance Budget Revenue（100 million yuan）	1204.33	128.15	149.61
#税收收入	Tax Revenue	1023.88	104.07	122.20
公共财政预算支出（亿元）	Public Finance Budget Expenditure（100 million yuan）	1113.47	128.27	142.92
年底金融机构存款余额（亿元）	Balance of Deposits of Financial Institutions at Year-end（100 million yuan）	17663.50	2031.19	2064.68
#城乡居民储蓄	Savings Deposits of Residents	5787.75	907.18	746.76
年底金融机构贷款余额（亿元）	Balance of Loans of Financial Institutions at Year-end（100 million yuan）	13626.86	1509.74	1490.75
规模以上工业企业主要指标	**Major Economic Indicators of Industrial Enterprises Above Designated Size**			
工业总产值（亿元）	Gross Industrial Output Value （100 million yuan）	28745.54	3369.21	4700.56
主营业务收入（亿元）	Main Business Income （100 million yuan）	28998.60	3356.42	4874.35
利润总额（亿元）	Total Profits （100 million yuan）	1252.70	172.30	84.48
利税总额（亿元）	Total Pre-tax Profits （100 million yuan）	1817.39	238.60	186.35
工业用电量（亿千瓦时）	Industrial Electricity Consumption （100 million kw.h）	982.66	123.65	246.75
社会消费品零售总额（亿元）	Total Retail Sales of Consumer Goods （100 million yuan）	3240.97	499.54	370.73
进出口总额（亿美元）	Total Imports （USD 100 million）	3056.92	197.49	319.62
#出 口	Exports	1746.89	129.21	128.11
实际到帐注册外资（亿美元）	Foreign Capital Actually Utilized （USD 100 million）	91.65	9.56	9.52
城镇居民人均可支配收入（元）	Per Capita Disposable Income of Urban Residents（yuan）	39079	39561	39695
城镇居民人均消费支出（元）	Per Capita Consuming Expenditures of Urban Residents（yuan）	25157	25003	27695
农民人均纯收入（元）	Per Capita Net Income of Rural Residents（yuan）	19396	19467	19460
农民人均生活消费支出（元）	Per Capita Living Expenditure of Rural Residents （yuan）	14381	14685	15129

注：城市居民人均可支配收入、城市居民人均消费性支出数据为全市口径。
Note：The data of per capita disposable income and per capita nonproductive expenditure of urban residents is subject to the municipal caliber.

Appendix 5 Continued 2

昆山市 Gunshan City	太仓市 Taichang City	南通市 Nantong City	海安县 Haian County	如东县 Rudong County	启东市 Qidong County	如皋市 Rugao City	海门市 Haimeng City
73.76	47.26	765.20	93.87	104.60	112.38	142.50	99.97
163.89	70.68	729.73	86.60	98.60	96.00	126.00	90.23
932	823	8001	1108	1733	1208	1492	939
2725.32	955.12	4558.67	480.14	478.00	589.14	590.17	663.10
24.46	33.61	319.09	47.69	56.56	61.48	52.77	46.50
1631.25	520.36	2414.11	246.30	243.03	306.09	318.49	377.60
1551.28	491.50	1992.11	204.33	197.87	240.62	269.01	315.74
1069.61	401.15	1825.47	186.15	178.41	221.57	218.90	239.00
165291	134439	62506	55443	48364	61127	46801	73473
767.62	459.93	2886.47	322.66	310.79	359.53	329.86	370.86
220.28	90.15	419.72	37.53	32.17	52.21	53.60	51.61
189.82	72.63	339.51	30.75	25.85	42.37	44.72	41.79
195.15	86.16	513.01	55.30	54.44	59.59	71.08	55.96
2364.12	1018.88	6297.19	681.06	504.06	691.33	670.20	719.57
787.13	377.17	3588.06	426.65	348.72	481.71	436.10	481.84
1601.39	863.41	3837.14	454.33	247.82	402.73	354.53	421.40
7686.82	1831.88	9890.12	1257.50	1243.68	1156.90	1360.88	1425.03
7703.16	1777.51	9690.95	1206.92	1231.69	1127.38	1280.49	1424.61
401.64	85.40	786.59	113.09	102.55	93.59	65.91	153.80
523.10	133.35	1160.15	147.71	148.32	142.32	108.78	233.81
146.47	68.79	222.96	30.61	27.88	15.96	31.02	22.36
493.62	195.07	1719.27	181.98	202.18	228.73	229.85	237.12
865.68	126.21	263.01	14.99	12.81	20.28	35.88	16.92
555.17	56.60	187.86	12.79	9.99	14.43	23.72	12.38
17.54	8.11	22.05	2.52	3.20	2.39	2.14	1.22
39740	39422	28292	26771	26768	26875	26010	29631
27634	27129	17858	16742	16734	17575	15889	18996
19563	19411	13231	12663	12156	14127	11663	15162
16122	13091	9839	9988	9309	10619	8165	11117

附录5 续表3

	指 标 Item	连云港市 Lianyun-gang City	赣榆县 Guanyu County	东海县 Donghai County
年末总人口（万人）	Year-end Population （10000 persons）	510.99	115.58	118.02
年末常住人口（万人）	Year-end permanent population（10000 persons）	440.69	94.81	94.96
土地面积（平方公里）	Area of Land （sq.km）	7615	1514	2037
地区生产总值（亿元）	Gross Domestic Products （100 million yuan）	1603.42	331.36	277.30
第一产业	Primary Industry	232.40	50.46	51.02
第二产业	Secondary Industry	736.14	166.07	127.37
#工 业	Industry	583.31	129.54	109.04
第三产业	Tertiary Industry	634.88	114.83	98.91
人均地区生产总值（元）	Per Capita GDP （yuan）	36470	34996	29233
固定资产投资完成额（亿元）	Investment in Fixed Assets（100 million yuan）	1280.88	202.31	189.35
公共财政预算收入（亿元）	Public Finance Budget Revenue（100 million yuan）	208.94	29.21	27.46
#税收收入	Tax Revenue	160.92	22.97	21.35
公共财政预算支出（亿元）	Public Finance Budget Expenditure（100 million yuan）	312.55	53.69	48.00
年底金融机构存款余额（亿元）	Balance of Deposits of Financial Institutions at Year-end （100 million yuan）	1503.66	188.93	186.71
#城乡居民储蓄	Savings Deposits of Residents	723.59	121.39	121.83
年底金融机构贷款余额（亿元）	Balance of Loans of Financial Institutions at Year-end （100 million yuan）	1196.58	140.69	133.41
规模以上工业企业主要指标	**Major Economic Indicators of Industrial Enterprises Above Designated Size**			
工业总产值（亿元）	Gross Industrial Output Value （100 million yuan）	3413.23	816.05	481.20
主营业务收入（亿元）	Main Business Income （100 million yuan）	3346.45	810.10	476.05
利润总额（亿元）	Total Profits （100 million yuan）	273.08	43.63	38.26
利税总额（亿元）	Total Pre-tax Profits （100 million yuan）	423.96	71.63	58.19
工业用电量（亿千瓦时）	Industrial Electricity Consumption （100 million kw.h）	75.91	19.48	10.79
社会消费品零售总额（亿元）	Total Retail Sales of Consumer Goods （100 million yuan）	575.49	108.28	107.89
进出口总额（亿美元）	Total Imports （USD 100 million）	80.04	3.91	2.76
#出 口	Exports	36.03	2.79	2.12
实际到帐注册外资（亿美元）	Foreign Capital Actually Utilized （USD 100 million）	7.34	1.30	1.39
城镇居民人均可支配收入（元）	Per Capita Disposable Income of Urban Residents（yuan）	20816	19533	19726
城镇居民人均消费支出（元）	Per Capita Consuming Expenditures of Urban Residents（yuan）	12726	11165	11819
农民人均纯收入（元）	Per Capita Net Income of Rural Residents（yuan）	9589	10310	9910
农民人均生活消费支出（元）	Per Capita Living Expenditure of Rural Residents （yuan）	6210	6790	6432

注：城市居民人均可支配收入、城市居民人均消费性支出数据为全市口径。
Note：The data of per capita disposable income and per capita nonproductive expenditure of urban residents is subject to the municipal caliber.

Appendix 5 Continued 3

灌云县 Guanyun County	灌南县 Guannan County	淮安市 Huaian City	涟水县 Lianshui County	洪泽县 Hongze County	盱眙县 Xuyu County	金湖县 Jinhu County	盐城市 Yancheng City	响水县 Xiangshui County
102.01	78.73	546.81	111.39	38.59	78.30	35.71	822.40	61.48
78.99	62.19	480.30	83.78	33.27	64.30	33.13	721.63	50.33
1840	1025	10072	1676	1394	2497	1394	16972	1461
220.29	210.47	1920.91	228.64	155.09	221.88	142.39	3120.00	181.35
50.34	39.39	247.98	45.01	25.17	40.49	22.94	456.13	35.58
102.23	105.28	889.20	93.66	66.89	96.50	58.42	1472.87	89.85
77.90	89.46	737.20	73.68	55.55	75.39	50.43	1258.22	80.33
67.72	65.80	783.73	89.97	63.03	84.89	61.03	1191.00	55.92
27401	33914	39992	27138	46707	34267	43077	43172	35907
164.46	163.04	1247.99	139.31	92.34	173.33	85.37	1940.89	141.99
25.86	25.59	233.61	21.62	17.10	23.15	15.35	312.78	19.73
20.67	20.30	180.93	17.92	13.66	18.01	13.25	251.38	15.20
41.02	41.88	339.86	43.66	28.43	40.26	25.33	473.48	35.86
143.28	88.23	1502.79	176.46	97.25	171.07	128.70	2699.33	99.66
87.16	62.06	806.86	104.47	48.70	89.96	76.69	1519.33	57.76
97.79	69.26	1173.18	107.17	78.65	134.80	103.64	1831.44	81.40
392.11	410.99	3952.61	433.06	367.28	485.65	303.60	5553.85	438.23
386.36	406.49	3953.91	421.52	359.86	498.82	300.13	5561.88	435.04
30.42	31.06	209.13	19.01	22.51	17.44	12.40	396.91	41.50
41.93	51.80	378.48	30.49	34.21	25.95	18.47	690.89	55.67
5.20	15.14	95.50	8.26	11.81	8.81	7.30	164.49	28.44
78.69	54.01	633.24	64.48	58.88	62.52	55.75	1023.20	42.18
2.35	1.62	42.41	3.31	1.93	4.21	3.09	57.54	4.56
2.15	1.34	33.66	3.04	1.36	3.97	3.04	34.65	3.53
0.55	0.23	21.21	2.10	2.25	2.80	2.00	21.11	1.32
15943	18535	20950	18116	21717	22230	22075	21940	18208
9553	10650	14458	12651	14414	13887	13419	15430	14503
8929	8472	9838	9185	10838	10031	10624	11898	9861
4921	5948	6493	5751	5862	5099	8167	6998	5630

附录5 续表4

指 标	Item	滨海县 Binhai County	阜宁县 Huning County	射阳县 Sheyang County
年末总人口（万人）	Year-end Population （10000 persons）	120.05	110.88	96.66
年末常住人口（万人）	Year-end permanent population（10000 persons）	94.48	83.96	89.22
土地面积（平方公里）	Area of Land （sq.km）	1915	1439	2855
地区生产总值（亿元）	Gross Domestic Products （100 million yuan）	267.69	274.99	320.31
第一产业	Primary Industry	49.70	46.34	69.59
第二产业	Secondary Industry	117.89	131.61	129.38
#工 业	Industry	99.78	98.40	117.54
第三产业	Tertiary Industry	100.10	97.04	121.34
人均地区生产总值（元）	Per Capita GDP （yuan）	28245	32731	35841
固定资产投资完成额（亿元）	Investment in Fixed Assets（100 million yuan）	187.32	163.00	168.31
公共财政预算收入（亿元）	Public Finance Budget Revenue（100 million yuan）	24.94	25.48	20.80
#税收收入	Tax Revenue	19.49	20.28	16.40
公共财政预算支出（亿元）	Public Finance Budget Expenditure（100 million yuan）	48.09	46.55	43.83
年底金融机构存款余额（亿元）	Balance of Deposits of Financial Institutions at Year-end （100 million yuan）	158.33	202.08	204.49
#城乡居民储蓄	Savings Deposits of Residents	97.14	135.70	132.17
年底金融机构贷款余额（亿元）	Balance of Loans of Financial Institutions at Year-end （100 million yuan）	109.94	138.82	153.51
规模以上工业企业主要指标	**Major Economic Indicators of Industrial Enterprises Above Designated Size**			
工业总产值（亿元）	Gross Industrial Output Value （100 million yuan）	426.55	436.90	465.14
主营业务收入（亿元）	Main Business Income （100 million yuan）	430.25	443.67	461.13
利润总额（亿元）	Total Profits （100 million yuan）	31.63	19.70	18.35
利税总额（亿元）	Total Pre-tax Profits （100 million yuan）	52.68	39.48	38.03
工业用电量（亿千瓦时）	Industrial Electricity Consumption （100 million kw.h）	16.01	20.48	9.90
社会消费品零售总额（亿元）	Total Retail Sales of Consumer Goods （100 million yuan）	69.98	82.09	110.00
进出口总额（亿美元）	Total Imports （USD 100 million）	2.14	1.69	2.45
#出 口	Exports	1.95	1.45	1.82
实际到帐注册外资（亿美元）	Foreign Capital Actually Utilized （USD 100 million）	1.50	1.68	1.60
城镇居民人均可支配收入（元）	Per Capita Disposable Income of Urban Residents（yuan）	19090	18253	19373
城镇居民人均消费支出（元）	Per Capita Consuming Expenditures of Urban Residents（yuan）	11975	13955	16028
农民人均纯收入（元）	Per Capita Net Income of Rural Residents（yuan）	10429	10545	11726
农民人均生活消费支出（元）	Per Capita Living Expenditure of Rural Residents （yuan）	5820	5490	6039

注：城市居民人均可支配收入、城市居民人均消费性支出数据为全市口径。
Note：The data of per capita disposable income and per capita nonproductive expenditure of urban residents is subject to the municipal caliber.

Appendix 5 Continued 4

建湖县 Jianhu County	东台市 Dongtai City	大丰市 Dafeng City	扬州市 Yangzhou City	宝应县 Baoying County	仪征市 Yizheng City	高邮市 Gaoyou City	镇江市 Zhenjiang City
80.41	113.59	72.53	458.42	90.31	56.24	81.74	271.40
73.77	98.59	70.12	446.72	75.11	56.27	73.90	315.48
1160	3221	3059	6591	1462	857	1922	3847
324.47	506.69	393.36	2933.20	323.03	370.27	336.00	2630.42
42.13	78.33	63.34	205.19	55.43	19.30	55.96	115.77
154.35	231.89	173.82	1554.46	151.85	212.86	156.05	1419.54
133.83	204.71	151.25	1344.66	121.50	187.73	126.29	1309.54
127.99	196.47	156.20	1173.55	115.75	138.11	123.99	1095.11
43916	51342	56014	65692	42982	65843	45436	83651
177.75	278.41	216.56	1783.65	197.69	247.45	234.29	1500.67
32.94	43.67	40.01	225.00	20.71	24.66	21.72	215.48
26.54	34.57	30.85	180.61	16.61	19.89	17.41	174.12
53.29	62.75	55.42	284.80	37.04	26.44	36.98	235.25
231.59	442.73	321.76	3310.84	262.79	333.11	296.25	2850.51
161.89	324.20	198.10	1697.51	171.88	194.23	203.41	1301.36
171.83	231.17	203.48	2006.50	163.41	183.58	167.79	2073.29
529.69	748.45	564.17	7198.48	607.60	1049.86	726.84	6105.69
525.10	746.19	557.02	7037.79	588.65	1012.94	717.50	5975.34
32.10	40.85	28.41	498.81	28.96	92.59	46.81	363.11
59.62	76.01	52.46	865.25	51.81	133.39	80.51	567.37
10.50	27.03	28.02	123.20	8.95	23.79	12.07	151.62
108.32	158.09	108.80	973.97	105.35	114.75	110.57	766.46
3.22	4.53	8.46	101.73	6.20	9.32	3.27	114.13
2.81	4.10	4.68	81.72	4.72	4.53	3.01	77.37
1.60	3.10	3.10	21.38	1.00	3.52	0.98	22.14
21215	23868	22471	25712	18988	26658	22588	30045
14115	14617	14704	16492	12730	16529	15196	17897
11705	13647	13517	12686	11670	12244	11828	14518
7014	7982	8729	8714	8269	8533	8405	10530

附录 5 续表 5

指 标	Item	丹阳市 Danyang City	扬中市 Yangzhong City	句容市 Jurong City
年末总人口（万人）	Year-end Population （10000 persons）	81.17	28.09	58.84
年末常住人口（万人）	Year-end permanent population（10000 persons）	97.40	34.01	62.22
土地面积（平方公里）	Area of Land （sq.km）	1047	331	1387
地区生产总值（亿元）	Gross Domestic Products （100 million yuan）	830.51	360.20	336.86
第一产业	Primary Industry	44.79	11.50	31.71
第二产业	Secondary Industry	447.76	202.69	177.89
#工 业	Industry	428.85	195.20	164.64
第三产业	Tertiary Industry	337.96	146.01	127.26
人均地区生产总值（元）	Per Capita GDP （yuan）	85549	106269	54275
固定资产投资完成额（亿元）	Investment in Fixed Assets（100 million yuan）	280.53	147.03	174.39
公共财政预算收入（亿元）	Public Finance Budget Revenue（100 million yuan）	50.09	22.57	25.02
#税收收入	Tax Revenue	41.92	18.13	21.29
公共财政预算支出（亿元）	Public Finance Budget Expenditure（100 million yuan）	54.31	25.36	35.86
年底金融机构存款余额（亿元）	Balance of Deposits of Financial Institutions at Year-end（100 million yuan）	725.50	350.86	318.78
#城乡居民储蓄	Savings Deposits of Residents	372.35	198.60	176.17
年底金融机构贷款余额（亿元）	Balance of Loans of Financial Institutions at Year-end（100 million yuan）	588.11	239.03	216.10
规模以上工业企业主要指标	**Major Economic Indicators of Industrial Enterprises Above Designated Size**			
工业总产值（亿元）	Gross Industrial Output Value （100 million yuan）	1931.79	877.53	896.48
主营业务收入（亿元）	Main Business Income （100 million yuan）	1899.27	846.29	893.04
利润总额（亿元）	Total Profits （100 million yuan）	92.91	60.09	40.73
利税总额（亿元）	Total Pre-tax Profits （100 million yuan）	141.19	95.78	85.11
工业用电量（亿千瓦时）	Industrial Electricity Consumption （100 million kw.h）	46.70	9.99	13.80
社会消费品零售总额（亿元）	Total Retail Sales of Consumer Goods （100 million yuan）	202.38	90.32	93.31
进出口总额（亿美元）	Total Imports （USD 100 million）	26.51	4.81	6.11
#出 口	Exports	21.84	3.63	4.45
实际到帐注册外资（亿美元）	Foreign Capital Actually Utilized （USD 100 million）	4.76	1.67	4.26
城镇居民人均可支配收入（元）	Per Capita Disposable Income of Urban Residents（yuan）	30120	33442	29625
城镇居民人均消费支出（元）	Per Capita Consuming Expenditures of Urban Residents（yuan）	16136	18008	18132
农民人均纯收入（元）	Per Capita Net Income of Rural Residents（yuan）	15171	16631	13235
农民人均生活消费支出（元）	Per Capita Living Expenditure of Rural Residents （yuan）	11722	10158	9486

注：城市居民人均可支配收入、城市居民人均消费性支出数据为全市口径。
Note: The data of per capita disposable income and per capita nonproductive expenditure of urban residents is subject to the municipal caliber.

Appendix 5 Continued 5

泰州市 Taizhou City	兴化市 Xinghua City	靖江市 Jingjiang City	泰兴市 Taixing City	姜堰市 Jiangyan City	宿迁市 Suqian City	沭阳县 Shuyang County	泗阳县 Siyang County	泗洪县 Sihong County
506.35	157.28	66.66	119.83	79.31	560.26	186.82	103.60	105.45
462.98	125.40	68.58	107.60	72.92	479.80	155.30	84.90	92.30
5787	2395	656	1170	928	8555	2298	1418	2731
2701.67	512.36	600.85	543.55	405.86	1522.03	480.50	273.74	264.63
191.75	81.54	18.88	42.80	31.68	226.80	71.76	46.21	49.17
1434.53	222.50	335.88	291.15	210.80	716.85	220.49	137.97	111.14
1237.05	190.40	310.80	253.82	172.44	589.82	194.31	113.88	89.17
1075.39	208.32	246.09	209.60	163.38	578.38	188.25	89.56	104.32
58378	40853	87639	50537	55635	31827	31000	32357	28780
1454.59	189.30	283.38	261.10	215.62	1025.56	258.16	184.46	160.65
223.62	29.46	44.01	32.61	23.54	158.13	48.79	21.76	19.76
179.73	24.08	35.28	26.13	18.90	130.07	38.30	17.79	15.26
300.90	58.68	47.77	50.58	34.95	272.40	78.20	42.00	44.42
3032.63	412.47	654.18	466.13	424.96	1226.87	280.00	206.18	181.74
1546.53	275.48	314.65	294.54	254.23	621.02	183.96	111.75	109.26
2007.97	264.26	408.86	272.19	305.79	1002.86	223.84	157.32	159.41
7127.49	957.08	1726.63	1429.91	800.41	2248.28	683.82	377.88	345.68
6918.60	950.94	1626.93	1414.05	757.96	2213.14	676.76	379.42	322.47
538.06	53.59	148.20	139.49	53.11	250.83	67.10	33.12	36.30
900.98	93.38	214.64	225.32	83.94	346.68	100.35	45.42	53.84
164.81	46.08	27.15	39.16	20.17	79.90	22.48	7.57	6.19
737.57	112.69	123.25	142.95	122.15	388.23	108.34	63.58	65.24
103.70	5.82	35.10	20.36	7.71	27.93	5.29	5.93	3.58
69.45	4.65	23.44	10.77	6.32	23.18	4.76	5.78	3.42
14.50	1.35	2.61	2.52	1.12	4.52	1.01	0.64	0.64
26574	24165	28803	26338	26714	16991	17215	16474	15935
16499	14262	19669	16456	15688	11864	12181	11208	11939
12493	11827	13715	12505	12228	9495	9557	9541	9327
8990	7658	11176	8209	8785	6594	7060	7109	4720

附录 6 长江三角洲地区各城市主要经济指标（2012 年）
MAIN ECONOMIC INDICATORS BY CITY IN THE YANGSE RIVER DELTA（2012）

指 标	Item	上海市 Shanghai City	南京市 Nanjing City	无锡市 Wuxi City
土地面积（平方公里）	Area of Land （sq.km）	6341	6587	4627
年末户籍人口（万人）	Year-end Population （10000 persons）	1426.93	638.48	470.07
年末常住人口（万人）	Year-end permanent population （10000 persons）	2380.43	816.1	646.55
地区生产总值（亿元）	Gross Domestic Products （100 million yuan）	20181.72	7201.57	7568.15
第一产业	Primary Industry	127.80	185.06	137.22
第二产业	Secondary Industry	7854.77	3170.78	4012.03
#工 业	Industy	7097.76	2748.46	3717.88
第三产业	Tertiary Industry	12199.15	3845.73	3418.90
人均地区生产总值（元）	Per Capita GDP （yuan）	85373	88525	117357
规模以上工业总产值（亿元）	Total Output Value of Industry above Designated Size （100 million yuan）	31896.88	11473.80	14446.85
社会消费品零售总额（亿元）	Total Retail of Consumer Goods （100 million yuan）	7412.30	3103.82	2443.24
固定资产投资完成额（亿元）	Investment in Fixed Assets （100 million yuan）	5254.38	4558.49	3618.07
#房地产投资	Real Estate Investment	2404.53	971.96	974.37
进出口总额（亿美元）	Total Imports and Exports（USD 100 million）	4367.58	552.35	707.72
#出 口	Exports	2068.07	319.16	413.13
实际到帐注册外资（亿美元）	Foreign Capital Actually Used （USD 100 million）	151.85	41.30	40.10
公共财政预算收入（亿元）	Public Finance Budget Revenue （100 million yuan）	3743.71	733.02	658.03
公共财政预算支出（亿元）	Public Finance Budget Expenditure （100 million yuan）	4184.02	769.66	648.61
金融机构本外币存款余额（亿元）	Deposits Balance in Foreign Currencies of Banking Institutions （100 million yuan）	63555.25	16540.43	10740.38
#储蓄存款	Savings Deposits	20247.24	4532.02	3763.82
金融机构本外币贷款余额（亿元）	Loans Balance in Foreign Currencies of Banking Institutions （100 million yuan）	40982.48	13079.32	8024.00
城市居民人均可支配收入（元）	Per Capita Disposable Income of Urban Residents （yuan）	40188	35092	35663
城市居民人均消费性支出（元）	Per Capita Consuming Expenditures of Urban Residents （yuan）	26253	22446	23000
农民人均纯收入（元）	Per Capita Net Income of Rural Residents （yuan）	17401	14786	18509
农民人均生活消费支出（元）	Per Capita Living Expenditure of Rural Residents （yuan）	12096	11114	12795
全社会用电量（亿千瓦时）	Total Electriccity Consumed （100 million kw.h）	1353.45	424.96	578.01
#工 业	Industrial	786.25	265.64	464.51

注：城市居民人均可支配收入、城市居民人均消费性支出数据为全市口径。
Note：The data of per capita disposable income and per capita nonproductive expenditure of urban residents is subject to the municipal caliber.

常州市 Changzhou City	苏州市 Shanghai City	南通市 Nantong City	扬州市 Yangzhou City	镇江市 zhenjiang City	泰州市 Taizhou City	杭州市 Hangzhou City	宁波市 Ningbo City	嘉兴市 Jiaxing City	湖州市 Huzhou City
4372	8488	8001	6591	3847	5787	16571	9816	3915	5820
364.77	647.81	765.20	458.42	271.40	506.35	700.52	577.71	344.52	261.38
468.68	1054.91	729.73	446.72	315.48	462.98	880.20	763.90	454.40	290.50
3969.87	12011.65	4558.67	2933.20	2630.42	2701.67	7802.01	6582.21	2890.57	1664.30
126.37	195.08	319.09	205.19	115.77	191.75	255.11	268.52	151.39	122.65
2100.76	6502.25	2414.11	1554.46	1419.54	1434.53	3572.63	3516.84	1603.08	886.42
1900.55	6055.10	1992.11	1344.66	1309.54	1237.05	3168.75	3170.07	1443.02	796.75
1742.74	5314.32	1825.47	1173.55	1095.11	1075.39	3974.27	2796.85	1136.10	655.24
85039	114029	62506	65692	83650	58378	88962	86228	63704	57350
8970.30	28745.54	9890.12	7198.48	6105.69	7127.49	12962.28	12155.08	6039.93	3333.83
1413.33	3240.97	1719.27	973.97	766.46	737.57	2944.63	2329.26	1083.74	703.87
2621.56	5142.51	2886.47	1783.65	1500.67	1454.59	3722.75	2901.43	1642.31	970.73
597.01	1263.36	481.74	235.84	205.48	223.62	1597.36	884.35	415.88	211.17
290.46	3056.92	263.01	101.73	114.13	103.70	616.83	965.73	287.44	87.37
199.62	1746.89	187.86	81.72	77.37	69.47	412.62	614.45	196.03	73.96
33.61	91.65	22.05	21.38	22.14	14.50	49.61	28.53	17.82	10.26
378.99	1204.33	419.72	225.00	215.48	223.62	859.99	725.50	257.73	138.55
391.22	1113.47	513.01	284.80	235.25	300.90	786.28	828.44	260.70	167.51
5789.88	18796.06	6478.01	3365.22	2903.48	3076.17	20148.00	11980.50	4597.34	2285.66
2489.97	5845.91	3605.65	1705.76	1308.93	1550.76	6089.00	4208.80	2155.49	1082.79
4018.21	14877.84	4001.62	2042.98	2128.23	2080.66	18090.90	11961.00	3670.52	1912.40
33326	39079	28292	25712	30045	26574	35704	38043	35696	32987
20918	25157	17858	16492	17897	16499	22518	22887	21720	19898
16737	19396	13231	12686	14518	12493	17017	18475	18636	17188
12027	14381	9839	8714	10530	8990	13612	12699	12326	11077
351.51	1189.93	301.79	173.63	193.47	211.31	591.72	514.09	351.42	165.84
277.88	982.66	222.96	123.20	151.62	164.81	396.19	384.59	289.23	126.50

附录 6 续表 Appendix 6 continued

指 标	Item	绍兴市 Shao xing City	舟山市 Zhoushan City	台州市 Taizhou City
土地面积（平方公里）	Area of Land （sq.km）	8256	1455	9411
年末户籍人口（万人）	Year-end Population （10000 persons）	440.83	97.18	590.95
年末常住人口（万人）	Year-end permanent population （10000 persons）	494.30	114.00	600.50
地区生产总值（亿元）	Gross Domestic Products （100 million yuan）	3654.03	853.18	2911.26
第一产业	Primary Industry	184.80	83.06	200.91
第二产业	Secondary Industry	1962.41	382.94	1419.47
#工 业	Industy	1751.79	295.81	1273.64
第三产业	Tertiary Industry	1506.82	387.18	1290.87
人均地区生产总值（元）	Per Capita GDP （yuan）	73991	74939	48505
规模以上工业总产值（亿元）	Total Output Value of Industry above Designated Size（100 million yuan）	8551.25	1199.83	3530.81
社会消费品零售总额（亿元）	Total Retail of Consumer Goods （100 million yuan）	1158.66	290.54	1304.30
固定资产投资完成额（亿元）	Investment in Fixed Assets （100 million yuan）	1722.56	570.60	1242.56
#房地产投资	Real Estate Investment	467.71	158.94	357.38
进出口总额（亿美元）	Total Imports and Exports（USD 100 million）	320.98	153.56	206.22
#出 口	Exports	255.57	92.24	172.39
实际到帐注册外资（亿美元）	Foreign Capital Actually Used （USD 100 million）	9.54	1.83	4.75
公共财政预算收入（亿元）	Public Finance Budget Revenue （100 million yuan）	265.76	85.56	220.42
公共财政预算支出（亿元）	Public Finance Budget Expenditure （100 million yuan）	278.71	155.22	287.93
金融机构本外币存款余额（亿元）	Deposits Balance in Foreign Currencies of Banking Institutions （100 million yuan）	5923.60	1389.97	4509.17
#储蓄存款	Savings Deposits	2503.32	508.59	2385.14
金融机构本外币贷款余额（亿元）	Loans Balance in Foreign Currencies of Banking Institutions （100 million yuan）	5129.15	1295.83	3893.16
城市居民人均可支配收入（元）	Per Capita Disposable Income of Urban Residents （yuan）	36911	34224	33979
城市居民人均消费性支出（元）	Per Capita Consuming Expenditures of Urban Residents（yuan）	22204	20958	20643
农民人均纯收入（元）	Per Capita Net Income of Rural Residents （yuan）	17706	18601	14567
农民人均生活消费支出（元）	Per Capita Living Expenditure of Rural Residents （yuan）	11107	13589	10148
全社会用电量（亿千瓦时）	Total Electriccity Consumed （100 million kw.h）	337.71	41.77	227.33
#工 业	Industrial	276.83	22.29	156.67

注：城市居民人均可支配收入、城市居民人均消费性支出数据为全市口径。
Note：The data of per capita disposable income and per capita nonproductive expenditure of urban residents is subject to the municipal caliber.

附录 7　主要统计指标解释

1. 地区生产总值　指一个国家（地区）所有常住单位在一定时期内生产活动的最终成果。国内生产总值有三种表现形态，即价值形态、收入形态和产品形态。从价值形态看，它是所有常住单位在一定时期内所生产的全部货物和服务价值超过同期投入的全部非固定资产货物和服务价值的差额，即所有常住单位的增加值之和；从收入形态看，它是所有常住单位在一定时期内所创造并分配给常住单位和非常住单位的初次分配收入之和；从产品形态看，它是最终使用的货物和服务减去进口货物和服务。在实际核算中，国内生产总值的三种表现形态表现为三种计算方法，即生产法、收入法和支出法。三种方法分别从不同的方面反映地区生产总值及其构成。

2. 可比价格　指对不同时期的价值进行对比时，扣除了价格变动的因素，以确切反映物量的变化情况。按可比价格计算的方法有两种：一是直接按产品产量乘不变价格计算；二是用物价指数换算。

3. 不变价格　指以同类产品某年的平均价格作为固定价格，用于计算各年的产品价值。按不变价格计算的产品价值消除了价格变动因素，不同时期对比可以反映生产的发展速度。新中国成立后，随着工农业产品价格水平的变化，国家统计局先后五次制定了全国统一的工业产品不变价格和农业产品不变价格。从1952年到1957年使用1952年工（农）业产品不变价格，从1957年到1970年使用1957年不变价格，从1971年到1980年使用1970年不变价格，从1981年到1990年使用1980年不变价格，从1991年开始使用1990年不变价格。

4. 各个计划时期　各个计划“时期”代表的年份如下：恢复时期为1950-1952年；第一个五年计划时期（简称“一五”时期）为1953-1957年；第二个五年计划时期（简称“二五”时期）为1958-1962年；调整时期为1963-1965年：第三个五年计划时期（简称“三五”时期）为1966-1970年；第四个五年计划时期（简称“四五”时期）为1971-1975年；第五个五年计划时期（简称“五五”时期）为1976-1980年：第六个五年计划时期（简称“六五”时期）为1981-1985年；第七个五年计划时期（简称“七五”时期）为1986-1990年；第八个五年计划时期（简称“八五”时期）为1991-1995年；第九个五年计划时期（简称“九五”时期）为1996-2000年；第十个五年计划时期（简称“十五”时期）从2001-2005年；第十一个五年计划时期（简称“十一五”时期）为2006-2010年；第十二个五年计划时期（简称“十二五”时期）为2011-2015年。

5. 平均增长速度　指某种现象在一个较长时期中逐年增长的平均速度。其计算方法有两种：一是习惯上经常使用的“水平法”，又称几何水平法，是以间隔期最后一年的水平同基期水平对比来计算平均每年增长（或下降）速度；二是“累计法”，又称代数平均法或方程法，是以间隔期内各年水平的总和同基期水平对比来计算平均每年增长（或下降）速度。在一般正常情况下，两种方法计算的数值比较接近，但在经济发展不平衡，出现大起大落时，该两个数值差别较大。

本《年鉴》内所列的平均每年的增长速度，均用“水平法”计算。从某年到某年平均每年增长速度的年份，均不包括基期年在内。如改革开放34年以来的平均每年增长速度是以1978年为基期计算的，则写为1979-2012年平均每年增长速度，其余类推。

6. 企业（单位）登记注册类型　是以在工商行政管理机关登记注册的各类企业为划分对象，以工商行政管理部门对企业登记注册的类型为依据，将企业登记注册类型分为内资企业、港澳台商投资企业和外商投资企业三大类。内资企业包括国有企业、集体企业、股份合作企业、联营企业、有限责任公司、股份有限公司、私营公司和其他企业;港澳台商投资企业和外商投资企业分别包括合资经营企业、合作经营企业、独资经营企业和股份有限公司。对不在工商行政管理部门进行登记注册的行政机关、事业单位和社会团体，主要按其经费来源和管理方式进行划分。

7. 国有企业　指企业全部资产归国家所有，并按《中华人民共和国企业法人登记管理条例》规定登记注册的非公司制经济组织。不包括有限责任公司中的国有独资公司。

8. 集体企业　指企业资产归集体所有，并按《中华人民共和国企业法人登记管理条例》规定登记注册的经济组织。

9. 股份合作企业　指以合作制为基础，由企业职工共同出资入股，吸收一定比例的社会资产投资组建，实行自主经营，自负盈亏，共同劳动，民主管理，按劳分配与按股分红相结合的一种集体经济组织。

10. 联营企业　指两个及两个以上相同或不同所有制性质的企业法人或事业单位法人，按自愿、平等、互利的原则，共同投资组成的经济组织。联营企业包括国有联营企业、集体联营企业、国有与集体联营企业和其他联营企业。

11. 有限责任公司　指根据《中华人民共和国公司登记管理条例》规定登记注册，由两个以上、五十个以下的股东共同出资，每个股东以其所认缴的出资额对公司承担有限责任，公司以其全部资产对其债务承担责任的经济组织。有限责任公司包括国有独资公司以及其他有限责任公司。

12. 股份有限公司　指根据《中华人民共和国公司登记管理条例》规定登记注册，其全部注册资本由等额股份构成并通过发行股票筹集资本，股东以其认购的股份对公司承担有限责任，公司以其全部资产对其债务承担责任的经济组织。

13. 私营企业　指由自然人投资设立或由自然人控股，以雇佣劳动为基础的营利性经济组织。包括按照《公司法》、《合伙企业法》、《私营企业暂行条例》规定登记注册的私营有限责任公司、私营股份有限公司、私营合伙企业和私营独资企业。

14. 其他企业　指上述企业之外的其他内资经济组织。

15. 港、澳、台投资企业　指港、澳、台地区投资者参照中华人民共和国有关涉外经济的法律、法规，以合资、合作或独资的形式在祖国大陆举办的企业。包括合资经营企业、合作经营企业和独资企业。

16. **外商投资企业** 指外国投资者根据中华人民共和国有关涉外经济的法律、法规，以合资、合作或独资的形式在中国大陆境内开办的企业。包括中外合资经营企业、中外合作经营企业和外资企业。

17. **三次产业** 根据社会生产活动历史发展的顺序对产业结构的划分，产品直接取自自然界的部门称为第一产业，对初级产品进行再加工的部门称为第二产业，为生产和消费提供各种服务的部门称为第三产业。它是世界上通用的产业结构分类，但各国的划分不尽一致。我国的三次产业划分是：

第一产业：农林牧渔业（包括农业、林业、畜牧业、渔业和农林牧渔服务业）。

第二产业：工业（包括采掘工业、制造业、自来水、电力、蒸汽、热水、煤气）和建筑业。

第三产业：除第一、第二产业以外的其他各业。

18. **人口数** 指一定时点、一定地区范围内的有生命的个人的总和。年度统计的年末人口数是指每年12月31日24时的常住人口数。不包括户籍不在本市的外来人数。

19. **出生率（又称粗出生率）** 指在一定时期内（通常为一年）出生的人数与同期平均人数（或期中人数）比率，一般用千分率表示。计算公式：

出生率=年出生人数/年平均人数×1000‰

出生人数是指活产婴儿，即胎儿脱离母体时（不管怀孕月数），有过呼吸或其他生命现象。

目前出生率的计算，在市级有公安的户籍口径、计生委的常住人口统计口径；国家、省级还有年度人口抽样调查公布口径等。本年鉴用的为公安口径出生数，包括补报往年出生数在内。

年平均人数是年初、年底人口数的平均数，也可用年中人口数代替。

20. **死亡率（又称粗死亡率）** 指在一定时期内（通常为一年）一定地区的死亡人数与同期平均人数（或期中人数）之比，一般用千分率表示。计算公式：

死亡率=年死亡人数/年平均人数×1000‰

21. **人口自然增长率** 指在一定时期内（通常为一年）人口自然增加数（出生人数减死亡人数）与该时期内平均人数（或期中人数）之比，一般用行千分率表示。计算公式：

人口自然增长率=（本年出生人数—本年死亡人数）/年平均人数×1000‰

人口自然增长率=人口出生率—人口死亡率

22. **人口预期寿命** 指在一定年龄组死亡率水平下，对某一确定的年龄日后平均还能继续生存的年数（或该年龄组未来的平均预期寿命）。

23. **从业人员** 指从事一定社会劳动并取得劳动报酬或经营收入的人员。包括：（1）国有、集体、其他经济类型中的全部在岗职工和其他从业人员；（2）城镇私营及个体劳动者；（3）农村社会劳动者。

各单位的从业人员是指在各级国家机关、政党机关、社会团体及企业、事业单位中工作，取得工资或其他形式的劳动报酬的全部人员。包括：在岗职工、再就业的离退休人员、在各单位中工作的外方人员和港澳台方人员、兼职人员、借用的外单位人员和第二职业者。不包括离开本单位仍保留劳动关系的职工。

24. **职 工** 指在内资（国有、集体、股份合作、联营、有限责任公司、股份有限公司）单位、港澳台投资单位和外商投资单位及其附属机构工作，并由其支付工资的在岗人员以及不在岗但劳动关系在本单位的离岗人员。

25. **在岗职工** 指在本单位工作并由单位支付工资的人员，以及有工作岗位，但由于学习、病伤产假等原因暂未工作，仍由单位支付工资的人员。

26. **离岗职工** 指由于各种原因，已经离开本人的生产或工作岗位，并已不在本单位从事其他工作，但仍与用人单位保留劳动关系的职工。

27. **从业人员工资总额** 指各单位在一定时期内直接支付给本单位全部从业人员的劳动报酬总额。包括在岗职工工资总额、劳务派遣人员工资总额和其他从业人员工资总额三部分。

28. **在岗职工工资总额** 指各单位在一定时期内直接支付给本单位全部在岗职工的劳动报酬总额。

工资总额的计算原则应以直接支付给职工的全部劳动报酬为根据。各单位支付给职工的劳动报酬以及其他根据有关规定支付的工资，不论是计入成本的还是不计入成本的，不论是按国家规定列入计征奖金税项目的，还是未列入计征奖金税项目的，不论是以货币形式支付的还是以实物形式支付的，均包括在工资总额内。

29. **在岗职工平均工资** 指各单位的在岗职工在一定时期内平均每人所得的货币工资额。它表明一定时期内职工工资收入高低程度，是反映职工工资水平的主要指标。计算公式为：

在岗职工平均工资=报告期实际支付的全部在岗职工工资总额/报告期全部在岗职工平均人数

30. **城镇登记失业人员** 指在劳动年龄（16周岁至退休年龄）内，有劳动能力，有就业要求，处于无业状态，并在公共就业人才服务机构进行失业登记的城镇人员。

31.**居民消费价格指数** 居民消费价格，指城乡居民支付生活消费品和服务项目消费的价格，是社会产品和服务项目的最终价格，同人民生活密切相关，在整个国民经济价格体系中具有极为重要的地位。居民消费价格指数，就是指反映一定时期内居民消费价格变动趋势和变动程度的相对数。

32.商品零售价格指数 商品零售价格，指工业、商业、餐饮业和其他零售企业向城乡居民、机关团体出售生活消费品和办公用品的价格。商品零售价格指数，就是指反映一定时期内商品零售价格变动趋势和变动程度的相对数。

33.服务项目价格指数 指居民非商品服务性支出的相对数。服务项目包括：电信费、邮费、交通费、洗理美容费、文娱费、学杂保育费、修理及其他服务费、医疗保险服务费8个大类。

34.城镇居民家庭就业人口 指城镇居民从事社会劳动并取得劳动报酬或经营收入的人口。就业人口包括通过国家统筹规划和指导由劳动部门介绍就业，自愿组织起来就业和自谋职业等方式，在国有单位、集体单位、中外合资、中外合作、外资在华独资的企业事业单位和私营企业单位工作或从事个体劳动的有固定性职业或临时性职业的人口。被聘用或留用的离休人员也记入就业人口。它是反映城镇居民的就业情况，计算就业面、负担系数的资料之一。

35. 城镇居民家庭总收入 指调查户中生活在一起的所有家庭成员在调查期得到的工薪收入、经营净收入、财产性收入、转移性收入的总和,不包括出售财物和借贷收入。收入以实际发生数额为准。无论收入是补发还是预发，只要是调查期得到的都应如实计算，不作分摊。

财产性收入指家庭拥有的动产（如银行存款、有价证券）、不动产（如房屋、车辆、土地、收藏品等）所获得的收入。包括出让财产使用权所获得的利息、租金、专利收入；财产营运所获得的红利收入、财产增值收益等。

转移性收入指国家、单位、社会团体对居民家庭的各种转移支付和居民家庭间的收入转移。包括政府对个人收入转移的离退休金、失业救济金、赔偿等；单位对个人收入转移的辞退金、保险索赔、住房公积金、家庭间的赠送和赡养等。

36. 城镇居民家庭可支配收入 指调查户可用于最终消费支出和其他非义务性支出以及储蓄的总和,即居民家庭可用于自由支配的收入。计算公式为：可支配收入＝家庭总收入-交纳个人所得税-个人交纳的社会保障支出-记帐补贴。

37. 家庭总支出 指家庭除借贷支出以外的全部实际支出。包括消费性支出、购房建房支出、转移性支出、财产性支出、社会保障支出。支出统计是以实际购得的商品或服务的总价值填报，不论其付款方式是一次性付清、分期付款，还是赊购，只要商品或服务已被消费就要按其总价值计量。如果采用分期付款或赊购形式，则要在借贷收入类相应的项目填入实付款与总的应付款的差额。

38. 城镇居民家庭消费支出 指被调查的城镇居民家庭用于日常生活的全部支出，包括食品、衣着、家庭设备用品及服务、医疗保健、交通和通信、教育文化娱乐服务、居住、杂项商品和服务八大类。包括用于赠送的商品或服务。

39. 农村居民家庭纯收入 指农村常住居民家庭总收入中，扣除从事生产和非生产经营费用支出、缴纳税款和上交承包集体任务金额以后剩余的，可直接用于进行生产性、非生产性建设投资、生活消费和积蓄的那一部分收入。它是反映农民家庭实际收入水平的综合性主要指标。农民家庭纯收入，既包括从事生产性和非生产性的经营收入，又包括取自在外人口寄回带回和国家财政救济、各种补贴等非经营性收入，还包括自产自用的实物收入。但不包括向银行、信用社和向亲友借款等属于借贷性的收入。

40. 农村居民家庭整半劳动力 指农村常住居民家庭成员中有劳动能力并经常参加实际劳动的人员。是生产的基本要素指标之一，是发展生产增加农民家庭收入的重要源泉。按规定，农村男18周岁至50周岁、女18周岁至45周岁为整劳动力；男16周岁到17周岁、51周岁到60周岁，女16周岁到17周岁、46周岁至55周岁为半劳动力。农民家庭整半劳动力，既包括在上述规定劳动年龄内和劳动年龄以外有劳动能力并经常参加实际劳动的男女整半劳动力，也包括农民家庭常住人员中属于职工的劳动力。但不包括在劳动年龄内已丧失劳动能力的人员。

41. 农村居民家庭生活消费支出 指农村常住居民家庭年内用于日常生活的全部开支。它是用来反映和研究农民家庭实际生活消费水平高低的重要指标。包括用于吃、穿、住、烧、用等生活消费品开支和文化、生活服务费用开支两大部分。

42. 全社会固定资产投资 固定资产投资是社会固定资产再生产的主要手段。固定资产投资额是以货币表现的建造和购置固定资产活动的工作量，它是反映固定资产投资规模、速度、比例关系和使用方向的综合性指标。全社会固定资产投资包括各种经济类型的投资，其投资总额分为：城镇投资、房地产开发投资、农村投资。

43. 房地产开发投资 指各种登记注册类型的房地产开发公司、商品房建设公司及其他房地产开发单位统一开发的包括统代建、拆迁还建的住宅、厂房、仓库、饭店、宾馆、度假村、写字楼、办公楼等房屋建筑物和配套的服务设施、土地开发工程（如道路、给水、排水、供电、供热、通讯、平整场地等基础设施工程）的投资。还包括非房地产企业实际从事房地产开发或经营活动，不包括单纯的土地交易活动。

44. 固定资产投资的资金来源 根据固定资产投资的资金来源不同，分为上年末结余资金、本年资金来源。其中本年资金来源又分为国家预算内资金、国内贷款、债券、利用外资、自筹资金和其他资金来源6种。

45. 固定资产投资按构成分 固定资产投资活动按其工作内容和实现方式分为建筑工程，安装工程，设备、工具、器具购置，其他费用4个部分。

46. 新增固定资产 指通过投资活动所形成的新的固定资产价值。包括已经建成投入生产或交付使用的工程价值和达到固定资产标准的设备、工具、器具的价值及有关应摊入的费用。它是以价值形式表示的固定资产投资成果的综合性指标，可以综合反映不同时期、不同部门、不同地区的固定资产投资成果。

47. 固定资产交付使用率 指在一定时期所增固定资产与同期完成投资额的比率。它是反映各个时期固定资产动用速度，衡量建设过程中投资改革的一个综合性指标。

48. 施工项目 指报告期内曾进行建筑或安装工程施工活动的建设项目。包括报告期内新开工项目、报告期以前开工跨入报告期继续施工的项目以及报告期施过工并在报告期内全部建成投产或停缓建的项目。

49. 全部建成投产项目 工业项目是指设计文件规定形成生产能力的主体工程及其相应配套的辅助设施全部建成，经负荷试运转，证明具备生产设计规定合格产品的条件，并经过验收鉴定合格或达到竣工验收标准，与生产性工程配套的生产福利设施可以满足近期正常生产的需要，正式移交生产的建设项目。非工业项目是指设计文件规定的主体工程和相应的配套工程全部建成，能够发挥设计规定的全部效益，经验收鉴定合格或达到竣工验收标准，正式移交使用的建设项目。

50. 房屋建筑面积 指从房屋外墙线算起的各层平面面积的总和，包括房屋结构（如柱、墙）占用的面积和地下室面积。多层建筑按各自然层面积总和计算，包括房屋内的楼隔层、突出墙面的眺望间、门斗、有柱雨罩的面积。不包括突出墙面结构的构件、艺术装饰等所占的面积，如台阶等。凹阳台，挑阳台按其水平投影面积一半计算建筑面积。

51. 房屋施工面积 指在报告期内施工的全部房屋（包括地下室、半地下室以及配套房屋）建筑面积。包括本期新开工的面积和上年开工跨入本期继续施工的房屋面积，以及上期已停建在本期恢复施工的房屋面积。本期竣工和本期施工后又停建缓建的房屋面积仍包括在施工面积中，多层建筑应填各层建筑面积之和。

52. 房屋竣工面积 指在报告期内房屋建筑按照设计要求已全部完工，达到住人和使用条件，经验收鉴定合格或达到竣工验收标准，可正式移交使用的各栋房屋建筑面积的总和。

53. 住宅面积 指施工和竣工房屋建筑面积中供居住用的施工房屋建筑面积。

54. 农林牧渔业总产值 是以货币表现的农、林、牧、渔业全部产品的总量和对农林牧渔业生产活动进行的各种支持性服务活动的价值。它反映一定时期内农林牧渔业生产的总规模和总成果。农、林、牧、渔业的统计范围是：

（1）农业 包括农作物种植业和其他农业。

农作物种植业包括谷物、豆类、薯类、棉花、油料、糖料、麻类、烟叶、蔬菜、药材、瓜类和其他农作物的种植以及茶园、桑园、果园的生产经营。

其他农业包括采集野生植物的果实、纤维、树胶、树脂、油料以及柴草、野生药材、菌类等及农民家庭兼营的商品性工业。

（2）林业 包括林木的栽培（不包括茶园、桑园和果园的栽培、管理和收获等活动）、林产品的采集和村及村以下合作经济组织和农户的竹木采伐。

（3）牧业 包括除渔业养殖以外的一切动物饲养和放牧以及野生动物的捕猎和饲养。

（4）渔业 包括水生动物和海藻类植物的养殖和捕捞。

（5）农林牧渔服务业 包括灌溉服务、农产品初级加工服务、其他农业服务、林业服务、兽医服务、其他畜牧服务、渔业服务业等。

55. 粮食产量 指全社会的粮食产量。包括国有经济经营的、集体统一经营的和农民家庭经营的粮食产量，还包括工矿企业家属办的农场和其他生产单位的产量。（粮食除包括稻谷、小麦、玉米、高粱、谷子及其他杂粮外，还包括薯类和豆类）。1989年以前全国粮食产量数据主要靠全面报表取得，1989年开始使用抽样调查数据。

56. 油料产量 指全部油料作物的生产量。包括花生、油菜籽、芝麻、向日葵籽、胡麻籽（亚麻籽）和其他油料。不包括大豆，也不包括木本油料和野生油料。花生以带壳干花生计算。

57. 水产品产量 指人工养殖的水产品和天然生长的水产品捕捞量，包括海水的鱼类、虾蟹类、贝类和藻类以及内陆水域的鱼类、虾蟹类和贝类，不包括淡水生植物。

58. 猪、牛、羊肉产量 指当年出栏并已屠宰后除去头蹄下水后带骨肉的重量（即胴体重）。

59. 耕地面积 指可以用来种植农作物、经常进行耕锄的田地，除包括熟地、当年新开荒地、连续撂荒未满三年的耕地和当年的休闲地（轮歇地）外，还包括以种植农作物为主并附带种植桑树、茶树、果树和其他林木的土地，以及沿海、沿湖地区已围垦利用的“海涂”、“湖田”等面积。但不包括属于专业性的桑园、茶园、果园、果木苗圃、林地、芦苇地、天然或人工草地面积。

60. 农作物播种面积 指实际播种或移植有农作物的面积。凡是实际种植有农作物的面积，不论种植在耕地上还是种植在非耕地上，均包括在农作物播种面积中，同时还包括因遭灾而重新改种和补种的农作物面积。目前，农作物播种面积主要包括粮食、油料、棉花、麻类、糖料、烟叶、药材、蔬菜、瓜类和其他农作物等十大类。

61. 有效灌溉面积 指具有一定的水源，地块比较平稳，灌溉工程或设备已经配套，在一般年景下当年能够进行正常灌溉耕地面积。在一般情况下，该面积应等于灌溉工程或设备已经配套，能够进行正常灌溉的水田和水源地面积之和。

62. 农用化肥使用量 指本年内实际用于农业生产的化肥数量，包括氮肥、磷肥、钾肥和复合肥。并要求按折纯量计算数量。折纯量指氮肥、磷肥、钾肥分别按氮、五氧化二磷、钾的100%成分进行折纯后的数量，复合肥按其所含主要成分折算的。

63. 农业机械总动力 指主要用于农、林、牧、渔业的各种动力机械的动力总和。包括耕作机械、排灌机械、收获机械、农产品加工机械、运输机械、植物保护机械、牧业机械、林业机械、渔业机械和其他农业机械[内燃机按引擎马力折成瓦（特）计算，电动机按功率折成瓦（特）计算]。不包括专门用于乡、镇、村、组办工业、基本建设、非农业运输、科学试验和教学等非农业生产方面用的动力机械与作业机械。但从事农副产品初级加工的村户工业的机械动力统计在内。

64. 期初（末）畜禽存栏数 指本期期初（末）农村各种合作经济组织和国营农场、农民个人、机关、团体、学校、工矿企业、部队等单位以及城镇居民饲养的大牲畜、猪、羊、家禽等畜禽的存栏数。从1997年起，猪及家禽调查方法，由全面调查改为抽样调查。

65. 工 业 指从事自然资源的开采，对采掘品和农产品进行加工和再加工的物质生产部门。具体包括：（1）对自然资源的开采，如采矿、晒盐、森林采伐等（但不包括禽兽捕猎和水产捕捞）；（2）对农副产品的加工、再加工，如粮油加工、食品加工、轧花、缫丝、纺织、制革等；（3）对采掘品的加工、再加工，如炼铁、炼钢、化工生产、石油加工、机器制造、木材加工等，以及电力、自来水、煤气的生产和供应等；（4）对工业品的修理、翻新，如机器设备的修理、交通运输工具（包括小卧车）的修理等。

66. 轻工业 指主要提供生活消费品和制作手工工具的工业。另一定义为：指生产消费资料的工业。包括：（1）以农产品为原料的。如棉、毛、麻、丝的纺织及缝纫，皮革及其制品，纸浆及造纸，食品制造等工业；（2）以非农产品为原料的。如日用金属、日用化工、日用玻璃、日用陶瓷、化学纤维及其织品、火柴、生活用木制品等工业。轻工业产品大部分是生产消费品，一部分作为原料和半成品用于生产，如化学纤维、工业用布、纸张、盐等。

67. 重工业 指为国民经济各部门提供物质技术基础的主要生产资料的工业。按其生产性质和产品用途，可以分为下列三类：（1）采掘（伐）工业，是指对自然资源的开采，包括石油开采、煤炭开采、金属矿开采、非金属矿开采和木材采伐等工业；（2）原材料工业，是指向国民经济各部门提供基本材料、动力和燃料的工业。包括金属冶炼及加工、炼焦及焦炭化学、化工原料、水泥、人造板以及电力、石油和煤炭加工等工业；（3）加工工业，是指对工业原材料进行再加工制造的工业。包括装备国民经济各部门的机械设备制造工业、金属结构、水泥制品等工业，以及为农业提供的生产资料如化肥、农药等工业。

根据上述划分原则，修理业中以重工业产品为修理作业对象的划为重工业，反之划为轻工业。

68. 工业总产值 指工业企业在报告期内生产的以货币形式表现的工业最终产品和提供工业劳务活动的总价值量。包括：生产的成品价值、对外加工费收入、自制半成品在制品期末期初差额价值。

69. 工业销售产值 指以货币表现的工业企业在一定时期内销售的本企业生产的工业产品总量。包括已销售的成品、半成品价值，对外提供的工业性作业价值和对本单位基本建设部门、生活福利部门等提供的产品和工业性作业及自制设备的价值。已销售的成品、半成品不论是本期生产的、还是上期生产的，只要是本期销售出去的均包括在内。对外提供的工业性作业是指企业按合同对外提供的工业性劳务。企业为本单位基本建设部门、生活福利部门等提供的产品和工业性作业及自制设备也应视同销售，这部分也作为销售统计。

工业销售产值的计算范围、计算价格和计算方法与工业总产值一致，但两者计算的基础不同；工业销售产值计算的基础是产品销售总量，工业总产值计算的基础是工业产品生产总量。

70. 应收账款 指企业因销售商品、提供劳务等经营活动，应向购货单位或接受劳务单位收取的款项，主要包括企业销售商品或提供劳务等应向有关债务人收取的价款及代购货单位垫付的包装费、运杂费等。

71. 实收资本 指企业各投资者实际投入的资本（或股本）总额，包括货币、实物、无形资产等各种形式的投入。按投资主体可分为国家资本、集体资本、法人资本、个人资本、港澳台资本和外商资本。

72. 资产总计 指企业过去的交易或者事项形成的、由企业拥有或者控制的、预期会给企业带来经济利益的资源。

73. 流动资产合计 资产满足以下条件之一应归为流动资产：（1）预计在一个正常营业周期中变现、出售或耗用，主要包括存货、应收账款等；（2）主要为交易目的而持有；（3）预计在资产负债表日起一年内（含一年）变现；（4）自资产负债日起一年内，交换其他资产或清偿负债的能力不受限制的现金或现金等价物。

74. 固定资产合计 指企业为生产商品、提供劳务、出租或经营管理而持有的，使用寿命超过一个会计年度的有形资产。

75. 固定资产原价 指固定资产的成本，包括企业在购置、自行建造、安装、改建、扩建、技术改造某项固定资产时所发生的全部支出总额。

76. 累计折旧 指企业在报告期末提取的历年固定资产折旧累计数。

77. 本年折旧 指企业在报告期内提取的固定资产折旧合计数。根据会计“财务状况变动表”中“固定资产折旧”项的数值填报。

78. 负债合计 指企业过去的交易或者事项形成的，预期会导致经济利益流出企业的现时义务。负债一般按偿还期长短分为流动负债和非流动负债。

79. 流动负债合计 负债满足下列条件之一的应归为流动负债：（1）预计在一个正常营业周期中清偿；（2）主要为交易目的而持有；（3）自资产负债表日起一年内到期应予清偿；（4）企业无权自主地将清偿推迟至资产负债表日后一年以上。包括短期借款、应付票据、应付账款、应付职工薪酬、应交税费等项目。

80. 非流动负债 指流动负债之外的负债。包括长期借款、应付债券等。根据会计“资产负债表”中“非流动负债合计”项目的期末余额数填报。

81. 所有者权益合计 指企业资产扣除负债后由所有者享有的剩余权益。公司的所有者权益又称股东权益。包括实收资本、资本公积、盈余公积、未分配利润等。

82. 主营业务收入 指企业确认的销售商品、提供劳务等主营业务的收入。

83. 主营业务税金及附加 指企业经营主要业务应负担的营业税、消费税、城市维护建设税、教育费附加等。

84. **利税总额**　指企业产品销售税金及附加、应交增值税和利润总额之和。

85. **工业成本费用利润率**　该指标反映工业投入的生产成本及费用的经济效益，同时也反映企业降低成本所取得的经济效益。计算公式为：

工业成本费用利润率=利润总额/成本费用总额

86. **工业产品销售率**　该指标反映工业产品已实现销售的程度，是分析工业产销衔接情况、研究工业产品满足社会需求的指标。计算公式为：

工业产品销售率＝（现价工业销售产值/现价工业总产值）×100%

87. **建筑业总产值**　是以货币表现的建筑业企业在一定时期内生产的建筑业产品和服务的总和。建筑业总产值包括三部份内容：

①建筑工程产值：指列入建筑工程预算内的各种工程价值。

②设备安装工程产值：指设备安装工程价值。

③其他产值：指房屋构筑物修理产值、非标准设备制造产值、总包企业向分包企业收取的管理费以及不能明确划分的施工活动所完成的产值。

88.**竣工产值**　一般是以单位工程为对象,当该工程按照设计所规定的工程内容全部完成,达到了设计规定的交工条件,经有关部门检查验收鉴定合格的单位工程价值工程,即为竣工产值。竣工产值包括范围应是报告期内竣工单位工程从开工到竣工的全部自行完成的价值，如果一个单位工程跨两个年度施工,其竣工价值应当包括上年度完成的价值。有些大型单位工程，如大型厂房、高级宾馆、各种管道、公路、铁路等，能够分跨、分层、分段施工并按合同规定，能够分开交付使用的，可以分开计算竣工产值。竣工产值不包括附属辅助企业或内部核算的其他单位为外单位生产和服务的价值。

89.**房屋建筑施工面积**　指报告期内施过工的全部房屋建筑面积，它包括本期新开工的面积、上期跨入本期继续施工的房屋面积、上期停缓建在本期恢复工的房屋面积、本期竣工的房屋面积以及本期施工后又停缓建的房屋面积。

90.**房屋建筑竣工面积**　指在报告期内房屋建筑按照设计要求已全部完工，达到了使用条件，经检查验收鉴定合格的房屋建筑面积。计算房屋竣工面积，必须严格执行房屋竣工验收标准。对民用建筑来讲，一般应按设计要求在土建工程和房屋本身附属的水、卫、气、暖等工程已经完工，通风、电梯等设备已安装完毕，做到水通、灯亮、经验收鉴定合格，并正式交付使用单位后，才能计算竣工面积。对于工业及科研单位等生产性房屋建筑：一般应按设计要求在土建工程（包括水、暖、电、卫、通风）及属于房屋组成部分的生活间、操作间等已经完成，经验收合格后才计算竣工面积。只差安装工艺设备、管线工程的亦可以计算竣工面积。

91. **自有机械设备年底总台数**　指归本企业（或单位）所有，属于本企业固定资产的生产性机械设备年末总台数。包括施工机械、生产设备、运输设备以及其他设备。

92. **自有施工机械设备年底总功率**　指本企业（或单位）自有施工机械、生产设备、运输设备以及其他设备等列为在册固定资产的生产性机械设备年末总功率，按设定能力或查定能力计算。包括机械本身的动力和为该机械服务的单独动力设备，如电动机等。计量单位用千瓦，动力换算可按1马力＝0.735千瓦折合成千瓦数。电焊机、变压器、锅炉不计算动力。

93. **工程结算收入**　指企业（或单位）按承包工程实现的工程价款结算收入，以及向发包单位收取的除工程价款以外的按规定列作营业收入的各种款项，如临时设施费、劳动保险费、施工机械调迁费等以及向发包单位收取的各种索赔款。

94. **工程结算利润**　指已结算工程实现的利润。如为亏损以“-”号表示。其计算公式为：

工程结算利润＝工程结算收入-工程结算成本-工程结算税金及附加。

95. **公路里程**　指在一定时期内实际达到《公路工程技术标准JTJ0l—88》规定的等级公路，并经公路主管部门正式验收交付使用的公路里程数。其计算单位为：KM。它包括大中城市的郊区公路以及通过小城镇街道部分的公路里程，也包括桥梁、渡口的长度，但不包括大中城市的街道、厂矿、林区生产用道和农业生产用道的里程。两条或多条公路共同经由同一路段，只计算一次，不得重复计算里程长度。公路里程是反映公路建设发展规模的重要指标，也是计算运输网密度等指标的基础资料。

96. **内河航道里程**　也称“内河通航里程”，是反映内河水运网规模、水平和发展情况的主要指标，是指在一定时期内，能通航运输船舶及排筏的天然河流、湖泊水库、运河及通航渠道的长度。包括全年季节性通航累计三个月以上的航道，但不包括仅供零散流放竹、木排的河道。

97. **货（客）运量**　指在一定时期内，各运输部门实际运送的货物（旅客）数量。是反映运输业为国民经济和人民生活服务的数量指标，也是制定和检查运输生产计划，研究运输发展规模和速度的重要指标。货运按吨计算，客运按人计算。货物不论运输距离长短，货物类别，均按实际重量统计；旅客不论行程远近或票价多少，均按一人一次作为客运量统计。半价票、小孩票也按一人统计。

98. **货物（旅客）周转量**　指在一定时期内，由各种运输工具运送的货物（旅客）数量与其相应运输距离的乘积之总和，是反映运输业生产总成果的重要指标，也是编制和检查运输生产计划，计算运输效率、劳动生产率以及核算运输单位成本的主要基础资料。通常以吨公里和人公里为计算单位。计算货物周转量通常按发出站与到达站之间的最短距离，也就是计费距离计算。

99. **邮电业务总量**　指以价值量形式表现的邮电通信企业为社会提供各类邮电通信服务的总数量。邮电业务量按专业分类包括函件、包件、汇票、报刊发行、邮政快件、特快专递、集邮、固定电话、出租电路、移动电话、分组交换数据通信、出租代维等。计算方法为各类产品乘以相应的平均单价（不变价）之和，再加上出租电路和设备、代用户维护电话交换机和线路等的服务收入。

100. 移动电话用户 是指通过移动电话交换机进入移动电话网、占用移动电话号码的电话用户。用户数量以报告期末在移动电话营业部门实际办理登记手续进入移动电话网的户数进行计算，一部移动电话统计为一户。

101. 英特网用户数 指办理登记手续且已接入国际互联网的用户数，包括局域网、城域网和广域网，包括拨号上网用户和专线上网用户。

102. 社会消费品零售总额 指各种经济类型的批发零售贸易业、住宿餐饮业和其他行业对城乡居民和社会集团的消费品零售额总和。这个指标反映通过各种商品流通渠道向居民和社会集团供应的生活消费品来满足他们生活需要，是研究人民生活、社会消费品购买力、货币流通等问题的重要指标。

103. 批发零售贸易业 指不直接从事商品的生产，而是从工农业生产者或从商品流通企业购进商品，不做任何加工，或只做简单的加工（如清洗、整理、分类、包装等），通过转卖以获取经济利益的单位。

104.住宿业 指有偿为顾客提供临时住宿的服务活动。

105. 餐饮业 指在一定的场所内，以烹饪、调制等手段，向购买者提供各种主要供现场消费的食品、饮料，并且所提供的这种服务要大于所提供的其他服务（如娱乐）的单位。

106. 限额以上批发企业 指年主营业务收入在2000万元及以上的批发贸易企业。

107. 限额以上零售企业 指年主营业务收入在500万元及以上的零售企业。

108. 限额以上餐饮企业 指年主营业务收入在200万元及以上的餐饮企业。

109. 商品销售总额 指对本企业以外的单位和个人出售的商品（包括售给本单位消费用的商品）金额。这个指标反映批发零售贸易企业在国内市场上销售商品以及出口商品的总量。包括：（1）售给城乡居民和社会集团消费的商品；（2）售给工业、农业等各行业作为生产、经营使用的商品；（3）售给批发零售贸易业作为转卖或加工后转卖的商品；（4）对国（境）外直接出口的商品。

110. 商品交易市场成交额 指在消费品市场与生产资料市场买卖双方（包括农民、非农业居民、机关、团体、工商企业、个体商贩）成交的全部商品金额，是反映商品交易市场规模的综合性指标。

111. 私营企业注册资本 指私营企业办理开业登记，或变更登记时核准的资金数，不包括银行贷款。

112. 个体工商业户数 指已经领取《营业执照》或《临时营业执照》的个体工商户的数量。

113. 个体工商业从业人员 指经过工商行政管理部门核准的、参加经营活动并领取报酬的所有人员，包括个体经营者本人、帮手、学徒等。

114. 个体工商业注册资金 指申请登记或变更登记时核准的资金。

115. 利用外资 指我国各级政府、部门、企业和其他经济组织通过对外借款、吸收外商直接投资以及用其他方式筹措的境外现汇、设备、技术等。

116. 外商直接投资 是指外国企业和经济组织或个人（包括华侨、港澳台胞以及我国在境外注册的企业）按我国有关政策、法规，用现汇、实物、技术等在中国大陆开办外商独资企业、与中国大陆的企业或经济组织共同举办中外合资经营企业、合作经营企业或者合作开发资源的投资（包括外商投资收益的再投资）以及经政府有关部门批准的项目投资总额内，企业从境外借入的资金。

117. 对外承包工程 包括各对外承包公司以招标议标承包方式承揽的下列业务（1）承包国外工程建设项目。（2）承包我国对外经援项目。（3）承包我国驻外机构的工程建设项目。（4）与外国承包公司合营或联合承包工程项目时我国公司分包部分。（5）以服务成果向业主收费的技术服务项目（包括承担地形地貌测绘；地质资源勘探与普查；建设区域规划；提供设计文件、图纸、生产工艺技术资料和工程技术经济咨询；工程项目的可行性考察、研究和评估；进行技术指导和培训人员等）。（6）对外承包兼营的房屋开发业务。对外承包工程的营业额是以货币表现的本期内完成的对外承包工程的工作量，包括以前年度签订的合同和本年度新签订的合同在报告期完成的工作量。

118. 对外劳务合作 指以收取工资的形式向业主或承包商提供技术和劳动服务的活动。我国对外承包公司在境外开办的合营企业，中国公司同时又提供劳务的，其劳务部分也纳入劳务合作统计。劳务合作营业额按报告期内向雇主提交的结算数（包括工资、加班费和奖金等）统计。

119. 国际旅游人数 指来中国大陆参观、访问、旅行、探亲、访友、休养、考察、参加会议和从事经济、科技、文化、教育、体育、宗教等活动的外国人、华侨、港澳和台湾同胞的人数。不包括外国在我国的常驻机构，如使领馆、通讯社、企业办事处的工作人员；来我国常住的外国专家、留学生以及在岸逗留不过夜人员。

120. 全社会用电量 指全年用电的总量，按用户的用电性质分为："农村用电"、工业用电"、"交通运输用电"和"城乡居民生活用电"等，各类用电中均包括电力企业售给本市用户的电量、自备电厂自发自用电量（包括余热发电量）和自备电厂售给附近用户的电量以及趸售电量。

121. 工业企业能源消费量 指工业企业在生产过程中作为燃料、原材料、动力、辅助材料使用的能源、工艺用能及非生产用能。

122. 财政总收入 指国家财政参与社会产品分配所取得的收入，包括一般预算收入和基金预算收入。一般预算收入主要包括：

（1）各项税收，包括增值税、消费税、营业税、企业所得税、个人所得税、资源税、固定资产投资方向调节税、城市维护建设税、房产税、印花税、土地增值税、城镇土地使用税、关税、契税和耕地占用税等。

（2）行政性收费收入，指按规定纳入预算管理的行政性收费收入。

（3）专项收入，包括排污费收入、水资源费收入、教育费附加收入等。

（4）其他收入，包括基本建设贷款归还收入、基本建设收入、捐赠收入等。基金预算收入主要包括工业交通部门基金收入、社会保险基金收入、土地有偿使用收入、政府住房基金收入等。

123. 财政支出 指国家财政将筹集起来的资金进行分配使用的数额。以满足经济建设和各项事业的需要，主要包括：

（1）一般公共服务：反映政府提供一般公共服务的支出。

（2）国防：反映政府用于现役部队、国防后备力量、国防动员等方面的支出。

（3）公共安全：反映政府维护社会公共安全方面的支出。

（4）教育：反映政府教育事务支出。

（5）科学技术：反映用于科学技术方面的支出。

（6）文化体育与传媒：反映政府在文化、文物、体育、广播影视、新闻出版等方面的支出。

（7）社会保障和就业：反映政府在社会保障与就业方面的支出。

（8）医疗卫生：反映政府医疗卫生方面的支出。

（9）环境保护：反映政府环境保护支出。

（10）城乡社区事务：反映政府城乡社区事务支出。

（11）农林水事务：反映政府农林水事务支出。

（12）交通运输：反映政府交通运输方面的支出。

（13）工业商业金融等事务：反映政府工业、商业、金融等事务支出。

（14）其他支出：反映不能划分到上述功能科目的其他政府支出。

124. 中央财政收入和地方财政收入 指按财政体制划分的中央本级收入和地方本级收入。1994年税制及财政体制改革以后，属于中央财政的收入包括关税，消费税，海关代征的进口货物增值税，铁路运输企业、国有银行、国有邮政企业所得税，铁道营业税，金融保险营业税（中央），海洋石油资源税，车辆购置税（费）等；属于地方一般预算的收入包括一般营业税，固定资产投资方向调节税，房产税，城镇土地使用税，土地增值税，车船使用税，屠宰税，耕地占用税，契税等；属于中央和地方共享的收入主要有：增值税，企业所得税，城市维护建设税，个人所得税，印花税等。需要指出的是，由于近几年来中央收入和地方收入的分配方式、比例发生了较大的调整，因此，历年的数据不完全可比。

125. 存 款 指企业、机关、团体或居民根据可以收回的原则，把货币资金存入银行或其他信用机构保管并取得一定利息的一种信用活动形式。根据存款对象的不同可划分为企业存款、财政存款、机关团体存款、基本建设存款、城镇储蓄存款、农村存款等项目。它是银行信贷资金的主要来源。

126. 城乡储蓄存款余额 城乡储蓄存款，包括城镇居民储蓄存款和农民个人储蓄存款两部分，不包括居民的手存现金和工矿企业、部队、机关团体等集团存款。城乡居民储蓄存款余额指城乡居民存入银行及农村信用社储蓄的时点数（存入数扣除取出数的余额），如月末、季末或年末数额。

127. 贷 款 指银行或其他信用机构根据必须归还的原则，按一定利率，为企业、个人等提供资金的一种信用活动形式。我国银行贷款，分流动资金贷款、固定资产贷款、城乡个体工商户贷款以及农户贷款等科目。

128. 承保额（保险金额） 指保险人对被保险人负担损失补偿或约定给付的金额。它是保险合同上的最高责任额，也是计算保费的依据。

129. 保费（保险费） 指保险人根据保险合同的有关规定，为被保险人取得因约定危险事故发生所造成的经济损失补偿（或给付）权利，付给保险人的代价。

130. 保险赔款 指保险事故发生后，经查证确属保险责任范围以内的保险标的损失，保险人根据保险合同的规定履行赔偿义务，给予被保险人的款项。

131. 年底实有铺装道路长度 指除土路外，路面经过铺装宽度在3.5米以上的道路，包括高级、次高级道路和普通道路。

132. 城市桥梁 指城市范围内，修建在河道上的桥梁和道路与道路立交、道路跨越铁路的立交桥，以及人行天桥。包括永久性桥和半永久性桥，不包括临时性桥、铁路桥、涵洞。

133. 城市下水道总长度 指所有排水总管、干管、支管及暗渠、检查井、连接井进出水口等长度之和。

134. 城市污水日处理能力 指污水处理厂每昼夜处理污水量的设计能力。

135. 城市园林绿地面积 指城市公共绿地、专用绿地、生产绿地、防护绿地、郊区风景名胜区的全部面积。

136. 公园绿地 指城市中向公众开放的、以游憩为主要功能，有一定的游憩设施和服务设施，同时兼有健全生态、美化景观、防灾减灾等综合作用的绿化用地。

137. 年底自来水生产能力 指年底城建部门管理的自来水厂和自备水源的社会单位取水、净化、送水、出厂输水干管等环节的实际生产能力。

138. 年底实有公共汽车 指年底可参加营运的全部车辆数，包括年底营运车辆和库存查封未参加营运的车辆，不包括非营运车辆，如架线车、油罐车、工程车、货车及其他专用车辆和借入的客运车辆。

139. 营运线路长度 指设置的固定营运的线路长度，包括郊区营运线路长度。不包括临时行驶的线路长度。

140. 年底供水管道长度 指从送水泵到用户水表之间所有管道的长度。

141. 全年供水总量 指公用自来水厂和自备水源的社会单位全年的供水总量，包括有效供水量及损失水量。

142. 生活用水量 指居民日常生活与公共福利设施的用水量。包括居民、饮食店、旅馆、医院、理发店、浴池、洗衣店、游泳池、商店、学校、机关、部队等单位的用水量。

143. 城市人口用水普及率 指城市用水的非农业人口数（不包括临时人口和流动人口）与城市非农业人口总数之比，计算公式：

用水普及率＝城市用水的非农业人口数/城市非农业人口数×100%

144. 输气管道长度 指由压缩机、鼓风机、储气罐的出口到用户立管之间的全部管道长度。

145. 全年供气总量 指全年售给各类用户的全部煤气量。包括工业用量、家庭用量和其他用量。

146. 城市用气普及率 指使用煤气（包括人工煤气、液化石油气、天然气）的城市非农业人口数（不包括临时人口和流动人口）与城市非农业人口总数之比。计算公式：

城市用气普及率＝城市用气的非农业人口数/城市非农业人口数×100%

147. 废水排放总量 指生产废水和生活污水的排放总量。生产废水指企、事业单位在生产、科研过程中向外排放的所有排放口的废水量总和。生活污水指城镇居民区和企、事业单位职工集中居住区排放的污水量。

148. 工业废水排放总量 指经过工业企业厂区所有排放口排到企业外部的工业废水量。包括外排的直接冷却水、超标排放的矿井地下水和与工业废水混排的厂区生活污水，不包括外排的间接冷却水（清浊不分流的间接冷却水应计算在内）。

149. 工业废气排放总量 指企业厂区内燃料燃烧和生产工艺过程中产生的各种排入空气中有污染物的气体总量，以标准状态（273k，101325Pa）计。

150. 一般工业固体废物综合利用量 指通过回收、加工、循环、交换等方式，从固体废物中提取或者使其转化为可以利用的资源、能源和其他原材料的固体废物量（包括当年利用的往年工业固体废物累计贮存量）。如用作农业肥料、生产建筑材料、筑路等。指燃料燃烧和生产工艺过程中排放的各种废气总量，以标准状态下每年万标立方米表示。

151. 一般工业固体废物处置量 指调查年度企业将工业固体废物焚烧和用其他改变工业固体废物的物理、化学、生物特性的方法，达到减少或者消除其危险成分的活动，或者将工业固体废物最终置于符合环境保护规定要求的填埋场的活动中，所消纳固体废物的量。处置方式如：填埋、焚烧、专业贮存场（库）封场处理、深层灌注、回填矿井及海洋处置（经海洋管理部门同意投海处置）等。

152. 工业烟（粉）尘排放量 指企业在燃料燃烧和生产工艺过程中排入大气的烟尘及工业粉尘的总质量之和。

153. R & D 是“研究与发展”（Research and development）的英文缩写。其含义是指在科学技术领域（包括自然科学、农业科学、医药科学、工程与技术科学、人文与社会科学领域），为了增加知识的总量，以及运用这些知识而进行的系统的、创造性的活动。R&D包括基础研究、应用研究、试验发展三类活动。

154. 独立研究与开发机构 指有明确的任务和研究方向，有一定学术水平的业务骨干和一定数量的研究人员，具有研究、开发、开展学术工作的基本条件，主要进行科学研究与技术开发活动，并且在行政上有独立的组织形式，财务上独立核算盈亏，有权与其他单位签订合同，在银行有单独户头的单位。

155. 科学家和工程师 指具有大学本科以上学历的人员和不具备上述学历但已评定为高、中级职称的人员。

156. 独立研究与开发机构职工 指在科学研究与技术开发机构工作，并由其支付工资的各种人员。包括长期职工和临时职工，不包括编制以外的离休、退休人员和停薪留职人员，但包括招聘人员。

157. 研究与发展经费支出 指报告期内用于研究与实验发展课题活动（基础研究、应用研究、实验发展）的全部实际支出。包括用于研究与发展课题活动的直接支出，还包括间接用于研究与发展活动的一切支出。

158. 发　明 专利法及其实施细则所称的发明是指对有关产品、方法或其改进所提出的新的技术方案。

159. 实用新型 专利法及其实施细则所称的实用新型是指对产品的形状、构造或者其结合所提出的适于实用的新的技术方案。

160. 外观设计 专利法及其实施细则所称的外观设计是指对产品形状、图案、色彩或者其结合所作出的富有美感并适于工业上应用的新设计。

161. 网上登记技术合同数 指本地区在全国技术合同网上登记系统中登记的技术合同数。

162. 网上登记技术合同成交金额 指本地区在全国技术合同网上登记系统中登记的技术合同成交金额。

163. 科技企业孵化器 是指以促进科技成果转化、培养高新技术企业和企业家为宗旨的科技创业服务机构。包括科技创业服务中心、大学科技园、归国留学人员创业园、软件园等综合型、专业技术型科技企业孵化器。

164. 在孵企业总收入 指在统计年度内由孵化器孵化的企业所实现的技、工、贸等各种收入之和。

165. 在孵企业从业人员 指本报告期末在孵化器孵化的企业的人员总数。

166. 毕业企业 指经孵化器扶持，发展到一定规模后脱离孵化器实现独立发展的企业。（毕业企业的数据仅按毕业时的数据累计，不进行跟踪）。

167. 普通高等学校 是指按国家规定的设置标准和审批程序批准举办的，通过全国普通高等教育统一招生考试，招收高中毕业生为主要培养对象，实施高等学历教育的全日制大学、独立设置的学院和高等专科学校、高等职业学校及其他机构（独立学院和分校、大专班）。

168. 成人高等学校 是指按国家规定的设置标准和审批程序批准举办的，通过全国成人高等教育统一招生考试,招收具有高中毕业或同等学历的人员为主要培养对象，利用函授、业余、脱产的多种形式对其实施高等学历教育的学校。包括：职工高等学校、农民高等学校、管理干部学院、教育学院、独立函授学院、广播电视大学、其他机构。

169. 专任教师数 教师是指专职从事教学工作的人员，包括临时调去帮助做其他工作的人员，不包括调离教学岗位担负行政领导工作的原教学人员。

170. 文化事业机构 指从事专业文化工作和为专业文化工作服务的独立建制的单独核算的单位。不包括这些单位另外举办独立核算的其他机构和各部门的业余文化组织。

171. 艺术表演团体 指从事戏曲、音乐、舞蹈、杂技等专业艺术表演，有独立账户，实行单独核算的团体。不包括半工半艺、半农半艺的业余剧团。

172. 艺术表演观众人数（人次） 指售票、包场演出或民族地区免费演出的艺术表演观众人次数。不包括彩排审查和内部观摩演出的观看人次数。

173. 医　院 指名称为医院，设有固定床位能收容病人住院并能为病人提供医疗、护理服务的医疗机构。包括县及以上医院、其他医院两部分。按所属性质分为卫生部门、工业及其他部门、集体所有制单位3类。其中县及以上医院按业务性质分为综合医院和专科医院。

174. 卫生技术人员 指卫生事业机构支付工资的全部固定职工和合同制职工中现任职务为卫生技术工作的专业人员。包括中医师、西医师、中西医结合高级医师、护师、中药师、西药师、检验师、其他技师、中医士、西医士、护士、助产士、中药剂士、西药剂士、检验士、其他技士、其他中医、护理员、中药剂员、西药剂员、检验员、其他初级卫生技术人员。

175. 医　生 指经卫生部门审查合格，从事医疗工作的专业人员。分为中医医生和西医医生。包括卫生技术人员中的中医师、西医师、中西结合高级医师、中医士、西医士和其他中医。

176. 等级运动员人数 指经考核正式批准授予等级运动员称号的人数。运动员等级分为国际级运动健将、运动健将、一级运动员、二级运动员。

177. 等级裁判员人数 指经考核正式批准授予等级裁判员称号的人数。裁判员等级分为国际裁判、国家级裁判、一级裁判、二级裁判、三级裁判。

178. 社会福利事业单位 指集中收养社会孤老、残、幼的机构。包括由民政部门管理的社会福利院、儿童福利院、精神病人福利院和城镇集体办的福利院，以及农村集体办的敬老院。

179. 社会福利事业单位收养人数 指由民政部门管理的和城镇及农村集体举办的社会福利事业单位中收养的老人、少年儿童、缺乏生活自理能力的残疾人员和精神病人。

180. 社会福利企业单位 指以安置城镇有一定劳动能力的盲、聋、哑和肢体残疾人员就业为目的，享受国家减免税待遇的国有或集体经济性质的企业。包括福利工厂、福利商品服务业、假肢厂和安置农场等单位。

181. 律　师 指受聘参加法律顾问处工作，担任法律顾问、刑（民）事代理人、刑事辩护人，办理非诉讼事件、解答法律询问，代写法律事务文书等主要从事律师业务的专职法律工作者和兼职律师。

182. 公证人员 指在国家公证机关依法办理公证事务的司法人员。包括公证员、助理公证员和在公证处工作的其他人员，

183. 办理公证文书 指公证处在一定时期内办结的公证文书件数。公证文书应按司法部规定或批准的格式制作。包括国内公证和涉外公证两部分。其中国内公证分为经济合同公证和民事法律关系公证两大类。

184. 调解人员 指在人民调解委员会担负调解民间一般民事纠纷和轻微违法行为所引起的纠纷的工作人员。包括调解委员会的委员和调解小组的调解员。

185. 调解民间纠纷 指调解委员会依照法律规定，根据自愿原则，用说服教育的方法调解民间发生的有关民事权利和义务的争执，促成当事双方达到协议和谅解，解决纠纷. 包括婚姻家庭纠纷，财产权益纠纷等。不包括法院受理的纠纷案。

APPENDIX7 EXPLANATORY NOTES ON MAIN STATISTICAL INDICATORS

1. Gross Domestic Product (GDP) refers to the final products of all resident units in a country (or a region) during a certain period of time. Gross domestic product is expressed in three different forms, i.e. value, income, and products respectively. The form of value refers to the total value of all products and services produced by all resident units during a certain period of time minus total value of intimidate input of materials and services of the nature of non-fixed assets or the summation of the value-added of all resident units; the form of income includes all the income created by all resident units and distributed primarily to all resident and non-resident units; the form of products refers to the value of all final goods and services for final use by all resident units plus the value of net exports of goods and services during a given period of time. In the practice of national accounting, gross domestic product is calculated with three approaches, i.e. production approach, income approach, and expenditure approach, which reflect gross domestic product and its composition from different aspects.

2. Comparable Prices refers to prices that removed the factors of price change so as to exactly reflect the change of aggregate when comparing the value of different periods. Two methods are used for calculating comparable prices: 1. Multiplying the output of products by their fixed prices of certain year; 2. Converting prices by relevant price index.

3. Constant Price refers to the average price of a given product in certain year, which is used for comparison of output value over time. As the output value at constant prices removes the factor of price changes, it reflects the trend of production development over time. Since 1949, with the changes in general price level, National Bureau of Statistics has issued nationally unified constant prices five times: the 1952 constant prices for 1949-1957; the 1957 constant prices for 1957-1971; the 1970 constant prices for 1971-1981; the 1980 constant prices for 1981-1990; and the 1990 constant prices have been used since 1991.

4. Various Planning periods The conventional division of time period in this statistical yearbook is as follows: Economic Rehabilitation Period, 1950-1952; the First Five-Year Plan period, 1953-1957; The Second Five-Year Plan period, 1958-1962; The Third Five-Year Plan period, 1966-1970; The Fourth Five-Year Plan period, 1971-1975; The Fifth Five-Year Plan period, 1976-1980;The Sixth Five-Year Plan period, 1981-1985; The Seventh Five-Year Plan period, 1986-1990;The Eighth Five-Year Plan period, 1991-1995;The Ninth Five-Year Plan period, 1996-2000;The TenthFive-Year Plan period,2001-2005;The Eleventh Five-Year Plan period,2006-2010;The Twelfth Five-year plan period ,2011-2015.

5. Average Annual Growth Rate refers to the average growth rate year after year in a long period of time. There are two methods for calculating: one is "level approach" , or the method of geometric level calculation, is the annual average growth (decrease)rate, which derived by comparing the level of the last year of the interval with that of the beginning year; the other is called "accumulative approach" , or algebraic average or equation method, is the annual average growth (decrease) rate, which is derived by summation of the actual figure of each year in the interval divided by the figure in the base year. Usually, the results calculated by the two methods are fairly close, but they differed sharply when uneven economic development occurred with striking fluctuations in growth.

The average annual growth rates listed in this statistical yearbook are all calculated by "level approach" . The base years are not listed when the years are listed for average annual growth rates. For example, the average annual growth rate of the 34 years since reform & opening-up implemented is listed as 1979-2012 without listing the base year 1978, the rest of the years are analogized as the same.

6. Registration Status of Enterprises Enterprises are classified into 3 categories, namely domestic-funded enterprises, enterprises with investment from Hong Kong, Macao and Taiwan, and enterprises with foreign investment, in the light of the registration status of an enterprise in industrial and commercial administration agencies. Domestic-funded enterprises include state-owned enterprises, collective-owned enterprises, cooperative enterprises, joint ownership enterprises, limited liability corporations, share-holding corporations Ltd., private enterprises and other enterprises. Included in the enterprises with investment from Hong Kong, Macao and Taiwan and enterprises with foreign investment are joint-venture enterprises, cooperative enterprises, sole investment enterprises and share-holding corporations Ltd. For government agencies, institutions and social organizations, which are not requested to be registered in industrial and commercial administration agencies, they are classified mainly by their sources of funds and way of management.

7. State-owned Enterprises refer to non-corporation economic units where the entire assets are owned by the state and which have registered in accordance with the Regulation of the People' s Republic of China on the Management of Registration of Corporate Enterprises. Excluded from this category are sole state-funded corporations in the limited liability corporations.

8. Collective-owned Enterprises refer to economic units where the assets are owned collectively and which have registered in accordance with the Regulation of the People' s Republic of China on the Management of Registration of Corporate Enterprises.

9. Cooperative Enterprises refer to a form of collective economic units (enterprises) where capitals come mainly from employees as their shares, with certain proportion of capital from the outside, where production is organized on the basis of independent operation, independent accounting for profits and losses, joint work, democratic management, and a distribution system that integrates remuneration according to work with dividend according to capital share.

10. Joint Ownership Enterprises refer to economic units established by two or more corporate enterprises or corporate institutions of the same or different ownership, through joint investment on the basis of equality, voluntary participation and mutual benefits. They include state joint ownership enterprises, collective joint ownership enterprises, joint state-collective enterprises, and other joint ownership enterprises.

11. Limited Liability Corporations refer to economic units established with investment from 2-50 investors and registered in accordance with the Regulation of the People' s Republic of China on the Management of Registration of Corporations, each investor bearing limited liability to the corporation depending on its share of investment, and the corporation bearing liability to its debt to the maximum of its total assets. Limited liability corporations include exclusive state-funded limited liability corporations and other limited liability corporations.

12. Share-holding Corporations Ltd. refer to economic units registered in accordance with the Regulation of the People' s Republic of China on the Management of Registration of Corporations, with total registered capitals divided into equal shares and raised through issuing stocks. Each investor bears limited liability to the corporation depending on the holding of shares, and the corporation bears liability to its debt to the maximum of its total assets.

13. Private Enterprises refer to profit-making economic units invested and established by natural persons, or controlled by natural persons using employed labour. Included in this category are private limited liability corporations, private share-holding corporations Ltd., private partnership enterprises and private-funded enterprises registered in accordance with the Corporation Law, Partnership Enterprises Law and Interim Regulations on Private Enterprises .

14. Other Domestic-funded Enterprises refer to domestic-funded economic units other than those mentioned above.

15. Enterprises with Investment from HongKong, Macao and Taiwan refers to enterprises set up in mainland China in the forms of joint investment,cooperation or solely-owned investment by investors from HongKong, Macao and Taiwan in accordance with foreign-related economic laws & regulations of China. They include joint-venture enterprises, cooperative enterprises & solely-owned enterprises.

16. Enterprises with Foreign Investment refers to enterprises set up in mainland China in the forms of joint investment, cooperation or solely-owned investment by foreign investors in accordance with foreign-related economic laws & regulations of China. They include joint-venture enterprises with foreign investment, cooperation enterprises with foreign investment and enterprises with sole (exclusive) foreign investment.

17. Three Industries Industry structure has been classified according to the historical sequence of development. Primary industry refers to extraction of natural resources; secondary industry involves processing of primary products;and tertiary industry provides services of various kinds for production and consumption. The above classification is universal although it varies to some extent form country to country. Industry in China comprises:

Primary industry: Farming, Forestry, Animal Husbandry and Fishery (including farming, forestry, animal husbandry ,fishery and Services).

Secondary industry: industry (including mining and quarrying, manufacturing, production and supply of electricity, water and gas) and construction.

Tertiary industry: all other industries not included in primary or secondary industry.

18. Total Population refers to the total number of people alive at a certain point of time within a given area.The annual statistics on total population is taken at midnight, the 3lst of December, excluding migrant population without household register in Changzhou city.

19. Birth Rate (or Crude Birth Rate) refers to the ratio of the number of births to the average population (or mid-period population) during a certain period of time (usually a year) which is often expressed in ‰. Birth rate in the chapter refers to annual birth rate. The following formula is used:

Birth Rate = Number of Births/Average Number of Population × 1000‰

Number of births refers to live births i.e. the births when babies had showed any vital phenomena regardless of the length of pregnancy.

The current calculation of birth rate is based on data residency by the public security data of permanent residency by the family planning commission at city levels, and can also be based on annual population sampling at country and provincial levels, including the late registration for births of previous year.

Annual average number of population is the average of the number of population at the beginning of the year and that at the end of the year, and can be substituted with the mid-year population.

20. Death Rate (or Crude Death Rate) refers to the ratio of the number of deaths to the average population (or mid-period population) during a certain period of time (usually a year) which is often expressed in ‰. Death rate in the chapter refers to annual death rate. The following formula is used:

Death Rate= Number of Deaths/Annual Average Number of Population × 1000‰

21. Natural Growth Rate of Population refers to the ratio of natural increase in population (number of births minus number of deaths) in a certain period of time (usually a year) to the average population (or mid-period population) of the same period which is often expressed in ‰. The following formulas are applied:

Natural Growth Rate of Population = (Number of Births-Number of Deaths)/Average Number of Population × 1000‰

Natural Growth Rate of Population = Birth Rate-Death Rate

22. Life Expectancy refers to the average number of years a person of a certain age will live (or the average life-span of an age group if the pattern of morality for this age group remains as it is.)

23. Employed Persons refers to the persons engaged in social labor and receive remuneration payment or earn business income, including:(1)fully employed staff & workers in state-owned, collective-owned or other kinds of economic sectors and otherwise employed persons; (2)private and individual economic laborors in towns; (3)rural social laborers.

Persons employed in various units refers to all the persons working in government agencies of various levels, political and party organizations, social organizations, enterprises and institutions, and receiving wages or other forms of payment. They include fully-employed staff and workers, re-employed retirees, foreigners and Chinese compatriots from Hong Kong, Macao, and Taiwan working in various units, part-time employees, employees of other units working temporarily at current posts, and employees holding the second job, but exclude staff and workers who have left their working units while keeping their labour contract(employment relation) unchanged. This indicator reflects the total number of laborers actually engaged in production or other operations in various units.

24. Staff and Workers refer to the persons who work in (and receive payment therefrom) enterprises and institutions of state ownership, collective ownership, joint ownership, share holding, foreign ownership, and ownership by entrepreneurs from Hong Kong, Macao, and Taiwan, and other types of ownership and their affiliated units and get paid also include the staff and workers who have left their working units while keeping their labour contract/employment relation unchanged.

25. Fully Employed Staff and Workers refer to persons who work in, and receive wages from their working units, as well as persons who have their work posts, but are temporarily absent from work for reasons of study or on sick, injury or maternal leave and still receive wages from their working units.

26. Staff and Workers Who Have Left Working Units but Still Remaining the Relationship with the Units refer to those who have left the production or working posts due to various reasons and are not taking other positions in the same units, but whose labor relationship still remained in the units.

27. Total Wages of Persons Employed refer to the total remuneration payment to the whole staff and workers in various units during a certain period of time, including the total wages of fully employed staff and workers, the total salaries of assigned personnel and the total earnings of other employed persons.

28. Total Wages of Fully Employed Staff and Workers refers to the total remuneration payment to fully employed staff and workers in various units during a certain period of time. The calculation of total wages is based on the total remuneration payment to the staff and workers. Therefore, all the wages and salaries and other payments to staff and workers are included in the total wages regardless of their sources, category, and forms(in kind or cash).

29. Average Wage of Fully Employed Staff and Workers refers to the average wage in monetary terms per person during a certain period of time for fully employed staff and workers in various units, which is one of the main indicators reflecting the general level of wage and is calculated as follows:

Average Wage of Fully Employed Staff and Workers = Total Wages of Fully Employed Staff and Workers in Given Period / Average Number of Fully Employed Staff and Workers in Given Period.

30. Registered urban unemployed people refer to unemployed people at working age (from 16 years old to retirement age) in urban areas that have the ability to work and the need for jobs and have registered at public employment service agencies.

31. Consumer Price Index Consumer price, refers to the price that consumer goods and services purchased by urban and rural residents, is the final price of social products and services, which influences the people' s livehood and lay a prominent role in the whole national economic price system. Consumer price index reflects the trend and degree of changes in prices of consumer goods purchased by residents.

32. Retail Price Index The retail price refers to the price that the residents afford for the living consumer and service. It is the final price of social products and service has a direct bearing on the people' s lives and has a fairly important states in the whole national economy system.

33. Service Price Index refer to the comparative number of the expenditure of non-commercial and service consumption. The items involve: telecommunication expense, postal expense, transportation expense, hairdressing & beautification expense, culture and entertainment expense, school and baby-sitting expense, mending and other expense, medical insurance service expense, total classifications.

34. Employment Population in Urban Households refer to urban residents engaged in certain work and receiving payment for the labor or income from their business operation, including those who work in state-owned or collective units, joint ventures, foreign-owned units and private with permanent or temporary jobs. The self-employed individuals and re-employed retirees are also included. This indictor reflects the situation of urban employment and is the basic data for calculating employment rate and dependency ratio.

35. Total income of urban families refers to the total income of sample families living in urban areas, which is comprising of salary income, net income from business operation, earnings from properties and income of transfer, not including the income of rent and sale of their properties. The income is calculated on what is actually occurred. The figure, whether redeemed or paid in advance, will not be further divided when calculated.

The income from properties refers to the income from the family owned chattel (saving deposits in banks, securities), real estate (such as housing, automobiles, land and personal collections). This includes the remising of one' s own properties, such as interests, rents, earning from patents, dividends from one' s property circulation, added profits of properties.

The income of transfer refers to the income of sample families, made up of the country' s payment transfer and inter-family payment, including retirement pension, unemployment welfare, compensation etc. The unit' s transfer of payment, including job compensation, insurance premium, public reserve of housing and inter family donations.

36. Disposable income of Urban Households refers to the total amount of sample urban residents' income, which is comprised of income direct available for consumption, non-compulsory expenditure plus savings deposits, i.e. the income which could be disposed of freely. The formula of calculation is: disposable income=total income of the family – personal income tax – expenditure on social insurance – received subsidiary.

37. Total expenditure of Households refers to total actual expenditure of a household excluding that from rending, which includes all daily expenditure, housing expenditure, transfer expenditure, property expenditure and expenditure on social insurance. The statistical calculation is based on actual value of commodities or service bought, regardless of the means of payment, whether on installment or not, so long as the commodity and service has been consumed. If the commodity or service was bought on tally or installment, the difference of actual payment and payment due is put into the categories under the title of income from debit and credit.

38. Consumer Expenditure of Urban Households refers to total daily expenditure of residents, including the expenditure on foods, clothing, household appliance and service, health, education, cultural and entertainment service, housing, occasional costs and service. including goods or services used for donation.

39. Net Income of Rural Households refers to the total income of the permanent residents of the rural households during a year after the deduction of the expenses for productive and non-productive business operation, the payment for taxes and the payment for collective units for their contracted tasks, which can then be spent for investments in productive and non-productive construction, for consumption in daily life and for savings deposit. It is a comprehensive indicator to show the actual level of the income of the peasants' household. The net income of the rural households includes not only the income from the productive and non-productive business operation, but also the income from the non-business operation, such as the money remitted or brought back by the members of the household who are in other places, the government relief payment and various subsidies. It includes not only the money income, but also the income in kind. But the income from borrowing from banks, friends and relatives is excluded.

40. Able-bodied and Semi-able Bodied Laborers of Rural Households refers to permanent residents of rural households who are able to work and actually engaged in social labor, which is one factor of production and sources of rural households income. According to the relevant regulations, male aged 18-50, female aged 18-45 are considered as able bodied laborers; male aged 16-17 and 51-60, female aged 16-17 and 46-55 are considered as semi-able bodied laborers. Those who are not in above age but able to work and actually engaged in social labor are also considered as able-bodied or semi-able bodied laborers, while those who are within the above age range but unable to work are not counted as able-bodied or semi able bodied laborers.

41. Expenditure of Rural Households for Consumption refers to total expenses of rural households on daily life, including expenses on food, clothing, housing, fuel, articles for daily use, and expenses on cultural life and services. This indicator is used to show the actual consumption level of peasants, including expense on food, clothing, housing, fuel, articles for daily use, and expenditure on daily life and services.

42. Total Investment in Fixed Assets in the Whole Municipality Investment in fixed assets is the essential means for social reproduction of fixed assets. Amount of investment in fixed assets refers to the volume of activities in construction and purchases of fixed assets in monetary terms. It is a comprehensive indicator which shows the size, pace, proportional relations and use orientation of the investment in fixed assets. Total investment in fixed assets in the whole society is classified into the following parts investment as categorized by ownerships. Total value of investment: city &town collective units, real estate development, investment in rural area.

43. Investment in Real Estate Development refers to the investment by the real estate development companies, commercial buildings construction companies and other real estate development units of various types of ownership in the construction of house buildings, such as residential buildings, factory buildings, warehouses, hotels, guesthouses, holiday villages, office buildings, and the complementary service facilities and land development projects, such as roads, water supply, water drainage, power supply, heating, telecommunications, land leveling and other projects of infrastructure. It excludes the activities in simple land transactions.

44. Sources of Funds for Investment in Fixed Assets refer to various funds received during the year by fixed assets investment for construction and purchase of fixed assets. They include balance of funds bought forward from the previous year, subtotal of sources of funds in this year, and various payable funds. The subtotal of the sources of funds in this year is further divided into six categories: state budgetary investment, domestic loans, bonds, foreign investments, self-raised funds, and other sources of funds.

45. Investment in Fixed Assets by Structure refers to the three major parts of investment activities, i.e. construction and installation, purchase of equipment and instrument, and other expenses.

46. Newly Increased Fixed Assets refer to the newly increased value of fixed assets through investment, including the value of projects completed and put into production, the value of equipment, tools, and vessels considered as fixed assets, as well as the relevant expenses as investment in fixed assets. This is a comprehensive indicator of investment in fixed assets, reflecting the achievements of investment in fixed assets in different periods, different sectors, and different regions.

47. Rate of Projects of Fixed Assets Completed and Put into Operation refers to the ratio of the newly increased fixed assets to the total investment made in the same period. This is a comprehensive indicator, reflecting the speed of the employment of fixed assets and the investment efficiency.

48. Projects under Construction refer to projects having construction and installation activities undertaken in the reference period, including projects started in the reference period, or continued from the previous period, or completed and put into production or suspended in the reference period.

49. Projects Completed and Put into Use Industrial projects refer to the major projects and accessory facilities completed which result in forming production capacity and have been checked and accepted while the living and welfare facilities have been completed and can ensure normal production and formally put into production. Non-industrial projects refer to the major projects and accessory facilities completed which possess the designed capacity and have been checked, accepted and formally put into production.

50. Floor Space of Buildings under Construction and Completed refers to total floor space in each story of buildings calculated from the outside line of building walls, including both usable space and the space occupied by constructions like pillars or walls. The floor space of multi-story buildings includes the total floor space of each story (including basement).

51. Floor space under construction refers to the floor space of all buildings (including basement, semibasement and supporting buildings) is being constructed within the period of the report. It consists of the floor space newly constructed in current phase and the floor space constructed from last year to current phase, and the floor space which stopped constructing in the previous phase but restarted to construct in current phase. The floor space completed in the current phase and the floor space stopped constructing or delayed construction of the current phase shall be included in the floor space under construction. As to multi storey building, floor space completed shall be filled in the total floor space of each storey.

52. Floor space completed refers to the total of building area of all buildings which are completed as per design requirement, meet the requirements for residence and use, and are inspected and accepted as qualified or meeting the completion acceptance criteria and can be transferred to normal use.

53. Floor Space of Residential Buildings refers to the floor space of the residential buildings under construction and completed among the total space of buildings under construction and completed.

54. Gross Output Value of Farming,Forestry,Animal Husbandry and Fishery refers to the total volume of products of farming, forestry, animal husbandry and fishery in value terms and the value of all kinds of supporting serving activities to farming, forestry, animal husbandry and fishery producing activities, which reflects the total scale and total result of agricultural production during a given period of time.The statistical scopes for Farming, Forestry, Animal Husbandry and Fishery are:

(1)Farming include crop cultivation and other farming crop cultivation, include planting of grain, beans, tubers, cotton, oil bearing crops,sugar crops,fiber crops,tobacco,vegetables,medicinal materials, melons and others, as well as tea,mulberry and fruit plantation.

Other farming include gathering of wild plant fruits, fiber,gum, oil, firewood, wild medicinal materials, fungi and commodity industry run by rural household.

(2)Forestry include planting of trees (not including planting,management & harvest of tea, mulberry and fruit plantation), collection of forest products,cutting and felling of bamboo and trees by villages and other cooperative organizations under villages.

(3)Animal Husbandry include raising and grazing of any kind of animal and hunting and raising of wild animal, excluding fish breeding.

(4)Fishery include cultivation and catches of acquatic animals and seaweed.

(5) The trade of farming, forestry, animal husbandry and fishery, including irrigation service, elementary processing service of farming products, other agricultural service, forestry service, veterinarian service, other animal husbandry service, fishery service, and so on.

55. Grain Yield refers to the yield in the whole country including grains produced by state farms, collective units, industrial enterprises and mines.(Grain includes rice, wheat, corn, sorghum, millet and other miscellaneous grains as well as tubers and beans). Data on grain production before 1989 were obtained through the Comprehensive Statistical Reporting System.Since 1989,data from sample sunveys are used.

56. Yield of Oil-bearing Crops refers to the total yield of oil bearing crops of various kinds, including peanuts, (dry, in shell) rapeseeds, sesame, sunflower seeds, flax seeds, and other oil bearing crops. Soybeans, oil-bearing woody plants, and wild oil-bearing crops are not included.

57. Output of Aquatic Products refers to catches of both artificially cultured and naturally grown aquatic products, including fish, shrimps, crabs and shellfish in sea and inland water as well as seaweed. Freshwater plants are not included.

58. Output of Pork, Beef, and Mutton refers to the meat of slaughtered hogs, cattle, sheep and goats with head, feet, and offal taken away.

59. Cultivated Area (Area under cultivation) refers to farmland which is plowed constantly for growing crops, including cultivated land, newly cultivated land in the current year, farmland left without cultivation for less than three years and fallow land in the current year, rotation land, rotation land of grass and crops, farmland with some fruit trees, mulberry trees and other trees and cultivated seashore land, lake land, and etc. The land of mulberry fields, tea plantations, orchards, nurseries of young plants, forestland, reed land, natural and man-made grassland and other land are not included in cultivated land.

60. Sown Area of Crops refers to area of land sown or transplanted with crops regardless of being in cultivated area or non cultivated area. Area of land re-sown due to natural disasters is also included.At present ,the sown area of crops:grain,oil-bearing crops ,lotton,hamp,sugar crops,tobacco,medicinal materials,vegetables,melons and other farm crops.

61. Irrigated Area refers to areas that are effectively irrigated, i.e. level land which has water source and complete sets of irrigation facilities to lift and move adequate water for irrigation purpose under normal conditions. Under normal conditions, irrigated area is the sum of watered fields and irrigated fields where irrigation systems or equipment have been installed for regular irrigation purpose.

62. Consumption of Chemical Fertilizers in Agriculture refers to the quantity of chemical fertilizers applied in agriculture in the year, including nitrogenous fertilizer, phosphate fertilizer, potash fertilizer, and compound fertilizer. The consumption of chemical fertilizers is required in calculation to convert the gross weight into weight containing 100% effective component (e.g. 100% nitrogen content in nitrogenous fertilizer, 100% phosphorous pentoxide contents in phosphate fertilizer, 100% potassium oxide contents in potash fertilizer). Compound fertilizer is converted with its major component.

63. Total Power of Farm Machinery refers to total mechanical power of machinery used in farming, forestry, animal husbandry, and fishery, including ploughing, irrigation and drainage, harvesting, transport, plant protection, stock breeding, forestry and fishery. The power of internal combustion engines is required to convert horsepower into watts and the power of electric motors is required to be converted into watts. Machinery employed for non-agricultural purposes, such as the machines used in township run and village-run industry, construction, non-agricultural transport, scientific experiments and teaching, is excluded.But mechanical power that engage in agriculture and sideline products for primary processing of villiage industrial mechanical power are included.

64. Number of Livestock or Poultry in Stock at Beginning (or End) refers to the total number of large animals, pigs, sheep, fowls, etc. raised by rural cooperative organizations, state farms, rural individuals, government agencies, schools, industrial and mining enterprises, army, and urban residents at the beginning (or end) of the reference period. The investigated method of the pigs and poultry has changed from overall investigation to sampling investigation since 1997.

65. Industry refers to the material production sector which is engaged in extraction of natural resources and processing and reprocessing of minerals and agricultural products, including (1) extraction of natural resources, such as mining, salt production, logging (but not including hunting and fishing); (2) processing and reprocessing of farm and sideline produces, such as rice husking, flour milling, wine making, oil pressing, cotton ginning, silk reeling, spinning and weaving, and leather making; (3) manufacture of industrial products, such as steel making, iron smelting, chemicals manufacturing, petroleum processing, machine building, timber processing; water and gas production and electricity generation and supply; (4)repairing of industrial products such as the repairing of machinery and means of transport (including cars).

66. Light Industry refers to the industry that produces consumer goods and hand tools. It also refers to the industry that produces consumer goods. The light industry consists of the following two branches: (1) the industrial sectors using agricultural products as raw materials, such as textile and sewing of cotton, wool, hemp and silk, leather and relative products, pulp and paper production, food production, etc.; (2) the industrial sectors using non-agricultural products as raw materials, such as metal, chemicals, glass, porcelain and ceramics, chemical fiber and relative fabric, matches, wood products and so on for daily use. Most of the light industrial products are production consumer goods, while some of them are used in the production of raw materials and semi-finished products, such as chemical fibers, industrial fabrics, paper products, salt, etc.

67. Heavy Industry refers to the industry, which produces capital goods, and provides various sectors of the national economy with necessary material and technical basis. It consists of the following three branches according to the purpose of production or the use of products:(1) Mining, quarrying and logging industry refers to the industry that extracts natural resources, including extraction of petroleum, coal, metal and non-metal ores and logging.(2) Raw materials industry refers to the industry that provides various sectors of the national economy with raw materials, fuels and power. It includes smelting and processing of metals, coking and coke chemistry, chemical materials and building materials such as cement, plywood, and power, petroleum refining and coal dressing. (3) Manufacturing industry refers to the industry that processes raw materials. It includes machine-building industry, which equips sectors of the national economy, industries of metal structure and cement products, industries producing means of agricultural production, such as chemical fertilizers and pesticides.

According to the above principle of classification, the repairing trades, which are engaged primarily in repairing products of heavy industry, are classified into heavy industry while these engaged in repairing products of light industry are classified into light industry.

68. Gross Industrial Output Value refers to the total volume of final industrial products produced and industrial services provided during a given period in monetary terms, including the value of finished products, the income of processing rendered to other units and the changes in the value of home-made semi-finished products between the beginning and closing of the period.

69. Industrial Sales Output Value refers to the total volume of industrial products sold by an industrial enterprise during a given period and in the form of currency. It includes the value of finished products, semi-finished products, and industrial operations rendered to other units, products, industrial operations and self-made equipment provided to the basic construction department, welfare department, etc. of the enterprise. As to those finished products and semi-finished products, no matter whether products are manufactured in this calculation period or the previous one, so long as they are sold out in this calculation period, they should be included. The industrial operations are industrial services rendered to other units according to contracts. The products, industrial operations and self-made equipment provided to basic construction department, welfare department, and etc. of the enterprise should be regarded as act of sale, and included in sales statistics.

The scope, price and method of calculation of industrial sales output value are the same as those for gross industrial output value. However, the calculation base are different: the base for sales output value is the total volume of products sold; the base for gross industrial output value is total volume of production of industrial products.

70. Accounts Receivable refer to money owed to a business on the sale of products, services and other business activities by its customers that have purchased goods or received services, mainly including money owed by concerning debtor(s) to a business on the sale of products or services, as well as the packaging costs, transport charges and so on paid in advance by a purchasing agent.

71. Paid-in Capital refers to the total capital (or equity) actually contributed to a corporation by investors in monetary terms, in kind, with intangible assets, etc. The investment entities can be divided into state capital, collective capital, corporate capital, personal capital, Hong Kong, Macao and Taiwan capital, and foreign capital.

72. Total Assets refer to all resources collected via past transactions or events of a business, owned or controlled by the business and expected to bring economic benefits to the business.

73. Total Circulating Assets refer to assets that meet one of the following conditions: (1) assets expected to be liquidated, sold or consumed within a normal business cycle, including inventory, accounts receivable, etc.; (2) assets held for trading purposes; (3) assets expected to be liquidated within one year (including one year) after the balance sheet date; and (4) cash or cash equivalents that have unrestricted ability for exchange of other assets or to pay off the liabilities within one year after the balance sheet date.

74. Total Fixed Assets refer to tangible assets, with service life over one fiscal year, held by a business for production, services, rental or operation and management.

75. Original Value of Fixed Assets refers to the cost of fixed assets, including the total amount of all expenses incurred at the time of purchase, construction, installation, reconstruction, expansion and technical improvement of a particular fixed assets.

76. Accumulated Depreciation refers to the accumulated amount of depreciation on fixed assets of a business during the past years drawn in the end of given period.

77. Depreciation Drawn in Current Year refers to the total amount of depreciation on fixed assets of a business drawn within given period, the data of which is collected according to the "Depreciation of Fixed Assets" of "Statement of Changes in Financial Position" in accounting.

78. Total Liabilities refer to the current obligations that are expected to result in outflow of economic benefits of a business incurred from past transactions or events of the said business. Liabilities are generally divided into liquid liabilities and non-liquid liabilities based on the length of the repayment period.

79. Total Liquid Liabilities refer to liabilities that meet one of the following conditions: (1) liabilities expected to be settled within a normal business cycle; (2) liabilities held for trading purposes; (3) liabilities that shall be settled within one year after the balance sheet date; and (4) liabilities that a business has no right to defer the settlement to more than one year after the balance sheet date by their own. Such liabilities include short-term borrowings, bills payable, accounts payable, remuneration payable to employees, taxes payable and other items.

80. Non-liquid Liabilities refer to liabilities other than in current liabilities, including long-term loans, bonds payable and so on, the data of which is collected according to the ending balance of "Total Non-liquid Liabilities" of "Balance Sheet" in accounting.

81. Total Creditors' Equity refers to residual interest owned by creditors in corporate assets after deducting liabilities. Company creditors' equity is also known as shareholders' equity, including paid-up capital, capital surplus, earned surplus, undistributed profits, etc.

82. Main Business Income refers to income of sales of goods and services and other main business recognized by a business.

83. Main Business Tax and Surcharges refer to the business tax, consumption tax, urban maintenance and construction tax, education surtax, etc. that should be borne by a company from main business.

84. Total Value of Profit and Tax (pre-tax Profits) refers to the total sum of profits, products sales tax and surcharges and the value added tax payable of industrial enterprises. It is also called pre-tax profits.

85. Ratio of Profits to Total Industrial Costs refers to the ratio of profits realized in a given period to the total costs in the same period, which reflects the economic efficiency of input cost and is calculated as follows:

Ratio of Profits to Total Industrial Cost(%)=(Total Profits/ Total Costs) × 100%

86. Sales Ratio of Industrial Products refers to the sales of industrial products to the gross industrial output value in given period, which is important in reflecting the linkage between production and sales and the extent of the needs of the society that has been met by the supply of industrial products. It is calculated as follows:

Sales Ratio of Industrial Products = [Industrial Sales / Gross Industrial Output Value (at current prices)] × 100%

87. Gross Output Value of Construction refers to total output value as expressed in monetary terms of the production and service of construction enterprises within certain period of time. The total value consists of three parts:

(1) Output value of construction projects, that is the value of projects covered by the project budgets;

(2) Output value of installation projects, that is the value of the installation of equipment, (excluding the value of the equipment to be installed);

(3) Other output value: refers to the value of production including repairing of auxiliary parts of housing, non-standard equipment manufacturing, administration cost of contractor on sub-contractor and other construction output which cannot be clearly categorized.

88. Output Value of Completed Projects usually refers to output value of single construction project concerned within reference period, calculated when the projected is completed as required by the plan of the project, meeting the requirements of turning over to the user and pass the examination of authorized department. The scope of output includes: the value created from start to completion of the projects. If the construction of the projects took more than one year, the output value should include the value completed in previous year. The output can be calculated on section by section bases on large projects if they can be divided by sections, levels of construction. Large plants, deluxe hotels, pipe work, highway, railway etc are examples of these large projects.

89. Floor Space of Buildings Under Construction refers to all the floor space of buildings in construction reported in reference period, including those starting construction, construction relayed from previous period, construction resumed after the delay of the previous period, completed construction and construction started in present period and stopped at present.

90. Floor Space of Buildings Completed refers to floor space of construction project concerned within reference period, calculated when the projected is completed as required by the plan of the project, meeting the requirements of turning over to the user and pass the examination of authorized department. The calculation of the floor space should strictly adhere to the standard requirements for check up the completion of the construction projects. For civil construction projects, generally speaking, the floor space should be calculated when the building itself and its water, sewage, gas, heating, ventilation, elevator etc have been completed according to the construction plan, passed the examination for completion and turned over to the user. For the industrial construction as well as the construction of R&D buildings, the floor space should be calculated, generally speaking, when the building was completed with water, heating, sewage and ventilation as well as auxiliary parts in living quarter and operational quarter, even without the installation of manufacturing equipment as well as pipelines.

91. Total Number of Machinery and Equipment Owned by the End of Year refers to the number of machines and equipment owned by the enterprises, and listed as the fixed assets of the enterprises by the end of the year, including machinery and equipment for construction, production and transportation.

92. Total Power of Machinery and Equipment Owned by the End of Year refers to the total power of machinery and equipment owned by the enterprises, and listed as the fixed assets of the enterprises by the end of the year, including machinery and equipment for construction, production and transportation. The power of the machinery is calculated on basis of the designed or verified capacity, covering the power of the machinery/equipment and the separate power equipment serving the machinery/equipment (such as electric motors), but excluding welders, transformers and boilers. The unit used for the calculation of power is kilowatt, with horsepower converted to kilowatt by 1 horsepower=0.735 kilowatt.

93. Income from Settlement of Projects refers to the income received by the construction enterprise from the contracted project through settlement procedures, and other charges to the contractoree as operational costs in addition to the value of the project, such as temporary facility fee, labour insurance premium , moving cost of construction equipment, as well as various types of claims to the contractee.

94. Profit from Settlement of Projects refers to profit realized through settled projects.- expresses loss-incrring.It is calculated with the following formula:

Profit from Settlement of Projects=Income from Settlement of Projects-Settled Cost-Settled Taxes and Extra Charges

95. Length of Highways refers to the length of highways which are builted in conformity with the grades specified by the Highway Engineering Standard JTJ01-88 formulated by the Ministry of Communications,and have been formally checked and accepted by the departments of highways and put into use. The length of highways includes that of the suburb highways at large and medium-sized cities, highways passing through streets at small cities and towns, and also the length of bridges and ferries. It does not include the length of streets in big and medium-sized cities and highways built for the production purpose at factories, mines, forest areas and agricultural areas. If two or more highways go the same section of the way, the length of the section is only calculated for once and no duplication is allowed. The length of highways is an important indicator to show the development of the highway construction and to provide essential information to calculate the transport network density.

96. Length of Navigable Inland Waterways an indicator reflecting the size and development of inland water network, it refers to the length of the natural rivers, lakes, reservoirs, canals, and ditches open to navigation during a given period, which enables the transport by ships and rafts. It includes the channels open to navigation for over an accumulative 3 months in a year, yet this does not include the river courses which are only used to float odd logs and bamboo rafts.

97 Freight(Passenger)Traffic refers to the volume of freight (passenger) transported with various means. Freight transport is calculated in tons and passenger traffic is calculated in the number of persons. Despite the type of freight and travelling distance, the freight transport is calculated in the actual weight of the goods: and despite the travelling distance and ticket price, the passenger traffic is calculated by the principle that one person can be counted only once in one travel. The passenger who travels with a half price ticket or a child ticket is also calculated as one person. The freight (passenger) traffic provides a quantitative measure to show how the transport industry serves the national economy and people, and is also an important indicator for planning the transport industry and for studying the development scale and speed of the transport industry.

98. Freight Ton-kilometers(Passenger-kilometers) refer to the sum of the products of the volume of transported cargo (passengers) multiplying by the transport distance, usually using ton-kilometer and passenger-kilometer as units for measurement. Normally, the shortest distance between the departure station and the destination station (i.e., the payable distance) is the basis to calculate the freight ton-kilometers. This is an important indicator to show the total results of the transport industry, to prepare and examine the transport plan and to measure the efficiency, the labor productivity and the unit cost of transport.

99. Business Volume of Post and Telecommunications Services refer to the total amount of services provided to society by post and telecommunications enterprises with the form of value. Post and telecommunications services can be divided by category as letter, parcel, bill of draft, newspaper and magazine distribution, EMS, philately, fixed telephone, lending circuit, mobile phone, packet switched data traffic and lending telephone switchboard maintenance. The calculation method shall be the sum of various kinds of product time average unit price (fixed price) then plus the service incomes from lending circuit, telephone switchboard and circuit maintenance on behalf of customers.

100. Mobile Telephone Subscribers refer to subscribers of the telephone using mobile telephone network, and occupying mobile telephone number. The number of subscribers shall be calculated as per the number dealt with the formalities of mobile telephone network at cell-phone business office as of the report date, each cell-phone shall be recorded as one subscriber.

101. Number of Internet Subscribers refers to the number of subscribers who have registered and accessed into the international network, including local network area, metropolitan area network, wide area network, and dial-up network subscribers and private wire network subscribers.

102. Total Retail Sales of Consumer Goods refers to the sum of retail sales of consumer goods sold by all sectors of the national economy to urban and rural residents and social groups. This indicator is used to show the supply of consumers goods through various channels to households and institutions, and is very important for the study on people's livelihood, on the purchasing power of consumer goods and on the circulation of money.

103. Wholesale and Retail Sales Trade refers to units not directly involved in the manufacturing of commodities, rather purchasing the commodity from manufacturers or circulating units without processing, or with simple processing (cleaning, tidying, categorizing, packaging, etc) and achieving benefits by reselling the commodities.

104. Accommodation refers to service provided to clients with payment.

105. Catering trade refer to the units offer various food and drinks consumed at once in certain places and this kind of service is more important than other services (entertainment, e.g.) offered.

106. Wholesale enterprises above designated size refer to wholesale companies with the main business income of more than RMB 20 million yuan.

107. Retail enterprises above designated size refer to retail companies with the main business income of more than RMB 5 million yuan.

108. Catering enterprises above designated size refer to catering companies with the main business income of more than RMB 2 million yuan.

109. Total Sales of Commodities refer to value of commodities sold by the establishments to other establishments and individuals (including direct export). This indicator reflects the total value of sales of commodities at domestic markets and export, including: (1)commodities sold to urban and rural residents and social groups for their consumption;(2)commodities sold to establishment in all industries for their production and opration;(3)commodities sold to wholesale and retail establishments for re-selling with or without further processing;(4)commodities for direct exprt to abroad.

110. Value of Business Transaction in Trading Markets refers to the total volume between the buyers of consumption market and sellers of production goods market, which includes farmers, non-agricultural people, government offices, organizations, industrial and commercial enterprises and individual sellers, and which serves as the comprehensive index of the dimensions of trading markets.

111. Registered Capital of Private Enterprises refer to the checked registered capital when the private enterprises do the start or change registered, exclude the bank loans.

112. The Units of the Private owned industrial and Commercial Enterprises refers to the amount of the private owned industrial and commercial enterprises, which have got the business licence or the temporary business licences.

113. Staff and Workers in the Private Owned Industrial and Commercial Enterprises refer to the whole people take part in the business and get paid, which are checked by the industrial and commercial department, involved the manager of the private industrial and commercial enterprises, helper and the apprentices.

114. Registered Capital of the Private owned Industrial and commercial enterprises refer to the checked registered capital when apply for or change the registration.

115. Utilization of Foreign Capital refers to remittance, equipment and technology financed from abroad, by loans, foreign direct investment and other forms undertaken by the Chinese governments at all levels, by various departments, enterprises and other economic units.

116. Direct Investment by Foreign Entrepreneurs refers to the investments inside China by foreign enterprises and economic organizations or individuals (including overseas Chinese, compatriots from Hong Kong and Macao, and Chinese enterprises registered abroad), following the relevant policies and laws of China, for the establishment of ventures exclusively with foreign own investment, Sino-foreign joint ventures and cooperative enterprises or for cooperative exploration of resources with enterprises or economic organizations in China. It includes the re-investment of the foreign entrepreneurs with the profits gained from the investment and the funds that enterprises borrow from abroad in the total investment of projects which are approved by the relevant department of the government.

117. Contracted Projects with Foreign Countries refers to projects undertaken by Chinese contractors (project contracting companies) through bidding process. They include: (1) overseas civil engineering construction projects financed by foreign investors. (2) overseas projects financed by the Chinese government through its foreign aid programs. (3) construction projects of Chinese diplomatic missions, trade offices and other institutions stationed abroad. (4) construction, projects in China Financed by foreign investment.(5) sub-contracted projects to be taken by Chinese contractors through a joint umbrella project with foreign contractor(Including bear terrain mapping; geological resource exploration and census ;construction regional planning; provide the design documents, drawings, production technology and engineering technical economic advice; feasibility investigation, research and evaluation of project;carry out technical guidance and training personnel);(6) housing development projects. The business income from international contracted projects is the work volume of contracted projects completed during the reference period, expressed in monetary terms, including completed work on projects singed in previous years.

118. Service Cooperation with Foreign Countries refers to the activities of providing technology and labor services to employers or contractors in the forms of receiving salaries and wages. Labor services providing by contractual joint ventures of Chinese international contracting corporations should be included in the statistics of service cooperation with foreign countries. The business income of labor service cooperation is the income in the form of wages and salaries, overtime pay, bonuses and other remuneration received from the employers during the reference period.

119. International Tourists refers to foreigners, overseas Chinese, Chinese compatriots from Hong Kong, Macao and Taiwan coming to China for sightseeing, visits, tours, family reunions, vacations, study tours, conferences and other activities of a business, scientific and technological, cultural, educational and religious nature. It does not include representatives and employees of resident institutions of foreign countries in China such as embassies, consulates, news agencies and offices of foreign companies and organizations, nor does it include long term foreign experts or students residing in China, or persons in transition without spending a night in China.

120. Total Electricity Consumption refer to the total amount of electricity consumed, it can be divided into "countryside used electricity", "industry used electricity", "transportation used electricity", "urban and rural residents used electricity" and so on, all kinds of the electricity consumption all involved the electricity sold to the city's consumer by power stations, the electricity produced for self use (involved the electricity made by the waste heat).

121. Energy Consumption of Industry Enterprises refer to the energy, artificial used energy and energy used in other fields as fuel, material and supplementary material.

122. Total Fiscal Revenue refers to the revenue obtained of the government finance by means of participating in distribution of social products, including normal budgetary revenue and fund budgetary revenue. The normal budgetary revenue mainly includes as follows:

(1) Taxes, including VAT, consumption tax, business tax, business income tax, individual income tax, resources tax, tax of adjustment for the orientation of fixed investment, urban maintenance and construction tax, housing property tax, stamp duty, land value increment tax, city and town land use tax, tariff duty, contract tax and tax on occupancy of cultivated land, etc.

(2) Administrative charges revenues refer to administrative charges revenues included in budgetary management in accordance with related stipulations.

(3) Special revenues, including revenue collected from imposing fee on sewage treatment, revenue collected from imposing fee on urban water resources, and extra-charges for education, etc.

(4)Other revenues, including revenue from the repayment of capital construction loan, revenue from capital construction projects, and donations and grants.

Fund budgetary revenue mainly consists of fund revenue from industrial and communication authorities, social insurance fund revenue, income from compensated use of land and government housing fund revenue, etc.

123. Government Expenditure refers to the distribution and use of the funds the government finance has raised, so as to meet the needs of economic construction and various causes. It includes the following main items:

(1)General public services indicating the expenditure on general public services provided by the government.

(2)National defense indicating the government expenditure on active military, reserve forces of national defense and national defense mobilization, etc.

(3)Public Security indicating the government expenditure on maintaining public security.

(4)Education indicating the government expenditure on education.

(5)Science and technology indicating the expenditure on science and technology.

(6)Culture, sports and media indicating the government expenditure on culture, sports, radio and film and news publishing, etc.

(7)Social security and employment indicating the government expenditure on social security and employment.

(8)Medical treatment and health indicating the government expenditure on medical treatment and health.

(9)Environmental protection indicating the government expenditure on environmental protection.

(10)Urban and rural community affairs indicating the government expenditure on urban and rural community affairs.

(11)Agriculture, forestry and water affairs indicating the government expenditure on agriculture, forestry and water.

(12)raffic and transportation indicating the government expenditure on traffic and transportation.

(13)Industrial, commercial and financial affairs indicating the government expenditure on industry, commerce and finance.

(14)Other expenditures indicating other government expenditures that cannot be categorized in the above function subjects.

124. State revenue and local government revenue refer to the revenue owned by the central government and the revenue belongs to local government in accordance with the financial system.

Since the reform of tax system and financial system in 1994, the revenue belonged to the central government includes tariff, consumption tax, value added tax of imported goods levied by the customs, income tax of railway transportation enterprises, state-owned banks, state-owned post enterprises, sales tax of railway and banking and insurance (central government), offshore petroleum resources tax and vehicle purchasing tax (charges), etc. The taxes belong to the general budgetary revenue of local governments include regular sales tax, vehicle and vessel usage tax, animal slaughter tax, tax on occupation of cultivated land and deed tax, etc. The revenue shared by the central government and local governments includes value added tax, business income tax, urban maintenance and construction tax, individual income tax and stamp tax, etc. One point demands explanation is that the data over the years can' t be compared fully due to the changing revenue-sharing pattern and sharing proportions between the central government and local governments in recent years.

125. Deposit is a form of credit by which enterprises, institutions, organizations or households can put money into banks and other credit institutions for safekeeping and interest earning under the principle of free withdrawal. According to different depositors, deposits are divided into enterprise deposits, treasury deposits, deposits of government agencies and organizations, capital construction deposits, urban savings deposits, rural deposits and other deposits. Deposits are major sources of the credit funds of banks.

126. Saving Deposits Balance of Urban and Rural residents Saving deposits include the bank savings deposits of organizations such as industrial and mining enterprises, army units, institutions, ect. The outstanding amount of savings deposits refers to the money put into banks and rural credit unions at certain time points (balance between deposit and withdrawal), such as the end of the month, quarter or year.

127. Loan is a form of credit by which banks and other credit institutions provide funds at certain interest rate to enterprises and individuals in the light of the principle of unconditional repayment. Loans from Chinese banks include circulating capital loans, fixed assets loans, loans to urban and rural individuals engaged in industrial and commercial business and agricultural loans.

128. Amount Insured refers to the maximum that the insurant will get for the claim of the case insured.

129. Premium is the fee paid by the insurant to the insurer to obtain the obligation of compensation from the insurance within the agreed terms.

130. Insurance Indemnity refers to the compensation paid by the insurer to the insurant in accordance with the stipulations of the insurance contract after confirmed the insured event within the scope of insurance coverage by means of verification.

131. Length of Paved Roads at the Year-end refers to the length of roads with a paved surface, and with a width of more than 3.5 meters, including high quality, medium quality and ordinary roads.

132. Urban Bridges refer to bridges over river courses, great separated junctions and overpasses in urban areas. Permanent bridges and semi-permanent bridges are included. Temporary bridges, railway bridges and culverts are excluded.

133. Length of Urban Sewage Pipes refers to the total length of general drainage, trunks,branch and blind drainage, inspection wells, connection wells, inlets and outlets, etc.

134. Daily Disposal Capacity of Urban Sewage refers to the designed 24-hour capacity of sewage disposal at the sewage treatment works.

135. Floor Space of the Park, Gardens and Green Area Of Urban refers to the total area of urban public green land, special green land, production green land, protection green land and suburban scenic spots.

136. Green Space in Park refers to the green area with main function of opening for the public, and recreation, which possesses certain recreation facilities and service facilities, integrated the effects of ecology perfection, scenery beautification, prevention and mitigation of the effects of disasters.

137. Production Capacity of Tap Water at the Year-end refers to the actual comprehensive production capacity of the waterworks administered by the urban construction department and those owned by enterprises or institutions, taking the capacity of the main links, such as water inflow, purification, conveyance and outflow of the trunk pipelines into account.

138. Number of Public Vehicles (Buses and Trolley buses) at the Year-end refers to the total number of operational buses available at the year-end, including the year-end operational vehicles and vehicles in stock. Non-operational vehicles such as stringing cars, tank cars, machine shop cars, trucks and other special vehicles and the borrowed passenger vehicles are excluded.

139. Length of Roads in Operation refers to the length of designated regular routes in operation, including the length of suburban routes in operation. The length of temporary operational lines is not included.

140. Length of Water Supply Pipelines at the Year-end refers to the total length of all the pipelines between the water pumps and the users water meters.

141. Annual Volume of Water Supply refers to the total volume of water supplied by the public water-works and those owned by individual enterprises and institutions during the whole year, including both the effective water supply and loss during the water supply.

142. Consumption of Water for Residential Use refers to the water consumption of households for daily life and the water consumption of public welfare facilities, including the consumption of restaurants, hotels, hospitals, barber shops, public bathhouses, laundries, swimming pools, shops, schools, institutions, army units and other units.

143. Percentage of Urban Population with Access to Tap Water refers to the ratio of the urban non-agricultural population (excluding temporary and mobile population) with access to tap water to the total urban non-agricultural population. The formula is:

Percentage of Population with Access to Tap Water=(Urban Non-agricultural Population with Access to Tap Water) / (Urban Non-agricultural Population) × 100%

144. Length of Gas Pipelines refers to the total length of pipelines between the outlet of the compressor, blower or gas tank and the gas meters of users.

145. Volume of Gas Supply refers to the total volume of gas sold to users in a year, including the volume for industrial use, residential use and other uses.

146. Percentage of Urban Population with Access to Gas refers to the ratio of the urban non-agricultural population with access to gas (including gas, liquefied petroleum gas and natural gas) to the urban non-agricultural population (excluding temporary and mobile population). The formula is:

Percentage of Population with Access to Gas =(Urban Non-agricultural Population with Access to Gas) / (Urban Non-agricultural Population) × 100%

147. Total Amount of Waste Water refers to the total amount of industrial waste water and resident waste water. The industrial refers to the total of the waste water produced in the producing, studying period of the enterprises and institutions. The resident waste water refers to the waste water produced in the residences.

148. Volume of Industrial Waste Water Discharged refers to the volume of industrial waste water discharged, through all outlets, to the outside of industrial enterprises, including waste water produced, direct-cooling water, underground water from mines that does not meet the standard of discharge, and the domestic sewage mixed up with industrial waste water when discharged, but excluding discharged indirect-cooling water.

149. Total Amount of Industrial Waste Gas Discharged refers to the total volume of all kinds of gas containing pollutants discharged to the air by factories in the process of fuel combustion and production, which is measured by standard conditions (273K, 101325Pa).

150. Volume of General Industrial Solid Wastes Utilized in a Comprehensive Way refers to the volume of solid wastes from which useful materials can be extracted or which can be transformed to utilizable resources, energy or other raw materials through recycling, processing, circulation, exchange, and so on, including the volume of industrial solid wastes stored up in the previous years and utilized in the current year, such as the solid wastes utilized as fertilizers, building materials, road construction materials, etc.

151. Volume of General Industrial Solid Wastes Treated refers to the amount of solid wastes eliminated by enterprises in the survey year through incineration of industrial solid wastes and other methods of changing the physical, chemical and biological properties of the industrial solid wastes, to reduce or eliminate their risk components, or by means of burying the industrial solid wastes in the landfill meeting the requirements for environmental protection. Such treatments include: burying, burning, piling in designated sites (warehouses), pouring water into the deep strata, filling of old mines, ocean disposal (as approved by Ocean Management Authorities), and so on.

152. Total Amount of Industrial Smoke, (Powder) and Dust Discharged refers to the total amount of smoke and industrial dust discharged to the air by enterprises in the process of fuel combustion and production.

153. R & D is the abbreviation of research and development, and refers to the systemic and creative activities for the purpose of increasing knowledge and applying the knowledge within the field of science and technology (including the fields of natural science, agricultural science, medical science, engineering and technological science and humanities and social science). R & D consists of three kinds of activities, including fundamental research, application research and experimental development.

154. Independent Research and Development Institutions refer to the state- owned institutions which have direct mission and research purpose, a certain number of core members with higher research level and certain number of research personal, favourable conditions for R&D and engaging in scientific research and technological development. The institutions also have their own independent organization and finance, authority to sign contracts with other units, their bank accounts. Independent research and development institutions include the institutions attached to central government agencies, Chinese Academy of Sciences, Chinese Academy of Social Sciences and the institutions attached to the local government.

155. Scientists and Engineers refer to persons who have completed university or higher education or obtained titles of senior and middle level professional positions.

156. Personnel of Independent Research and Development Institutions refers to the persons working in and receiving payment from research and development institutions. It includes regular full-time and temporary staff and workers and employees working on contracts, but excludes retirees and persons leaving their work without payment but still retaining their posts, who are not on the employee list.

157. Total Expenditure on Research and Development refers to all actual expenditure made for R&D (basic research, applied research and experimental development)in reference period. It includes direct expenditure on R&D and indirect expenditure on R&D (including management and necessary administrative expenses of research institutes, investment in capital construction relating to R&D).

158. Inventions refer to the inventions as specified by the patent law and its detailed rules and regulations for implementation. They refer to the new technical proposals to the products or methods or their modifications.

159. Utility Models The utility models specified by the patent law and its detailed rules for implementation refer to the new technical proposals on the shape, structure or combination of shape and structure of product, which is suitable for practical use.

160. Designs refer to the designs as specified by the patent law and its detailed rules and regulation for implementation. They refer to the aesthetics and industry applicable new designs for the shape, pattern and color of the product, or their combinations.

161. Number of online registered technology contracts refers to the number of local technology contracts registered via the national technology contracts on-line registration system (http://www.ctmht.net.cn/).

162. Business volume of online registered technology contracts refers to the business volume of local technology contracts registered via the national technology contracts on-line registration system (http://www.ctmht.net.cn/).

163. Science and Technology Enterprises Incubator refers to the scientific and technological innovation service organization aiming to promote the transfer of scientific and technological achievements, and to nurture high-tech enterprises and entrepreneurs. It includes technological innovation service center, university technology parks, innovation (venture) park for returned overseas students, software parks and professional technological enterprises incubators.

164. Total income of enterprises under incubation refers to the sum of various incomes achieved from technology, industry and trade by the enterprises under incubation within the statistical year.

165. Persons employed by enterprises under incubation refer to the total number of persons employed by the enterprises under incubation at the end date of this report.

166. Incubated Enterprises refer to the enterprises realize independent development after developed to a certain scale so that divorce from the incubator. (The data of incubated enterprises is only accumulated based on the data of graduation time, without tracking).

167. Regular Institutions of Higher Learning refer to educational establishments set up according to the government evaluation and approval procedures, enrolling graduates from senior secondary schools via national entrance examination and providing higher diploma education. They include full time universities, independent colleges and senior professional schools, senior vocational universities and other institutions (such as independent institutes, branch schools and junior colleges).

168. Institutions of Higher Learning for Adults refer to educational establishments set up according to the government evaluation and approval procedures, enrolling personnel with senior secondary school or equivalent education via national entrance examination and providing higher diploma education by means of correspondence, part time or full time. They include workers' colleges, peasants' colleges, institutes for administration, educational colleges, independent correspondence colleges and etc.

169. The number of Full-time Teachers refers to the number of personnel engaged in education as full-time teachers, including those who are temporarily designated (within one year) to assist in other fields. The former teachers transferred from teaching to undertake administrative management are excluded.

170. Cultural Institutions refer to units which have their own organizational system and independent accounting system and specialize in or serve cultural development. They exclude other establishments run by these cultural institutions and amateur cultural groups established by various departments.

171. Art Troupe refers to the troupe which is engaged in drama, opera, music, dance, acrobatics or other art performance, opens independent accounts with banks and has self-supporting accounting system; excluding the troupes which are engaged partly in industrial or agricultural activities, partly in art performance and the professional troupes organized by the people.

172. Number of Spectators at Art Performance refers to the number of attendants at commercial shows, completely booked shows or free shows given in minority national areas, and does not include the number of spectators at rehearsals for examination and internal shows for study.

173. Hospitals refer to medical institutions with permanent hospital beds, which are able to take in patients and provide them with medical and nursing services. Hospitals are classified into three categories: hospitals at or above the county level, hospitals of rural townships, and other hospitals. According to their ownership, hospitals can be classified into three categories: hospitals under the public health departments, hospitals under industrial and other departments and collective-owned hospitals. Hospitals at or above county level are divided into comprehensive and specialized hospitals.

174. Medical Technical Personnel refers to all medical staff and workers employed by medical institutions, including doctors of Chinese and Western medicine, senior doctors who integrate traditional Chinese therapeutics with Western therapeutics in practice, senior nurses, pharmacists of Chinese and Western medicine, laboratory specialists, other specialists, paramedics of Chinese and Western medicine, nurses, midwives, druggists in Chinese and Western medicine, laboratory technicians, other technicians, other practitioners of Chinese medicine, nursing attendants, pharmacological workers of Chinese and Western medicine, laboratory workers, and other primary medical personnel.

175. Doctors refer to qualified professional medical workers approved to practice by public health departments. They are classified into doctors of Chinese medicine, doctors of Western medicine, senior doctors who integrate traditional Chinese therapeutics with Western therapeutics in practice, paramedics of Chinese medicine and Western medicine, and other specialists of Chinese medicine.

176. Number of Athletes in Grades refers to the number of athletes who have been given titles through examination. The titles of athletes include international masters of sports, masters of sports, first-grade and second-grade.

177. Number of Referees in Grades refers to the number of referees who have been given titles after examination. They are classified as international referees, national referees and referees of the first, second and third grades.

178. Social Welfare Institutions refer to institutions taking care of old people without children,handicapped people and orphans. They include social welfare institutions run by civil affairs departments, children welfare institutions, social welfare institutions for mental patients, and collective-owned old peoples homes in rural areas.

179. Number of People Taken in by Social Welfare Institutions refers to the number of old people, children, totally dependent handicapped people and mental patients taken in by social welfare institutions run by civil affairs departments and those run by collective units in urban and rural areas.

180. Social Welfare Enterprises are collective owned enterprises which employ the blind, deafmute, and other handicapped people who are able to work in cities and towns and enjoy exemption from state taxes, including welfare plants, welfare commercial services, artificial limb plants and farms, etc.

181. Lawyers are legal workers who are employed full time by legal counseling firms to act as legal advisers, agents in criminal or civil lawsuits, or defenders in criminal lawsuits, or to handle non-litigious legal affairs, to advise on matters of law or to write legal papers for others. Both full-time and part time lawyers are included.

182. Notary Personnel refers to judicial workers of the state notary offices handling notarization work according to law. They include notaries, assistant notaries, and other people working for notary offices.

183. Notarized Documents refer to the documents settled by notary offices in a year. The notary documents are drawn up in accordance with the regulations of the Ministry of Justice, including domestic documents and foreign-related documents. Domestic documents are divided into two major categories, documents on economic contracts and documents on civil legal relations.

184. Mediators refer to workers on peoples mediation committees responsible for mediating in civil disputes and cases of slight infraction of the law. They include members of the mediation committees and mediators of mediation groups.

185. Mediation of Civil Disputes refers to mediation committees work in mediating in civil disputes concerning civil rights and duties through persuasion and education in accordance with the provisions of law on a voluntary basis, so as to solve disputes by helping the parties involved come to an agreement and understanding. These disputes include divorce cases and disputes over property ownership, but exclude the civil cases to be handled by the court.

图书在版编目（CIP）数据

常州统计年鉴 . 2013 / 常州市统计局 国家统计局常州调查队编 .
-- 北京 : 中国统计出版社，2013.7
ISBN 978-7-5037-6826-2

Ⅰ . ①常…
Ⅱ . ①常… ②国…
Ⅲ . ①统计资料 – 常州市 – 2013 – 年鉴
Ⅳ . ① C832.533-54

中国版本图书馆 CIP 数据核字 (2013) 第 123938 号

常州统计年鉴 -2013

作　者 / 常州市统计局　国家统计局常州调查队
责任编辑 / 陈越月
责任校对 / 徐　戌
封面设计 / 青之鸟设计
出版发行 / 中国统计出版社
通信地址 / 北京市西城区月坛南街 57 号
邮政编码 / 100826
办公地址 / 北京市丰台区西三环南路甲 6 号
邮政编码 / 100073
电　话 / 邮购（010）63376909 书店（010）68783171
网　址 / http://csp.stats.gov.cn
印　刷 / 常州市武进第三印刷有限公司
经　销 / 新华书店
开　本 / 880mm × 1230mm 1/16
字　数 / 1150 千字
印　张 / 34 印张
版　别 / 2013 年 7 月第 1 版
版　次 / 2013 年 7 月第 1 次印刷
定　价 / 300 元

本书附同版本 CD-ROM 一张，光盘内容以书面文字为准。
如有印装差错，由本社发行部调换。